PATTERNS OF LANGUAGE

Structure, Variation, Change

PATTERNS OF LANGUAGE

Structure, Variation, Change

ROBBINS BURLING
Program in Linguistics
Department of Anthropology
University of Michigan
Ann Arbor, Michigan

ACADEMIC PRESS
San Diego   New York   Boston   London   Sydney   Tokyo   Toronto

Copyright © 1992 by ACADEMIC PRESS, INC.

All Rights Reserved.

No part of this publication may be reproduced or transmitted in any form or by any means, electronic or mechanical, including photocopy, recording, or any information storage and retrieval system, without permission in writing from the publisher.

Academic Press, Inc.
A Division of Harcourt Brace & Company
525 B Street, Suite 1900
San Diego, California 92101-4495

United Kingdom Edition published by
Academic Press Limited
24–28 Oval Road, London NW1 7DX

Library of Congress Cataloging-in-Publication Data

Burling, Robbins.
    Patterns of language : structure, variation, change / Robbins
Burling.
        p.   cm.
    Includes bibliographical references and index.
    ISBN 0-12-144920-3
    1. Language and languages.   2. Linguistics.   I. Title.
P106.B778   1992
410--dc20   91-28918
                                                                  CIP

PRINTED IN THE UNITED STATES OF AMERICA
   94 95 96   MM 9 8 7 6 5 4

CONTENTS

4. Lexical Variation and Change

PART TWO   Sounds

5. Phonetics

6. Phonology

7. Phonological Variation

8. Variation through Time: Phonological Change

PART THREE   Sentences

9. Generative Grammar

10. The Functions of Syntax

11. Syntactic Typology

17. Language and Civilization

PREFACE

Many introductions to linguistics have been written, and I would like the reader to know what persuaded me to write still another. In several respects I have tried to treat the subject a bit differently than other introductions to linguistics do.

First, I felt that our understanding of linguistic variation has reached the point where it can be integrated more closely with other linguistic topics. Since variation is the raw material from which the various changes develop, language variation forms the natural bridge between language structure and language change, between synchrony and diachrony. Instead of isolating variation as a separate topic, therefore, I have treated it along with other aspects of language. Admittedly, this arrangement comes at the price of breaking up the treatment of variation and change into several parts—lexical, phonological, and syntactic—but I believe the advantages of this arrangement offset the cost.

Second, I believe functional and typological approaches to syntax can now play a larger role in an introductory treatment than has been possible in the past. Our rapidly expanding knowledge of syntactic typology gives a sense of the diversity of the world's languages, which is in danger of being obscured in more exclusively formal approaches. The related functional perspective can add context and provide some understanding of the reasons why syntax assumes the forms found in various languages. Of course, students deserve to enjoy the beauties of formal approaches to syntax, and I introduce generative syntax in Chapter 9. However, I have tried not to let the technicalities of the more formal syntactic frameworks lead to the slighting of other topics and points of view.

I have used examples from a wide variety of languages. I understand the attractions and advantages of working with one's native language, and it is certainly true that any book on linguistics written in English must give ample examples from the only common language of all its readers. Nevertheless, both the intrinsic interest of diversity and my hope of conveying a sense of the range of similarities and differences among the world's languages argued for the plentiful use of examples from other languages.

I have tried to avoid dogmatism and to offer alternative ways of looking at language. I point out areas where linguists disagree, where our knowledge is still limited, and where important work remains for the next generation of linguists, some of whom, I hope, will be among the readers of this book. I also wanted to demonstrate the logic of theory construction and theory testing. I wanted to be clear about the relationship between observation and theoretical claims, to ask not only how data lead us to build theories, but also how our theories define what we take to be data. An introduction is not too early a point to raise questions about the relation between observations and theory and about the structure of our knowledge. In no other subject is it more profitable to raise such questions than in linguistics.

This book may seem advanced to some readers because I include a number of topics that most introductory books avoid. Others may find it elementary because I focus less than some introductions on the technical apparatus of linguistics. I have used technical terms, symbols, and formulas where they added clarity, but technical apparatus has an unfortunate way of becoming an end in itself, and where no precision is lost I have preferred to write in prose, rather than in symbols and formulas. I deeply believe that there is little in any field that cannot be made clear to interested beginners, and it is beginners, of any age or from any background, for whom I have written. At the same time, beginners should learn about the issues that linguists themselves find interesting. They do not need to be restricted to elementary topics. Language is endlessly fascinating, not only to linguists but to every speaking human being, and linguistics does not have to be presented with such obscurity that it becomes inaccessible to the average student, scholar, or interested general reader. Readers deserve to know what linguists quarrel about and what issues make them quarrel. I do not find it contradictory to suggest that I have written an advanced book for beginners.

Far too much is known about language to be squeezed into a single book, and anyone venturing to write an introduction to linguistics faces some awful choices about what not to include. Often, I had to resist the temptation to include too much, but only firm resistance kept the size of the book from growing completely out of control. In the end, I made choices that reflect my own particular interests and biases. I have surely omitted or skimped on topics that are the favorites of other linguists, but even if there were a clear consensus about what should be found in an introduction to linguistics, I would rather write a book that conveys an enthusiasm for my own favorite topics than a book that represents a flat consensus.

The chapters are divided among four parts. The first three deal with what many linguists still consider to be the core areas of the field: words, sounds, and sentences, or, in the jargon of linguistics, lexicon, phonology, and syntax. Within each of these I deal not only with synchronic structure but also with variation and change. I have written these three parts so that they can be read in any order. This requires a modest amount of repetition, but I believe the advantages of flexibility will outweigh whatever awkwardness this repetition brings. The topic of language change, as linguists generally understand it, is divided among Parts I–III, but Part IV, ''Growth,'' deals with several other kinds of language development. These include pidgins, creoles, language acquisition in the child, and the evolution of language in the species. In all of these a more elaborate kind of language has grown from simpler beginnings.

A number of conventions are helpful when writing about language. When words and sentences are cited in their conventional spelling they are written in italics. Single quotes are used for translations of words or sentences into another language or a different dialect. Square brackets surround phonetic symbols that indicate pronunciation. Slanting brackets surround phonemic transcriptions. In a few places small curly brackets are used around the transcription of morphemes. Important technical terms are written in bold face when they are first introduced and occasionally when reintroduced later.

This book is the result of a long fascination with language and of repeated attempts to convey my fascination to students. I am indebted to the many students who have helped me to understand my subject better, even as I have tried to learn how to help them. Several of my students have done much more than just push me to make better sense. Jay Coskey, Tim McDuff, and Paul Wang each gave detailed comments on earlier drafts. Cheryl Carter and Naomi Gurt not only corrected my commas and spelling but spent many hours patiently pointing to the places where I was awkward or unclear. Regina Johnston turned out to be a slang expert. The largest part of the work on the manuscript was done during several long visits in Oslo, Norway, where the Department of Social Anthropology at The University of Oslo offered me a desk and warm hospitality. To the Oslo anthropologists and also to the Oslo linguists, in whose fine reading room I spent many hours, I owe a debt that will be difficult to repay.

Friends and colleagues, many of them at the University of Michigan and the University of Oslo, have read parts of the manuscript and offered their criticism, allowed me to use their examples, discussed linguistic issues, tried to straighten out my confusions, and even experimented with parts of the manuscript with their students. My warm thanks go to Patrice Beddor, Kirsti Koch Christensen, Norma Diamond, Steven Dworkin, Deborah Jackson, Deborah Keller-Cohen, Elizabeth Lanza, Ernest McCarus, John Myhill, Paz Naylor, Helen Ottaway, Emanuel Polioudakis, Roy Rappaport, Hendrik Sinding-Larsen, Hanne Gram Simonsen, Thomas Toon, Frances Trix, and Anna Wierzbicka. Bente Odner and Nancy Hansen drew the fine diagrams and drawings. I am also indebted to several anonymous reviewers who were recruited by Academic Press and who offered their sage criticism. Suzanne Kemmer was an anonymous reviewer who, after offering wonderfully detailed, thoughtful, and helpful comments, revealed her identity so now I can thank her by name. Kari Gluski spent far more time than she should have had to spend squeezing phonetic symbols out of computer programs. And, finally, my ideas have been repeatedly clarified by many long hours of talk about language with Anne Hvenekilde. None of these good friends should be blamed for my continued confusions. To all of them, my thanks.

While I have had help from all these people, I would welcome additional help from others. I would be pleased to have comments from students, from teachers, or from anyone else who happens to pick up the book. Reader's reactions will be important to me whether they concern a misplaced comma or a linguistic theory that I have misunderstood, and I invite correspondence: Robbins Burling, Program in Linguistics, University of Michigan, Ann Arbor, Michigan 48109 USA.

CHAPTER ONE

The Uses of Language

KNOWING A LANGUAGE

All of us can speak at least one language with easy fluency. Speaking and understanding our first language seems to be such a natural process that we hardly notice its complexities. Indeed, we may not even suspect how complex a language can be until we study a foreign language and discover how much we have to learn. What do we have to learn in order to speak and to understand a language? What is it that we know when we "know" a language?

To understand and to speak a language, we must, for one thing, know a vast number of words. Nobody knows how to count words well enough to give a reliable estimate of total vocabulary size, but adults certainly know tens of thousands of words, and we continue to add to our vocabularies throughout our lives. As far as anyone can judge, people from all corners of the world, even those without writing or formal education, have vocabularies that compare to our own in size.

Our stock of words represents a huge investment of learning, but words form only the most obvious component of what we need to know in order to use a language. We also need to know how to move our tongues, lips, and other organs of speech, and we need to move them with a speed and precision that goes beyond that of any other muscular activity over which we have conscious control. The delicate movements of a surgeon's hands do not surpass the delicate movements of our tongues. We need our lingual acrobatics in order to produce the sounds of speech that are capable of keeping our thousands of words distinct from one another.

In addition to a large vocabulary and to the speech sounds with which we form our words, we need to be able to relate our words to one another. A language would not be very useful if we could not organize its words into phrases and sentences. If our listeners are to understand our meaning, we must know how to assemble words in ways that make sense to them. It is the patterns by which words are combined that linguists call syntax.

The vocabulary, the sounds, and the syntax of a language have formed the central concern of the discipline of linguistics, but in order to speak like the other members of our language community, we need to know still more. We must have a sense of what style is appropriate for the time and place in which we speak. Sometimes slang will be admired as clever, but at other times, nothing will do except formal expressions. We need to know which topics are suitable for which occasions. We need to know how to launch a conversation, how to ask questions, and how to respond. We need to know how to get a turn when others are already talking and how to break off a conversation when we have had enough. We need to be able to make realistic estimates of how much our listeners already know so that we can judge what we need to say and what we can safely omit. We need to know even when to speak and when to remain silent. The conventions for using language vary from one language to another and from one culture to another. Since they have to be learned anew by each new speaker, it is little wonder that both children and adults require many long years in order to master a language.

WHAT IS LANGUAGE FOR? HOW CAN IT MEET OUR NEEDS?

What does language do for us? What must a language be like if it is to be capable of meeting our needs? A few preliminary and tentative answers to these questions can be suggested now, but the rest of the book will be needed to flesh these answers out.

Communication and Cognition

First, of course, a language is a system of communication. To say this, however, is to say very little, for the barking of a dog, the arched back of an angry cat, and the crying of a human baby also communicate. Like dogs and babies, adult humans communicate with their facial expressions, their gestures, and their voices, quite apart from language. With a frown, a grunt, a smile, a puzzled brow, or a tensed body we show each other how we feel. We can even understand some of the cries and gestures of other species. We are properly warned by a dog's growl and curled lip. We relax at the sight of his wagging tail. For some sorts of messages, both human and animal, a mew, a hiss, a chuckle, a smirk, or a trembling lip convey meanings more subtle even than language.

The human nonverbal communication of cries and gestures, like the nonverbal communication of animals, is an excellent tool for conveying messages about one's inner emotional state. Our anger, hunger, fatigue, or excitement may be more easily and more subtly conveyed by facial expressions and gestures than by words. Nevertheless, the information conveyed by frowns, sighs, and even trembling lips has narrow limits, and for some messages, only language will do. Nonverbal communication is nearly useless when we want to convey information about the state of the world outside our own bodies. Only with language can we tell someone what happened a year ago or describe affairs on the other side of the mountain. Only with language can we agree to meet for lunch at 12:30 at the Fleetwood Diner. Human beings need a language that is capable not only of expressing emotion, but also of describing the state of the world around us. The ability of human language to convey factual information goes far beyond the capacity of any known form of animal communication, and far beyond the capacity of our own nonverbal communication.

Language permits us to cooperate and to organize more complex social systems than are available to other animals, and it is by means of language that we express and perpetuate our cultural differences. The language that permits this kind of communication is what sets us apart most clearly from other animals. It is hardly too much to say that it is language that makes us human.

Language offers us a unique form of communication, but, when we emphasize its communicative use, we may forget that language also has another important function: the organization of human cognition. A mind that can convey information to another mind must also be capable of organizing this information for its own use. Human beings not only communicate with language but, at least in some degree, they also think with the help of language. Perhaps we could not even use language for communication if we were not also capable of using it to organize our ideas. Language, then, is a tool for both communication and for thought, and we can ask what kind of a tool language must be if it is to satisfy our cognitive, communicative, and social needs.

At a minimum, a language needs a vocabulary of meaningful expressions, a means of keeping the words of its vocabulary distinct, and a means of showing how these words are related. These are the three areas of language that linguists refer to as **lexicon** (the vocabulary), **phonology** (the system of distinctive sounds), and **syntax** (the organization of words into phrases and sentences). Each of these is the topic of one part of this book, but each deserves to be introduced briefly here.

A Lexicon: Words

To be used for either communication or cognition, a language must, first of all, have a **lexicon,** a stock of meaningful words of some sort, and these words must be distinct from one another and recognizable to the user. The words of most human languages are expressed by noises that we form with our vocal organs and receive with our ears, but there are specialized forms of human language that use other kinds of words. We translate the noises of spoken language into the visible marks of written language, and deaf people communicate with hand gestures instead of with noises, but whether it is seen or heard, every language must have a stock of words.

A language must have words that stand for the things that its users want to talk about. Thus all human languages have words for the objects, qualities, actions, and events that people perceive in the world around them; the vocabulary of a language is a reflection of the interests of its speakers. Every natural language, for instance, has words for the objects and events of nature, for its inanimate rocks and its living plants and animals, but since people everywhere are interested, most of all, in people, every language has even more words for people and for their activities. We need proper names like *Nelson* and *Detroit* that refer to particular people and places, but we also need more general words like *table* or *walk* or *blue* that can be applied to a range of objects or events. We need words for concrete visible and audible objects, and other words for less tangible, more abstract, ideas.

A language that could be used only to talk about objects and events that are within the sight or hearing of the speaker would allow only a very limited means of communication. A richer language must allow its speakers to talk about things that are out of sight or distant in time and, of course, all natural human languages make this possible. All languages, then, must have ways of locating objects and events in time and space. If a language is rich enough to describe hidden objects, or events that have not yet happened, it is also likely to be rich enough to express ideas of pure imagination. We need words not only for *cows* and *horses,* but also for *mermaids* and *unicorns.* Imaginary worlds can be described by all human languages; all languages can be used for lies.

However large its vocabulary, no language can have an entirely distinct word for everything that is of interest to its speakers. This means that languages need ways of constructing longer and more complex words from shorter and simpler parts. Every language has both simple words like *boy, lamp,* and *desire* and complex words like *boyfriend, lamppost,* and *undesirability.* **Morphology** is the branch of linguistics that investigates the ways in which complex words are built from smaller pieces.

Syntax: Ways of Joining Words

Adults know tens of thousands of different words, but they want to talk about more than tens of thousands of different things. Though large, our stock of words is hardly infinite, and we gain real freedom of expression only by joining words together in phrases and sentences. By using words in groups, we gain the ability to talk about a limitless range of affairs. We cannot, however, string our words together in a haphazard way. We can create complex meanings only if we join them according to a systematic plan. We need to agree on consistent patterns of word order, and we need a means of showing how words are related to each other. In other words, a language needs **syntax,** a set of conventions by which its stock of words can be combined.

It is possible to imagine a communication system that could do no more than express facts, true or false, about the world. Some systems of formal logic and mathematics come close to this, but natural human languages do much more.

They also provide ways of emphasizing what the speaker regards as important and ways of conveying the speaker's attitude. They provide ways of calling attention to changes of topic and ways of limiting repetition. They offer devices by which a long discourse or conversation can be given continuity. All of these are made possible, in part, by the syntax that organizes the words of a language.

Phonology: Ways of Distinguishing among Words

A language with thousands of words needs a means of keeping all these words distinct from one another. Of the huge number of possibilities, a listener needs to know exactly which words a speaker has chosen. Natural spoken languages keep their words distinct by means of a complex system of speech sounds. These must, of course, be the kinds of sounds that can be made by the human vocal apparatus and distinguished by the human ear. Other types of languages represent their words in other ways. Sounds can be represented on paper by visible symbols, and the sign language of the deaf uses visible gestures of the hand rather than audible noises, but any language that has thousands of words requires a complex coding system by means of which these words can be conveyed from one person to another.

The calls and gestures of an animal communication system must also be recognizable, of course, but the number of separate signs in an animal's "vocabulary" is far smaller than the number of words in a natural language. The means of keeping animal signs distinct from one another can be correspondingly simple. It is the complexity of the means used for representing the words of a natural spoken language that makes **phonology,** the study of the sound systems of languages, such an important part of linguistics.

Learnability

If a language is to be used by human beings, it must be learnable by a small person who grows up among larger people who already know the language, even though these others have no self-conscious knowledge of how to teach it. By exposure, practice, trial, and error, children must be able to work their way into the vocabulary and into the syntactic patterns of the language. They must be able to move, step by step, from simple beginnings to the full language of adulthood.

If a language is to be used by human beings, it will have to be adapted to the human attention span and to the human ability to process information. It will need a syntax that can be learned and processed by the human mind. Its vocabulary must be no larger than the human mind can store, and its words must be defined in ways that conform to the mind's conceptual abilities. Linguists now believe that many of the specific characteristics of natural languages are molded by the equally specific characteristics of our minds.

Perhaps the characteristics of natural languages can be brought into sharper focus by an analogy with computer programming languages. Anyone who has used a programming language should recognize that much of what has been said in the previous paragraphs would apply to programming languages as well as to natural languages. First, in the constants and variables that enter into computer commands, computer languages have something very much like words. Like natural languages, computer languages have to keep their words distinct. They do this, not by the distinctive noises of the human voice, but by the symbols on a screen or, ultimately, by the zeros and ones, the bits and bytes, that lodge in computer memory. The bytes of a computer, like the sounds of a human language, provide a code that can keep large numbers of words distinct.

In addition to its words, and the code by which these words are expressed, a computer language also needs a syntax, including both special symbols and rules of order. The special symbols help to show the relationship of the constants and variables to one another. The rules of order define how the constants and variables must be arranged if the computer is to understand them. As every novice programmer learns all too quickly, words cannot be entered in any random order. Indeed, computers are far less tolerant of syntactic mistakes than are human listeners.

The similarities between natural languages and the programming instructions used for computers are close enough to make it reasonable to describe programs like FORTRAN, BASIC, and Pascal as "languages," but people are not computers, and the languages used by people and computers must be correspondingly different. Computer languages must be suitable for computers, electronically readable, painfully explicit, and allow for great speed. Natural languages must be suitable for human beings, suitable for our vocal organs and for our ears, of course, but suitable above all for our brains. It is obvious that the sound patterns of a natural language must be adapted to our voice and ears. It may not be quite so obvious that its syntax must be adapted to our minds. Just as the syntax of a computing language must conform to the computer with which it is used, so must the syntax of a natural language conform to the nature of the human speakers and listeners.

Adaptability

Human beings are capable of great diversity, and our languages need to be adaptable enough to meet a range of changing needs and interests. When new conditions arise, people need new words to describe them. When people migrate to new climates, they need words for new plants and animals. When technology changes, they need words for the new machines and procedures that the technology brings. Even within a single society, different groups of people have different needs. Occupational groups need their own technical terms. Men and women, children and old people, have their special ways of talking. A language has to be adaptable enough to meet all the varied needs of its speakers; this means that languages are always variable. Being variable, they are also subject to change.

The chapters that follow will give examples from many languages, and suggest ways in which their words and their syntax can satisfy the needs of their users. Some tasks can be accomplished in many different ways, and this allows languages to have surprisingly varied organization. At the same time all languages share a basic ground plan, and this ground plan must be appropriate to the shared nature of the animal that speaks. Even the variability of language is an expression of human nature, perhaps the most dramatic evidence of the ability of human beings to adapt and to learn. Both the ways in which languages differ and the ways in which they resemble each other need to be examined. The field of linguistics can even be defined as the investigation of the similarities and differences among the world's languages.

LEARNING LANGUAGE AND DOING LINGUISTICS

Gaining a mastery over one's first language is a task that requires all the years of childhood. Five-year-old children are sometimes credited with already having achieved this mastery, but their job is by no means finished. Five-year-olds may have outgrown their baby talk so they can avoid the obvious errors of smaller children, but they still have thousands upon thousands of words to learn and, by adult standards, even their grammatical skills remain limited. In our literate society, five-year-olds still face the task of learning to read, but even in societies without writing, people continue, right through childhood and even beyond, to gain increasing facility with their language.

Each child surely begins the process of language learning with a mind that, under the pressures of natural selection, has been specifically designed for the task. The potentialities of the human mind must be stimulated by the rather imperfect evidence of the language that envelops the child. One way to interpret what children do when they learn their first language is to consider them to form a series of hypotheses about the nature of the language they hear. They can be described as making, unconsciously of course, some hypotheses—guesses—about how the language works. Sometimes they will guess badly, and this will lead to mistakes, but as they revise their hypotheses, they gradually move closer to the form of the language that others use.

In some degree, linguists discover the patterns of a language in the same way that children do, but unlike children, they work self-consciously. Like every child who ever learned to speak, a linguist deals with some data from a language and tries to make sense of it. Certain patterns seem to be discernible in the data, and the linguist gets a hunch about them. The hunch can then be tested to see whether the same pattern can be found in additional data. Sometimes it can, and the hunch ("hypothesis" is only a more elegant word for "hunch") will be confirmed. At other times, the hunch will fail, and it will have to be abandoned, but other hunches, other hypotheses, can then be tried until one is found that works more consistently.

In this way, we continually move back and forth between the data of languages and hypotheses about how languages work. When we put enough hypotheses together, and when they seem to hold reasonably well for a large enough body of data, we may even dignify what we have constructed by calling it a "theory." Then, as our theories develop, they, in turn, suggest what sorts of data we should look for next. We learn to ask new and different questions, and our theories even suggest what we should accept as data. Our theories suggest what we should expect, and as our theories change we become surprised by different things, for surprise comes when an expectation is not met, when the predictions of a theory are not fulfilled. Always, we move back and forth between data and theory, drawing inferences, forming hypotheses, and building theories on the basis of our data, but at the same time letting our theories determine what sorts of data we will look for and even what evidence we will accept as data.

This moving back and forth between data and theory is characteristic of all the systematic intellectual enterprise known as "science," but in no field is it easier to get a clear sense of how data and theory depend on one another than it is in linguistics. Linguists may not seem to conduct the kinds of deliberate and controlled experiments that are characteristic of most scientific disciplines. Physicists fling particles around their accelerators to see whether or not their behavior confirms a physical theory. Chemists mix bits into their beakers to test whether they join as theory says they should. Psychologists compare samples of experimental and control subjects, once again as a means of putting their theories to the test. Linguists do not usually conduct the kind of controlled experiment that psychologists conduct, but they have their own form of experiment. Linguists do inspect data—the sounds, words, and sentences of languages. They do form hypotheses about the patterns into which these words and sentences fall, and they do construct theories that seem to account for their data. Armed with hypotheses and theories they then search for the specific linguistic examples that will put their theories to the test. In its testing of theories by the collection and inspection of data, linguistics is as firmly grounded in experiment as is any scientific field.

As they move between the data of languages and theories about how to explain and understand their data, linguists conduct thousands of miniexperiments by which they gradually refine their ideas about the nature of language. Many such experiments will be reviewed in this book, though they will rarely be referred to explicitly as experiments. Readers should find themselves making the same kinds of experiments as they search their own minds for exactly the right examples that will confirm, or contradict, a claim that they have heard or an idea of their own about how some aspect of language works. Linguistics is the ideal subject for getting a feel for the way in which theories are formed and tested, for getting a sense of the dependence of theories on data and of data on theories.

RICHNESS AND IMPOVERISHMENT

Linguists are convinced that all people, whatever their technology and whatever their culture, have rich and complex languages. People who have never had a chance to examine diverse languages sometimes suppose that people with little formal education are able to get along with a vocabulary of only a few hundred words, or that the languages of remote tribes lack terms for abstract concepts, but when languages are examined carefully, they all turn out to have many thousands of words and to give their speakers the means to express subtle abstractions. People without modern technology, to be sure, do not need words to describe our machinery but, reciprocally, we do not need words to describe their hunting practices. Languages differ in the words their speakers use, but all can be readily adapted to changing conditions. As soon as people need to talk about nuclear energy or Amazonian insects or computer programming, they invent the vocabulary that allows them to do so.

All languages are characterized by complex but orderly rules by which words are constructed and combined. The belief that some languages are able to get along without grammatical rules is as fanciful as the belief that some languages get along with only a few hundred words. As far as we are able to tell, the grammatical apparatus of all languages gives speakers everywhere the ability to express their ideas with equivalent richness, freedom, and subtlety. We have never been able to find linguistic criteria by which one language could be described as "simpler" or more "primitive" than another.

What is true of different languages is also true of different forms of the same language. All dialects appear to have equivalent resources. By the time people find their way to a book or to a class in linguistics, they have already passed through a good many years of schooling, and our schools are remarkably successful in conveying the idea that some sorts of language are "better" or "more correct" than others. As with different languages, however, linguists have never been able to find linguistic criteria by which the dialect of one group could be judged as richer or more expressive than any other dialect, or more capable of conveying information with logic and efficiency.

The failure to find linguistic criteria for judging one language or dialect to be superior does not mean that popular attitudes about the superiority of some languages are unimportant. We have to listen to what people tell us about their language. The very fact that people often have very strong feelings about what is right and what is wrong makes attitudes both fascinating and important, but we learn more about attitudes than about language when people insist on "correct" ways of talking that hardly anyone follows in practice. It is sometimes said, for example, that prepositions should not be used to end sentences with. Since almost everyone ends a sentence with a preposition now and then, the rule cannot be taken seriously as a description of real language, but it does suggest something about people's attitudes toward language. The popular belief that some expressions are "wrong" depends more on people's attitudes toward the speakers who use such expressions than on any inherent linguistic deficiencies.

Linguists are generally more interested in how people really talk than in how some authority says they *ought* to talk, and linguists look on all the varied styles and dialects of a language as equally worthy of linguistic analysis. To a linguist *They ain't seen no one* is just as valuable a sentence, and just as "good" a sentence, as *They haven't seen anyone*. Whatever people can say must be accepted as part of their language. Linguists even tend to be a bit impatient with those who presume to instruct others about what they should and should not say.

VARIABILITY AND CHANGE

All languages that are spread over a wide area exhibit dialectal variation, and all languages offer their speakers a varied range of styles. We also find that all languages keep changing. While it is sometimes convenient to think about a language as if it is a stable and even homogeneous system, languages are, in reality, always variable and always changing. Linguists have traditionally divided their field into synchronic and diachronic parts. Synchronic linguistics is the study of the organization and structure of a language at a single time. Diachronic linguistics is the study of the ways in which languages change through time. What connects synchronic structure and diachronic change is variation. As we look more closely at a language we find endless variability. Its words, its sounds, and its syntax vary not only from one region to another but also from one social group to another and from one situation to another. As some variants gain favor and spread, others decline and then disappear. In this way, the language gradually changes.

One dimension of linguistic variability lies in the difference between written and spoken language. The reader may already have noticed that the terms used in these paragraphs have referred more often to spoken language than to writing, and when linguists use the unmodified word "language," they almost always refer to talk rather than to marks on paper. There are several reasons for this focus on spoken language. In part, linguists have wanted to compensate for the vast amount of attention that other scholars give to written language. They have also recognized that people everywhere have always talked, while writing is limited to a relatively recent period of history and is still far from universal. Most of all, however, the linguist's attention to spoken language stems from the conviction that it has developmental priority. Every written language is based on a spoken language. Some writing systems represent the spoken language quite faithfully, and others much less so, but no fully autonomous written language has ever been invented. In the long course of human history, in the history of each language, and even in the experience of each human individual, spoken language has always come first. Linguists give it priority.

This should not imply that written language is unimportant. Writing is indispensable in a society like our own. It can even have a strong influence on the spoken language from which it first grew. Linguists do, sometimes, include written languages in their studies, and some aspects of writing will be reviewed in the final chapter of this book. Nevertheless, when "language" is referred to here without qualification, the word should always be understood to mean "spoken language." When writing is discussed, the explicit expression "written language" will be used.

Each of the first three parts of this book begins with chapters that focus on the synchronic organization of language, and each goes on to discuss variation and change. These three parts deal respectively with the three topics into which the facts of language most naturally divide: lexicon (words), phonology (sounds), and syntax (the organization of words into phrases and sentences). Part IV has a different organization. It deals with a number of ways in which languages can grow or develop, whether within the few years of a single child's maturation, the thousands of years of writing, or the millions of years of human evolution. Such topics can be most profitably considered only after a grounding in the more central linguistic topics of phonology, syntax, and the lexicon.

Words

INTRODUCTION TO PART ONE

A language needs a grammar, and it has to be pronounced, but speakers are usually more clearly aware of the words of their language than of either its syntax or phonology. We discuss words with our friends; we explain words to our children; we continue to learn new words for as long as our minds remain clear. When in doubt about their language, literate speakers turn easily to the authority of a dictionary.

Vocabulary articulates with every other aspect of a language. Each word has a characteristic pronunciation, and each word joins with others in distinctive syntactic patterns. Good dictionaries include information not only about the meaning of words, but also about their pronunciation and syntactic use. This means that words will never be out of view, even in the sections of this book that focus on phonology and syntax, but this first group of chapters is concerned, more specifically, with the words themselves. Chapter 2 considers the way we use words to convey meaning. Chapter 3 deals with the more formal aspects of vocabulary, with the various kinds of words that are found in a language, and with the way in which complex words can be built from smaller parts. Chapter 4, which concludes this group of chapters, reviews vocabulary variability and the changes that come to vocabulary with the passage of time.

CHAPTER TWO

Meaning and the Lexicon

WORDS AND MEANINGS

Every language has tens of thousands of words, and we call this stock of words the **lexicon.** These words name the things that the speakers are most concerned with. People need hundreds and even thousands of words to name the objects of their natural world, the sun and the clouds above, and the land with its rocks and sand and water below. They need names for the wild plants of their homeland, for the parts of these plants, and for the stages of their growth. People who are farmers also need names for their domestic plants and for the techniques that they use to grow them. Everyone has names for animals, both wild and domestic, for the tools used in their daily lives, for their houses, their clothes, their food. Everyone uses a complex vocabulary to locate activities in time and in space, and to describe sizes, shapes, color, and texture. Everyone has ways of talking about quantity, quality, and probability.

To judge by the extent of vocabulary, the overriding interest of people everywhere is people. Everyone can describe people by their age, sex, status, skills, and temperament. With kinship terms people can describe their relationship to one another. Everyone has a detailed set of terms that label the parts of the human body, along with words for the human emotions and for the senses of sight, sound, touch, taste, and smell. Everyone can describe human activities in detail, how people position and move their bodies and how they manipulate objects. Everyone has words for their miseries and their pleasures and for the stages of their lives from birth to death. They have abstract words to express their ideas about their livelihood, about their social system, rules, and customs, and about their religious and cosmological beliefs. Everyone has words that describe language and speech. Everyone can describe unseen and imaginary worlds. Every language allows its speakers to lie.

Wherever we travel and whatever language we study, we find that people have the words to talk about these universal concerns, but not everyone is concerned with exactly the same matters, and as interests change, so does vocabulary. A century ago, our great-grandparents had an extensive vocabulary for horses, the body parts of horses, their harnesses, and the kinds of carriages that horses pulled. Only a few people who have a special interest in horses still control this older vocabulary, but we now have an equally extensive vocabulary for automobiles, their types, and their parts. The shift in vocabulary simply mirrors the cultural shift from the horse and buggy to the automobile. People who live without modern industry or its products have no need for the words that describe industrial goods or activities, but they can be expected to have a rich vocabulary for the activities that are important to them, and as far as we can tell, the average vocabulary of nonindustrial and non-literate people is no less extensive than the average vocabulary of those who live in the modern industrial world. More than two thousand words that name various kinds of plants have been counted in the language of the Hanunóo, a tribe of shifting farmers of the Philippines. This rich vocabulary reflects the importance of plants in the people's lives.

People cannot resist giving names to things. Newly discovered mountains, stars, and species, like newly born children and newly adopted animals, all need verbal labels. The first thing we want to know about a newly observed type of bird is its name. We imagine that we have learned something concrete about the bird itself simply by learning what people have called it. A large part of mastering any new subject or skill is to gain control over its vocabulary. In order to frame a house, carpenters need to know not only how to use their hammers and saws, but they need also to know the meaning of *joist, boxing, stud, plate, header, rafter, gable, pitch,* and *ridge.* Everything we consider important has been given a name. Whenever something becomes important, we name it.

Except for proper names, such as *Billy* or *Mt. Everest,* most words name not just a single object or event, but an entire class of objects or events. *Tree* can refer to any one of millions of large plants of quite varied shapes, sizes, and colors. *Run* can name an activity engaged in by people and animals of every degree of speed, style, and skill. Even machines are said to "run." In addition to naming, then, words classify. The word *tree* classifies some objects as trees and, at the same time, it excludes other objects. In order to use the word *tree,* we need to be able to make a distinction between trees and nontrees. We need to have a sense of the criteria for deciding what is, and what is not, a tree. The classificatory aspect of words is crucial to language, for if we could not apply a single word to a whole range of phenomena, we would need a different word for every single thing that we wanted to talk about. We would need one word for your right index finger, one word for mine, one word for the oak tree in your yard, and another word for the pine tree in my yard. It is in the nature of human language that varied phenomena must be grouped together and recognized as "the same," or at least as enough alike to be named by the same word. Too many distinct names for too many phenomena would make a language impossible to learn, but too few words would deny us precision. We need enough words to make the distinctions that are important to us, but not so many that we are forced to make unnecessary distinctions. A language must balance the need for adequate precision against the danger that its vocabulary might expand beyond manageable bounds.

Anyone who studies a foreign language soon learns that the words of one language frequently lack exact equivalents in another language. The English word *change,* for example, can be translated by several different Norwegian words: *forandre, shifte, bytte, veksle. Forandre* means 'change' in the sense of 'alter,' as in *forandre* the wording of a sentence. *Shifte* or *bytte* is used when replacing one thing by another, so that one can *shifte* or *bytte* trains, clothes, or even languages, as when one changes from Norwegian to English. When times change, they can either *shifte* or *veksle*. Only *veksle* can be used for changing (exchanging) money.

We should expect languages less closely related to each other than Norwegian and English to differ more widely in the way they assign meanings to words. Nevertheless, words do not vary without limits, and examples from the lexicon can be used to illustrate a point that we will return to again and again in the course of this book: languages differ from one another in many ways, but they also show fundamental similarities. One goal of linguistics is to chart the extent to which languages differ, and the extent to which they are all alike. In this chapter we will consider several examples from the lexicon that illustrate both linguistic uniformity and linguistic variation.

BODY PART TERMS

We can start by considering the terminology for parts of the human body. Few areas of the lexicon are more concrete than body part terms, and in few areas do languages resemble each other more closely. We all need to talk about our similar bodies, and we talk about them in rather similar ways. Travel to the most remote corner of the globe, and you will easily find equivalents for all of the ordinary body part terms of your own language. The same body parts have salience everywhere, and people always give them names. Nevertheless, we find variation even here.

Everyone, it seems, has words that, in their literal meaning, correspond closely to English *head, eyes, nose,* and *mouth.* No parts of our bodies are more salient, more ready to be named. Everyone also has ways of talking about *hands, arms, legs,* and *feet,* though not everyone has four words that correspond exactly to ours. Some languages have a single word that covers both our *hand* and our *arm* and a second that covers both *foot* and *leg.* The meaning of the word that is closest to English *leg* may end at the ankle, extend to the beginning of the toes, or include the toes as well. In some languages fingers and toes are referred to by the same word, and in others the toes are named by a compound expression that means "fingers of the foot." Individual fingers are more likely to have their own names than are individual toes. English has a special word for *thumb,* and most Americans recognize *pinky* as equivalent to *little finger,* but we have no choice except compound expressions for the corresponding toes: *big toe, little toe.* We have conventional expressions, though no separate words, for *index finger, middle finger,* and *ring finger,* but we have to resort to a more elaborate description on the rare occasions when we need to refer to one of our three middle toes: *the toe next to my little toe.* Our vocabulary is always more elaborate in areas that we find important. Our words confirm the fact that we find fingers more important than toes, and that some fingers are more important than others.

We extend a few terms to let them apply to more than a single part of our anatomy. Used by itself, *back* refers to the back of the torso, but we can use the same word for the *back of the hand* and the *back of the head* to say nothing of the *back of the mind* or *back of the closet.* Since it has its own word, we may suspect that the back of the torso is a rather more important and salient part of the body than the back of the hand. Other languages make other terms do double duty. The wrist and ankle may be called the *neck of the arm* and the *neck of the leg* because, like the proper neck, they refer to regions where the body narrows. Fingers and toes are sometimes called *noses of the hand* and *noses of the feet.* Being round, the bones that protrude from the sides of the ankle are sometimes called *eyes* of the leg, and, because it is round and at the top, a buttock may be called the *head of the leg.* Some languages suggest closer parallels between arms and legs than does English. *Elbow* and *knee, ankle* and *wrist, palm* and *sole,* and other corresponding pairs may be called by the same words. Of course, the people can distinguish these when they need to. Just as we can distinguish *left arm* from *right arm* or even the *toe next to the little toe,* when that becomes important, so others can distinguish *arm elbows* from *leg elbows* whenever there is a danger of being misunderstood.

Less-salient body parts are sometimes referred to with the help of words drawn from other parts of the vocabulary. We have *eyelid, shoulder blade, kneecap,* and *rib cage,* and other languages use *head leather* for 'scalp,' *eye egg* for 'eyeball,' *ear leaf* for 'earlobe,' and even *arm shovel* for 'hand.' It is even more common to draw on the vocabulary of body parts to describe inanimate objects. In English, and probably in most languages, body part terms are a rich source of metaphor. We speak of the *foot* of a mountain, the *arms* and *legs* of a chair, the *eye* of a needle or a potato, the *mouth* of a cave or a river, a *neck* of land, and the *back* of almost anything. An angled pipe is called an *elbow.* We get a *toe* hold, we *back* off. Children can be *cheeky,* and adults can display *spleen,* but they can also be *hearty.* Things can get *hairy.* Other languages have their own body part metaphors, often quite different from ours. In some languages, a person who is immodest or who speaks out too freely is described as *having no eyelids.*

It is clear that not even a domain as concrete and universal as the human body is treated uniformly by all languages. More abstract areas of the lexicon, and areas that refer to more culturally variable phenomena, can be considerably more varied.

VERBS OF PERCEPTION

Just as all human beings share the same kind of body, so they share the same kind of sensory apparatus, and whatever language people speak, they need to be able to refer to the five senses of sight, hearing, touch, taste, and smell. For the sense of sight, English has three important verbs: *look at, see,* and *look.* *Look at* is used for a viewer who acts deliberately, while *see* refers to a more passive experience. We cannot *look at* something unintentionally, but we can *see* something quite by accident. *Look* describes a quality of an object, rather than an activity or experience of an observer. Objects may *look* ugly or beautiful. Thus when we *see* (notice) how fine something *looks* (appears), we may decide to *look at* (examine) it more closely.

For the sense of hearing, we have three words that parallel our three words for sight: *listen to, hear,* and *sound.* Thus, when we *hear,* how beautiful a bell *sounds* we may decide to *listen to* it more carefully. For the senses of touch, taste, and smell we are content with just one word each, whether we refer to an activity, to an experience, or to a quality. Thus when I *feel* (notice) how nice the velvet *feels,* I may decide to *feel* (examine) it some more. When I *taste* (notice) that soup *tastes* both hot and sour, I may decide to *taste* (test, examine) it more carefully. When I *smell* (notice) something in the refrigerator that *smells* rotten, I *smell* (test by smelling) more carefully so that I can find what it is and throw it away. The finer distinctions made for sight and hearing presumably reflect the greater importance that we attach to these senses. The English verbs of perception are shown in Table 2–1.

All languages provide ways of expressing these meanings, but they are by no means uniform in the way that they apportion these meanings to words. Although Swedish is closely related to English, it organizes its verbs of perception rather differently, as shown in Table 2–2. Like English, Swedish makes a three-way distinction among the verbs of sight and hearing, but it makes finer distinctions than English for touch, taste, and smell. *Känna* can often be translated as 'feel' as in 'I feel (notice) a cold draft,' but for 'feel' in the more active sense, of 'examining the feel of' *känna på* is required. A passive form, *kännas,* is used for describing the quality of how something feels. Swedish differs more strikingly from English in its treatment of taste and smell. *Smaka* and *lukta* describe the quality of how things 'taste' and 'smell,' but the preposition *på* must be added when an activity rather than a quality is referred to. For the experience of tasting and smelling, Swedish has expressions that can be literally translated as 'feel the taste of,' and 'feel the smell of.' Thus the verb *känna* can be used not only for the sense of feel, but for the senses of taste and smell as well, and this means that 'feel' is not always a good translation of *känna.* A word such as 'sense' or 'notice' might seem to express its meaning

Table 2-1
English Verbs of Perception

	Activity	Experience	Quality
Sight	look at	see	look
Hearing	listen to	hear	sound
Touch		feel	
Taste		taste	
Smell		smell	

From Viberg (1984).

more accurately, but English has no single word that covers exactly the same area of meaning as *känna*.

Table 2–3 gives the verbs of perception in Quechua, an Indian language widely spoken in Peru. Sight, probably the most important of our senses, is represented by three verbs in Quechua, just as it is in English and Swedish, but as can be seen in the table, Quechua gets along with just two verbs for each of the other senses. For the senses of hearing, touch, and taste, the activity and the experience are expressed by the same verb, while quality is expressed by a related but distinct verb. For the sense of smell, it is the activity that is kept distinct. Each of these three languages divides the realm of sense perception in a somewhat different way, but it is difficult to see any advantage that one language has over another. Each language gives its speakers the resources needed to express the same meanings.

Table 2-2
Swedish Verbs of Perception

	Activity	Experience	Quality
Sight	titta på	se	se ut
Hearing	lyssna på	höra	låta
Touch	känna på	känna	kännas
Taste	smaka på	känna smaken av	smaka
Smell	lukta på	känna lukten av	lukta

From Viberg (1984).

Table 2–3
Quechua Verbs of Perception

	Activity	Experience	Quality
Sight	qhaway	rikuy	rikukuy
Hearing	uyariy		uyarikuy
Touch	sientey		sientekuy
Taste	llamiy		llamikuy
Smell	muskhiy		q'apay

From Viberg (1984).

VERBS OF MOTION

The ways in which languages describe the movements of objects through space offer a more subtle example of linguistic variation. As English speakers, we are accustomed to verbs of motion that suggest something about the cause of the motion or the manner in which something moves. When we say *hammer in the nail, throw me the ball,* or *blow it off the table,* the verbs *hammer, throw,* and *blow* indicate the cause of the motion. In *float into the cave, slide down the hill, swing on its hinges, squeeze through the crack, bounce it into the room,* and *chop down the tree,* the verbs *float, slide, swing, bounce,* and *chop* all indicate something about the manner of the movement.

Verbs like these seem so natural to English speakers that we may find it hard to imagine any other way of talking, but even a language as much like English as Spanish deals with motion in a quite different way. Most Spanish verbs of motion suggest nothing at all about the cause or the manner of motion, but they indicate, instead, something about its direction or path. Thus to translate 'The bottle floated into the cave,' a Spanish speaker would have to say something like *La botella entró a la cueva flotando,* literally 'The bottle moved-into the cave floating.' The verb in this sentence, *entró,* describes the path of movement. The manner of the movement, if it is expressed at all, can be indicated only by an adverb, *flotando.*

Other Spanish verbs that describe other paths are easily illustrated: *La botella salió de la cueva flotando* 'The bottle floated out of the cave,' literally, 'The bottle moved-out from the cave floating'; *El globo subió por la chimenea flotando* 'The balloon floated up the chimney,' literally, 'The balloon moved-up through the chimney, floating'; *Las dos botellas se juntaron flotando* 'The two bottles floated together,' literally, 'The two bottles moved-together floating.' Cause is also more likely to be indicated by a Spanish adverb than by the verb itself: *Tumbé el árbol a hachazos* 'I chopped the tree down,' literally, 'I felled the tree by axe chops'; *Saqué el corcho de la botella retorciéndolo* 'I twisted the cork from the bottle,' literally, 'I moved-out the cork from the bottle twistingly.'

To indicate the path of motion, English speakers generally use prepositions such as *into* or *out of*. When Spanish speakers want to indicate the manner of motion, they must generally use an adverb. The languages exploit different machinery to accomplish the same ends. Spanish and English are not totally different, however. English does have verbs, such as *enter, rise,* and *fell,* that describe the path of motion, but they are not typical. *I chopped the tree down* certainly comes more naturally to the English tongue than *I felled the tree by axe chops*. The opposite pattern is more natural in Spanish.

If the Spanish treatment of verbs of motion seems a bit strange to English speakers, a third pattern may seem stranger still. Instead of indicating something about manner, cause, or path of motion, some languages use motion verbs to suggest the nature of the moving object. Atsugewi, an Amerindian language of northern California, is such a language. Atsugewi verb roots always have prefixes and suffixes so the following verb roots are written with hyphens:

-lup- 'move like a small shiny spherical object,' (e.g., a round piece of candy, an eyeball, a hailstone).

-t'- 'move like a smallish flat object that can be attached to something,' (e.g., a postage stamp, a clothing patch, a button, a shingle, the sunshade of a cradle).

-caq- 'move like a slimy lumpish object,' (e.g., a toad, a cow dropping).

-swal- 'move like a limp linear object suspended at one end,' (e.g., a shirt on a clothesline, a hanging dead rabbit, a flaccid penis).

-qput- 'move like loose dry dirt.'

-st'aq'- 'move like runny icky material,' (e.g., mud, manure, rotten tomatoes, guts, chewed gum).

Verb roots like these can be preceded by prefixes that indicate the kind of instrument that is causing the motion. Atsugewi has dozens of these including: *ca-* 'by the wind blowing on it'; *cu-* 'by being pushed or poked by a linear object'; *ma-* 'by the action of a foot'; *phu-* 'by the action of the mouth.' Verb roots also take suffixes that can show the path or destination of the motion: *-ic't* 'into a liquid'; *-cis* 'into a fire'; *-ipsnu* 'into an enclosed volume (e.g., a house, oven, crevice, stomach)'; *-mik* 'into someone's face or eye.' Finally, the verb root, along with its instrumental prefix and its path of motion suffix, is preceded by, or even surrounded by, additional affixes that indicate something about the subject of the verb and the tense.

Atsugewi verbs are difficult to illustrate accurately because when all these pieces are combined in actual words, the pieces influence each other's pronunciation in intricate ways. For present purposes, we can illustrate verbs by writing the parts separately, as if they retain their pronunciation. A verb such as the following, then, could be used in a sentence that describes what happens when guts are blown into a creek.

> *'w-   ca-   st'aq'   -ic't-a*
> it   by-wind   move-ickily   into-liquid
> 'It, moves, as icky stuff, by the wind, into a liquid.'

The next verb could describe how the speaker uses a stick to poke guts into a fire.

> *s'w-   cu-   st'aq'   -cis-a.*
> I   by-long object   move-ickily   into-fire
> 'I cause icky stuff to move into a fire with a stick.'

Finally, the following verb could describe the action of spitting a candy ball into someone's face.

> *mw-   phu-   lup   mik-a.*
> you   by-mouth   move-small-spherically   into-face
> 'With your mouth, you move a small spherical object into his face.'

If we are to characterize motion in all its detail, we must be able to express something about the kind of object that moves, the path or direction of the movement, the manner in which it moves, and the cause of its motion. Every language provides its speakers with ways of describing all of these, but the means that are used are varied. Characteristically, English verbs of motion indicate manner or cause; Spanish verbs, the path or direction; and Atsugewi verbs, the type of object that moves. Still, total consistency is hardly to be expected. When we say *he entered the room,* our English verb indicates the path of motion as clearly as any Spanish verb. When we say *it flowed over the edge of the table,* our verb indicates the kind of object that is moving, much as do Atsugewi verbs. Nevertheless, different languages do emphasize different aspects of motion, and even if we find the English pattern most familiar, we should not imagine it to be any more "natural" than the other patterns.

COMPONENTIAL ANALYSIS

Some sets of words fall more easily into orderly arrangements than do body-part terms or verbs of motion. In particular, the organization of pronouns and kinship terms is often clearly revealed by recognizing that each term combines several components of meaning. Consider, for example, the pronouns of Palaung, a language that is spoken in northeastern Burma and that belongs to the Austro-Asiatic family of languages. The Palaung pronoun system differs from ours in two important ways. First, the language has a set of "dual" pronouns. This means that speakers must chose a different pronoun when speaking about two people ('we two,' 'you two,' 'they two') than when speaking about a single person ('I', 'he,' etc.) or when speaking about three or more people. Second,

Palaung pronouns leave no ambiguity about whether or not the hearer is included. English *we* can mean either 'you and I' or 'they and I' so when a listener hears someone say *we,* she has to judge from the context whether or not she is included herself. Palaung pronouns allow no such ambiguity. 'You and I,' 'he or she and I' and 'they and I' are all carefully distinguished from one another. Palaung ignores the gender distinction between *he* and *she* that is forced on speakers of English, but the distinct set of duals and the careful avoidance of ambiguity about the hearer mean that Palaung needs more pronouns than English. These pronouns are given in Table 2–4. 'Thou,' as used in the translations in this table, implies no archaic or religious connotations. It is to be understood as simply meaning 'you, singular.'

The table is arranged in a way that implies that each Palaung pronoun can be clearly defined according to three cross-cutting **components** of meaning: (1) The number of people (singular, dual, plural); (2) whether or not the hearer is included; and (3) whether or not the speaker is included. *Mi,* for instance, means (1) singular; (2) hearer included; and (3) speaker not included, i.e., 'thou.' *Gar* means (1) dual; (2) hearer not included; and (3) speaker not included, i.e., 'they two.' These three components allow the universe of personal reference to be clearly apportioned among eleven pronouns. Notice that there is no "singular" pronoun in the quadrant of the table that includes both speaker and hearer. No pronoun could include them both and still be singular.

Palaung pronouns apportion people quite differently than do English pronouns. Where English speakers are content with the single word *we,* Palaung speakers must choose among no less than four different terms: *ar, e, yar, ye.* The choice among these depends on whether two people or more than two people are included, and on whether or not the hearer is among them. English *you* can correspond to *mi, par,* or *pe,* and English *they* can correspond to either *gar* or *ge.* To anyone who is acquainted only with English pronouns, the Palaung system may seem needlessly intricate, but it is at least as orderly and logical as our own system of pronouns, and speakers of Palaung might find English pronouns to be dangerously ambiguous.

Table 2–4
Palaung Pronouns

	Speaker included		Speaker not included	
Hearer included				
Singular			*mi*	'thou'
Dual	*ar*	'thou and I'	*par*	'he or she, and thou'
Plural	*e*	'thou, I, and he, she or they'	*pe*	'they and thou'
Hearer not included				
Singular	ɔ	'I'	ʌ	'he or she'
Dual	*yar*	'he or she, and I'	*gar*	'they two'
Plural	*ye*	'they and I'	*ge*	'they, three or more'

Languages have so few pronouns that a very simple analysis by components can usually distinguish their meanings. Kinship terminologies invite a similar kind of analysis, and they are complex enough to be more interesting. The meaning of a kinship term, like the meaning of a pronoun, can generally be decomposed in an intuitively natural way by several components of meaning. The meaning of English *father* might be decomposed into something like (1) male; (2) one generation up; and (3) lineal (i.e., related in the direct line as an ancestor or direct descendant). *Uncle* differs from *father* in being a "collateral" rather than a lineal relative (i.e., not a direct ancestor or descendant): *Mother* differs from *father* by sex, and *son* differs by generation. *Mother, father, aunt, uncle, son, daughter, nephew,* and *niece* can all be defined by differing values of the three semantic components of sex, generation, and lineality.

Other kinship terms force us to recognize additional semantic components. *Brother, sister,* and *cousin* are all collateral rather than lineal relatives, just as *uncle* is, since they are neither direct ancestors nor direct descendants. In order to distinguish *brother* and *sister* from *cousin,* we also need to specify the degree of collaterality. We might say that *brothers* and *sisters* have the first degree of collaterality, while *first cousins* have the second degree. More distant cousins have correspondingly higher degrees of collaterality. For *in-laws,* and even for some kinds of *uncles* and *aunts,* we also need to recognize a distinction between *consanguineal* relatives (those related by "blood") and *affinal* relatives (those related by marriage). We can pursue an analysis of this sort until every kinship term is defined by a set of values that lies along a series of components. Thus a *great uncle* would be (1) 'male' (on the component of sex); (2) 'two generations up' (on the component of generation); and (3) 'first degree of collaterality' (on the component of collaterality).

All people have kinship terms, but languages organize them in quite varied ways. Sex and generation seem always to play a role, but other components of meaning are less consistently needed. Some people distinguish *older brother* and *older sister* from *younger brother* and *younger sister,* and some even distinguish *father's older brother* from *father's younger brother.* Such languages can be said to make use of a component of relative age. Some languages distinguish kinsmen according to the sex of a linking relative. Thus they may distinguish *mother's sister* from *father's sister.* For such languages we would have to recognize the sex of the linking relative as a significant component of meaning. On the other hand, some people ignore differences that English speakers carefully recognize. Thus *younger sister* and *younger brother* may be called by the same term, ignoring the component of sex, just as it is ignored for English *cousin.* Other languages fail to distinguish between *grandfather* and *grandfather's brother,* thus ignoring the component of lineality. Some people use the same terms that they use for *brother* and *sister* for some, or all, of their *cousins,* thus ignoring the component of degree of collaterality. Whatever the differences in detail, however, all people are able to apportion their kinsmen into categories that are defined by some sort of genealogical network.

Definitions like these, which cleanly decompose the meanings of a set of terms by means of cross-cutting components, have a satisfying degree of precision. Just as Palaung ɔ can be defined as (1) one person; (2) speaker included; (3) hearer not included, so English *brother* can be defined as (1) own generation; (2) male; (3) first-degree collateral. Such definitions can be used to divide the world of kinsmen into tidy categories just as they can be used to divide the world of personal reference to which pronouns refer. A term can be found for every logically possible position in the system, and we could use definitions like these to help us decide what kinship term or which pronoun to use in a foreign language that we were trying to learn.

It was once hoped that the kind of analysis that has been used so successfully with pronouns and kinship terms would let us decompose the meaning of many other areas of the vocabulary into meaningful elements. A remarkable amount of discussion, for instance, went into a debate about whether or not the meaning of *kill* could be decomposed into *cause to die*. So far, it seems fair to say, the bulk of vocabulary has proved firmly resistant to any such variety of componential analysis, and it has important limitations even when used with pronouns and kin terms.

When we distinguish pronouns or kinship terms by cross-cutting components, we seem to imply sharply defined differences in the meanings of words. The method invites us to draw precise boundaries, to search for the exact conditions that allow a term to be used. But the meanings of words are often more slippery than these distinctions imply, and we violate the way we use language if we insist on too sharp distinctions in meaning. Even within the domain of kinship, the kinds of formal componential definitions suggested here miss something important about the way in which terms are used. For one thing, they miss the connotations of the words, the feeling of *brotherliness* that is implied by *brother* or the tenderness that we expect of a *mother*. They also miss the extended meanings that kinship terms acquire. Although no one would confuse his status with that of genuine kinship, a priest may be addressed as *father,* presumably because he acts in some ways that recall the behavior expected of a biological father. American children sometimes use *aunt* and *uncle* for friends of their parents, even though they lack real ties of kinship. A purely genealogical analysis misses these extended uses, but these meanings are part of the terms' broader sense, and we overlook an important aspect of meaning if we fail to take these extended usages into account.

COLOR TERMS

The boundaries between the meanings of some words are much fuzzier than the boundaries that separate kinship terms or pronouns. Color terms are a good example. Physically, the color spectrum is an unbroken continuum. No physical boundaries divide the range of wave lengths that spans the visible spectrum from red to purple. Languages assign names to parts of this continuum, but different languages name different parts. Since no lumps or narrow places define points on the spectrum in the way that they define points on the human body, we might expect that one segment of the spectral continuum would be as easily named as any other.

We can give people a color chart with patches of color that range from red at one end to purple at the other, and from light at the top to dark at the bottom. We can ask them to draw boundaries that separate the areas named by the various color terms of their language, and obtain a kind of map of the terms. The results of such mapping turn out to be disappointingly unreliable. We are not surprised when people who speak different languages draw their boundaries in different places, but even people who speak the same language are far from consistent. It is even more disturbing to find that the same individual may, on different occasions, draw the boundaries in quite different places. The boundaries between color terms are distressingly unstable.

Instead of asking people to draw boundaries, we can ask them to point to the "truest" or "best" representative of the various color terms, and their responses then become more consistent. The boundary between *red* and *orange* seems uncertain, but the locations of the "best" *red* and the "best" *orange* are more stable, not only for a single individual but also for different speakers of the same language. People may argue about the boundary between *blue* and *green,* but they usually agree quite well on the position of the "best" *green* or the "best" *blue,* or on what can be called the **focus** of the meaning of each term. More surprisingly, even people who speak utterly different languages generally point to quite similar spots on a color chart as being the best representatives of their color terms. Most languages, for instance, have a color term with a focus at the same spot that English speakers point to as the best *red.* Many languages also have terms with the same foci as English *green, yellow,* and *blue.* Whatever the physical facts of the spectral continuum, people seem much more inclined to assign labels to some points along that continuum than to others. The spectrum may have no physical divisions, but observers of the spectrum find some of its points more salient than others, and so easier to name.

If we want to compare the color terms of different languages, we need to decide which words to count as color terms, and which to set aside. Some terms hardly deserve to be considered as "basic," and the following are best excluded: (1) words that name a particular variant of another term (such as *scarlet* or *crimson,* which are kinds of *red*); (2) words that can refer only to a limited range of objects (such as *blond,* which is used only for hair and wood); (3) words that are unknown to a substantial number of the people who speak the language (such as *chartreuse* and *fuchsia*); (4) expressions that name a color by citing an object that has the color (such as *sky blue* or *lemon*). If we eliminate all these nonbasic terms, each language has basic terms for only a small number of points on the color chart. English has just eleven terms that fit this definition as "basic": *black, blue, brown, gray, green, orange, pink, purple, red, yellow, white.*

Languages differ more than might be expected in the number of their basic color terms. Some languages apparently have only two. These seem always to have black and white as their foci, though perhaps 'light' and 'dark' would translate the range of their meanings more accurately. Languages with three terms seem always to add a term for 'red' to those for 'black' and 'white.' This strikes most people as intuitively reasonable because, apart from black and white, people generally regard red as the most salient color. Red would seem to be the color that cries out most insistently to be named. Languages with four color terms add either 'yellow' or 'green' to the first three, and languages with five color terms have both 'yellow' and 'green.' The sixth term to be added is 'blue,' the seventh 'brown,' and a few languages add from one to four additional terms: 'pink,' 'purple,' 'orange,' and 'gray.'

The most surprising thing about this sequence is that it seems to be closely correlated with the level of economic and technical development of the people who speak the languages. Only a few languages, all spoken by people who have very simple technology, are limited to two terms. Only the languages of a few technologically developed people of European and East Asian origin have as many as eleven. Other languages fall between these extremes. The Tiv, a West African tribe with a relatively simple technology, have three terms; the Hanunóo, shifting cultivators of the Philippines, have four; the Eskimo have five; some more developed African groups have six; the Burmese have seven.

The reason for this correlation between color terms and technological development is not entirely clear, but it may be due to nothing more subtle than the advancing technology of colored dyes. Only with dyes can we produce objects that are identical except for their color. The only convenient way to distinguish two pieces of cloth that differ only in their color is to have words for those colors. In a world to which dyes have not yet penetrated, objects differ in many ways other than by color alone. It is hardly necessary to call leaves 'green' or the sky 'blue' since everyone knows their colors. Why should people need a word for 'yellow' if everything in their world that is yellow already has a name that distinguishes it from everything else? Nor does a limited number of basic color terms prevent people from describing and referring to colors, for they can always describe one thing as having the color of something else. Every language gives its speakers a way to say such things as "the color of a daffodil," or "a little darker than the bark of that tree." We must never imagine that the absence of a color term in a language implies the inability of its speakers to perceive, or to talk about, the color.

The organization of color terms has two important implications. First, the range of phenomena to which a word such as *red* can be applied is by no means an undifferentiated field. Some *reds* are *better reds* than others. Among the many kinds of *reds* that we find in the world, we can distinguish one *prototypical red,* an ideal color that is the best of all possible reds. In addition to this ideal red, we are able to recognize a range of similar colors that we are willing to call *red,* or at least *reddish.* These resemble, more or less, the prototypical red, but they are not the best representatives of the color. The boundaries that divide *red* from other named colors are inevitably fuzzy. We are more confident of the focus.

The second implication to draw from the organization of color terms is more subtle. Recognizing the variability by which languages assign meaning to words, some people have argued that it is only language that imposes order on our world. An extreme form of this position even suggests that the world of our perceptions is little more than a kaleidoscopic jumble until language comes along and assigns words to segments of our perceptions. In assigning words, language creates order and even creates the "things" of our world. In the face of what we now know about color terminology, it is difficult to maintain such an extreme "relativistic" view. The physical spectrum may be an unbroken continuum, but the human perceptual apparatus makes some colors particularly easy for us to recognize and to name. Naming is by no means infinitely variable from one language to another, and the world, as we perceive it, has a good deal of organization even without the help of language.

In rejecting an extreme relativistic view of meaning, we do not have to move to the opposite extreme. We might expect an opposite "realistic" view to regard the perceived world as being securely fixed, quite apart from language. The world, in this view, would contain discrete objects that are almost waiting to be named. From this realistic point of view, language would have no role at all in organizing our perceptions, but it would simply assign meanings to preexisting phenomena. Languages, however, are so varied that an extreme realistic view is no more defensible than an extreme relativistic view. Anyone who has studied a foreign language knows that the "things" that are named in another language are often quite different from those named in one's own. Language does help us to bring order to our world, and different languages impose somewhat differing orders. We can only conclude that language varies, but that it varies within limits. Our biological nature gives considerable organization to our perceptions, but language helps to give this organization its final refinements.

PROTOTYPES

Color terms have prototypical meanings, and we find that the meanings of many other words can also be clarified by recognizing prototypicality. Americans can easily describe a prototypical *breakfast*. It is the first meal of the day, and it may consist of eggs, or possibly cereal or waffles, together with toast, orange juice, and, very likely, coffee. Although the prototypical breakfast comes in the morning, we have no trouble understanding a sign on a restaurant wall that says "Breakfast Served at any Time of Day." This can only mean "ignore the typical time for breakfast, but remember its typical foods." On the other hand, if Billy comes home from a friend's house and tells us "Johnny Chang's family eats wonton soup for breakfast," we may share Billy's surprise, but it will not be surprise at the way he has used the word *breakfast*. In understanding Billy, we ignore the typical American breakfast menu, while focusing on its typical hour. The midafternoon restaurant meal and the soup at the Chang home deviate in opposite directions from the prototypical morning eggs, but we easily understand both as extensions from what is prototypical.

In the same way, a prototypical *climb* might describe a small boy clambering up a tree. The boy moves upward, and he exercises his limbs in the rather complex way that comes naturally to small boys. Boys can also climb down from a tree, and mountaineers and mountain goats can climb down from their peaks, so an upward direction is not always implied by *climb*. On the other hand, airplanes can climb up into the clouds, and automobiles, like mountaineers, can climb to the top of a mountain pass, so climbing is sometimes possible without any limbs at all. However, airplanes and automobiles cannot *climb down* again. It seems that for an action to count as *climbing,* it must involve at least one of the two characteristics of prototypical climbing: movement upward, and clambering. If both components are missing, we have moved so far from prototypicality that the word can no longer apply.

Once we start to see prototypes we see them everywhere. Shirts and skirts are more prototypical items of clothing than are shoes, socks, or hats. Earmuffs and aprons are even more marginal. Saws and screwdrivers are better examples of tools than are tape measures, or crowbars. Chairs and tables are prototypical pieces of furniture. Pianos and television sets are more marginal. Pianos, of course, are as much musical instruments as they are furniture, but they are hardly prototypical musical instruments either. Violins and clarinets seem closer to prototypicality.

Strangely, even classes with unambiguous boundaries are still felt to have more and less prototypical members. We know that, by scientific reckoning, there is no such thing as a partial bird. A color may be *sort of red* and a piano may be *sort of furniture,* but there is nothing in the world today that is *sort of a bird*—except that we act as if there were. Some birds strike us as more birdlike than others. For Americans, robins and sparrows are prototypical birds. They are thoroughly birdlike in all respects. Owls and parrots seem a bit less prototypical, and peacocks and ducks even less so. Out on the edges of birdishness are penguins and ostriches, still perfect birds by every biological criterion, but less like birds in our everyday thinking. Perhaps we first learn the word *bird* by associating it with robins and sparrows, and only later learn to extend the meaning to less and less typical birds. Perhaps we never quite outgrow the feeling that we have to stretch the meaning of *bird* if we are to make it apply to a penguin.

The field to which a word refers, then, is not uniform. Words apply better to some things than to others. Words sometimes apply quite literally, but at other times we cheerfully stretch them away from their literal meanings. As they are stretched first one way and then another, words sometimes acquire such a complex network of related meanings that we find it difficult to point to a single prototypical center. Consider, for instance, the English word *over,* which is used with a bewildering range of meanings. *Overeating, all over the ceiling,* and *it's all over between us* have so little in common that we might be tempted to call these three *over*s entirely separate words, with no more in common than a *seal* that swims and a *seal* that closes a letter. Unlike the two unrelated meanings of *seal,* however, the many meanings of *over* are linked by intermediate senses that make it impossible to separate them clearly.

Sometimes, as in *a bird flew over the field, over* combines the idea of motion in a line with a position that is above and separated from a reference area, the reference area in this case being *the field.* In *the bird flew over the wall,* the reference area is reduced to a point. In *Sam walked over the hill,* the reference area has disappeared, and in *Sam jumped over the wall,* the line of motion is no longer a straight line, but some sort of curve. In *he knocked over the chair, the fence fell over,* and *he rolled over,* rotary movement entirely replaces movement in a line. With *New Jersey is over the bridge* and *Sam lives over the hill,* we have lost almost all sense of movement. Perhaps Sam travels *over* the hill now and then, although we cannot know that for certain. New Jersey surely never travels *over* the bridge. By this time *over* has come closer in meaning to *across* than to *above.* Neither a straight line, a high position, nor any motion at all proves to be essential to *over.*

The sense of *overflow* is related to *go over the wall* or *over the edge* but *overflow* often adds an implication of excess. It suggests that it was not intended to flow so far. The sense of excess becomes unambiguous in *overeat, oversleep,* and *overstimulate.* If these imply passing some wall-like boundary they may echo other uses of *over* that suggest movement, but the movement has become entirely metaphorical.

The wires stretched over the field implies much the same position as *the bird flew over the field,* but the idea of movement is lacking. *The painting hangs over the fireplace* retains a reference to location but without the linear sense of either *wires* or *flying birds. The board is over the hole* is related to *the picture hangs over the fireplace,* but it adds the idea of 'covering' or even 'hiding.' *The city clouded over* also implies covering, and perhaps *A pall hangs over the city* does too. *The ice spread over the window* retains the sense of 'covering,' but we lose any sense of 'position above' since most windows are vertical, and the ice is not 'above' the glass. Similarly *she wore a veil over her face* does not imply that the veil is 'higher' than the face.

Windows, faces, holes, and cities may be fully covered or even hidden by ice, veils, boards, and clouds, but if *I walk all over the hill,* I never risk hiding the hill, and I do not have to cover every square centimeter. To say that *there were freckles all over her face* has to mean that some gaps showed through between the freckles. Even when *there are flies all over the ceiling,* we expect bits of the ceiling to show through between the flies. The flies need not be in motion, and they are actually below the ceiling at the same time that they are all over it. We seem to have entirely lost touch with the meaning of *over* with which we began in *the bird flew over the field.*

Many quite separate ideas may be conveyed by *over*: motion in a straight or circular path; location above, sometimes but not always separated from a reference point; excess; partial or complete covering. None of these ideas is essential. All are missing from some of the uses to which *over* is put. Nevertheless, the meanings of all these *over*s are connected by so many intermediate steps that we would find it difficult to draw boundaries that would let us count the number of "different" meanings that *over* can convey.

Over is an extreme example. The meanings of most words are more constrained, but no word is immune to the pulling and stretching that allows us to adapt our language to our needs. Different languages, of course, gather quite different ranges of meanings together to be labeled by a single word. We would be astonished to find a word in another language that had exactly the same range of meanings as English *over*. When we first encounter a foreign language, some of its words can seem to sprawl chaotically over unfamiliar ranges, and learning these ranges is one of the major challenges of second-language acquisition.

METAPHOR

Our ability to stretch the meanings of words, to use old words in new ways, is an essential feature of our language. We need to be able to talk about new things, and we have only our old familiar words with which to do so. If we could not stretch the meanings of words, talking about things that we had never encountered before would be far more difficult. In fact, we stretch meanings all the time, and when we stretch them far enough we call our expressions **metaphors.** We recognize some uses of words to be prototypical, some to be less prototypical but still reasonably literal, and others to be increasingly metaphorical.

No sharp line can be drawn between literal and metaphorical usage. Where does literal use end and metaphorical use begin in human *head*, fish *head*, *head* of cabbage, *head* of a cane, *head* of a pin, *head* start, *head*master, *head*line? Or *catch* in *catch* a ball, *catch* a word or expression, *catch* a cold. If we have always lived in northern climates where oaks or pines are prototypical trees, we may feel that we have to stretch the meaning of *tree* just slightly even to apply it to a palm. We stretch the word further when we use it for a banana "tree" or for bamboo, and perhaps, when we stretch it all the way to *coat tree, family tree,* or to the *tree structures* with which linguists describe the syntactic organization of sentences, we reach the domain of metaphor. We could hardly talk if we could not extend the meanings of words far beyond their central, prototypical use.

A kinship term such as *uncle* refers prototypically to the brother of one's parent and only slightly less literally to the husband of one's aunt. When children use *uncle* and *aunt* for the friends of their parents, the meanings have been stretched somewhat, and when we reach *Uncle Sam* with all its political connotations, we have moved far from the prototypical meaning. Fraternity *brothers* and sorority *sisters,* founding *fathers,* and *daughter* languages are far enough from prototypicality to be called metaphors.

A *brilliant* sound, a *dark* frown, a *heavy* heart, and *screaming* orange paint all extend the meanings of adjectives from their most literal, prototypical domain to other, more metaphorical, domains. Anger *boils*, words *fly*, defense *caves in*, insight is *penetrating*. The line between literal and metaphorical use is not only fuzzy but also shifts with time as metaphors fade and their meanings become conventional. Is the word *fuzzy*, in the previous sentence, a metaphor, or has it been used so often in this way that the abstract sense of "imprecise" has been added to a more literal meaning that describes a texture? When *screaming* is used to describe paint, it must be considered metaphorical, but what about *blunt* when used to describe a person or *dull* when applied to either a person or a color? Perhaps the line between literal and metaphorical use is too fuzzy to allow any clear answer to these questions.

We have whole families of related metaphors. We describe an argument with many of the terms that we use for a physical battle. We *attack* an *opponent's* position, and we *defend* our own. We *barrage* people with questions, and try to *shoot down* their arguments. We describe someone's position as *indefensible* but admit that another's criticisms were *right on target*. We try to *win*, but we sometimes *lose*. Or consider all of the ways in which the expression *time is money* is echoed in the manner in which we talk about time. We can *waste* or *save* time, just as we can *waste* or *save* money. We can even *lose* time, *budget* time, *run out* of time, *invest* time, or *spend* our time *profitably*.

Metaphors like these are everyday expressions, and they even seem to reveal ways of thinking that are part of our culture. We do not yet know the extent to which other cultures express similar ideas through their metaphors. Some metaphors are certainly widespread. It is common, perhaps universal, for example, to extend spatial terms to temporal concepts. We do this in English when we use *in, around, back, go,* and *come,* in phrases like *in the afternoon, around five o'clock, look back to days gone by, going to scream,* and *coming attractions*. Everyone must deal with time and space, but where cultures differ, we may suspect that their everyday metaphors will also differ. That, however, remains a topic for future research.

Poets search, more or less self-consciously, for particularly striking metaphors, and we sometimes think of metaphor as a somewhat esoteric specialty of certain kinds of literature. We certainly delight in the new metaphors that we discover in fine writing. Such metaphors catch our imagination by pointing to unexpected or unconventional relationships, but metaphor is by no means limited to self-conscious literature. Rather, it is a pervasive feature of everyone's language. Metaphors represent the most extreme way in which speakers and writers can stretch the meanings of words to express new ideas, but they are an essential part of everyone's creative use of language.

OSTENSIVE AND VERBAL DEFINITIONS

We learn the meanings of our words in two quite different ways. A child's earliest words have to be learned without the help of a developed language, and this means that they must be learned within the context of the child's nonlinguistic experiences. From the time of their earliest encounters with language, children seem to be prepared to associate sounds made by the human voice with objects and events in their world. Surely this is one way in which the human mind is endowed with the potential for learning a language. A child's earliest words, such as *mommy, dada, doggie, hot,* and *bye-bye,* all begin to be learned along with the experience of things that can be seen, heard, and touched. Of course it requires more than a single pointing for the meaning of a word to be learned in all its detail. Many points to what is and is not a dog may be needed before a child can use the word as others use it. As more is learned, both about the world and about other related words, explanations can help with the final refinements of even these most basic words.

Nevertheless, the setting within which language is used is essential. It is hard to imagine learning the meaning of *red* without seeing the color and associating it with the sounds of the word. One could hardly grasp the meaning of *heavy* without experiencing what happens to one's muscles when trying to lift something that is called *heavy.* Even as adults, the experience with objects and events contributes to the way we learn some new words. When we see a flower that we had never noticed before and hear someone call it a *blue gentian,* we learn a new word more effectively than we could ever learn it from a dictionary alone. Words that are defined by pointing, by direct experience with the world within which language is used, are said to be defined **ostensively.** We all learn many hundreds of words ostensively, and we could not even begin to learn the words of our first language without experiencing them in a context of sight, sound, and touch.

Once our language has grown sufficiently complex, however, we add to our vocabulary when we hear new words defined by means of words that we already know. We might learn the meaning of *unicorn* with the help of a picture, but we could also learn it with the help of a verbal definition. We are more likely to learn the meaning of *electron, hydrogen, virus, saber-tooth tiger, neutron star, civilization, third cousin, fairy,* and *god* by having them explained with words we already know than by having any direct experience with the objects to which they refer. Once children have learned enough basic words, they add to their vocabulary with endless questions: "What does *incomplete* mean, Daddy?" Adult Americans continue to add to their vocabulary by turning to the verbal definitions of a dictionary.

Perhaps we learn even more words by hearing them used in a verbal context than by either ostensive or verbal definitions. Small children may be given a chance to hear a few new words in isolation from other words (*hot! bye-bye*) but, like the rest of us, they hear most of their new words embedded in sentences and surrounded by other words. Even such common words as *and, but, in,* and *now* are rarely defined explicitly for children, and they are not so easily defined by pointing as are words like *doggie* or *mommy.* They are frequently heard in a context that includes other words, and their meanings can be gradually inferred with the help of both the linguistic and the nonlinguistic context.

As adults, we continue to learn new words in the context of familiar words. If we know enough words, we can often make plausible guesses about the meaning of the few that remain. We may not guess exactly right the first time, but as we hear a word used in a variety of contexts, our sense of its meaning grows more exact until we are finally able to use it ourselves. Without ever before having encountered the word *axon*, a reader would gain a rough idea of its meaning from this passage:

> Growing axons are thought to make their way to specific parts of the rudimentary brain by following a chemical trail whose production is probably determined genetically. After the leading tip of an axon reaches its destination, it elaborates an arbor of branches, each of which has a bulbous terminal (Kalil, 1989, p. 38).

These sentences do not explicitly define *axon*, but by encountering the word in passages like this, its meaning would gradually come into focus. Neither seeing an axon nor hearing an explicit definition would be needed, although both might help. By pointing, by verbal definitions, and by hearing words used in context, each speaker gradually builds up a vocabulary of many thousands of words.

MEANING, CULTURE, AND THOUGHT

All languages give their speakers words by which to talk about kinsmen, sensations, colors, body parts, and the many other phenomena in which people are interested, but the details vary endlessly, and we must ask why languages assign words in such varied ways. Do the differences among languages grow out of the varied cultures in which they are spoken? Do the differences reveal varied ways in which the speakers conceptualize their world? If a single term is used for both 'younger brother' and 'younger sister' does this suggest something important about the culture? Does it suggest that people who speak the language think of these kinsmen as more similar than do people who use distinct words? These questions have been endlessly debated, and while unambiguous answers are still hard to find, the questions are too important and too interesting to be ignored.

The relation of language to culture is easier to deal with than the relation of language to thought, and in gross terms we can hardly doubt that the vocabulary of a language reflects the culture of its speakers. Americans really do have many words for automobiles, and the Hanunóo really do have many words for plants. At a more detailed level, kinship terms surely reflect, in some degree, the kinship practices of the society in which the terms are used. The fact that *aunt* can refer either to the sister of our father or to the sister of our mother, and even to the wives of our uncles, suggests that we expect to have roughly the same sort of relationship with all these women. We have a different term for *mother*, and this reflects the different expectations that we have of a mother. In societies where the various "aunts" are called by different terms, we would expect the different "aunts" to have different roles. In a society where the same term is used for mother and for mother's sister, but where a different term is used for father's sister, we would expect a mother's sister to act, in some respects, more like a mother than like a father's sister.

It is more difficult to see how differences in body part terms, pronoun usage, or verbs of perception reflect cultural differences. What subtle nuance of Swedish culture could explain why Swedes should use an expression that translates literally as "feel the smell of " while English prefers the simple verb *smell*? It is not clear that Palaung culture is better suited than European or American culture to a pronoun system that interpolates duals between singulars and plurals. If a term like "neck of the leg" for ankle has cultural significance, it is by no means obvious. It is worth pursuing such terminological quirks to see whether some kind of cultural significance might be found, but we have to expect a good many of the detailed differences among languages to rest on little more than chance. Meanings can be assigned in many different, but equally efficient, ways; thus, our judgment about the importance of culture for determining vocabulary distinctions must be mixed. In broad terms and in some details, vocabulary surely reflects the culture in which the language is used, but it would be rash to expect cultural significance in every word.

Does the way we use words reveal the way in which we conceptualize our world? Do people who use the same word for their younger brother and younger sister *think* of them as more similar than we do? It seems intuitively obvious that a linguistic distinction would help speakers to conceptualize a difference. Learning the terminology of a new subject seems to help us to think clearly about it. Linguistic distinctions seem to aid our perceptions. Learning the names of wildflowers helps us to recognize them when we see them again. It proves to be very difficult to pin these feelings down, however, or to prove any sort of consistent relationship between language and conceptualization. Certainly the failure to make a consistent linguistic distinction implies neither an inability to recognize the distinction, nor an inability to invent a linguistic distinction when one is needed. People with a single term for *younger brother* and *younger sister* are not ignorant of their differences. We can distinguish among our various aunts when it becomes important to do so. We must never suppose that a failure to maintain a conventional terminological distinction implies a deficiency in perception.

But does the habitual use of a linguistic distinction make it easier to think of the things referred to as distinct? Does the Spanish habit of using verbs of motion that refer to the direction of movement, or the Atsugewi habit of suggesting the type of object that is moving, mean that Spanish and Atsugewi speakers conceive of motion in different ways than English speakers do? It has been difficult to give firm answers to questions like these. Some linguists are deeply skeptical about the cognitive implications of such linguistic differences, and they see no convincing evidence that they are anything more than superficially different ways of talking. On the other hand, fluent bilinguals often maintain that some things are more natural to express in one language than in another, and that the differing availability of words is one factor in the different feeling they have about their languages. It may seem very different to say *I feel the smell of garlic* than to say *I smell garlic*. People have quite varied attitudes about these issues, however, and it has not been easy to find clear evidence that would help to sort them out.

CHAPTER THREE

Morphology

MORPHEMES, FREE AND BOUND

To the people who speak a language, the most important thing about words is their meaning, and some of the ways in which meaning is assigned to words were surveyed in the previous chapter. In addition to looking at meaning, linguists also like to consider what they call the **form** of words. As linguists use the word, "form" includes the patterns by which words are constructed from smaller pieces, and the patterns by which they are joined together into larger phrases and sentences. This chapter will consider the more formal aspects of words, in particular the patterns by which they are built up from smaller parts.

Like the words of most languages, English words are often constructed from shorter meaningful parts: *go-ing, walk-ed, boy-s, mean-ing-ful, un-flap-abil-ity, re-fresh-ing-ly*. The smallest pieces, those that can no longer be divided into even smaller meaningful bits are called **morphemes.** Some words, such as *walk, ankle,* and *Mississippi* are themselves morphemes because they have only one indivisible meaningful part, but many of our words have several morphemes. Languages differ widely both in the number of morphemes that they join to form a single word and in the arrangements by which they are joined. **Morphology** is the study of the way words are built up from smaller parts.

Morphemes that can stand alone as words are called **free** morphemes. Those that must be attached to something else are called **bound** morphemes. In the examples just given, *go, walk, boy, mean, flap,* and *fresh* are free morphemes. *-ing, -ed, -s, -ful, un-, -abil-, -ity, re-* and *-ly* are bound morphemes. These examples, then, are all constructed from one free morpheme together with one or more bound morphemes. The free morphemes around which these words are built can be called **roots,** and the peripheral pieces are **affixes.** Roots in English are generally free morphemes, but this is not true of all languages.

Latin *am-o* 'I love' consists of a root *am-* 'love' and a suffix *-o* 'I', but *am-* is no more capable of standing alone than is *-o*.

In addition to words formed from a root and affixes, English also has a great number of words that are formed from two, or occasionally three or more, roots. We call these **compounds**: *baseball, blackmail, fathead, playmate, baby-sit, off-color*. Affixes can generally be attached to compounds just as they can be attached to single free roots: *baseball-s, blackmail-ing*. English also has a few words that are constructed from two bound morphemes with no free morphemes at all: *Anglophile, astrology*. We also have a few words constructed from one easily interpretable morpheme joined to a piece that has no independent existence at all. The most famous examples are several *-berry* words, including *huckleberry, boysenberry* and *raspberry*. We generally consider *huckle-, boysen-* and *rasp-* to be morphemes, even though they are never found except in these compounds.

An affix that is attached to the beginning of a word is called a **prefix.** One that is attached at the end is a **suffix.** English has fewer prefixes than suffixes, but our stock of prefixes includes *un-, anti-, dis-, non-, counter-, miss-, ex-, mini-, mono-, step-, sub-, semi-,* and *re-*. Anyone can easily collect a much larger sample of suffixes simply by keeping one's ears open or by scanning a few written paragraphs and looking at the ends of words.

A few languages allow affixes to be inserted into the middle of words where they are known as **infixes.** In Bontok, a language of northern Luzon island in the Philippines, for example, *-um-* is infixed to convey a sense of 'becoming.'

fikas	'strong'	fumikas	'he is becoming strong'
kilad	'red'	kumilad	'he is becoming red'
bato	'stone'	bumato	'he is becoming stone'
fusul	'enemy'	fumusul	'he is becoming an enemy'

Some languages also use a process known as **reduplication** in which words, or parts of words, are doubled. In Ilocano, like Bontok spoken in northern Luzon, plurality is shown by doubling the first syllable of a word.

píŋgan	'dish'	piŋpíŋgan	'dishes'
tálon	'field'	taltálon	'fields'
bíag	'life'	bibíag	'lives'
nuáŋ	'carabao'	nunuáŋ	'carabaos'

Morphemes, including both roots and affixes, are the blocks from which words are built. Words, in turn, are the building blocks for the larger structures of language.

WORD CLASSES: PARTS OF SPEECH

Different sets of suffixes can be joined to different kinds of English words, and the suffixes give us a convenient way to classify the words. For example, a large number of English words can be used with the plural suffix -s: *cows, trees, bricks, ideas, complications.* We call these words **nouns.** Another large class of English words can be followed by the past tense suffix -ed, by the progressive suffix -ing, or by the third person singular suffix -s: *walk, walked, walking, walks; try, tried, trying, tries.* We call this second set of words **verbs.** (Remember, the spoken language has priority over the written language, so the vagaries of English spelling, such as the rule that derives *tries* from *try* can be ignored). A third set of English words, called **adjectives,** can take the suffixes -er and -est: *big, bigger, biggest, quick, quicker, quickest.* Each suffix is generally limited to one class of words. Verb suffixes cannot be freely attached to nouns; noun suffixes, to adjectives, or adjective suffixes, to verbs. **Girling, *bigs* and **walkest* are not English words. (The asterisk is used to indicate that these forms are judged to be impossible.) Notice that the distinctions we make among nouns, verbs, and adjectives, are **formal** distinctions based on the forms that the words can assume. They are not based on meaning. We do not have to know what a word means in order to decide whether it is a noun or verb, but we do have to know what affixes it can be used with. English nouns, verbs, and adjectives are built up from different sets of morphemes, so we say that they differ in their morphology.

When we distinguish among classes of words by their suffixes we make a **morphological** distinction. The major classes of words that we identify in this way, such as nouns, verbs, and adjectives, are called **parts of speech.** Sometimes, in order to refine our definitions of the parts of speech, we have to add **syntactic** criteria to the morphological criteria. That is, we must consider not only the patterns by which the words are constructed, but also the patterns by which words are combined into larger phrases and sentences. Consider, for instance, *beautiful* and *complicated.* These cannot be used with the "adjectival" suffixes, -er and -est. **Beautiful-er* and **complicated-est* are quite impossible. This means that, by morphological criteria, *beautiful* and *complicated* are not adjectives. Nevertheless, they act like adjectives in most respects other than their affixes. Like *big* and *quick,* they can be preceded by *very,* and they can be used to modify a noun. *Very complicated machine* and *very big machine* are equally acceptable. The two pairs of words, in fact, are used in nearly the same way, except that where *big* and *quick* can be followed by the suffixes -er and -est, *beautiful* and *complicated* can be preceded by *more* and *most.* Their syntactic patterns, but not their morphology, allows us to include words like *beautiful* and *complicated* in the class of adjectives.

English nouns, verbs, and many adjectives can be distinguished by their suffixes, but some of our most common words, such as *we, my, that, of, all, and, but, the,* and many others, allow no prefixes or suffixes at all. These words fall into several parts of speech of their own but, lacking affixes, these parts of speech can be defined only according to the larger syntactic patterns in which the words are used. In English, these words can be divided among such parts of speech as *pronouns, prepositions, determiners, conjunctions,* and several kinds of *adverbs.* We will return to syntax in later chapters, and in this chapter we will be primarily concerned with what happens inside words.

The distinction we have made among nouns, verbs, and adjectives is, of course, specific to English, and it is by no means self-evident that all languages need equivalent classes. In fact, not all languages do have a formally distinct class of adjectives. All languages, to be sure, have ways of expressing the meanings that are expressed by English adjectives— *hot, black, long, difficult, weird,* etc.—but in some languages these meanings are expressed by words with the same formal characteristics as either nouns or verbs.

In Garo, a language spoken in eastern India and distantly related to Burmese, for example, most words with meanings that correspond to our adjectives and most words with meanings that correspond to our verbs enter exactly the same kinds of constructions. Both can take suffixes that are somewhat like tense endings, and both can be used to modify nouns.

kat-a	'run'	da'l-a	'be big'
kat-ja	'not run'	da'l-ja	'not big'
kat-jok	'has run'	da'l-jok	'got big, grew'
kat-gen	'will run'	da'l-gen	'will be big'
kat-gip-a mande	'person who runs'	da'l-gip-a mande	'big person'

In a language like Garo we find no formal reason to recognize separate classes of adjectives and verbs. Garo has words for actions that correspond in meaning to our verbs, and it has words for qualities that correspond in meaning to our adjectives, so Garo speakers are in no way handicapped in expressing their ideas, but they must express them with different formal machinery. As long as we define parts of speech by the forms of a particular language, we must expect parts of speech to differ from one language to another.

Clearly the parts of speech of each language will have to be defined by criteria that are specific to that language. The particular affixes that join with roots, and the particular phrases into which words enter will necessarily differ from one language to another. It then becomes partly an empirical question and partly a matter of definition whether different languages have parts of speech that are similar enough to warrant the same name. Although some languages lack a formally distinct class of adjectives, it will be argued in Chapter 10 that all languages do have classes of words that are enough like our own parts of speech to deserve the names ''nouns'' and ''verbs.'' Nevertheless, we can decide on which parts of speech we need only by a close investigation of each language, and we have no reason to expect all languages to have exactly the same word classes.

CONTENT WORDS AND FUNCTION WORDS

In addition to the distinctions among parts of speech, linguists find it useful to recognize a different and somewhat more general distinction among words. Words that refer to the objects and ideas that people want to talk about, whether real or imaginary, are called **content** words. These include most nouns, verbs, and (if the language has such things) adjectives, and these words are used to convey the messages that people want to convey. We have other words that are used to organize the content words and to show how they are related to each other. These are called **function** words. Our English determiners (*the, an, this, those,* etc.), conjunctions (*and, but, or,* etc.), and many of our prepositions (*on, at, in, by,* etc.) are function words. They are needed to mark the structure of the sentences, but they refer only indirectly to the things we want to talk about.

The line between content words and function words is not sharp. Pronouns (*I, it, we,* etc.) and some prepositions (*above, between,* etc.) do refer to things that people want to talk about, but they also help to organize other words. Despite the fuzzy boundary, the distinction between content words and function words is an important one. Relatively pure content words such as *boy, rock, run,* and *purple* play a very different role in the language from relatively pure function words such as *the, of, if,* and *or.*

Languages have many more content words than function words, but the individual function words tend to be used more frequently. Only a small proportion of the words listed in a dictionary are function words, but their proportion is much higher in running text or conversation. In any word count, the function words tend to cluster among the words of highest frequency, while all the words of low frequency are content words.

New content words are easily added to the language. Nouns, verbs, and adjectives are said to be **open** classes because new words are readily accepted into them. Whether they are borrowed from another language, constructed from parts already found in the language, or simply made up new, most words added to English enter as nouns, verbs, or adjectives. The classes of function words, by contrast, are relatively **closed.** We cannot add a new pronoun or conjunction to the language as easily as we can add a new noun or verb. Affixes are, in this and in other ways, similar to function words. Affixes also belong to relatively closed classes, they are high in frequency and, like function words, they help to mark out the relationship among the content words. No class of words and no class of affixes, to be sure, is completely closed. In the long course of a language's history, new words do find their way into every class, and new affixes are occasionally formed, but the difference between relatively closed and relatively open classes of words remains clear.

The function words are important to the syntax of the language, and we will consider their use more closely in the chapters that deal with syntax. Here we will be concerned primarily with the content words.

INFLECTION AND DERIVATION

A slippery but still useful distinction can be made between two kinds of affixes known as **inflectional** and **derivational** affixes. The suffixes that we used to define the parts of speech, such as the plural *-s,* the past tense *-ed,* and the comparative -er, are inflectional affixes. Suffixes such as -ment, -ive, -ize are derivational. Intuitively, though loosely, we can think of derivational suffixes as forming new words (boy-hood, invent-ive, dark-en), whereas inflectional suffixes result in new forms of the same words (boy-s, invent-ed, dark-er). Unfortunately this is not an entirely reliable distinction, since it is not always clear how to decide which words are "new."

Inflectional affixes never change the part of speech of the word to which they are attached. Tries, trying, and tried are verbs just as is try; bigger, and biggest, like big, are adjectives; boy and boys are both nouns. Derivational affixes, on the other hand, often change a word's part of speech. Eras-ure is a noun, but it is derived from the verb erase. Black-en is a verb derived from an adjective. Rock-y is an adjective derived from a noun. Not all the suffixes that we want to call derivational change the part of speech, however. King-dom is a noun formed from another noun. Green-ish is an adjective formed from another adjective. Mis-understand is a verb formed from another verb. Since kingdom, greenish, and misunderstand seem to be different words than king, green, and understand, we consider -dom, -ist, and mis- to be derivational affixes, even though they do not change the part of speech.

Inflectional affixes tend to be used in a relatively regular way. They can usually be joined to most, or all, of the words that belong to the correct part of speech. Thus all verbs can take the third person singular suffix or be put into the past tense. Derivational affixes, on the other hand, each tend to be used with fewer words, and they exhibit more irregularities. We can form cannibalism, hooliganism, cubism, racism, careerism, and many other similar words by suffixing nouns with -ism, but we cannot freely attach -ism to every noun in the language. *Dinnerism, *burglarism, *spherism, *colorism, and *jobism seem to be unknown, although we can certainly imagine ways that they might be used. (The * means that these are not really words that occur in the language.)

Like the other criteria, regularity and widespread use do not always reliably distinguish inflection from derivation. Some languages have fearsomely irregular affixes that we want, on other grounds, to call inflectional. Not even in English are inflectional suffixes used with complete regularity. Not all English adjectives can take the adjective suffixes, -er and -est, but still want to call -er and -est inflectional suffixes. We also have at least one derivational suffix that can be used as freely as our inflectional suffixes. The "agentive" suffix -er can be attached to any verb: read, reader; explore, explorer. Since -er changes the part of speech from verb to noun, we want to call it a derivational suffix rather than an inflectional suffix in spite of its free use.

New derivational affixes can be added to the language more easily than can new inflectional affixes. Another way of saying this is that the class of derivational affixes is more open than the class of inflectional affixes. When alcoholic encourages the use of drugoholic, chocolaholic, and coffeeholic, we may be witnessing the emergence of a new derivational suffix. When hamburgers were followed by cheeseburgers, wimpyburgers, onionburgers, and all sorts of other -burgers into our culture and into our language, another derivational suffix seemed to be in the making, but since *burger* has now emerged as an independent word, it can no longer be regarded as simply a bound suffix. New derivational suffixes are not added to English so easily as new nouns, but the class of derivational suffixes is not quite closed, and new derivational suffixes do nothing to upset the equilibrium of the language. The addition of a new inflectional suffix, to join our plural and past tense suffixes, would amount to a far more profound change in the grammar of English.

The two kinds of suffixes have one final difference: derivational suffixes tend to be more closely attached to the root word than are inflectional suffixes. In a primarily suffixing language like English, this means that derivational suffixes come first. In *run-er-s, custom-ize-ing,* and *liquid-ate-ed, -er, -ize,* and *-ate* are derivational suffixes, while *-s, -ing,* and *-ed* are inflectional suffixes. This relative ordering of derivational and inflectional suffixes makes sense if we think of the derivational suffixes as forming new words. Inflectional suffixes can then be added to these new words. We have a few exceptions even here. If *-in-law* in *mother-in-law* is a derivational suffix, those who pluralize the word as *mothers-in-law,* as their school teachers instructed them, are placing an inflectional suffix before a derivational one. The fact that some people say *mother-in-laws,* in defiance of their teachers, suggests that they find it more natural to place the inflectional suffix last. This is a case in which separate words have been losing their former independence, and *in* and *law* are merging into a derivational suffix. As long as *in* and *law* were separate words it was natural to say *mothers,* but as *mother-in-law* comes to seem more and more like a single word, speakers grow less comfortable with the increasingly archaic order of the morphemes. Teachers may be waging a losing battle against the natural pressures of the language to place the inflectional suffix last.

Table 3–1 gives examples that show how a few English derivational suffixes shift words among the major parts of speech. Notice that some of the derivational suffixes can be used in more ways than one, and at least one suffix (*-ing*) appears in some situations as an inflectional suffix (*I am go-ing*) and in other situations as a derivational suffix (*their com-ing-s and go-ing-s*). A bit of experimentation will demonstrate that some of these derivational suffixes can be used much more freely than others. Verbs are less easily derived in English than adjectives, and our language is especially rich in noun derivation.

English is generally credited with exactly eight inflectional suffixes: the plural *-s* and the possessive *-'s* are used with nouns; *-er* and *-est* with adjectives; and third person singular *-s,* progressive *-ing,* past *-ed,* and the perfect suffix *-en* (as in bitten, ridden, forbidden) with verbs. Like many languages, English has far more derivational affixes than inflectional affixes, but the individual inflectional affixes are more common. We sometimes manage to use several derivational affixes in the same word, as in *form-al-ize-ation, social-ist-ic-al-ly,* and *un-help-ful-ness.* Some languages also allow a single word to take several inflectional affixes, but one is all that an English word can manage.

Table 3–1
English Derivational Affixes

	From	Noun	Adjective	Verb
To				
Noun		steward-ess	dark-ness	flirt-ation
		king-dom	free-dom	run-ner
		man-hood	warm-th	depart-ure
		step-mother	social-ist	arriv-al
Adjective		derivation-al	red-ish	destruct-able
		fault-less	good-ly	count-less
		wood-en	un-helpful	mourn-ful
Verb		winter-ize	black-en	un-fold
		class-ify		re-think

PRODUCTIVITY

A construction that speakers can use freely to produce new forms is said to be **productive.** The plural morpheme can be productively suffixed to English nouns, and the past tense morpheme can be productively suffixed to verbs. Most inflectional suffixes are highly productive, although the adjective suffixes *-er* and *-est* cannot be suffixed to adjectives such as *complicated,* so they are less productive than the others. The agentive *-er* is highly productive. The suffix *-ment* was productive at one time but is no longer. Its period of productivity left us with a large number of nouns derived from verbs (*arrangement, discernment, development, alignment*), but we can no longer use it to form new words. *Advancement* and *containment* are fine, but **retreatment* and **includement* are not. Similarly, the *-th* of *warmth, depth,* and *length* is no longer productive, so we cannot form new words such as **coolth, *tallth,* or **bigth.*

Like so many other distinctions we have made, productivity is a matter of degree. Even the least productive suffixes must, at one time, have been sufficiently productive to be used to form new words. For better or worse, *-ize* is considerably more productive today than *-ment,* but it is by no means as productive as the agentive *-er.* Everyone is probably willing to *pulverize, modernize,* and *fertilize,* and these days it is difficult not to *computerize, winterize,* and *Americanize.* Many people resist *containerize* and *finalize* and even more would be repelled by *bottlize, garmentize,* or *paperize,* but it would be rash to deny their possibility. Transitive verbs (see Chapter 10) can be productively suffixed with *-able,* as in *breakable, advertizable, mountable, programmable,* etc., but intransitive verbs cannot: **sleepable, *weepable, *dieable.*

The derivational suffix *-ful* is also semiproductive. We can add *-ful* to any word for a container in order to indicate the amount held in the container. If a new word *glorg* 'a container for liquid nitrogen' came into English, no one would hesitate about *glorgful*. *-ful* is not so productive that it can be easily added to every English noun, however. *Tableful, wallful,* and perhaps even *floorful* seem possible, but **ideaful* and **speedful* are, at best, dubious. A *draftee* is one who is drafted, and we would understand someone who talked about a *hugee* or a *kissee*. An *escapee* is one who escapes, but we might resist *sleepee* as one who sleeps or *eatee* as one who eats. *-ee*, like *-ize*, is partially, but not fully, productive.

As these examples suggest, new words can be coined, but not all coinages are equally acceptable. A few catch on and become a part of the language, but even highly productive constructions can be blocked in various ways. Productive though the agentive *-er* may be, we may be reluctant to use *stealer* in the sense of 'one who steals' because *thief* is already available. We can add *-ness* to many adjectives to form abstract nouns such as *dampness, firmness,* and *redness*. If we are reluctant to accept **longness* or **hotness*, it is probably because of the availability of *length* and *heat*.

There is a necessary relationship between productivity and the transparency of meaning. If a speaker can freely produce a new word or a new form of a word, others must be able to understand its meaning the first time they hear it. Pluralization is highly productive in English, and no one finds it difficult to understands a new plural when a new noun enters the language. Anyone who knows the meaning of *quark, diskette,* and *nucleotide* finds the meaning of *quarks, diskettes,* and *nucleotides* transparent. Less productive constructions may have less consistent meanings, so that the meanings of derived words are often less transparent than are the meanings of inflected words. Precisely the same process seems to be used to derive *tasty* from *taste* as is used to derive *smelly* from *smell,* but we cannot know that *tasty* tastes good but that *smelly* smells bad, except by learning these words individually. An *achievement* is something that is *achieved* and an *assignment* is something that is *assigned,* but a *containment* is not something that is *contained*. We can imagine an English dialect in which people would talk about the *containment that is in that box,* and the fact that we do not use the word this way is simply an accident of our English. We have to learn the meaning of these derived words individually. The unproductivity of *-ment* allows it to confer quite different meanings on different words. Thus unproductive constructions frequently have quite idiosyncratic meanings, and speakers of a language simply have to learn each one of them.

MORPHOPHONEMICS

Until now we have made the implicit assumption that each morpheme always retains a single stable pronunciation. For many morphemes, this is a reasonable first approximation. *Black, walk, -er, -est* and a great many other English morphemes are very stable. Other morphemes, however, undergo substantial changes. For reasons that will become clear later, the processes by which morphemes change their pronunciation are known by the jawbreaking term **morphophonemics.** A detailed study of morphophonemics requires a more extensive understanding of phonology than can be assumed now, but we need to consider some of the ways in which morphemes vary in their pronunciations.

Consider, first, the English plural -s. As the words in Table 3–2 demonstrate, this suffix has three distinct pronunciations. The plurals of the first column are pronounced with the /s/ of *sew,* while those of the second column have the sound of /z/ in *zoo.* The plurals of the third column are pronounced with a vowel followed by a /z/. Linguists call vowels that are pronounced like this one "schwa" and they write the vowel as /ə/. We can, therefore, write the three alternative pronunciations of the plural as /-s/, /-z/, and /-əz/. The slanting brackets indicate that the letters inside represent pronunciations, not spellings; traditional spellings will be shown by italics.

English speakers are not free to select any form of the plural that they happen to fancy, but must make their choice according to the final sound of the word to which it is attached. Words that end in "voiceless" consonants (see Chapter 5), including /p, t, k/, and some others, require /-s/ as their plural. Words that end in vowels or in "voiced" consonants, including /b, d, g, r/, and some others, require /-z/. Words ending in /s/, the *ch* sound of *church,* and a few other consonants require /-əz/.

These three forms of the English plural are all considered "regular" because the choice among them is automatic, based entirely on the pronunciation of the word to which it is attached. The choice is so automatic that many speakers are not even aware that they pronounce their plurals in different ways, and yet no native speaker can be in doubt about the proper plural of a new word. The plurals of *glorg* and *druss* would certainly have to be *glorg*/-z/ and *druss*/-əz/.

The three forms of the plural suffix differ in pronunciation but, in an abstract sense, they are all varieties of the "same" suffix. The individual forms /-s/, /-z/, and /-əz/ are said to constitute three **allomorphs** of the plural **morpheme,** and allomorphs are written between slanting brackets: "/ /". It will sometimes help clarity to write more abstract representations of morphemes between curly braces: "{}". Thus the allomorphs of the plural morpheme will be written

Table 3–2
English Plurals

/-s/	/-z/	/-əz/
cats	dogs	finches
trucks	cars	busses
boots	shoes	laces
pats	hugs	kisses
oaks	pines	larches

as /-z/, /-s/, and /-əz/, but {-z} can be used for the morpheme without regard to its specific pronunciations. Each allomorph has its own pronunciation, but a morpheme, as such, has no single pronunciation of its own. It can be pronounced only by means of one or another of its allomorphs. For morphemes with stable pronunciations, like {black} or {-er} , we sometimes speak loosely as if the morpheme itself has a certain pronunciation, but even for morphemes that have only one allomorph, (that is, those always pronounced the same way), it is more accurate to say that it is the allomorph that is actually pronounced.

Presenting patterns like these as formal rules can serve as a check on the accuracy of our understanding. Starting with the morpheme {-z}, three rules will describe the conditions under which each of the three allomorphs is used.

$$\{-z\} \rightarrow /\text{-əz}/ \Big/ \{ \text{ /s, z, č, ǰ, ʃ, ʒ/} \} \underline{\qquad}$$
$$\{-z\} \rightarrow /\text{-s}/ \Big/ \text{ [voiceless] } \underline{\qquad}$$
$$\{-z\} \rightarrow /\text{-z}/ \Big/ \text{ [elsewhere] } \underline{\qquad}$$

The first of these formulas should be read as meaning "The morpheme {-z} is pronounced with the allomorph /-əz/ in the context where it follows /s, z, č, ǰ, ʃ/, or /ʒ/. The arrow means "becomes" or, in this case "is pronounced as"; the large slant line means "in the context of"; and the dash shows the position of the sound that is being changed. The large curly braces indicate that any one of the speech sounds (phonemes) given inside calls for the allomorph /-əz/. As will be explained in Chapter 5, /č, ǰ, ʃ/, and /ʒ/ stand, respectively, for the final sounds of *hatch, bridge,* and *rash,* and for the middle consonant of *measure.* The second formula says that the plural morpheme will be pronounced /-s/ when it follows a voiceless speech sound. The third simply says that it will be pronounced /-z/ everywhere else. Notice that these rules must apply in the order given. The second rule should apply only to those voiceless consonants that are not included in the first rule. If the second rule applies too soon it will incorrectly allow such plurals as *bus/-s/, *match/-s/. If the third rule applies before the others, it will produce plurals like *bus/-z/ and *cat/-z/. In many other cases, also, rules have to apply in a particular order so as to yield the right results.

The plurals of the overwhelming majority of English nouns are formed with one of these three regular allomorphs of {-z}, but we have a handful of nouns that are irregular: *ox, oxen; man, men; foot, feet.* It is possible to describe the *-en* of *oxen* as an additional allomorph of the plural suffix that happens to be used only in *oxen* and, with some extra complications, in *children* and *brethren,* but it is difficult to identify a segment of *men* or *feet* that represents the plural morpheme. Somehow the plurals are so thoroughly dissolved in the roots of these words that the parts can no longer be separated. We will do best to avoid worrying about which part of *feet* represents the pedal extremity and which part represents the plural, and simply describe the situation by saying that the combination of the root *foot* and the plural suffix {-z} results in *feet*:

foot + {-z} → *feet*

A few English words lack any distinctive plural form at all, but since the overwhelming majority of English nouns do have distinctive plurals, we do not want to deny a plural to the few that lack them. *Sheep* needs a plural as badly as *goat*. We need only point out that the plural of *sheep* has the same form as the singular:

sheep + {-z} → *sheep*

We now have rules that let us describe English plural formation, but we have had to base the choice among plurals on two quite different factors. In a full description of the plurals we would first set aside the limited number of irregular nouns, and specify the plural for each. These plurals can be said to be **morphologically conditioned** because, in order to know which form of the plural to use, we need to know what particular morpheme is being pluralized. Once the irregular words are taken care of, the choice among the remaining "regular" plurals depends on the phonology. For these regular words, all we need to know in order to choose the right plural is its final sound. Since it depends on the sound, the choice among the regular allomorphs is said to be **phonologically conditioned.**

Selection among the forms of English verb suffixes follows principles similar to those of selection among plural forms, but several verb suffixes are very irregular. The progressive suffix *-ing* does not vary and can be added to all verbs: *laugh-ing, go-ing, com-ing.* The third person singular suffix *-s* has three regular allomorphs that are selected by exactly the same rule as the three allomorphs of the plural suffix: *catch*/-əz/, *walk*/-s/, *row*/-z/. The past tense and the perfect tense are much less regular. A few examples are given in Table 3–3.

Just as some nouns have "regular" plurals, some verbs have "regular" past and perfect suffixes. As with the plurals, the selection among the regular verb suffixes depends only on the pronunciation of the final sound of the root. The first six examples in Table 3–3 illustrate the three regular allomorphs of the past tense morpheme and, for regular verbs like these, the past and perfect forms are identical. English has far more irregular verbs than it has irregular nouns, however, and a small selection of these are also listed in the table. For many irregular verbs the past and perfect forms are different, and we can deal with this complexity only by saying that the past tense and the perfect tense are formed by different suffixes. Both past and perfect verb forms are very diverse, but {-d} can stand for the past tense suffix. The perfect suffix can be written as {-en}, reflecting its pronunciation in words like *bitten,* but it is often pronounced /-əd/, /-t/, or /-d/. The perfect suffix must be kept distinct from the past {-d}, and {-en} suggests its most common distinctive pronunciation.

Table 3–3
English Past and Perfect Forms

Present	Past	Perfect
walk	walked (walk/-t/)	have walked
stop	stopped (stop/-t/)	have stopped
beg	begged (beg/-d/)	have begged
cry	cried (cry/-d/)	have cried
glide	glided (glid/-ed/)	have glided
chat	chatted (chat/-ed/)	have chatted
fly	flew	have flown
bring	brought	have brought
see	saw	have seen
bite	bit	have bitten
ride	rode	have ridden
go	went	have gone

Various irregular pasts and perfects can be described as follows:

get + {-d} → got   get + {-en} → gotten
forget + {-d} → forgot   forget + {-en} → forgotten
see + {-d} → saw   see + {-en} → seen
write + {-d} → wrote   write + {-en} → written
bring + {-d} → brought   bring + {-en} → brought
go + {-d} → went   go + {-en} → gone
hit + {-d} → hit   hit + {-en} → hit

English has dozens of irregular verbs, and anyone who wants to speak the language must simply learn them. In the same way, a full description of the language would require every irregular form of every verb to be listed. Once all these irregular verbs are taken care of, the regular past and perfect forms can be described more efficiently. The pronunciation of each regular allomorph must be described along with the conditions under which each occurs. This can be easily done by means of the same kinds of formulas already used for describing plurals, but this time the same rules can apply both to the past {-d} and to the perfect {-en}.

$$\{\{\text{-d}\}, \{\text{-en}\}\} \rightarrow /\text{-əd}/ \; \big/ \; \{/t, d/\} \underline{\quad}$$
$$\{\{\text{-d}\}, \{\text{-en}\}\} \rightarrow /\text{-t}/ \; \big/ \; \begin{bmatrix} \text{voiceless} \\ \text{consonant} \end{bmatrix} \underline{\quad}$$
$$\{\{\text{-d}\}, \{\text{-en}\}\} \rightarrow /\text{-d}/ \; \big/ \; [\text{elsewhere}] \underline{\quad}$$

The first of these rules accounts for words such as *plotted, saluted, flirted, loaded,* and *flooded*; the second, for *walked, sipped, hatched, chased, pushed,* and *laughed*; the third, for *loved, robbed, buzzed, judged, loaned, longed, sawed,* and *paid*.

Just as some suffixes change according to their surroundings, so do some root words. Many English words change their vowels or final consonants when followed by certain derivational suffixes: *decide, decision; flame, inflammable; concede, concession.* For some speakers, some consonants change when a plural is added: *house, houses; leaf, leaves; loaf, loaves.* (Again: it is pronunciation, not spelling, that matters.) The location of the accents, or as linguists say, "stress" may depend on the suffix. Wherever stress originally falls, suffixes such as -seque and -ette attract the stress themselves: *picturésque, statuésque, majorétte, luncheonétte.* Suffixes such as -ity shift the stress to the last syllable before the suffix: *majórity, absúrdity, placídity, destrúctibility.* Finally, suffixes such as -able leave the stress unchanged: *pícturable, destrúctable, undecídable, fáshionable, ánswerable.*

In simple cases it seems natural to identify each morpheme with both a distinctive meaning and with a reasonably stable sequence of sounds. *Dis-like-s* has three morphemes that follow each other in simple sequence, each with both a distinct meaning and a distinct pronunciation. In other cases, as with *feet* and *flew,* the constituent morphemes seem to dissolve into each other. A word like English *went* shows that even more dramatic changes are possible. *Went* shows no phonological resemblance whatsoever either to *go* or to any other past tense form, but we still want to say that *went* is the past of *go.* It seems reasonable to say that *went* results from some sort of fusion of *go* and {-d}. In cases like these, it no longer seems useful to think of morphemes as being represented in any simple way with an identifiable sequence of sounds. In simple cases we can identify stable sequences of speech sounds with specific meanings, but our analytical techniques need to be flexible enough to take account of words like *went,* in which the relationship of sound and meaning is more complex.

The rules that describe how plurals and verb tenses are expressed in English are examples of a broad class of morphophonemic rules that begin with morphemes and describe how these morphemes are pronounced under various conditions. In many languages the morphophonemic rules are complex and idiosyncratic. Children continue to make morphophonemic errors, such as regularizing past tenses, until they are about 5 years old, and morphophonemic complexities contribute greatly to the burden of second-language learners. Too many foreign language classes spend a large and dreary proportion of their time drilling students in the language's morphophonemic irregularities. We might do better to remember that children, whom we sometimes imagine to be such masterful language learners, need 5 long years of nearly full-time immersion in their language before they master its morphophonemics. We deceive ourselves if we expect an adult to learn as much in one or two years of part-time study.

Since we like to suppose that linguistic complexity is limited only by the nature of the human mind, and that the average mind of one population is pretty much the same as the average mind of another, we might expect all languages to exhibit more or less the same amount of morphophonemic complexity. Rather surprisingly, they do not. As an example of just how different

Table 3–4
Chinese Numbers

1 yī	11 shí-yī	23 èr-shí-sān
2 èr	12 shí-èr	etc.
3 sān	13 shí-sān	30 sān-shí
4 sì	14 shí-sì	31 sān-shí-yī
5 wǔ	15 shí-wǔ	etc.
6 liù	etc.	40 sì-shí
7 qī	19 shíjiǔ	etc.
8 bā	20 èr-shí	98 jiǔ-shí-bā
9 jiǔ	21 èr-shí-yī	99 jiǔ-shí-jiǔ
10 shí	22 èr-shí-èr	100 bǎi

languages can be, consider the numerals from one to 100 in Mandarin Chinese, the most important language of China, and in Hindi, the most widespread language of India. These are shown in Tables 3–4 and 3–5.

Chinese has distinct words for the numbers from 1 to 10, and combinations of these 10 words are used with no modification at all to form the numerals all the way up to 100. The numerals are constructed with such utter regularity that readers can easily derive most of them by analogy with those given in the table. Hindi, by contrast, is riddled with irregularities. It is generally possible to perceive that each Hindi numeral is composed of two parts, the first standing for the digit and second for the multiples of ten, but both parts are idiosyncratically variable. Knowing every number from 1 to 98 would still not be enough to predict the word for 99. English and other familiar European languages lie between these extremes. English shows Hindi-like irregularity through the teens, but for the higher numbers, it settles gradually into a more Chinese-like regularity.

We have no explanation for the greater morphophonemic complexity of some languages. It might be supposed that the simplicity of Chinese numbers would be balanced by morphophonemic complexity in some other corner of the language, and that Hindi numerical complexity might be offset by morphophonemic simplicity somewhere else, but this is not the case. Chinese morphophonemics is more regular throughout. This is not to say that Chinese does not have other sorts of complexities, and perhaps these balance, in some way, its morphophonemic regularity. Chinese does not, after all, have the reputation of being an ''easy'' language. In spite of the striking morphophonemic differences among languages, we have no general measures of complexity and no firm basis for claiming that, overall, one language is more complex than another. We will return to morphophonemic rules in the chapters that deal with syntax.

WHAT IS A WORD?

Throughout this chapter, we have been working with the unstated assumption that we know what words are. Is this fair? Do we always know where one word

Table 3–5
Hindi Numbers

1 ĕk	21 ikkīs	41 iktālīs	61 iksaṭh	81 ikkāsī
2 dō	22 bāīs	42 bayālīs	62 bāsaṭh	82 bayāsī
3 tīn	23 teīs	43 tĕtālīs	63 trēsaṭh	83 tirāsī
4 cār	24 caubīs	44 cauvālīs	64 caūsaṭh	84 caurāsī
5 pãc	25 paccīs	45 paītālīs	65 paīsaṭh	85 pacāsī
6 che	26 chabbīs	46 chiyālīs	66 chiyāsaṭh	86 chiyāsī
7 sāt	27 sattāis	47 saītālīs	67 sarsaṭh	87 sattāsī
8 āṭh	28 aṭṭāis	48 aṛtālīs	68 aṛsaṭh	88 aṭṭāsī
9 nau	29 untīs	49 uncās	69 unhattar	89 navāsī
10 das	30 tīs	50 pacās	70 sattar	90 navvē
11 gyārā	31 iktīs	51 ikyāvan	71 ik-hattar	91 ikkānvē
12 bārā	32 battīs	52 bāvan	72 bahattar	92 bānvē
13 tera	33 tĕtīs	53 trēpan	73 tihattar	93 tirānvē
14 caudā	34 caūtīs	54 cauvan	74 cauhattar	94 caurānvē
15 pandrā	35 paītīs	55 pacpan	75 pac-hattar	95 paccānvē
16 sōlā	36 chattīs	56 chappan	76 chihattar	96 chiyānvē
17 satrā	37 saītīs	57 sattāvan	77 satattar	97 sattānvē
18 aṭṭārā	38 aṛtīs	58 aṭṭāvan	78 aṭh-hattar	98 aṭṭhānvē
19 unnīs	39 untālīs	59 unsaṭh	79 unāsī	99 ninnānvē
20 bīs	40 cālīs	60 sāṭh	80 assī	100 sau

ends and the next begins? Can we define "word" in a way that will allow us to compare words in different languages? The answers to these questions turn out to be far from clear, and it is surprisingly difficult to define "word" in a consistent way. The words we recognize in one language do not always seem to be the same sorts of objects as the words we find somewhere else. It is hardly enough, for instance, to define a word as a stretch of language with a characteristic meaning, since morphemes that are smaller than words, as well as phrases that are larger, surely have characteristic meanings. Words are neither the smallest nor the largest bits of language with meaning.

Are words the smallest units of a language that can be used alone? This comes closer to what we are looking for, since it safely removes suffixes such as *-ous, -ment*, or the plural *-s* from the category of words. Unfortunately, some other bits of language that we might very well like to call words are in danger of being excluded along with suffixes. We write *the* and *a* as separate words, but it is hardly more natural to pronounce *the* alone than to pronounce *-ous* alone. The ability to stand by itself is not quite enough to define a word.

Is a word a unit that cannot be interrupted by other words inserted into its middle? We might consider *the house* to consist of two separate words because we can insert so many other words between its parts: *the big house, the ghastly big ugly house,* etc. Unfortunately this is not quite satisfactory either, for by this definition we risk labeling some things as words that we would prefer to call suffixes. *The Queen of England's horse* does not belong to *England* but to the *Queen*. We have no hesitation about inserting *of England* into *The Queen's horse*. Do we, then, have to call the possessive *-'s* a word?

So difficult is it to give a fully consistent definition of "word" that linguists have occasionally doubted that it is a real unit of language. Even more desperately, someone once suggested that a word is simply whatever is conventionally written with white spaces before and after, forgetting, perhaps, that some languages have been written with no separation between the words at all. Any resort to the white spaces of paper relegates words entirely to the written language, and this definition cannot be taken seriously.

In spite of all these problems, the marginal cases are, in fact, relatively few. Most often, the units that we can pronounce alone are also the units that resist the insertion of additional words, and these units come reasonably close to what we want to call a word. The best rule of thumb may also be the simplest. We can pause between words much more easily than we can pause within a word. We might say *What uh- are the uh- carpenters uh- doing?*, but we would be unlikely to say *What are the car uh- penters do uh- ing?* Any place where we can easily pause can be considered a word boundary.

Perhaps, moreover, we should not expect to find a single definition of "word" that works for all languages and under all circumstances. Languages change in the course of the centuries, and we know that independent words sometimes become glued together. Most prefixes and suffixes probably began as independent words. English contractions, such as *can't, didn't, I'll, would've, we'd, they'd've,* may show the first stage of the squeezing of two, or even three, words into one. It can take centuries for words to lose their independence completely, and throughout these centuries, we should expect to find bits that no longer act like fully independent words but that have not yet been quite reduced to mere affixes. This means that we should not expect that the units of a language will always be clearly classifiable as either free or bound morphemes. At any point in history, a few are likely to be marginal.

The number of marginal cases is small enough that in most, perhaps all, languages it seems to be useful to recognize a unit that can include more than a single morpheme, but less than a sentence, and such units can be called words. These are generally units that speakers find easy to pronounce by themselves, without the support of other words before or after, and they are the units within which pauses are difficult or impossible. We generally find that the grammatical processes that take place within these "words" are quite different from the grammatical processes that join them together into larger phrases. The order of morphemes within a word is generally quite rigid; the order of words within a sentence often has more freedom. Some aspects of pronunciation also lead us to recognize words. In many languages each word carries one primary stress. In some languages, stress always comes at the beginning of the word, while in others it is always at the end and, in such cases, word boundaries are clearly marked. Where vowel harmony is found, it is typically limited to the vowels of a single word (see Chapter 6). It is the fact that we have to recognize that the patterns of both grammar and pronunciation within words are often quite different from the patterns of larger stretches of language that constitutes the final justification for recognizing the word as a significant linguistic unit. This is also the justification for the distinction we make between **morphology,** the study of the way words are constructed, and **syntax,** the study of the way words are joined to others.

Even if we can find units in all languages that we can reasonably call words, this does not mean that words everywhere are exactly the same kind of unit. Vietnamese words are very short, rarely more than one morpheme long, so it hardly seems necessary to make a distinction between morphemes and words. At the other extreme, some languages squeeze far more into a single word than does English. Eskimo is famous for its giant words. The single Eskimo word *iqalussuarniariartuqqusaagaluaqaagunnuuq* means 'It is said that we have admittedly got a strict order to go out fishing for sharks.' Clearly, a "word" in Eskimo and a "word" in Vietnamese are not exactly the same thing, and neither is strictly comparable to an English word. Nevertheless, we so regularly find *some* unit that deserves to be recognized as distinctive, that linguists easily use the term "word" for all languages.

COMPOUNDS

Words like *crybaby* and *barnstorm,* which are formed from two or more roots, are called **compounds.** English spelling is far from consistent, and sequences that we have to recognize as compounds may be written as if they are a single word (*fingernail, cardboard, highbrow*), as hyphenated words (*card-carrying, high-rise, blue-collar*), or as two words separated by a space (*finger bowl, high chair, blue book*). The uncertainty that we so often have about when to write compounds as one "word," when to use a hyphen, and when to write two separate "words" suggests that the conventions of our writing do not reflect any real difference in the spoken language. We will ignore the variation of the written language, and treat all of these as compounds.

It is not always easy to distinguish between a compound and a two-word sequence, but many compounds are pronounced like single words. As compounds, *bláckbird* 'a species of bird,' and *hót dog* 'frankfurter' are stressed on the first of their two roots, and this distinguishes them from freely constructed phrases that are stressed on the second root: *black bírd* 'a bird of any species that is colored black,' *hot dóg* 'a dog that is hot.' Stress is not always a reliable criterion for distinguishing compounds, however, for many sequences of morphemes that deserve to be called compounds have stress on the second member: *glass eye, knotty pine, ill will, acid rain, lone wolf.* A better criterion of a compound is the impossibility of inserting additional words between its parts. We cannot insert additional words into *city wall, world war,* or *motor city,* and this encourages us to consider them to be compounds, in spite of their stress, and in spite of our habit of writing them as if they were two words.

The meaning of a compound cannot generally be understood simply from the meanings of its parts. *Ice cream* has a far more specific sense than anything we could understand directly from the meanings of *ice* and *cream*. The same is true of *hardware, jet-propelled, door prize,* and thousands of other English compounds. Compounding is not a fully productive process in English, and we have to learn the meaning of each compound, just as we have to learn the meanings of all our other words. We expect to be able to figure out the meaning of longer phrases and sentences from their constituent words, and from the way in which the words are joined together, but we cannot count on understanding the meaning of compounds the first time we hear them.

Compounds can be formed in a bewildering variety of ways. In English, compound nouns are the most common. *Girlfriend, clothespin, bath towel, fishing rod,* and hundreds of others are formed from two nouns. *Cut-throat, kill-joy, towline,* and *blowtorch* are formed from a verb followed by a noun. *Nosebleed, sunshine,* and *birth control* have a noun followed by a verb. *Hold up, count down,* and *blowout* are nouns formed from a verb and a preposition. *Fast-food, software,* and *fat cat* are formed from an adjective and a noun. Since adjectives generally precede nouns in English, it is not always easy to know when an adjective–noun phrase has become so fixed that it deserves to be called a compound. To the extent that a sequence acquires a specialized meaning not directly derivable from its parts, to the extent that it becomes difficult to insert other words between its halves, and to the extent that it is pronounced as a single word, we have to regard it as a compound rather than as a simple phrase.

Compounding can also form new adjectives. *Childproof, card-carrying,* and *leadfree* include nouns. *Bitter-sweet, deaf-mute, open-ended,* and *ready-made* are formed from two adjectives. Several other types of compound adjectives are illustrated by *overqualified, roll-neck, white-collar, make-believe, quick-change, see-through,* and *over-night*. English verb compounds are not quite so common but *carbon-date, stir-fry, freeze-dry, free-associate, fine-tune, jump-start, panhandle,* and *make-do* can all be used as verbs.

Compounding supplements derivation to allow a language to build up an enormous vocabulary from a somewhat less enormous stock of morphemes, but the line between compounding and less fixed but still conventional expressions is by no means sharp. Every language has vast numbers of phrases that are constructed by entirely normal syntactic rules but that have gained conventionalized meanings that can no longer be fully understood from their parts. *Take it for granted, answer the phone, mow the lawn, express an interest in, unwed mother, natural selection, bread and butter, mitigating circumstances, last resort,* and even *I don't care* fail to meet most of the criteria of single words, so we hardly want to consider them to be compounds, but we have all heard these phrases many times, and the meanings they convey to us come more from the experience of hearing them used together than from our ability to analyze them into their separate parts. Examples can be found that range from freely constructed phrases (*break a window pane*), through conventional expressions (*break a promise*), to fixed compounds (*breakneck*). Finally, as we will see in the next chapter, through the course of time the constituents of a compound may sometimes so completely lose their independence that we may finally forget that they began, long ago, as compounds (*breakfast*).

WORDS IN OTHER LANGUAGES

We can identify words in all languages, but we must not expect words to have the same characteristics everywhere. In fact, the structure of words, the kinds of affixes that they take, and the amount of information that is squeezed into a single word all vary greatly from one language to another.

Garo verbs can take much longer strings of suffixes than we find in English. At a minimum, every Garo verb must have one suffix that is drawn from a class that can be called "tense markers." The most common tense marker is *-a*, and it most often indicates present time. *-jok* is used to convey some of the same meanings that we convey with *have* as in *we have seen, we have gone*. *-gen* indicates the future. *-bo* forms an imperative. Thus *ni-a* means 'look,' *ni-jok* 'have looked,' *ni-gen* 'will look,' and *ni-bo* 'look!'

The complexities begin with a large class of optional suffixes that can be inserted between the verb root and the tense marker. In the following example, the suffixes *-ku-* 'yet,' *-ja-* 'negative,' and *-eng-* 'progressive' (with roughly the same meaning as English *-ing*) come between the verb root and the tense marker.

ni-	*ku-*	*ja-*	*eng-*	*a*
look	yet	not	progressive	present

'is not yet looking'

Still more complex verbs are possible. The verb root *kat-* 'run' can be used with the suffixes already given and with several others as well: *-ba-* 'in this direction, to here,' *-pi'l-* 'back, return,' *-tai-* 'again.'

kat-	*ba-*	*pi'l-*	*tai-*	*ku-*	*ja-*	*eng-*	*a*
run	here	back	again	yet	not	progressive	present

'is not yet running back here again'

Most of these suffixes can be freely attached to any verb root and, although their order is fixed, they can be used in any combination. It is right to wonder whether a sequence as long and complex as *kat-ba-pi'l-tai-ku-ja-eng-a,* with its eight easily recognizable morphemes, should even be counted as a single "word." The two obligatory constituents, the verb root and the tense suffix, come first and last, however, and it is difficult to find any reasonable spot between them for a word break. Speakers, moreover, pronounce these sequences with an intonation that implies their unity, and they rarely interrupt them with a pause. Since these stretches of morphemes satisfy the requirements that we expect of words, we need not hesitate to call them words, even though it takes several English words to translate them.

These Garo suffixes act like inflections. They are productive and very regular. Some verbs can also be used with additional suffixes that act more like the derivational suffixes of English. These occur directly after the verb root, before all the other suffixes, and they cannot be productively attached to all verb roots. Their meanings are generally more difficult to pin down than those of the later suffixes, and the meaning of the derived verb is not always immediately understandable from the meaning of its parts. The suffix -chak- appears in such words as *dak-chak-a* 'help' from *dak-a* 'do'; *a-gan-chak-a* 'answer' from *a-gan-a* 'talk'; *don-chak-a* 'put or place on something' from *don-a* 'put, place'; *o'n-chak-a* 'give on behalf of another' from *o'n-a* 'give.' Generally, -chak- implies 'doing something for someone else, or to something else' but the meanings of these verbs are not fully predictable from the meanings of their parts. These verbs can, of course, be used with the full battery of inflectional suffixes: *dak-chak-tai-gen* 'will help again.'

Finally, Garo also has a few suffixes that follow the tense suffix. Questions are formed by adding -*ma* to the end of the verb, and -*kon* conveys the sense of 'probably.' *A-gan-chak-jok-ma?* 'Has (he) answered?' *A-gan-chak-ku-ja-eng-a-kon* '(He) is probably not answering yet.'

Words of a very different type from those of either English or Garo are found in Arabic. Many Arabic words are formed from a root consisting of three consonants and a set of vowels that alternate with the root consonants and that act rather like an affix. Consider, for instance, the set of related words that are formed around the consonantal root *k-t-b*. All these words have something to do with writing.

kátab	'he wrote'
yíktib	'he writes, will write'
káatib	'clerk'
kátaba	'clerks'
kitáab	'book'
kútub	'books'
maktúub	'written'
máktab	'office, desk'
maktába	'library'

Káatib, for example, can be said to be formed from the root, *k-t-b,* and the "radical," -*áa-i-*. When the two parts are joined, the meaning becomes 'clerk, one who writes.' The radical -*áa-i-*, carries an agentive meaning (something like the English -*er*), and this can also be seen in words that it forms with some other roots: *ráakib* 'rider,' *náaʃir* 'publisher.' The radical *má-a-* indicates the place where something is done: *máṭbax* 'kitchen,' *máxzan* 'store,' as well as *maktába* 'library.'

It should be clear that the kinds of words that we find in English are far from representative of the full range of words that are possible in human languages.

THE STRUCTURE OF THE LEXICON

Anyone who learns a language needs to know several kinds of facts for each of many thousands of words. First, each word has a unique range of meanings; second, it has a characteristic pronunciation; third, it enters into characteristic morphological and syntactic constructions. The facts of meaning, pronunciation, and syntax that are characteristic of each word add up to a vast amount of detail, much of it highly idiosyncratic. Linguists search for regularities in their data, but languages have irregularities as well, and the lexicon can be looked on as a kind of storehouse for the irregular details. Good dictionaries give information about the meaning, pronunciation, and grammatical patterns of each word, and the lexicon that we carry in our heads must contain an even more detailed version of the same information.

The fact that each word has a unique meaning and a unique pronunciation seems obvious. The fact that the morphological and syntactic characteristics of each word also need to be specified may not be quite so obvious, but the simple assignment of each word to one or another part of speech is only the beginning. In English, for example, a distinction must be made what are known as "mass nouns" and "count nouns." *House, cloud, rock,* and *oat* are count nouns. They can easily be used with plurals, with numbers, and with the indefinite article, *a/an*: (*houses, two clouds, a rock*). Words like *water, air, sand,* and *wheat* are mass nouns. They cannot be used with *a/an* or with numbers unless a measure word is used at the same time (*a cup of water, a puff of air, two grains of sand*), and they take plurals less easily than do count nouns. The plural of a mass noun generally means "kinds" so that *waters* suggests several *kinds* of water. Words for unbounded substances, like water and air, tend to be mass nouns, while more clearly bounded objects are generally named by count nouns. We can say *one oat,* however, even though we have to say *one grain of wheat,* so *oat* is a count noun, but *wheat* is a mass noun. This shows that the distinction between mass and count nouns is, in part, quite arbitrary, and a complete lexicon would have to label each noun as either "mass" or "count."

Nouns also differ on a scale of animacy. Animate nouns such as *cow* or *accountant* can be used in sentences such as *the cow is hungry* or *the accountant is sleepy,* while inanimate nouns like *bus* and *piano* cannot. Words for animals are, in some ways, intermediate between words for people and for inanimate objects. We can say *the midwife is honest* or *the coach is sorry,* but we cannot easily describe *horses* as *honest* or *mice* as *sorry.* As we will see in Chapter 10, the semantic role of "Agent" generally requires an animate noun.

Verbs are divided among even more categories than are nouns. The distinction between intransitive verbs like *sleep* and *run* and transitive verbs like *build* and *watch* is a familiar one. Transitive verbs take an object (*build a house, watch the circus*), while intransitive ones do not. As will be seen in more detail in Chapter 11, verbs need to be classified in much more complex ways than a simple distinction between transitive and intransitive implies. A verb like *give,* for example, requires not only a subject and a direct object, but an indirect object as well: *I gave the white elephant to my cousin* where *elephant* is the direct object and *cousin* is the indirect object. *Put* requires a location to be specified as well as an object: *I put the chutney on the table* is fine, but **I put the chutney* is not. Each verb requires or allows a characteristic range of nouns that represent the subject, object, indirect object, location, and various other elements. Every item in the lexicon of a language, then, must be characterized by its meaning, its pronunciation, and by the morphological and syntactic constructions into which it can enter.

In spite of the differences among languages, parts of speech with similar meanings tend to attract similar kinds of affixes and modifying words. Nouns often take plural affixes, definite articles, and case markers (that show such things as what is the subject and what is the object). Verbs, instead, often have affixes that show tense (past, present, etc.) and agreement (such as the third person -*s* of English). Some languages convey these meanings by independent words rather than by affixes, and even languages that do have affixes generally supplement these with independent words with parallel meanings as well. Thus English has plural affixes, but these do not keep us from using numbers or adjectives like 'many' and 'some' that convey meanings related to plurality. Case markers can be supplemented by independent prepositions and agreement markers by independent pronouns. Adverbs can express meanings that supplement and expand on the meanings of tenses.

It is not surprising that independent words and affixes do parallel jobs. When we know the history of affixes we generally find that they have been derived from independent words that have been gradually attached to another word. In spite of some ambiguity about what to call a "word," we have to recognize that languages differ significantly in their amount of affixation. Some allow luxuriant affixation; a few have almost none. Whether with affixes or with independent words, however, all languages have the machinery to accomplish the same kinds of tasks and to convey most of the same kinds of meanings.

VOCABULARY SIZE

Now and then we hear a claim that some impoverished and poorly educated rural population or some remote tribe has to manage with a meager dialect of no more than a few hundred words. At the other extreme, English is sometimes described as particularly rich, with the most extensive vocabulary of any language. Are these claims justified?

It turns out to be surprisingly difficult to count vocabulary or to compare the vocabulary size of two languages. For one thing, we have to distinguish between the total number of words in a language, and the total number of words that are known, or used, by a single speaker. Even a dictionary of moderate size holds many more words than the head of any single person. A dictionary summarizes the language of many speakers or, more often, writers. They may have written in widely differing times and places, on many different subjects, and in many different styles. Since English has been written for a long time and used for a wide range of subjects, and since English lexicographers have been industrious collectors of words, it is hardly surprising that English dictionaries are notably bulky. By this rather special criterion, it is correct to credit English with having a very large vocabulary. The size of our dictionaries, however, gives us no evidence at all that the vocabulary of the average English speaker is larger than the vocabulary of the average Basque or Hopi.

To test an individual's vocabulary, it might seem that we could take a random sample of, let us say, 1% of the words in a dictionary, and then test people to find out how many they know. We would then simply multiply our results by 100 to obtain a reasonable estimate of vocabulary size. It is far more difficult than this to get a reliable estimate of vocabulary, and the reasons for the difficulty deserve to be considered.

The worst problem is to decide what to count. What should we call the "same" word and what must we admit to be "different" words? Inflectional forms, such as *walks, walked,* and *walking* should probably count as forms of the same word, while derivational forms like *bookish* and *constitution* probably deserve to be considered different from *book* and *constitute.* But what about *work, worker; climax, climactic; smoke, smoky; visible, visibility; happy, unhappy; specific, non-specific; bad, badly; nation, national, nationality, nationalize, nationalization,* and thousands of similarly related sets. Do all of these count as separate words? Or can we regard some of them as different forms of the same word? We do not know how to make principled and consistent decisions in all these cases.

Do compounds count among the words of an individual's vocabulary? Learning to use compounds like *hot dog, firefly,* or *thumb tack* seems hardly different from learning to use roots like *sausage, mosquito,* or *nail.* If the latter count as words, should not compounds also count? But how widely must the meaning of a compound diverge from the meaning of its parts in order to count as a separate item of our vocabulary? What about *necktie, blue jeans, top coat, mini-skirt, sport shirt, tie clasp, top hat, long pants, short sleeves, belt buckle, high heel, shirt button, white shoes, leather shoes, plaid shirt, yellow shirt? Necktie* is certainly a compound and *yellow shirt* is not, but where, between these extremes, do we draw the line? Which should count as separate words in our vocabulary? Once again, there seems to be no way of making consistent and principled decisions. We could, to be sure, simply follow the decisions already made by the authors of a dictionary, and count as a separate word whatever the dictionary lists as a separate entry. Unfortunately different dictionaries make different decisions on such matters, and we really should not solve our problems by leaving the decisions to someone else. When tested on dictionary samples, moreover, it turns out rather consistently that the larger the dictionary used, the larger the "vocabulary" of the people we test. Larger dictionaries simply list more words, so people have more chances to recognize those they know. When results depend so closely on the choice of tools, we have to be cautious about accepting them too easily.

Counting morphemes instead of words would avoid some of the worst problems. If we count morphemes we can stop worrying about derived words and compounds. We would omit a vast amount of the lexical information that everyone needs to know, but the task of counting would become more tractable. Even if we limit ourselves to counting morphemes, however, we face the problem of homophones, different morphemes that are pronounced alike. We can agree that *bank* as the edge of a river must count as a different morpheme from *bank* as a place to store money. *Seal* as an animal counts as a different morpheme from *seal* as a way of closing an envelope. But what about *horn* as a musical instrument and as an adornment on an animal? Etymologically these are related, since animal horns were once used to make blowing horns, but for many people today the two meanings have probably drifted far enough apart to count as separate words. Etymological history alone is not enough to qualify words as still related in the modern language. What about *park* as a grassy or woodsy place for recreation and as something we do with an automobile? Again, these are connected historically, but they have only a feeble residual connection today. What about *stead* in *steady, steadfast, instead of, in good stead, homestead, bedstead*? Like the different meanings of *horn*, these uses of *stead* are etymologically related. The meaning of 'place' can still be discerned, sometimes a bit dimly, in all of them, but the surviving uses of *stead* have pulled far apart. How many morphemes do they now represent? Many sets of words that are historically related would no longer count as sharing a morpheme, and yet some retain obvious similarities in both form and meaning. Should any of the following count as sharing a morpheme? *frail, fragile; timber, lumber; soluble, solvable; sorry, sorrow; tight, taught; drawer, draw, drag; valley, vale; crevice, crevasse; loathe, loath; mead, meadow; beseech, seek; flavor, savor; socket, sprocket; evade, avoid; junction, joint; wink, wench; lentil, lens; snore, sneeze, snooze, snout*. If we can find no consistent way to decide when words have drifted so far apart that they no longer share a morpheme, how can we count how many someone knows?

We face still another problem. How do we judge whether someone "knows" a word or a morpheme? If we want to count someone's vocabulary, we have to decide whether a word is known well enough to be included in the count, but people have only a partial knowledge of many words. They know a word in some of its uses but not in others. They understand some words that they would not use themselves. They understand some words in context that they would not understand in isolation. We might try to define vocabulary narrowly by saying that people have to be able to use the word productively before we will count it as a part of their vocabulary, but we cannot simply follow people around and check to see how many words they use. A word can lie dormant in memory for a decade, but be immediately available when it is needed. We know some words well enough to use even if we have never yet found the right occasion for them.

Even if we could find a way to solve all these problems for a single English speaker, and even if we could find a way to average the results for different speakers to give us an average English vocabulary, we might be no closer to being able to compare two languages. The words of one language are by no means directly comparable with those of another. A language like Eskimo, that allows its speakers to construct new words with great freedom, will clearly have more "words" than another language in which word creation is more restricted. Once again, counting morphemes instead of words might seem to avoid some of these problems, but it might introduce others. The flexibility and richness of a language depend, in part, on its derived words and compounds. Perhaps some languages compensate for a limited number of derived words and compounds by having a larger number of separate morphemes. Counting only morphemes might be unfair to the language with rich derivation and compounding.

Comparing individuals who speak the same language might seem easier than comparing languages. If we do not care about the total number of words, but only about whether one person has more than another, the difficulties may be fewer. The designers of verbal aptitude tests and even of general intelligence tests apparently believe that individuals differ in their stock of words, and that the differences can be measured. At least their tests often include measures of vocabulary. Most verbal aptitude tests emphasize the vocabulary of certain kinds of writing, and a good many linguists harbor a suspicion that these tests give no useful measure of total vocabulary. People who do not read well, or who do not read much, generally do badly on these tests, but it is quite possible that some of these low performers make up for their limited literary vocabulary by a lively oral vocabulary, including a rich range of slang. All these factors make the vocabulary of an individual difficult to measure, and without measures for individuals, we can hardly estimate the average vocabulary of the speakers of a language. This, in turn, leaves us with no way to make systematic comparisons among different languages or even among dialects of the same language.

Are there *un*systematic ways of trying to decide whether one language has a richer vocabulary than another? All we can do is to fall back, rather feebly, on the experience of people who have actually invested the time and effort to learn other languages. Their testimony, at least, seems clear: No language lacks expressive power. No language lacks a rich vocabulary. No language, and no dialect, limits its speakers' ability to talk about the subjects they are concerned with. Within the limits of such informed judgment, no language community appears to use a richer vocabulary than any other. Judgment, however, is not measurement. Linguists tend to believe that average vocabulary size is more or less constant from one language to another, but this belief rests more on faith than on knowledge. The faith comes not from counting words, but from more generalized experiences with diverse languages, from the presumption that vocabulary size is limited only by the limits of the human mind, and from the conviction that the mind must set the same limits everywhere.

The problems of measurement such as those that have been raised in this section are the reason that this book includes a good many sentences that run something like this: "As far as we can tell, no language has more . . . than any other language." Claims of this kind are feeble, but they are often all we can safely assert. Nevertheless, in the case of vocabulary size, it is also important to state that the opposite claim, the claim that some languages or dialects, or even some individual people, manage with a vocabulary of only a few hundred words, is mere fantasy. That much, at least, we can insist on with confidence.

CHAPTER FOUR

Lexical Variation and Change

A VARIABLE AND CHANGING LANGUAGE

In the last two chapters, an implicit assumption has been made that languages can be looked on as reasonably stable systems. This is a plausible assumption for many purposes, but when looked at closely, languages always turn out to be variable, and they are always in a state of restless change. Change is vividly illustrated by successive translations of a passage from the Bible into English.

The King James translation, published in 1611, looks archaic to a twentieth century reader but, as shown by the familiar opening of the book of Genesis, its language can still be understood.

> **I. 1.** In the beginning God created the Heaven, and the Earth. **2.** And the earth was without forme, and voyd, and darkenesse was vpon the face of the deepe: and the Spirit of God mooued vpon the face of the waters. **3.** And God said, Let there be light: and there was light. **4.** And God saw the light, that it was good: and God diuided the light from the darkenesse. **5.** And God called the light, Day, and the darkenesse he called Night: and the euening and the morning were the first day. (Pyles and Algeo, 1982, p. 211).

Two and a half centuries earlier, in the 1380s, John Wycliffe or his followers had translated the same passage into English. We still find much that is familiar, but some words and phrases are different enough from modern English to interfere with easy understanding.

> **I. 1.** In the first made God of nought heuen and erth. **2.** The erth forsothe was veyn withinne and voyde, and derknesses weren vp on the face of the see. And the spirite of God was yborn vp on the waters. **3.** And God seid, "Be made light," and made is light. **4.** And God sees light that it was good and dyuidide light from derknesses. **5.** And clepide light day and derknesses night, and maad is euen and morn, o day. (Pyles and Algeo, 1982, p. 165).

Still earlier, in about the year 1000, Ælfric translated the same passage into the West Saxon dialect of his time. Many words remain recognizable, but the language is so different from modern English that it scarcely counts as the same language. A modern reader needs special study to understand it.

I. 1. On angynne gescēop God heofonan and eorðan. **2.** Sēo eorðe sōðlīce wæs īdel and æmtig, and ðēostra wæron over ðære nywelnysse brādnysse; and Godes gāst wæs geferod ofer wæteru. 3. God cwæð ðā: Gewurðe lēoht, and lēoht wearð geworht. **4.** God geseah ðā ðæt hit gōt wæs, and hē tōdælde ðæt lēoht fram ðām ðēostrum. **5.** And hēt ðæt lēoht dæg and ðā ðēostru niht: ðā wæs geworden æfen and morgen ān dæg (Pyles and Algeo, 1982, pp. 132–133).

These translations illustrate a fundamental trait of all languages: they always change. The further we reach back in time, the greater is the gulf that divides the language from the one we know today. Languages change slowly enough to allow the oldest grandmother to talk easily with her youngest grandchild and, except for the regular arrival of new words, people take little note of the accumulating changes. Still, slowly but relentlessly, languages change in every way, in pronunciation and in grammar as well as in vocabulary, until, after enough centuries have passed, the language becomes transformed. Modern English has moved so far from Old English that it is usually counted as a different language.

Languages not only change, they also diversify. Whenever the speakers of a language are separated, whether by geography or by social barriers, we find that they develop linguistic differences, and the longer they are separated, the more these differences grow. Thus, when a language spreads over a wide territory, it always develops dialects, and with the passage of time the dialects may gradually develop into languages whose speakers can no longer understand each other.

Changes in language begin when a few people try out a new sound or word or expression. Many such innovations die almost as soon as they are born, but a few catch on and spread. For a time, the old and new forms compete. Some people continue to use the old expression, some use the new, and many shift back and forth, but as long as a change is underway, the language exhibits variation. Looked at closely, a change can be seen as a shift in the frequency with which competing forms are used. Some of the variation that we observe in any language is destined to die out, leaving the language where it was before, so we cannot assume that all variability represents change in progress, but an understanding of how languages change must always rest on an understanding of how they vary.

We cannot resist the analogy of a variable and diversifying language with a variable and diversifying biological species. Just as every species shows genetic diversity, so every language shows diversity in pronunciation, syntax, and vocabulary. Just as the genetic variability of a species is the raw material for biological evolution, so linguistic variability is the raw material for language change. Just as a species can diversify until it splits into two or more daughter species, so a language can split into two or more daughter languages. By comparing related species we can infer some characteristics of the common but extinct ancestor; by comparing related languages we can infer some characteristics of their extinct parent. In linguistics, as in evolutionary biology, we even use genealogical terms. We talk about "sister languages" that are "daughters" of the same "parent" language. We draw "family" trees that show the connections among "related" languages. We even speak of languages as **genetically related** when they are descended from the same ancestor.

Only with the theory of selection does the biological analogy break down. Selection of the fittest individuals provides the mechanism that drives biological evolution, but we know of no comparable mechanism that drives linguistic change. We do not even know of any measures by which we might judge one language to be better adapted than another. Languages, like species, keep changing, but we do not interpret the changes that we can observe as demonstrating progress, better adaptation, or even increasing complexity.

In language, as in biology, then, change depends on variation, and we cannot understand change without understanding variation as well. Words, sounds, and syntax are all used differently by different people, in different places, and under different circumstances, and all aspects of language are subject to change. We will postpone an examination of variation and change in phonology and syntax until later chapters, and the remainder of this chapter will focus on variation and change in the lexicon.

VARIATION

The lexicon varies by geographical region, by social group, and by the situation in which people talk. Of the three, regional variation may be the easiest to notice. The varieties of a language that are characteristic of a particular geographic area are known as **regional dialects** or simply **dialects.** We can speak of the dialects of New York, London, the Midwest, or Yorkshire. As linguists use the word, all spoken varieties of a language are "dialects," not just those that are thought of as rustic, or that deviate from some recognized standard. The Queen of England, the Kentucky mountaineer, and the reader and writer of this book are all said to speak dialects, simply because we all speak some particular variety of the language. Dialects can differ from one another in every way, but to count as belonging to the same language, they must be enough alike to be mutually comprehensible.

Language reflects the social divisions as well as the geographical divisions of a society. Age, sex, occupation, social class, and ethnic background all affect peoples' choice of words, and the term **social dialect** refers to the distinctive language variety of a social group. Each of us also adjusts our language, including our vocabulary, to suit the particular situation in which we speak. We select more formal words on some occasions, more colloquial words on others. Varieties that depend on the situation can be called **styles.** Regional, social, and stylistic variation can be regarded as three dimensions of variability. All three can be illustrated by variation in vocabulary.

English speakers are well aware of the vocabulary differences that separate Britain and America. *Lift/elevator, goods/freight, lorry/truck, spanner/ wrench, petrol/gas, puncture/flat, flat/apartment,* and *leader/editorial* are only a few of the hundreds of pairs of words that divide British and American English. Even in an era of mass communication, different words describe the machinery that makes the communication possible: *Telly/TV, cinema/movie theater.* Even when British and American speakers use the same words, they sometimes use them in different ways. Englishmen say *corn* where Americans say *grain,* but they say *maize* where Americans say *corn.* A *vest* is an 'under-shirt' to an Englishman but a 'waistcoat' to an American. Englishmen are more likely to *walk about in the aircraft,* Americans to *walk around in the airplane.* When an Englishman offers to *knock you up in the morning* he is promising only to awaken you, not to make you pregnant.

Differences are also found within each nation. New Yorkers may *stand on line* to buy *soda* but Midwesterners *stand in line* for a *pop,* and Bostonians drink *tonic* rather than either *pop* or *soda.* What most Americans call a *milk shake* becomes a *frappe* in Boston and a *cabinet* in Providence, R. I. *Pavement/sidewalk, bubbler/water fountain, johnnycake/corn bread/corn pone, dragonfly/darning needle, blinds/shades, pigsty/pigpen, baby carriage/ baby buggy/baby coach/baby cab* are only a few of the words that have been identified by dialectologists as being variously favored in different parts of the United States. The dialects of Great Britain may be even more varied. Scottish dialects are distinguished from most English dialects by such words as *kirk* 'church,' *yin* 'one,' *yon* 'that,' and many others.

Regional dialects are distinguished from one another by phonological and syntactic differences as well as by lexical differences, but we are often most vividly aware of words. The words of our home region seem "natural," and we may chuckle at the words we hear from other places, but it is impossible to find any deep significance in calling something a *spanner* rather than a *wrench.* The choice is merely a matter of convention. If we want to be understood we have to use the words that our neighbors will recognize, so people who live close together and who cooperate regularly need to use the same words. An American would be silly to talk about a *goods lift* but an Englishman would be just as silly to talk about a *freight elevator.* Since people have to adjust their language to conform to the people among whom they live, words come to characterize the communities in which they are used.

Communities can be divided in many other ways than by geographical barriers, and every sort of social division comes to be marked by differences in language. Age, sex, occupation, social class, and ethnic group all influence vocabulary choice.

Age

Older people sometimes cling to words that their juniors regard as old fash-ioned. Any American who, in the 1990s, still says *phonograph* must be well past the fiftieth birthday. Some younger Americans regard *ice box* as distinctly quaint when applied to the standard household appliance. At the other end of the age scale, every generation of young people seizes on words that set them off from their elders. These words change so quickly that convincing examples are in danger of being outdated by the time they appear in print, but some young people in Detroit in the late 1980s took pleasure in words such as *to diss* 'to talk about someone in a bad way,' *crew* or *posse* 'the people one hangs out with,' *get busy* 'be part of an exciting event,' and *dipping* 'listening in or butting into other's affairs.' Readers should be able to think of their own more current examples.

Sex

Burmese has two different words for 'I'. Men say *čúndò* while women say *čummà*. No words are assigned to men and women quite this rigidly in English, but we do have words that are more characteristic of one sex than of the other. Women are often more knowledgeable than men about fabrics and colors, and they more often use words like *beige* and *chartreuse*. American men probably use *buck* in the sense of 'dollar,' more often than women, and if anyone still uses *two bits* to mean 'a quarter' it is probably a man.

A half century ago, a woman could grow up in the United States without even hearing, let alone learning, some of the obscenities that men, even then, used more freely. Men guarded their language when in the presence of women, and "protected" them from the rougher words. The sexual revolution of the 1960s brought a defiant breaking of these old taboos and, with wider use, those terrible words have grown less terrible. It is hard to imagine a woman growing up in the United States in the nineties without learning the specialized vocabulary of obscenity but, even in this more liberated era, most women still use these words less freely than men.

Occupation

Just as we signal our age and sex by our words, we also signal our occupation. We all need technical terms in our work, but words can also serve as a kind of badge of occupational membership. Medical jargon allows accurate communication among physicians, but it can also be used to validate membership in the profession and even to intimidate patients. Latin legal terms help lawyers and judges to make careful distinctions, but they also confer an aura of dignity on the courts. The words of less learned professions are no different. To be accepted among truck drivers one must know how to use words as other truck drivers use them.

Criminal argot offers particularly rich examples of a distinctive occupational vocabulary. It is sometimes supposed that the special words of the argot are used in order to allow criminals to speak with each other in public without being understood by outsiders, but a free use of criminal argot would give the speakers away even if it were not understood. Criminals, like the members of other professions, do need technical terms, but argot is used more as a badge of group membership than as a means of secrecy, and it is more often spoken in private than in crowds. Criminals, though living in a larger society and dependent on that society for their livelihood, are still threatened by it. They can depend only on one another for help, and their argot is one means of forging solidarity.

Social Class

Social class differences can introduce barriers to communication that are nearly as effective as geographical barriers. If people talk mostly with others of their own social class, we should expect each class to be characterized by its own distinctive words. Perhaps because vocabulary is relatively easy for the speaker to control, convincing examples of words that are limited to just one social class are more difficult to find than distinctive regional words. As soon as a word becomes stereotyped as lower class, people try to avoid it. People are often less ashamed of the distinctive words of their region, and they may be quite proud of their occupational words, so such words need not be avoided. A word that is perceived to be characteristic of a lower social class may invite such scorn that people search for a more respectable, "classier," alternative.

In some parts of the United States, and at some periods, people have felt strongly about the choice among words such as *curtains/drapes, doily/place mat, couch/sofa/davenport,* or *dinner/lunch* as the name of the noon meal. A man tells us something about his background and even about his class by the way in which he refers to his wife: *my wife, Carol, Mrs. Jones, the Mrs., my old lady.* By linguistic criteria the choice between *curtains* and *drapes,* or between *my wife* and *the Mrs.* is no more significant than the choice between *spanner* and *wrench,* but this does not stop people from reacting more strongly to *the Mrs.* than to *spanner.*

Ethnic Group

As long as American ethnic groups remain distinct, they are likely to retain a few characteristic words. A few terms may be needed for a group's distinctive religious observances or special cuisine, but ethnic groups also develop their own slang. *Chutzpah* 'nerve, self confidence' and *yenta* 'a gossip' come from Yiddish, and we recognize *bad* in the sense of "good" and *man* as used to call to someone as having originally been black slang. If the slang terms escape their ethnic origins and come to be adopted by the general population, they lose their value as marking an in-group ethnic style, but new words can always be invented to replace them. Black slang has regularly escaped into the general American vocabulary, but black speakers have always been inventive about finding new words.

Even very small communities develop their own distinctive expressions. The *anthro* and *econ* of one campus are replaced by *anth* and *ec* on another. Business organizations, clubs, even families, have words that members use to mark themselves off from others. The family that vacations by driving in Mexico but continues to use the Mexican Spanish word *topos* for 'highway speed bumps' even after returning to Missouri, acquires not only a useful word, but also a badge of in-group membership. The delighted parents who adopt their baby's word *pepe* for potatoes have found another badge of family solidarity. Vocabulary is an irresistible means for marking the social distinctions that people find important. We constantly use vocabulary to demonstrate our membership in some groups, at the same time that we use it to exclude others.

The third dimension of linguistic variability, to place beside regional and social variability, is **style.** Each of us chooses our words to suit the particular circumstances in which we speak. A relaxed family gathering calls for a different way of talking than a banquet or a religious service. A night out with the boys calls for a still different selection of words. *Kids* and *guys* refer to the same kinds of people as *children* and *men,* but there are times when *children* and *men* would sound hopelessly pompous to Americans and other more serious occasions when *kids* and *guys* would be embarrassingly casual. Anyone who fails to adjust his vocabulary to different situations deserves the accusation of insensitivity.

We give the word **slang** to expressions with a distinctly informal flavor. These are words that would be out of place in a serious document or in any kind of formal language. Everyone uses slang on some occasions, but we also know when to avoid it. Slang often changes rapidly. People seize on a clever or vivid expression, use it until it grows stale, and then replace it with something new. This means that any printed description of slang, with its examples of yesterday's favorites, is likely to look a bit tired, but certain meanings consistently attract slang. Many slang terms confer general approval: *neat, great, swell, cool, groovy, bold, swish, yummy.* As many suggest human deficiencies: *jerk, twit, boob, dunderhead, bird brain, flea brain, dim wit, sad sack.* Every reader can surely add to these lists.

Stylistic, social, and regional differences interact and overlap. Words like *tote* 'carry' and *reckon* in the sense of 'think, suppose' were once more characteristic of southern American dialects than of the north, but they have been carried into northern cities by poor Southerners, and there they have come to be associated with lower-class speech rather than simply with regional speech. If people limit the circumstances in which they use the vocabulary of their occupations, their vocabulary will mark a style as well as a social group. When we hear a policeman respond to a question posed by a television interviewer by saying *The accused was apprehended as he emerged from the cleaning establishment,* we suspect that he might have spoken differently had he been less conscious of being a policeman. We also suspect that he will describe the events in a different way when, later over a cup of coffee, he tells his wife what happened. The polysyllabic words mark the man's occupation at the same time that they characterize the very special situation in which he is called upon to speak.

The wealth of our vocabulary lets each of us search widely for the words we want. Of course we have to choose words that will express the ideas we are concerned with, and we only look foolish when we use words from a very different region or a very different social group than our own. Still, speakers have an enormous range of words to choose from, and the selection marks many things: the social groups with which speakers would like to identify, their sensitivity to the situation, their wit and imagination. The vocabulary of popular people and of admired social groups is imitated by others, and so new words may spread through the population and change the language. It is in this way that variation serves as the raw material out of which linguistic change can grow. In the remainder of this chapter we will turn to this fourth type of variability, and consider the way in which vocabulary changes with the passage of time.

LEXICAL INNOVATION

Languages change steadily and in every way. Some kinds of changes advance so slowly that we hardly notice them, but lexical changes are clearly apparent to everyone. Adult speakers of English all recognize words that, in the course of their own lifetime, have entered the language, acquired new meanings, or simply become more common. During our era of rapid technological change, the most productive source of new vocabulary has probably been the arrival of new technologies. Most recently, the computer revolution has spawned swarms of new terms. Some of these are old and well-established words now appropriated for a new use: *file, chip, program, memory, floppy, BASIC*. Others are new terms constructed from old parts: *software, hard disk, random access memory, microprocessor, work station, mainframe*. Still others come closer to being entirely new words, though most ring with at least a few familiar echoes: *byte, gigabyte, megaflop, transistor, FORTRAN*.

Computer terminology is only the latest example of technical jargon to flood our language. Older waves of technological change have brought us the vocabulary of photography, railroads, automobiles, and motion pictures. Our technical vocabulary alone would make our language incomprehensible to a Rip Van Winkle who returned from the last century, but technology is not the only source of new vocabulary. Psychoanalysis has given our language new words and new meanings for old words: *repression, frustration, ego,* and *superego*. Music has given new meanings to *acid, rock,* and *soul*. Environmental concerns yield *ozone hole* and *greenhouse effect,* and they turn an adjective, *green,* into a noun and give it a new meaning.

Periods of rapid social change generally require new words. In the late 1960s the advocates of radical change drew attention to themselves and symbolized their own participation in the changes by adopting new words. Among other sources of new vocabulary was black slang. Seeing their own position as oppressed, the radicals of the 1960s were attracted by the vocabulary of another oppressed group, so terms from black slang found their way to wider and wider social groups. The most unlikely people learned to say *up tight, far out, right on,* and *ya dig?*

New words can be created in several ways. The two most productive sources of new words, derivation and compounding, were considered in Chapter 3. These are both reasonably transparent processes, and the meanings of new compounds and derived words are usually rather clearly related to the meaning of the parts from which they are formed. Nevertheless, once formed, new words can acquire a life of their own and, when we look at well-established words, we often find that they have drifted far from their origins. In meaning or in pronunciation, or both, new compounds and derived terms may grow distinct from the pieces that make them up. Well-established derivational forms like *institution* and *expedition* have some sort of residual connection with *institute* and *expedite,* but the connection is such a distant one that the meanings of the derived nouns are only loosely related to the meanings of the underlying verbs. *Hothouse* first became specialized to mean a building where plants are grown, and not simply a 'house that is hot.' Then, since a hothouse exerts pressure for things to happen quickly, the word could be extended further to describe other working conditions where the pressure is high and where talent and creativity are forced into bloom. *Chairman* is an obvious compound of *chair* and *man,* but both its meaning and its pronunciation have become specialized. It would sound quite strange to pronounce the second *a* in *chairman* in the same way that we pronounce it in *man.*

If the pronunciation and meaning of a compound or a derived word diverge far enough from the pronunciation and meaning of its parts, it may finally lose all connection with its original constituents. As separate words, the original constituents may even be lost from the language and survive only in compounds. The parts of a compound may then merge into a word that speakers no longer recognize as a compound. *Breakfast* originally referred to the breaking of a fast, but that sense has become so obscured that people are usually surprised the first time it is pointed out. The first syllable of *husband* was originally derived from *house,* but its meaning and pronunciation have diverged so far that no one is any longer likely to recognize the connection without being told. Even more remotely, the word *nice* is derived from a Latin word *ne-scius* 'not know,' and *nest* goes back to an even older compound of 'sit' and 'down.' The older parts of these words have been so totally fused as to be unrecognizable.

Derivation and compounding are the most productive sources of new words, but several others also deserve notice.

Back formation amounts to a kind of reverse derivation in which shorter words are created from longer words by analogy with established grammatical patterns. The child who announces that he intends to take his hammer and *ham that nail* has made a back formation from *hammer. Ham* is not likely to become part of the language, but some back formations have become well established. *Donate* was originally a back formation from *donation,* constructed on the analogy with existing pairs such as *creation, create. Enthuse* and *televise* are more recent back formations that seem likely to gain a respectable place in the language. We still recognize *burgle* as either a mildly amusing or mildly stale witticism, but our grandchildren may accept it as an entirely normal word and imagine that *burglar* is derived from *burgle* instead of the other way round.

Clippings result from more random abbreviations. Some eminently respectable English words, such as *piano, bus,* and *fan,* began as clippings. These have gained considerable independence from their original sources, *pianoforte, omnibus,* and *fanatic,* but many other clippings are still regarded as colloquial or slangy equivalents of the fuller form: *exam, bio, lab, burger.* By abbreviating long but frequently used words, clippings allow a changing vocabulary to maintain an efficient distribution of long and short words. It is efficient for the most common words of the language to be short, since the total length of utterances can then be kept to a minimum. Uncommon words can be longer, since they less often slow things down. As soon as a long word becomes common, speakers generally find a way to abbreviate it.

Blends occur when two words are blended into one, as when *brunch* is blended from *breakfast* and *lunch,* or when *smoke* and *fog* blend into *smog.*

Proper names have been the source of many new words. *Volts, curies, amperes,* and *coulombs* are all named for scientists who helped to develop the theories that require these concepts. Place names sometimes become attached to their products. *Cognac, china,* and *cayenne* all began as place names. *Gin* comes from *Geneva,* and *cashmere,* from *Kashmir.* Our names for the planets, many originally the names of Roman gods, have given us names for human temperaments that were believed to be under the planets' dominance: *mercurial, martial, jovial, saturnine. Venereal* comes from *Venus,* the name of a planet and of the Roman goddess of love, and *lunatic* and *loony* are based upon Latin *luna* 'moon,' once associated with the instability of insanity.

In a number of modern languages, including English, sequences of initial letters have become a particularly rich source of new words. Sometimes these are pronounced by the letter names, but they deserve to be called words, particularly when we no longer remember what the individual letters stand for: *DDT, LSD, BLT, NBC, TNT, IBM.* We seem to be particularly fond of three-letter combinations, but universities graduate their *BA*s and *BS*s, and research is conducted at the *NIMH* (National Institute of Mental Health). A sequence of initial letters pronounced as if they actually spell a word is called an **acronym**: *UNESCO, NATO, AIDS.* Like clippings, these abbreviations increase the efficiency of a language by shortening long but frequently used phrases into what amount to single words.

The **coinage** of a totally new word is an unusual event. The trade name *Kodak* is said to have been created new, and some new drugs are given names unrelated to older words, but more often it is easier to construct new words with the help of bits that are already familiar and that make the new word easier to recognize and remember. Even new drug names have to be chosen with due attention to the symbolism that sounds have for speakers. Drug companies want their drugs to be taken seriously, so they give them names with sounds that suggest their importance, reliability, and potency: *Sumatriptan, Leukine, Neupogen, buspirone.*

We have a handful of words that are **onomatopoetic,** based, often rather loosely, on noises. *Cock-a-doodle-doo* has a certain resemblance to the sound of a cock's crow, while *moo* and *baa* have a somewhat looser resemblance to the cries of cows and sheep. Words such as *swish, bang,* and *crash* may seem to echo the sounds that they name. The words with these meanings in other languages are often very different from our own, however, and when we learn that Norwegian pigs say *nøff-nøff,* instead of *oink-oink* like good English pigs, we must suspect that even words for animal noises are more conventional than onomatopoetic.

One additional source of new words must be added to the sources that have been discussed in this section: borrowing from other languages. Borrowing is so important that it deserves a section of its own.

BORROWING

Other languages are the final source of new words. Whenever two languages come into contact, they are likely to affect one another. Speakers who know two languages can easily carry features from one language into the other, and these bilingual speakers, in turn, can influence monolingual speakers. The process by which the features of one language are incorporated into another is known as **borrowing.** Under the right conditions, virtually anything can be borrowed, but words move across language boundaries most easily. Words that are borrowed into a new language are called **loan words** and, as we all know, English is particularly rich in loan words that have been drawn from many languages.

The kinds of words that are borrowed give clues to the social conditions under which the borrowing took place. English borrowed many Scandinavian words at the time when Scandinavian-speaking settlers, known as "Danes," lived in parts of Britain. Most of these Danes were farmers whose way of life was not much different from that of their Anglo-Saxon contemporaries. The Scandinavian and English languages of the period were closely related, and farmers with similar languages and similar technology could easily borrow each other's words. Most of the words that the Danes gave our language name ordinary objects and activities of daily life, and they fit so easily among words of older Anglo-Saxon origin that most English speakers are not even aware of their Scandinavian source: *gift, root, skill, skin, sky, wing, happy, low, same, wrong, call, die, get, give, hit, take, want.* Even the pronouns *they, them,* and *their* come from Scandinavian, and they have replaced, or almost replaced, the older English equivalents. In informal English, when we say, *I can't find 'em,* the *'em* is actually a remnant of the older English pronoun *hem,* meaning 'them.' Perhaps the word had been so severely shortened that a weightier synonym was needed for careful language, and a pronoun with a bit more substance could be borrowed from Scandinavian. Another surprising Scandinavian borrowing is the verb form *are*. Someone who says *They are happy* uses a sentence in which all three words were originally Scandinavian.

English has borrowed even more freely from French. French influence was strongest in the centuries following the Norman conquest, and the kinds of words that were taken from French during that period were very different from the words borrowed earlier from Scandinavian. After the Norman conquest, English continued to be spoken by the majority of the people, but French became the language of the court and the upper classes. This gave French great prestige, and French words poured into English. French was the language of government, and we still use French words for matters of state: *council, country, crown, government, minister, nation, parliament, people, state.* Most noble titles were French: *Prince, duke, marquis, viscount, baron. King, queen,* and *earl* remained English, but French *royal* still sounds a bit more serious and stately than English *kingly.* Most terms of heraldry are French (*sable, gules, vert, etc.*) as are most military terms (*armor, army, banner, navy, siege, war*) and legal terms (*court, crime, defendant, judge, jury, justice, plaintiff*). The title *attorney general* and the phrase *malice aforethought* even retain French word order with their adjectives in second place.

In some domains, English words survive alongside French words, and the differences in their meaning can reveal the nature of society in Norman England. Barnyard animals were cared for by English farmers, and they still have English names (*cow, calf, sheep, pig*), but once the animals were brought to the table, where the cultivated language was French, the animals acquired French names (*beef, veal, mutton, bacon, pork*). We still eat a humble English *breakfast,* but we have taken over the more elegant French *supper* and *dinner.* The lower artisans were English (*baker, fisherman, miller, shepherd, shoemaker, smith*). The higher artisans, who were likely to serve the French-speaking upper classes, more often acquired French titles (*carpenter, mason, painter, tailor*). Even the humble crime of *theft* was English, while the more sophisticated crime of *larceny* was French. Sports and games, being the prerogative of the upper classes, often brought along their French terminology: *chase, falconry, ace, deuce, tray.* The word *sport* itself comes from French *desport.*

French words began their invasion during the period when French speakers held a dominant social position in England, but the prestige that French then acquired survived long enough to encourage later writers to exploit the scholarly vocabulary of French. Well over half the words in our dictionaries are now loan words, and we still think of English as particularly open to borrowing, but the loan words that most dramatically transformed the lexicon of English entered the language many centuries ago. As English-speaking peoples grew in power, borrowing into English slowed, though it has never stopped. As the language of a conquering people, English had become less receptive to new words by the time it reached the Americas. The handful of words that have been accepted into English from American Indian languages are limited to names for things that had been unknown to Europeans until they reached the Americas, such as *potato, tomato, tobacco, skunk,* and *teepee.* We still welcome an occasional new word from other languages, such as *sputnik* and *glasnost* from Russian and *sushi* from Japanese, but words are now more often borrowed *from* English than *into* English. For really dramatic examples of borrowing today, we must go to other parts of the world.

When the speakers of a minority language, like the Garo of Bangladesh, begin to absorb the technological and social inventions of the modern world, their language may undergo massive borrowing. The one hundred thousand Garos of Bangladesh constitute less that one tenth of 1% of the nation's population, and almost everyone else speaks Bengali as their first language. All education is in the Bengali medium and, except for the traditional farming, every occupation demands a knowledge of Bengali. Even to buy a few objects in the market requires at least a few Bengali words. As a result, by the time they reach the age of 5, all Garos who live in Bangladesh have begun to learn Bengali, and by the time they are grown, almost all can carry on a conversation. A few become fluent bilinguals. Garos now farm with techniques that were learned from Bengali farmers, and their words for tools, for land measurements, and even for many plants and animals have been borrowed from the Bengali language. The Garos are too poor to have joined the modern consumer society, but they know about busses, trucks, automobiles, watches, and even tape recorders. The words for all this new machinery and the words for their parts and for the way in which they are used, all come to the Garos from Bengali, though a good deal of it comes ultimately from English. A handy means of transportation that the Garos call a *baisikol* has parts that are called *hendel, bel, sit, pedel, chen, brek, karier,* and *tair.* When a *tup* gets a hole, it is called a *lik.* Like this technical terminology, the vocabulary of the schools, of the subjects learned in school, and of politics, government, the law, and the courts is all borrowed.

As a result of nearly universal bilingualism, Garos feel free to use any Bengali word that they think will be understood. They readily incorporate Bengali words into the matrix of a Garo sentence, adding Garo suffixes and embedding the words into larger constructions as if they had always been Garo. Under these circumstances, hundreds of Bengali words pour into Garo. Since it is the language of education, learning, good jobs, powerful people, and an easier life style, Bengali comes to be associated with a higher status, and people begin to borrow words not only because they need to talk about new things, but also as a means of associating themselves with all that is prestigious. Even prepositions, demonstratives, and personal pronouns find their way into Garo from Bengali. Arithmetic is learned in school, and thus through the medium of the Bengali language, and one of the most important uses for numbers is in the market, where the traders always speak Bengali. As a result, Bengali numbers have driven most older Garo numbers out of the language. Many Garos in Bangladesh do not even know the older Garo numbers above 5.

The impact of Bengali on Garo is far more profound than anything in the linguistic experience of living English speakers. It is impossible for a Garo to speak without using Bengali words. Like the French loan words in English, some Bengali loan words have become well enough established in Garo to have acquired their own conventional pronunciation and sometimes even their own conventional meaning. Other words are borrowed on the spot, used in Garo sentences either because they are the only words the speaker knows, or because they seem like elegant equivalents for ordinary Garo words. Loan words may retain a good deal of their original Bengali pronunciation, and the phonological habits of Garos become modified as a result. If we wanted to count the total vocabulary of a Garo speaker, it would be misleading to count only the words of native Garo origin. Garo speakers can draw so easily on the full range of Bengali vocabulary, that these words too must be counted as part of their vocabulary. Like speakers of many other languages that are subjected to heavy borrowing today, thoughtful Garos worry about the corruption that all these new words seem to be bringing to their language. As English speakers, we value the well-established French loan words of our language and feel that English is richer because of them, but during the period when a language is undergoing massive borrowing, its speakers are more likely to look on the invading words as a source of corruption than of enrichment.

Profound borrowing can bring such radical changes that we may wonder whether the languages that emerge after heavy borrowing might sometimes be regarded as having more than a single parent. Biological species cannot borrow genes from one another, so the branches on a family tree of related species can divide, but they can never rejoin. Does the possibility of borrowing allow the branches of a family tree of languages to grow back together?

Linguists have most often presumed that, in spite of borrowing, two languages are no more capable of genuine merger than are two species. We generally expect each language, like each species, to have just one single ancestral line. Even a heavy overlay of borrowing should not alter the older genetic affiliation of a language. Under extreme social conditions, however, we do find languages that have drawn so heavily on two or more earlier languages that they lack the unambiguous descent from just one ancestral language that we generally expect. Occasionally we even have to recognize what amounts to new languages. These may show the influence of several earlier languages but lack the more usual kind of historical continuity with just one of them. Such extreme conditions will be considered along with pidgins and creoles in Chapter 14.

Breaks in linguistic continuity of this sort happen only under extreme conditions, and more often languages do exhibit continuity with just one single ancestral line. In spite of borrowing, we are usually able to recognize the underlying relationships among languages, and it is this that allows us to arrange the great majority of the world's languages in family trees where branches divide repeatedly but do not grow back together again.

NEW MEANINGS FOR OLD WORDS

The vocabulary of a language changes not only by the addition of new words, but also by expanding the meanings of old words. *Chip, disk, program,* and *memory* are old words appropriated by a new technology. Slang is often created from established words by giving them new senses: *right on, groovy, bad, beat.* Metaphors, too, give new meanings to familiar words and phrases: *He cleaned up the remaining problems. She cut through to the heart of the matter. He peppered his language with pungent expressions. She sailed into the room with a bright smile.*

When words expand their meanings, the newer meanings are often more general or abstract than their older meanings. Metaphorical meanings of words are, typically, more abstract than their literal meanings. A *waltz* is a lively dance, but when we say *he waltzed through the problem,* we generalize away from the specific dance, even while we maintain a more abstract sense of 'liveliness' or 'ease.' Similarly, the slang sense of words also tends to be more abstract than the literal sense. In its literal sense, *cool* refers to a reasonably specific temperature. Its slang sense suggests only a very generalized approval.

Many other words have abstract meanings that we consider neither slang nor metaphorical but that have nevertheless been added to older, more concrete, meanings. The relatively concrete older meaning of *feel* that implied "touching" has been joined by a more subjective meaning that implies no touching at all: *I feel differently about it now. Observe* retains an older sense of "watch" but it can now also mean either "state" or "follow a custom" as in *He observed that he had had quite enough* and *They always observe the Sabbath.* The meaning of *assume* has been extended from "take on" as in *assume a role* to "presume, take for granted," as in *I assume that you are going.* To the older temporal meaning of *while* as in *He sat while he ate* has been added a more abstract sense of 'although' as in *While she would like to go, it is quite impossible.*

It is not always easy to pin down exactly what we mean by "concrete" and "abstract," but perhaps we can agree that causation is somewhat more abstract than time and that time is more abstract than space. There does, at any rate, seem to be a tendency for spatial terms to develop temporal meanings, and for temporal terms to develop causal meanings. *Go,* a verb that describes a relatively concrete movement through space, has acquired a temporal meaning in *he is going to come here.* The older meaning of *since,* as in *since this morning,* was temporal. Its causal meaning, as in *since you insist,* developed later.

Among the most abstract words of all are our function words, and when we know their history, we often find that function words grew out of older content words. *Have* can still indicate a relatively concrete sense of "possession" but it is also used as an auxiliary verb in phrases such as *He has gone* or *he has to go,* in which all sense of possession has been lost. *Be* retains an older sense of "exist" but the forms of *be* are now more often used to indicate more abstract grammatical relationships, as in *she is going* or *he was suspicious. In back of* appropriates a term for a concrete body part and incorporates it into a phrase that is used like a preposition with a relatively abstract spatial sense. We will return, in Chapter 13, to the conversion of content words to function words and to the way in which these words can be drawn more tightly into the syntax of the language. This conversion is a part of a much more general process by which the meaning of relatively concrete words can be gradually stretched toward more abstract senses.

ETYMOLOGY

Because languages diverge into daughter languages, and because these daughters, in their turn, can continue to diverge, we can recognize families of related languages, all of which trace their origins to a single ancestral language. The world's most widespread language family is known as **Indo-European** which, in addition to most of the languages of Europe, includes Armenian, Persian, and the languages of Northern India.

While the ancestral language that gave rise to the modern Indo-European languages left no written records, we can make a number of plausible inferences about the parent by comparing its daughters. Techniques will be described in Chapter 8 that allow us, even without the direct evidence of writing, to use our knowledge of words in the daughter languages to "reconstruct" the forms that these words had in the ancestral language. A reconstructed language that is unknown from written records is called a **protolanguage** and **Proto-Indo-European** is the name given to the language that was ancestral to all the later Indo-European languages.

The branch of Indo-European to which English, Dutch, German, and the Scandinavian languages belong is called **Germanic.** The common ancestor of the modern Germanic languages left no more written records than did the earlier Proto-Indo-European, so it is known as **Proto-Germanic.** Because Proto-Germanic split into its daughters more recently than Proto-Indo-European, the Germanic languages share more words than do the more distantly related Indo-European languages. Words in related languages that are descended from the same word in their ancestral language are known as **cognates,** and the study of cognates can tell us a good deal about how words change and develop, and even about the development of the cultures in which the languages have been spoken. The study of the history and development of words is called **etymology,** and the way words develop through time can be illustrated with an example of a single ancient Indo-European word.

Indo-Europeanists reconstruct a root **ped-* for the Proto-Indo-European ancestor of the English word *foot.* (Reconstructed words for which we have no direct written evidence are indicated by "*", the same symbol that we used to mark an ungrammatical expression. Both usages suggest that the form is "unattested," in one case because it cannot occur, in the other because the language left no written records.) A form of *ped- was passed down, with a somewhat altered pronunciation, to Proto-Germanic where it is reconstructed as *fōt-. This eventually evolved into our modern word *foot,* still retaining the meaning it had several thousand years ago and still, apparently, having a somewhat similar pronunciation.

A suffixed form of this word became the Germanic *feterō, and this developed into the English word *fetter,* originally a 'leg iron' but now more generally a 'restraint.' Another suffixed form led through Germanic to the English word *fetlock* 'the projection on the back of a horse's leg, just above the hoof.' A related Germanic word *fetēn 'to bring back,' presumably originally meaning 'on foot,' gave rise to the English *fetch.*

In addition to these words that have come to English directly through Proto-Germanic, Proto-Indo-European *ped- also gave rise to related words in both Latin and Greek and, through borrowing, these have developed into still other English words. Indo-European *ped- developed into *pes* in Latin, but in some circumstances the root was used in the form *ped-.* Latin forms of the word are found in such modern English words as *pedal, pedestrian, pedicel, pioneer,* and *millipede,* all of which have something to do with feet or with the lower part of an object. *Pawn,* originally 'foot soldier,' is derived from the same word. The word also entered various Latin compounds. *Expedīre* originally meant 'to free from a snare' ('out the foot') but it gave rise to our *expedite.* Latin *impedīre* 'to put in fetters, hobble' has become our *impede.* English *dispatch* and *impeach* come from a Latin word *pedica* 'fetter, snare.' Latin *pējor* 'worse' originally meant 'stumbling' but it gave rise to English *pejorative* and *impair.* The related Latin *pessimus* 'worst' has led to our *pessimism.* From Latin *peccāre* 'to stumble, sin,' we get English *peccadillo* and *impeccable.*

A Greek form of the same word, *pod* was borrowed into English in such words as *podium, antipodes, octopus, platypus, podiatry, podzol* and many others. A related Greek word *pēdon* 'rudder' gave rise to English 'pilot.' A Persian form of the same word, *pāī* 'leg, foot' entered a compound with *jāma* 'garment' and became the source of our word *pajamas.*

Only a few words multiply quite as luxuriantly as Indo-European *ped- but we can follow the development of hundreds of words in the Indo-European languages, and we are able to trace the history of words in many other language families as well.

RECONSTRUCTION OF CULTURAL CONTENT

If we can be confident about enough reconstructed words of a proto-language, we may be able to use these words to infer something about the culture of the people who spoke the language. No early proto-language has been reconstructed in more detail than Proto-Indo-European, and the reconstructions allow a number of plausible guesses about the way of life of its speakers several thousand years ago. Proto-Indo-European words have been reconstructed that must have meant *day, year, winter, spring, summer, fall, moon/month, sun, star,* but these tell us little about their customs, since words for these concepts are nearly universal. Nor, since everyone also has pronouns and body part terms, do we learn much when we notice that modern Indo-European languages share a number of cognate pronouns and words for body parts.

On the other hand, the fact that Proto-Indo-European seems to have had a word for *snow,* reconstructed as **sneig^wh-,* suggests something about the climate of the region where the language was spoken. There were words for *beech tree, apple,* and *cherry* and, like *snow,* these northern species suggest a relatively northern origin. The language also had a general word for *tree/wood,* but this reveals little about their homeland. Wild animals included names for northern species like *wolf, beaver, mouse, salmon, eel,* as well as a general word for *bird* and for several types of bird: *crane, thrush, starling, sparrow, finch, woodpecker.* Insects are represented by *wasp, hornet, fly, bee, louse,* and a word that probably meant either *bedbug* or *moth.*

Domestic animals tell us more than wild animals about the people's way of life. The people who spoke Proto-Indo-European seem to have had words for *cow/bull, sheep, lamb, goat, swine, dog,* and *horse.* The fact that they not only kept domestic animals but also raised crops is suggested by words for *grain,* including one that may have meant *wheat.* Two words for *grinding* confirm the suspicion that they were grain farmers, and there are words for *furrow, plowshare, yoke, sickle,* and *gather/pluck.* There were also words for *fire, cook, raw,* and *meat.*

The numerals for *two* through *ten* can be reconstructed and the speakers of Proto-Indo-European must, like us, have had a counting system based upon multiples of ten. A word meaning *copper* and, somewhat more tentatively, words for *bronze, gold,* and *silver* have been attributed to the Proto-Indo-Europeans. These suggest a knowledge of metallurgy, but since no word for iron can be traced back so far, they have often been thought of as Bronze Age farmers who had not yet learned to use iron. There was a word for *axle* that seems to have been derived from a word for the 'navel,' and a word for *wheel* that may have been derived from a word meaning 'revolve.' The transparent sources of these words suggest that wheeled vehicles may have still been a relatively recent invention at the time when Proto-Indo-European was spoken. There was a word for *boat,* and probably one for *oar,* so the people seem to have known about water transport, but they are not thought to have been a seafaring people.

They had a number of words that dealt with religious matters, *preach, worship/honor,* and *praise aloud.* The ancestor of our word *sing* meant not only *sing* but also *prophesy, make incantations.* There was a word that seems to have meant something like *venerate the dead.* There was a word for *god* and a compound *god-father,* as in the Greek *Zeus patēr* and the related Latin

Jupiter. Perhaps they conceived of the family of the gods in the image of their own families. A word possibly meaning something like *tribal king* survived both as Latin *rēx* and Hindi *raja*. Words for *law, bond,* and *pay compensation* give us hints about their economic and legal system. A few longer fixed phrases occur in more than a single daughter language so it seems likely that they were also found in the parent language: *imperishable flame, holy force,* and *weaver of words*. This last describes the Indo-European poet.

Many kinship terms can be reconstructed. There were a number of terms for a woman's relatives by marriage through her husband, including a term for *husband's brother*, but fewer terms can be reconstructed for relatives by marriage through the wife. This fact has been interpreted to imply that their families were patriarchal and patrilocal. If daughters moved to their husbands' households at marriage, in-laws would be more important for in-marrying women than for their stay-at-home husbands. There is a term for *mother* but the term for *father* seems also to have meant head of the household. It is believed that the term for *brother* could be used for some cousins as well as for real brothers, and our word 'sister' seems to derive from a word having the more general meaning of *female member of one's kinship group*.

The picture that we are able to build up by collecting the meanings of reconstructed vocabulary gives no more than a sketch of the culture, but when we lack written records, we must be grateful for whatever hints we can find. The picture that has emerged from the study of Proto-Indo-European vocabulary is of a people who farmed and raised animals and who lived sometime after bronze was invented (at least three thousand years before the beginning of the modern era) but before the invention of iron smelting about two thousand years later. Their homeland has been variously located anywhere from the Baltic Sea in the north to Anatolia (modern Turkey) in the south, or to Central Asia farther east.

This picture leaves us with one mystery: What power could have allowed a Bronze Age people to carry their language so far? Indo-Europeans were not the first, or only, Bronze Age people, and they have even been pictured as occupying a rather peripheral position in early Bronze Age times. How could they have imposed their language on such a huge area? Recently the archeologist Colin Renfrew has suggested that Proto-Indo-European may have been spoken even longer ago than the Bronze Age. He suggests that it dates from the time of the earliest agriculture more than six thousand years before our era. He places Proto-Indo-European in Anatolia, one of the earliest centers of agriculture, and he proposes that the early Indo-European languages may have been carried northward and westward across Europe along with farming. Farming could have given its speakers such a technological advantage that they and their language could have absorbed or displaced the earlier population.

To many linguists, 6000 BC seems too early for the common ancestor of the Indo-European languages, especially since the earliest farmers did not have copper, wheels, axles, or horses and would hardly have needed words for them. To accept Renfrew's proposal we would have to suppose that these words were not a part of the original Indo-European vocabulary at all, but spread by later borrowing. Nevertheless, the proposal does suggest a powerful social force that could have driven the spread of the language. Archeological remains allow us to follow the two-thousand-year advance of agriculture across Europe, and the population expansion and resulting power that came with agriculture could easily have been enough to pull language along with it. This proposal is still new, however, and it remains controversial.

RELATED LANGUAGES

Tracing etymologies is possible only if we know whether languages are related. Judging relationship is often difficult, however, and it is an area where linguists often disagree. After thousands of years of accumulated changes, we might expect the diverging descendants of a language to grow so far apart that we could no longer recognize their common origin. This possibility means that we can never prove that two languages are unrelated. Their differences may simply be the result of such a long separation that their relationship has become obscured. Nevertheless, great efforts have been made to judge the relationships among the world's languages since, even in the absence of written records, linguistic relationships give us clear evidence about historic and prehistoric contacts among long-separated peoples. We know, for example, that the languages of the island of Madagascar, which lies off the east coast of Africa, are related to the languages of Indonesia and even to languages spoken as far east as Hawaii. At some point during prehistory, people must have traveled from someplace in the east, possibly from Indonesia, all the way around the Indian Ocean to Madagascar, bringing their language with them. Without our knowledge of this linguistic relationship, we might never have guessed at this migration.

Languages are counted as genetically related when they show similarities we judge to have been inherited from their common ancestor. Before we can have confidence in the relationship, we need to rule out three other sources of similarity. These include phonological and syntactic similarities as well as lexical ones, but we can consider them together here.

1. Universals. The fact that two languages both have verbs tells us nothing about their relationship since we can recognize verbs in every known language. We learn no more from the presence of consonants, vowels, question words, negations, subjects, or objects since these are also found everywhere.

2. Chance. Every pair of languages shows a few chance similarities. With thousands of words to choose from, it would be remarkable if a few of these words did not resemble each other. The history of amateur linguistics is littered with wonderful discoveries of words in distant languages that are tantalizingly similar, and with erroneous conclusions about ancient historical connections. Before we can conclude that two languages have a common history, we must be confident that their similarities are greater than can be expected by simple chance.

3. Borrowing. The most difficult evidence to untangle when judging genetic relationship comes from the influence that one language, even a totally unrelated language, can have on another. Under the right social conditions, borrowing can radically transform the vocabulary of a language, and it can even bring such extensive changes to phonology and syntax that older genetic relationships become obscured. Under extreme conditions, people may even draw on the resources of two or more languages and create what amounts to a new language, one that has no real genetic continuity with any earlier language (see Chapter 14). In the more usual situation, even with extensive borrowing, languages retain clear continuity with just one ancestral language. One example is English which, in spite of all its borrowing from French and elsewhere, remains unambiguously a Germanic language.

Ordinarily we can discount the minimal degree of similarity that is due to universals and chance, and with sufficiently careful comparison, even borrowing can usually be recognized. The most common, or "core," vocabulary is less likely to be borrowed than are rarer or more specialized words. Loan words and native words may differ in their phonological characteristics. English words that were originally borrowed from French, for example, are often phonologically distinct from the older Germanic words. Sometimes loan words are so much like their originals in the loaning language that their source is obvious. Sometimes loan words are recognizable because they are used in specialized cultural or technical areas where the influence of another society has been strong. In any case, if family relationships among languages are to be judged successfully, loan words must, in one way or another, be set aside. Only if we can rule out universals, chance, and borrowing can we have confidence that the similarities between two languages give evidence of their genetic relationship.

A natural question to raise is whether *all* the languages of the world are ultimately related to one another. A small minority of linguists have proposed that we may have enough evidence to suggest that they are, but most linguists have believed that, even if they are related, their original divergence would have taken place many times too long ago to be recognizable by the available methods. The judgments that linguists make today about the relationships among the languages of the world are summarized in Table 4–1 in the Appendix to this chapter.

The greatest linguistic diversity in the world today is found in areas like New Guinea, where modern technology has only recently penetrated. Modern communications and the geographical extent of modern political units tend to encourage a few major languages to spread at the expense of most others. The native languages of the Americas remain very diverse, but they are dying out rapidly under the onslaught of English, Spanish, and Portuguese, and under the homogenizing pressures of modern technology and communication.

Throughout Asia and Africa, a few languages that happen to be spoken in strategic areas or by powerful peoples are gaining speakers while the minority languages of weaker societies retreat. To linguists, the disappearing languages offer precious testimony of the rich diversity of which the human intellect is capable. Linguists can only struggle to record as much as possible of the full range of the world's linguistic diversity before it is smothered under the homogenizing pressure of a few dominant languages.

REASONS FOR LEXICAL CHANGES

As we will see in Chapters 8 and 13, the reasons for changes in phonology and syntax are often in dispute, and occasionally mysterious. The reasons for changes in vocabulary are less obscure. Technical and social innovations, migration to a new environment where there are new things to talk about, and borrowing from the languages of prestigious neighbors all call for new vocabulary.

Speakers are able to manipulate their lexicon more easily and more self-consciously than they can manipulate their phonology or syntax. We deliberately choose our words so as to demonstrate our cleverness, our alertness, our awareness of the seriousness or frivolity of the situation, our status in society, or the status to which we aspire. Far from always wanting to sound like others, we often seek to sound just a bit more clever or modern or important or serious or tough or, indeed, a bit more of whatever quality we happen to find desirable. Since many people are likely to be striving for these same qualities, we must always compete with others. Admired words are easily imitated, but the fresh innovations of one period quickly become the stale clichés of the next. We all have to keep changing our language simply to keep up with the crowd.

Individuals and groups have their favorite words that they use as badges of their social roles and aspirations. The words of admired groups are easily imitated but, with wide imitation, these words soon lose their special standing. Newer words must then be found in order to keep oneself or one's group in the lead. This cycle of innovation–imitation–innovation can be seen most clearly in the restless replacement of slang as each generation and each social movement seeks to differentiate itself from its predecessors, but the same forces drive changes in other areas of the lexicon as well. More clearly than phonology or syntax, the lexicon shows how innovation and imitation work together as an engine that can bring continual change to a language. Many lexical innovations and lexical fads will fade with time, but a few become established and leave the language permanently changed.

Borrowing, the need for new technical terms, the search for novelty, and all the many processes by which new words can be formed result in a restlessly changing vocabulary. Phonology and syntax also change, but they change at a more stately pace. The lexicon demonstrates more clearly than any other linguistic domain that languages never stay in one place.

APPENDIX: LANGUAGE FAMILIES OF THE WORLD

Table 4–1 summarizes our present knowledge of linguistic classification, but much work remains to be done. Linguists differ greatly in their judgments about language relatedness, and some of the uncertainties and disagreements are suggested in the entries of the table. The languages of some "families," such as "Indo-Pacific," have not yet been well classified, and it is possible that they are no more than convenient labels under which, in the absence of firm evidence for their relationship, all the languages of an area can be grouped. It must be remembered that it is never possible to demonstrate conclusively that two languages are *not* related. The most we can ever know is that no relationship has, so far, been demonstrated. Some related languages have probably drifted so far apart that we will never know of the connection between them.

A special comment is called for concerning the classification of the Native American or "Amerindian" languages. Joseph Greenberg has recently proposed that all Native American languages, except for Eskimo-Aleut in the far north and the Na-Dene languages of western Canada and the United States are ultimately related to each other in one enormous and diverse language family. He divides this family into a half dozen subgroups and these in turn into smaller sub-subgroups. These smaller divisions correspond in part, though by no means exactly, to language families that others have recognized. Greenberg's new classification has not received general acceptance by linguists working on Amerindian languages, but it brings a welcome organization to a very complex field, so it is Greenberg's classification that is given here. At the very least, it will be his classification that people argue *against* in the coming years, even if it is not finally accepted. Readers should be warned that many linguists who work most closely with American Indian languages are very skeptical of this classification, and they continue to argue in favor of several entirely independent Amerindian families.

No one has proposed a scheme for classifying the languages of the Old World languages that is quite so comprehensive as Greenberg's classification of the New World languages, but a number of suggestions have been made for wider groupings than are shown in Table 4–1. One proposal that has aroused a good deal of recent interest originated with Soviet linguists. They have argued that several of the language families listed in the table, including Indo-European, Dravidian, Uralic, Altaic, and possibly Afro-Asiatic are all united in one enormous family to which they give the name "Nostratic." A few people have gone so far as to suggest that Eskimo is also related to these. However, with languages as diverse as these, there is always room for strong differences of opinion. So far, only a small minority of linguists outside the Soviet Union are prepared to accept Nostratic.

In Table 4–1 the language families are ordered geographically, starting in southern Africa, moving northward to Europe and then across Asia and the Pacific, and finally down through the Americas. Where subgrouping is reasonably clear, subgroups are shown. Names in bold face type stand for groups of related languages or for "language isolates," i.e., single languages with no known relationship to any other language. Names in Roman type are the individual languages within larger language families. A dagger (†) indicates an ancient language that is now extinct. The figures in parentheses give an estimate of the number of native and non-native speakers, in millions, in 1990. An attempt has been made to include most of the world's languages that are spoken by three million or more people. Also included are all the languages from which examples have been drawn elsewhere in this book, as well as other languages that may have a special interest for readers. Languages not followed by a number are spoken by fewer than one million people. The number of languages spoken today has been variously estimated at between 3000 and 8000, so the table is far from exhaustive.

Table 4-1
Language Families of the World

Africe

Khoisan. The languages of the San (formerly known as "Bushman") and Khoikhoi peoples of Southern Africa.

Niger-Kordofanian. An extensive family of several hundred languages that covers much of sub-Saharan Africa. It has several branches.

  Benue-Congo. Includes the sprawling group of Bantu languages that covers most of southern Africa and much of eastern Africa: Zulu (7), Xhosa (7), Sotho (7), Thonga (3), and Tswana (3) of South Africa; Shona (7), Makua (3), Nyanja (4), Nyamwezi-Sukuma (4), and Mbundu (6) of southeast Africa; Bemba (2), Rundi (6), Rwanda (8), and Kinyarwanda of south-central Africa; Kikuyu (5) Luhya (3), Swahili (43), Kamba (3), and Luganda (3) of east Africa; Kituba (4), Kikongo (3), Luba-Lulua (6), Lingala (6), and Sango (3) of central Africa. The **Benue-Congo** group also includes many non-Bantu languages, including Efik (6) and Tiv (2) of Nigeria.

  Kwa. A large group of west African languages, including Akan-Twi-Fante (7) and Ewe (3) of Ghana, and Igbo (16) and Yoruba (18) of Nigeria.

  Mande. Includes Malinke-Bambara-Dyula (9) and Mende (2) of Sierra Leone.

  West-Atlantic. Includes Wolof (6) of Senegal, Fuuta Jalon (3) of Guinea, and Fula (13).

  Gur. Includes More (4) of Burkina Faso.

Nilo-Saharan. A family embracing a number of languages spoken along the upper Nile in Sudan and to the west and south, including the **Nilotic** languages such as Luo (3), Dinka and Nuer, and the **Saharan** languages such as Kanuri (4) in Chad and Niger.

Near East, Europe, Central and South Asia

Afro-Asiatic. A language family of northeastern Africa and the Near East, known both from ancient times and from still-vigorous modern languages. It is divided among several subgroups, including:

  Chadic. A number of languages of the area around Lake Chad and northern Nigeria, including Hausa (34).

  Berber. Several languages of Morocco and Algeria, including Kabyle (3), Shilha (3), and Tamazight (3).

  Cushitic. Galla-Oromo (10), Somali (7) and other languages in and near Ethiopia.

  † Ancient **Egyptian** and its later descendant † **Coptic.**

Table 4-1 (continued)

Semitic. † Akkadian, † Aramaic, † Phoenician, Arabic (197), and Hebrew (4) of the ancient and modern Near East, as well as several languages of Ethiopia including Amharic (17) and Tigrinya (4).

† **Sumerian.** An extinct language of Mesopotamia, famous as the first language to leave extensive written records. No known linguistic affiliation.

Caucasian. Several highly diverse languages of the Caucasus which may fall into more than a single language family. Includes Georgian (4).

Altaic. A language family spread from Turkey all across central Asia. Similarities have been noted with **Uralic,** Korean, and even Japanese. Three subgroups are recognized:

Turkic. Turkish of Turkey (55); Azerbaijani of Iran and the USSR (14); Turkoman (3), Kazakh (8), Kirghiz (2), Tatar (7), Uzbek (13), all of the USSR; and Uighur (7) of Chinese Turkestan.

Mongol (5).

Tungus. Includes a few minor languages of Eastern Siberia, and also Manchu, the language of the conquering people who founded the last Imperial dynasty of China.

Uralic. Sami (formerly called "Lapp"), Finnish (6), Estonian (1), Hungarian (14), and various minority languages of the Soviet Union including Samoyedic, Ostyak, Mordvin, and others. Some linguists have suggested a distant genetic relationship between **Uralic** and **Altaic.**

Basque. A language spoken in northwestern Spain and adjacent regions of France with no known linguistic affiliation.

† **Etruscan.** An extinct language of Italy with no known affiliation.

Indo-European. The most widespread and most thoroughly studied language family of the world, with several well-defined subgroups:

Celtic. Formerly distributed across much of Western Europe but now confined to small remnant groups: Breton in France, and Welsh, Irish, and Scots Gaelic in the British Isles.

Germanic. English (443), Dutch-Flemish (21), Afrikaans (10), German (118), Yiddish (less than 1), Danish (5), Swedish (9), Norwegian (5), Icelandic (less that 1). The affiliation of English-based pidgins and creoles can be questioned, but they can be placed here for convenience: Tok Pisin of Papua, New Guinea, and the English-based creole languages of Hawaii and many parts of the Caribbean.

Romance. † Latin and its modern descendants: Portuguese (173), Galician (3), Spanish (341), Catalan (9), French (121), Italian (63), Romanian (25). The Romance-based creoles, including Haitian Creole French (6) and others, should also be noted.

Slavic. Serbo-Croatian (20), Bulgarian (9), Macedonian (2), Slovenian (2), Czech (12), Slovak (5), Polish (43), Ukranian (45), Byelorussian (10), Great Russian (293).

Albanian (5).

Armenian (5).

Greek. † Ancient and Modern (12).

Baltic. Lithuanian (3), Latvian (2).

† **Anatolian.** Extinct languages of Anatolia (modern Turkey), including † Hittite.

† **Tocharian.** Extinct languages known from sixth century AD inscriptions from Chinese Turkestan.

Indo-Iranian. Two branches: **Iranian** includes † Scythian, Kurdish (9), Farsi (Persian) (32), Pushto (21), Baluchi (4) and Tajik (4). The **Indic** branch includes ancient † Sanskrit and † Pali; Sinhalese (13) of Sri Lanka; Nepali (13) of Nepal; Sindhi (16) of Pakistan; Kashmiri (4) and Punjabi (84) of Pakistan and India; Bhili (3), Gujerati (38), Konkani (4),

(continued)

Table 4–1 (*continued*)

Marathi (64), Oryia (30), and Assamese (22) in India; Bengali (184) in India and Bangladesh. The most extensive Indic language is Hindi/Urdu (444) of both India and Pakistan. Urdu is written with the Arabic alphabet and Hindi with Devanagari, but the spoken forms are so similar that they count as one language.

Burushaski. A language of the Hunza area of northern Pakistan with no known linguistic affiliation.

Dravidian. Several important languages, mostly of South India: Telegu (68), Kannada (41), Malayalam (34), and Tamil (65), the latter spoken in Sri Lanka as well as India. This family also includes a number of smaller languages, such as Oraon (2) and Gondi (2) in central India, and still others spoken as far to the northwest as Pakistan.

Austro-Asiatic. Two main branches are recognized:

Munda. Several languages of Central India, including Mundari and Santali (5).

Mon-Khmer. Scattered languages distributed from eastern India across mainland Southeast Asia and south to Malaysia, including Khmer (7), the language of Kampuchea, Mon and Palaung of Burma, and many others.

The Pacific

Austronesian. Hundreds of languages spoken over a huge area from Madagascar, through Indonesia and all across the Pacific, as far east as Hawaii. Its geographical range is rivaled only by Indo-European. The subclassification of the Austronesian languages is not yet clear. The **Western Indonesian** languages seem to be relatively closely related. In addition to Indonesian-Malay (138), the very similar official languages of Indonesia and Malaysia, they include Achehnese (3), Batak (4), and Minangkabau (6) of Sumatra; Iban of Kalimantan; Javanese (58), Balinese (3), Madurese (10), and Sundanese (24) of other Indonesian islands, and probably distant Malagasy (11) of Madagascar. Bugis (4) of Sulawesi seems to be more distantly related. All the languages of the Philippines are Austronesian. They include Tagalog (36), Cebuano-Bisayan (12), Bikoi (4), Ilocano (7), Panay-Hillgaynon (6), Samar-Leyte (3), and many others of more restricted distribution, including Bontok and Hanunóo. The **Polynesian** languages form a reasonably well-defined subgroup and include Hawaiian, Samoan, Maori, and others. The greatest diversity within this family seems to occur in New Guinea and neighboring areas, but other related languages are found throughout Micronesia, among the native people of Taiwan, and among a few of the minority peoples of southern Vietnam. Various proposals have been made for relating **Austronesian** to **Mon-Khmer** to **Kam-Tai,** and even to Japanese.

Indo-Pacific. A highly diverse group of "non-Austronesian" languages, spoken in parts of New Guinea and the neighboring islands. These languages are often called "Papuan," and linguists are by no means agreed that they all fall into a single family. They may be related to Andamanese spoken in the Andaman Islands in the Bay of Bengal, and possibly to the extinct † Tasmanian language of the island off southeastern Australia.

Australian. About 200 surviving languages of the native peoples of Australia. Includes Dyirbal.

Southeast and East Asia

Kam-Tai. Thai (48) of Thailand, Shan (3) of Eastern Burma, and Lao (4) of Laos are closely related. Somewhat more distantly related languages are found on Hainan island off the Chinese coast, and on the southern China mainland, including Zhuang (14). Attempts have been made to relate **Kam-Thai** to **Sino-Tibetan** on the one hand and to **Austronesian** on the other.

Viet-Muong. Vietnamese (57) and a few minority languages of mountainous northern Vietnam.

Table 4-1 (continued)

Various attempts, none entirely convincing, have been made to relate **Viet-Muong** to **Kam-Tai**, to **Mon-Khmer**, and to **Sino-Tibetan**.

Sino-Tibetan. Second only to Indo-European in total numbers of speakers, this family includes Chinese, and a large number of Tibeto-Burman languages to the south and west:

   Tibeto-Burman. Far more diverse than the Chinese branch of **Sino-Tibetan**, the **Tibeto-Burman** languages have only a fraction as many speakers. **Tibeto-Burman** includes dozens of languages spoken from Nepal and Tibet in the west, across northeastern India, throughout Burma, and into northern Thailand and southwestern China. In addition to Tibetan (5) and Burmese (30), this subgroup includes Newari and Sherpa in Nepal, Karen in Burma, Garo and its close relatives Atong, Wanang, and Kachari in India, and many others.

   Chinese. Far less diverse than **Tibeto-Burman, Chinese** nevertheless includes at least five mutually unintelligible languages. (1) Various dialects of Mandarin (864) are spoken throughout northern and western China. Putonghua, the official spoken language of China, is a standardized form of Mandarin based primarily on the dialect of Beijing. Mandarin is spoken by more people than any other language in the world. (2) Wu (62) is spoken in the lower Yangtze area and includes the important urban dialects of Shanghai, Wenzhou and other cities. (3) Min (48) includes the dialects of Taiwan, as well as those of Fujien, Fuzhou, and Amoy provinces along the adjacent China coast, and it is spoken by many overseas Chinese. (4) Hakka (32) is spoken in scattered agricultural enclaves throughout southeastern China. (5) Yue, widely known as "Cantonese" (63), is the language of the southern coastal provinces, including the cities of Guangzhou (Canton) and Hong Kong.

Hmong-Mien. Also known as **Miao-Yao**, this group comprises several languages of southern China, and northern Southeast Asia, including Hmong (5) and Yi (6). Hmong is the language of many Vietnamese refugees in the United States. It has often been supposed that **Hmong-Mien** is related to **Sino-Tibetan**, but the evidence is not convincing.

Korean (71). No certain linguistic affiliation has been established for Korean, but attempts have been made to demonstrate a relationship to **Altaic** on the one hand and to Japanese on the other.

Japanese (125). As with Korean, no certain linguistic affiliation is known for Japanese, though several have been proposed, including a relationship to Korean, or even **Altaic** in one direction, and to **Austronesian** in the other.

Ainu. An aboriginal language of Japan, with no known linguistic affiliation.

Paleo-Siberian. Several scattered languages of Siberia that may, or may not, be related to each other, including Chukchee, Kamchadal, Koryak, Ket, Yukaghir.

The Americas

Eskimo-Aleut. Aleut of the Aleutian islands, and at least two Eskimo languages: Yupik of Eastern Siberia and Alaska, and Inuit spoken from the Yukon eastward to Greenland.

Na-Dene. Haida and Tlingit of the Pacific Coast, and the **Athabaskan** group that includes several languages of inland Western Canada as well as Navajo and Apache of the southwestern United States.

Amerind. This extensive grouping of languages, recently proposed as a family by Joseph Greenberg, includes all of the native languages of the Americas except for **Eskimo-Aleut** and **Na-Dene.** Greenberg recognizes six major subgroups. The first of these he calls **Northern Amerind.** It is so extensive and includes so many familiar North American Indian languages that its three major branches are listed separately here.

(continued)

Table 4–1 (*continued*)

Almosan-Keresiouan. The first of the three branches of **Northern Amerind** is, in turn, divided into two parts. The **Almosan** half includes the **Algonquian** languages such as Cree, Ojibwa, Delaware and others, that once covered most of northeastern North America, and the Salish and Wakashan languages of the Pacific Northwest. The **Keresiouan** half includes the Iroquoian languages of the northeast, the Siouan languages of the plains, and Keresian in the southwest.

Penutian. The second of three branches of **Northern Amerind** includes a large number of languages spread from Tsimshian, Chinook, and others of the northwest Pacific coast; through Maidu, Miwok and others of California; Zuni of the southwestern United States; Natchez, Choctaw and others of the Gulf states; all the way to the Mayan languages of southern Mexico.

Hokan. The third of the three branches of **Northern Amerind** is found primarily in California and Baja California. It includes Pomo, Washo, Atsugewi, and others.

Central Amerind. This group includes Hopi, Tewa, Kiowa, and other languages of the southwestern United States as well as important languages of Mexico: Zapotec, Mixtec, Aztec, and many others.

Chibchan-Paezan. A number of scattered languages spoken from southern Mexico through central America and the northwestern portion of South America as far south as Argentina.

Equatorial-Tucanoan. A group scattered from the Caribbean to beyond the Amazon as far south as Uruguay. It includes the important Paraguayan language Guarani (4), as well as Tupi, Arawakan, and many others.

Ge-Pano-Carib. Many languages from the Caribbean coast of Venezuela across tropical lowland South America and as far south as Uruguay.

Andean. Spoken in pockets from Ecuador to the southern tip of South America, this group includes two of the most widespread surviving American languages, Quechua (8), and Aymara (2), both spoken in Peru and Bolivia.

PART TWO

Sounds

INTRODUCTION TO PART TWO

The chapters of Part Two are concerned with speech sounds, the most directly observable aspect of language. Chapter 5 describes the sounds themselves, and the way we use our vocal organs to produce them. Chapter 6 deals with the organization of speech sounds in particular languages, with the way they affect one another, and with the patterns into which they fall. Chapter 7 is concerned with the variability of speech sounds, the way in which pronunciation varies from one regional dialect to another, from one social class to another, and even from one occasion to another. Finally, Chapter 8 considers the way in which the sounds of languages change with the passage of time.

CHAPTER FIVE

Phonetics

INTRODUCTION

Much of the process of talking and understanding takes place in the minds of speakers and listeners, well beyond any area where it can be directly observed. We can watch a person's gestures and we can look at the context within which the speech occurs, but we cannot peer into the minds of speakers or listeners to find out how they form their sounds or words or sentences. The only parts of the language itself that we can observe directly are the articulation of the sounds by the vocal organs, the passage of the sounds through the air, and, to a very limited extent, what happens in the ear. The study of speech sounds forms the most concrete branch of linguistics.

Technically, speech sounds are known as **phones,** and **phonetics** is the science that studies them. In principle, it should be possible to study speech sounds at three points: the vocal organs where they are produced, the air through which the sound waves of speech are carried, and the ear. In practice, too little is known about the workings of the ear to make its study useful. The study of sound waves that carry language through the air is known as acoustic phonetics. This is a well-developed specialty, but too technical a subject to be treated in this book. This leaves **articulatory phonetics,** the study of the mechanics of the vocal organs, and of their positions and movements during speech, as by far the most useful way of learning about, describing, and understanding the sounds of speech. The study of phonetics, in other words, begins with a lesson in anatomy.

AIRFLOW

Most speech sounds begin with the lungs. It is the lungs that control the flow of air as it passes up the trachea (windpipe) and through the **larynx** (the voice box, or "Adam's apple"), on through the **pharynx** (the space above the larynx), into either the **oral tract** or the **nasal tract,** and finally out through the mouth or the nose (see Fig. 5–1).

After the air leaves the lungs, the first point where anything can happen is the larynx, and the crucial part of the larynx is a pair of small muscular folds, the vocal cords, that stretch along either side of the air passage. The space between these vocal cords is called the **glottis.** In their most relaxed and open position, as in normal silent breathing, the vocal cords allow the air to pass freely and quietly through the glottis in both directions, but they can also be closed tightly together so that no air at all can get through. We open and close the glottis repeatedly as we speak, but it takes a bit of practice to become aware of its position and to control its movements consciously.

If the lungs exert gentle pressure to exhale, the air can still be held back by a closure in the throat, and it is the glottis that is closed. The air is released and allowed to escape when the vocal cords open. Typically, English words such as *apple* or *orange,* that are spelled with an initial vowel, really begin when the glottis opens to allow air to pass out through the vocal organs. English speakers

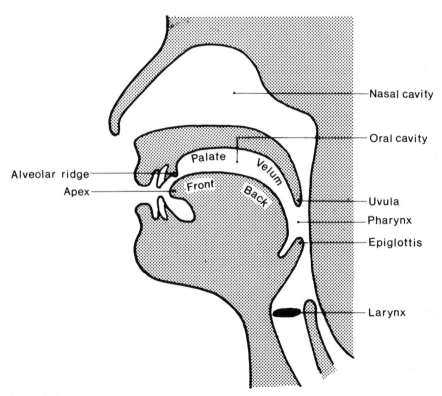

Figure 5–1
The organs of speech are shown.

close and then reopen the glottis in the middle of the noise of dismay that we sometimes spell *oh-oh*. With a bit of practice, it is possible to learn to close and reopen the vocal cords at will.

The vocal cords can do more than simply open and close. If they are given just the right tension, the passing air stream will set them into vibration, much as the air stream causes the reed of a musical instrument to vibrate. It is the vibration of the vocal cords that gives the musical pitch to a hum. You can feel the vibration by placing your fingers on your Adam's apple and saying a prolonged *zzzzzz* (not whispered, but out loud!). If you say *ssssss* there will be no vibration. If you alternate *s* and *z* by saying *sssszzzzsssssszzzz* you will both hear and feel the vibration being turned on and off. The vibration will be especially clear if you pinch your ears shut, for the resonance of the *z*'s will then contrast more strongly with the relative silence of the *s*'s.

When the string of a guitar or violin is tightened and then let loose again, it vibrates at varying frequencies and, as a result, its pitch rises and then falls. In much the same way, the vocal cords can be adjusted to vibrate at different frequencies and to impose a range of musical pitches on the passing air stream. The greater the frequency of vibration, the higher the pitch. When humming a tune, the vocal cords must be adjusted to a new frequency for each new note.

The humming sound imposed on the air stream by the vibrating vocal cords is called **voice.** The English vowels, and many of its consonants, including *b, d, g, v, z,* and *n,* are accompanied by vibration of the vocal cords and are therefore said to be "voiced." During the production of other consonants, such as *p, t, k, f, s,* and *sh,* voicing is briefly interrupted (that is, the vocal cords stop vibrating), and such consonants are described as **voiceless.**

After the air stream has passed through the larynx, it moves on up through the pharynx and toward the part of the vocal tract that can be seen in a mirror. With your tongue or finger, you can feel that the front part of the roof of your mouth is hard. This is the **hard palate,** and its firmness is due to underlying bone. Farther back, at about the point where too vigorous a probe can cause gagging, the bone ends and the soft palate or **velum** begins. The velum is a muscular gateway that can be raised or lowered to direct the path of the air stream. By lowering your velum, you open the nasal tract and direct some or all of the air out through your nose. When your velum is up, on the other hand, it articulates against the back wall of the pharynx, and it can then close off the nasal tract completely and direct all of the air out through the oral tract. A look in the mirror will give you a surprisingly good view of the velum and of its movements.

When your mouth is shut during normal breathing, the velum must be lowered so that the air can pass in and out through your nose, but for the majority of speech sounds, the velum is up, so all the air passes out of the mouth. For **nasal** sounds such as *m* or *n,* however, or when humming with the lips closed, the velum must be lowered, to let the air pass out through the nose. A good test for the position of the velum is to pinch your nose closed while trying to articulate a speech sound. If the sound is normal, it can only mean

that your velum is up, so that it prevents the air from moving into the nasal tract
where it would be obstructed by the pinched nose. If the sound is distorted, on
the other hand, it is because air tries to escape through the nose but fails to do
so, and this can happen only if the velum is down and the nasal tract is open.

Most of the remaining complexities of speech sounds are introduced by the
movements of the tongue and lips. With them, we guide or obstruct the passage
of air and change the resonance properties of the oral tract. In that way, we
alter the acoustic quality of our speech sounds.

CONSONANTS

Speech sounds fall into two broad categories. For **vowels** the articulators are
relatively open so that the air can escape easily. **Consonants** are the speech
sounds in which the vocal tract is more constricted or even closed off entirely.
The consonants, in turn, can be further distinguished from one another in two
ways, first by the **point of articulation** and second by the **manner of articulation.**
The point of articulation is the place in the mouth where the articulation takes
place, from lips at the front to glottis in the rear. The manner of articulation
refers to the type of closure that is achieved. The types of consonants that
are described in the following paragraphs, such as stops, nasals, and fricatives, are distinguished by the characteristic manners in which they are
articulated.

Stops

The greatest possible restriction of the air flow is to stop it off completely.
Speech sounds in which the vocal tract is fully closed are known, appropriately, as **stops,** and they can be made at many points along the vocal tract.
Farthest to the front are the lips, and by closing the lips you can articulate a
bilabial stop. If you say *apapapa* you produce a series of bilabial stops separated by vowels. The English sound that is written with the letter *p* is a
voiceless bilabial stop. It is called "voiceless" because the vocal cords stop
vibrating during the stop. If vibration continues without interruption through a
series of bilabial stops, they will sound more like *abababa,* and these are called
"voiced bilabial stops."

Symbols have to be used in a particularly careful way when describing
speech sounds, but familiar letters can often be used. Thus linguists accept the
convention of English, and of many other languages, and use *p* for voiceless
bilabial stops, and *b* for voiced bilabial stops. Since people can articulate many
more sounds than can be distinguished by the meager 26 letters of the English
alphabet, however, the usual letters have to be supplemented by a considerable number of **phonetic symbols,** including both specially designed letters and
various hooks, lines, and accents that are added to the letters and that linguists
call **diacritical** marks. Phonetic symbols are conventionally written within
square brackets: [ ]. Anything written in these brackets must be interpreted as

having the value assigned to it within the study of phonetics. As in the case of [p] and [b], this is often similar to the sound that the symbols represent in English or in some other language, but many of the symbols will be new. Not even familiar symbols can always be assumed to represent exactly the sounds of English.

It is important to realize that the relationship between a speech sound and its symbol is entirely arbitrary. Any symbol can be used for any sound as long as we are clear about how we are using it, but our task will be easier if we can agree on common conventions. Most of the phonetic symbols used in this book are among those recommended by the International Phonetic Association (IPA), an organization that tries to standardize usage. The most useful consonant symbols are shown in Table 5–1, which is constructed so that points of articulation are placed along one dimension and manners of articulation along the other. Where two symbols occur together, the one on the left stands for a voiceless phone and that on the right for a voiced one. All these symbols are needed so that the sounds of all languages can be represented, and standardization helps linguists to understand each other's work. To start with, we are on familiar ground: [p] stands for a voiceless bilabial stop; [b] for a voiced bilabial stop.

The English bilabial stops differ from each other in one other way than just voicing. [p] is usually followed by a slight puff of breath, while [b] is not. You can feel the difference with your hand or see the difference by letting a small strip of paper flutter in front of your mouth while saying pairs of words like *pie* and *buy*. The puff of air that accompanies the [p] is called **aspiration,** and when we want to be precise we describe English [pʰ] as a voiceless, bilabial, aspirated stop, where [ʰ] stands for aspiration. English [b], by contrast, is a voiced, bilabial, *un*aspirated stop.

Voicelessness and aspiration often occur together. Aspiration seems to reinforce a voiceless sound such as English [p] and make it more clearly different from a voiced [b]. Not all languages have aspirated stops, however. The voiceless stops of French have little aspiration, and even in English, a few voiceless stops are unaspirated. The paper strip test with *spy, spoor,* and *spit* should convince you that their *p*'s are considerably less aspirated than those of *pie, poor, pit.*

[pʰ], [p], and [b] are all bilabial, but the bilabial position is only one of many points where stops can be articulated. Behind the lips, they can next be conveniently produced with the tip, or **apex,** of the tongue. The apex can stop off the air flow anywhere from the teeth at the front to a point quite far back on the hard palate, and all such stops can be called **apical.** In English we make most of our apical stops at approximately the area of the **alveolar ridge,** the ridge of gums behind the upper teeth that you can easily find with the tip of your tongue. Since the apex of the tongue can hit the roof of the mouth in several places, particular kinds of apical stops are often named by the location where the tongue hits. The typical English **alveolar** stops are one variety of apical stop. [tʰ], [t], and [d] are used to symbolize the English alveolar stops of words such as *toe, stow,* and *dough.*

Table 5–1
Consonants

	Bilabial	Labiodental	Dental	Alveolar	Retroflex	Palatal	Velar	Uvular	Pharyngeal	Glottal
Stops	p b		t̪ d̪	t d	ʈ ɖ	c ɟ	k g	q ɢ		ʔ
Nasals	m	ɱ	n̪	n	ɳ	ɲ	ŋ	ɴ		
Fricatives	ɸ β	f v	θ ð	s z		ʃ ʒ	x ɣ	χ ʁ	ħ ʕ	h ɦ
Approximant	w			ɹ		j				
Lateral approximant				l						
Affricates		p͡f		t͡s d͡z		t͡ʃ d͡ʒ	k͡x			
Trills	ʙ			r				ʀ		
Taps or Flaps				ɾ	ɽ					
Implosives	ɓ			ɗ			ɠ			
Clicks	ʘ			ǃ						

Some languages have apical stops at slightly different positions. French stops are usually **dental** rather than alveolar, with the tongue touching the teeth, considerably farther front than in English. Even the English word *width* usually has a dental rather than an alveolar stop. Hindi has both dental stops and **retroflex** stops. Retroflex stops are made by curling the tongue quite far back and articulating the apex against the hard palate well to the rear of the alveolar ridge. When dental and retroflex stops need to be distinguished on paper, dental stops can be written with a small open box beneath the letter, [d̪] and [t̪]. The retroflex stops are written as [ḍ] and [ṭ].

The initial stops of *cold* and *gold* are articulated still farther to the rear of the mouth by articulating the **back** part of the surface of the tongue against the velum. These are called **velar** stops, and [kʰ] and [k] are used for the aspirated and unaspirated voiceless velar stops in *cool* and *school*. [g] is used for the voiced velar stop in *ghoul*. If you repeat *keep* and *cool* several times while paying careful attention to the position of your tongue and lips, you will notice that your tongue is pushed considerably farther forward for *keep* than for *cool*. At the same time, you round your lips more for *cool* than for *keep*. By adjusting the tongue and lips in this way, you anticipate the position that they will need to assume during the following vowel. Some languages have stops made with the surface of the tongue articulating very far forward against the hard palate. These **palatal** stops can be written as [c] and [ɟ].

Stops can be made as far back as the uvula, the small lobe of flesh that hangs from the rear edge of the velum in the back of the mouth. English does not have uvular stops, and English speakers often find them difficult to articulate. The flow of air must be stopped off very far back in the mouth, well back of the rearmost English [k]. [q] and [ɢ] are used for voiceless and voiced uvular stops.

The rearmost point where a stop is possible is the glottis. A **glottal stop** is made by closing the vocal cords, and its symbol looks like a question mark without a dot: [ʔ]. In addition to the glottal stops in *oh-oh*, which is generally pronounced [ʔoʔo] or [ʔʌʔo], English speakers usually close the glottis briefly when they articulate voiceless stops after vowels. Words such as *ape, ate,* and *ache* generally have a glottal stop just before the final [p], [t] or [k]. In some urban dialects in Britain, such as London's Cockney, these glottal stops have become especially prominent and have even replaced the other consonants. Glottal stops can also be heard clearly in some New York City pronunciations of the *t* in words such as *bottle* and even *glottal*. Since the vocal cords cannot vibrate while closed, glottal stops can never be voiced. This means that only one symbol is needed for the glottal stop.

It is possible to make simultaneous closures at two points along the vocal tract. Some African languages have what are known as **labiovelar** stops in which the air stream is stopped simultaneously at both the lips and velum. Labiovelar stops are written with a pair of letters connected with a tie, as in Yoruba [ak͡pá] 'arm,' and [àg͡bà] 'old.'

It is important to understand that stops can be articulated anywhere along the continuous range of the vocal tract. Of course the sounds used in any language must be distinct enough to be readily discriminated by the listener, and this means that no single language can exploit more than a small number of the points where stops are possible. Many languages, in fact, have stops at just three or four positions, with the bilabial, apical, and velar positions the most common. Nevertheless, the total range of points exploited by one or another of the world's languages is very large.

Nasals

During the production of both [p] and [b], the velum is raised, closing the nasal tract and forcing all the air out through the oral tract. If, instead, you lower the velum during a bilabial stop, the air stream will escape through your nose. If your vocal cords keep vibrating, the result will be a voiced bilabial nasal, conveniently symbolized by [m]. Notice that we have no voluntary control over any part of the nasal tract past the velum. If the velum is lowered, the only way to prevent air from escaping through the nose is to pinch the nostrils closed with the fingers or to catch a good nose cold, which clogs up the passage and distorts the sounds. Ordinary English [m] is voiced, but it is easy to produce voiceless nasals. The sound (or the lack of sound) of ordinary exhalation with the mouth closed might even be described as a "voiceless bilabial nasal." A few languages do make use of voiceless nasals, and these phones are symbolized by a small circle written below the letter. A voiceless [m] would be written as [m̥]. Burmese has a voiceless bilabial nasal in [m̥má] 'mirror.' This [m̥] amounts to a voiceless puff of air through the nose, and it is followed immediately by a voiced [m] when the vocal cords start to vibrate. To an English speaker, the acoustic impression of this word is somewhat like [h] followed by [ma].

   Apical nasals of various sorts are also possible: dental, alveolar, or retroflex, and voiced or voiceless. Phoneticians use [n] to stand for voiced apical nasals and, where precision is required, [n̪] can be used for a dental nasal and [ɳ] for a retroflex nasal. Most English apical nasals are alveolar, but *tenth* usually has an apico-dental [n̪]. Burmese has a voiceless apical nasal in [n̥ni?] 'two.'

   English has velar nasals in words such as *sing, bang, wrong, flung,* and linguists write this sound as [ŋ], an *n* with a *g*-like tail. English words never begin with a velar nasal, but many languages have no such restriction. Burmese has both voiced and voiceless initial velar nasals: [ŋâ] 'fish', [ŋ̥ŋe?] 'bird'. The phonetic symbols used for nasals at several other points of articulation are shown in Table 5–1.

Fricatives

Instead of stopping off the oral passage completely, the **articulators,** (as the vocal organs that move and come into contact are called) can be pressed together only tightly enough to produce a hiss as the air passes through. The result will be a **fricative** rather than a stop. Fricatives can be articulated in all the same places as stops, and fricatives allow some extra complications of their own.

English has several fricatives. [f] and [v] of *ferry* and *very* are made by pressing the lower lip against the upper teeth, but allowing some air to be squeezed out between them. Since these sounds involve both the lip and teeth, they are known, respectively, as voiceless and voiced **labiodental** fricatives. **Bilabial fricatives,** with the air hissing between the two lips, are also possible. Spanish has a bilabial voiced fricative that is spelled *v* as in the name, *Havana*. Voiceless and voiced bilabial fricatives are written as [ɸ] and [β].

English has a second pair of fricatives that are usually described as **interdental.** The term implies that the apex of the tongue goes between the teeth, and so it may, but sometimes the tongue is squeezed tightly behind the upper teeth instead. In either case air hisses over and around the tongue and against the upper teeth. These are the "th" sounds in such words as *thigh* and *thy*. Although we spell both these words with *th*, they have distinct initial sounds, for English has two interdental fricatives. We use [θ] for the voiceless interdental fricative in *thing, three, ether, bath,* and *thigh,* and [ð] for the voiced interdental fricative in *them, these, either, bathe,* and *thy*.

Next, English has two pairs of fricatives that are known as **sibilants** and that are articulated by squeezing the tongue against the alveolar ridge or palate. A voiceless [s] is found in *soup, city, bossy, kiss* and a corresponding voiced [z] in *zoo, buzzard, cheese.* In addition, we have voiceless [ʃ] in *show, nation,* and *flash* and a corresponding voiced [ʒ] in *measure, leisure,* and, sometimes and for some speakers, in *garage, beige,* and *rouge.* Notice, however, that English does not have [ʒ] initially, except rather marginally in a few borrowed words like *genre* and in names like *Jacques.* [ʒ] is a bit unusual even at the end of a word, and some speakers pronounce *rouge* and *garage* with the final sound of *judge* rather than with [ʒ]. Everyone has a [ʒ] in *measure.*

A careful description of [s], [z], [ʃ], and [ʒ] is made difficult by the fact that speakers differ from one another in the way they articulate these sounds. Some speakers point the tip of their tongues upward while articulating them, producing friction with the apex of their tongues. Others point their tongues downward, pressing the apex behind the lower teeth and making the friction with the **front** of the tongue, the surface just behind the apex. Still others point their tongues up for one set, down for the other. These varied positions seem to produce no perceptible acoustic difference, and apparently each of us stumbles into one or the other articulation when we first learn our language. Once a tongue habit is established, there is never any reason to change.

In either case, [s] and [z] are alveolar or even dental, while [ʃ] and [ʒ] are postalveolar or palatal, but the acoustic quality of all sibilants is produced in considerable part by shooting the air in a fast and narrowly directed stream against the teeth or lips. In English, [s] and [z] are not only articulated farther forward than are [ʃ] and [ʒ], but more of the air is blown against the teeth. Slight differences in articulation can sharply redirect the air flow so that it blows against a quite different area and produces a different acoustic quality.

Most languages have at least one sibilant. Some, like English, have sibilants at two points of articulation, and a few languages have more.

Fricatives can be articulated farther back in the mouth than [ʃ] and [ʒ]. German has a voiceless velar fricative, as in *Bach,* that is symbolized as [x]. A corresponding voiced velar fricative is found in some pronunciations of Spanish *g,* in words such as *pago* 'I pay,' and is symbolized by [ɣ]. The standard Parisian dialect of French has a uvular fricative which is spelled *r* but which is symbolized phonetically as [ʁ]. This French *r* is usually voiced, as in *rouge* [ʁuž] 'red,' but it is occasionally voiceless as in *quatre* [kætʁ̥] 'four.'

Even further to the rear, Arabic has pharyngeal fricatives made by restricting the air flow through the pharynx. Pharyngeal consonants are difficult for English speakers to learn, since we are not accustomed to controlling the shape of the pharynx, but they occur freely in Arabic as in [ħammaam] 'bath' with an initial voiceless pharyngeal fricative [ħ], and [ʕamm] 'uncle' with an initial voiced pharyngeal fricative [ʕ].

[h] is used for a voiceless glottal fricative. English [h] usually has some glottal friction, but it has less friction than the similar phones of some other languages, so it is not the best possible example. Since English [h] has little restriction on the passage of air, it is sometimes described as an approximant rather than a fricative (see below). Occasionally it is even called a voiceless vowel that has the same tongue and lip position as the voiced vowel that follows. The [h]'s of *he* and *who,* for instance, are very different from each other, but they are both like the vowels that follow. In words like these, the transition from [h] to the vowel may be marked primarily by the onset of voicing, so that the most important characteristic of [h] is simply the absence of voicing. Usually, however, even English [h] does have a touch of friction, and the only way to make a loud [h] is give it more friction. A voiced glottal fricative is found in a few languages and is symbolized by [ɦ].

Nasal fricatives are not impossible, but they are rare. The air that escapes through the nose during any nasal phone reduces the air pressure in the mouth, and this makes it difficult to produce satisfactory friction. This is probably why they are rare.

Affricates

A simple stop is ordinarily released quite decisively, often into a vowel, but if a stop is released more gradually so that friction occurs during the release, we call the resulting phone an **affricate.** The initial and final consonants of *church* are voiceless affricates, and those of *judge* are voiced affricates. The affricate of *church* begins with a voiceless alveolar stop, similar, but not quite identical to [t]. The stop is then released into [ʃ]. Sometimes this affricate is symbolized as [tʃ], with a separate symbol for each of its parts, but often it is more convenient to have a single symbol, and [č] can be used. The corresponding fluent combination of voiced phones, [d] and [ʒ], produces the affricates of *judge,* and this can be symbolized as either [ǰ] or [dʒ] depending on whether its unitary or its complex character needs emphasis.

Not all languages have affricates, and it is rare for a language to have as many affricates as it has stops or fricatives, but affricates can be articulated wherever both a stop and a fricative are possible. The initial sound of German *pferd* 'horse' is an affricate, [p͡f], that combines a voiceless bilabial stop with a labiodental fricative. German *zu* 'to' and *zwei* 'two' begin with an affricate formed by releasing an apical [t] into a fricative [s]. Although spelled *z*, it is pronounced [t͡s].

Approximants

Stops require the articulators to close completely, and fricatives bring them close enough together to produce friction. Consonants in which the articulators are even less tightly closed, and in which the air can move freely enough through the vocal tract to avoid friction, are known as **approximants.** English has several approximants, and these can be taken as representative of a wider range of possibilities.

English [w] is a **labiovelar** approximant and, as the term "labio-velar" suggests, it has some degree of constriction at both the lips and at the velum. English speakers may notice the rounding and compression of the lips more than the narrowing at the velum, but by checking the tongue position carefully while articulating [w], the velar narrowing should also become apparent. The articulation of English [w] is very similar to that of the vowel [u] (see below).

In most dialects of English, *r* is an approximant made by bunching the tongue upward and backward, and sometimes by curling the apex into a more or less retroflex position, often with some lip rounding. Different dialects, and even different speakers, produce their *r*'s in rather different ways, so it is difficult to give a single description that is satisfactory for everyone. Some of the articulatory differences seem to produce very little auditory difference, but others are quite noticeable. The Scottish *r,* for instance is often an apical trill (see below). The most widespread type of English *r* can be represented by [ɹ]. Generally [ɹ] is voiced, but it can be voiceless when following a voiceless stop as in *pray* and *cream.*

The initial sound of words such as *yes, yellow,* and *young* is a **palatal** approximant, made with the tongue humped up toward the hard palate. The letter *y* must be reserved for a vowel, so the palatal approximant is written with [j], the letter that is used for this sound in German and the Scandinavian languages. Just as [w] is similar to the vowel [u], so the articulation of [j] is very much like that of the vowel [i] (see below).

Laterals are phones in which the tongue is articulated against the roof of the mouth, but air is allowed to escape quite freely around one or both sides. Several varieties of laterals are possible depending on which part of the tongue makes the articulation and the exact point where it strikes. English [l] is a lateral, usually made by articulating the apex of the tongue against the alveolar ridge. Like English [ɹ] and like the laterals in most languages, English [l] is usually voiced, although when following a voiceless stop, as in *play* or *clay,* it may be partially voiceless. Welsh has a distinctive voiceless [l̥]. In their original Welsh pronunciations the proper names *Llewelyn* and *Lloyd* begin with voiceless laterals. The air can escape so freely in a voiceless [l̥] that it may make little noise, and perhaps this is why voiceless laterals are less common than voiced laterals. It may also be the reason why, when they do occur, voiceless [l̥]'s typically have a good deal more friction than voiced [l]'s. The friction gives them enough substance to be heard. Even in English, the voiceless [l̥] of *plaque* is likely to have more friction than the voiced [l] of *black*. [l̥] is similar to [ɹ] in a number of respects and they are sometimes grouped together as **liquids.** The air passes down the center of the mouth for [ɹ], while it passes down the side for [l].

Phones very much like approximants are sometimes tightly joined to another consonant, and they are then known as **secondary articulations. Palatalized** consonants, for instance, are made by raising the tongue toward the palate at the same time that some other articulation is made. The effect is to add a [j] like sound to the consonant, and palatals can be symbolized by a small raised [ʲ]. Russian has several palatalized consonants as in [bratʲ] 'to take' and [krɔfʲ] 'blood.' **Labialized** consonants are accompanied by lip rounding, and they can be symbolized by adding a [ʷ] to the basic symbol. American [ɹ] is generally somewhat labialized when it is first in a word, and English [k] is labialized in words like 'quick' and 'quilt.' **Velarized** consonants have the back of the tongue raised toward the velum in a position similar to that used for the vowel in English *food* (see below). Final [l] in English words such as *ball* or *bill* is usually velarized.

Trills and Flaps

A trill is made when one of the articulators is set into vibration by the passing air stream. The most common trill, the so-called rolled *r,* is apical. The trick about an apical trill is to place a very relaxed apex against the palate in the area of the alveolar ridge, and give it just the right amount of muscular tension so that the air pressure from the lungs is strong enough to blow it away but not strong enough to keep it away. The apex is then repeatedly blown away from the palate, only to flop back again. The individual flaps of the tongue are not under direct muscular control. The voiced apical trill can be symbolized by simple [r]. Spanish has an apical trill in words such as *perro* [pero] 'dog.'

Some dialects of French and German have uvular trills. Here it is the uvula, rather than the apex of the tongue, that interrupts the flow of air. The uvula is blown away from the back of the tongue and then flops back against it, so that the air passage opens and closes rapidly. If a special symbol for a uvular trill is needed, [ʀ] can be used.

A third possible trill is bilabial. We sometimes make a bilabial trill to show how cold the weather is, and we even try to spell it as *brrr.* Bilabial trills are surprisingly rare in the world's languages, though they are not quite unknown. If you aspire to real phonetic virtuosity, you might try to articulate bilabial, apical, and uvular trills simultaneously. It is not quite impossible.

A flap, [ɾ], amounts to a minimally short apical trill. The tongue brushes just once against the palate or alveolar ridge but is immediately blown away. Most Americans use a flap for the *d* in words like *ladder, bidder,* etc. In addition to its apical trill in *perro* [pero] 'dog,' Spanish has an apical flap, in words such as *pero* [peɾo] 'but.'

Implosives and Clicks

The great majority of speech sounds in the world's languages, and all that have been considered so far, are made under outward pressure of the air from the lungs. Understandable, though distorted, speech can also be produced by pulling the air in with the lungs instead. Swedes often say *ja* 'yes' with in-drawn air, but sounds made in this way have no important part in the world's languages.

Apart from the lungs, it is also possible to produce significant inward air pressure either by moving the larynx quickly downward, or by pulling the tongue sharply backward, and such sounds are important in some languages. The downward movement of the larynx can produce sounds known as **implosive** stops. If the movement of the larynx is fast enough, voicing can continue during the release of the articulators. This is because air can pass upward through the descending larynx even while inward pressure is created at the articulators. A distinctive acoustic quality is produced as the articulators open. The easiest implosive stop to make is bilabial, but implosives are also possible at other positions. Bilabial, apical, and velar implosives can be symbolized by [ɓ], [ɗ], and [ɠ] respectively. They are important in many African languages.

Like implosives, **clicks** are produced under negative pressure, but instead of pulling the air inward with the larynx, the negative pressure is produced by the backward movement of the tongue. Enough pressure can be created in this way to pull the articulators apart with a sharp clicking noise. The sound of a smacked kiss is a bilabial click. The chucking noise used to encourage a horse is a lateral click. The *tsktsk* with which we can indicate gentle disapproval is an apical click. Clicks are included among the ordinary consonants of the Khoisan languages and some neighboring Bantu languages of southern Africa.

VOWELS

This survey of speech sounds began with the stops, and it then reviewed sounds with progressively less constriction of the vocal tract. The speech sounds with the least constriction of all, those that let the air escape most freely, are the vowels. Indeed, **vowels** can be defined as speech sounds that are produced with little obstruction to the passage of air. The line between vowels and consonants is not sharp, for speech sounds can show every intermediate degree of obstruction. Later, vowels and consonants will be distinguishable according to the different roles they play in the sound systems of particular languages, but for now, the important distinction between them is the articulatory one.

The most important distinctions among vowels are made by varying the position of the tongue and the shape of the lips. The differences among the English vowels in *beam, boom,* and *calm* can illustrate these distinctions. First, and perhaps most obviously, the lips are pursed together for the vowel in *boom* but not for those in *beam* or *calm.* Vowels with the lip shape of *boom* are said to be **rounded,** while vowels with the lip shape of *beam* and *calm* are **unrounded.** Second, the tongue is pushed considerably farther to the front for *beam* than for *boom.* You should be able to feel your tongue move front and back if you pronounce these words repeatedly, one after the other. The vowel of *beam,* therefore, is described as a **front** vowel while the vowel of *boom* is said to be a **back** vowel. For most speakers, the vowel of *calm* is neither as far front as for *beam* nor as far back as for *boom,* so it is said to be **central,** neither far front nor far back, but in between. Third, *beam* and *boom* are usually formed with the highest part of the tongue closer to the roof of the mouth, and with the mouth less widely open, than is *calm. Beam* and *boom* are said to have **high** vowels, while the vowel in *calm* is called **low.**

Front/back, high/low, and rounded/unrounded describe the three most important distinctions among vowels. *Beam* can be described as having a "high-front unrounded" vowel; *boom* has a "high-back rounded" vowel; *calm* has a "low-central unrounded" vowel. The three articulatory features can occur in any combination, however, so many vowels other than just these three are possible. Moreover, since we can move our lips and tongue gradually from any vowel position to any other vowel position, no sharp breaks divide one vowel quality from another. As a result, we can recognize many vowels that are intermediate between these first three.

Table 5–2 shows the most commonly used vowel symbols. [i] is shown in the upper left as standing for the high-front unrounded vowel. This symbol is sometimes used for the English vowel in *beam,* but this English vowel has an

Table 5–2
Vowels

	Front unrnd.	Front rnd.	Central unrnd.	Back unrnd.	Back rnd.
High	i	y	ɨ	ɯ	u
	ɪ				ʊ
Mid	e	ø	ə	ɤ	o
	ɛ	œ	ʌ		ɔ
Low		æ			
			a	ɑ	ɒ

additional complication that makes it a less than perfect example. The French vowel in *ici* 'here' is a better candidate for the ideal [i]. Other front unrounded vowels that are pronounced at progressively lower positions are [ɪ] of English *bid*, [e] of French *été* 'summer,' (the vowel of English *fate* is similar, but not identical), [ɛ] of English *head*, and [æ] of English *fat*. Just as **central** is used to describe vowels that are halfway between front and back, so **mid** is used for vowels that are halfway between high and low. [ɛ] is a "mid-front unrounded" vowel. When precision is needed, vowels such as [e] and [ɛ] can be described as "higher mid" and "lower mid" respectively.

In the upper right corner of Table 5–2, [u] stands for a high-back rounded vowel. The vowel in French *nous* 'we,' which has the tongue drawn up very high and pulled far to the back is an even better example of a high-back rounded vowel than the vowel in English *boot*. The vowel of English *good* is just a bit lower but also back and rounded, and it is symbolized by [ʊ]. Still lower is the [o] of French *mot* 'word,' similar, though not identical, to the vowel of English *hope*. [ɔ] is used for a lower mid-back rounded vowel that some, but not all, English speakers have in *law* and *paw*. [ɒ] represents a rounded vowel that is lower and farther back than anything found in most varieties of English. The vowel of Norwegian *lån* [lɒn] 'loan' is such a low-back unrounded vowel. **Central** vowels lie halfway between "front" and "back," and in addition to [a], English has a central vowel in words such as *cut* and *butter*. This is a **mid-central** vowel, and is represented by [ʌ]. English has another mid-central vowel that is similar to [ʌ] but usually just a bit higher. This is the vowel that linguists call *schwa* and write as [ə]. English schwa is always short and weakly stressed. The first (unaccented) syllables of *collapse, condition, banana,* and *about* usually have schwas. Some phoneticians have interpreted the vowel of *just,* when unaccented and spoken quickly in a phrase like *just a minute,* to be an even higher central vowel, the so-called barred *i,* written as [ɨ].

Alert readers will have noticed that all the English front vowels are unrounded, while its back vowels are all rounded. Many languages share this characteristic with English, probably because backness and rounding produce somewhat similar acoustic effects. They tend to reinforce each other, so that back rounded vowels are maximally distinct from front unrounded vowels. Nevertheless, both front rounded vowels and back-unrounded vowels are found in some languages. Both French and German have front rounded vowels. French *tu* 'you' and German *fünf* 'five' have high-front rounded vowels, and [y] is used to represent this vowel. Some dialects of French have a mid-front rounded vowel in *feu* [fø] 'fire,' and a slightly lower mid-front rounded vowel in *oeuf* [œf] 'egg.' Turkish has a high-back unrounded vowel. Turks write this as a dotless *i* (ı), while linguists use [ɯ]. A high-back unrounded vowel like Turkish [ɯ] has the tongue in approximately the same position as [u], but the lips are unrounded as if for [i]. A Turkish example is *adım* [adɯm] 'my name.' A low-back unrounded vowel, farther back than the [a] in English *calm* can be written as [ɑ]. Norwegian has a low-back unrounded vowel in *land* [lɑn] 'land.'

Table 5–2 can be looked on as a conventionalized diagram of the human mouth, with front vowels at the left and the high vowels at the top. Notice that, by convention, the cross section of the vocal organs in Figure 5–1, and both the consonant and vowel charts in Tables 5–1 and 5–2, place the front of the mouth at the left. Since the difference between front and back vowels seems to be greatest for the high vowels and to be progressively reduced for lower vowels, the diagram is often drawn in the form of a trapezoid that narrows toward the bottom. Additional symbols could, of course, be assigned to the remaining spaces in the vowel chart or for even finer distinctions, and occasionally such symbols are needed, but for most purposes those shown in Table 5–2 are enough.

Rounding, height, and backing are not the only features that can keep vowels distinct. Most vowels are voiced, for instance, but voiceless vowels are by no means impossible. One of the things we do when we whisper is to cut off our voicing completely. The result is less noise than ordinary talking, which is what we want when we whisper, but for most purposes we prefer the noise that voicing provides. More important than voiceless vowels are **nasal** vowels. These are made by lowering the velum during the vowel so that part of the air stream passes through the nasal tract. Nonnasal or **oral** vowels, by contrast, have the velum raised so that all the air passes through the oral tract. Any combination of tongue and lip position can be articulated with a lowered velum, so it is possible to produce as many nasal vowels as oral vowels, but since it is harder for a listener to distinguish nasal vowels, languages rarely have as many nasal as oral vowels. A tilde [˜] is placed over the symbol to signify a nasal vowel. French has nasal vowels, such as the one in *fin* [fæ̃] 'fine', which is lower mid-front unrounded and nasal, and in the one in *mon* [mɔ̃] 'my,' with a lower mid-back rounded nasal vowel. Nasal vowels have a less prominent role in English than in French but, particularly in American English, vowels that are followed by a nasal consonant, [m], [n], or [ŋ], tend to be somewhat nasalized. The velum drops during the vowel in anticipation of its lowered position during the consonant.

Vowels become still more complex if the tongue or lips move during their production. Almost all the vowels of American English have some movement, although the tongue holds fairly steady for the vowels in *bit, bet, but,* and *pot* and we can describe these as **monophthongs,** at least as pronounced in most dialects. Vowels such as those in *buy, bough,* and *boy,* on the other hand, require the tongue, and sometimes the lips as well, to move as the vowel is pronounced. The vowel in *buy* begins at a low-central or low-back position, not far from [a], but the tongue then moves decisively upward and to the front. The vowel of *bough* also starts low, but the tongue then moves up and to the rear and, at the same time, the lips are rounded. The vowel of *boy* begins at a mid- or lower-back rounded position, and the tongue then moves upward and to the front while the lips unround somewhat. A great variety of tongue and lip movements are found in the vowels of other languages.

Vowels in which there is movement of the tongue or lips are called **diph-**

thongs. Most of the articulatory movement of English diphthongs takes place during their second half, and this final portion is called a **glide** or, sometimes, a **semivowel.** The English glides are enough like the approximants [j] and [w], to lead some linguists to transcribe *buy, bough,* and *boy* as [ba^j], [ba^w], and [bɔ^j] or even as [baj], [baw], and [bɔj], the choice depending on whether the linguist wants to emphasize their unitary or their complex character. English vowels will be considered more carefully in Chapter 6.

SUPRASEGMENTALS: PITCH, STRESS, LENGTH

It is natural to think of vowels and consonants as segments that occur one after another in the stream of speech. Like the letters of our written language, each segment of our spoken language seems to have a clear order in a long sequence of similar segments, following some, preceding others. Later we will consider some serious problems with this view of phonology, but we often speak of vowels and consonants as **segmental** units, as if they occur in simple, linear, order. We also use other speech sounds that can only be pronounced simultaneously with the segmental vowels and consonants. These additional speech sounds include length, stress, and pitch, and they are known as **suprasegmentals.**

Unlike the segmental consonants and vowels, the phonetic quality of the suprasegmentals can be described only on a relative scale. The highest pitch used by a low-voiced man may be lower than the lowest pitch of a high-voiced woman. Nevertheless, everyone can move between (relatively) high and (relatively) low pitches. Similarly, when speaking quietly, one's loudest sounds may be quieter than one's softest sounds on other occasions, but it is the relative volume that is important, not the absolute volume. So also with length: In languages where vowels or consonants are distinguished from one another by their length, it is their relative length, rather than their absolute length, that matters.

Pitch

Pitch is determined by the frequency that is imposed on the air stream by the vibrating vocal cords. By maintaining a steady frequency we can easily speak in a monotone, but this is a totally unnatural way to talk. Ordinarily our pitch swings constantly up and down.

We refer to the melody of a phrase or sentence as its **intonation.** If you say *He's going tomorrow* with a gently falling intonation, you will be understood as offering a simple statement of fact. If you say the same sequence of words with a pitch rise at the end of *tomorrow,* it will be heard, instead, as a question. If the pitch tends downward, but there is a sharp rise on *-mor-* followed by an equally sharp fall on *-row,* it will be heard as irritation or, if the pitch change is sufficiently great, as anger. An even more pronounced rise on *-mor-* will indicate surprise.

Even a single syllable can be given widely varying meanings by changing its intonation. Consider the following examples of *no*, in which the contour of the pitch is imitated by a waving line above the word.

nõ   Simple denial

nò   Firm denial

nô   Annoyed denial

nó   Do you really mean ''no?''

nõ   I think not, but I'm not sure

no   Oh, please, not that!

All languages have intonational patterns like these that flow along with the words and sentences. Some languages also use pitch differences in a second and quite different way. As we will see in more detail in the next chapter, **tone** languages such as Chinese distinguish otherwise identical words or syllables by nothing other than their relative pitch, or ''tone.'' In these languages the tone differences are much more closely tied to particular syllables or words than are the intonational patterns of English. The transcription of intonational patterns is not well standardized. Sometimes the only way to make things clear is by such devices as the wavy lines used here with ''no.'' Tones are often distinguished by accents on the vowels or by numbers attached to the syllables.

Stress

In English, as in many but by no means all languages, one syllable of most words has a heavy stress or ''accent'' that sets it off from the other syllables. Thus *Peter, pumpkin,* and *eater* are stressed on the first syllable, while *Irene, delays,* and *enough* are stressed on the second. Stressed syllables can, when necessary, be marked by an acute accent above the vowel: *únder, belów.* Like pitch, the stress of a syllable can be recognized only by comparison with the surrounding syllables. In addition to the stress that marks one syllable of most English words, stress also joins with pitch in forming the longer patterns of intonation that stretch over phrases and sentences.

It is tempting to think of stress as equivalent to volume or loudness, but the phonetics of stress is not quite so simple. In fact, in view of the easy confidence with which English speakers can identify stressed syllables, it is surprisingly difficult to pin down its exact acoustic nature. Several things apparently happen together, and listeners may be able to take clues from all of them. Stressed English syllables do tend to be a bit louder than other syllables, but they may also, and perhaps more significantly, be pronounced with a slightly higher pitch. They may also be a bit longer than the surrounding syllables. Perhaps the fundamental characteristic of stressed syllables is that the speaker expends more muscular energy in their production, so that the greater volume of air that emerges from the lungs makes it both higher and louder. In some languages, such as Norwegian, however, stressed syllables tend to have a *lower* pitch than unstressed syllables, so the relationship of stress and pitch is not straightforward. Much remains to be learned about the nature of stress and about the way that loudness is used in language.

Length

The third suprasegmental feature is relative length. English vowels tend to be pronounced somewhat longer when followed by a voiced consonant than when followed by a voiceless consonant, and they are even longer when followed by no consonant at all. This is easiest to observe in sets of words such as *beat/ bead/bee, boot/booed/boo, plate/played/play* that differ primarily in what follows the vowel. The difference in vowel length, in fact, is one of the clues that listeners use to distinguish voiced and voiceless final stops. If words that vary in the voicing of their final stops are recorded on tape, and if the tapes are then cut and spliced so as to remove the stop altogether, listeners can still hear the difference between voiced and voiceless finals simply by the length of the preceding vowel. Thus, at least in English, the acoustic signals by which listeners distinguish what we usually describe ''voicing'' include the length of the preceding vowel.

In most American dialects, vowel length depends primarily on what follows the vowel, and vowel length alone is not enough to keep two words distinct. The difference between vowels traditionally called ''long'' and ''short'' in English, such as the difference between the vowels of *beat* and *bet,* is primarily a difference in tongue position rather than of actual temporal duration. In Norwegian, on the other hand, different words can be distinguished from one another simply by the length of their vowels: *takk* [tak] 'thanks,' *tak* [taak] 'roof;' *nytte* [nytə] 'use,' *nyte* [nyytə] 'enjoy.' In their usual spelling, Norwegians show that vowels are short by doubling the following consonant letter. The phonetic transcription used here and enclosed by brackets shows vowels to be long by doubling the vowel letter. Long vowels may also be transcribed with a [ː] following a vowel: [taːk] 'roof.' Short vowels can be left unmarked if long vowels are consistently marked in some way. Some languages also distinguish long and short consonants. Italian *nono* [nonɔ] 'ninth' and *nonno* [nonnɔ] 'grandfather' are distinguished by the length of the second consonant. Long consonants are most often written with a doubled letter.

Suprasegmentals differ from vowels and consonants in one other way: they mimic features of nonlinguistic sounds. The sounds of music and the sounds of the natural world around us are characterized by pitch, length, and loudness, just as are the sounds of language. The qualities of segmental vowels and consonants are more narrowly confined to language.

SYLLABLES

Some phones are difficult to pronounce in isolation. Length, pitch, and stress can have no expression apart from the segmental sounds with which they co-occur. Even a [p] needs to be attached to a vowel, at least on one side, if it is to sound at all natural. Vowels are more independent. We can pronounce a lonely [a] or [i] and expect a listener to recognize what we are saying, but even this is an artificial exercise, more likely to be attempted by a linguist than by an average speaker. In real speech, sounds always come in groups. We hear each of the sounds of our language only in the context of other sounds. They bump into each other, and they affect one another.

In particular, speech sounds come to us organized in syllables. Speakers all have a good idea of what syllables are, and in 99 cases out of 100 we readily agree on the number of syllables in any particular word. Still, many English speakers feel uncertain about how many syllables are found in at least a few of the following words: *fire, flour, feel, error, chasm, desirable, mysticism, cuddling, median*. In spite of such marginal cases, we can appeal to our intuitive sense of the syllable, and when we do so, we note that most syllables are built around a vowel. In most languages, a few syllables consist of nothing else. It is not easy to articulate more than a few consonants in a row, so before a consonant sequence gets very long, it is likely to be interrupted by a vowel; this requires vowels to occur quite regularly in connected speech. It is easier to produce a long string of vowels than a long string of consonants, but vowel sequences, too, seem to call for intervening consonants. At any rate, it is characteristic of all languages that vowels alternate with consonants or with short strings of consonants, and each alternation most often counts as a syllable.

Not quite every syllable has a vowel, however. The second syllables of *kitten* and *button* have no vowels, at least if we mean by "vowel" a speech sound that is made with an unobstructed vocal tract. (Remember, we are considering the spoken language, not the written language. We write vowel letters in these words, of course, even when we do not pronounce vowel sounds.) In speech, the [n] can directly follow the [t] with no intervening vowel. The [n] of these words is said be a **syllabic** consonant, a consonant that is capable of acting as the nucleus of a syllable, a role more often filled by a vowel. Syllabic consonants are written with a small vertical line beneath them, so *button* can be transcribed as [bʌtn̩]. English [l] is a syllabic consonant in such words as *cattle* [kætl̩] or *bottle* [batl̩]. In rapid speech, syllabic [m] and [ŋ] are also possible: *He went jumping* [jʌmpm̩] *past me* or *I'm backing* [bækŋ̩] *the car*. Syllabic consonants are found in many languages. As in English, they are frequently nasals or liquids that, being more resonant than stops or fricatives, are also a bit more vowel-like.

Table 5-3
Diacritics

t^h	Aspirated
t^j	Palatalized
t^w	Labialized
ţ	Dental articulation
ņ	Syllabic consonant
õ	Nasalized
o̥	Voiceless
oː	Long

CONCLUSIONS

The most important of the many thousands of different speech sounds that human beings can produce with their vocal organs have now been surveyed. It must be clear that we could not possibly devise a separate phonetic symbol for every phone that we can produce. When precision is necessary, we can simplify the task of transcription by using **diacritical** marks (**diacritics**) to modify the phonetic symbols. The diacritics that have been used in this chapter are listed in Table 5-3.

The more precisely we try to transcribe, the more likely we are to decorate our notation with diacritics. We could continue to describe and transcribe sounds in ever greater detail, increasing the accuracy of our measurement of air pressure and air flow, of the point and manner of articulation, of the relative timing of the cooperating articulators, of voice and nasality, and of much more, but we cannot possibly catch everything in the stream of speech, and there can be no absolute standard of accuracy. The accuracy of a transcription can be judged only in relation to the purposes for which it is to be used, and as we reach for ever more detail, we should begin to ask ourselves whether there is not some reasonable stopping place. How much detail do we really want? For some purposes, too much detail will simply obscure our view of the most interesting problems. Practical analysis must deliberately omit a good deal. Can we find principles by which we can decide what to include and what to leave out?

No single language uses more than a fraction of the total number of possible speech sounds, and it is by focusing on the sounds of individual languages that we will escape from limitless complexity. It is the task of the next chapter to consider how the sounds of individual languages are organized and the ways in which they can be described.

CHAPTER SIX

Phonology

CONTRAST AND THE PHONEME: ALLOPHONES, COMPLEMENTARY DISTRIBUTION, AND DISTINCTIVE FEATURES

The study of articulatory phonetics leads us to recognize thousands of possible speech sounds, and it is from this vast potential that each language draws its particular repertory. Each language then organizes its sounds in its own way. When we shift our attention from the sounds themselves to the organization of sounds in specific languages, we shift from phonetics to the study that linguists call **phonology.** We consider the sounds of particular languages, and ask how these sounds are organized, how they interact with each other, and into what sorts of patterns they fall.

Phonology is one of the core topics of linguistics, and it is essential for any understanding of how language works, but there is a more general reason for studying phonology. No better topic can be found with which to convey a feeling for the way we construct theories, and for the way these theories then help us to explain our data. It is easier in phonology than in virtually any other discipline to gather and inspect data and to consider alternative theoretical perspectives by which these data can be interpreted. Additional data can then be collected so as to test the theories. This chapter, therefore, is intended not only to introduce the principles of phonology, but also to demonstrate the strategy of theory building. Often we will consider data and then ask how the data can be understood. We will devise and try out theoretical principles that help to make sense of the data. Occasionally this may seem to be a somewhat laborious and indirect approach. It might seem easier to give the theories first and then illustrate them with examples, but by starting with data and then constructing theories so as to make sense of the data, we reflect the logic of discovery and the procedures by which linguists themselves must always work. The chapter starts where phonetics left off, with the relatively concrete world of sounds, but it progresses step by step to increasingly abstract ways of describing sounds. It will gradually move away from the audible noises of speech toward increasingly abstract units and theoretical principles that are not themselves observable but that help us to make the data understandable.

A good starting place is an example from English that is superficially quite simple. The words *tore, store,* and *door* begin with three different kinds of alveolar stops. *Tore* begins with a voiceless and aspirated stop; *store* has a voiceless but unaspirated stop; *door* has a voiced stop. Speakers of English, however, perceive the aspirated [t^h] of *tore* and the unaspirated [t] of *store* to be more like each other than either is like the voiced [d] of *door.* Our feeling is a reflection of a principle that linguists call **contrast.** We say that [t^h] and [d] contrast in English because they are different enough, all by themselves, to distinguish different words. *Tore* and *door* differ *only* in their initial stops. The remainder of the words are identical, but the initial stops are enough to keep them distinct. Nor is this pair alone, for scores of other pairs of English words are distinguished by this same contrast: *tie/die, town/down, toe/dough, bat/bad,* and many others. We call these **minimal pairs** because, while they differ in pronunciation, they do so only to the minimal extent necessary to be recognized as distinct English words. It is by means of minimal pairs that we prove to ourselves that two phones, such as [t^h] and [d], are in contrast.

The [t^h] of *tore* and the [t] of *store* are also phonetically different, but a search for two English words that form a minimal pair by differing only in the aspiration of their *t*'s is doomed to failure. It will be discovered, instead, that [t^h] never occurs directly after initial [s], while [t] never occurs as a word initial. [t^h] and [t] differ from one another, but English does not exploit this difference to distinguish different words. When two sounds like [t^h] and [t] never contrast, but occur under different phonological conditions (i.e., one occurs first in a word while the other is found only after [s-]), they are said to be in **complementary distribution.** To say that [t^h] and [t] are in complementary distribution means that [t^h] never occurs in those positions where [t] occurs, and vice versa.

We need a way of talking about [t^h] and [t] that will correspond to the feeling of English speakers that they are, in some sense, the "same" sound in spite of the clear fact that they are phonetically different. We need to recognize that they are different in one respect, but similar in another, different phonetically, but not different enough to mark an English contrast. They are not different enough to distinguish a minimal pair of English words. All this is recognized by saying that two **phones** (two phonetically distinguishable speech sounds) that are in complementary distribution (occur under different conditions) are **allophones** (variants) of the same **phoneme.** To call them "allophones" is to recognize their phonetic difference, but at the same time to join them as members of the same phoneme and thus to recognize their special relationship to one another within the language.

[t^h] and [t] are allophones of a phoneme that we will write as /t/. The phoneme is a more abstract unit than its allophones but, so long as we recognize that /t/ has somewhat different pronunciations under differing circumstances, it is certainly natural to think of English as having just one phoneme /t/. The same symbols can be used for phonemes that have been used for phones, but slanting brackets will be used to enclose phonemic symbols instead of the square brackets that enclose phonetic symbols. Thus /t/ can be understood to mean the English phoneme that is sometimes aspirated and sometimes not. Since allophones are particular pronunciations of their phoneme, they are symbolized by phonetic symbols and, like all phonetic symbols, they can be placed within square brackets.

The phoneme /t/, then, is a set of somewhat differing allophones that are in complementary distribution with each other. It is the phoneme /t/ that contrasts with other English phonemes, such as /p, d, s/ and /ð/, because /t/ is capable of keeping a word like *toe* distinct from words like *Poe, dough, sow,* and *though*. On the other hand, the allophones [tʰ] and [t] do not contrast with each other. Rather, the choice between them depends on the neighboring sounds, or on what linguists call the **environment.** It is by recognizing contrasting phonemes, each comprising a number of noncontrasting allophones, that linguists capture the feeling of English speakers that the difference between [tʰ] and [d] is much more significant in the language than the difference between [tʰ] and [t]. [tʰ], [t], and [d] are all phonetically different, but only [d] contrasts with the others. The three phones (speech sounds) group into just two contrasting phonemes.

One way of getting an intuitive feeling for the meaning of "phoneme" is to imagine an ideal spelling system. If English spelling were more regular, each phoneme might always be represented by the same letter, and the same letter might always represent the same phoneme. *Feel, telephone,* and *laugh* would all be spelled with an *f*. *Guest, ghost,* and *example* might all be spelled with *g*'s (no *h* would be needed in *ghost*) but *George* and *budget* would require a different letter, perhaps *j*. The letter *t* could be used in both *top* and *stop* even though it would not stand for identical phones. Since these are allophones of the same phoneme, and selected in accordance with the surrounding phonemes, the ideal writing system could ignore this allophonic difference. It is crucial to understand, however, that letters are units of a writing system, while phonemes are units of the spoken language. Letters can be used as symbols that stand for phonemes, but letters are not, themselves, phonemes.

The principle of contrast is the fundamental principle of phonology, and the word "contrast" is used in several different, though closely related, ways. At the most concrete level, we often speak of two words contrasting, as when we say that *buy* and *pie* contrast in English. More generally, we also speak of two phonemes contrasting, since /b/ and /p/ keep not only *buy* and *pie* distinct but can be used to keep many other pairs of words distinct as well. At an even more abstract level, we can also speak of the contrast provided by a **distinctive feature.** We say that English has a distinctive feature of voicing (or a "voiced/voiceless contrast") and that this feature serves not only to keep /b/ distinct from /p/, but also to distinguish /d/ from /t/, /g/ from /k/, /v/ from /f/, and several other pairs.

By searching through the vocabulary of a language, it is possible to work out its system of contrasts, and to learn how it uses these contrasts to keep its phonemes distinct. Every phoneme of a language must differ from every other phoneme by at least one distinctive feature. Thus English /p/ and /b/ differ in the distinctive feature of voicing; /p/ and /t/ differ in their point of articulation; /p/ and /f/ differ both in their point of articulation and their manner of articulation; /e/ differs from /i/ in height, and so forth.

Contrast, complementary distribution, allophone, phoneme, and *distinctive feature* form a set of interrelated concepts that are fundamental to the understanding of phonology. If the set of concepts seems to be rather heavy baggage for describing some fairly obvious facts about English, that is because we are so familiar with English that we hardly need to have the facts explained. When we look at other languages, or even at other dialects of English than our own, we will see that some of their contrasts are quite different from those we are accustomed to. They group allophones into phonemes in unfamiliar ways. These terms will then provide tools by which to explore and describe both the ways in which languages are alike and the ways in which they are different. The following sections will give additional examples, and explore some of the implications of this set of concepts.

CONDITIONED AND FREE VARIATION

The complementary distribution of English [t^h] and [t] is just one of many examples in which the pronunciation of a phoneme can be said to be **conditioned** by the surrounding phonemes. A preceding /s/ is the "condition" under which the phoneme /t/ is pronounced without aspiration. Another example of conditioning is the lengthening of vowels before voiced consonants that was discussed in Chapter 5. In the new terminology, English vowel lengthening can be described as follows: The length of vowels is conditioned by the following consonant in such a way that vowels have longer allophones before voiced consonants and shorter allophones before voiceless consonants. *Bad* and *bat* can be transcribed phonetically by writing [bæːd] and [bæt], where [ː] indicates length. Phonemically, however, we can write these two words as /bæd/ and /bæt/. The phonemic transcription indicates that the same phoneme, /æ/, is found in both words. Of course, it is pronounced differently, but that fact is not indicated directly in the phonemic transcription. Rather, the allophonic variation in vowel length will have to be described as part of the general description of the phonological system. This will require a generalization, somewhere in the grammar, to the effect that vowels such as /æ/ are longer before voiced consonants than before voiceless consonants. That fact is part of the description of the allophones of /æ/.

We saw in Chapter 5 that English /k/ is articulated in different positions depending on the following vowel. It is pronounced farther front before a front vowel, as in *keep,* than before a back vowel, as in *coop.* The front and back allophones of /k/, therefore, are in complementary distribution, the choice between them depending on the position of the following vowel. Nasalized and non-nasalized English vowels are also in complementary distribution, with a following nasal consonant conditioning the nasalization of the preceding vowel. English /r/ and /l/ are usually voiced, but they have voiceless (and somewhat fricativized) allophones when immediately following voiceless consonants, as in *try, please, crush, clip*. Most allophones of English /t/, /d/, and /n/ are alveolar, but dental allophones are used before /θ/ as in *eighth, width,* and *tenth*. When looked at closely, most phonemes have a range of allophones that vary in accordance with their phonological environment.

We often find that phonemes take on some of the phonetic characteristics of their neighboring sounds. The fronting and backing of /k/, for instance, conforms to the position of the following vowel. /r/ and /l/ become voiceless after a voiceless stop. When one phoneme takes on a characteristic of its neighbors, we say that it **assimilates** to them. English vowels assimilate to the nasality of the following consonant. English /k/ assimilates to the position of the following vowel. English /r/ and /l/ assimilate to the voicing of the preceding consonant. It is always tempting to look on assimilation as a way of making articulation easier. Speakers do not have to move their tongues quite so far if /k/ can adapt its position to suit the following vowel. If the velum must come down for a following nasal consonant, it may be easier to let it come down just a bit early, and this means that the vowel will also be nasalized. We must be cautious about "explaining" too much on the basis of ease of articulation, however. Not all languages have nasal assimilation of the kind that we find in American English, so we cannot "explain" American English nasal assimilation without simultaneously creating a puzzle out of its absence in some other languages. What is easier for the speaker, moreover, sometimes makes things more difficult for the hearer, so ease of articulation has to be balanced against ease of discrimination and comprehension.

Because of assimilation, phonemes come to be pronounced in different ways under different circumstances, and this implies the complementary distribution of their allophones. The phonetic variability of a phoneme does not always depend on its environment, however. Sometimes variation is much more free. Consider word-final voiceless stops, such as the /p/ of *top*. When a word ends with /p/, English allows us a good deal of freedom in how vigorously we release our lips when we have finished with it. We may release a final /p/ with a certain amount of aspiration, though rarely with as much as an initial /p/. Alternatively, however, we can close our lips and leave them closed. Not only is there no aspiration, but the lips may not be released at all, so such stops are called "unreleased." The same variability is found in final /t/ and final /k/, and readers can experiment with the pronunciation of words such as *soap, soot,* and *sick* in order to determine the range of variation that they allow themselves. Since the environment is not a major determinant of how much aspiration we give to our final voiceless consonants, or of how quickly we release them, we call this an example of **free variation** to distinguish it from the

conditioned variation that we describe as complementary distribution. Free variation is an expression of the freedom allowed to a speaker. The differing pronunciations allowed by free variation are counted, along with those governed by conditioned variation, as allophones. Together, free variation and conditioned variation provide for the range of sounds that can express a phoneme.

A certain amount of free variation is inevitable, simply because it is impossible for speakers to repeat themselves precisely. At the same time, each language allows relatively wide variation in some areas but sets tighter limits in others. One of the early problems that every second-language learner has to cope with is to learn whether two slightly different sounds are in free variation, in complementary distribution, or in contrast. If it is possible to select freely between the alternatives, they are in free variation. If the variant forms always occur in differing phonological environments, they are in complementary distribution. If the two sounds can distinguish separate words, they are in phonemic contrast.

ENGLISH CONSONANT PHONEMES

We can discover the consonant phonemes of English by searching among minimal pairs and near-minimal pairs. Ideally we would like to find sets of words that differ only in a single consonant, but we can supplement these with words whose differences are not quite so minimal. Consider the examples in Table 6–1. Words that are true minimal pairs with other words in the same column are shown without parentheses. Near-minimal pairs have parentheses. The table includes minimal pairs for most, though not quite all, of the consonant contrasts in English, and most of the gaps are easy to fill. No perfect minimal pair for /j/ and /v/ is included in the table, for instance, but examples can be found: *Yale/vale, yokel/vocal.*

Several of the gaps in the table are accidental. There *could* be an English word pronounced /jæt/, but there happens not to be. A few gaps, however, are real. First, /h/ never occurs finally in English so we cannot hope to find a word to go in the final column for /h/. The situation of /j/ and /w/ is a bit more complex, but unless diphthongs such as those in *bay* and *bow* are considered to end in /j/ and /w/, these consonants are also forbidden as word finals.

On the other hand, /ŋ/ never occurs initially. This means that the only position in which /h/ and /ŋ/ could possibly contrast would be in the middle of a word, and as long as we confine our search to monosyllables, a minimal pair for /h/ and /ŋ/ is impossible. In fact, no minimal pairs are found among longer words either. Strictly speaking, /h/ and /ŋ/ are in complementary distribution. Does this make them allophones of the same phoneme? Logically we might be tempted to group them together, but they are so different phonetically that linguists have not yielded to the temptation. Instead, we feel that we should not group phones together in the same phoneme unless they have a reasonable

Table 6–1
Consonant Phonemes

	/-aʲ/	/-in/	/-æt/	/-uʷ/	/ri-/
/p/	pie	pin	pat	Pooh	rip
/b/	buy	bin	bat	boo	rib
/t/	tie	tin	tat	too	writ
/d/	die	din	(dad)	do	rid
/k/	chi	kin	cat	coo	Rick
/g/	guy	Guin(ea)	gat	goo	rig
/m/	my	minn(ow)	mat	moo	rim
/n/	nigh	ninn(y)	gnat	knew	rin(se)
/ŋ/	—	—	—	—	ring
/f/	fie	fin	fat	phoo(ey)	riff
/v/	vie	Vin(ce)	vat	voo(doo)	riv(er)
/θ/	thigh	thin	That(cher)		(pith)
/ð/	thy	that			(with)
/s/	sigh	sin	sat	sue	wris(t)
/z/	Zi(on)	Zin(fandel)	(zap)	zoo	(whiz)
/ʃ/	shy	shin	shat	shoe	(wish)
/ʒ/	—	—	—	—	(rouge)
/h/	high	hin(der)	hat	who	—
/č/	Chi(nese)	chin	chat	chew	rich
/ǰ/	ji(ve)	gin	(Jack)	Jew	ridge
/j/	yi(pe)	yin(&yang)	(yak)	you	—
/w/	"y"	win	(wax)	woo	—
/r/	rye	Rin(TinTin)	rat	rue	rear
/l/	lie	Lynn	(lap)	loo	rill

phonetic similarity. It is by no means obvious how much phonetic similarity is required to make them "reasonable" allophones of the same phoneme, but the case of /h/ and /ŋ/ seems clear. They are too different to be grouped comfortably together.

We face another problem with /ʒ/. The table contains a line for /ʒ/ but only one entry, *rouge,* and even this word is not pronounced with a /ʒ/ by all English speakers. English /ʒ/, in fact, is a bit rare. It occurs as a word initial only in a few borrowed words such as *genre* and *Jacques,* and it is not at all common as a word final. This makes it difficult to find minimal pairs in which /ʒ/ contrasts with other consonants. We have a few: most speakers have minimal contrasts in *beige/bait/base* and *allusion/Aleutian. Leisure/ledger* is a minimal pair for some. We also have some near minimal pairs such as *measure/nether/ledger* that support the phonemic status of /ʒ/ even if they do not prove it.

If we wanted to eliminate /ʒ/ from the list of English phonemes, we would have to show that it is in complementary distribution or in free variation with some other phone. Since there is some alternation between [ʒ] and [ǰ] in words such as *garage* ([garaʒ] or [garaǰ]), and *rouge* ([ruʷʒ] or [ruʷǰ]), one possibility might be that [ʒ] and [j̆] are free variants of the same phoneme. However, both /j̆/ and /ʒ/ are secure and stable between vowels in words such as *pleasure, treasure, ledger, badger,* and this is enough to convince us that /ʒ/ and /j̆/ have to be considered as separate phonemes. One other argument for considering them to be separate phonemes will be considered in the next section. All the other consonant phonemes listed in Table 6–1 are in clear contrast with one another.

DISTINCTIVE FEATURES

By searching out enough minimal pairs we arrive at a list of the consonant phonemes of English. Table 6–1 lists these phonemes, with stops first, followed by fricatives, affricates, and then approximants. This is a conventional and reasonably logical order for such a list, but nothing in the process of finding minimal pairs requires, or even suggests, this arrangement. As far as a minimal pair search goes, the phonemes might be listed in any sequence at all.

To list the phonemes in random order would clearly miss something important about the relationships among them. We know that some phonemes have special similarities to each other, and we need a way to recognize these similarities. We know that /b/ and /d/ have more in common with each other than they have with /h/, both because they have common phonetic features (e.g., they are both voiced and both stops) and because they have similar effects upon surrounding phonemes (e.g., they both cause the previous vowel to be long). We need some way to classify phonemes that takes account of their relative degree of similarity and difference.

One way of classifying phonemes is by the point and manner of their articulation. Linguists have traditionally displayed the phonemes of a language in a chart that reflects this classification. Table 6–2 displays, in a rather conventional way, the English consonants that we have identified, and the arrangement of the table parallels that of Table 5–1 in Chapter 5. In both cases, the columns represent the points of articulation and the rows represent the manners of articulation. Since Table 6–2 is limited to the sounds of just one language, it can be both simpler and more complete than Table 5–1.

A certain amount of artistry is involved in producing even a simple chart of this sort. We like our charts to be as symmetrical as possible, and sometimes more symmetry can be achieved by rearranging some of the classes of phonemes. Whether affricates are grouped with stops (as in the table) or with fricatives, for instance, involves some judgment and even taste. Linguists like to arrange their data in a way that reveals the regularities and symmetries, but there can be a danger of forcing more symmetry onto the data than they really deserve. Arrays of consonants, such as Table 6–2, characteristically achieve a fair symmetry for stops and nasals, and a reasonable symmetry for fricatives, but they have a discouraging tendency to end with a more or less miscellaneous left-over category that defies easy or simple arrangement. Thus the English

Table 6–2
English Consonant Phonemes

p		t		č	k
b		d		ǰ	k
m		n			ŋ
f	θ	s	ʃ		
v	ð	z	ʒ		
w	j	l		r	h

approximants that are listed in the last line of Table 6–2 are less easily arranged into a symmetrical pattern than are the stops and fricatives, and they line up less perfectly in the same columns.

Charts such as Table 6–2 give a useful overview of the distinctive sounds of a language, but they are inevitably limited by the two dimensions of a sheet of paper. Phonological systems are multidimensional, and the problems in drawing a chart come from the need to reduce the many dimensions to just two. A more satisfactory way of recognizing the relationships among phonemes comes by recognizing **distinctive features.** By classifying the phonemes of a language by means of their distinctive features, we gain a more consistent way to recognize groups of similar phonemes. Those that share one or more features, such as voicing, velar articulation, or nasalization, will then fall into natural groups. Phonemes that share several features will be particularly closely related.

The following distinctive features, among others, can be used to divide the English consonants into contrasting sets. These same features turn out to be useful for distinguishing the consonants of many other languages as well.

1. Obstruent/sonorant. Oral stops, affricates, and fricatives are all classified as **obstruents.** These are sounds in which the flow of air from the lungs is relatively obstructed. Nasals and approximants, on the other hand, are classified as **sonorants,** implying that they have a relatively resonant or sonorous quality. Voiceless obstruents are common; voiceless sonorants are less so.

2. Continuant/noncontinuant. Although fricatives are classed as obstruents, they are the only obstruents that do not include a stop. Like nasals and approximants, fricatives can be prolonged or "continued." Fricatives, therefore, are classed together with nasals and approximants as **continuants,** while affricates and stops are **noncontinuants.**

3. Strident/nonstrident. Affricates and most fricatives are called strident and characterized by greater noise than are other phones. Stops, sonorants, and /θ/ and /ð/ are said to be **nonstrident.**

4. Nasal/nonnasal. The consonants /m, n, ŋ/ are set apart from all others by a lowered velum. Since this allows air to pass through the nasal tract, they are called **nasals.**

5. Voiced/voiceless. The voiced/voiceless contrast divides the English obstruents into two sets.

These five distinctive features give us a useful initial classification of English consonants. In Table 6–3 "+" indicates that a set of consonants has the characteristic, while "−" indicates that it does not.

Few linguists can resist the temptation of adding distinctive features to an analysis like this until every phoneme is distinguished from every other phoneme by at least one feature. Unfortunately, it is not always clear how to select the best additional features. Since distinctive features should apportion the phonemes into sets whose members act in parallel ways, debates over the best choice of distinctive features hinge on which set yields the most reasonable classification of phonemes. Since obstruents in many languages tend to act in similar ways, it is useful to recognize obstruents as a distinctive category of consonants and to set them apart from sonorants. If bilabial and velar stops act in ways that are different from dental and alveolar stops, it is also useful to set them apart by a distinctive feature.

We want to be able to speak of groups of phonemes that are defined by two or more features and that behave in parallel ways. Thus the voiceless noncontinuant obstruents of English, namely /p, t, k/, and /č/, all have aspiration initially before a vowel, and all are likely to be glottalized finally. Readers may find it interesting to experiment with the consonants, and with a variety of distinctive features, to see what sort of order they can bring to them, but linguists are not yet agreed about the best way to assign distinctive features, even for a language as well known as English. Not even the five features used in Table 6–3 are universally accepted.

These five features are all **binary.** This simply means that each feature has only two possible values. Consonants are either voiced or voiceless, either nasal or nonnasal, either obstruent or sonorant, etc. Many linguists have hoped to limit features to binary ones, while others have been more willing to accept multivalued features. Three-way distinctions may seem more natural in some cases, such as the English distinction among bilabials, apicals, and velars, though it is easy to suggest two binary features (e.g., bilabial versus nonbilabial, and apical versus nonapical) that will make the same distinctions.

The attraction of binary features is, to some extent, an aesthetic one. There can be something very satisfying about reducing all of the complexities of a

Table 6–3
Classifications of Consonants

	Vcls. stops (ptk)	Vcd. stops (bdg)	Vcls. afrs. (č)	Vcd. afrs. (ǰ)	Vcls. frics. (fsʃ)	Vcls. intdl. (θ)	Vcd. frics. (vzʒ)	Vcd. intdl. (ð)	Nsls. (mnŋ)	Aprxs. (lrwy)	h (h)
Obst.	+	+	+	+	+	+	+	+	−	−	−
Cont.	−	−	−	−	+	+	+	+	+	+	+
Strd.	−	−	+	+	+	−	+	−	−	−	−
Nas.	−	−	−	−	−	−	−	−	+	−	−
Vcd.	−	+	−	+	−	−	+	+	+	+	−

sound system to a set of simple and decisive binary features. Multivalued features may seem to violate the symmetry and uniformity that a description might otherwise have. If we believe that our linguistic descriptions are leading us toward an understanding of how the human mind operates, we may even ask ourselves whether there is something about the human mind that works on binary principles, but since we know less about the functioning of the human mind than we do about the organization of language, we are not likely to be helped to decide between binary and multivalued features by an appeal to psychology. Still, aesthetic criteria should not be ignored. Linguists do search for solutions to their problems that are simple or elegant, just as biologists and chemists do, and this goal implies criteria that are, in the end, aesthetic.

Beyond aesthetics has been the hope of finding a single set of distinctive features that would be applicable to all languages. Distinctive features would then provide a universal framework within which all phonological systems could be described and compared. This would mean, however, that no single language could provide all the evidence that would be needed for deciding on the best set of features.

Having presented the justification for distinctive features, it is possible, at last, to return to /ʒ/ and to offer the additional argument for its phonemic status that was promised in the last section. This is an argument based on symmetry. All other obstruents in English come in voiced/voiceless pairs. Our description of English phonology becomes more symmetrical by recognizing /ʒ/ to be the voiced partner of /ʃ/. If there were no /ʒ/ in English, there would be a gap in the system. We *ought* to have a /ʒ/. The case of English /ʒ/ is hardly in doubt, but other languages present more ambiguous cases, and criteria of symmetry sometimes persuade us to decide in one way rather than another. The importance given to criteria of symmetry is, once again, partly a matter of aesthetics and personal preference. It remains a stubborn fact of English that /ʒ/ is set apart from all other obstruents by its restricted distribution. No search for symmetry should be allowed to obscure that fact.

AMERICAN VOWELS

English vowels are far more variable from one dialect to another than are consonants, and this makes vowels much more difficult to describe on silent paper. Vowels vary so much that it is artificial to propose any single or unified system as if it could be appropriate for English speakers everywhere. A different approach is to begin with one particular variety of the language and then to use that variety as a reference point when looking at others. We will begin, therefore, with a description of what can be called an "idiolect," since it represents the speech of one particular person. This idiolect is one variety of upper Midwestern American English which, by the 1990s, had probably become just a bit old fashioned. The selection of this idiolect is, admittedly, a bit arbitrary, but it is convenient for the author since it is his. To focus on a single idiolect has the disadvantage that it will require most readers to pay close attention so as to understand how their own vowels compare with the vowels being described. It is not always easy to follow a description of a dialect different from one's own, but by focusing on just one variety, we avoid the artificiality and superficiality of a description that pretends to be generally valid.

The stressed vowels of this idiolect are listed here, symbols are assigned to each contrasting vowel phoneme, and a number of illustrative words are given for each vowel. Unstressed vowels would unnecessarily complicate the picture, so the examples are limited to stressed vowels. Few people will have a dialect exactly like this one, but readers should be able to compare their own vowels with the author's, and they should ask themselves how their own vowels differ from his. Almost everyone will find that some particular words will have to be assigned to different phonemes. Most people will also find that they lack some of the author's contrasts or make contrasts that the author lacks.

/i/	bit, bid, bin
/e/	bet, pen, bed
/æ/	bat, ant, have
/a/	alms, balm, father, spa, ha, hot, cot
/ʌ/	but, bud, hut
/o/	want, wash, log, bought, caught, paw, raw
/u/	put, good, foot
/iʲ/	bee, beat, idea
/eʲ/	bay, bait
/aʲ/	buy, bite
/oʲ/	boy, Boyd
/aʷ/	bough, bout
/oʷ/	no, boat
/uʷ/	boo, boot
/ir/	spirit, syrup, fierce, feared, beard, spear, dear, beer, zero, eerie, dearie
/er/	merry, ferry, very, spared, bared, air, spare, hair, Mary, hairy, vary, fairy, marry, Harry, carrot
/ar/	heart, arms, aren't, far, star, are, starry, sorry, borrow, tomorrow
/ʌr/	hurry, worry, courage, bird, fern, verge, burr, sir, fur, furry
/or/	horse, court, border, pour, for, store, story
/ur/	poor, pure, poorest

The transcription used here is a phonemic one, and it is deliberately different from the phonetic transcription we have used up to now. Here, when describing a phonological system, the system of contrasts is more important than the phonetic detail and, where no ambiguity results, conventional letters are easier to use than phonetic symbols. The vowel in *paw, raw,* etc., was written with [ɔ] in earlier examples, but it is written here as /o/. Since we have no other need for plain *o,* it can substitute comfortably for ɔ. Still, English has too many vowels for the five vowel letters of the conventional alphabet, so there is no avoiding a few special symbols.

Some rather arbitrary decisions must be made about which vowels deserve to be written with single letters and which are better written with a **digraph,** a pair of letters. Ideally, single letters should be used for simple vowels, and digraphs for diphthongs, since diphthongs are complex vowels consisting of a simple vowel plus a glide. Unfortunately the line between simple vowels and diphthongs is not always sharp. Dialects differ, and linguists draw different conclusions about them. Whether, for instance, we choose to transcribe the vowel of *fate* as /e/ /eʲ/ or /ej/ depends, in part, on whether we want to emphasize its unitary or its complex nature. In many respects it acts like a single unit, but some speakers, including the author, have enough of a glide to invite comparison with the vowel of *fight* where the glide is clearer. /eʲ/ represents something of a compromise. In the transcription used here, even the vowels of *beat* and *boot* are written as /ɪʲ/ and /uʷ/ and this may give a misleading impression that they are diphthongs as clearly as are /aʲ/ and /aʷ/. This arrangement is much better suited to some varieties of English than to others. Some speakers do have slight glides even in the vowels of *beat* and *boot,* but other speakers seem not to.

Writing /ɪʲ/ and /uʷ/, however, has one other advantage. It liberates simple /i/ and /u/ to be used for the vowels of *bit* and *good* and this means, in turn, that we can dispense with ɪ and ʊ entirely. Practical considerations, such as what can be written on a typewriter, make it difficult, even undesirable, to insist on too much standardization of phonetic symbols. Different examples and different goals call for somewhat different choices, and it must always be remembered that any symbol can stand for any phone (or any phoneme) as long as we are clear about what we mean.

Whatever symbols are chosen, the vowels of *beat* and *boot* do share some characteristics with the (other) diphthongs. Most simple vowels like the /i/, /e/, and /u/ of *pit, pet,* and *good,* for example, can never end a word, but always require a following consonant. /iʲ/ and /uʷ/, on the other hand, occur easily in word-final position just as do the unambiguous diphthongs /aʲ/, /aʷ/, and /oʷ/. /iʲ/, /uʷ/, and the (other) diphthongs are sometimes described as **tense,** suggesting that they require more tension in the muscles of the vocal organs than is needed for the simple vowels that, by contrast, are called **lax.** These shared characteristics suggest that it is reasonable to group /iʲ/ and /uʷ/ with the diphthongs, however feeble their glide.

The most variable phone in English is the /r/ that follows vowels. Many British and some American dialects lose /r/ after vowels and, with or without an /r/, the vowels in these words are extremely variable. Speakers of some r-pronouncing dialects may find that the role of /r/ when it follows a vowel is similar to that of /ʲ/ and /ʷ/. Like /ʲ/ and /ʷ/, /r/ affects the preceding vowel phonetically and forms a tight unit with it. Listing these r-colored vowels here along with the other vowels will facilitate the comparison with an *r*-less dialect that is described in Chapter 7.

The low vowels form another area of great dialectal variability. Most American readers will find that they use /a/ in some words that are listed here as having /o/. A few readers will have no contrast at all between the vowels listed here as /a/ and /o/. A few Americans and many British speakers will find that they have three vowels in this area. We are now, however, encroaching on the topic of language variability, and this is best left for the next chapter.

English has one other important vowel but, since it occurs only in unstressed syllables, it is omitted from this list. This is the **schwa** that linguists write as /ə/ and that occurs in the first syllables of *collapse, above,* and *concern.* In addition to being unstressed, /ə/ is generally quite short.

CONTRASTS IN OTHER LANGUAGES

The significance of phonological contrast shows up most vividly when we consider languages other than our own. It is then that we become aware of just how different languages can be and how much the conceptual machinery that we have been developing is needed. The sound systems of all languages can be analyzed into a few dozen phonemes that are distinguished by an even smaller number of distinctive features, but the particular features and the particular phonemes differ widely.

Like many languages of India, Hindi has two striking contrasts that English lacks. First, a contrast between aspirated and unaspirated stops means that /tʰik/ 'okay' and /ʈik/ 'teak, a kind of tree' are as clearly distinguished in Hindi as are *tick* and *Dick* in English. Because this contrast is not a part of the English phonological system, and because English speakers are not trained to recognize it, it can be difficult for an English speaker even to hear, let alone reproduce. Nevertheless, it is crucial in Hindi and it is used to distinguish many pairs of words. Second, Hindi also has a contrast between dental and retroflex stops so that /aṭa/ 'come' with a dental stop is different from /aṭa/ 'flour' with a retroflex stop. These two contrasts, neither of which is found in English, allow Hindi to have four consonant phonemes, /ṭ/, /ṭʰ/, /ʈ/, /ʈʰ/, all of which are likely to sound to English speakers like their own /t/.

The dental/retroflex contrast of Hindi has no parallel in English. The articulatory position of our own /t/ is usually alveolar and thus intermediate between the position of the two Hindi stops. Since our tongues and ears have not had practice in making or hearing the Hindi contrast, English speakers tend to interpret both the dentals and the retroflexes as if they were alveolars, like the closest English phoneme.

The Hindi contrast between aspirated and unaspirated stops does echo a familiar characteristic of English. The difference between aspirated English [tʰ] in words such as *top, take, tick* and unaspirated [t] in words such as *stop, steak, stick* parallels the Hindi contrast, but the two sounds are in complementary distribution in English rather than in contrast. English words are never distinguished by the presence or absence of aspiration alone. Since the phonetically similar stops of Hindi can be used to distinguish minimal pairs, we

Table 6–4
Hindi Voiceless Stops

	Bilabial	Dental	Retroflex	Velar
Aspirated	p^h	$t̪^h$	$ʈ^h$	k^h
Unaspirated	p	$t̪$	$ʈ$	k

must recognize them as being in contrast. Moreover, it is not only the dental and retroflex stops that contrast in aspiration, but the bilabials and velars as well. Thus /p/ contrasts with /p^h/, and /k/ contrasts with /k^h/. As a result, Hindi has the eight voiceless stops, as shown in Table 6–4, while English has only three. Presence versus absence of aspiration is as pervasive a distinctive feature of Hindi as is the presence versus absence of voicing in English.

It is by no means unusual to find phonetic differences that, like aspiration, are in complementary distribution in one language but in contrast somewhere else. French, for example, has nasal vowels that contrast with oral (non-nasal) vowels: /œ/ *eux* 'them,' /œ̃/ *un* 'one'; /bo/ *beaux* 'beautiful,' /bõ/ *bon* 'good.' The nasalization of American English vowels occurs only when the vowels are followed by a nasal consonant, and this means that nasal and oral vowels are in complementary distribution rather than in contrast. French vowel nasalization, on the other hand, is not predictable from the surrounding phonemes, so French must be analyzed as having an oral/nasal contrast.

In Chinese, words with identical vowels and consonants can be distinguished by their relative pitch. We call these different pitches **tones,** and the Beijing dialect of Chinese has four contrasting tones that we can identify on paper by means of accents written over the vowels. *Shī* 'louse' is pronounced with a high and fairly level tone. *Shí* 'time' begins quite low and then rises to approximately the same pitch as the first tone. *Shǐ* 'history' first falls a bit to a very low level and then rises again, finishing slightly higher than it began. Finally, *shì* 'is, are' starts high but immediately falls abruptly. With some minor exceptions, every Chinese syllable has one of these four tones. The tones are just as capable of distinguishing words from each other as are the vowels or consonants of English.

Languages exploit an ingenious range of contrasts. Swedish has a contrast between two kinds of high, front, rounded vowels. The vowel which Swedes spell *y* has the lips pushed outward almost as in a good smacking kiss. The vowel that they spell *u* has the tongue in much the same position and the lips are again rounded, but this time they are pinched inward, rather as if tasting something sour: *ny* 'new,' *nu* 'now.' Zulu, a Bantu Language of South Africa, distinguishes clicks, made by pulling the tongue sharply backward by inward air pressure, from stops made with ordinary outward air pressure from the lungs. Quechua, a Native American language spoken in the Andes, is one of many languages that distinguish velar from uvular stops. Garo contrasts plain nasals with nasals that are interrupted by a glottal stop. Malayalam, a South Indian language, contrasts alveolar and dental trills.

Just as other languages make contrasts that seem exotic to speakers of English, so they fail to make contrasts that we take for granted. Our contrast between /r/ and /l/ seems easy and obvious to us, but many languages make no such contrast. Some have either an [r]-like phoneme or an [l]-like phoneme but not both. Korean has a single phoneme with differing allophones, one of which strikes our ears as rather like our /r/, another more like our /l/. Although Koreans have these varying allophones, they have only one of them in any single environment, and they often have considerable difficulty learning to use them contrastively in a way that seems so easy and natural to English speakers. The contrast between the vowels of *beat* and *bit,* which comes easily to English speakers, is missing from Spanish. This makes it difficult for Spanish speakers to learn the English contrast, which is why native speakers of Spanish can be heard to say things like *The dog beat me on the leg.* One difficult task faced by all students of a foreign language is to learn the unfamiliar contrasts of their new language.

Charts of a language's phonemes give a quick summary of their phonological system, and they can demonstrate just how different languages can be. The original Polynesian language of Hawaii has a notably restricted number of phonemes. With only eight consonants, just two of them stops, it has one of the simplest consonant systems known. It does not even allow consonant clusters or any syllable final consonants at all. With five short and five long vowels and the possibility of vowels coalescing into diphthongs, Hawaiian vowels surpass Hawaiian consonants in complexity, but not even its vowels reach the complexity of many other languages. With such a limited choice of phonemes, Hawaiian has a limited number of distinct syllables, so it is little wonder that most Hawaiian words are polysyllabic (see Table 6–5).

The phonemes of Navajo given in Table 6–6 are very different. Navajo has three series of stops. Those in the middle series, /t/, /k/, and /k^w/, are aspirated and voiceless. /b/, /d/, and /g/, are characterized as much by the absence of aspiration as by voicing. The third series is glottalized, as indicted by the apostrophe. Navajo has a particularly rich array of affricates, including several that are released as laterals, and it has glottalized affricates along with its glottalized stops. Fricatives can be either voiced or voiceless, and /l/ has

Table 6–5

Hawaiian Phonemes

p		k	h	ʔ	
m	n				
w	l				
i	u	iː		uː	
e	o	eː		oː	
a		aː			

Table 6–6
Navajo Phonemes

Glottalized			t'	ts'	tʃ'	tɬ'	k'		ʔ
Voiceless			t	ts	tʃ	tɬ	k	kʷ	
Unaspirated		b	d	dz	dʒ	dl	g		
Voiceless				s	ʃ	ł	x	xʷ	
Voiced				z	ʒ	l	ɣ	ɣʷ	
Glottalized		'm	'n		'y				
Voiced		(m)	n		y				
i			iː		ī		ĩː		
e	o	eː		oː	ẽ	ō	ẽː		ōː
a			aː		ã		ãː		

enough friction to warrant its classification among the fricatives. Nasals and *y* can be either voiced or glottalized. Voiced *m* is placed in parentheses because it is unusual in Navajo. Navajo has vowels in only four positions, but these can be short, long, nasalized, or both long and nasalized. In addition to these vowels and consonants, Navajo has contrasting high, low, rising, and falling tones. People who have not grown up with the language do not find it easy to pronounce.

THE PHONEMES AS A CODE

It is time to summarize the main points that have been developed in this chapter so far. The phonology of any language can be described by means of contrasting phonemes that organize its speech sounds. Phonemes become the significant units of a description, but they are far more abstract units than the articulatory noises with which we began the study of speech sounds. Typically, each phoneme of a language can be represented by a number of varying allophones. English /k/ may be either aspirated or unaspirated. Korean /r/ sometimes sounds more like [r] and sometimes more like [l]. A phoneme, then, does not have a single pronunciation. Rather, it is a collection of pronunciations, a set of similar sounds that do not contrast with each other but that, taken collectively, contrast with other sets. Allophones are grouped into phonemes according to quite different patterns in different languages, and this means that a phoneme, unlike an articulated and audible phone, can be defined only with reference to a particular language.

Since phonemes are defined by their contrast with other phonemes in the same language, it makes little sense to compare a phoneme in one language directly with a phoneme in another language. No other language is likely to group exactly the same allophones together. We will need new techniques when we want to compare the phonological systems of several languages.

The phonemes constitute a language's coding system, and they can even be compared to the zeros and ones of a digital computer. Just as the information in a computer memory is coded by means of a series of zeros and ones, so the information conveyed in the messages of a natural spoken language is coded by a series of phonemes. The units of both coding systems are discrete or, as a linguist would say, they "contrast" with one another. This means that you can choose between two phonemes such as a /t/ and a /k/ but you cannot compromise between them. There is no such thing as something halfway between /t/ and /k/ any more than there is a halfway point between a zero and a one in computer memory. Computers with this kind of coding system are called "digital" computers, and the phonemes give a digital organization to the sound system of a human language.

Not all of human communication has this discrete, digital quality. We communicate important messages with our laughter, and a giggle and a belly laugh certainly mean different things. Nevertheless, we can find no sharp dividing lines between a giggle, an average laugh, and a full belly laugh. Rather, our different kinds of laughter grade into each other. They are connected by a continuous range of intermediate forms. A continuous range of intermediate phonetic steps also connects a phonetic [t] and a phonetic [k], but English phonology imposes such a sharp boundary between them that no phonological compromise is possible. No such boundary separates the different kinds of laughter, and this means that laughter, along with the rest of our nonverbal communication, is built on nondiscrete principles. Language is discrete and digital.

Other mammalian communication is more like the human nonverbal communication of giggles, laughs, whimpers, and cries than it is like language, for it is based on nondiscrete rather than on discrete and digital principles. Long before human beings invented the digital computer and the discrete coding systems with which we communicate with computers, we had already evolved a digital language. It is one of the most dramatic innovations with which evolution has endowed human beings, and it has allowed language to be constructed along very different principles from those of any other animal communication system that we know anything about.

The type of sound system provided by contrasting phonemes gives human language two distinct levels of patterning, one at the level of phonology, and the other at the level of syntax. In other words, language has both a level of contrasting but meaningless phonemes and a different level of meaningful units such as morphemes and words. The phonology provides the code from which the larger units of language can be built. Like the four nucleic acids that form the DNA of all living cells and that provide the codes for a score of amino acids and thousands of different proteins, the few dozen phonemes of a natural language can be linked together into thousands of different words and into more sentences than we can ever list. As far as we know, this coding system is unique to human language, and it distinguishes language sharply from human non-verbal communication such as laughter, as well as from the communicative signals used by other animals.

PHONOTACTICS AND SYLLABLES

/blit/, /čoŋk/, /grifəl/, /pnor/, /strʌnp/, and /čloh/ are sequences of English phonemes. As speakers of English, we know that they are not English words, but we also know that they fail to qualify as English words in two quite different ways. The first three examples could have been English words, and they might become English words in the future. Their phonemes occur in sequences that are permissible within the patterns of our language. We can easily imagine that a new brand of soap could be called *blit* or a child's game called *griffel*. On the other hand, /pnor/, /strʌnp/, and /čloh/ could never become English words because their phonemes occur in impossible sequences. No English word can begin with /pn/ or /čl/, and no word can end with /np/ or /h/. **Phonotactics,** the study of the permitted order and arrangement of the phonological units of a language, is concerned with such restrictions.

As we saw in Chapter 5, each alternation of consonants and vowels tends to count as one syllable. Most syllables have a vowel at the center, with one or more consonants coming before or after. The possible syllable types of a language can be shown by sequences of "C" and "V" indicating the number and order of consonants and vowels. Thus many languages have syllable types such as V, CV, CVC, and CCVC.

English is unusual among languages in the freedom with which consonants can be joined into the sequences that linguists call **clusters.** Such words as *strength* /streŋkə/ (CCCVCCC), *twelfths* /twelfəs/ (CCVCCCC), and *worlds* /wʌrldz/ (CVCCCC) have consonant clusters that would defeat the tongues of speakers of most languages. Sometimes they defeat our own tongues. At the opposite extreme from English are languages like Hawaiian in which every syllable consists of a single consonant followed by a vowel (CV). Hawaiian does have diphthongs and a contrast between long and short vowels, but it has no clusters of two or more consonants, and it has no syllable-final consonants at all. Most languages fall somewhere between the English and Hawaiian extremes in the complexity of their syllables.

All English consonants except /ŋ/ and /ʒ/ can occur at the beginning of a word. The stops and some fricatives can also form clusters with one of the voiced approximants /r/, /l/, /w/, or /j/ in second position. Thus typical English clusters such as /kr/, /kl/, /kw/, and /kj/ in *crick, click, quick,* and *cute* are formed from a stop plus an approximant, but not all stop–approximant combinations are possible. /*tl/ and /*dl/, for example, are impossible in English. An English speaker may feel that this is because they would be difficult to pronounce, but the Tlingit Indians of the Pacific Northwest have no trouble with their /tl/, and our impression of difficulty is probably the result, rather than the cause, of the gaps in English. In addition to clusters consisting of a stop plus an approximant, English has a large set of clusters that begin with /s/ such as those that are found in *spill, stop, school, split, strap,* and *squeeze.*

Except for /h/, /j/, and /w/, all English consonants can also occur at the end of a syllable or word, but the inventory of final clusters is quite different from the inventory of initial clusters, and it is considerably more diverse. In *r*-pronouncing dialects, /r/ can form a cluster with almost every other consonant. /l/ can form clusters with nearly as many: *self, filth, false, valve, elm, mulch, bulge, bulk, bold,* etc. In addition, we have clusters formed from a nasal plus another consonant (*tent, lunch, nymph, thank*), /s/ plus a stop (*lisp, last, task*), and various stop–fricative and stop–stop pairs (*width, adze, raft, task, box, lapse, apt, protect*). Final clusters can be made still more complicated by adding /s/, /z/, /t/, or /d/ in plurals and past tenses.

Large though our inventory of permitted clusters is, it has strict limits. Many English clusters, both initial and final, include an approximant, and the approximant is generally found next to the vowel. This seems natural if we think of a syllable as opening up toward the vowel and then closing again. An approximant can serve as a transition between the more closed obstruents at the edges of the syllable and the more open vowels at the center. Even the /n/ and /s/ of the clusters in *tent* and *nest* are intermediate in closure between the central vowels and the final stops. Many languages share this English pattern of obstruent–approximant clusters, but the particular inventory of clusters varies greatly from one language to another. In English our obstruent–approximant clusters are supplemented by clusters that have /s/ at the periphery, as in *streets, spooks,* and *scalps,* but these are lacking in many languages.

It should be obvious that the adjacent consonants of a cluster often share articulatory features. Final /mp, nt/, and /ŋk/, as in *lamp, rent, sink,* for instance, are called **homorganic,** meaning that the point of articulation of both members of the clusters is the same: bilabial, alveolar, and velar, respectively. These three are all possible clusters in English, while nonhomorganic combinations such as /*np/, */nk/, */mk/, and /*ŋp/ are not. (The asterisk indicates that these clusters are impossible in English.) Here is a place where ease of articulation offers an irresistible explanation. The vocal organs do not have to undergo such difficult articulatory acrobatics when producing homorganic clusters as they would for mixed clusters such as /*mk/.

In the same way, both members of a cluster tend to share the same value for voice. English allows /sp/, /st/, and /sk/ in which both constituents are voiceless, but not /*sb/, /*sd/, or /*sg/ where voicing would be mixed. The devoicing of /r/ and /l/ in /pr/, /kl/, and elsewhere can be understood as a way of giving consistent value for voicing, in this case voicelessness, to the entire cluster. Even the clusters that we form with suffixed consonants have consistent voicing. The plural of *bed* is pronounced /bedz/, while the plural of *cat* is pronounced /kæts/. The past of *tug* is pronounced /tʌgd/ while the past of *tuck* is pronounced /tʌkt/. Articulation is made easier by keeping the voicing consistent throughout the cluster.

Because English final clusters are so varied, an English speaker can easily be misled into supposing that the two sides of a syllable are more or less symmetrical, with roughly the same possibilities on both sides. A closer look at the inventory of English clusters shows that what is found at the beginning of a syllable is actually quite different from what is found at the end, and in many languages the difference is much greater. The extreme case is a language like Hawaiian that has no final consonants at all, but many languages permit more consonants, or more consonant clusters, before a vowel than after it. The Beijing dialect of Chinese allows 21 initial consonants and consonant clusters but only 3 finals. Japanese has about 28 different initials but, like Hawaiian, no finals at all.

Recognizing syllables as units with a systematic organization offers a new way to distinguish vowels from consonants. Up to now, we have distinguished them by the ease with which air flows through the vocal passage, but it is now possible to define a consonant as any phoneme that occupies a consonantal position in a syllable—typically at its margins—while a vowel is a phoneme that occupies the central, or nuclear, position. This gives a sharper distinction between the two, but it is a distinction that will vary from one language to another. Phones that count as consonants in one language could very well turn up as vowels some place else.

By the criterion of syllable position, /w/, /j/, /r/, and /l/ are unambiguously consonants when they occur initially in English words, such as *west, yes, rest, less,* because this is a position where other consonants can also occur. On the other hand, similar phones occur after vowels in words such as *tow, toy, tore, toll,* and we may want to count these, or some of them, as a part of the vowel rather than as consonants. The /w/- and /j/-like phones that come at the end of some English vowels, as in *pie, cow,* and *boy,* are so closely united with the vowel that most linguists find it natural to consider them to be part of the vowel rather than separate consonants. They are often called "semivowels" or "glides." The /r/ that follows vowels is also joined closely to the vowel, but in *r*-pronouncing dialects it seems a bit more like a consonant than the glides in *pie* and *cow,* so /r/ is generally considered a consonant in this position as well as initially. /l/ is even more consonantlike. Still, there is room here for differing interpretations, and it may be that different descriptions are appropriate for different dialects.

DEAF SIGNS

To what extent are human languages shaped by the medium of sound through which they are transmitted? The phonemes and words of a language that is transmitted by sound must occur one at a time, but what form would a language take if several things could happen simultaneously? Recently, linguists have become aware of the sign languages of the deaf, which take place in three-dimensional visible space rather than in one-dimensional time. Sign languages resemble spoken languages in many ways, but because they depend on sight rather than sound, they are dramatically different in other ways. The similarities of signed and spoken languages can be attributed to the common human potential to speak. The differences result from the contrasting media in which they occur.

The language known as American Sign Language, or ASL, is the most widely used means of communication among deaf Americans. ASL is not, as is sometimes supposed, a signed version of English. Neither the phonemes, words, spelling, nor syntax of English are represented directly in ASL. Rather, ASL is an independent language with its own vocabulary and its own syntax. Until recently educators of the deaf in the United States tried to discourage ASL because they were afraid it would interfere with their goal of teaching English. In spite of its discouragement, seriously deaf children have always found sign language so much easier than English, or than any signed version of English, that signing has always been used outside of the classroom. Many deaf people learn ASL from other children when attending schools for the deaf, and sign languages have flourished wherever deaf people have sought each other's company. More recently many educators have changed their attitude about signing and have begun to encourage it, believing that the best possible foundation for future education is confident skill in the only type of language that can come easily and naturally to deaf children. By all reports, a sign language like ASL gives its users a means of expression that is as rich as a spoken language.

Like a spoken language, a sign language needs words that can represent the things and ideas that people want to talk about. Like a spoken language, also, it needs both a means of keeping these words distinct from one another and a syntax to show how the words are related. The visual medium imposes different restrictions on the formation and use of words than does sound, but it offers advantages as well as disadvantages. This section will describe a few of the ways in which words are distinguished in a signed language—the signed equivalent of phonology. Some aspects of signed syntax will be described in Chapter 11.

The words or **signs** of ASL are formed with the hands, and they can be distinguished from each other in several ways. Most important are the shape of the hand or hands, their location with respect to other parts of the body, and the way in which they move. In addition to these three characteristics, signs can be distinguished in at least three other somewhat more subtle ways: the particular part of the signing hand that touches another part of the body, the direction in which the hand is turned (its orientation), and the arrangement of the hands in relation to each other. Shapes, positions, movements, and orientations can be combined in many ways, and they allow a large vocabulary of the sort that every language needs. For example, Fig. 6–1, shows the sign for CANDY, which is made with the index finger pressed against the cheek. In the sign for TRAIN, two fingers of one hand move across the two fingers of the other. YEAR is made with an active fist making a circle around a stationary fist. (The English translations of signs are conventionally written in capital letters.)

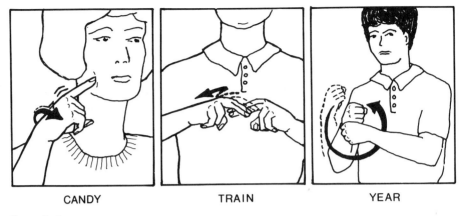

CANDY   TRAIN   YEAR

Figure 6–1
Arbitrary ASL signs. From Klima and Bellugi (1979).

    Like phonemes, the hand shapes, positions, and movements that distinguish signed words are in contrast with one another. Minimal sign pairs can be found that are alike in every way except, for example, hand shape. Just as no spoken language uses every possible sound, ASL does not use every possible hand shape, position, or movement. Certain shapes and positions are exploited, but others are not. All this makes the various features of the signs quite like the phonemes of a spoken language, but unlike phonemes, the hand features occur simultaneously. It is natural to think of the consonants and vowels of spoken language as occurring in sequence, but the shape, position, movement, and orientation of a sign all take place together. More things can happen simultaneously in visible space than in audible sound.

    Spoken and signed words also differ in the ease with which they can imitate the world outside of language. Spoken languages have a handful of onomatopoetic words, like *cock-a-doodle-doo*. These imitate sounds of the world, but speech sounds are too specialized, too different from other sounds, to encourage extensive onomatopoeia. Imitative gestures are much easier to produce than imitative sounds, and many of the signs of ASL recall, in some way, the things that they stand for. Words of this sort are said to be **iconic,** and iconicity is much more widespread in ASL than in English. Figure 6–2 shows the ASL word for EGG, which suggests a stylized breaking of an egg, and VOTE suggests the act of dropping a ballot into a box. Both of these are clearly iconic, but it would be wrong to suppose that signing is simply a kind of pantomime. Many signs of ASL are as arbitrary as any word of spoken language. Even while being equally iconic, moreover, different sign languages can have quite different signs for the same meaning. Figure 6–3 shows the sign for TREE in Danish sign language, which is made by outlining the shape of the tree with the palms of the hand. Chinese signers extend the fingers and thumbs and outline the shape of a trunk. The ASL TREE is made with forearm vertical, the fingers

Figure 6–2
Iconic ASL signs. From Klima and Bellugi (1979).

flared at the top and twisting, like branches shaking in the wind. None of these signs for TREE would be transparent to a first-time viewer.

With the passage of time, some signs lose their earlier iconicity. The sign for HOME (Figure 6–2) is now made by tapping the fingers of one hand against two spots close together on the cheek. Nothing about this sign is obviously iconic, but it began as a sequence of two other signs, one meaning EAT and the other SLEEP, both of which clearly are iconic. The sign for EAT is made with the finger tips close to the mouth, and SLEEP is made with the palm of the hand against the side of the head. When used together to mean HOME these separate signs gradually fused into a distinct and noniconic sign. The hand shape for EAT is now retained throughout, and the locations of the two original signs moved closer until they were finally reduced to two quick taps on the

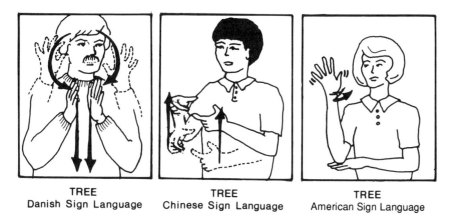

TREE	TREE	TREE
Danish Sign Language	Chinese Sign Language	American Sign Language

Figure 6–3
Signs for TREE in three sign languages. From Klima and Bellugi (1979).

cheek. No longer is it so clear that HOME is the place where one eats and sleeps.

Most signing is not pantomime, but signing does allows the incorporation of pantomime in a way that is more difficult in spoken language. When deaf people need to talk about something new, for which they have no conventional signs, they may be able to describe it in pantomime. People who use spoken language also outline things with their hands, of course, but there is no way to incorporate descriptive gestures into a spoken language. They can be incorporated into signing, but with repeated use even pantomimes tend to become conventionalized. Gradually they come to be made with a combination of the conventional hand shapes, locations, and types of movement that are already in use. As will be pointed out in Chapter 17, several early writing systems went through a similar process of conventionalization. Written symbols that began iconically, as pictures, gradually became stylized beyond any possible recognition. In both signing and in writing, ease of production has taken precedence over ease of recognition.

The opportunity for iconicity might suggest that signs have an advantage over spoken words. They are less arbitrary so they might be easier to learn. Signs have compensating disadvantages, however. Apart from the obvious drawback that it is difficult to sign in the dark or while working with the hands, signing probably requires more energy than speaking. In addition, in spite of the simultaneity of the features that make up a sign, each sign takes almost twice as long to produce as a spoken word. We can produce and recognize distinctive sounds much more rapidly than we can produce or recognize distinctive gestures. Some of the ways in which the syntax of signing compensates for the slower rate of sign production will be described in Chapter 11.

In spite of the differences between spoken and signed language, both have rich and expressive vocabularies. Like spoken languages, sign languages have thousands of distinct words, and these cover the full range of meanings that the speakers of any language require. New words are readily developed whenever people want to talk about new things, and there is no reason to suppose that signing restricts, in any way, the expressive powers of its users.

SEGMENTATION AND ITS PROBLEMS: TONE LANGUAGES

The unstated assumption has been made in this chapter that phonemes occur sequentially, that they follow each other like the letters on a printed page or, as a timeworn comparison would have it, like beads on a string. This has been a reasonable point of view to start with, but two types of evidence have already been considered that ought to make us cautious about too easy an acceptance of this tempting point of view. First, there is clearly plenty of overlap of the phonetic material by which we identify adjacent phonemes. We distinguish voiced and voiceless consonants partly by the length of the preceding vowel. An /h/ anticipates the shape of the vowel that follows. All the assimilations by which one phoneme adapts to its neighbors blur the boundaries between them. Instrumental analysis of the sounds that pass from speaker to hearer shows that sounds change continually with few clear breaks between phonemes. One way of acknowledging the mutual influence that neighboring phonemes have on one another is to recognize their overlapping nature. The beads on this phonemic string melt into each other.

An even more serious objection to the beads-on-a-string view arises with tone languages like Chinese. In the example given earlier, Chinese tones were written by accents over the vowels: shī 'louse' with a high-level pitch; shǐ 'history' with a falling–rising pitch. Writing tones this way may seem to imply that they occur more or less simultaneously with the vowels. Since the vowels are usually the most resonant part of the syllable, this is certainly the easiest place for tones to be heard. Still, it is difficult to find clear grounds for insisting that the tone is attached specifically to the vowel rather than to the syllable as a whole and, wherever we hear it, the tone hardly fits sequentially among a string of linearly arranged consonant and vowel segments.

Burmese, also a tone language, raises an additional complication. For syllables that end with a vowel, Burmese has a three-way tone contrast. Syllables that end with a glottal stop, on the other hand, show no tone contrast at all. It is tempting to look on these stopped syllables as constituting a fourth tone. Syllables with glottal stops certainly contrast with syllables having one of the other three tones. If we consider the final glottal stop to be one part of the phonetic realization of one of four Burmese tones, however, we must also acknowledge that the phonetic scope of tone extends to the very end of the syllable. There can be no doubt that tone is phonemic in Burmese. Just as in Chinese, contrasting tones are enough to distinguish otherwise identical Burmese words, but it would be entirely artificial to try to force the tone into a linear sequence along with the vowels and consonants. Burmese tone is better characterized as a feature of the entire syllable. The linear, one-dimensional, beads-on-a-string view of phonology can no longer be maintained.

Consider another language, Mende of Sierra Leone in West Africa, where tones seem to be spread across an entire word. One-syllable Mende words can have one of five contrasting tone patterns: High [´], Low [`], Falling [ˆ], Rising [ˇ], and Rising-Falling [˜]:

High:	/kɔ́/	'war'
Low:	/kpà/	'debt'
Falling:	/mbû/	'owl'
Rising:	/mbǎ/	'rice'
Rising-Falling:	/mbã̂/	'companion'

If each of these five tone patterns could occur freely on any syllable, we would expect to find 25 different tone sequences on two-syllable words, but these turn out, like one-syllable words, to allow only five distinct tone patterns: High-High, Low-Low, High-Low, Low-High, and Low-Falling.

High-High:	/pέlέ/	'house'
Low-Low:	/bὲlὲ/	'trousers'
High-Low:	/ŋílà/	'dog'
Low-High:	/fàndé/	'cotton'
Low-Falling:	/nyàhâ/	'woman'

The correspondence between two-syllable tone patterns and one-syllable tone patterns is obvious. High-High corresponds to High, Low-Low to Low, High-Low to Falling, Low-High to Rising, and Low-Falling to Rising-Falling. Even three-syllable words have five similar tone patterns.

High-High-High:	/háwámá/	'waistline'
Low-Low-Low:	/kpàkàlì/	'tripod chair'
High-Low-Low:	/félàmà/	'junction'
Low-High-High:	/ndàvúlá/	'sling'
Low-High-Low:	/nìkílì/	'groundnut'

We can describe Mende phonology as consisting of two parallel but distinct segmental levels, one formed by the sequence of vowels and consonants, and the second by a sequence of tones. As a tone sequence becomes attached to a word, it spreads across the word and adapts to its length. A three-syllable word allows the pattern to spread out widely enough so that each syllable will have a level tone. With shorter words, two level tones may have to be squeezed together onto a single syllable, and in that case, a rise or a fall takes place within the length of that syllable. In the most extreme case, where an entire tone sequence has to fit onto a one-syllable word, it can even happen that three tones must be placed on a single syllable. The Low-High-Low tone pattern of a three-syllable word then becomes the rising-falling pattern of a one-syllable word.

Tone languages like Mende give us particularly insistent evidence that a phonological system has to be interpreted as including more than a simple linear sequence of segmental phonemes. The theory that allows for two or more parallel segmental levels is known as **autosegmental phonology.**

ENGLISH STRESS

The simple segmental view of phonology breaks down even in English once we look beyond the consonants and vowels and consider stress, for it is no more possible to locate stress than to locate tone at a particular point in a sequence of vowels and consonants. To make sense of English stress, we must first recognize that it is used in several distinct ways. First, stress joins with pitch as one component in the larger patterns of sentence intonation. Sentence intonation is used for such purposes as distinguishing questions from statements and showing the speaker's attitude. Second, particular words can be emphasized by means of what is known as **contrastive stress.** By stressing different words, very different meanings can be given to a sentence such as *George shouldn't bite his nails*. Placing the stress on *George* suggests that it may be all right for someone else to bite his nails, but with stress on *bite* its meaning becomes *George should do something else to his nails*. If *nails* is stressed, the sentence suggests that *He should bite something else*. It is clear that contrastive stress occurs simultaneously with the segmental vowels and consonants, and it would be artificial to try to locate it at some particular point in the sequence.

In addition to sentence intonation and contrastive stress, English assigns **word stress** to one particular syllable of most words. Along with the vowels and consonants, the position of stress helps to identify the word and to keep words distinct from one another. Two-syllable English words must carry stress on either the first syllable (*cárry, wáter, quíckly*) or on the second syllable (*attráct, discréte, advíce*). Stress can even indicate whether we are dealing with one word or two. The phonological difference between *bláckbird*, a species of bird, and *black bírd*, a bird that happens to be colored black, lies in the position of stress. We have a few minimal, or near-minimal, pairs in which the position of stress is the primary distinguishing feature. Most of these are noun/verb pairs in which the noun has stress on the first syllable, and a related verb has stress on the second: *insult, contract, permit*.

Three-syllable words offer three locations for stress:

First syllable	Second syllable	Third syllable
dífficult	contráption	enginéer
décimate	enáble	understánd
glórify	fantástic	contradíct
hándyman	impórtant	forty-fóur

Linguists have found it surprisingly difficult to specify the precise phonetic characteristics that distinguish stressed syllables. Nevertheless, speakers of English are rarely in doubt about where the stress belongs and, when words are pronounced carefully and by themselves, one important phonetic cue for the position of stress is the pitch contour, the pattern by which the pitch rises and falls. Consider first, a three syllable word like *contráption* that is stressed on the second syllable. Here, the pitch is usually highest on the second syllable, and it drops decisively on the third. The first syllable seems closer in pitch to the second syllable than to the third, but perhaps it is best described as Mid. *Contráption* can, then, be characterized as having a Mid-High-Low tone pattern, with the peak in tone marking the stressed syllable.

A word like *enginéer*, with the stress on the final syllable, also has a decisive drop in pitch, but the drop seems to be squeezed onto the last syllable, which begins high but then falls. The first two syllables can be characterized as Mid, so these words have a Mid-Mid-Falling pattern, in which the Falling syllable combines High and Low. This pattern differs from the pattern of *contráption* not in the sequence of pitches, but in the way in which the sequence is spread across the word. In *enginéer* just as in *contráption*, the peak in pitch is located on the stressed syllable. In both words, the syllables before the pitch peak are Mid.

In *difficult,* the stress is on the first syllable, which is high, and the pitch drops between the first and second syllables. In all three cases, then, the High pitch marks the stressed syllable, and it is followed by a sharp drop in pitch. Any syllables preceding the High and stressed syllable have a Mid pitch. All three words could be described as having a (Mid)-High-Low pitch pattern, if we understand that Mid pitch is spread over all the syllables before the High and is missing if there are no such syllables.

A similar pitch contour can be recognized on shorter words, if we allow it to be squeezed from one or both ends. In words such as *wáter* the pitch drops between the first and second syllables, while in *advíce* the entire drop occurs on the final syllable. Only when stress occurs on the final syllable is an earlier syllable available to show a Mid pitch. When a one-syllable word is stressed, the entire fall occurs on the only available syllable, and of course there is nothing to carry an initial Mid pitch.

In words that are longer than three syllables, we find the same pattern, but it is stretched even more. *Cardiováscular* has six syllables, with primary stress on the fourth. The first three have a Mid pitch that is higher than the pitch of the final two syllables, but not quite so high as that of the fourth, stressed, syllable. When stress comes late in a long word, there are more initial syllables with Mid tone, and when stress is early, more trailing syllables have a Low pitch. Words of any length can be interpreted as having a (Mid)-High-Low pattern as long as we know that the initial Mid is lost whenever stress is on the first syllable, as it always is in one-syllable words.

English word stress shares more with the Mende tones than might at first have been supposed. In both languages a single pattern of tone or stress can spread out over words of varying numbers of syllables. In English, at least three syllables are needed to display the pattern fully, though shorter words show it in squeezed versions. Three syllables are also needed in Mende if each syllable is to have a level tone, but squeezed tone sequences appear on shorter words in Mende also. Of course, the two languages also differ in important ways. English has only a single "tone" pattern, while Mende has five. On the other hand, the single English pattern can be attached to words at different places, while the Mende tone patterns are always distributed across the syllables in the same way. The choice in Mende is among different tone patterns, while the choice in English is among the syllables at which to anchor it.

TURKISH VOWEL HARMONY

Having recognized the nonsegmental nature of tone and stress, it is reasonable to ask whether other aspects of phonology might not also be clarified by breaking away from too rigid a segmental view. An example comes from Turkish, which has strict limits on which vowels can occur together in the same

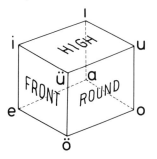

Figure 6-4
The Turkish vowel cube.

word. The vowels of a Turkish word can be said to "harmonize" with one another, and vowel harmony can be described by recognizing vowel features that, like tone or stress patterns, extend across an entire word.

Turkish has eight vowels that are distinguished from each other by the three binary features of height, backing, and rounding. These can be interpreted as forming an elegantly symmetrical vowel system. Half the vowels are high and half are low, (or at least nonhigh); half are front and half are back; half are rounded and half are unrounded. No linguist can resist thinking of these vowels as if arranged in a conceptual cube. In Figure 6-4 the four high vowels are shown on the corners of the top plane; the nonhigh vowels are on the bottom. The four front vowels are on the left front vertical plane, and the four rounded vowels are on the right front vertical plane. Conventional Turkish spelling is so well adapted to the phonology of the spoken language that the standard spelling can be used in this example. The vowels that are spelled *ü* and *ö* in standard Turkish orthography are front rounded vowels, high and low respectively. The vowel that is written as ı ("dotless *i*") is high, back, and unrounded. *e* and *o* are low (or "nonhigh") vowels that contrast with the high vowels. The high vowels *i* and *u* and the low back vowel *a* complete the corners of the cube.

Contrasts among all eight vowels can be found in monosyllables and in the initial syllables of longer words, so there can be no doubt about their phonemic status. In noninitial syllables, however, the choice of vowels is narrower. The limitations show up most clearly in the vowels of suffixes, of which Turkish has a great many, for each suffix has several forms. The alternating forms of each suffix differ in their vowels, and the vowels of the suffixes must "harmonize" with the earlier vowels of the word. Some suffixes have two alternate pronunciations, and others have four. For example, the plural suffix is sometimes pronounced *-ler* and sometimes *-lar*:

evler   'houses'
yollar   'roads'

The first person possessive suffix has four alternative forms, *-im*, *-ım*,

-üm, -um:

evim	'my house'
adım	'my name'
köyüm	'my village'
kolum	'my arm'

Notice that the vowels of the plural suffix (*a, e*) are both low, while all four vowels of the first person possessive suffix (*i, ü, u, ı*) are high. Other suffixes fall into two groups. Some are like *-lar/-ler*, with vowels that alternate between *a* and *e*, both of which are low and unrounded; others are like im/üm/um/ım, and alternate among the four high vowels. These limitations can be more carefully described as follows:

1. Some suffixes always have low vowels, and others always have high vowels. Suffixes never alternate between low and high.

2. When a suffix has a low vowel, the vowel is always unrounded, i.e., either *a* or *e*. The low rounded vowels, *o* and *ö*, are never found in suffixes. A suffix with a low vowel always has *e* (front) when it follows a front vowel in an earlier syllable. It has *a* (back) when it follows an earlier back vowel. Notice that vowels of *yollar* are both back, while vowels of *evler* are both front. All this leads to the generalization that suffixes having low vowels must harmonize with earlier vowels in backing.

3. When a suffix has a high vowel, this vowel takes both its rounding and its backing from the earlier vowels of the word. Thus both the vowels of *evim* are front, and both are unrounded. Both vowels of *adım* are back and unrounded. Readers can check that the two vowels of both *köyüm* and *kolum* also show harmony in both backing and rounding. Suffixes with high vowels, then, harmonize with the earlier vowels in rounding as well as in backing.

All this boils down to the fact that the vowels of a Turkish word have to agree, or "harmonize," with each other. All the vowels of a word must be back or all must be front, and high vowels must harmonize in rounding as well. It is revealing to look on Turkish rounding and backing in somewhat the same way that we have already looked on Mende tone and English stress, as features of the whole word. The features of backing and rounding can be said to characterize an entire Turkish word, and not simply individual vowels within the word. The entire word is either back or front, and either rounded or unrounded. The only feature that has to be specified for each individual vowel is its height, either high or low. The six words of the earlier examples can then be rewritten with their features of Backing ("B" or "F") and Rounding ("R" or "U") pulled away from the individual vowels and written at the beginning, where they are meant to refer to the entire word. The individual vowels need to be defined only as high ("H") or low ("L"). Remember, however, that low rounded vowels are allowed only in the first syllable. All later low vowels will be unrounded.

FU(LvlLr)	evler	'houses'
BR(yLllLr)	yollar	'roads'
FU(LvHm)	evim	'my house'
BU(LdHm)	adım	'my name'
FR(kLyHm)	köyüm	'my village'
BR(kLlHm)	kolum	'my arm'

In each case the features of backing and rounding are spread across the entire word, just as the features of tone are spread across an entire Mende word and the features of word stress are spread across an entire English word. Thus both vowels of the word for 'houses' are shown to be Front, Unrounded and Low, namely an *e*. The word meaning 'my arm' has a Back Rounded Low vowel, *o,* in the first syllable, but a Back Rounded High vowel, *u,* in the second. In all cases, the local feature of height combines with the backing and rounding features of the word to produce the phonetic quality that characterizes each vowel. A few additional examples show that the same patterns are characteristic of longer words. These examples are formed with two suffixes, the past participle, *-dHk-,* and the third person possessive suffix *-lLrH.*

FU(vLrdHklLrH)	verdikleri	'their giving'
BU(LrLdHklLrH	aradı kları	'their looking'
FR(yHrHdHklLrH)	yürüdükleru	'their walking'
BR(LkHdHklLrH)	okuduklaru	'their reading'

We are so accustomed to writing with a sequence of letters that it seems cumbersome to extract vowel features in this way, but to do so expresses a regularity in Turkish phonology that is missed by more conventional spelling. In particular, it allows suffixes to be written in the same way in every word. Since the alternate forms of the suffixes are determined only by the characteristics of the root word to which they are attached, writing them in this way expresses an important generalization about the language, the harmony that unites the vowels of Turkish words. Of course words must be spoken in real time, and they have to consist of a connected flow of sounds, but this flow can be understood as the expression of a more abstract underlying pattern. Like the tone patterns of Mende or the stress pattern of English, Turkish vowel features are best understood as extending across an entire word.

ALTERNATIONS AND UNDERLYING FORMS

The analyses offered for Mende tones, English stress, and Turkish vowels suggest that relatively abstract forms can be looked on as "underlying" the more concrete "surface" forms. No one can hear Mende tones, English stresses, or the patterns of Turkish vowel harmony apart from the segmental vowels and consonants of the language, but in each case we can postulate more abstract units that account for what we observe. The surface forms that we hear can be derived from more abstract units that seem to underlie them. The next step is to focus more specifically on ways in which relatively diverse surface forms can be related to more uniform underlying forms, and this will lead to a "process" view of phonology in which uniform underlying forms will be described as "changing" into the surface forms that we pronounce and hear.

First, we can restate some of the English patterns of alternation that have already been considered. The pronunciation of a phoneme often depends on its environment: English voiceless stops are aspirated initially, but unaspirated after /s/; vowels are lengthened before voiced consonants; /k/ is fronted before front vowels. These alternations can be summarized by means of brief rules whose conventions are similar to the morphological rules used in Chapter 3. The large curly braces mean that the rule applies equally to any item on the inside; the arrow can be read as "is pronounced as"; "#" marks a word boundary; the large dash indicates the location of the item being described. Thus, the first formula means that the phonemes /p/, /t/, and /k/ are aspirated when they occur as word initial (following a word break) and preceding a vowel. When features are stacked vertically within braces, it means that both features must be present for the generalization to hold. Thus a vowel is long when it occurs before a segment that is *both* voiced *and* a consonant. To characterize the pronunciation of all the phonemes of a language under all possible conditions would require a large number of such rules.

$$\{/p, t, k/\} \quad \rightarrow \quad \{[p^h, t^h, k^h]\}/ \#\underline{\quad} \text{ vowel}$$

$$\{/p, t, k/\} \quad \rightarrow \quad \{[p, t, k]\}/ \text{ /s/}\underline{\quad} \text{ vowel}$$

$$\text{vowel} \quad \rightarrow \quad \text{long} / \underline{\quad} \begin{bmatrix} \text{voiced} \\ \\ \text{consonant} \end{bmatrix}$$

$$/k/ \quad \rightarrow \quad [\underset{\sim}{k}] / \underline{\quad} \begin{bmatrix} \text{front} \\ \\ \text{vowel} \end{bmatrix}$$

These rules describe straightforward allophonic variation, but languages also have considerably more radical kinds of phonological alternation. Consider what happens to a word final /t/ or /d/ when the next word begins with /j/. In relaxed speech, the pronunciation becomes /č/ or /ǰ/. *Bet you* becomes /bɛču^w/. *Had you* becomes /hæju^w/. As English speakers can verify with their own examples, this is a regular and pervasive process of colloquial English. It can be described by a straightforward rule:

$$\{/t, d/\} + /y/ \rightarrow \{/č, ǰ /\}$$

Notice that this rule differs in a crucial way from those given just above. The earlier rules described the circumstances under which a phoneme comes to be represented by a particular allophone. This new rule suggests that one phoneme can be transmuted into an entirely different phoneme, a much more radical kind of alternation.

Consider, next, the possessive of the name *Len* and the third person singular of the verb *lend*. Most English speakers pronounce *Len's* and *lends* identically, even though the words from which they are derived have contrasting pronunciations. Adding /z/ to either /len/ or /lend/ results in /lenz/. Similarly, *fines* and *finds* are both pronounced /faʲnz/, even by speakers who clearly distinguish *fine* and *find*. The plural of *cent* is pronounced /sens/, exactly like *sense*. Some missing /d/'s and /t/'s need to be accounted for, and this can be done by another rule that says that /t/ or /d/ disappears when coming between /n/ and either /s/ or /z/. "Ø" means "zero." It stands for something that has disappeared:

$$\{/t, d/\} \rightarrow \emptyset \; / \: /n/ \underline{\quad} /s, z/$$

Unlike English, German has no voiced stops at the end of words. Thus even though the German words *Rat* 'council,' and *Rad* 'wheel, bicycle' are spelled differently, both are pronounced identically as /rat/. When these words are used with certain suffixes, however, their pronunciation is different:

	'council'	'wheel'
Nominative singular	/raːt/	/raːt/
Genitive singular	/raːtəs/	/raːdəs/
Nominative plural	/reːtə/	/reːdər/

The word for 'wheel' has /d/ in its inflected forms but /t/ in the uninflected form. The word for 'council' has /t/ under all circumstances. If 'wheel' were the only German word to behave this way we would simply describe it as irregular and move on to other matters, but German has a very large number of words that act like *Rad,* having a voiceless consonant when used without a suffix, but a voiced consonant when followed by some suffixes. The simplest way to understand this voiced/voiceless alternation is to infer that the basic form of a word like *Rad* 'wheel' has a voiced stop, but that this stop is devoiced when there is no suffix. In other words, instead of saying that one /raːt/ but not the other mysteriously changes to /raːd/ when a suffix is added, we take /raːd/ as basic and say that it changes to /raːt/ when a suffix is *not* added. *Rat* 'council' begins as /raːt/ and never changes. Again, the alternation can be summarized by a rule that describes a process of change: /d/ turns into /t/ before a word break:

$$/d/ \quad \rightarrow \quad /t/ \; / \underline{\quad} \#$$

Since devoicing in final position affects not just /d/ but all voiced obstruents, we can write a more general rule:

$$\begin{bmatrix} \text{voiced} \\ \text{obstruent} \end{bmatrix} \rightarrow \begin{bmatrix} \text{voiceless} \\ \text{obstruent} \end{bmatrix} / \underline{\quad} \#$$

A more precise rule would state that all the features of the obstruent except for voicing are preserved. Thus bilabial voiced stops remain bilabial stops but merely lose their voicing when they show up finally. A less formal rule will be sufficient here, as long as what happens is understood.

When the conditions are right, underlying /t/ and /d/ also lose their contrast in many dialects of American English. Many Americans pronounce *writer* and *rider* identically, although the words from which they are formed, *write* and *ride,* are different. For these speakers, when either /t/ or /d/ occurs between vowels and before an unstressed syllable, it is pronounced as an alveolar flap:

$$\{/t, d/\} \quad \rightarrow \quad [\mathrm{r}] \; / \; [\text{vowel}] \underline{\qquad} \begin{bmatrix} \text{vowel} \\ \\ \text{unstressed} \end{bmatrix}$$

These rules all suggest that we need to recognize an abstract level that is not only "deeper" than the audible sounds of the language, but "deeper" even than the level of its phonemes. German *Rad* 'wheel' is certainly pronounced with a voiceless final stop, so it must be interpreted as having the phoneme /t/, but the wider patterns of the language lead us to interpret this /t/ as having derived, in turn, from a "deeper" or more "underlying" /d/. Similarly, the final clusters of *cents* and *sense* are certainly identical at the phonemic level, but they derive from different underlying sources.

Many other examples lead to the similar conclusions. The words *telegraph, telegraphy,* and *telegraphic* are pronounced /télǝgræf/, /tǝlégrǝfiʲ/, and /telǝ-grǽfik/. The most weakly stressed syllables of these words, like the most weakly stressed syllables of countless other English words, have the vowel /ǝ/, but the stressed syllables have other vowels. The most efficient way of describing all these vowels is to consider the /ǝ/'s to be surface vowels only, all of them derived from quite different underlying vowels. Once again, we are led to postulate underlying forms that can be different from the surface forms that we can actually hear. The underlying forms of the words could be regarded as /télegræf/, /telégræfiʲ/, and /telegrǽfik/. These differ from each other only in their suffixes and in the position of stress. This way of writing the three words shows that they are related to each other, but it does so at the cost of distancing the transcription from the phones that we hear. As we actually produce them and hear them, the vowels certainly differ from word to word, but spelling them alike surely reflects our intuitions as English speakers that the words are very closely related. If the same symbols are used to represent the underlying vowels in all three words, rules will be needed that describe how similar underlying forms yield different surface vowels under different circumstances. Roughly speaking, the underlying vowels survive in syllables that are stressed, but they are reduced to /ǝ/ in the most weakly stressed syllables.

Sometimes rules are needed that delete whole segments. Consider these examples:

damn   damnation
condemn   condemnation

column	columnar
autumn	autumnal
sum	summation
form	formation
reclaim	reclamation

The difference between these pairs of words might be described by saying that *damn, condemn, column,* and *autumn* add an /n/ when followed by a suffix, while *sum, form,* and *reclaim* do not. To express the rule in this way would mean that each word would need to be labeled in some way to show whether or not the addition of a suffix calls for an added /n/. If, however, the underlying form of the word is taken to be the pronunciation found in the second column, the situation is easy to describe: /n/ is deleted whenever an underlying word ends with /mn/.

$$/n/ \quad \rightarrow \quad \emptyset \ / \ m \underline{\quad\quad} \#$$

Notice that this rule does not depend on a knowledge of conventional English spelling. Similar phenomena can be found even in unwritten languages. It is true, of course, that conventional English spelling reflects some of the same underlying forms that we want to recognize, but a knowledge of the spelling is not needed in order to discover the patterns.

Similar reasoning suggests that an underlying /g/ is lost under certain circumstances. Ignore, for the moment, the vowel changes in the following pairs:

sign	signify
paradigm	paradigmatic
phlegm	phlegmatic
design	designate

As before, the underlying forms of these words can be considered to include a cluster, /gn/ or /gm/, but the /g/ is lost when the word lacks a suffix:

$$/g/ \quad \rightarrow \quad \emptyset \ / \underline{\quad\quad} \text{[nasal]} \#$$

where "nasal" stands for either /n/ or /m/.

It is now worth considering a more complex example in which the derivation from underlying forms requires several interrelated rules. To start with, notice that English has many word pairs in which /aʲ/ and /i/ alternate:

divine	divinity
expedite	expeditious
ignite	ignition
contrite	contrition
divide	division
satire	satirical

An accurate account of this alternation requires a rule that carefully points to particular suffixes, but an informal statement will be sufficient here:

$$/aʲ/ \quad \rightarrow \quad /i/ \ / \underline{\quad\quad} \text{[various suffixes]}$$

Next comes a set of words that partially overlaps the preceding set, in which /t/ alternates with /ʃ/:

ignite	ignition
expedite	expeditious
construct	construction
donate	donation
rotate	rotation
locate	location

This alternation seems to be covered by still another rule:

$$/t/ \quad \rightarrow \quad /ʃ/ \ / \ \underline{\quad}\{\text{-ion, -ious}\}$$

Now, however, a new kind of problem arises, for by looking just a bit further, we find examples that condradict this rule. In the following pairs, many speakers have /č/ in the derived words even though the previous examples, and the rule that accounted for them, would lead us to expect /ʃ/:

quest	question
Christ	Christian
tempest	tempestuous
contempt	contemptuous

These apparent exceptions offer a good occasion to pause and be more explicit about how linguists work, and even to consider how they conduct small-scale experiments. First, we notice an apparent regularity according to which /t/ turns into /ʃ/ under certain circumstances. Thus /ekspədaʲt/ gives rise to /ekspədišʌs/. Noting that /t/ becomes /ʃ/ before -ious amounts to a tiny theoretical generalization, a statement of apparent regularity that we discover in our data.

Next we deliberately look for more data as a means of testing that theoretical generalization, and we follow exactly the same logic that any scientist follows when performing an experiment that is designed to test a theory. When we put this rule to the test, we soon encounter words such as *question* that are apparent exceptions. Exceptions like this sometimes force us to abandon a generalization. We then have to admit that our earlier hunch was wrong and start over again. We look for a different way to describe the facts. But sometimes we can salvage something from our earlier generalization and, instead of abandoning it completely, find a way to modify and improve it so that it will account for the exceptions as well as for the original data. So we inspect our apparent exceptions to see if they differ, in some significant way, from the examples that fit the original rule. When we do this, we notice that each of the new examples, unlike the old ones, has a continuant, either an /s/ or /m/, before the /t/. The /t/ of our first set of examples followed a vowel or /k/. Thus we can rewrite our rule in a way that will account for both the old and the new data:

$$/t/ \quad \rightarrow \quad /č/ \quad / \ [\text{continuant}] \ \underline{\quad}\{ \text{-ion, -uous}\}$$

/t/   →   /ʃ/ / [elsewhere] ___ { -ion, -ous}

We have carried out a miniexperiment. We have proposed a generalization (formed a hypothesis), searched for data to test it, found data that do not fit, and then proposed a revised generalization in the form of a revised set of rules. Logically, the next step is to search for still more data, and when we do so we find another problem:

right /raʲt/   righteous /raʲčəs/

Here is a word where the /t/ becomes /č/ rather than /ʃ/ even though it lacks a continuant. (Pronunciation rather than spelling is at issue here, of course). It might have been expected that *righteous* would be pronounced with /ʃ/, perhaps as [*rɪʃəs]. Inconveniently, it is not. Can the rules be modified again so as to take account of the anomalous *righteous*?

What about considering the underlying form of *right* and *righteous* to have some sort of continuant that would be analogous to the /s/ of *quest* or the /m/ of *contempt*? This underlying continuant could trigger the conversion of /t/ to /č/, and later it could be deleted in the same way that /n/ was deleted from the underlying /dæmn/ in *damn*. The appropriate symbol for an unheard segment would seem to be the unknown variable "x" so let us consider *right* and *righteous* to have the underlying forms /raʲxt/ and /raʲxtəs/. The rules will first change /t/ to /č/ after a continuant and before a suffix like *-ious*. This rule will yield /raʲxčəs/. Once this change has been made, another rule deletes the /x/ to yield /raʲčəs/, exactly what we want.

This derivation works. These rules can account for the forms that we actually use. With these rules, however, we have climbed to a new level of abstraction. For one thing, this derivation requires rules to be applied in a particular order. /x/ cannot be deleted until it has done its job of helping turn /t/ into /č/. More worrisome is the fact that we have now proposed an underlying segment, /x/, that never appears on the surface at all. The other segments that have been deleted do appear in some circumstances where they can actually be heard. The /n/ gets deleted from *damn,* but we may be comfortable about calling this a deletion because we can hear the /n/ in *damnation*. The /x/, on the other hand, has been inserted into /raʲxt/ only to make a rule work, and there is nothing in the modern language to tell us what /x/ might sound like. Surely this is one stage more artificial than the other rules we have proposed, and it may even seem disturbingly tricky. Maybe it is only a bit of sleight of hand to save an otherwise convenient rule. At this point, we may grow nervous. How abstract should we allow our rules to become?

What we have actually done with this example is to reconstruct a fragment of the history of the English language. There was a time when words such as *right* and *righteous* really did have a continuant where we placed our /x/. It was a velar fricative and, except in a few Scottish dialects, it has completely disappeared from modern English. Our rule turns out to reflect the history of the language, as does the "gh" of our spelling. Must we conclude that rules like this are still alive today, and that they still account for the forms of words like *righteous*?

Some linguists seem to have felt that such rules do continue as an active part of our language and that they constitute part of the knowledge that speakers carry with them in their heads. It has even been supposed that children continue, somehow, to learn such rules. Otherwise, how could they get *righteous* right? Does this mean that we all carry a bit of the history of our language around with us? Other linguists have been more skeptical. They have felt that an analysis such as this gives too much life to the now-dead residue of a long-forgotten historical process, a process that has little continuing relevance for the living language. Such linguists find it easier to believe that children simply learn some words, including *righteous,* as units. Such words would not need to be derived from other words by abstract rules.

The type of phonology that has been introduced briefly in this section and that makes use of a sequence of rules to derive the surface phones of a language from more abstract and regular underlying forms is known as **generative phonology.** This type of phonology uses an ordered sequence of rules that starts from a relatively abstract and relatively regular "underlying" level, and moves step by step in the direction of a more concrete, but also less regular, "surface" level. Generative phonologists have been willing to accept very abstract underlying forms and complex derivational processes to turn these into surface forms.

Some other linguists have been more cautious, and they have wanted to distinguish living rules of the language from the residue of ancient but now dead rules. The English rule that derives /č/ from a /t/ followed by a /j/, as in /hičuʷ/ from *hit you,* is healthy and productive. People say /gača, dijə, pikčər/, for *got you, did you,* and *picture,* so easily and automatically that they are rarely even aware of what they are doing. The rule that derives /i/ from /aʲ/ in words such as *ignition* from *ignite* still seems to be alive, though it is surely less vigorous. By comparison, the rule that deletes an underlying /x/ from *right* is moribund. We find a range of rules that have varying degrees of vigor, and how far we want to go in accepting such rules into a grammar of contemporary English remains, in part, a matter of judgment, or even of taste. Perhaps as we learn more, we will find firmer criteria for deciding where the line should be drawn.

RULES AND ABSTRACTIONS

The word "rule" has been used freely in this chapter, but it should not be passed by without comment. Rules, such as those that derive surface forms from deeper levels, can be looked on in two quite different ways. Conservatively, a rule can be thought of as no more than a succinct summary of the regularities that we find in our data. It is always tempting, however, to take rules a bit more seriously than this, and even to attribute them to speakers of the language. Linguists can hardly avoid hoping that they are doing more than simply devising gimmicks that somehow account for data. It seems more important to be learning something about the way in which real speakers organize their language. We have to wonder whether, or to what degree, ordinary speakers use a grammar in a way that parallels the generalizations of linguists.

Intense arguments have been waged about the psychological reality of our linguistic generalizations. If linguistics is, as many of us hope, one means of learning something about the nature of the human mind, we would like our generalizations to reflect the way in which real speakers speak. On the other hand, no one would propose that our mental rules have precisely the form that linguists write on paper. We are far from a consensus on such matters or even on how we might try to resolve our disagreements.

The abstract formulations that linguists devise also suggest difficult questions about how children learn to speak. To the extent that the abstract structures are a real part of the language, do we have to believe that children, like linguists, must learn them? This might seem to be an almost impossible task, for it suggests that children, like linguists, take the concrete but fragmentary samples of language that they hear, and draw very abstract conclusions from them. Does this not force children into the role of little linguists? Or, could it be, instead, that children can avoid learning some of these rules because they come to the task of language learning with rules already built into their own minds by their genetic inheritance? Perhaps it is in the nature of the human mind to "expect" (unconsciously, of course) that languages will have a certain form. Perhaps our minds are designed as language learning devices.

From one point of view this is a perfectly banal claim. We can have little doubt that a human child is endowed with a mind that predestines it to learn a language. A young chimpanzee has a different kind of mind and cannot learn a language in the way a human child does. To say that we learn differently from chimpanzees says nothing concrete about our minds, however, and many linguists would like to give a much more precise characterization to the mind that is designed for language learning. To be sure, children have to learn the idiosyncratic features of the language that happens to be spoken in their community, but if we believe all languages to be built according to sufficiently similar plans, we may suppose that learners come to the task with most of the plan already built into their heads. It is reasonable to suppose that the task of language learning would be made much easier by having a great deal already built in.

This chapter has moved toward an increasingly abstract conception of phonology. Starting with concrete sounds, we have been led, step by step, first to phonemes and then to phonological units like tones or the features of vowel harmony that stretch across entire syllables or words. We have been led to propose abstract underlying forms that are never heard themselves but that help us to account for the surface forms that we do hear. The surface forms are derived from the underlying forms by a series of phonological rules, and forms are processed from relatively uniform underlying forms to differentiated surface forms. The "same" phoneme comes to be pronounced in varied ways because of the allophonic rules by which it assimilates to its neighbors. Uniform underlying vowels are pronounced differently in *telegraph* and *telegra-*

phy because they have been processed in different ways. The "same" Turkish suffix is pronounced in different ways in harmony with the root word to which it is attached. The "same" underlying vowel is pronounced one way in *ignite* and another way in *ignition.*

In proposing these abstractions, we are proposing theories about how a language works. The units of these theories, whether they are segmental phonemes, rules, underlying forms, or the patterns of vowel harmony, are theoretical constructs rather than data that can be directly observed. These theoretical constructs help us to make sense of our data, but they are not themselves data, and we must always remain open to the possibility that other more useful or more powerful theoretical constructs will be devised that will make our present theories obsolete. We should also remind ourselves periodically that our theoretical constructs help to define what we accept as data. We have no choice but to interpret our data in terms of abstract units and rules of some sort, but when we do so we always risk a circularity, for our abstractions may lead us to count some observable phenomena as data but to ignore or dismiss other phenomena as irrelevant. The best defense against this circularity is to submit our generalizations to the scrutiny of other linguists. Some of them will be eager to find flaws in our arguments and to propose alternative theories that account for a wider range of data.

Whatever our theories, however, they ought to accomplish two things. First, we need theories of particular languages. It is reasonable to look on a description of the sound system of a language as a theory of that sound system. In making generalizations about the sounds of a language, we make predictions about the kinds of noises that count as samples of that language, and these predictions can be tested against additional data that are drawn from speakers of that language.

But in addition, we hope that by learning how one language works we will also learn something about how all languages work. We expect that languages are enough alike so that the methods and the theories that are developed to account for one language can be fruitfully applied to others. Of course, it will always be an empirical challenge to explore the ways in which languages are similar and the ways in which they are different, but we have looked at enough languages by now to feel confident that they can all be illuminated by many of the same concepts. We do not expect to find vowel harmony everywhere, but we do expect sounds to influence their neighbors. We do not expect to find tone everywhere, but we do expect to find intonation. We expect to find syllables constructed from vowels and consonants, and we even expect to find some of the same familiar classes of vowels and consonants. We are not surprised to find phonological alternations that can be described by rules whose form is similar to those we have used here for English. In addition to developing theories of the ways in which particular languages work, then, we want to develop a theory that tells us something more general about the nature of human language. We can even hope that as we come to understand more about the nature of language we will also discover something important about the species that speaks.

CHAPTER SEVEN

Phonological Variation

INTRODUCTION

In Chapters 5 and 6, the sound systems of languages were treated as if they were reasonably uniform, as if the pronunciation of English, or of any other language, could be thought of as stable and unvarying. This is a useful simplification to make when first considering phonology, but we cannot maintain such a view for long without misrepresenting the nature of language. The truth is that no language, certainly not English, has uniform pronunciation.

First, everyone is aware of the distinctive pronunciations of **regional dialects.** British pronunciation differs from American pronunciation, and regions within each country differ from each other. New Yorkers do not pronounce their words just like Bostonians nor do Londoners pronounce theirs like the people of Glasgow. If we listen carefully enough, we find still subtler differences. Even within a single city, people from different neighborhoods may show slight differences in their speech. All of us are likely to reveal our origins by the way we pronounce our words. Everyone speaks a dialect.

Dialectology began as the study of regional differences, but, like vocabulary, pronunciation varies in other ways than by geography. It is by belonging to a community and by participating in a network of communication that people are able to imitate each other's speech and to keep their dialect uniform. Conversely, barriers to communication allow dialect differences to emerge and survive. In our own complex society, differences in social class throw up barriers to communication that are even more effective than geography. In a society as complex as that of the United States we should not be surprised to find that people of different ethnic backgrounds and of different social classes speak in different ways. Indeed, language variation can reflect a society's social divisions with embarrassing clarity. For this reason linguists have grown increasingly interested in **social dialects** in the last two decades, and social variables have been added to regional variables as a second dimension of dialectal variability.

Like vocabulary, phonology varies along a third dimension, that of **style.** Just as we choose our words to suit the occasion, so do we vary our pronunciation. It would be an insensitive speaker who failed to adjust his or her language to fit the situation.

Variation in the lexicon was considered in Chapter 4, and variation in syntax is the topic of Chapter 12. This chapter is concerned with phonological variation: the way in which pronunciation varies from place to place, from social group to social group, and from occasion to occasion. The fourth important dimension of variation, change through time, will be reserved for the next chapter.

GEOGRAPHICAL DIALECTOLOGY

Pronunciation can differ from one dialect to another in three ways. First, dialects may make use of differing contrasts and, as a result, have different inventories of phonemes. Second, even where the same contrasts are found, a phoneme may be pronounced in varied ways. Third, even when speakers pronounce their phonemes in the same way, they may choose different phonemes for particular words. English dialects differ in all three ways.

Variation in Contrast

Dialects often differ somewhat in their phonological contrasts. Consider the following pairs of words: *wear/where, witch/which, wine/whine, Y/why, we/ whee, weather/whether.* For some speakers, the words in each pair contrast; for others, they are homophones. For those who make the contrast, the second member of each pair has an initial *h*-like aspiration (since the puff of breath that forms the aspiration comes at the beginning of the words, linguists often write the initial sounds of *where* as /hw/). The aspiration may sometimes be lost in rapid speech, but there is no question that, for some speakers, the words contrast when carefully articulated. Speakers who do not make a contrast between these sounds have no aspiration in any of these words, and they pronounce the pairs as homophones. Such speakers are sometimes said to have "lost a contrast," but of course the individual speakers never had a contrast, and it is really the language or the dialect that has lost the contrast in the course of its history.

Americans are often totally unaware of this dialectal difference. People for whom these pairs are homophones can be startled to discover that some of their friends make the contrast and, conversely, those who make the contrast can be equally startled to find that some of their friends do not. Somehow, each English speaker learns, very early and very deeply, either to make this contrast or to ignore it, but once our language becomes fixed, we seem to become almost deaf to the difference between contrasters and noncontrasters. Our ears have such tolerance for this kind of dialect difference that we can speak to each other for decades without becoming aware of our differing pronunciation.

We are more often aware of some other differences in contrast. Many Englishmen and a few Americans, particularly those from eastern New England, have contrasting vowels in words like *Mary, marry,* and *merry.* Other Americans, including most of those who grow up in the Midwest and far west, lack these contrasts entirely and pronounce all three words as homophones. Still others, including many New Yorkers, pronounce *Mary* and *merry* as homophones, but pronounce *marry* differently. Those who pronounce *Mary, marry,* and *merry* identically, use the same vowel in *ferry, fairy, hairy, Harry, carry, Kerry, very,* and *vary.* Others divide this list into two or three groups, each with its own contrasting vowel.

Most Americans have a three-way contrast that distinguishes /or/, /ur/, and /o/ in words like *pour, poor,* and *paw.* A few Americans and many speakers from England have no contrasts in the words and pronounce them all as homophones. These speakers have no /r/ in *pour* or *poor* and the vowels of all three sets of words converge as low, or mid, back, and rounded. The difference between the dialects is not limited to these three words, of course. All words that have /or/, /ar/, or /o/ in typical American dialects have the same vowel in typical dialects of England. Other contrasts that are observed in some dialects but not in others are represented by such pairs as *cot/caught, ladder/latter, (tin)can/can(be able), hoarse/horse, pin/pen, bomb/balm, you/Hugh.* All of these are homophones for some speakers; all are in contrast for others. Most speakers of English make some of these contrasts; perhaps no one makes them all. Each of us feels that some of these pairs are clear homophones, while others are in clear contrast. An inquiry among people from varying backgrounds will certainly reveal varying views about which words are obviously different and which words are, just as obviously, the same.

It can be difficult to grasp the fundamental linguistic truth that someone else's contrasts can be different from one's own. The sounds that each of us contrasts are likely to seem so transparently different as to make it seem weirdly implausible that anyone could ignore that difference. Conversely, it can seem just as implausible that someone else would make a contrast that seems unnecessary. Those who make the /hw, w/ contrast are likely to find it just a bit slovenly to neglect it, but it may seem fussy and pedantic to those who are not accustomed to it.

So firmly are we in control of our own particular system of contrasts that it can be difficult to hear the contrasts that others make, even in a careful demonstration. Those who pronounce the vowels of *horse* and *for* identically with those of *hoarse* and *four,* may have to listen very attentively to detect a difference in the speech of someone who contrasts them, and yet the contrast seems self-evident to those who make it. If one is to understand the nature of dialect variation, it is essential to grasp the fact that people really do differ in their contrasts, and that we all find our own contrasts equally real.

Most speakers either make the /hw, w/ contrast in all the words where the contrast is possible, or they merge them all into homophones. The merger of /hw/ and /w/ is an all-or-none matter. The comparison of dialects is made vastly more complex by the fact that many other mergers are only partial. Phonemes that are in contrast in one dialect may fall together in another dialect under some conditions but remain in contrast elsewhere. Consider, for instance, the contrast between /i/ and /e/. Most, perhaps all, English speakers have this contrast in pairs like *pick/peck, Sid/said,* and *big/beg.* Dialects of the northern United States and Britain have the same contrast in *pin/pen, bin/Ben* and *sinned/send.* In most of the American south, however, this contrast is lost before /n/, with the result that *pin/pen, bin/Ben, sinned/send* and many other pairs become homophones. Southern speakers maintain the /i, e/ contrast faithfully in most positions, but it disappears before /n/.

A similar example is provided by /d/ and /t/. For many Americans, the contrast between these consonants is lost between vowels when the next syllable is unstressed, as in *ladder* and *latter,* but the contrast is maintained in other positions. Partial mergers like these, in which a contrast is lost under certain conditions but maintained in others, are more common than complete mergers, and they greatly complicate the description of dialect differences.

Variation in the Phonetic Realization of a Phoneme

Even when they have no difference in contrast, two dialects may differ in the pronunciation of some of their phonemes. Consider, for instance, the vowel found in *go, home, dope, show, Joe, no, jokes,* and in dozens of other words. This vowel is pronounced somewhat differently in different dialects, but any one speaker is generally consistent, using the same vowel in all these words. In most dialects of American English, the vowel begins in a fairly low and quite far back rounded position, and it then becomes more sharply rounded as it moves higher and farther to the back. Many British English speakers use a vowel that begins well to the front of the typical American vowel, and in a distinctly less rounded and slightly higher position. Like the American version of the vowel, it then moves up and back and to a more rounded position, but it may not go quite so high or be quite so rounded as in America. Anyone who cannot remember hearing the differing American and British pronunciations of this vowel might search out someone from the other side of the Atlantic and listen to the difference.

The British/American difference is an entirely systematic one. It extends to all of the many scores of words in the language that have this vowel. We do not need to hear the transatlantic pronunciation of the word *scope* in order to offer a confident prediction of its pronunciation. We know how it will be pronounced in the other dialect because we already know about *soap, rope,* and *float. Scope* will surely rhyme with *soap* over there, just as it does at home.

In much of the southern United States, and as far north as Philadelphia, the vowel of the words *How now brown cow?* begins in a low front position, near to the vowel /æ/. The vowel then moves up and back and the lips round, so that it ends as high, back, and rounded. Americans who live farther north and west may begin, instead, with a vowel that is farther back, closer to the position of the /a/ in *father,* but their vowel also ends as high back rounded. Once again, this is a systematic difference. Knowing how someone pronounces *how, now,* and *brown,* makes it easy to predict how he or she will pronounce *cow.*

In the jargon of linguistics these systematic differences are described by saying that the phoneme has different **phonetic realizations** in different dialects. It is reasonable to consider the different dialects to have the same phoneme, but the phoneme shows up in different dialects with varied phonetic forms. The phoneme remains in contrast with other phonemes, so this is not a case like /w/ and /hw/, or /i/ and /e/ before /n/, where dialects differ in a contrast, but the differences are no less systematic. Anyone who wants to mimic another dialect must rely on systematic dialect differences like this. Good mimics do not have to learn a new pronunciation for every word in the language. Rather, they learn to modify the realization of their phonemes to conform to the patterns of the imitated dialect. This allows them to pronounce a word as it should be pronounced even if they have never heard that word from the mouth of a native.

Variation in Phoneme Selection

The third way in which dialects vary in pronunciation is much less systematic than the others. Even when both the contrasts and the phonetic realization of the phonemes are the same, particular words may be pronounced with different phonemes. People whose dialects are otherwise very similar, for instance, may select different phonemes for words such as *route* or for *orange.* Where some say /ruᵂt/ and /orənǰ/, others say /raᵂt/ and /arənǰ/. *Laboratory* and *schedule* are generally pronounced as /læbrətoriʲ/ and /skéjuᵂəl/ in America, but as /ləbórətriʲ/ and /ʃéjuᵂl/ in Britain. Most Americans pronounce *beautiful forsythia* as /bjuᵂtəful forsiθiʲə/, but Philadelphians are more likely to say /bjutiʲful forsaʲθiʲə/. Northerners are more likely to say /griʲsiʲ/, Southerners to say /griʲziʲ/. Anyone who has spoken with people from other parts of the English-speaking world should be able to think of many similar examples.

Differences of this sort imply no extensive differences in the phonological system of the dialects. People with the same set of phonemes and the same contrasts simply choose different phonemes for a few of their words. Individual words that vary in this way are easy to imitate. We have no difficulty imitating another's pronunciation of *route* or even a transatlantic pronunciation of *schedule* because our dialect gives us the phonemic resources to pronounce them either way. Where contrasts differ or where the phonetic realization of phonemes differs, we find our phonological skills less adaptable. It may be exceedingly difficult to make a contrast that we lack in our native dialect, or even to articulate a phoneme in a position that is not found in our own dialect.

Differences in phoneme selection, however, are much less systematic than differences in contrast or phonetic realization. Words like *schedule* and *greasy* vary in unique ways, and a mimic would have to learn the idiosyncrasies of each of these words in order to render the dialect accurately. About all that a linguist can do with such words is to list them, describe their varying pronunciations and, perhaps, draw maps to show where the differing pronunciations are used. Since linguists like to look for patterns, they tend to find variation of this sort comparatively uninteresting. They have more often put their effort into studying the more systematic kinds of dialect differences.

In clear cases, contrast, phonetic realization, and phoneme selection are nicely distinct from one another, but we find many mixed cases. Consider, for example, the pronunciation of low central and back vowels in the dialects of North American English. Most speakers in the United States have at least two contrasting vowels in this part of the mouth. Words such as *father, balm,* and *calm,* and often words such as *hot, cot,* and *pop* as well, are pronounced with a low central unrounded vowel, /a/. Words like *paw, fought,* and *caught,* on the other hand, are pronounced with a vowel that is somewhat farther back, a bit higher, and more rounded. (This vowel was written as /o/ in Chapter 6, but for the sake of phonetic accuracy it must be written here as /ɔ/.) Most Canadians and some Americans, especially those from California and some parts of the Midwest, pronounce all these words with the same vowel. They lack a contrast between *cot* and *caught* and so have lost a contrast that others continue to make. At a first level of approximation, this is simply one more example of the variability that regional dialects show in their contrasts.

There are complications. First, speakers who lack the contrast do not all pronounce their single vowel in the same way. Canadians tend to use a vowel that is farther back and more rounded than the Californian vowel, more like the [ɔ] of people who maintain the contrast. The merged California vowel, on the other hand, is more like the vowel that nonmerging Americans use for *father* and *calm,* more like [a]. Roughly speaking, the two vowels have merged as [a] in California, but as [ɔ] in Canada. If we ignored all the dialects where the contrast is still maintained, and compared only the dialects of Canadians with Californians where the contrast is lost, we could describe the dialects as having different phonetic realizations of a single phoneme. Canadians pronounce this phoneme as [ɔ] and Californians pronounce it as [a], but they use their differing pronunciations for the same set of words.

This is not the end of the complications. Even people who observe the /a, ɔ/ contrast differ considerably in the words they pronounce with each vowel. Almost everyone who makes the contrast has the relatively front and unrounded [a] in *father* and the relatively back and more rounded [ɔ] in *paw.* However, *dog, log, Chicago, want, wash, gone, on, off, awful, wrong, hot* and dozens of other words are assigned in chaotically varied ways to these two vowels. This variation makes it difficult to write about the vowels in a way that will be clear to all speakers. In some parts of the country, there seems to be a fairly steady drift of individual words from a pronunciation with /ɔ/ to one with

/a/. Thus most Chicagoans used to pronounce their city's name as /ʃəkɔgoʷ/, but more and more are coming to say /ʃəkagoʷ/ instead. If the drift from /ɔ/ to /a/ continues until no more words are pronounced with /ɔ/, the result will be a loss of contrast between the two vowels. It may be the long term fate of all North American English to follow the lead of Canadians and Californians and to lose this contrast. In the mean time, many individual words are variable.

This type of drift, in which individual words shift from one pronunciation to another, is known as **lexical diffusion,** and it is an important mechanism by which changes in pronunciation accumulate in a language. We will return to lexical diffusion in Chapter 8.

DIALECT GEOGRAPHY

If we surveyed the geographical distribution of the two pronunciations of *greasy* we would find areas where each was favored. To summarize our findings, we could draw a line across the map of the eastern United States that would show the boundary between the two pronunciations. Most people north of the line would say /griʲsiʲ/ while most people south of the line would say /griʲziʲ/. We could draw a second line across the eastern half of the United States that would separate the northern area where words such as *pin* and *pen* contrast, from a more southern area where they are homophones. Linguists call such lines **isoglosses,** and they use this word to describe the boundary between the differing forms of any variable linguistic feature. Dialects can differ in many thousands of ways, and since isoglosses can be drawn to show the areas that use different words or different grammatical rules as well as different pronunciations, it would be possible to draw thousands of isoglosses that would cover a map with an intricate web of crisscrossing lines.

Every time we cross an isogloss, the dialect changes slightly, and as one travels farther and farther from home, and as changes accumulate, the language can be expected to grow less and less familiar. It is possible to travel eastward from the Indus valley in Pakistan, all across the north Indian plain and as far as the Ganges delta in Bangladesh, and find that neighboring villagers can always understand each other easily. People from the extreme east and west cannot understand each other at all. Literate residents of the Indus valley and of the lower Ganges write with different alphabets and count themselves as speaking entirely separate languages, and yet no sharp linguistic boundaries divide them, only a network of isoglosses.

The same thing is true, or was true, of the traditional dialects of many parts of Europe. One can travel from Belgium to southern Spain or all the way to the tip of the Italian boot, and find that people of adjacent areas can readily communicate. This whole Romance-speaking area can be called a **dialect continuum,** an area without sharp linguistic boundaries, an area in which neighbors can always understand each other. Like the chain of mutually intelligible dialects that connected Anglo-Saxon to modern English, there is a

chain of mutually intelligible dialects connecting the French of Brussels to the
Portuguese of Lisbon and to the Italian of Palermo. We hardly notice the
differences between adjacent forms of the language, but at the extremes of
either time or space, French, Portuguese and Italian, like Anglo-Saxon and
modern English, must count as separate languages.

Another dialect continuum joins Austria, Germany, and the German speaking areas of Switzerland, with the Dutch-Flemish speaking areas of the Netherlands and Belgium. Once again, there are no sharp linguistic boundaries, only
gradual but steady changes. The Scandinavian languages, Danish, Swedish,
and Norwegian, form a third dialect continuum, while Polish, Czech, Slovak,
Ukrainian, and Russian form a fourth (see Map 7–1). The borders between
these dialect continua are sharp. Romance does not grade gradually into
Germanic, nor Germanic into Slavic, but no such sharp boundaries are found
within these areas.

National boundaries can disturb a dialect continuum. Education that is

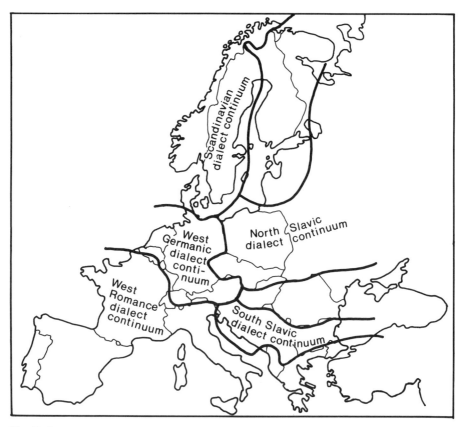

Map 7–1
European dialect continua. From Chambers and Trudgill (1980).

controlled by national authorities, literacy that is dominated by a national standard, and by the prestige of the capital and its way of talking all tug border dialects in opposite directions. Thus in the neighboring regions of France and Italy, it is the dialect of more conservative and less educated rural people that shows continuity across the international border. Those who are better educated and who are oriented toward Paris and Rome for their learning and prestige are likely to adjust more or less successfully to a national standard that is set elsewhere. Thus political boundaries can modify local dialects, and they can even attract isoglosses. Statesmen sometimes try to draw political boundaries in a way that corresponds to linguistic boundaries. Linguists are more likely to feel that language adapts to politics.

A political border, or any other social or geographical barrier that interrupts communication, can cause isoglosses to cluster and run parallel. We can then identify a more significant division between two dialects than one formed by a single isogloss. Isoglosses can also outlive the political conditions under which they became established. Southern Swedish resembles Danish in many ways. This reflects the geographic proximity of southern Sweden to Denmark, but it also reflects the centuries when the southern part of modern Sweden was included within the Danish kingdom. At that time, the inhabitants would probably have identified their language as Danish. When the political boundary changed their descendants began to call their language Swedish, but this reflected changed political identification rather than a switch to a new language. Dialect geographers recognize a bundle of isoglosses that cut across France and that serve to divide the French language into two major dialect areas. It is believed that the division between north and south that is marked by this bundle reflects cultural and political differences that go all the way back to Roman times.

Dialect diversity in the United States is greatest on the east coast where English settlement has the longest history. The differences tend gradually to fade as one moves west. Linguists have divided east coast dialects into Northern, Midland, and Southern forms, with Boston and New York characteristically Northern, Philadelphia characteristically Midland, and the cities from Washington southward characteristically Southern. Map 7–2 represents one attempt to show dialect areas for the east coast, though any map like this is bound to be something of an idealization. Clearly differences are found within any so-called dialect area, just as similarities unite adjacent areas. One may doubt whether New York English is really more like Bostonian than it is like Philadelphian. Isoglosses do not always cling together so as to form sharp boundaries between dialect areas.

Still, cities introduce discontinuities in the American dialect map that recall the discontinuities formed by the national borders of Europe. Cities form communication hubs, and people orient themselves toward them. Cities have sometimes been so badly scorned that people have tried to resist their influence by keeping their own pronunciation untainted, but as centers of power and prestige, their dialects have as often been admired and imitated. Each city is

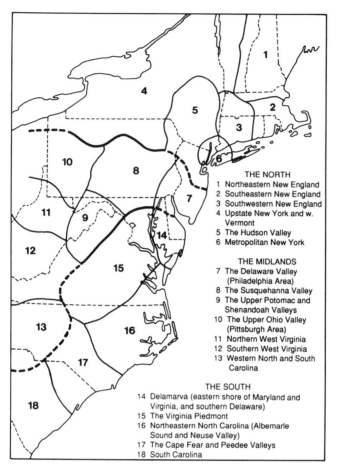

THE NORTH
1 Northeastern New England
2 Southeastern New England
3 Southwestern New England
4 Upstate New York and w.
  Vermont
5 The Hudson Valley
6 Metropolitan New York

THE MIDLANDS
7 The Delaware Valley
  (Philadelphia Area)
8 The Susquehanna Valley
9 The Upper Potomac and
  Shenandoah Valleys
10 The Upper Ohio Valley
  (Pittsburgh Area)
11 Northern West Virginia
12 Southern West Virginia
13 Western North and South
  Carolina

THE SOUTH
14 Delamarva (eastern shore of Maryland and
  Virginia, and southern Delaware)
15 The Virginia Piedmont
16 Northeastern North Carolina (Albemarle
  Sound and Neuse Valley)
17 The Cape Fear and Peedee Valleys
18 South Carolina

Map 7–2
American dialects. From Kurath (1949).

most apt to influence the dialects of its own hinterland. The areas of New Jersey that lie near to New York reflect the New York dialect. Areas closer to Philadelphia are more likely to show the influence of that city.

Dialect maps like Map 7–2 are a useful way to summarize a great deal of information, but they also risk considerable oversimplification. People do not change their pronunciation every time they step across an isogloss, and we should never expect everyone on one side of a line to pronounce a word differently from everyone on the other side. Rather, all sorts of compromises are made. Neighbors may differ. Some people may use an intermediate pronunciation, and others may vacillate. As we recognize the kinds of variation that blur these boundaries, we move to a recognition of stylistic differences and of social dialects.

ENGLISH VOWEL SYSTEMS

The techniques of dialect geography are best suited to investigating the detailed but unsystematic differences among dialects. Dialects also exhibit more pervasive and systematic differences, and these call for a different kind of description. The variation among English vowels provides a good example.

English vowels, particularly as they interact with a following /r/, form the most intricately variable aspect of English phonology. The dialect known in Britain as "RP" (from "Received Pronunciation") differs in several respects from the author's midwestern vowel system that was described in Chapter 6, and this makes comparison between the two dialects worthwhile. The words that were used to illustrate the midwestern dialect are listed here, grouped this time as they are pronounced by some RP speakers.

/i/	bit, pin, bid, spirit, syrup
/iː/	bee, beat
/iə/	fierce, feared, beard, spear, dear, beer, idea, eerie, dearie, zero
/e/	bet, pen, bed, merry, ferry, very
/eə/	spared, bared, spare, hair, air, Mary, hairy, vary
/æ/	bat, ant, flat, marry, Harry, carrot
/ə/	but, bud, hut, hurry, courage, worry
/ɑ/	laugh, aunt, heart, aren't, arms, alms, balm, father, far, star, are, spa, ha, starry
/ɔ/	hot, cot, bomb, want, wash, lot, borrow, sorry, tomorrow
/ɔː/	bought, caught, horse, court, border, paw, raw, pour, store, for, poor, boor, sure, story, poorest
/u/	put, good, foot
/uː/	boo, boot
/əː/	bird, fern, verge, burr, fur, sir, furry
/ei/	bay, bait
/ai/	buy, bite
/ɔi/	boy, Boyd
/ou/	no, boat
/au/	bough, bout

The symbols used for the British phonemes generally follow those used by the British phonetician Daniel Jones, and they differ enough from the symbols used for the midwestern vowels to give a somewhat exaggerated impression of differences between the dialects. To use /i/ and /u/ in place of /iʲ/ and /uʷ/, for instance, amounts to little more than a notational variant. In some cases, however, the transcriptions actually hide differences. The same words are sometimes grouped together in both dialects but pronounced in rather different ways. *No, boat, row, go, flow,* and *dough,* for instance, are typically pronounced quite differently in England and in America, and the English realization of this phoneme might be more accurately symbolized by /əu/ than by

/ou/. What is important here, however, is not the choice of symbols but the way in which the words are grouped and the system of contrasts that the grouping reveals.

The differences among low central and back vowels that we considered earlier for North American dialects can be traced in this list of RP vowels. Where some Americans pronounce *father, hot,* and *caught* with a single vowel, and where other Americans have two vowels, one in *father* and *hot* and the other in *caught,* many British speakers have three contrasting vowels, symbolized here as /ɑ/, /ɔ/, and /ɔː/.

The greatest dialect differences are related to /r/ and its loss. Even dialects where the /r/ is pronounced, differ in the contrasts that they maintain before /r/. *Mary/marry/merry, for/four,* and *pour/poor* all contrast in some dialects but merge in others. More dramatic differences separate dialects that do pronounce "preconsonantal r" from those that do not. All English dialects have /r/'s before and between vowels, in such words as *red, already,* and *berry.* Some dialects, including RP, forbid /r/'s before other consonants, so that words like *fort* and *harm* lack /r/'s. For many British speakers, and for many New Englanders as well, word final /r/ comes and goes depending on the next word. When the next word begins with a consonant the /r/ is missing, but when the next word begins with a vowel the /r/ reappears. Thus some speakers use a vigorous /r/ in *four of them* even while pronouncing *four men* with no /r/ at all. Spelling, of course is irrelevant. For many speakers, /r/ comes and goes as relentlessly in *idea* and *Cuba* as it does in *four.*

As a first and very crude approximation, we can describe most dialects of American English as /r/ pronouncing, even in *start, firm,* and *four times,* where the /r/'s follow vowels and precede consonants. At the same crude level of approximation, we can describe the dominant dialects of England, including RP, as lacking these "preconsonantal" /r/'s. The word **rhotic** describes dialects that pronounce the preconsonantal /r/, while those that do not are called **nonrhotic."** Broadcast American is almost always rhotic, and broadcast British is almost always nonrhotic, but both rhotic and nonrhotic dialects are found on both sides of the Atlantic. Eastern New England and much of the lowland south is nonrhotic, while Scotland, much of Wales, and parts of northern and western England are as vigorously rhotic as any variety of American.

When preconsonantal /r/ disappears, the vowels it leaves behind are often quite different from the other vowels in the dialect. In many nonrhotic dialects, some vowels end with a glide that moves the vowel toward the mid-central position and that amounts to a sort of distant echo of the lost /r/. This means that *bid* and *beard* continue to contrast as do *bed* and *bared.* The /r/ is gone from *beard* and *bared* but the echoing /ə/ remains. In other cases the loss of /r/ in nonrhotic dialects leads to the loss of contrasts. Speakers who lack preconsonantal /r/'s generally pronounce such pairs as *arms/alms* and *court/caught* as homophones.

STYLES AND FAST SPEECH

Here is a moderately detailed phonetic transcription of a rapidly articulated colloquial English sentence.

[ʔajəlaʲʔgːɔʷɾəmuviṇṇaʲʔ]

Not even a trained phonetician finds a transcription like this easy to interpret, although it represents an utterly ordinary sentence. If each word is written as it might be pronounced alone and more carefully, the sentence might look more like this:

[haʷ wuːd juʷ laʲʔk tʰə gɔʷ tʰə ə muʷːviʲ tʰənaʲʔt]

Even this has more phonetic detail than we find easy to deal with on paper, and we can simplify it even further with a more abstract phonemic transcription:

/haʷ wʊd juʷ laʲk tuʷ goʷ tuʷ ə muʷviʲ tuʷnaʲt/

By this time, it should become clear that the sentence is simply the question *How would you like to go to a movie tonight?,* and the example is intended to suggest the gulf that separates natural fast speech from the careful pronunciation that is more often analyzed by phonologists. We can say anything at all in a wide range of increasingly rapid and abbreviated ways.

He is going to look for her.
He's goin' t'look for 'er.
[izənəlukfʌɹː]

I do not know
I don't know
[aṇnoʷ]

"I don't know" can even be shorn of everything except its intonation. It is possible to answer a question by humming the tune of "I don't know" with the lips firmly closed and, in the right context, a listener is still able to understand easily. The phonological reductions of fast speech can include the loss of many contrasts and even of entire segments. People interested in mechanical speech recognition as a means, among other things, of communicating with computers have occasionally suggested that we might be able to build a speech recognition device that would work by recognizing each phoneme as it occurs sequentially in the stream of real speech. The massive phonological reductions of fast speech so thoroughly obscure the phonemes that such proposals must be regarded as quite fanciful.

It is a greatly reduced phonology that we hear in our daily conversation, but we hear it as if it is built out of a sequence of much fuller sounds. In ways that are not yet well understood, we are able to use our profound knowledge of our language to reconstruct a full phonological form from severely reduced sounds. It is not simply our spelling system, and it is not simply the analysis of linguists, that lead us to interpret the fast speech of daily life as if it is a reduction from some fuller form. People can, after all, slow down and pronounce their words with all the segments that a linguist recognizes. Even nonliterate speakers can pronounce their words carefully enough to demonstrate all their segments and to show clear contrasts with minimally different words. Nonliterate people, like those who can read and write, produce language samples that can be readily interpreted as consisting of abstract phonemes that are in contrast with one another and that, for the most part, follow each other in linear sequence.

It is fast speech that a tape recorder catches, however, and it is fast speech that we generally produce and hear. We have to recognize that a phonological analysis that describes speech as if it is a sequence of phonemes is a theoretical construct of considerable abstraction. Since children generally hear only the fast colloquial forms of daily conversation, it is still a bit mysterious just how they manage to learn the full forms of their language. Linguists find it easier to describe the process by which an underlying sequence of phonemes is reduced to fast speech than to describe how a hearer reconstructs a sequence of phonemes from what is perceived in fast speech. We can think of fast speech as the output of a sequence of rules that work on the underlying full forms, and we can ask what sorts of rules we apply to the full forms when we speak rapidly. How do we move from full forms to fast speech?

First, of course, we have the ordinary rules of phonological assimilation by which neighboring phonemes influence one another. These rules result in a selection of particular allophones to represent the phonemes. English vowels become nasalized, initial stops become aspirated, and so forth. Second, many high-frequency words have common abbreviations. Some of these abbreviations are recognized by conventional contractions, *aren't, I'd, we're, could've, gonna,* etc., but other contractions are almost as common, although less often written. Expressions such as *bread n' butter* and *you c'n go* have vowels deleted so that *n*'s become syllabic. Many grammatical words in English have their vowels reduced to schwa when they are unstressed in rapid speech: *She'd ə gone* 'she'd have gone.' In *He said* [ðæʔəd] *happen* 'He said that would happen,' *that* can have its final /t/ pronounced as a glottal stop, the /w/ can disappear, and the vowel can be reduced to a very short schwa.

Other phonetic processes of fast speech yield sounds that we do not normally consider even to belong to English, and that speakers of English find difficult to articulate when learning a foreign language. The *to* of *like to go,* in the example with which this section began, can be reduced to little more than a lengthening of the initial *g* of the following word. The vowel of *to* is lost, and when the *t* is assimilated to the following *g,* the result is a long consonant. A voiceless nasal can appear in a fast pronunciation of *tonight.* As vowels are reduced to schwa and then lost entirely, exotic consonant clusters appear. Syllabic consonants become common.

Fast speech is not, as is sometimes imagined, slovenly speech. On the contrary, it requires a high degree of skill to speak quickly. Second-language learners speak slowly at first, because they lack the expertise for anything else. Fast speech is "easier" than more deliberate and "careful" speech, only in the same sense that it is quicker and "easier" for a highly skilled technician to perform a delicate manipulation than for someone without training. The skillful technician wastes fewer motions and concentrates on the essentials. This may allow the task to be finished more quickly and so use less total energy, but if this appears easy, it is a deceptive appearance that hides long practice. Skillful speakers waste less motion and energy in fast speech than they might in slower speech, and this is, in a sense, "easier," but it is an ease that is gained though skill rather than through carelessness.

Speakers must judge their audience and use speech that is no faster than their hearers are capable of understanding. The better we know our listeners, and the more familiar they are with our topic and with our way of talking, the more quickly we can speak and the more phonological reductions we can safely make. If we speak too fast we risk losing our audience, so the needs of the hearer to understand must be balanced against the desire of the speaker to finish with efficiency. Casual conversation often teeters on the brink of unintelligibility, so listeners must regularly interrupt with "what?" in order to slow the speaker down. This means that learning to understand rapid natural speech can be one of the most challenging tasks facing a foreign language learner. When speech is in danger of becoming unintelligible even for the natives, it is likely to be well beyond intelligibility for foreigners. Even a foreigner who reads easily and who can understand a formal lecture may be defeated by fast colloquial chatter.

It is probably true of all languages that speed and phonological reduction increase as the situation grows less formal and as the participants in a conversation become better acquainted. All languages seem to show a gradation of styles from formal to informal, and one of the characteristics of informal speech is the fluent reduction of phonological detail, but we know even less about phonological reduction in other languages than we know about English.

SOCIAL DIALECTS

Dialect differences arise and persist because people talk less with members of other communities than with members of their own. The need or the desire to communicate within one's own community limits the possible variation, but when people do not communicate, their dialects are certain to diverge. Social distance can be as effective as geographical distance in hindering free communication. In geographically mobile but socially complex societies like that of the United States, social differences begin to rival regional differences as the primary determinant of dialect variation.

In the 1960s, William Labov studied social dialects in New York City and showed that people of varied social-class background have correspondingly varied pronunciation. One of the variable features of English that is most closely related to social class in New York is the pronunciation of the famous "preconsonantal /r/." In words such as *guard* and *board*, where the /r/ follows a vowel and precedes a consonant, and in words like *car* and *beer* where the /r/ may be followed by an initial consonant in the next word, New Yorkers sometimes pronounce the /r/ and sometimes do not. Labov investigated the factors that lead New Yorkers to pronounce /r/ on some occasions but to omit it on others, and he found that pronunciation is influenced by both style and social class.

Almost all New Yorkers pronounce preconsonantal /r/ on at least some occasions, but few pronounce it consistently wherever it is found in spelling. The likelihood that /r/ will be pronounced depends on both the social status of the speakers and the care with which they speak. Social class can be defined by such factors as education, income, and type of employment, and the higher we look on the New York social-class ladder, the more /r/'s we find. At the same time, whatever their class, people manage to increase their production of /r/'s when they are careful. Labov listened to the speech of people who differed in class, and he observed how their speech changed under varying conditions of formality. He recorded their pronunciation when reading lists of minimal pairs (which invites the most careful possible style), when reading word lists (which requires an only slightly less careful style), when reading a connected passage, when responding to questions in a relatively formal interview, and when engaging in more relaxed conversation (which encourages the most informal style of all). The proportion of possible occasions in which the preconsonantal /r/ was actually pronounced, for each of several classes and under these five conditions of formality, is shown in Figure 7–1.

The slopes of the lines show clearly that as speech becomes more careful, the proportion of pronounced /r/'s climbs steadily. In addition, more /r/'s appear with each jump in social class. The pattern demonstrates forcefully that preconsonantal /r/ is a prestigious pronunciation in New York City. "Better" people, those with better education, better jobs, or more money, use more /r/'s than those lower on the social scale. At the same time, when being careful and when able to pay attention to their own speech, everyone is able to boost the rate of /r/'s. Several factors may help those of higher social class to pronounce more /r/'s. First, they may have paid more attention to the admonitions of their teachers. It is regarded as "better" to pronounce these /r/'s, and some effort is made in New York schools to persuade children to speak in a more "correct" way. Second, people of higher social class may have more contact with, and so be more influenced by, speakers from other parts of the country where preconsonantal /r/ is better established. Many people with high status move to New York, bringing their dialects, including their /r/'s, with them. They help to set, and to change, the standards within the city. Third, higher-class speakers certainly have more contact with each other, and this gives them more opportunity to adjust their language to conform to the standards of their own class. Classes, in some degree, are communities with their own standards,

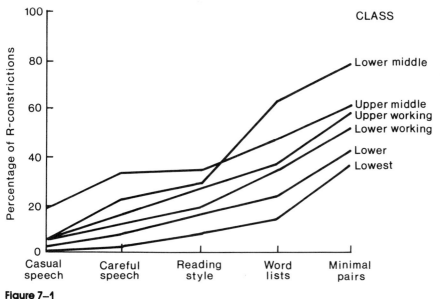

Figure 7–1
Pronunciation of /r/ in New York City. From Labov (1964).

and their members influence each other's speech. Finally, upper-class speakers may simply be more careful because the prestige of "speaking well" matters more to them.

Whatever factors influence the individual speaker, the symbolism of /r/ is clear. Since /r/ is characteristic of higher social classes, it comes to be associated with upward mobility, and it is a style toward which ambitious people strive. Notice the single case in which the lines of Figure 7–1 cross. In the two most careful styles, members of the second highest class pronounce even more /r/'s than those in the highest class. They seem to be "overachieving." Their behavior can probably be attributed to the insecurity of speakers who have not quite reached the top. Those above them need not worry so much about their position. The second highest class includes the strivers who modify their language most strongly when they have an opportunity to be especially careful.

Preconsonantal /r/ is by no means the only variable that is sensitive to both class and style. Under the right circumstances, all English speakers delete some word-final consonants. Most Americans can probably omit final /t/ from *best one* and final /d/ from *send for it*. The triple consonant sequence /stw/ in *best one* invites the dropping the middle /t/, and the /ndf/ of *send for it* can be more easily pronounced without the /d/. Although most speakers are able to make these deletions, deletion is not usually obligatory. The /t/ and the /d/ can be pronounced if the speaker is careful, and like the pronunciation of preconsonantal /r/ in New York City, the pronunciation of /t/ and /d/ in these clusters is, for many English speakers, a variable.

Best and *send* are less likely to lose their final consonants if a vowel follows. Thus deletion is less likely in *best of them* and *send it to me* than in *best one* and *send for it*. Nevertheless, some English speakers are able to omit /t/'s and /d/'s even before a vowel, though they may omit them less regularly there than when a consonant follows. We can try to ask ourselves how often, and under what circumstances, we make these deletions, but we are not always accurate judges of our own speech. A tape recording is likely to reveal that we omit consonants considerably more frequently when they are followed by another consonant than when followed by a vowel. At the same time, consonants are more likely to be retained under formal conditions or when the speaker finds it important to be careful. They are more likely to be deleted in relaxed and informal circumstances. All this is reminiscent of the way /r/ comes and goes in New York City.

Some Americans, however, *never* pronounce a /t/ in *best* or a /d/ in *send*. Such speakers simply lack the final /st/ and /nd/ clusters. For such speakers, *best* becomes homophonous with *Bess,* and *wind* is identical to *win*. As with /r/ in New York City, the loss and retention of /t/ and /d/ varies with social class, and there is some tendency for more consonants to be pronounced as one moves up the social scale, although even those at the very top delete them occasionally. Once again, it must be insisted that there is nothing "careless" about consonant deletions. It requires considerably more skill to vary one's speech in careful recognition of the formality of the situation than to speak with exactly the same style at all times.

The interacting influence of social class and careful style that Labov discovered in New York City has been found in dozens of other cases and in several languages. Many phonological variables have turned out, like /r/ and /t, d/ deletion, to be sensitive both to class and to style. Speakers from all social classes may show stylistic variability, but each class has its own range of variation along the scale. As with the loss of preconsonantal /r/ in New York City and the deletion of other consonants, the lower-class speakers in their most careful style may achieve no more than some higher-class speakers manage in their least formal speech.

We still know relatively little about language variation in societies with less sharp class distinctions than ours. We might expect that a society with less social stratification would also show less variability in its language. Not even the simplest or most homogeneous tribal society escapes divisions between old and young or between male and female, however, and these are often reflected clearly in the way language is used.

One part of the world where social dialects have been carefully studied is India. Indian society is very different from our own, but it is hardly a society that is characterized by social equality. Caste affiliation remains important in India, and in rural areas the members of a single village may be divided into as many as a dozen or more separate castes. People generally marry within their own caste, and since each caste has its own ceremonies and its traditional occupation, castes combine some of the characteristics of kinship groups, trade unions, and religious denominations. The divisions between the castes are often sharp, and castes are rigidly ranked. Some are ritually and socially superior to others.

Knowing how sharply castes are divided, a linguist should expect their differences to be reflected in the way people speak, and indeed they are. Even within a single village of a few hundred or a few thousand people, members of different castes are likely to use slightly different forms of the language. Perhaps it is inevitable that members of the higher castes look on their own language as superior, and feel that members of the lower castes speak in vulgar or uncouth ways. To an outsider, there may seem no rational reason why /baḷl/ should be a more elegant way for Hindi-speaking villagers to pronounce the name of 'an ear of corn' than /bal/, but people are quite capable of scorning others for their pronunciation of such a word. Americans can be just as scornful of a fellow citizen who says /æks/ instead of /æsk/ for *ask*.

The language variation that distinguishes the dialects of Indian castes, like the variation that distinguishes American social classes, serves to mark out the social divisions that are important within their respective societies. We have come to expect that whatever social distinctions are important will be reflected in language. Class, caste, age, sex, occupation, and even the degree of one's political liberalism may influence the way one speaks. Speakers are sensitive to these differences, and use them to judge others and to fit them into the social niches that they recognize.

CONCLUSIONS

We all have very strong feelings about our own language, and no one can entirely escape the sense that some dialects or styles are more natural, or more appropriate, or more beautiful, or simply "better" than others. All people strive, in some degree, to emulate those whom they admire and to adopt their speech styles. Those who are fortunate enough to have grown up in a community where a prestigious dialect is spoken, and who thereby gain such easy proficiency in this dialect as to make it seem entirely natural, sometimes wonder why people from other backgrounds fail to use the same "better" language. If we recognize the complexity of the social and psychological pressures that converge on each one of us and that influence the way we speak, we must see that the advantages are by no means all on the side of adjusting one's speech in the direction of the higher social classes. To abandon the speech of one's own childhood and community may be personally traumatic and socially disloyal. By using language that sounds snooty, both children and adults risk ridicule or severe criticism from their family and friends. For some people, particularly young men, upper-class speech may seem impossibly sissyish. Lower-class speech may connote masculinity and toughness, and it can be abandoned only at considerable personal risk.

Middle-class Americans can get some idea of the wrench that would be required to abandon lower-class speech in favor of the forms favored by school teachers if they imagine what they would have to endure in order to learn a "better" British English dialect. Even when living in England, few Americans are eager to abandon the comfortable dialect of their childhood, and few Americans take kindly to the occasional British suggestion that American dialects are a bit provincial or second class. Hints along these lines may do nothing but strengthen the American's determination to resist Anglicization. Children whose families speak a nonprestigious dialect may react in the same stubborn way to a teacher's criticism of their speech, and the criticism may only persuade them to dig in their heels and resist the pressures of the school. When we criticize people's speech and urge them to "improve," we may threaten their deepest levels of self-esteem. We should not be surprised when they resent such criticism and reject it.

Regional and social class differences are only the most obvious of the social factors that divide us into dialect groups, and we should expect that other sociological differences will also be reflected in language. Women do not speak in exactly the same way as men. Old people do not speak identically to young people. Rural and urban dialects are different. We all speak differently on different occasions. Speech differences, in fact, serve as a remarkably precise map of social differences, and charting language variation can be grimly diagnostic of the cleavages in a society. People who would never admit to prejudices against the members of an ethnic group may, nevertheless, be highly critical of their language. Their attitudes about language can be a chilling reflection of their suppressed attitudes toward the people who use the language. Americans usually reserve their sharpest criticism not for pronunciation but for grammar, however, and we will return to social variation when we consider the relation of grammar to social class in Chapter 12.

English speakers tend to think of their language as a rather stable and well-defined system. Even when we are unsure of our own usage, we suppose that an authority can be found who can tell us what the correct English should be. We settle arguments by referring to the ultimate authority of the dictionary. We expect school grammar lessons to help us, somehow, to use our language more "correctly." People regularly grieve over what they feel to be the accumulating corruptions of their beloved language. But the stability and uniformity of language is an illusion. Each region, social group, and occasion calls for a different kind of speech, and our language is immeasurably richer for being so varied. Nor does pronunciation remain stable through time. As the decades and centuries pass, the pronunciation of our language, like that of every other language, inexorably changes. In the next chapter, we turn to this final dimension of variability, the changes that take place over time.

CHAPTER EIGHT

Variation through Time: Phonological Change

THE COMPARATIVE METHOD

The **comparative method** is a set of techniques that can be used to infer the characteristics of an earlier language from the known characteristics of its daughter languages. The method can be used to make inferences about languages that left no written records, and this gives us a distinctively linguistic method for learning about the past. The development of the comparative method in the nineteenth century established the basis for our understanding of phonological change, and it remains one of the triumphs of linguistics. One goal of this chapter is to introduce the techniques of the comparative method and present a few of its results.

The comparative method starts by observing correspondences between the phonemes of related languages. Every English-speaking student of German notices the regularity with which English /t/ corresponds to German /ts/, the phoneme that Germans spell with z: to/zu, toe/Zehe, two/zwei, ten/zehn, tooth/Zahn, and many others. Similarly English /p/, under some circumstances, corresponds to German /pf/: pepper/Pfeffer, paw/Pfote, plum/Pflaume. English /d/ often corresponds to German /t/: door/Tür, day/Tag, dough/Teig. These correspondences reflect both continuity and change from the earlier Germanic language that was ancestral to both English and German. That ancestral language had consonant phonemes that were ancestral both to modern English t, p, and d and to modern German z, pf, and t. They and several other consonants are believed to have changed their pronunciation in the southern and eastern German dialects that form the basis of modern standard German. Thus the sound correspondences among modern languages reflect earlier changes, and this change is known as "the High German consonant shift."

The comparative method can be illustrated by the small set of words shown in Table 8–1. These come from four languages of the Bodo group, the subgroup of Tibeto-Burman to which Garo belongs, and all these languages are spoken in northeastern India. Syllables play an important role in these languages, and while syllables join to form larger words, only the syllables that are directly relevant to the correspondences are shown in the table. One characteristic of these languages is that syllable initials often have quite different correspondences than syllable finals.

This is only a tiny and carefully selected sample of words, but several similarities among the languages are immediately apparent. All the syllables meaning 'dry' and 'cloud' begin with *r,* and this suggests that the ancestral language from which these all derive probably had an initial *r as well. ("Reconstructed" phonemes, i.e., those inferred from later languages rather than known from written records, are indicated by an asterisk.) The words for 'long' and 'drink' have *l* in two of the languages but *r* in the other two. One possible explanation is that the ancestral language had another phoneme, perhaps *l, that was distinct from *r, but that has come to be pronounced in the same way as *r* in Garo and Atong. The words for 'bird' and 'hit' suggest an ancestral *d, but Wanang has *t.* Perhaps an earlier *d was devoiced to become *t* in Wanang. 'Flower' is the only word given in the table that begins with *b* in most of languages, but it follows the pattern of 'bird' and 'hit' since Wanang, once again, has a voiceless initial that corresponds to the voiced initials of the other languages.

These syllables give fewer examples of final consonants, but *m, n, ŋ, r,* and *k* correspond in examples from at least three languages, and we can guess, tentatively, that the ancestral language had final *m, *n, *ŋ, *r, and *k as well. Of course we do not know how *m and *k developed in Kachari since cognates for the relevant words are missing. Three sets of words have glottal stops in Kachari, Garo, and Atong, but they are missing from Wanang. A tentative conclusion is that an ancestral *ʔ was lost in the development of Wanang. The vowel correspondences are less easy to discern from such a small sample. Vowels that could derive from *a are found in the words for 'dry' and 'flower,' but there is an unexplained irregularity in the Wanang word for 'cloud.' The

Table 8–1
Cognates in Bodo Languages

	Kachari	Garo	Atong	Wanang
dry	-raʔn	raʔn-	raʔn-	ran-
cloud		-ram	-ram	rəm-
long	-lauʔ	roʔ-	rauʔ-	-ləu-
drink	leŋ	riŋ-	reŋ-	ləŋ-
bird	dauʔ	doʔ-	dauʔ	təu
hit		dok-	dok-	tok-
flower	-bar	-bar	bar	par

more complex vowel correspondence found in the words for 'long' and 'bird' can probably be attributed to just one ancestral vowel phoneme, but it is risky, from the limited evidence of these few words, to guess its pronunciation. The vowels in the words for *hit* and *drink* hint at still other correspondences.

More examples from these four languages would give a fuller picture of their correspondences, and these would imply a set of phonemes of the ancestral language. With enough examples and enough painstaking comparison, we might hope to build up a tolerably good picture of the older phonological system. That is the goal of the comparative method.

GRIMM'S LAW

The crowning nineteenth century achievement of the comparative method was the growing understanding of the relations among the group of languages now known as **Indo-European.** The similarities among Greek, Latin, and the modern Romance and Germanic languages had long been recognized, but in the late eighteenth century it was also discovered that Sanskrit, the sacred language of Hinduism and the language that is ancestral to the modern languages of north India, was also related to the European classical languages. Other languages extending from Iceland across most of Europe, and on through Iran to India, were gradually recognized as belonging to a single immense family, all of them having descended from a single common ancestor. We have no records of this ancestral language, for presumably it was never written, but it has come to be known as **Proto-Indo-European.**

It has long been clear that the Indo-European languages fall into several well-defined subgroups. English, Dutch, German, and the Scandinavian languages show such clear similarities that the special relationship of these "Germanic" languages can hardly be questioned. Ancient Latin, Greek, and Sanskrit texts and somewhat later texts in Germanic, Slavic, and other languages give us information about earlier stages of several Indo-European languages, but the very earliest stages that were spoken before writing began can be known only by the comparative method. Linguists still disagree about where and when Proto-Indo-European was spoken, but we have learned a good deal about its linguistic characteristics.

Nineteenth-century scholars, notably Jakob Grimm, otherwise famous as a collector of fairy tales, noticed some regular sound correspondences that distinguish the Germanic languages from their Indo-European cousins. A particularly clear correspondence relates *f* of English and other Germanic languages, to *p* of more distantly related Indo-European languages. It is believed, in part because *p* is found in many more languages than *f*, that *p* represents the older pronunciation and that this changed to *f* in Germanic: Latin *pēs,* English *foot;* Latin *piscis,* English *fish;* Latin *pater,* English *father;* Latin *pecu,* English *fee;* Greek *pūr,* English *fire;* Latin *pullus,* English *foal.*

The Germanic *f* is a fricative, while the *p* of Latin and other Indo-European languages is a stop, but both are voiceless and both are articulated with the lips. Thus they are closely related sounds, and this makes it reasonable to suppose that one of them could have changed into the other. It turns out, moreover, that two other Germanic fricatives also correspond to Indo-European stops. Words that have *t* and *k* in other Indo-European languages turn up in Germanic languages with θ and *h*, as in Latin *trēs*, English *three* and Latin *caput*, English *head*. In three parallel cases, then, the voiceless stops found in other languages correspond to Germanic fricatives. The simplest explanation is that older stops were transformed into the corresponding fricatives as Indo-European evolved into Germanic.

A second set of correspondences relates voiced stops in the other Indo-European languages to the corresponding voiceless stops in Germanic. Earlier **b* became *p*, **d* became *t*, and **g* became *k*: Latin *labium*, English *lip*; Latin *duo*, English *two*; Latin *grānum*, English *corn*.

A third set of correspondences is somewhat more varied and more difficult to demonstrate. Words showing these correspondences are generally reconstructed as having had **bh*, **dh*, and **gh* in Proto-Indo-European, and perhaps these were voiced breathy stops, although that is not certain. Whatever the original phonetics, they gave rise to fricatives in Latin (*f, s, h*), to voiceless aspirates in ancient Greek (*ph, th, kh*) and, in two cases, to phones described as voiced aspirates in Sanskrit (*bh, dh*). In modern Germanic languages, the consonants that survive from these words often turn up as voiced stops (*b, d, g*). The most difficult part of this correspondence to establish is the one that should derive from ancient **gh*. No known language retains anything reasonably regarded as *gh*. The attested correspondence is between Sanskrit and Latin *h*, Greek *kh*, and Germanic *g*. Nevertheless, by reconstructing **gh* as a plausible ancestor for all these varied pronunciations, we nicely complete the pattern suggested by the other correspondences. Examples include Sanskrit *bhara:mi* 'I bear,' English *bear*; Sanskrit *madhu* 'honey, mead,' English *mead*; Latin *hostis* 'stranger, enemy,' English *guest*.

These consonants seem to have chased each other through phonetic space. Everything changed but, in the end, Germanic preserved its contrasts and even emerged with many of the same consonants as its Indo-European (or "I–E") ancestor. The changes are summarized in Table 8–2, where the first line shows that I–E **bh* became Germanic **b*; I–E **b* became Germanic **p*; and I–E **p* became Germanic **f*. The remaining lines can be read in a parallel way.

The discovery of these consonant correspondences was an impressive achievement. Their regularity even suggested that human behavior might be governed by the same kinds of orderly rules that are discoverable elsewhere in nature, and they acquired a somewhat pretentious label: **Grimm's law.** It is hardly a law in any of the usual senses of the term, but rather a summary of a set of historical events, a set of consonant changes that distinguish the Germanic languages from their Indo-European cousins.

Once the regularities had been discovered, a number of exceptions stood out. In several apparently related words, the Germanic languages have the

Table 8–2
Grimm's Law

Breathy		Voiced		Voiceless		Fricative
bh	→	b	→	p	→	f
dh	→	d	→	t	→	θ
gh	→	g	→	k	→	h

same consonant as the other languages. One example is the word for "is," where Sanskrit had *asti,* Greek *esti,* and Latin *est.* Gothic (the oldest Germanic language for which we have written records) had *ist.* According to Grimm's law, in order to correspond with the *t* of the other languages, Gothic should have had θ, but here it retained *t.* At first, this looked like a disturbing exception to an otherwise regular correspondence, but as additional examples were assembled, it was discovered that the second members of voiceless consonant clusters did not change according to patterns of Grimm's law, but instead retained their older pronunciation. What had looked like an exception proved to conform perfectly to a somewhat more carefully stated pattern of correspondences, and this new correspondence became known as Werner's Law.

Some other Germanic words that, according to Grimm's law, should have had the voiceless fricatives *f,* θ, or *h* (since they correspond to *p, t, k* in the other languages) appear in German with *b, d,* or *g* instead. An example is the *d* of Gothic *fadar,* Old English *feder* 'father' corresponding to Latin *pater* and Greek *patēr.* (The modern [ð] of English *father* developed later.) Germanic languages were then found to have voiced stops *b, d, g* in precisely those words where the preceding vowel is *un*accented in Greek and Sanskrit. Once again, apparent exceptions fell into a pattern that could be incorporated into the law by a more precise description of the environment in which the changes took place.

The gradual reduction in the number of exceptions to Grimm's law that was made possible by taking increasingly careful account of the phonological environment led some nineteenth century scholars to claim that sound changes were absolutely regular, and it encouraged the use of the word *law.* The belief in regularity amounted to the claim that if one could state the conditions with sufficient precision, then every word that met those conditions would change. In practice, the expectation of regularity meant that when apparent exceptions were discovered, scholars believed it to be worthwhile to sort through the data in the hope of finding features of the phonological environment that would account for the exceptions. In this way the exceptions might be brought under a revised rule where they would no longer count as true exceptions. The expectation of regularity implied that it was not the changes that needed to be explained. Rather it was often the failure of a sound to change in certain words that called for more investigation.

CHAIN SHIFTS

Another set of sound changes, this one known as the "Great Vowel Shift," transformed the long vowels of Middle English. The changes are summarized in Table 8–3. This table glosses over a good many complications, but generally speaking, most of the long vowels rose. However, the very highest vowels, $i\textrm{:}$ and $u\textrm{:}$, developed into diphthongs, $əi$ and $əu$. A striking feature of the Great Vowel Shift is that, in spite of all the changes, the contrasts found in the fifteenth century were maintained, at least under some circumstances, into the sixteenth century, and most of the contrasts still survive in Modern English. Phonological contrasts were needed to keep words distinct, of course, and it is hard to avoid the conclusion that the vowels were pushing and pulling each other about through the vowel space, almost playing a game of follow the leader. It is as if, with other vowels crowding up behind them, the top vowels could remain distinct only if speakers pronounced them as diphthongs. Speakers have to keep their contrasts in repair. The pattern of these changes is shown in Figure 8–1. Unfortunately, while we understand the mechanics of the Great Vowel Shift rather well, the reasons for the shift remain obscure.

The Great Vowel Shift left its residue in all later forms of English. The names of our vowel letters changed along with their pronunciation, so that our name for "A," [eʲ], now sounds nearly like the name for "E," [e], in other western European languages. The English name for "E" [iʲ], in turn, sounds quite like the name for "I," [i], in other languages. The Great Vowel Shift took place at a time when English had a clear difference between long and short vowels, and it affected only long vowels. The shift is the source of vowel alternations still found in English in such pairs as *derive/derivative, deceive/deception* and *cave/cavity.* Each of our vowel letters is now used for words with two quite different pronunciations, one for words with vowels that were short at the time of the great vowel shift and that did not change their pronunciation, the other for words with vowels that were long and that have changed: *pan/pane, pet/Pete, bit/bite, hop/hope, cut/cute.*

The comparative method can be used to make inferences backwards about changes that took place in the past, but it does not ordinarily give us a direct view of changes in progress. If we look closely enough at the variation we hear all around us, however, we can come closer to witnessing changes ourselves.

Table 8–3
The Great Vowel Shift

15th century		16th century		20th century	
iː	→	əi	→	aʲ	bite
eː	→	iː	→	iʲ	beet
ɛː	→	eː	↗		beat
aː	→	aː	→	eʲ	mate
uː	→	əu	→	aʷ	mouth
oː	→	uː	→	uʷ	boot
ɔː	→	oː	→	oʷ	boat

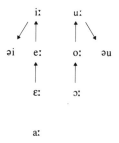

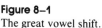

Figure 8–1
The great vowel shift.

In favorable cases, we can even hear the different pronunciations of older and younger speakers and judge the older speakers to use the more conservative pronunciations. One currently active sound change in American English has been named the "northern cities chain shift."

The term **chain shift** is used when two or more phonemes move in the same direction, as they did during the Great Vowel Shift, so that the contrasts between them are maintained. One vowel seems to be pushing another ahead or dragging another behind. As phonemes move about they do sometimes collide and lose their contrast, but there must also be pressures to maintain the contrasts even in the face of considerable movement. The contrasts, after all, are needed in order to keep words distinct, and comprehension would suffer if too many contrasts were lost too quickly. Movement of a vowel is not so risky if other vowels move to make room at the same time.

The northern cities chain shift describes the situation in a number of cities of northeastern and north central United States, including Buffalo, Detroit, and Chicago, where younger speakers tend to pronounce the vowels of words such as *hot, got, rod,* and *watch* quite far to the front. To people from other parts of the country, a Detroit *hot* can sound almost like their own *hat,* and a Detroit pronunciation of *John* can be mistaken for *Jan.* The northern cities fronting of this vowel is actually a continuation of a nineteenth century shift that moved the vowel forward from a low back and rounded position. Speakers in eastern New England and Britain often preserve a more backed and rounded vowel in words like *hot.* This means that the vowels of these words can be pronounced in several ways: In Britain and eastern New England the vowel is likely to be [ɔ], rounded and quite far back; in much of the United States and in the dialect of broadcasting, a low central vowel, [a], is most common; in several northern cities, younger speakers have moved it still further forward, where it approaches [æ].

The northern cities' fronting of /a/ is one part of a larger pattern. Indeed, we might wonder if too much fronting of this vowel might not risk a collision with /æ/. Could it become difficult to keep words like *hot* and *hat* distinct? Any such risk is avoided in the northern cities by the tendency for older /æ/ to rise from its more typically low front position. The vowel of words like *hat* and *cap* can climb at least to the mid position and sometimes even higher. On the other side of /a/ another change is possible. When /a/ moves front, it leaves more room in the back. The old /o/ of *bought* and *caught* can move somewhat forward, encroaching on the older but now vacated position of /a/. The movements of these vowels are reminiscent of the more dramatic movements of the Great Vowel Shift. In both cases, several vowels have moved in the same direction, and, the contrasts among them have generally been maintained.

MERGERS AND SPLITS

The comparative method rests on the assumption that a language's distinctive sounds can gradually change their pronunciation, but that the changes occur in an orderly way. In the examples we have considered so far, phonemes changed their pronunciation, but most of their contrasts with other phonemes were preserved. Sometimes, however, two phonemes may move so close together that they finally merge. When that happens, some words lose their contrasts. Under other circumstances, a single phoneme can also split, yielding two or more contrasting phonemes, but we expect that splitting will also take place in an orderly manner. The picture that emerges is of the phonemes of a language jostling each other in phonetic space, often keeping out of each other's way, but occasionally merging and occasionally splitting.

We can observe ongoing mergers in the variation that we hear around us. One of the few points where the initial consonants of modern English dialects vary is in the /w, hw/ contrast in words such as *wear* and *where*. Even if we had no written records of the history of English, we might suspect that this contrast was once more widespread than it is now, perhaps even a universal feature of English. We might guess that the distinction has been gradually reduced until, for many speakers, it has disappeared. Another example is the contrast that some, though not all, speakers maintain between *do* and *dew* or between the initials of *noon* and *new*. For some speakers there is as much of a /j/ in *dew* and *new* (/dju^w, nju^w/) as in *few* or *view,* while for other speakers the /j/ is completely gone. Once again it is plausible to infer that earlier dialects had a contrast between words with /j/ and words without, but that this contrast has been lost in some dialects. The principle followed here is that when some dialects have a contrast that others lack, the first explanation to consider is that we are witnessing the loss of a formerly more widespread contrast.

Contrasts are sometimes lost in limited environments but preserved in others. The loss of contrast between /i/ and /e/ in words such as *pin* and *pen* that is characteristic of most of the American South is generally confined to vowels that are followed by /n/, though occasionally the loss is extended to the position before /m/. *Jim* and *gem* then become homophones. The contrast survives in other positions so that /i/ and /e/ have to be recognized as distinct phonemes in all dialects, but not all dialects have both phonemes in all positions. The contrast has been lost in some circumstances but not in others.

A phonological system needs contrasts, and if too many contrasts are lost, others will be needed in compensation. The manner in which English fricatives once split, and thereby introduced a new contrast into the language, shows one way that new contrasts can arise. In Old English the phonemes /f/ and /s/ were often voiceless, but when occurring between vowels or before a voiced consonant, they were voiced. Thus [f] and [v] were in complementary distribution, as were [s] and [z]. When some final vowels were lost, however, fricatives that had preceded the vowels retained their voicing even though they no longer had vowels on both sides. Thus *cnafa* [knava] 'boy' lost its final vowel and became [knav], the modern *knave,* and retained its voiced [v]. Previously, only voiceless [f]'s had occurred in word final position but now, instead of being in complementary distribution, /v/ and /f/ were in contrast. A new English phoneme was born. /z/ split from /s/ at about the same time and in much the same way.

One assumption of the comparative method is that sound changes are absolutely regular, that if the conditions of change can be precisely enough defined, all words that meet the conditions will be found to have changed. Often, however, when we observe the correspondences between closely related dialects, this expectation of regularity does not seem to be satisfied. We regard dialect differences as the first step in the development of language differences, but dialect differences are sometimes characterized by more variability than the regularity of a Great Vowel Shift or a Grimm's law would lead us to expect. If we believe that the variability of /a/ and /o/ in North American English suggests that the vowels are in the process of falling together, we must also admit that this is happening in a chaotic fashion. It seems to be individual words that shift from one pronunciation to another. Different individuals use innovative pronunciations with varying sets of words. Some linguists have argued that **lexical diffusion** is a better way than regular sound change to describe the process by which these vowels are changing. Lexical diffusion implies that changes diffuse gradually from word to word, and that no regular sound shift affects every word simultaneously.

Lexical diffusion is a messy process, but even lexical diffusion can lead, in the end, to the appearance of regularity. If the contrast between /a/ and /o/ is finally lost, it will look to our descendants as though the sound change had been entirely regular. It might then appear that every word that formerly had an /o/ had changed its pronunciation to /a/. Some linguists now suggest, therefore, that the regularity of a sound change is finally established only after it is completed. Only then are the exceptions removed. The hypothesis of exceptionless sound change, nevertheless, has been a richly productive one, and it is still the best working hypothesis when studying sound correspondences. It invites scholars to investigate apparent exceptions and, as patterns are discovered in the exceptions, to find more and more regularity in their data.

We can recognize something more like a regular sound change in the systematic correspondence between different phonetic realizations of the same phoneme. The English and American pronunciations of the vowel in words like *go, foam, hope, road,* and *soap* correspond with utter regularity. By the rules of the comparative method we would judge that the English and American vowels must have developed from the same vowel in an earlier form of the language. In whatever way the ancestral vowel was pronounced, it must have moved in at least one of the modern dialects, but it has done so in a fully regular way, and its movements have not compromised its contrasts with other phonemes. This is one of many examples in which we interpret phonemes as moving about and changing their phonetic realization without upsetting the language's phonological system, and it is one of many cases where we can be more confident about the existence of an earlier phoneme than about its exact phonetic realization. A regular sound change has taken place in one or in both dialects, but the system remains intact.

When comparing dialects, we inevitably tend to focus on their differences rather than their similarities, but their similarities also tell us something about their history. English consonants are relatively uniform in all dialects, and this suggests that the ancestral form of English from which modern dialects derive also had similar consonants. Vowels that are uniform across dialects can also be judged to have derived from a similar ancestral vowel. Thus most English dialects have very similar vowels in *bid, hit, rich, hiss,* etc., so it seems reasonable to believe that the ancestral dialect had much the same vowel in much the same set of words. By enough diligent comparison we can hope to reconstruct most, or even all, of the phonemes of an ancestral dialect or language, and thus to reconstruct its phonological system.

Some phonological changes, including many vowel changes, can be thought of as gradual and cumulative. Others, particularly those that result in the falling together of formerly distinct phonemes, seem to be inherently abrupt. Phonemes either contrast or they do not contrast, and there is no halfway point. Do we need to puzzle about whether sound change is steady or abrupt, or whether phonemes fall together gradually or suddenly? This question was once regarded as something of a riddle, but our present understanding of language variation dispels any mystery about the process.

When speech is sufficiently rapid, almost every contrast in a language must occasionally be lost. A long-term change that we summarize as the loss of a phonemic contrast actually takes place by a gradual expansion of the circumstances in which the contrast is ignored. In careful speech, some English speakers still make a contrast between /w/ and /hw/ but, for most of them, the contrast probably becomes obscured, at least occasionally, in fast speech. For other speakers the contrast is completely gone. The long-term trend seems to be for the contrast to disappear from the language. It may not be long before only the most stubbornly conservative speakers ever make the contrast, and its final loss will then soon follow. A similar process must once have brought the loss of the /k/ that used to distinguish words such as *knight* from *night.* Like the /w, hw/ contrast, the /n, kn/ contrast may have survived longer in careful speech than in fast speech, and there must surely have been a time when some older and more conservative people retained the contrast, while others ignored it. We may even suspect that those who hung onto the contrast deplored the "careless" speech of those who lost it. Gradually, however, the occasions in which the contrast was maintained grew fewer, until it finally disappeared.

We might expect that vowel changes could take place gradually, but even they are more likely to involve variation. Some people, on some occasions, pronounce a vowel in an innovative way. It is likely to be more often, or more radically changed, in some phonological environments than in others. Change takes place as the proportion of variants used under varied circumstances gradually shifts. The differences that we observe when we compare American and British dialects are the result of all sorts of shifting patterns of variation. In the linguistic variation of our language, we can see changes in progress, but we cannot predict which variants will accumulate and become established as permanent changes. We have no way of knowing which of today's trends will continue and which will reverse.

Sometimes, however, we can interpret today's variation by reference to long-term trends. The variation in preconsonantal /r/ in New York City can now be understood in historical perspective. Sometime during the eighteenth century, respectable people in London began to omit their preconsonantal /r/'s. The prestige of the city and of its speakers lent prestige to its dialect, and its nonrhotic pronunciation spread not only to other parts of England but to several cities of the American East Coast as well. Boston, New York, and much of the coastal and plantation south became nonrhotic. Philadelphia, Baltimore, the Midwest and West remained firmly rhotic.

In the twentieth century, rhotic pronunciation acquired renewed prestige in New York. This may have been encouraged by the rise of radio networks and their choice of a rhotic dialect as an inoffensive pronunciation that would be acceptable throughout the country. Rhotic speakers, some of them with power and prestige, moved to New York from other parts of America, and they may have helped to set the new standard. At any rate, even in formerly nonrhotic New York City, the influence of a more "national" standard, a form of English that was less marked by regionalisms, began to be felt. Many New Yorkers came to feel that it was "better" to pronounce /r/ than to leave it out.

In parts of Britain the prestige of preconsonantal /r/ is just the reverse of its prestige in New York. For many Englishmen a preconsonantal /r/ seems distinctly rustic, and as they acquire their education British speakers sometimes learn to leave /r/ out. In New York City, educated speakers struggle to put it in. Nothing could illustrate more perfectly the arbitrary nature of linguistic norms, for there is certainly nothing either inherently good or inherently bad about an /r/. In New York today, preconsonantal /r/ seems to be spreading, but we have no way of knowing whether the spread will continue until New York moves securely back to full rhoticism.

CHARACTERISTIC SOUND CHANGES

Some sound changes take place easily in one direction but almost never in the reverse direction. Voiceless stops, for instance, sometimes become voiced between vowels, but we would be surprised by a case in which stops were devoiced between vowels. Many examples are known in which velar stops have been "palatalized," giving rise to sibilants or affricates. English /č/ in *chin* and *chicken* developed by palatalization from an older /k/. The many English words spelled with *g* but pronounced as /ǰ/ are a legacy of a parallel palatalization of an older /g/. It is unusual for palatals to move in the reverse direction and became velar stops. The unidirectionality of some phonological changes means that we can sometimes infer the direction of change from the correspondences that we find between two languages. When velar stops in one language correspond to palatal affricates in another, we suspect, even without other evidence, that the velar stops are older.

Some unidirectional sound changes leave characteristic results. Four specific phonological features so frequently arise from characteristic sound changes that they deserve special note: syllables that end in vowels, nasal vowels, long vowels, and tones.

1. Final vowels and the loss of final consonants. The final bits of a word seem to be particularly subject to erosion. In a great many languages we find evidence that final consonants have weakened or disappeared. We have seen that English speakers drop final consonants under some circumstances. French spelling reflects an earlier stage of the language when final consonants were more regularly pronounced than they are today. The loss of contrast among final consonants amounts to a sort of halfway point in the path to disappearance. The loss of final-consonant voicing in German has reduced the repertory of word-final consonants and led to the homophony of such words as *Rad* 'wheel' and *Rat* 'council,' even though no consonant has been completely lost.

If a language lost all its word-final or syllable-final consonants, all its words or syllables would end in vowels. Initial consonants are by no means immune to loss, but they tend to be more resistant than finals. The more frequent erosion of finals fits with the fact that many languages have a richer array of initial consonants and consonant clusters than of final consonants and clusters. Languages without final consonants are reasonably common. Languages without initial consonants are unknown. To be sure, final vowels can also be lost, and this can bring earlier consonants into final position again. In either case, we see a gradual nibbling away at the ends of words.

2. Nasal vowels and the loss of final nasal consonants. One specific loss, that of final nasal consonants, often leaves a characteristic trace: nasal vowels. Indeed, nasal vowels have so often arisen in this way that whenever we find nasal vowels, we suspect that an earlier stage of the language had final nasal consonants. As in English, nasal consonants often condition nasalization of the preceding vowel. If the consonants disappear while the vowel nasalization remains, then distinctive nasal vowels will have made their appearance in the language. As long as the consonants remain, we can consider vowel nasalization to be simply the result of assimilation of the vowels to the consonants. When the consonants are lost, nasalization of the vowels becomes contrastive. French nasal vowels arose in this way, and so did the nasal vowels of a number of other widely scattered languages.

This mechanism for the development of nasal vowels helps to explain a regularity that might otherwise be mysterious. It appears that no language has more nasal vowels than nonnasal vowels. Why should this be? If nasal vowels arise by transferring the feature of nasalization from consonants to preexisting oral vowels, there can be no more nasal vowels than there had previously been oral vowels. The relative number of nasal and oral vowels in a language, like the frequency of syllables without final consonants, can be understood as the result of a typical kind of phonological change.

3. **Vowel length and the loss of final voicing contrast.** A phonological contrast between long and short vowels can develop in a way that parallels the development of nasal vowels. We have seen that English vowels are longer when followed by a voiced consonant than when followed by a voiceless consonant, and many other languages have a similar pattern. It seems that the lengthening emphasizes the voicing, and makes voiced consonants easier to distinguish from voiceless ones. In English, of course, the difference between the vowel length of such words as *pat* and *pad* is purely allophonic, for it depends entirely on the voicing of the following consonant, but we can imagine that if the voicing contrast were lost, the difference in vowel length might remain. In that way, a new phonological contrast of vowel length would develop. Contrastive vowel length seems to have arisen in exactly this way in a number of languages, though it is not the only way in which length contrasts can develop.

4. **Tones and the loss of initial voicing contrasts.** In many languages, including English, syllables with voiced initial consonants tend to be pronounced with a somewhat lower pitch than syllables with voiceless initials. Thus, English, *pat* is likely to be pronounced with a somewhat higher pitch than *bat*. A frequent way in which languages have developed tone contrasts is by losing the contrast between initial voiced and voiceless consonants while retaining the older difference in pitch. A tone contrast replaces the older voicing contrast as a way of distinguishing words.

Nasal vowels, vowel length, and tones allow some contrasts to be maintained, even in the face of significant phonological change. Nasal consonants can leave their echoes behind in nasal vowels. Voiced final stops can leave their echoes as long vowels, and voiced initials leave theirs as low tones. As in the case of the Great Vowel Shift and Grimm's law, where many contrasts were preserved in spite of extensive sound changes, we can see that phonological systems can undergo extensive reorganization while continuing to keep most words in contrast. It is difficult to avoid the conclusion that there is pressure for preserving contrasts. Phonemes can move about, and old features can be transmuted into new features, but contrasting phones often manage to keep out of each other's way. We can understand some of the kinds of reorganizations that we observe as ways of preserving the contrasts that any language needs.

But, finally, contrasts do sometimes get lost. Words that were once pronounced differently become homophones. Vowels fall together. All the final stops of an earlier stage of Burmese have fallen together as the modern Burmese glottal stop. Even in some dialects of British English, voiceless final stops also merge as glottal stops. We know of other languages where final glottal stops have disappeared leaving behind nothing but short vowels or a particular tone as their echo. If the distinctive vowel length or the distinctive tone is later lost, that may amount to the final stage in a long process by which the earlier consonants have faded away. With the passage of sufficient time, anything at all can be lost. Time appears to grind away relentlessly at the sounds of every language.

When too much is lost, compensating changes are needed. The loss of phonemes from the ends of words can mean the loss of meaningful suffixes, and speakers may have to add words elsewhere in the sentence to make up for the loss. When contrasts are lost, homophones develop, and people will have to invent new ways to make their meanings clear. Too many contrasts cannot be lost unless new contrasts arise to do the old job.

PHONOLOGICAL BORROWING

One important source of innovation is the influence of another language. Borrowing of traits from one language to another is less important for phonology than for the lexicon, but when languages are in sufficiently intimate contact, borrowing can influence phonology as well. If enough words like *tsetse fly* were to come into English we might acquire a new affricate phoneme. If enough words like *Jacques* and *genre* were borrowed, and if they retained their original /ʒ/, an established phoneme would no longer be restricted to non-initial position. If enough words like *Vladimir* and *Vladivostok* were borrowed, we would have a new cluster.

The split between voiced and voiceless English fricatives took place during the period when English was under strong French influence. As we have seen, the split occurred when words lost suffixes, and preceding voiceless fricatives were brought into word-final position, but the new contrast was also helped along by borrowing. French words with voiced initial [v] and [z] were borrowed into English at about the same time, and the prestige of the French language encouraged people to retain the French voicing of the originals instead of adapting them to older English phonetic habits. The influence of French, then, contributed to the splitting of the older English phonemes.

The term borrowing is most often used when people incorporate features from another language into their own native language. Languages can, however, influence one another in a different way. When an entire population shifts from one language to another, features of the old language can be easily carried into the new one. If language shift happens quickly, and in circumstances where the new speakers lack close contact with native speakers, learning may be imperfect, and many traits of the older language can then be carried into the new one. Adult learners usually speak a new language with what we would call a foreign accent. If their children have to model their own developing language on the accented language of their parents these phonological patterns can stabilize into what amounts to a new dialect. Usually we expect words to be the most easily borrowed features of language, but when people shift their language the phonological influence of another language can be even more extensive than lexical influence. The phonological similarities that we find, even today, between the Dravidian languages of south India and the modern descendants of Sanskrit are generally attributed to the time when Sanskrit first arrived on the Indian subcontinent. The earlier residents, some of whom had probably spoken Dravidian languages, are thought to have retained some of their older phonological habits even after shifting to the Sanskrit of the ruling minority.

Sounds can occasionally be borrowed even when neither language shift nor borrowed words play a decisive role. A dramatic example is the spread of the "uvular" r across Europe. Most earlier European languages had apical r's that were either flapped or trilled, but by the eighteenth century, a uvular fricative or trill found its way into Parisian dialects as a replacement for the older apical pronunciation. Paris was a center of power. Its new pronunciation acquired a metropolitan prestige and it began to spread. It moved out to other dialects of French, and then leapt across language boundaries until some dialects of Dutch, German, Danish, Swedish, and Norwegian all came to be characterized by the uvular r. It always spread first to the cities, and it must have carried an aura of sophistication. Everywhere the rural dialects lagged behind. The uvular r is still spreading in Norway. Its distribution, shown in Map 8–1, only partially conforms to the boundaries between languages.

The distribution of front rounded vowels in Europe is shown in Map 8–2. As with uvular r, front rounded vowels are shared by a number of adjacent languages and dialects. Only those dialects of Italian that lie closest to French have front rounded vowels, and the more distant dialects of German lack them. We cannot trace the origins of front rounded vowels to a single time and place in the way we can trace the origin of the uvular r, but distributions like these force us to recognize that languages can influence each other's pronunciation, just as they can influence each other's vocabulary.

REGULAR SOUND CHANGE AND IRREGULAR GRAMMAR

It sometimes happens that an entirely regular sound change gives rise to grammatical irregularities. Many of the irregularities that we find in modern English are the residue of regular but ancient sound changes.

An ancestral form of English can be reconstructed in which some plurals

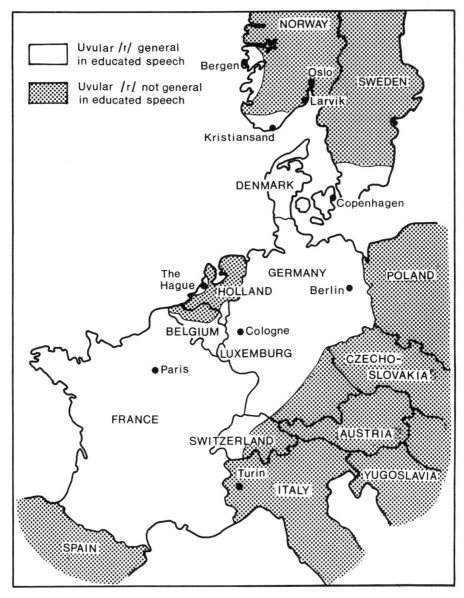

Map 8-1
Distribution of uvular *r*. After Chambers and Trudgill (1980).

were formed by the straightforward process of adding an *i* to the singular form, as shown in the first column of Table 8-4. It then happened that front vowels, including *i*, influenced the vowels of the preceding syllables. The preceding vowels were fronted, making them conform to the articulatory position of the following vowel. This kind of vowel fronting occurred in many Germanic

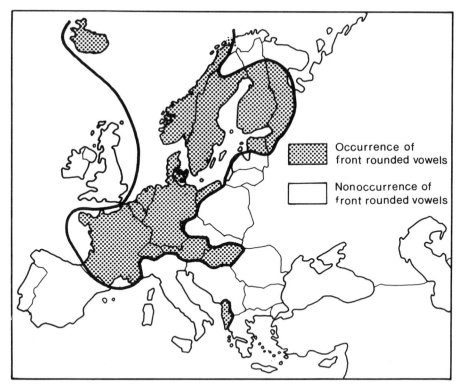

Map 8–2
Front rounded vowels in Europe. After Bynon, 1977.

languages, where it is known as **umlauting.** Umlauting is reminiscent of Turkish vowel harmony, which was described in Chapter 6, except that umlauting affects the preceding vowel while Turkish vowel harmony affects subsequent vowels. Under the pressure of umlauting, the -*i* of the plural could change the vowel of the word to which it was attached, and some plurals came to have different vowels than the singulars of the same word. These are shown in the second column of Table 8–4.

Table 8–4
Umlaut and Irregular English plurals

Pre-Eng. 1	Pre-Eng. 2	Old Eng.	Modern Eng.
muːs	muːs	muːs	mouse
muːsi	myːsi	myːs	mice
foːt	foːt	foːt	foot
foːti	føˑti	føːt	feet
gans	goːs	goːs	goose
gansi	gøːsi	gøːs	geese

At first, this vowel fronting must have been an entirely regular phonological process, governed simply by the character of the later vowel. By the stage of Old English, however, the *i* of the older plural had been lost from the language, and only the fronted vowels of the root remained as its echo. The difference between singular and plural was then marked only by the vowel change. As English continued to develop, the vowels of these words changed along with all the other vowels of the language, but the residue of the ancient and regular process of umlauting survives in the irregular plurals of modern English.

Modern English has a more widespread pattern of alteration in singular–plural pairs such as *half/halves, loaf/loaves, path/paths, and house/houses,* and also in adjective–verb and noun–verb pairs such as *safe/save, abuse/abuse, choice/choose, cloth/clothe, bath/bathe.* In these pairs, the singulars, adjectives and nouns have unvoiced fricatives, /f, θ, s/ while the plurals and verbs have the corresponding voiced fricatives /v, ð, z/. (Some speakers regularize certain plurals and now say /haʷsəz/ rather than the older /haʷzəz/.) These alternations date from the time when English voiced and unvoiced fricatives were in complementary distribution, unvoiced when final, but voiced between vowels. A suffix that began with a vowel, as the plural and some other suffixes then did, had the effect of surrounding a final fricative with vowels, and so changing it from unvoiced to voiced. Later, when these suffixes were simplified or lost, the voicing of the fricative was left behind as an echo of the lost vowel. As in the case of umlauting, the modern irregularities can be understood as the residue of regular but ancient sound changes.

The vowel alternations that resulted from the Great Vowel Shift have left an even more vigorous residue in the modern language. English still has scores of word pairs that are distinguished by vowels separated by the Great Vowel Shift. *Divine/divinity, satire/satirical, serene/serenity, meter/metrical, profane/profanity,* and *grateful/gratitude,* all reflect the changes that carried /iː/ to /aʲ/, /eː/ to /iʲ/, and /aː/ to /eʲ/ while leaving the original short vowels unchanged. Many other examples should come easily to mind.

In the course of time, irregularities introduced by phonological changes may be slowly regularized again. When more common or more regular patterns spread at the expense of patterns that are less common or less regular, we recognize what is known as **analogical** change. *Formulas* and *auditoriums* take over from *formulae* and *auditoria. Leaped* and *dived* are used in place of *leapt* and *dove.* Irregular /ruʷvz/ and /haʷzəz/ can be replaced by regular /ruʷfs/ and /haʷsəz/. In all these cases, regular processes are extended by analogy to words that had once been exceptions to the regular rules. The regular forms may gradually drive older irregular forms from the language. Uncommon words are always more susceptible than common words to analogical regularization. Speakers hear the irregular forms of uncommon words less often and learn them less well, so they more often need to fall back on the regular rules. Thus only a few very common nouns such as *mouse, foot,* and *man* retain irregular plurals in Modern English. Most of our irregular verbs are among the more frequently used verbs of the language. With sufficient time, we may expect that more and more irregular words will be gradually regularized.

The three kinds of alternations represented by *foot/feet*, *safe/save*, and *divine/divinity* all began as regular sound changes, but these regular changes left the modern language with irregularities. At any stage of a language we expect to find some automatic and productive phonological rules along with others that have, in varying degrees, become fossilized as irregularities. A productive rule of modern American English assimilates /t/ to a following /j/ to produce /č/, so that *got you* is pronounced [gačuʷ]. Other rules, such as those deriving from the Great Vowel Shift, were once quite regular, but while their results remain widespread they are no longer fully productive. Still other rules, such as the umlauting that gave rise to our irregular plurals, have left no more than a tiny residue. In the end, these final irregularities may be completely ironed out of the language, but even as old irregularities are eliminated, others are likely to be introduced. We have a picture, then, of irregularities invading the language as a result of regular phonological processes, and then being slowly removed again by the irregular process of analogy. The phonology of a language seems always to be in a state of slightly unstable equilibrium, continually changing in its details, but always remaining the same kind of object. We cannot see that, overall, languages grow either more or less regular.

THE CAUSES OF PHONOLOGICAL CHANGE

Linguists have learned a good deal about the mechanics of phonological change, and we have some understanding of what types of changes are more or less likely. Unfortunately, we know much less about *why* phonology changes. There seems to be no obvious reason for a language to change in the dramatic ways that we have observed. Why should such changes as the Great Vowel Shift or the consonant changes summarized as Grimm's law take place? Why should some dialects of English lose their /r/'s? Several answers to such questions have been offered; none is totally satisfying.

Simplification

Perhaps the most obvious explanation for phonological change is that languages move in the direction of easier articulation. Often it is tempting to interpret changes as simplifying the task of the speaker. One obvious example is the widespread tendency, as the centuries pass, for consonants to be lost from complex clusters. Final clusters are especially likely to be worn away.

Ease of articulation, however, needs to be balanced against ease of comprehension. Sloughing off final consonants may make a language easier for the tongue, but it may simultaneously make it more difficult for the ears. Loss of contrasts may make a language easier to speak but harder to understand. Clearly a language could not get "simpler" forever without simplifying itself out of existence, and if simplification for the speaker merely shifts the difficulty to the listener, we may doubt that anything has been gained. Sometimes, moreover, changes can lead to increased complexity, even for the speaker.

Vowels are sometimes lost from betweeen two consonants with the result that new clusters develop, presumably an increase in complexity.

If we consider only phonology, it is difficult to insist that Hawaiian is as complex as Navajo, but when all aspects of language are taken into account, linguists have never found any measures that suggest that one language is more or less complex than another. We usually assume that the complexity of human language is set by the capacity of the human mind, and even if we are unable to measure it, we tend to expect that all languages should have, roughly, the same degree of complexity. Thus we expect that simplifications in some areas will have to be balanced by adding complications elsewhere. Why, then, should some areas simplify?

Simplification, moreover, provides no explanation at all for why dialects keep drifting apart until they become separate languages. If the changes of one dialect are explained on the grounds of simplification, how is the surviving complexity of some other dialect to be explained? Simplification offers a tempting post hoc explanation for some kinds of changes, but languages sometimes preserve extraordinary complexities for a very long time. At any one moment, there are hundreds of changes that would make a language simpler. Only a few of these changes actually take place, and we have no way of explaining why languages simplify in some ways but not in others. Simplification, then, provides no general explanation for language change.

Imperfect Learning by Children

Since each child must learn a language anew, a discontinuity separates the generations, and we should not take it for granted that children will be able to reproduce the language of their parents in every detail. If, in the course of learning, each generation brings slight revisions to the language, we might expect the revisions to accumulate into substantial changes.

As we saw in the last chapter, fast natural speech exhibits massive phonological reduction. If we assume that relatively abstract and full underlying forms lie behind the surface forms, each child will have to infer the underlying forms on the basis of the surface forms that can actually be heard. It may be that children make imperfect inferences. Children, who must model their own developing speech on a variable input, could fail to note those occasions when a variable contrast is maintained, and thus fail to learn the contrast. If this happened regularly enough, we would count the language as having changed.

Children's imperfect learning offers us a mechanism by which a linguistic variable could lose its variability. If we believe that people continue to add complexities to their language throughout their lives, we must also presume that children's earliest language is, at first, simpler than the more fully developed and mature language of their parents. Children must select a sample of their parents' rules, but they may not select exactly the same rules that their parents started with a generation earlier. Perhaps we should expect each child's language to be a bit different from that of the parents.

To explain language change by imperfect learning, however, risks being little more than an elaborate rephrasing of the explanation by simplification. Have we done more than point to a particular mechanism by which simplification might occur? The discontinuities introduced by childhood learning offer no better an explanation for the divergence of dialects than does simplification. Why should children in one place introduce different changes from those living somewhere else?

Filling out a Pattern

Linguists take pleasure in symmetrical phonological systems, and perhaps the people who use language do too. We do find languages with apparent asymmetries. Papago, a native American language of the southwestern United States, has four voiced stops: bilabial, dental, retroflex, and velar. It has voiceless stops at three of these same positions, but it lacks a voiceless retroflex stop. The absence of a voiceless retroflex stop seems to leave Papago with an obvious gap, a hole in the system that ought to be relatively easy to fill. Could there be internal pressures to fill such gaps?

We have seen that English /ʒ/ has a limited distribution. It occurs easily between vowels, as in *measure,* a bit uncertainly as word-final, as in *barrage* and *garage,* and only very marginally as an initial. English speakers who study French find it easy to learn to pronounce initial [ʒ] in words like *je* 'I,' and it would seem almost "natural" to add initial /ʒ/ to English, and in that way to make the array of English initial consonants more "complete."

The difficulty with symmetry arguments is that all languages have asymmetries as well as symmetries, and if we want to offer pressure toward symmetry as an explanation for change, we may find ourselves mystified by all the remaining asymmetries. Perhaps, after all, it is only an aesthetic ideal of linguistics that makes symmetry so attractive. Pressure toward symmetry, or at least pressure toward typological consistency, has been an even more popular explanation for change in syntax than for change in phonology, and we will return to the topic in Chapter 10.

Innovation and Cleverness

We often assume that people want to talk like those around them, and there is no doubt that imitation is crucial to language. We could hardly learn to speak a language if we could not imitate. Sometimes, however, people are more eager to set themselves apart from others than to sound like them, and language then provides a wonderful medium for innovation. In modern western societies, adolescence is a time of some rebellion, and adolescents frequently want to demonstrate that they are different from their parents. One expression of this urge to be different is rapidly changing clothing styles. Rapidly changing slang is another. An occasional phonological specialty of adolescence may have the same motivation. Many of the linguistic innovations so eagerly embraced by adolescents are, to be sure, destined to die as quickly as they are born, but a few may be more permanently incorporated into the language where they become a part of the accumulating long-term changes. We do not know enough about the social dynamics of societies very different from our own to have confidence in the universality of adolescent innovation, but it is certainly important in our society.

It is not only adolescents who want to set themselves apart. People everywhere strive not only to sound like others, but also to sound just a bit different. People try to be a bit more clever, a bit more imaginative, a bit more colorful. We seek not only familiarity but also novelty. Some of the clever bits stick and contribute to long-term change. Perhaps they also add new complexities to balance the simplifications occurring elsewhere.

We might expect the most rapid linguistic divergence to come when two groups are seized by mutual dislike. They should easily be able to engage in reciprocal linguistic innovation in order to demonstrate their mutual differences. Under such circumstances people might introduce innovations almost deliberately, in order to distance themselves and their group from the enemy.

Social Pressures

The constellation of social forces that exists in a society at any particular time, together with the social connotations of particular pronunciations, is surely one important factor in giving direction to phonological change. If all languages exhibit variation, and if some values of the variables connote prestige, we can expect people everywhere to feel impelled to imitate the individuals and the social groups that they admire. We can even imagine a sort of push–pull effect, in which people with prestige continually try to set themselves apart by adopting innovative forms of the language, while others just as relentlessly seek to imitate them. This "pursuit of the elite" is a well-known force for continued change in such areas as clothing styles, and the restless innovation of slang is also easily interpreted in this way. Could a similar mechanism lie behind phonological change?

We can at least speculate that if, for some reason, it became a mark of high status to raise one's vowels a bit, those with less status might try to elevate themselves by imitating their betters and raising their vowels too. To keep ahead, the people with status might then push their vowels up just a bit further. Once this process got started it would always be dangerous to lower one's vowels again, since they might sound vulgarly lower class. New York City /r/ and the vowels that are being affected by the northern cities chain shift may be changing under the pressures of prestige. It is not clear that these changes are impelled by the push–pull pattern of the pursuit of the elite, but if we let ourselves speculate, we might even ask whether changes as extensive as the Great Vowel Shift might not have been driven by such forces. We may never know the particular social meanings attached to phonological variation at the time of the Great Vowel Shift, but we are beginning to learn about the kinds of social forces that drive similar changes today.

Social pressures, however, hardly give us a complete explanation for sound change. In particular, they tell us nothing about why languages change in one direction rather than another. It seems to be a matter of mere chance that a particular form acquires prestige. In New York /r/ is admired, while in England it is the absence of /r/ that is admired. We may look at particular situations, such as the social-class system of New York City, and understand the forces that are driving the change, but we have no way at all to predict the direction of future changes. The kinds of social forces that we are coming to understand, moreover, are those that are found in modern and stratified societies like our own. We know that languages have always changed in all other kinds of society as well, even in the technologically simpler societies that were found everywhere before the last few thousand years. We still know little about the social forces that propelled language change in those societies.

Borrowing and Technological Innovation

Borrowing and new technology are well-understood forces that encourage linguistic change, but, as was discussed in Chapter 4, they are usually more important for introducing new vocabulary than for new pronunciation. If enough words are borrowed they can introduce new sounds into the language. Still, borrowing cannot be the primary cause of change. Borrowing can only lead languages to grow more alike, and other mechanisms must be responsible for introducing and maintaining the rich linguistic heterogeneity that we still find in the world.

Why Not Change?

Perhaps we can gain another perspective on language change by turning the question around. Instead of asking "Why do languages change," let us ask, instead, "Why are they so stable?"

We have an excellent partial answer to this reformulated question. Languages must be consistent enough to let us keep talking. They should probably change slowly enough so that grandchildren can talk easily with their grandparents. Beyond this, however, we should probably not expect anything as complex as language to remain fixed. The business of a language can be managed in so many ways that random variation in the behavior of its speakers might pull a language this way or that, with change restrained only to the extent that people want to make themselves understood. Within the limits of people's ability to communicate, variation and change may not be important. Perhaps this reformulated question is only a way of ducking the problem, but it is well to remember that it is not always change that calls for explanation. Consistency and conservatism may be just as mysterious.

Whatever its explanation, change is a permanent fact of language. Grandparents can talk with their grandchildren, but the grandchildren never learn the language of their grandparents in all its details. Languages are always in flux, and the conservatives of one generation, who lament the terrible language of the next, never have the power to stay the changes. Time and mortality always favor the language of the children.

Sentences

INTRODUCTION TO PART THREE

The five chapters of Part Three deal with syntax, the patterns by which words are combined into phrases, clauses, and sentences. In any treatment of syntax today, an important place must be given to the ideas of Noam Chomsky. Chomsky's impact on linguists began in 1957 with a little book called *Syntactic Structures* that dramatically reoriented the study of syntax. Chomsky gave linguists exciting new ways of looking at syntax, and new schools of syntax have been in restless competition every since. Chomsky's own thinking has undergone at least two major revisions since he wrote that first book, and many other competing views of syntax have flourished.

Chapter 9 introduces the basic ideas of "generative grammar" that began with Chomsky but that have come to be widely accepted as central to most types of modern syntax. Some of Chomsky's more recent proposals are outlined in the final sections of the chapter, but the technicalities of his latest proposals, in particular so-called Government and Binding syntax, are beyond the scope of this book. Chapters 10 and 11 approach syntax from so-called functional and typological perspectives that are less closely associated with Chomsky. As with the parts of this book that deal with the lexicon and phonology, this part on syntax concludes with a discussion of variation and change. Chapter 12 is devoted to regional, stylistic, and social variability, and Chapter 13 to syntactic change.

CHAPTER NINE

Generative Grammar

GRAMMATICAL AND UNGRAMMATICAL

Everyone who speaks a language fluently has a firm sense that words can properly combine in some ways but not in others. It is not likely that anyone ever used the following sequence of words before, but no one can doubt that they form an orderly English sentence: *These delicious little morsels are good enough to save for eventual distribution to the chimpanzees.* This is surely a very different kind of sequence than we get by arranging the same words backwards: *Chimpanzees the to distribution eventual for save to enough good are morsels little delicious these.* We cannot even read the reversed series of words with the intonation and rhythm that we expect in a sentence, let alone interpret it as having a coherent meaning.

Linguists would say that the first of these word sequences is **grammatical,** while the second is not. Only in the first are the words put together in a way that follows the rules of English grammar. The distinction between grammatical and ungrammatical sentences is a fundamental one in the study of syntax, and if the distinction is unfamiliar, an analogy may help to make it clear.

In the usual notation of elementary algebra, certain sequences of symbols are "well formed":

$$3 + 4 = 7$$

$$(4 + x)(4 - y) = 0$$

$$x^2 + y^2 = z^2$$

The same symbols can be rearranged into other sequences that are not all well formed:

$$x + = y =$$

$$-43 +$$

$$)x($$

Ill-formed sequences like these are more than simply false, and we need to distinguish well-formed formulas that happen to be false, from formulas that are ill formed, the latter sometimes so odd that it is impossible even to apply terms like "true" or "false" to them. Ill-formed sentences simply have no meaning. They are uninterpretable. The following equation is obviously false, but we would still want to call it "well formed."

$$5 + 2 = 6$$

It is possible to write a set of rules that state, precisely and explicitly, which sequences of algebraic symbols are well formed and which are not. With such a set of rules we can test any formula for its well-formedness. For a system as simple as ordinary algebraic notation we can usually take well-formedness for granted, and we rarely need to point out explicitly that a sequence like "=)x)y(=" is out-of-bounds. Nevertheless, the difference between a well-formed and an ill-formed formula is a crucial one in any formalized mathematical system.

Computer "languages," such as BASIC, FORTRAN, and Pascal, are sufficiently complex that it more often becomes useful to write explicit descriptions of their syntax and to use these as guides that tell us whether or not a particular sequence is legal within that language. The best programmer makes syntactic mistakes and writes formulas that the computer will not accept because they are not legal sequences. An explicit description that specifies which sequences are legal can help programmers to find their mistakes. Computer languages are simple enough to allow a precise and fully explicit definition of syntactically acceptable well-formed formulas, and at the same time they are complicated enough to make such a description useful.

Languages like English or Japanese (sometimes called "natural languages" to distinguish them from the deliberately invented languages of mathematics or computer science) are vastly more complex systems than even the most intricate computer language, but one of the early suggestions made by Noam Chomsky was that a natural language could also be looked on as a formal system. The goal of a grammar, he said, should be to account for the well-formed sequences of words (such as *we like to eat*), and to distinguish these from ill-formed sequences (such as **to eat like we*). Following this suggestion, many linguists became attracted by the goal of writing a grammar of a natural language that would be as clear, explicit, and complete as a syntactic description of a computer language or the rules for well-formedness of a mathematical system. They have wanted to work toward a description of a language that would state, explicitly and fully, which sequences of symbols (words and affixes) are well formed (grammatical) and which sequences are ill formed (ungrammatical). It is this kind of rigorous and explicit description that is called a **generative** grammar. We are still a very long way from achieving such an explicit grammar, but the nature and goals of the study of syntax have been greatly clarified by thinking of our subject in this way.

Of course, a natural language like English is very different from an artificial language like FORTRAN, to say nothing of a mathematical notation as simple as that used for algebra. Other than the sheer complexity of a natural language, the most important difference may be that a natural language is not a deliberate human invention whose rules are chosen to meet the explicit needs of the inventor and user. Instead, a natural language is, from the point of view of the investigator, an object of nature that calls for empirical investigation. We are free to design new computer languages and new systems of mathematics that have quite different syntactic patterns from those we have used before. Natural languages are also the product of human minds, but nobody invented English or any other natural human language in the way that FORTRAN and algebraic notation were invented. The linguist must take a language as given. It is a system that, like a biological organism or a rock formation, is there to be explored. The linguist tries to understand this natural object, to discover its regularities, and to devise theories that will help us to understand how it works.

When describing languages and when discussing linguistic theory, linguists use a number of words that are also used by nonlinguists, and it is important to be clear about the technical meanings that these words have within linguistics. In particular, "rule," "grammar," and "grammatical" have quite specialized meanings for linguists. For a linguist, a "rule" is nothing more than a statement that summarizes an observed regularity of language. In offering a "rule," a linguist does not mean to imply that it *ought* to be followed, and it is certainly not intended as any sort of guide to behavior. Rather, the rules of linguists are statements that describe, or in some way account for, the regularities that we discover in our data. Whether the rules are there in the language just waiting to be discovered by the linguist, or whether the linguist invents the rules as a helpful means of describing the language, is a difficult epistemological question, and it is a question about which linguists are by no means in full agreement, but linguists are agreed that their rules must never be interpreted as regulations for how a language *should* be used. If people use their own language in a way that is not accounted for by our rules, then it is the rules that need revision, not the language.

"Grammar" and "grammatical" are also used in special ways by linguists. The **prescriptive grammar** that has often been taught in our schools amounts to an attempt to persuade students that some grammatical forms are better, or more suitable for certain occasions, than other grammatical forms. The **descriptive grammar** of linguists, by contrast, has the goal of accounting for all the sentences that people can produce, and it accepts these as "grammatical" whether or not they would be accepted in a prescriptive grammar. When linguists talk about a "grammatical" sentence or construction, they do *not* mean that it conforms to a particular style that is taught in school as "correct." If a speaker can use sentences such as *He don't got none* or *I ain't never seen none of 'em,* these have to be accepted as valid examples of that speaker's language. They are grist for the linguistic mill, as valuable and "grammatical" as any other sentence.

We must avoid any association of the word "grammar" with the prescriptive rules that are taught to school children, but the word has two other uses, both of which are current within linguistics. First, linguists use "grammar" for the schemes, often a set of rules, that they use to describe a language. In this usage, a grammar has exactly the same status as a physical theory of light, or a biological theory of metabolism. It is an invention of linguists, and it amounts to a theory that describes, or accounts for, the natural phenomena that they investigate. When we work out grammatical rules for a language, we develop a theory of that language. Like any theory, our grammatical generalizations stand or fall in accordance with their ability to account for the data we observe. When our grammar fails to account for the data, we must revise the theory and hope that we can improve its "fit" with the data.

Unlike a physical or a biological system, however, a natural language is, in an important sense, a product of the human mind, and linguists talk as if all speakers have a "grammar" of their language tucked away up there in their heads. Linguists struggle to develop explicit grammars of the languages they investigate, but they also talk as if ordinary speakers also use something quite similar to this grammar, except that it is largely inexplicit and even unconscious. Biologists hope their theories will account for the form and function of biological organisms, but they hardly need to wonder whether these organisms have their own theories of biology. Physicists do not have to worry about whether electrons or quarks have their own theories of elementary particles, but there is a sense in which all human beings *do* have a theory of their language. The grammar of ordinary speakers, presumably, guides and directs their daily use of language. Certainly each individual's language follows orderly patterns, and these orderly patterns would seem to require some sort of guiding system, some kind of "grammar," some means for deciding whether or not a sequence of words should count as a sentence. If a speaker's language conforms to a set of rules, then it would seem that some kind of (largely unconscious) grammar that incorporates those rules must be lodged in the speaker's mind.

Or, at least, linguists talk as if people have such grammars. When we investigate a language, we even hope that the explicit grammar that we work out will correspond, in some way, to the unconscious grammar that ordinary speakers have in their minds. The word "grammar" can refer both to the set of unconscious rules that all speakers use, and to the explicit description that a linguist devises, but we must not be lulled into the unquestioned assumption that these two "grammars" must necessarily be the same kind of phenomena.

Some linguists doubt whether natural human languages like English or Thai are really well-defined formal systems in the way that programming languages or mathematical notations are. Looking on language in this way, however, has given linguists a rich and fruitful way of thinking about their subject. It has opened new ways of approaching syntax, and many syntacticians have found it entirely reasonable to work toward the goal of a fully explicit, "generative" grammar that would do for a human language what rules for well-formed formulas do for a system of mathematical notation.

GENERATION, COMPETENCE, AND PERFORMANCE

It is easy to devise rules that generate (i.e., account for explicitly) *only* grammatical sentences. Fragments of grammar that do this successfully are given in later sections of this chapter. The problem with such fragments is that they always leave out vast numbers of other sentences that are equally grammatical. It is just as easy to devise rules that generate *all* the grammatical sentences of a language: "Take some words of the language and arrange them in some order." The trouble with this rule, of course, is that it also allows a great many pseudo-sentences, sequences of words that are not grammatical at all. What is difficult, and what we are still a very long way from accomplishing, is to write a grammar that accounts for *all* the sentences and *only* the sentences of a language.

The hope that a grammar might generate all and only the grammatical sentences of a language implies a clear distinction between sentences that are grammatical and other sequences of words that are not. This corresponds to the unambiguous distinction between well-formed and ill-formed algebraic formulas. Natural languages, however, are never quite so simple, and one of the most difficult questions to decide is what to accept as data. In particular, where do we get the sentences that we want to account for? When we record ordinary conversation on tape and then transcribe what people have said onto paper, we always find a considerable proportion of fragments, false starts, and broken sentences: *Well, I thi-, why don't we-, at least I'd like to test-, I mean taste it.* Written transcripts of spoken conversations are notoriously difficult to read. They contain so much backtracking, so much hemming and hawing, that it is often difficult to extract the central message. No one would want to dignify such fragments by calling them "well formed."

Following Chomsky, many linguists have come to use the words **competence** and **performance** to express the difference between the orderly sequence of words that native speakers accept as well formed, and the less orderly output that they utter in daily conversation. These terms suggest that even if speakers interrupt themselves part way through a sentence only to start off again in a different direction, they can still recognize a more orderly language that lies behind all the surface irregularities. Chomsky proposed that it is their "linguistic competence" that allows native speakers to recognize grammatical (well-formed) sentences and to reject those that are ungrammatical (ill-formed), and he also argued that this competence has almost nothing to do with whether speakers have ever heard or uttered these sentences before. When we put our underlying competence to work in the real world of talk, the language we produce is subjected to all sorts of "performance" errors. We hesitate, we backtrack, we stumble. We forget where we began our sentence, and we end up where we had not intended. It is not this confusing performance, but the more orderly underlying competence, that many linguists have found most interesting.

We need a distinction such as that between "competence" and "performance." We have to recognize the importance of a speaker's sense of what is grammatical, even when much of the actual talk that we hear and produce deviates from grammaticality. For some purposes, it is important to study what is actually said, and some linguists do transcribe real conversations and examine the transcripts for regularities. More typical, especially of work done by those linguists who have been most strongly influenced by Chomsky, has been to use data drawn from judgments by native speakers about whether or not a proposed sequence of words is well formed. When linguists investigate their own language, the judgments are almost always their own. This means, however, that the decision about whether a sentence is, or is not, to be counted as well formed has nothing at all to do with whether it has ever actually been pronounced.

Although we can hardly avoid the distinction between competence and performance, we must also recognize its dangers. When we focus on linguistic competence, we do not obtain our empirical data from real conversations, but rather from judgments of grammaticality. We divide proposed sentences into grammatical and ungrammatical sets, not according to whether anyone has ever said them, but on the basis of someone's judgment, often our own, about whether or not they are well formed. Linguists even use the term ''intuition'' to describe the way in which they, and other native speakers, make their judgments about sentences, and linguistics can sometimes seem to be in danger of losing its empirical foundation and disappearing into subjective introspection. At worst, the distinction between competence and performance offers linguists a way to rid themselves of inconvenient data. If proposed sentences do not conform to one's theory of how a language should work, it may be tempting to dismiss them as nothing more than the result of ''performance errors.''

The problems with introspective data are aggravated by the fact that individual speakers find it difficult to decide about the grammaticality of a good many proposed sentences. Are, for example, the following sentences grammatical? *Where Philip drove the truck is to Wabash. This bus is gotten on right here, Your friends have all a lot of money. I requested Suzy help me. Morton saw a description by Hortense of himself.* People disagree in their judgments about such sentences. Many feel insecure. A generative grammar is supposed to decide on grammaticality in a fully explicit way, but if human speakers cannot always decide, can we expect a formal grammar to do better? Two responses are possible. First, the grammatically doubtful sentences are, in fact, only a small proportion of the total possible sequences of words, and we have plenty to keep us busy if we just try to explain the clear cases. More ambitiously, we might aim for more than a simple two-way distinction between grammatical and ungrammatical, but for a grammatical description that is subtle enough to show why the doubtful sentences are problematic.

The most serious problems with introspective data arise from individual differences in what people are willing to accept as grammatical. Any theory that locates grammar in individual minds must live with individual variability, but if we took our data from what people actually said, variability ought not to be a serious problem. Working out the grammar of a single speaker would be a legitimate linguistic goal, and individual variation could be studied in a straightforward manner. Unfortunately, variable judgments that are based on introspection are beyond the reach of other observers. If two linguists are arguing a point, and one insists "it is grammatical in *my* dialect even if not in yours," the data on which the judgment is based are inaccessible to public scrutiny. Each of us may have privileged access to our own intuitions, but we cannot base a general theory on data that will forever be hidden from others. When there is general agreement about introspective judgments, there is no problem about using introspective data. Caution is needed as soon as people disagree.

Fortunately, there are vast areas of agreement, areas where there can be no dispute whatever about what counts as a grammatical sentence and what does not. Broad regularities can be investigated in sentences of undisputed grammaticality. Other sequences of words are just as clearly ungrammatical. We should be able to begin by investigating the clear cases, and hope to close in gradually on those about which our judgments are less clear or less uniform.

PHRASE STRUCTURE RULES

One of the central components of any generative grammar is the part known as the **phrase structure.** This is the part of the grammar that provides for the constituents of a sentence, its words and phrases, and for their basic order. The nature of phrase structure will be illustrated here by English sentences. This example is offered less as a description of a fragment of English than as an illustration of the way linguists work and think. For this reason, instead of simply offering a polished and finished description, the presentation will be indirect, moving back and forth between examples and generalizations. We will consider sentences as sources for hunches about how verb phrases are formed, offer hunches in the form of rules, use the rules to predict additional data, and then search for more data that will allow us to test the rules and to propose modified and improved rules. The method of investigation is more important than the particular rules that emerge, but if the rules we develop seem convincing, that ought to give us confidence that we are on the right track.

Consider, then, the following sentences, stretched out into numbered columns so as to show their similarities:

1	2	3	4	5	6
The	*boy*	*watch*	*-s*	*the*	*man*
This	*girl*	*admire*	*-d*	*that*	*boy*
That	*man*	*chase*	*-s*	*this*	*cat*
The	*cat*	*scratch*	*-d*	*the*	*girl*
This	*elephant*	*fear*	*-s*	*that*	*elephant*

If a bit of tolerance is allowed for the spelling conventions by which the third person singular suffix *-s* and the past tense suffix *-d* are joined to the previous word, there can hardly be much dispute about the grammaticality of these sentences. These are not sentences about which individual speakers are uncertain or about which speakers disagree. We could easily add hundreds of other similar sentences, and a rudimentary grammatical rule will account for, or "generate," them all: Any sentence will be grammatical if it consists of one item from each of the six columns arranged in the order of the columns. This rule will, of course, generate not only the five sentences with which we began, but an additional 1,345 as well. (The product of the numbers of different items in each column is $3 \times 5 \times 3 \times 2 \times 3 \times 5 = 1350$, five of which have already been listed.) This is more sentences than anyone would want to list, but it is worth while trying a few of them to make sure that the rule really does yield English sentences. It is a rule that generates *only* English sentences. Obviously it is a very long way from generating all English sentences. Indeed, it covers only a most trivial fragment of the language.

Closer examination of the sentences reveals some further regularities. It is easy, for instance, to add dozens or even hundreds of additional items to columns 2, 3, and 6, but it is less easy to expand columns 1, 4, and 5. This difference suggests that the sentences contain two rather different types of words. We should also notice that column 1 contains the same items as 5, while 2 contains the same items as 6, and if we looked at a more diverse selection of English sentences, we would soon feel justified in making the generalization that the words we find in columns 1 and 5 are often found in front of the words we find in 2 and 6. We have located a pervasive pattern of English. To ease the burden on memory, the columns, and even the repetitive pairs of columns, 1–2, and 5–6, can be given traditional names. Let us call the words in columns 1 and 5 "Determiners," those in 2 and 6 "Nouns,' those in 3 "Verbs," and the two items in 4 "Tense Markers." Let us also call the pairs of words in columns 1–2 and 5–6 "Noun Phrases." The grammar that accounts for these sentences can now be expressed somewhat more carefully:

1. A Sentence consists of a Noun Phrase followed by a Verb, followed by a Tense Marker followed by another Noun Phrase.
2. A Noun Phrase consists of a Determiner followed by a Noun.
3. A Determiner can be *this, that,* or *the.*
4. A Noun can be *boy, man, girl, cat,* or *elephant.*
5. A Verb can be *watch, admire, chase, scratch,* or *fear.*
6. A Tense Marker can be *-s* or *-d.*

By using a number of fairly obvious abbreviations (S = Sentence, NP = Noun Phrase, Det = Determiner, → = "consists of" or "can be rewritten as") these rules can be written a bit more formally:

1. S → NP + Verb + Tense + NP
2. NP → Det + Noun

3. Det → *this, that, the*
4. Noun → *boy, man, girl, cat, elephant*
5. Verb → *watch, chase, admire, scratch, fear*
6. Tense → *-d, -s*

Rules 3, 4, 5, and 6 simply list the words or suffixes (morphemes) that can appear in each position. These are "Lexical Insertion Rules," and they list the available vocabulary. The number of sentences that this grammar will generate could be easily multiplied simply by adding more words. The operation of the set of rules can be illustrated by showing how they generate the first sentence in the sample, *The boy watches the man.* Start with rule 1 and then, by rule 2 expand the two NPs to Det + Noun to yield Det + Noun + Verb + Tense + Det + Noun. Then select a word or affix from the correct list for each position in the formula: *the* for Det, *boy* for Noun, etc.

A set of rules that provides only for simple sentences like these amounts to a dull and obvious grammar, but it does give us something on which to build. Consider, for instance, the patterns that can be found in sentences with somewhat more complex verbs.

The girl forgets the boy.
The girl forgot the boy.
The girl has forgotten the boy.
The girl had forgotten the boy.
The girl is forgetting the boy.
The girl was forgetting the boy.
The girl has been forgetting the boy.
The girl had been forgetting the boy.

The first thing to notice about these sentences is that the words that immediately follow the initial noun phrase come in pairs: *forget/forgot, has/had, is/was.* Our rules should reflect this pairing. Second, notice that *is, was,* and *been* are always followed by a word with the suffix *-ing.* Similarly, *has* and *had* are always followed by a word with a different, but distinctive, form, in these examples by a word having the suffix spelled *-en.* By experimenting with other words, it is possible to discover exactly what kinds of words can follow *has* and *had.* Our rules will have to show the relationship between *is, was, been, has,* and *had* and the suffixes of the words that follow.

All this can be accounted for by modifying the rules we have already proposed and by adding a few new conventions. One useful convention will be to use parentheses to surround items that are optional. Everything written within a single set of parentheses must be included, or everything must be omitted. Thus in Rule 1, below, *have* + *-en* is optional, but neither *have* nor *-en* can be used without the other. They require each other.

1. S → NP + Tense + (*have* + *-en*) + (*be* + *-ing*) + Verb + NP
2. NP → Det + Noun
3. Tense → *-d, -s*

4.–6. Other Lexical Insertion Rules (formerly rules 3, 4, and 5)

7. Hop affixes over the following word and suffix them to that word.

The only new parts of this tiny grammar are the words and suffixes in parentheses, and rule 7, which linguists have referred to, almost affectionately, as the "affix-hopping rule." This rule moves (or "hops") *-ing, -en, -s* and *-d* past the following word and attaches it there as a suffix. This is a new type of rule. Instead of simply stating what can occur and in what order, it moves things around.

To see how these rules work we can follow them as they process one sentence. We have to start at the top with rule 1, which has two optional parenthetical expressions. This gives us some choices, and we can simply select arbitrarily among the alternatives. From rule 1, we might select:

NP + Tense + *have* + *-en* + Verb + NP

This omits only the optional (*be* + *-ing*). Next, we apply rule 2, which splits the two NPs into Determiners and Nouns so that its output becomes:

Det + Noun + Tense + *have* + *-en* + Verb + Det + Noun

With rules 3 through 6 we select some lexical items, and this could yield the sequence:

The girl -d have -en forget the boy.

Finally, rule 7 tells us to hop the two affixes over the following words and attach them there as suffixes. *-d* must hop over *have* and produce *had,* the past of *have.* Similarly *-en* hops over *forget* and produces *forgotten.* The resulting sentence is:

The girl had forgotten the boy,

a sad event, perhaps, but a fine grammatical sentence.

A digression is needed in order to take care of some details that have been passed by rather quickly. The suffixation that just took place assumes some rather idiosyncratic adjustments that words and suffixes have to undergo when they are joined together. Somehow *had* emerges from the combination of *have* and *-d*; *forgotten* is the result of joining *forget* and *-en.* As English speakers, we are well aware that many words, especially verbs, show all sorts of fussy irregularities of this sort, and we need to provide for them. The rules that account for the forms that words and morphemes assume under the varied influence of their neighbors are the **morphophonemic** rules that were considered more carefully in Chapter 3. These rules show how a sequence of morphemes (words and the meaningful parts of words) is converted into, or represented by, a sequence of phonemes. In a full generative grammar, the morphophonemic rules would work on the output of the syntactic component of the grammar. This output would consist of a sequence of morphemes, and the morphophonemic rules would specify how these morphemes should be represented by the distinctive sounds of the language.

Morphophonemic rules can be annoyingly irregular. A complete description of English would need a long list of these rules in order to provide for all the irregularities. To spell these rules out here would divert our attention from the broader patterns of the language, and since all English speakers carry a knowledge of the morphophonemic rules in their heads, it is quicker to rely on everyone's intuitive knowledge. Let us simply accept the fact that the past of *have* is *had,* and that when *-en* is added to *forget* the result is not **forgeten* but *forgotten.* Many other morphophonemic rules like these will be taken for granted in the discussion that follows.

Notice that the rules do two quite different things. In some, a choice is offered, such as a choice among a list of words or morphemes, or the choice of whether or not to include (*be* + *-ing*). Some rules, such as the affix-hopping rule or the rule that says an NP consists of Det + Noun, give instructions for how something should be changed or expanded. Some rules do both.

Readers should try out the rules that have been given so far in order to satisfy themselves that they really do account for sentences that native speakers judge to be grammatical. Even if these rules do produce grammatical sentences, however, it may seem that there has been some sleight-of-hand in making them up, that the rules have been pulled like a rabbit from a conjurer's hat. Where, in particular, did rules 1 and 7 come from? We certainly did not reach them in any systematic manner. Anyone who finds this disturbing, however, misunderstands the nature of linguistic investigation. In fact, the method of discovering grammatical rules makes not a bit of difference, just as it makes not a bit of difference how the laws of any natural science are discovered. It matters not at all where our generalizations come from; it matters a great deal whether, once devised, they work.

Every reader can test these particular grammatical rules, and it is in the testing that the empirical side of linguistics, like the empirical side of any science, emerges. Of course we are more likely to come up with plausible hunches, generalizations, and hypotheses when we work in a reasonably systematic way, but in the end it requires insight, or just plain sensible or intelligent guessing, to arrive at good generalizations. But generalizations need to be tested, and it is well worth taking a few minutes to play with the rules in order to test whether they really do yield grammatical sentences.

If we are convinced that the rules work, it is time to look at additional sentences.

The girl should forget the boy.
The girl may have forgotten the boy.
The girl will be forgetting the boy.
The girl would have been forgetting the boy.

A vast number of similar sentences could be produced to show that *can, could, shall, should, will, would, may, might,* or *must* can be inserted into any of the sentences right after the first NP, so long as the verb, which follows immediately, is deprived of its Tense suffix. These words are known as

"Modal Auxiliaries," or simply "Modals," and it happens that English has exactly nine words that act in just this way.

Our sentences are growing in complexity. We can make this complexity more manageable if everything that can come between the first Noun Phrase and the Verb is grouped together. We can consider Modals, the marker of Tense, *have* and *be* all to belong together as part of what can be called the "Auxiliary." We will want to specify that a sentence must have either a Tense or a Modal, but not both. The convention for indicating a choice of this sort is to enclose the choices in curly braces: { }.

1. S → NP + Auxiliary + Verb + NP
2. Auxiliary → $\left\{ \begin{array}{l} \text{Tense} \\ \text{Modal} \end{array} \right\}$ + (*have* + *-en*) + (*be* + *-ing*)
3. NP → Det + Noun
4. Modal → *can, could, shall, should, will, would, may, might, must*
5. Tense → *-d, -s*
6.–8. Other Lexical Insertion Rules.
9. Hop all affixes over the following word and suffix them to that word.

The rules now provide for a choice between a Modal and a Tense marker, but only the latter is an affix. This means that, when a Modal is chosen rather than a Tense marker, the affix-hopping rule will not apply to it, and the Modal will retain its position as the first member of the auxiliary in front of the verb. The affix-hopping rule, in other words, applies only under certain conditions, and the rule must spell out those conditions. A *have* or *be* that directly follows a modal, therefore, will retain its original form as *have* or *be* because no affix is available to jump over it and to change it to *has, had, is,* or *was.* In many other sentences, however, the affix-hopping rule will do some modest rearranging. We will pass by the large number of morphophonemic rules that show how the sentences should be pronounced, but with this limitation, these grammatical rules should provide for all the sentences we have looked at and for a great many others.

The fact that these rules leave numerous options is crucial. The phrase structure rules include some items, such as (*be* + *-ing*) that are optional, and in the choice between Tense and Modal they offer alternatives. Even more options are provided by the Lexical Insertion Rules, which provide the choices among words. Several of these word lists could be easily expanded to give a much wider choice. Options are essential for any set of rules that is to apply to an interesting range of data. A sequence of rules that had no options at all could generate only a single sentence.

MOVEMENT RULES

We have already used one rule, the affix-hopping rule, that moves a few things about, and for other kinds of sentences it is often revealing to recognize more dramatic kinds of movement. It seems natural, for example, to use a movement rule as a way to derive questions from corresponding statements. Before reading further, readers might enjoy playing with questions like those listed here, trying to construct a rule that shows how they can be derived from statements.

Has the boy kissed the girl?
Is the girl kissing the boy?
Had the dog been chasing the man?
Can the man have forgotten the woman?
Must the dog have bitten the girl?
Hasn't the man eaten the stew?
Can't the schoolteacher teach the children?
Does this man admire that dog?
Did that woman chase the cat?
Didn't the principal fire the schoolteacher?

Most of these questions can be easily accounted for by saying that the first word of the auxiliary has been moved to the beginning of the sentence, in front of the initial Noun Phrase. Thus *Has the boy kissed the girl* seems to be derived from *The boy has kissed the girl* by the movement of *has*. In sentences with a negative, the negative moves too. The only real complication arises with statements that have no auxiliary at all. A sentence like *This man admires that dog* has no auxiliary, and so it has nothing to move to the front in order to make a question. If a sentence like this is to be turned into a question, it needs to be given *do, does,* or *did* as a kind of dummy auxiliary. It seems that English questions need some sort of Auxiliary to move to the front of the sentence and, if nothing else is available, a form of *do* will have to be supplied.

English has other questions that are formed with "question words" such as *what, who, where,* etc.

Who found the ghost?
What will John find in the closet?
What did John find in the closet?
Where did he find it?

The first of these is very similar to a simple statement such as *John found the ghost.* The only difference is that *John* has been replaced by *who.* The other questions differ more sharply from the corresponding statements. *What will John find in the closet?* might correspond to a statement such as *John will find the ghost in the closet,* but to get from the statement to the question, two changes are needed. First, *ghost* must be replaced by *what* to yield *John will find what in the closet?* This is not quite impossible, but normal English questions require a change in word order as well. The question word must move to the front of the sentence and, at the same time, the subject, *John,* must change places with the auxiliary, *will.* This results in a natural sounding question: *What will John find in the closet?* The third sentence, *What did John find in the closet?* is similar to the second except that it is presumably derived from something like *John found the ghost in the closet,* a sentence that has no auxiliary. *What* can replace *the ghost* and then move to the front of the sentence, just as it did in the previous sentence, but that would yield *What John found in the closet?* In a case like this, a dummy auxiliary must be added to fit into the auxiliary position. The affix will then hop over the auxiliary *do,* turning it into *did,* rather than over the verb *find.* Finally, *Where did he find it?* can be derived from *He found it in the closet.* This time the question word replaces *in the closet,* moves to the front of the sentence, and a dummy *do* is added to keep everything in the right place.

Passive sentences involve even more radical movements than questions. Consider a sentence such as *The girl is forgotten by the boy.* This sentence can be derived from the active sentence *The boy forgets the girl,* but to get from the active to the passive, several changes are needed: (1) The old object (*the girl*) moves to the beginning of the sentence where it becomes the new subject; (2) The old subject (*the boy*) moves to the end of the sentence, picks up the preposition *by* and forms a prepositional phrase. This prepositional phrase can be dropped, and this gives English speakers a way to avoid any mention of the old subject: *The girl is forgotten;* (3) Another word (*is* in this example) has to be added to the Auxiliary; (4) The Verb (*forget*) takes an *-en* suffix, which, by a morphophonemic adjustment, yields *forgotten.* All of this sounds rather complex when spelled out explicitly, but English speakers manage to create passives perfectly easily.

Questions, passives, and the affix-hopping rule can all be described as requiring words to be moved about. Movement rules are one way to show how some sentences are related to each other, but it is beyond the scope of this book to spell out the limits on what can and cannot be moved in English or in any other language. The important point is that we can often obtain a clearer understanding of the organization of sentences if we supplement phrase-structure rules with movement rules.

Technically, movement rules are said to convert the **deep structure** of a sentence (known in some of the more recent literature as "D-structure") to its **surface structure** (or "S-structure"). The terminology implies that the phrase structure generates an underlying level of deep structure and that movement rules readjust the output of the phrase-structure component of the grammar to produce the surface structure. The deep structure has been thought of as quite abstract, sometimes even as preserving underlying logical relationships or as lying relatively close to the conceptual structure. The surface structure of a sentence is closer to what we can pronounce and hear, and it is more accessible to direct observation. The deep structure is inferred as a means of accounting for the characteristics of the more directly observable surface structure.

A STRUCTURED LANGUAGE

Phrase structure and movement rules describe grammatical sentences and distinguish these from ungrammatical sequences of words. In doing so they specify the internal structure of sentences. In effect, they assign a structure by showing which words are nouns, verbs, prepositions, etc., and which sequences of words are noun phrases, prepositional phrases, etc.

For example, consider a sentence that is just a bit more complex than those considered so far: *The young pitcher should throw a ball to the batter.* To generate this slightly more complex sentence, the rules also have to be slightly more complex than those used earlier. This sentence has a Prepositional Phrase, and the rules that are given here group this with the Verb and the second Noun Phrase into a Verb Phrase. A rule that allows an Adjective to be added to a Noun is also given. VP 'Verb Phrase' stands for *throw a ball to the batter;* PP 'Prepositional Phrase' for *to the batter;* NP 'Noun Phrase' for *the young pitcher, a ball,* or *the batter.*

S → NP + Modal + VP
VP → Verb + NP + PP
PP → Preposition + NP
NP → Det + Noun
Noun → (Adjective) + Noun
Lexical Insertion Rules

A visually more intuitive way of showing the same derivation is by means of what is known as a **tree diagram** as in Figure 9–1. The tree diagrams that linguists draw always have their roots at the top and their twigs at the bottom. This tree diagram gives exactly the same information as the sequence of rules, with each split in the branches corresponding to one of the rules. Words are attached to the twigs at the last stage, and this corresponds to the stage of the Lexical Insertion Rules.

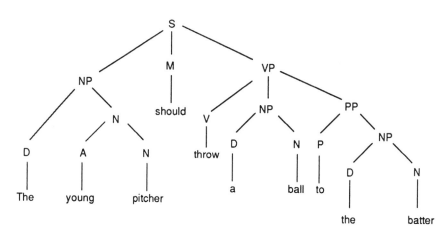

Figure 9–1
Tree structure diagram of "The young pitcher threw a ball to the batter."

Still another way of showing the same information is by means of what is known as a **labeled bracketing.** Brackets are used to enclose constituents of the sentence, and each constituent is labeled with its name. To save space, several additional abbreviations are needed: D 'Determiner,' N 'Noun,' A 'Adjective,' V 'Verb,' M 'Modal,' P 'Preposition.' A labeled bracketing is more compact than a tree diagram, but it is much more difficult to read.

[S[NP[D The] [N[A young] [N pitcher]]] [M should] [VP[V throw] [NP[D a] [Nball]] [PP[P to] [NP[D the] [N batter.]]]]]]

The rules, the tree, and the labeled bracketing are three equivalent ways of showing that a sentence is more than a simple sequence of words. A sentence has a structure and, in particular, some sequences of words within a sentence are real constituents, while others are not. *The young pitcher,* for example, is a constituent. It hangs from a single node of the tree, and it is surrounded by its own set of brackets labeled 'NP.' Other words or phrases (e.g., *she, the tired student*) can be substituted for *the young pitcher* leaving the structure of the rest of the sentence unchanged. Some other word sequences of this sentence, such as *ball to the* are not constituents, as can be seen by their scattered positions on different branches of the tree diagram and by the failure of these words to be enclosed by a single pair of brackets. The point is a simple but crucial one: a sentence is not a mere sequence of words but is a structured organization of words. Formal rules cannot be written to distinguish grammatical and ungrammatical sentences without recognizing the structured way in which the words of a sentence are organized.

Movement rules, for instance, can be described only in terms of the structure of a sentence. As we have seen, some English questions are formed by moving the Auxiliary to the front of the sentence. *Was he feeling cheerful?* is a question formed from *He was feeling cheerful.* In order to form questions like this, the Auxiliary needs to be identified and this, in turn, requires knowledge of the structure. The Auxiliary cannot be identified simply by its position in the sentence, since it may occur almost anywhere. *All the men who rode their horses have come* has the Auxiliary in eighth position, next to the last, but it must be moved all the way to the front to make a question: *Have all the men who rode their horses come?* Nor can a speaker simply select the first word that can act as an Auxiliary and move it. To make a question from *She is looking for the man who is scared* the first *is* must be moved: *Is she looking for the man who is scared?* To make a question from *The man who is scared is running,* the second *is* must be moved: *Is the man who is scared running?* Speaking requires an (unconscious) understanding of the structure of sentences, and the grammars of linguists must be written in ways that take account of this structure.

COMPLICATIONS AND INFINITY

The phrase-structure rules and movement rules that have been described account for a good many English sentences, but they do not begin to account for all of English. Some hint of the complexity that languages display can be gained by suggesting just a few of the many areas that would need to be taken into account in a fuller grammar of English.

One obvious limitation of the rules given so far is that they provide only for third person singular subjects. First and second person subjects (*I, we, you*) and third person plurals (*they, the horses, etc.*) require different verb forms. A more complete grammar would need to show how the verb is modified to conform to the subject. Third person singular subjects require verbs with a suffixed -*s*, but this suffix is impossible otherwise. Even more complex rules are needed in order to deal with the differences between *am, are, is, was,* and *were.*

A more serious limitation of the rules given earlier is that they fail to show how complex sentences can be built up from simple ones. English provides numerous ways in which two or more sentences can be united. These range from simple joining of two sentences with a conjunction, as in *Graham was sleeping, but I worked hard,* to various constructions in which one sentence is "embedded" in, and "subordinated" to, another. In each of the following sentences, the embedded sentence is enclosed in brackets. Some of these embedded sentences require, or allow, a "Complementizer" such as *that, whether,* or *for* to be added as a way of helping to mark the sentence as embedded. *I know [that Oswald hates to do that]. He wondered [whether he should come]. They are anxious [for us to get out of here]. They demanded [that we answer the questions]. I hope [that he can leave tomorrow].* Even *I plan on [leaving tomorrow]* can be regarded as containing an embedded sentence, something like *I am leaving tomorrow* from which the subject, *I,* has been deleted. The rules that determine whether a Complementizer is needed, which one is needed, whether the embedded sentence requires or allows a subject, what form that subject will have, and what form the verb will assume are exceedingly complex, as any speaker of English can discover by a bit of experimentation.

Still another area that would have to be dealt with in a more complete grammar is the topic that linguists call **anaphora.** Anaphors are words that refer back to an earlier word in the sentence or discourse, and languages have complex rules that govern what anaphors can be used and under what circumstances. Consider, for instance, the different usages of *her* and *herself.* In some cases the choice between these two words helps the hearer to know who is being referred to. Thus *Betsey dislikes her* and *Betsey dislikes herself* point to two quite different people. On the other hand, *Alexandra said she was embarrassed* is ambiguous, since we cannot tell whether it is Alexandra or someone else who is embarrassed. It might seem that a distinction similar to the difference between *her* and *herself* would be useful here, but we cannot say **Alexandra said herself was embarrassed.* The rules that explain which pronouns are ambiguous, and that determine when we can and when we cannot use the "*self*" pronouns turn out to be surprisingly complex. Much linguistic research is now being directed toward trying to understand the nature of these and other anaphors.

It sometimes happens that what looks like the same phrase or sentence can have two quite different structures. A simple example is *the son of Isabel and Don*. Two different derivations of this phrase are suggested by the two different tree diagrams shown in Figure 9–2. This sequence of words is, of course, ambiguous, and the differing derivations represented by the differing tree diagrams offer an explanation of the ambiguity. It even seems reasonable to look upon *I met the son of Isabel and Don* as representing two different sentences that happen to sound alike. When two different words sound alike, we say they are "homophonous." The individual words in these sentences are neither ambiguous nor homophonous but the two sentences that they form can be described as "structurally homophonous." The alternative meanings of ambiguous sentences such as, *The shooting of the hunters was terrible, Visiting relatives can be a bore,* or *Time flies like an arrow,* are other examples of structural homophony. In each case alternative derivational paths result in identical sequences of words. *She made the robot fast* has at least a half dozen different meanings, resulting from as many derivational paths.

Languages have another source of complexity that needs to be considered more carefully: recursive rules. We can construct a totally novel sentence whenever we like. Since there can never be a fixed limit to the number of sentences, we can speak of the number of possible sentences of a language as, quite literally, "infinite." One way of thinking about this infinity is to realize that we can start with any sentence at all and add more bits so as to make it longer or more complex. We can elaborate *I see a pretty little girl,* to *I see a pretty little girl who waved her hand,* to *I see a pretty little girl who waved her hand as she crossed the street,* to *I see a pretty little girl who waved her hand as she crossed the street against the red light . . .* and we could keep on adding phrases as long as stamina and interest held up. There is never a fixed ending point after which additional elaboration is impossible. Nor are we limited to adding bits at the end. We can also add them at the beginning and say *I tried hard to see a very pretty little girl who . . ., I wonder if I should try hard to see a very pretty little girl who . . .,* etc. We cannot ever *list* all the sentences of a language because, however long our list grows, we can always come up with another sentence that speakers will recognize as legitimate. A linguist's grammar ought to be able to recognize as many legitimate sentences as a speaker can.

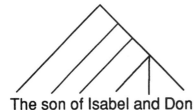   

The son of Isabel and Don   The son of Isabel and Don

Figure 9–2
Tree diagrams of "The son of Isabel and Don."

The grammar that speakers have at their disposal must have limits. However capacious our brains (or minds) may be, they are surely finite in size. This has to mean that the grammar that fits into our finite minds must also be finite. The only plausible way for a finite grammar to provide for an infinite number of sentences is by means of what are known as **recursive rules.** These are rules that can be applied over and over again. The simplest sort of recursive rule is illustrated by our ability to add "great" repeatedly to a phrase that finally ends in "grandmother." When children speculate about their "great great great great . . . great grandmother" they have discovered the joys of a recursive rule.

The rules that have been proposed in earlier sections of this chapter are capable of accounting for thousands of sentences—many millions if enough lexical items are included—but the number of these sentences is still finite. We need a way to account for still more sentences than these, and the grammars that linguists devise have many sorts of recursive rules, some a great deal more complex than the rule of "great." We can pile up adjectives in front of nouns: *The delicate little old brown wooden . . . spoons."* We can nest clauses inside one another, as in the famous dog *that chased the cat, that killed the rat, that ate the malt, that. . . .* We can join long strings of words, phrases, and even whole sentences with conjunctions such as *and.* By means of rules that can be applied repeatedly, the possibility of generating an infinite number of sentences can be built into a linguist's grammar.

The simplest of recursive rules can be expressed by a single formula:

Noun → Noun + *and* + Noun

This rule describes our ability to produce "Nouns" such as *melons and oranges* or *hammer and nails* from simpler nouns. Its recursive power is expressed by the fact that the same symbol appears on both sides of the arrow, and this allows the rule to be applied repeatedly: *melons and oranges and bananas and peas and peanuts and . . .*

A slightly more complex kind of recursion is made possible by a pair of rules:

S → NP + Auxiliary + VP
VP → Verb + S

The second of these rules is new, but it expresses our ability to incorporate entire sentences into a verb phrase. For instance, the Sentence *Victoria hopes Ambrose will leave* includes a Verb Phrase, *hopes Ambrose will leave,* and this Verb Phrase, in turn, incorporates the Sentence *Ambrose will leave.* In this case the recursive property is expressed by a pair of rules rather than by a single rule, but the result is the same, since "S" appears to the left of the arrow in the first rule but to the right in the second rule, and this allows us to apply the rules repeatedly: *Frank doesn't believe that Bill understands that Victoria hopes that Ambrose will leave.* Recursive rules like these expand the potential output of a grammar from a large but finite number of sentences to a range of sentences that can no longer be calculated. No grammar that lacked recursive rules could do justice to human language.

This section has given hints about a few of the many ways in which our grammar would have to be expanded before it would account for any significant portion of the English language. The start that has been made makes it seem reasonable to try to incorporate ever wider areas of a language into our description. This seems like a plausible way to carry on the task of constructing a formal grammar that will finally be able to generate all and only the sentences of a language. We might hope that it would be relatively easy to build on the rules that we already have and to move progressively closer to accounting for much, or even most, of the language. In fact, the rules we have seen are only the beginning. The more linguists explore, the more they realize remains unknown.

Notice that the rules that have been considered in this chapter provide no grounds for making particular choices. Alternatives are possible, but nowhere is a suggestion made as to why one choice should be preferred to another. In particular, meaning and context do not affect the choice among alternatives in the rules, so there is no way that a sentence can be selected to express a particular meaning. It is possible to program a computer to follow rules like these. It can select alternatives according to some scheme of random numbers, and it can churn out grammatical sentences in endless numbers. Rules that generate sentences without reference to anything outside of the rules themselves are described as constituting "autonomous syntax," and linguists have debated, indeed fought over, the advantages and disadvantages of autonomous syntax. Some linguists have tried to construct exceedingly formal grammars whose rules operate quite mechanically and without dependence on meaning or on the requirements of the conversation. A computer program to generate sentences uses a kind of ultimately autonomous syntax. A computer may help to check the accuracy and completeness of a set of rules, but a computer that produces a list of random sentences is a long way from duplicating a real speaker's skills.

In Chapter 10, a number of "pragmatic" considerations will be reviewed that suggest ways in which syntax responds to the requirements of conversation. These introduce external constraints on syntax that seem to restrict its autonomy. Nevertheless, the appeal of autonomous syntax is great. It has a formal elegance that would be undermined by the messy complexities of meaning and context, and some linguists believe it will be possible to devise autonomous rules that will account for a great many of the complexities that we find in language. As more and more data are considered, the grammatical rules that are necessary grow correspondingly more complex, but this may simply be evidence for the vast linguistic capacity of the human mind.

Should the rules that linguists construct be understood as providing a model for the way human beings really form their sentences and talk? It can hardly be an exact model. We should never suppose that our brains literally start by processing sentences through a set of phrase-structure rules, proceed by introducing lexical items, and finish by moving a few things around. Psycholinguists have experimented to see whether speakers need more time to process sentences that linguists describe as having a more complex derivation, but their experiments have not yielded consistently positive results. The fact is that we have little way of knowing how real sentences are formed in real people's minds, and we should be cautious about interpreting the rules that linguists devise as closely mirroring anything that takes place in the mind. Our claims must be more modest.

Is there some weaker sense in which these rules might be said to constitute an analog for the way people's minds work? If asked directly, many linguists are cautious about claiming any psychological reality for their rules, but it is difficult to deny their psychological reality too insistently without abandoning the hope that linguistics has something to tell us about the nature of the human mind. Nevertheless, there are other ways to justify the rules than by claiming that they model the mind. For some linguists, it is enough that they generate sentences that speakers accept as grammatical, especially if they do so in a satisfying, even elegant, way.

DISCOVERY PROCEDURES AND LEARNABILITY

There was a time when some linguists believed that, if they collected enough examples from a language, it should be possible to submit their data to an automatic and mechanical procedure that would yield a set of grammatical rules. It was believed, in other words, that there should be a systematic procedure (an ''algorithm'') by which language data could be processed without any contribution of imagination or insight from a human linguist. This would amount to what linguists have come to call a **discovery procedure.** If we had a full discovery procedure, linguistic analysis could be done in the same way that we all once learned to solve some kinds of mathematical problems. For this kind of problem, we start with a formula (a procedure), plug our data into the formula, grind the crank, and watch the answer come popping out. On a more elaborate scale, this amounts to a description of how a computer does its work. If a computer is properly programmed, we simply feed it some data, and when this has been automatically and thoughtlessly crunched, the computer spits out its answer. Had computers been available five decades ago, linguists might have imagined that it would be possible to develop a computer program that would receive and crunch the data from a language and then spit out the rules of a grammar. The creative part of linguistics would then have consisted of developing the program. Once written, the program could have been left to analyze the data by itself.

No one has ever come close to developing a discovery procedure, computerized or not, that could be used to analyze any significant amount of linguistic data in this way. Rather, our characteristic working method has always more closely resembled the steps by which some grammatical rules for a few fragments of English were developed earlier in this chapter. We collect some data, often a rather limited amount, inspect the data for regularities, make hunches (hypotheses) about how it might work and then go back for some more data to see whether our hunches are confirmed. It has never mattered where the hunches come from, for the hunches stand or fall only on how well they account for the data. Even the way in which linguists write technical articles for each other reflects this style of work. Data are offered, and some generalizations are proposed. Typically it is argued that these generalizations account for the data better than other competing generalizations. What linguists do *not* do in their articles is to justify their hypotheses by the manner in which they reached them. The hypotheses are justified only by their success in accounting for data.

For many linguists, one of the most convincing aspects of Chomsky's earliest contribution to the field was his insistence that there can, in principle, be no systematic discovery procedure. The discovery of the rules of language, he said, is like the discovery of the laws of nature. The formulation of hypotheses in all areas of science is a stumbling and unsystematic affair that calls primarily for insight and imagination. Only later when we test our hypothesis do we have any possibility of using careful and systematic procedures. A grammar of a language amounts to a theory of how the language works, and no more than biologists or physicists do linguists have a systematic way to develop a theory. All of us proceed by hunches and hypotheses, and these gain acceptance only as they are shown to account for data.

When we notice the regularity and assurance with which all human children learn the language of their community, however, our inability to develop a systematic discovery procedure presents us with a paradox. We can have no confidence at all that a linguist, presented with a mass of data, will be able to work out a systematic grammar. Indeed, scores of linguists have devoted lifetimes of labor just to English, and they are still a very long way from anything they would consider to be a complete grammar. By contrast, we have utter confidence that a collection of human cells weighing hardly more than 3 kg will, within a very few years, grow into a chattering child in free control of the community's language. Indeed, human children learn to chatter in spite of the fact that much of the language they hear is distorted by performance errors such as hesitations, and false starts. Do we have to credit all ordinary human children with an inbuilt discovery procedure that eludes every adult linguist? What does a child have that a linguist lacks? Why do children appear to learn so much more of their language in a single decade than linguists have learned after all their lifetimes of toil?

If a language really requires the kinds of complex rules that generative grammarians have proposed, then every speaker, including every child, would seem to need some sort of analog of these rules. We do not need to imagine that the rules of the linguist correspond exactly to the psychological reality of a speaker, but speakers do exhibit linguistic regularities, and they must have something in their heads that guides them. The somewhat fragmented and random selection of sentences to which the average child is exposed hardly seems like a promising source of data on which to base the rules that the child will need in order to speak. How, then, can a child possibly manage?

Chomsky's answer to this seeming paradox, an answer that many linguists find persuasive, is that our genetic inheritance provides children with a large part of the necessary grammar. If their grammar is built in, it does not have to be learned at all. Instead of having to be learned, much of language may simply be a reflection of the kind of mind that all normal human beings inherit as a part of their genetic birthright. If children come to the task of learning a particular language with a great deal of linguistic knowledge already built in, we can understand how language can develop so rapidly in childhood. Children may start with something very different from the "tabula rasa" or "blank slate" that behavioral psychologists once believed was the nature of the untaught child. Instead of being a mass of unstructured protoplasm that is ready to respond adaptively to any environmental influence, children's brains may be very specifically preprogrammed for language. This raises the possibility that an examination of language could be a means of learning something about the nature of the mind that can learn a language.

UNIVERSAL GRAMMAR

Much of Chomsky's recent writing addresses the puzzle of how a child can learn such a complex thing as a human language when presented with such inadequate input. Hearing a random selection of conversation, much of it fragmentary, all normal children manage, with apparent ease, to acquire the language of their community. The initial state of a child's mind lacks the characteristics of any particular language, but it must still be prepared, in very specific ways, to acquire some language. How is this initial state of the mind transformed into the steady state of language knowledge that is characteristic of adult speakers?

To put the question in this way focuses attention on what Chomsky has called the **Internalized language** or the **I-language** that characterizes the mind. Many other linguists, he suggests, have focused instead upon the **Externalized language** or **E-language,** the sentences that people actually speak. Linguists following an E-language approach examine what people say, sometimes even by recording their conversations, and they look for the regularities and patterns in these language samples. They are interested in how a speaker behaves, and they may look for correlations between the language they hear or record and such social factors as the class of the speakers or the setting in which they speak. Such linguists are more often concerned with linguistic performance than with linguistic competence.

Linguists who follow an I-language approach, on the other hand, are concerned with what the speakers know rather than with how they behave. They seek to understand what knowledge a speaker needs in order to judge the grammaticality of sentences. They are more concerned with linguistic competence than with linguistic performance. They hope to be able to use the evidence of language as a means of learning something about the unique nature of the human mind. In particular, linguists who are concerned with I-language would like to understand how children can pass from the initial state of language knowledge, the state of mind with which genetic inheritance endows them, to the steady state of language knowledge possessed by mature speakers. The initial state, it is assumed, must already be exceedingly complex, but by examining the data of languages we can hope to learn something about it. We can hope to learn not only something about particular languages but something about the universal nature of all languages. It seems plausible to suppose that whatever is common to all languages must be due to the universal, inborn, character of the human mind, so the search for linguistic universals becomes a means for investigating the mind, in particular the universal initial state from which the mind begins its task of language learning.

The mind is taken to dictate **principles** that all languages must follow. For example, English conforms to a principle known as **structure-dependency.** This means that its rules act in ways that depend on the structure of the sentence. As we have seen, some kinds of English questions are formed by moving the Auxiliary to the front of the sentence, and an understanding of the structure of the sentence is needed in order to move the Auxiliary in the correct way. Since English speakers know how to make questions, they must have a knowledge of the structure of sentences, and Chomsky has argued that the principle of structure-dependency applies to all languages. Indeed this principle is said to characterize the human mind, and to be one of many principles that children bring to the task of language learning. Structure-dependency is not something that children have to learn since it is built into their minds from the beginning. Children come to the task of language learning "expecting" (unconsciously, of course) that the language will have structure-dependency. Linguists who follow an I-language approach want to understand the principles that lie behind all languages. They investigate particular languages as a means of learning about these principles, but they are more interested in constructing a theory of language in general than a theory of how some particular language works.

But languages also differ from one another, and even an I-language approach must grapple with the way in which children learn the particular characteristics of one particular language. To deal with the differences, Chomsky proposes that our minds are provided with something that he calls **parameters** and that act rather like switches. The parameters must be set to conform to the particular language that a child learns to speak. For example, some languages, such as English and French, require every sentence to have a subject. Other languages, such as Spanish and Italian, allow a pronoun subject to be omitted or "dropped." Languages like Spanish are called "Pro-drop" languages. To account for the difference between Spanish and English, the mind is described as having a **Pro-drop parameter** that can be set in either of two ways. Children learning Spanish must have their pro-drop parameter set to the pro-drop position, while children learning English must have theirs set to non-pro-drop. Much attention has been paid to the kind of evidence that children would need in order to get their parameters set correctly. The presumption has been that there are a relatively limited number of parameters (though the specific number has been left vague) and that they are capable of being set by the limited evidence available to children. It has also been presumed that the parameters have pervasive effects as they lay down the patterns of the language, so that a particular setting for pro-drop, for example, should provide not only for whether or not pronouns can be dropped, but for other associated features of the language as well.

This view of language and of the way that particular languages are learned has been called the "principles and parameters" approach. The principles lay down universal constraints to which all languages must conform. The parameters provide for the differences among languages. Principles and parameters are properties of the mind. All languages must conform to the principles, and each language must conform to its particular parameter settings, but linguists who are interested primarily in I-language study languages as much to get an insight into the mind, and into its principles and parameters, as to gain an understanding of particular languages or particular rules.

The implication of Chomsky's teaching is that a great deal of language is built into our minds so that it does not have to be learned at all. In particular, the core of syntax is felt to result from the inherited nature of the human mind. Languages do differ from one another, and the particular characteristics of each language need to be learned by each individual child, but to Chomsky and to his students the universalities of language have always seemed most interesting. If our goal is to use language as a means by which we can discover something about the nature of the human mind, then it is the universals of language that seem to deserve the closest study.

Whatever is universal must be exemplified in every language, so it makes no theoretical difference what language we investigate, but in practical life, it is easiest to investigate one's own language. Linguists can penetrate to the deepest levels only in a language they control easily. It may even be difficult to offer subtle judgments about grammaticality in any language except one's own native language. Since Chomsky and the largest number of his students have been native speakers of English, extensive attention has been directed toward an ever deeper investigation of English syntax. The hope of ferreting out the deepest principles of universal grammar has lead many linguists to peer into their own minds and to try to understand their own linguistic competence. As more and more abstract patterns are found, many people working in this area have become increasingly convinced that the patterns they are discovering could not possibly be learned, and that they can be explained only on the basis of inborn human nature.

DOUBTS AND RESERVATIONS

Chomsky has always argued for his proposals with great rhetorical force, and he has never held back from a vigorous attack on those whom he perceives to hold opposing, or incorrect, views. In concluding this chapter, therefore, it is only fair to let the opponents have a word, for however influential Chomsky has been, a good many linguists remain unconvinced by some of his proposals, particularly by the more recent proposals that were sketched in the previous section.

Some linguists, for example, feel uncomfortable by what appears to be Chomsky's willingness to "explain" linguistic regularities by attributing them to our genetic inheritance. Perhaps this explains one mystery, language, only by means of an even greater mystery, the mind. As a metaphor for how the mind works, principles and parameters seem appealing though not particularly dramatic. They are one way of describing what we have known all along, that languages are alike in some ways but systematically varied in others. As a realistic description of the circuitry of the brain, on the other hand, principles and parameters are certainly dramatic, but in the absence of any serious knowledge of neuron circuitry, they are very far from persuasive.

Since we have no independent way of delving into anyone's mind or brain to find out whether it contains any close analog to the mechanisms that Chomsky proposes, we have no empirical way to test claims for the way in which linguistic phenomena depend on our inherited human nature. To some linguists, this makes the claims seem quite empty. Few people would deny that, in some loose sense, the mind is responsible for language, but insisting on the importance of human nature does not seem to tell us very much about either language or the mind. Worse, if we are content to "explain" so much by the mind, we may fail to look for or to recognize other kinds of explanations.

We can certainly imagine factors other than genetic inheritance that might constrain the form of language. The social system in which language is used, or the requirements of information exchange, or the legacy of historical change could all have some bearing on the patterns of syntax. Even the broader linguistic context may be more significant than is sometimes acknowledged by those who focus their attention on the structure of single sentences. If we focus too hard on constructing a grammar that generates sentences, we may miss the ways in which sentences are dependent on and influence each other within a larger discourse.

Nor are these "alternative" explanations in any way incompatible with a belief in the importance of the mind and in genetic inheritance. To say that the form of the human leg is genetically determined does not make it less true that the form of the leg is functionally appropriate for moving an animal of our size in a gravitational field like that of the earth. We would even expect that natural selection would result in animals that inherit functionally appropriate legs. In exactly the same way, we ought to expect natural selection to result in an animal with a mind that produces functionally adaptive language. We can agree that the form of language is constrained, even determined to some degree, by the inherited nature of the human mind, but too much insistence on genetic inheritance, when we know so little about its bearing on language, may be an unfortunate way of ending a discussion. Rather than explaining something, it may stop us from looking for other, complementary, kinds of explanations. Why, when there is no incompatibility between genetic and functional explanations, and when so few people dispute the significance of the brain for language, has the insistence on genetic inheritance been so shrill?

Some linguists have also been disturbed by the willingness of many formal syntacticians to limit their studies to their own languages. In the last few years Chomskyan linguists have shown a refreshing interest in a wider variety of languages, but for most of the years of Chomsky's influence, those most closely associated with him have felt confident that anything found universally will certainly be found in their own language. This has justified a concentration on the native language of the linguist, often English. Linguists who have been most interested in linguistic typology, on the other hand, have always found it essential to investigate a wide variety of languages before claiming some trait as universal.

Generative linguists have replied to the charge of looking at too few languages, by pointing out the risk that linguists who look at many languages must inevitably restrict themselves to relatively superficial features of those languages. An occasional generative linguist has even heaped scorn on other linguists who insist on "butterfly collecting" among the exotic languages of the world. Getting past the surface structure and penetrating to the more profound levels of language, they have argued, requires a deeper, even native, ability. To some other linguists, however, the generative focus on "deep structure" has gone too far. "Deep" suggests "important," as if the "mere" surface structure does not matter very much, as if only those linguists who attend to deep structure are pursuing the truly "profound" aspects of language. But all that any linguist can hear is the surface structure; the deep structure can be known only by inference. Linguists have always proposed abstractions that can be used to explain what we hear. Even the thoroughly pre-Chomskyan phoneme exists at a "deeper" level than more "surface" phonetics. Nevertheless, there is room for sharp differences of opinion about the most appropriate "depth" to work, and some non-Chomskyans find the surface structure more real and more revealing than any hypothetical deep structure. Some warn against forgetting the surface structure in the search for a "depth" that may, after all, be nothing more than the invention of the linguist.

Even the insistence on the importance of universals that has characterized much of generative linguistics has seemed one-sided to some linguists. The commonsense view would seem to be that languages share some features but differ in others. The attitude taken in this book is that we should be interested in both similarities and differences. Of course, Chomskyans recognize differences. Languages are not all exactly alike. Their vocabularies, for example, differ in all sorts of ways, and recent generative linguistics has turned increasing attention to the lexicon. Still, there has been an insistence on a high degree of universality, and this may stem from a special view of what is important, or what is central to language. Why has it been taken for granted by Chomsky and his students that syntax is the central component of language? Chomsky has even argued that some aspects of syntax are more central than others. He has used the terms **core** and **periphery** to distinguish different parts of the syntax. It is the core that is subject to the universal constraints of the principles and to the variability provided by the parameters. The periphery is acknowledged to contain all sorts of irregularities that are not laid down by universal grammar and that the individual simply has to learn. The periphery may show the distorting effects of linguistic history and of irregularities that come from borrowing from other languages. Is there a danger that whenever linguists encounter data that fail to fit their preconceptions of universal grammar, they can simply label that data as part of the periphery? To the skeptics, it does not seem particularly impressive to discover "universals" if the nonuniversal features of the language can be so easily dismissed as irrelevant by tossing them into the periphery.

Finally, Chomsky's focus on the problem of language acquisition sits uneasily with the kinds of evidence that he recognizes. Being concerned with I-language, Chomsky relies on judgments of grammaticality for his evidence rather than on what is actually said in conversation. Yet small children cannot be persuaded to give judgments about the grammaticality of sentences. Chomsky has recognized this clearly, for he has described the problem of language acquisition as a "logical problem" and not as something that can be solved by watching children. In order to study children's language empirically, it is necessary to listen to what they say, but this is E-language, not the internalized knowledge of language that Chomsky seeks to understand. To some linguists this puts Chomsky's pronouncements about children a very long way from the real chattering world in which children live.

This has been a long list of topics about which linguists differ. Should we be dismayed at the differences of opinion? To many linguists it is disputes like these that make their field so exciting, but the disagreements do mean that linguists have very different ideas about how to go about their business. Should they concentrate on investigating one language in as much detail as possible, or should they look at the widest possible variety of languages? Should they be most interested in the similarities among languages or in their differences? Should they seek explanations in biology, in human psychology, in human society, in history, in the logic of communication, or are there still other places to look? Those questions will be answered only as every method and every idea is tested by experiment in the decades ahead.

The next two chapters of this book will approach syntax from a functional and typological perspective rather than from Chomsky's. The assumptions made in these chapters and the questions they raise are often different from those of more formal syntacticians. We will be as interested in the differences among languages as in their similarities. We will not be content to call something universal without looking at many different languages. We will ask what functions syntax fills, and we will ask how syntax is constrained by conversational needs. In all these ways, the discussion will be distinguished from orthodox generative linguistics. It is important, however, to recognize the pervasive influence of generative grammar. Chomsky's arguments have brought a wonderful ferment to linguistics and have led us to ask a host of interesting new questions about language. Few of the questions that any syntactician asks today could have been asked with the same degree of clarity had Chomsky not so dramatically reoriented our view of the subject. The decades since Chomsky's influence first began to be felt have given us a far more extensive knowledge of syntactic patterns than we ever had before. Even linguists, who do not identify themselves, self-consciously, as "generative linguists," owe a great deal to Chomsky's ideas.

CHAPTER TEN

The Functions of Syntax

INTRODUCTION

Students who first embark on the study of a foreign language often find its organization to be surprisingly strange. The syntax, in particular, can seem almost unreasonably different from the familiar syntax of one's native language. Syntax does have important jobs to do, important functions to perform, but these are complex functions that require complex solutions, and they can be accomplished in many different ways. Each language, to some extent, supplies its own set of solutions. At the same time the needs that must be met by syntax are much the same everywhere, and these common needs also impose common patterns on the syntax of all languages. The purpose of this chapter is to suggest a few of the tasks that syntax must accomplish and to explore a few of the varied means by which these needs can be met.

We can start with a simple example. In Turkish, *My son threw the stone at that big dog* can be said in the following way: (D.O. means direct object; I.O., indirect object; Sub., subject; Loc., locative.)

Oğlu-m	*taş-ı*	*o*	*büyük*	*köpeğ-e*	*at-tı.*
Son-my	stone-D.O.	that	big	dog-I.O.	throw-3p.past

The same meaning can be expressed in colloquial Arabic of southern Lebanon as:

Rama	*ibn-i*	*l'-ḥaǰar*	*ʕa*	*ḥal'-kalb*	*al-kabir.*
Threw	son-my	the-stone	at	that/the-dog	the-big

Halfway around the world, the same idea can be put into Tagalog, the most widespread language of the Philippines, as:

Tinapon	*nang*	*anak*	*ko*	*ang*	*bato*	*sa*	*malaki-ng*	*aso.*
Threw	by	child	my	Sub.	stone	Loc.	big	dog

Whether these sentences strike us as surprisingly different from English or surprisingly similar depends largely on our point of view. Of course the particular words are different. We expect each language to have its own words to refer to a domestic canine and to a throwable piece of a common hard mineral. It is only slightly more surprising to find that the words of one language cannot always be directly translated into the words of another. Like most languages, these three have straightforward equivalents of *stone, dog,* and *throw,* but it is more normal in Tagalog to say 'my child' than 'my son.' To make the child's sex explicit would require several additional words. More abstract concepts are less likely to be expressed by closely equivalent words than are the concrete ideas of this sentence.

The differences in word order may seem more striking. The verb comes last in Turkish but first both in this Arabic sentence and in Tagalog. In all three languages, the possessive 'my' happens to come after the word for 'son' or 'child,' but 'big' comes before 'dog' in Turkish and after 'dog' in Arabic. In Tagalog the adjective can come either before the noun or after it, but -*ng* is always suffixed to the first word of the pair. Thus 'big dog' could be expressed as *asong malaki* as easily as *malaking aso.* In either case, the -*ng* links the two words together.

Perhaps the greatest differences among the languages lie in the bits that tie the major words together. In Turkish, the suffixes -*ı* and -*e* keep the missile safely distinguished from the target. Their role is similar to that of English prepositions, but they follow the noun instead of precede it. Arabic has a preposition *ʕa* that shows where the stone is going. Tagalog also has three particles, *nang, ang,* and *sa,* that are similar to prepositions, and that indicate the role of each noun in the sentence. In Arabic, both the noun *kalb* 'dog' and the adjective *kabir* 'big' are coupled with articles that mean, approximately, 'the.' Tagalog has no explicit translation for 'the,' but *bato* 'stone' is the subject of the sentence (as shown by the *ang* that precedes it), and this implies a definite meaning equivalent to that conferred by English *the.* The verbs in all three languages show the tense to be past, but they do so in different ways. The Turkish suffix -*ti* indicates both past tense and a third person singular subject. In Arabic it is the *absence* of any prefix or suffix that shows both third person and past tense. For other tenses and other subjects affixes would have to be attached to the verb. The Tagalog verb tells us nothing about the person or number of its subject, but it does show something about time. The root of the Tagalog verb, 'throw,' is *tapon* and the -*in*-, which is inserted into the middle of the verb, shows that the action has been completed.

If our first reaction to sentences like these is to be surprised at their differences, we must, on second thought, be almost as impressed by their similarities. To be sure, not everything that people talk about is as universal in human experience as the things referred to in this particular sentence. Stones, children, and dogs are found almost everywhere, and everyone past infancy can throw. Other similarities among these sentences may seem more noteworthy. Like English, all these languages have verbs. The meaning of 'throw' is, in every case, conveyed by a verb, and the markers of past time are always attached to it. All the languages have either function words or affixes that act like English prepositions, but these sometimes come after the noun and sometimes before it. In these three languages, as in all other natural human languages, words with coherent meanings combine into sentences. Everywhere simple sentences can be formed by combining a verb such as *throw*, with varying numbers of nouns, such as *rock*, *child* and *dog*, or with noun phrases such as *my son* and *that big dog*.

Languages have more subtle syntactic similarities than can be shown by simple sentences like these, but even this example is enough to suggest that all languages are built on a similar ground plan. One goal of linguistics is to chart the degree to which languages are similar and the degree to which they vary, and we can begin to understand the range of syntactic variation by considering the way in which simple sentences are formed.

NOUNS AND VERBS

A strategic starting place is with "nouns" and "verbs." Linguists believe that all languages have some words that can be reasonably called nouns and others that can be reasonably called verbs. They believe, moreover, that this amounts to an empirical claim about the nature of language, and that it is not merely a consequence of the way we define the terms.

Most of us were told in school that a noun stands for "a person, place, or thing" and that a verb stands for some sort of "action." This attributes the difference to the words' meanings, but meaning is not always a reliable guide. The word *explosion* seems to refer to an action rather than to a "thing" but no one would call it a verb. To understand why *explosion* is a noun we must appeal to the formal differences between nouns and verbs rather than to their semantic differences, and the most obvious formal distinction lies in the kinds of suffixes that each type of word takes. If a word can take plural and possessive suffixes (*boys, boy's, explosions*) we call it a noun. Words that can take past tense and third person singular suffixes (*walked, walks*) are called verbs. Using suffixes to distinguish parts of speech gives us a useful classification of English words. The classification is confirmed as a significant one as soon as we notice that the words we have called nouns and verbs on the basis of their affixes, also combine with other words in differing ways. Only the nouns, for example, can be preceded by adjectives and by articles: *a little boy, the brown cow, the terrible explosion* but not **the big believe* or **a red eat*. Only the verbs can be used with auxiliary verbs: *can believe, will eat* but not **can cow, *will boy*, or **must explosion*.

The study of English parts of speech is made complex by our ability to use a very large number of words as either a noun or a verb. In *The fire blazed cheerfully*, the word *fire* is a noun, but in *She fired up the furnace*, we use it easily as a verb. The following sentences testify to the freedom with which

English words can act as nouns (marked *n*) on one occasion and verbs (*v*) on another: *He slices(v) off two slices(n). They are manning(v) the ships(n). The men(n) shipped(v) the hammers(n). We hammer(v) the nails(n). She nails(v) the shingles(n). They shingle(v) the roof.* We can decide whether *slice, man, ship, hammer, nail,* and *shingle* are nouns or verbs only by the way they are used in particular examples. If we considered only meaning, we would not know how to classify them.

Meaning cannot be ignored, however. Although defined on formal grounds, nouns and verbs often do turn out to have their own characteristic kinds of meanings. In general, the English words that we call nouns (because they can be used with plurals, etc.) name relatively enduring phenomena. Prototypical nouns are names for concrete objects that survive through time: *rock, tree, book, child, horse.* Prototypical "verbs" name more transient phenomena, actions that quickly pass: *run, sit, fall.* English adjectives frequently name phenomena of intermediate duration: *red, hot, deep.* Duration is not always a reliable criterion for a word's part of speech. Many *sparks(n)* can occur in the time that the earth *revolves(v).* The tendency still seems clear.

The particular formal (as opposed to semantic) criteria by which we distinguish English "nouns" and "verbs" is specific to English, of course. It is based on English suffixes and English words. If parts of speech are defined by formal criteria like these, they will need different definitions for each language, and it could turn out that different languages would have quite different parts of speech. It was pointed out in Chapter 3 that some languages lack a distinct class of adjectives, for example, and that the meanings that English expresses by adjectives are expressed in some languages, such as Garo, by verbs.

In every language, however, we do seem to find at least two major classes of words that can be formally defined by the differing constructions into which they enter. More surprisingly, perhaps, we also find that all other languages assign words to these classes in much the same way as does English. One major class always seems to include words that are used for tangible and relatively enduring phenomena, such as *rock, sky, house, child,* and *water,* and it seems reasonable to call these nouns. A second major class always has words that refer to more transient phenomena such as *run, see, hit, wash,* and *give,* and we can call these words verbs. The claim that the noun/verb distinction is found in all languages, then, is an empirical one. It is based on the observation of many languages. Nevertheless, it is not the case that every single meaning is assigned in the same way everywhere. In some cases, meanings that are conveyed by nouns in one language are conveyed by verbs in another. We consider the English word *night* to be a noun, not because it refers to a "thing," which seems debatable, but because it takes noun suffixes and can be used in noun phrases. In Garo, the word that is closest in meaning to English "night" can be classed as a verb because it takes the same tense suffixes as other Garo verbs. It is not an accident that meanings like that of *night* are classified differently by different languages. The meaning of *night* is neither prototypically noun-like nor prototypically verb-like. It is neither an enduring physical object like a *rock* nor a fleeting action like *run*, but something in between. This makes it possible to group it with either class of words, and different languages assign it differently.

SENTENCE PATTERNS: THE GROUND PLAN

The syntax of a language must show how the words of a sentence are related to each other. Languages do not accomplish this task in exactly the same way, but the needs everywhere are enough alike to allow comparisons. One sentence pattern that is common in all languages consists of a single main verb together with one or more associated nouns or noun phrases, and this means every language needs ways that show how the nouns of a sentence are related to the verb. This section will explore some of the means by which this is accomplished.

In English, Turkish, Arabic, and Tagalog, a verb meaning 'throw' can be associated with nouns meaning 'son,' 'stone,' and 'dog' to form the sentences with which this chapter began. These sentences happen to have three noun phrases, but other sentences have more phrases or fewer. The number of noun phrases in a sentence is set, in part, by the verb of the sentence. All languages have some verbs that require only a single noun phrase. We call such verbs **intransitive.** *The man sleeps, The children cried*, and *Dogs bark* have intransitive verbs and just one noun phrase. Sentences like these can often be translated quite directly into other languages, although the word order may need to change, and various grammatical bits and pieces may be needed to complete the sentence. In addition to their nouns and verbs, for instance, these English sentences have several suffixes, the plural *-s*, the past tense *-ed* and the third person singular *-s*, as well as the article *the*. We call the noun phrase that is used with these intransitive verbs the **subject** of the sentence.

Some verbs in all languages require at least two nouns or noun phrases. We call these verbs **transitive,** and they require slightly more complex sentences than do intransitives. *The chimpanzee heard the snake, The boy washed the dishes*, and *The hardy axe-man chops the wood* are formed with the transitive verbs (*hear, chase,* and *chop*) that require two nouns or noun phrases. Once again, all languages have sentences that are constructed around transitive verbs. We give the name **object** to the second noun that is associated with transitive verbs.

It is less easy than might be supposed to find unambiguous criteria by which to decide which of two noun phrases is the subject and which is the object. In English, and in many other European languages, the subject is usually easy to identify because the subject is the noun phrase with which the verb agrees. For instance, the choice among *am, is,* and *are* depends on the subject. No such criterion is available in languages that lack verb agreement but, in practice, we generally find that sentences in all languages have noun phrases that are used in similar enough ways to the subjects of familiar European languages to invite us to call them subjects. Subjects are often the agents who perform the action represented by the verb. Objects tend to be the recipients of the action.

Languages differ in the order in which their subjects, objects, and verbs usually occur. In English the subject comes before the verb and the object follows, giving subject-verb-object or "SVO" order. Many other languages have quite different word orders. They are not always so fixed as in English, but it is usually possible to identify a single most common or "basic" order for each language. In particular, some languages place the verb first in the sentence, while others place it last. Since in almost all languages the subject usually comes before the object, the most common basic word orders in the languages of the world are Verb-Subject-Object (VSO) as in Gaelic, Tagalog, and some varieties of Arabic, Subject-Verb-Object (SVO) as in English and Chinese, and Subject-Object-Verb (SOV) as in Japanese, Hindi, and Turkish. Languages with customary VOS, OVS, and OSV word orders are much less common.

A sentence with two noun phrases poses a problem that sentences with just one noun phrase escape. The hearer needs to be shown which noun is which. In a sentence like *The cat chased the dog,* the hearer must be able to understand who is doing the chasing and who is being chased. We manage this in English primarily with word order. The chaser must be placed before the verb, and the one who is chased must follow. This seems easy and natural to an English speaker, but it requires a rigid word order that many languages lack.

When the subject and object are on the same side of the verb, as in VSO and SOV languages, word order offers a less secure means of keeping the subject and object distinct than in languages where the verb comes between them. If VSO or SOV order were rigidly adhered to, word order might still be able to do the job, but VSO and SOV languages generally allow more word-order flexibility than we are accustomed to in English. Typically, a language with SOV as its most common or basic word order allows OSV as an alternative, and this makes it essential to have some means, other than word order, that will keep the subject and object safely distinguished. There are two ways to manage this.

The most straightforward method is to attach some sort of mark to one or both of the noun phrases and let the marks indicate the roles of the noun phrases. When such marks are joined to the nouns as affixes, they are usually called **case** markers, and many languages, including Russian and Latin, mark their nouns with case markers. These let the listener know which noun to interpret as the subject of the sentence and which as object.

The suffix *-ı* that is attached to the word *taş-ı* 'stone,' in the Turkish sentence given earlier, is a case marker that shows that *taş* is the direct object of the verb. Similarly, the suffix *-e* of *köpeğ-e* 'dog' shows that its word is an indirect object, the recipient of the action. English has a remnant of a case system in the difference between the subjective and objective forms of some of our pronouns: *I/me, he/him, we/us,* etc. These allow us to make plausible guesses about meaning even when the usual word order of English is abandoned: *He me saw, Saw me he, Him saw I, I him saw.* In many languages, the normal method of distinguishing subjects from objects is to mark the noun phrases in some such way as this.

Even languages in which the verb usually comes between the subject and object may allow freer word order than does English. The most common Russian word order is SVO, exactly as in English, but Russian has a well-developed case system so that its word order can be more flexible. For example, the most straightforward Russian translation of *Tanya chose Masha* is:

Tanja vybrala Maſu.

Tanja has the nominative (subject) suffix *-a,* while *Maſu* has the accusative (object) suffix *-u.* It is these case suffixes, rather than the word order, that tells the listener who did the choosing and who was chosen. The case suffixes allow the words to be reordered without changing the basic meaning. In fact, the three words of this Russian sentence can be arranged in any of their six logically possible orders without obscuring the central fact of who chose whom. If however, the case markers are reversed, the meaning will be reversed even if the word order stays the same.

Tanju vybrala Maſa.
'Masha chose Tanya.'

Word-order changes do not leave the meaning untouched, however, for the emphasis shifts. Russian word order can be used to convey some of the subtleties that we convey in English by the way we place emphatic stress. Thus, in answer to the question *Who chose Masha?,* an English speaker might say *Tánya chose Masha* with stress on *Tánya.* A Russian could give the same emphasis to *Tanja* that we give with heavy stress, by changing the word order: *Maſu vybrala Tanja.* This moves the subject, which is still safely marked as the subject by the suffix *-a,* to a somewhat less common position in the sentence. In this way it is made to stand out, much as stress makes a word stand out in English. Word order, then, can be used to accomplish two quite different tasks. All languages have ways to show who it is who chases, bites, or chooses, and who is chased, bitten, or chosen. All languages also have ways to direct attention to one or another part of the sentence. English needs word order to identify the participants; Russian is freer to use word order to direct attention.

Word order and case marking give alternative means by which subject and object can be distinguished, and there is a third means of achieving the same end. This is to mark the verb so that it points to one or both of the noun phrases, and indicates which roles these noun phrases have in the sentence. Pointing to a noun phrase as a subject or an object is one of the functions of verb **agreement.** In many European languages, the verb must agree with the subject in both person and number, so that if the subject is third person and plural (e.g., *they, the alligators*) the verb must also be marked as third person and plural. English has a remnant of verb agreement in the verb suffix *-s.* We add *-s* to a verb only when it has a third person singular subject *she, a boy, the robin,* etc.: *The robin eat-s the worm,* but *The robins eat the worm.* If English had a less rigid word order, we would understand *robin* to be the subject of *eats* in *Eats the robin the worms* or even *The worms eats the robin* because *eats* requires a singular subject. *Eats* points to *robin,* not to *worms.* If person markers attached to the verb point effectively to the noun phrases and show their roles in the sentence, then the person markers can supplement, or even replace, word order and case marking.

In some languages verbs carry markers not only for subject agreement but for object agreement as well. Swahili, a widespread Bantu language of East Africa, is such a language, and it provides a good illustration of a complex agreement system that effectively shows the relationships between the verb and its noun phrases. Consider these four sentences:

Mimi   *ni-na-i-taka*   *nazi.*
I   I-pres.-it-want   coconut
'I want the coconut.'

Mimi   *ni-na-ya-taka*   *maembe.*
I   I-pres.-them-want   mangoes
'I want the mangoes.'

Yeye   *a-na-zi-taka*   *ndizi.*
He   he-pres.-them-want   bananas
'He wants the bananas.'

Yeye   *a-na-u-vunja*   *mlango.*
He   he-pres.-it-break   door
'He is breaking the door.'

Each verb in these Swahili sentences has three prefixes. The first agrees with the subject. The second (-*na*- in all these sentences) is a tense marker for present time. The third agrees with the object. The first and third prefixes, then, are agreement markers that point, respectively, to the subject and object of the sentence. They must agree in person, in number, and in what is known as "noun class." The illustrative sentences have examples of just two of several subject markers: *ni*- 'first person singular subject,' (I), and *a*- 'third person singular subject,' (he). These resemble the person markers that are suffixed to the verbs of many European languages.

While object markers are less familiar to speakers of European languages, those in Swahili work in a similar way to subject markers. The main complication is a result of the noun classes. Swahili nouns fall into a half dozen different classes. These differ from each other in several ways, but the important point here is that each class calls for a different set of subject and object agreement markers on the verb. -*i*- and -*u*- are singular object agreement markers for the noun classes to which 'coconut' and 'door' belong. -*ya*- and -*zi*- are plural object agreement markers for the noun classes to which 'mangoes' and 'bananas' belong. Hearing -*zi*- prefixed to the verb, a Swahili speaker knows that the object has to be plural and that it is a member of a particular class. The only possible noun in the third sentence that could be the object, then, is *ndizi* 'bananas.' By attending to the agreement markers, Swahili speakers can rarely be in doubt about what is the subject and what is the object of the sentences that they hear.

English word order, Russian case marking, and Swahili verb agreement illustrate three alternative methods by which subjects can be distinguished from objects. Some method of distinguishing subject and object is essential, but one method does not seem to have a clear advantage over the others. As the number of noun phrases in a sentence increases, however, the problem of distinguishing them from one another grows more acute, and word order and verb agreement both become less reliable. Even in English we must often resort to other techniques than word order when a sentence has more than two noun phrases. English verbs like *give* or *offer* generally require an indirect object in addition to the subject and direct object. In *I gave Miriam the squid* we continue to rely on word order to distinguish the recipient (*Miriam*) from the thing that is given (*squid*). We can also say *I gave the squid to Miriam*, but as soon as we reorder the objects in this way, we need to mark the second, or "indirect" object, with the preposition *to*. In this way we show that the noun phrases have been switched, and that we are not feeding *Miriam* to the *squid*. *To* marks the indirect object, the recipient of the gift. Like a Russian case marker, *to* shows the role of its noun phrase, and it gives English speakers a certain amount of freedom to vary the word order.

Intransitive verbs like *sit, die,* and *walk* require only one noun phrase; transitive verbs like *chase, hit,* and *choose* require two noun phrases; a few verbs such as *give, offer,* and *show* are typically used with three noun phrases. In addition to their required noun phrases, most verbs also permit additional optional noun phrases. Important among these are **locatives** that locate the action of the verb in time or space: *in the ball park, among the daffodils, on Tuesday, after the party.* As the number of noun phrases increases, verb agreement and word order are no longer enough to keep them distinct, and we make the role of most English locative noun phrases clear by marking them with prepositions such as *in, among, on, after.*

Every language has either **prepositions** that are placed at the beginning of noun phrases, or **postpositions** that are placed at the end. The term **adpositions** is used to cover both prepositions and postpositions. Like case markers, adpositions help to indicate the role that their noun phrases play in the sentence. It is not always easy to distinguish adpositions from case markers, but generally the term case markers is used for relatively small sets of markers, often for those that are attached firmly to their nouns or pronouns as affixes, and that indicate major roles in the sentence such as subject and object. The word adpositions is used for larger sets of words that have a bit more independence and that show more specific meanings, such as location in time or space. Not all languages have anything that we would want to call case markers, but all have adpositions—either prepositions or postpositions. Cases and adpositions both help to show the role that their noun phrases play in the sentence.

In summary, all languages have simple sentences consisting of a verb and varying numbers of associated noun phrases. Word order and verb agreement markers can help to show the role of the noun phrases, and noun phrases are sometimes marked by either case markers or adpositions as well. Examples could be drawn from every language in the world. The following sentences from five languages show this universal pattern, but they also demonstrate some of the varying orders that the words and their affixes can assume within their sentences.

Turkish:
Hasan   öküz-ü   aldı.
Hasan   ox-object   bought
'Hasan bought the ox.'
Welsh:
Lladdodd   y   ddraig   y   dyn.
killed   the   dragon   the   duckling
'The dragon killed the duckling.'
Garo (Eastern India):
Anga   biskut-ko   biʔsa-na   roʔn-a.
I   biscuit-object   child-to   give
'I give the biscuit to the child.'
Bemba (Southern Africa):
Umuana   a-a-lya   umukate   ne-ecimuti.
child   he-past-eat   bread   with-stick
'The child ate (the) bread with a/the stick.'
Chinese:
Wŏ   bă   zhuāngzi   dă-pò   le.
I   object   window   break   past
'I broke the window(s).'

SYNTACTIC AND SEMANTIC ROLES

Each noun phrase has its place in the syntax of its sentence, but each also conveys a meaning. It is useful to distinguish between what we can call the **syntactic role** of a noun phrase and its **semantic role**. The difference can be illustrated by sentences like the following, all of which are formed with the same verb but with differing arrays of noun phrases:

The men break the window with a hammer.
The hammer breaks the window.
The window breaks.

First, consider the ways in which these sentences differ. Each has a different subject, *men, hammer,* and *window,* respectively. The subjects are easy to identify, primarily because of the firm English rule that requires the subject to precede the verb, but verb agreement supports this identification. *Men* requires a plural verb, while *hammer* and *window* both require singular verbs. In the first and second sentences *break* must be considered transitive, since it is followed by an object, *window,* but in the third sentence, *break* has no object, so it counts as intransitive. In the first sentence, the preposition *with* is used along with *hammer* to form a prepositional phrase, *with a hammer,* but no prepositional phrase is found in either the second or the third sentence.

These are traditional, and accurate, ways of describing these three sentences, and they point to some obvious differences among them. At the same time, some equally important similarities have been missed. It is always the *window* that shatters. Where it is mentioned, it is always the *hammer* that comes into contact with the glass. In the only example where the *men* are mentioned, it is they who wield the hammer. When we point out that the three nouns of these sentences appear variously as "subject," "object," and "prepositional phrase," we risk losing sight of this deeper consistency. We need ways to refer both to the similarities among these sentences and to their differences.

The term **semantic role** can be used to describe the consistent sense that these noun phrases carry. We will say that *men* has the semantic role of **Agent** in the first sentence, that *hammer* has the semantic role of **Instrument** in both the first and second sentences, and that *window* has the semantic role of **Patient** in all three sentences. The nouns keep their semantic roles in the three sentences, but they fill the different **syntactic roles** of "subject," "object," and "prepositional phrase." By distinguishing semantic roles from syntactic roles, we make it possible to talk about both the similarities and the differences among the noun phrases of sentences such as these.

English has scores of verbs like *break* that can be used with the semantic roles of Agent, Patient, and Instrument: *shatter, split, dissolve, connect, open, close,* and many others. A bit of experimentation will show that all these verbs share with *break* the ability to form three kinds of sentences, each with a different constellation of semantic roles: *Florence opened the door with a key, The key opened the door, The door opened; The chemist dissolved the zircon in the acid, The acid dissolved the zircon, The zircon dissolved.* With these verbs, an Agent and an Instrument are both optional, but a Patient is always required.

How does a speaker decide which semantic roles to assign to the syntactic roles of subject, object, and prepositional phrase? In the case of these verbs, the rules are clear. When all three semantic roles are expressed, the Agent is always put into the subject. Indeed, the Agent can be regarded as a kind of ideal, or prototypical, subject. If there is an Instrument but no Agent, the Instrument becomes the subject. English has a strict requirement that every sentence must be provided with a subject, and a sentence with no semantic role except Patient must have the Patient as its subject.

Other sets of verbs require, or allow, other constellations of semantic roles. Verbs such as *put, set, place, lay* may have an Agent and a Patient, but they also require some sort of Locative, as in *Melody put the book on the table,* where *Melody* is the Agent, *book* is the Patient, and *on the table* is a Locative that shows where the Patient is *put.* Sentences with verbs like *put* can, optionally, include an Instrument, as in *Melody set the red hot iron onto the anvil with the tongs,* but it is awkward to omit the Agent and move the Instrument into subject position. Unless we are deliberately suggesting that these are magic tongs with a will of their own, **The tongs set the red hot iron onto the anvil* is of doubtful acceptability, though it is no less logical than *The key opened the door* or *The hammer broke the window.* It is simply an odd characteristic of English that verbs like *put* generally require animate subjects (human or animal), while verbs like *open* and *break* can easily take inanimate Instrumental subjects (such as *key* or *hammer*) as well. The classification of verbs by their semantic roles will be considered further in the next chapter.

We will avoid confusion if we reserve the words "subject" and "object" for syntactic roles that are defined by syntactic patterns, in particular by word order and verb agreement. Terms like "Agent," "Patient," and "Instrument" will be reserved for semantic roles. The traditional grammatical terms "nominative" and "accusative" are best reserved for still another distinction, that of **case.** The term case will be used only for languages in which the nouns or pronouns change their form in some way, generally either by affixing a case marker or by a more radical alteration such as the change from *I* to *me.* Case marking is one means (others are word order and verb agreement) by which a listener can identify the subject and object of a sentence and know which noun phrase stands for the Agent, Patient, and the other semantic roles. Case distinctions are closely related both to syntactic roles and to semantic roles, but they are not identical to either, and a separate word is needed for them.

Cases, syntactic roles, and semantic roles are easily confused with each other because both cases (e.g., nominative, accusative) and syntactic roles (e.g., subject, object) are used as a means of signaling the semantic roles of their noun phrases. The nominative case is typically used for the subject of a sentence. In English we can frequently identify the Agent of a sentence because of its subject position, and in some languages, a clearly marked nominative case will identify a noun as the subject and as the Agent. Similarly the accusative case is typically used for the object of a sentence, and objects are frequently the Patient. If case, syntactic role, and semantic role always corresponded (nominative = subject = Agent; accusative = object = Patient) we could avoid the triple terminology, but the correspondence is by no means exact. It is precisely because these three distinctions interact with each other in very complex ways that we need a terminology that will help us to keep them distinct.

English pronouns, for instance, have several different forms, so these forms deserve to be called "cases." *I* is nominative and *me* is accusative. Typically, *I* appears as the subject of a sentence, and *me* appears as the object. In addition, however, *me* and the other accusative pronouns (*him, her, us, them*) also serve as objects of prepositions (*with us, to me, beside her,* etc.). The concept of "case" allows us to point to the common features of *me, him,* etc., wherever they are used. The concept of syntactic role gives us a way to distinguish objects of verbs from objects of prepositions.

Agents often become the subjects of their sentences, but since other semantic roles sometimes replace the Agent, we must not fall into the trap of simply equating subjects and Agents. As the examples have shown, a Patient such as *door* can be used either as the object or subject of the verb *close*. An Instrument such as *key* can occur not only in a prepositional phrase but also as the subject of a sentence. Many of the intriguing complexities of languages, in fact, come from differing ways of reconciling case, syntactic role, and semantic role.

In summary then, we have three related concepts, and three sets of terms to stand for them. First, "case" is used when nouns or pronouns assume different forms. Languages with case systems may mark their cases by means of affixes or by more radical changes in the form of the word. Second, "syntactic role" refers to the syntactic relationship of nouns and noun phrases to other words in the sentence, in particular to the verb. Position before or after the verb is one obvious indicator of syntactic role, but others are verb agreement and the choice among adpositions. Third, "semantic role" refers to such concepts as Agent, Patient, and Instrument. Only by keeping these three distinct can their relationships to each other be made clear. We will want to ask which semantic roles are expressed by various syntactic roles and, in languages with cases, we will want to ask how the syntactic roles and the cases are related.

Linguists tend to assume that semantic roles are relatively uniform from language to language. Every language will surely need ways to let its speakers talk about Agents and Patients and Instruments. Is it possible, then, to identify a universal set of semantic roles? Certainly comparisons among languages would be made easier if we could recognize a set that is common to them all. Unfortunately it remains far from clear exactly which and how many such roles need to be distinguished. Agents, Patients, and Instruments seem to be needed everywhere, and many other semantic roles have also been proposed. In a sentence such as *I cooked the Peking duck for Tom, Tom* is sometimes considered a **Benefactive,** because *Tom* clearly benefits from my action (presuming that I have cooked well). An "Agent" is usually something that takes the initiative in performing the action, but what are *waves* in a sentence such as *The waves washed the shells onto the beach*? *Waves* can hardly take much initiative so they are not prototypical Agents, and yet they perform some rather Agent-like actions. One proposed solution is to assign *waves* to a new semantic role called **Force.**

Albert in *I gave the book to Albert* has sometimes been assigned the semantic role of **Recipient.** It is not always clear that Recipient needs to be distinguished from Benefactive, although *Benjamin wrote a letter to the Prime Minister for*

Joyce seems to have both. What about the semantic role of *Gertrude* in *Gertrude saw the pussy willow? Gertrude* is unquestionably the subject of this sentence but, since she is more acted on than acting, she is hardly an Agent. Perhaps *Gertrude* should be the Patient, or possibly even the Recipient. Or, perhaps a new semantic role is needed, that of **Experiencer.**

Noun phrases that locate events in time and space bring other complications. English noun phrases that are formed with prepositions such as *at, on, in, near, far from, on top of* might be grouped together as **Locatives,** but prepositions that show a fixed location might be distinguished from others that indicate something about the direction of motion, such as *toward* and *from.* Perhaps all these *spatial* Locatives should be distinguished from *temporal* Locatives formed with such prepositions as *until, since,* and *during.*

We face an uncomfortable degree of uncertainty here. How many semantic roles should be allowed? The sentences we considered that are formed with verbs like *break* and *close* convince us of the need for recognizing something like semantic roles, but linguists are far from any consensus about exactly which semantic roles are needed. We will return to the problems raised by semantic roles in the next chapter when we consider the classification of verbs.

PRAGMATICS: OLD AND NEW INFORMATION

If you are standing by a window with a friend who says *The bird is eating a worm,* she probably assumes that you are able to identify the bird. You may already have been talking about the bird, or perhaps your friend notices that you have been watching it. The worm, on the other hand, is presented as something new. Most likely it is entering the conversation for the first time, and perhaps your friend believes that you had not noticed it before. If you are already talking about a worm when a bird appears on the scene, your friend would be more likely to describe precisely the same visible event by saying *The worm is being eaten by a bird.* Now it is the worm that is being taken for granted and the bird that is being introduced as a new topic of conversation. The difference between *The bird is eating a worm* and *The worm is being eaten by a bird* has nothing to do with the objective situation of bird and worm. In both cases the worm disappears down the throat of the bird. Rather, the difference lies in what has been talked about previously, and in the speaker's expectation of what the hearer is already aware of.

As this simple example suggests, conversation requires us to do more than simply state objective facts about who does what and to whom. We must also present these facts in a clear and logical order. Even as we call attention to new information and to changes in topic, we also need to maintain continuity by referring back to what we have already said. We need to bring new information into the foreground while setting it in the context of familiar information. We need to give prominence to what is most important. The study of how we manage all this is one part of the branch of linguistics now known as

pragmatics. When considering Russian word order we touched on some pragmatic techniques, and we can now consider them more carefully.

One aspect of pragmatics that has received extensive attention is the way in which languages allow their speakers to distinguish between "new" and "old" information. As in the example of the *bird* and the *worm*, speakers are careful to distinguish information that they believe their hearer is already aware of from information they expect to come as new. Old information is always needed in order to give context to the new information, but the old information can often be put into the background so that the new information will stand out more clearly. Linguists have come to use the word **Topic** for the part of the sentence that is taken as given, often for information that is previously known. It is not the most fortunate choice of terms. "Topic" sounds as though it should stand for the central information of a sentence, but it has come to be used, instead, for the background information against which the new information is set. However infelicitous, there is no escape from this widely used term, and perhaps it can seem reasonable if the Topic is thought of as "what the sentence is about." A typical sentence states its Topic and then goes on to give some new information about that Topic. This added information is referred to as the **Comment.** The Topic, then, is what one makes a Comment about. "Topic" and "Comment," are **pragmatic roles** and they form a final pair of terms to be placed beside the other sets we have recognized: "nominative," "accusative," "dative," etc.; "subject," "object," "indirect object," etc.; "Agent," "Patient," "Instrument," etc. "Topic" and "Comment" give us a final way of distinguishing the roles played by the various parts of a sentence. The roles and the most typical ways in which they are expressed are summarized in Table 10–1.

In many languages, perhaps in all, there is a tendency for old information, the Topic, to be placed early in the sentence. New information, the Comment, generally comes later. The early position of *The bird* in *The bird is eating a worm* helps us to interpret it as old information. We understand *a worm*, which comes later, as new information. If it is the *worm* that has already been under discussion, we can maneuver it into first place and say *The worm is being eaten by a bird,* and in that way make it the Topic and show it to be old information. The new information, the *bird,* then comes as a later Comment. One of the reasons for using a passive sentence like, *The worm is being eaten by a bird,* instead of its active counterpart, *A bird is eating the worm,* is to move the noun phrases about so that the familiar information is put into the background, and the new information is highlighted.

English provides a second means of marking information as old. We usually use a definite article (*the*) when we believe that the hearer will be able to identify the object or the person we refer to. If someone cries out *I see the elephant,* the crier must assume that the hearer expects an elephant to turn up. The hearer may be surprised to know that it has already been spotted, but not that it is an elephant. If, instead, someone cries out *I see an elephant,* with the indefinite article *an,* the surprise may come because the hearer had been

Table 10–1
Cases and Roles

	Example categories	Typically shown by
Cases:	Nominative, Accusative, Dative	Affixes; Radically changed form (e.g., I/me)
Syntactic roles:	Subject, Object, Adpositional phrase	Word order; Case markers; Adpositions; Verb agreement
Semantic roles:	Agent, Patient, Instrument	Adpositions; Word order
Pragmatic roles:	Topic, Comment	Early or late position in a sentence; Articles; Stress

expecting a giraffe or a Volkswagen. *The* identifies something that the hearer can be expected already to hold in awareness. *A* introduces something new.

A definite article does not always imply that something has already been explicitly mentioned, but it does suggest that it can be readily identified. Previous mention in the conversation is one likely means by which something can be identified, but there are two other possibilities. First, the object may be visible or audible to the people who are talking: *Look at the tiger! Can you reach the forceps? What's the rumbling sound that I hear?* Second, the word may refer to the only one of its kind: *the Emperor of Japan, the sun, the last letter of the alphabet.* When neither previous mention, perceptibility, nor uniqueness can be used to identify the object, it is more appropriate to use *a*. In a series of connected sentences, we generally introduce new items with indefinite articles, but when the same item is referred to again, we use a definite article instead: *A man and a boy came into the room. The boy went to the window but the man sat down.*

Topics tend to set the scene with old information early in the sentence, and since old information tends to be marked with a definite article, we should expect that the subjects of English sentences (which come early and tend to be Topics) would more often have definite articles than do objects (which come later), and this expectation can easily be tested. In a sample of approximately 350 subjects and 350 objects that were drawn from a diverse set of written texts, less than one tenth of the subjects but almost half the objects were indefinite (Givon, 1979, p. 52).

	Subject	Direct object
Definite	91%	56%
Indefinite	9%	44%

Indefinite subjects do occur in English (*A man walked into the room, A book was on the table*), but these figures suggest that they are considerably less common than definite subjects (*The man walked into the room, The book was on the table*), and indefinite subjects are probably even less common in spoken

English than in written English. We accept *A book is on the table* as a grammatical English sentence, but in easy conversation it might be more natural to replace it with *There is a book on the table*. *There is* amounts to a way of signaling the introduction of new information and pushing it away from the very beginning of the sentence. *There is* is regarded as a bit inelegant, not quite suitable for writing, but the pragmatic pressures of conversation encourage its use in casual speech. It feels awkward for the new information to come too close to the beginning of a sentence. *There is* moves it to a more comfortable position.

Subjects tend to precede objects in most languages and, except when the verb comes first, a likely position for the subject is at the beginning of a sentence. In some languages it seems to be sufficiently awkward for new information to appear this early that indefinite subjects are not allowed at all. Although they are not excluded from English, indefinite subjects are not entirely natural either. The same pressures that make them unnatural in English are strong enough to exclude them entirely from some other languages.

An Agent so frequently becomes the subject of its sentence that we can consider the Agent to be the most natural or prototypical semantic role for the subject. Since the Agent–subject is likely to come early in the sentence, the sentence will have a certain harmony if the same noun phrase is also the Topic, the carrier of the old information. We find, indeed, that the prototypical subject, in English and in other languages, is not only the Agent but the Topic as well. We can make up a tedious story in which each sentence begins with a subject that is both the Topic (previously mentioned) and an Agent, but that goes on to introduce new information: *I will tell you a story about a fisherman. The fisherman selected a fishing pole. He walked to a river bank. There he used the fishing pole to catch a fish. The fish made a terrible splash.* The familiar information with which these dull sentences begin is usually given either by a pronoun, *I* or *he,* or by a definite article, *the.* Even *there* in the fourth sentence refers to the earlier *river bank,* so it counts as old information. After having been launched with old information, however, each sentence goes on to introduce some new information that is signaled by an indefinite article.

We can think of the dynamics of building a sentence by imagining that a speaker tries to push both the Agent and the Topic into the subject position. If the Topic is also the Agent then the speaker faces no problem, but if the Agent is not old information, Agent and Topic are necessarily different, and they must then compete for the subject position. All languages, including English, provide extensive machinery by which the conflicting demands of the Agent and Topic on the subject position can be reconciled. Indeed, many of the complexities of syntax can be understood as ways of coping with these conflicting demands. We can consider several of these mechanisms.

Word Order

When we considered Russian word order, we found that the three words of *Tanja vybrala Maſu* 'Tanya chose Masha' can be rearranged into any of the six logically possible orders and still yield a grammatical sentence. Whatever the order of the words, the case suffixes of the two nouns will always show who was chosen and who did the choosing. The case suffixes liberate word order to be used for expressing other meanings than the difference between Agent and Patient, and Russian word order responds more readily than English to pragmatic needs. *Tanja vybrala Maʃu* is a good answer to the question 'Who did Tanya choose?' since, when answering, *Tanja* will be old information and *Maʃu* will be new. A good answer to the question 'Who chose Masha?' would be *Maʃu vybrala Tanja*. Here, *Tanja* comes as the new information, so it is best moved to last place.

Russian nouns are not marked with definite and indefinite articles as they are in English, but since word order can be used to convey pragmatic information more easily in Russian than in English, articles are not so crucial. A language like Russian with reliable case marking can use word order for pragmatic purposes and thus dispense with definite and indefinite articles. A language like English that has reliable articles to mark old and new information can use word order to distinguish the most important semantic roles and thus dispense with case marking.

However, just as word order cannot do the entire job of marking all semantic roles in English, so word order is not always adequate for marking pragmatic roles in Russian. When English word order fails us, we fall back on prepositions to make sure the semantic roles are clear. When word order fails the Russians, and when they need to distinguish old and new information more carefully, they can use demonstratives (words such as *this* and *that*) to convey a sense of definiteness. Both languages need to accomplish the same tasks, but they use different means. Both languages provide optional alternative strategies as a supplement to word order. Word order, case marking, adpositions, articles, and demonstratives are all interdependent, and we can hardly hope to understand how one of these works without understanding all the others.

Passives and Cleft Sentences

Although word order is less easily used to convey pragmatic information in English than in Russian, we do have a number of means by which we can rearrange the constituents of a sentence so as to improve their fit with pragmatic requirements. We have already seen that one of the functions of the English passive is to redistribute noun phrases in a way that makes them conform more closely to the expectation that old information will come early in the sentence. Consider the following stereotypical pair of sentences from a news program: *We have been hearing the views of the Assistant Secretary of Defense. He was interviewed by John C. Jacobson.* The passive construction of the second sentence maneuvers the new information, the interviewer's name, into the Comment position at the end of the sentence. *John C. Jacobson interviewed him* would convey the same factual information, but it would be awkward because the new information would come too early.

Another way in which English can bring old information to the front of a sentence is by means of "cleft sentences," so called because they have a split or "cleft" between the topic and the rest of the sentence. *It was IBM that Florence used to work for* is a cleft sentence related to *Florence used to work for IBM,* but the *IBM* has been removed from the end and maneuvered into initial position. The cleft and the noncleft sentences express the same objective fact, but we would use them in different situations. If we had already been talking about IBM, *It was IBM that Florence used to work for* would be a reasonable sentence. If we had been talking about Florence, we would find it more natural to introduce *IBM* into the conversation by saying *Florence used to work for IBM.*

Stress

One important way by which we signal new information in English is by contrastive stress. Stress can even override other signals. In *Matílda investigated Matthew,* the heavy stress on *Matílda* shows us that she is the one who is now entering the conversation for the first time, while *Matthew* has probably already been mentioned. Stress on *tomorrow* in *I'm going to New York tomórrow* emphasizes its final position in the sentence and confirms the expectation that the trip was already under discussion. Most likely it is the date that is being revealed for the first time. If the stress is shifted to *I,* so that the sentence becomes *Í'm going to New York tomorrow,* it could be used in a context in which the time and destination had already been mentioned, but someone was still in doubt about who was traveling. The stress shows that the new information involves the traveler, even though that comes first in the sentence.

Written English provides no easy and reliable equivalent for the contrastive stress of the spoken language. This forces us, when writing, to find other ways of pointing to information as new. This is probably one reason that a number of constructions that seem a bit stilted in spoken conversation, including the passive, are used more freely in written English.

Placement of Adverbs and Prepositional Phrases

English adverbs can be moved about more easily than either subjects or objects, and we can deemphasize *tomorrow* in *I'm going to New York tomorrow* by moving it to the beginning of the sentence. *Tomorrow I'm going to New York* and *I'm going to New Yórk tomorrow* (with heavy stress on *New Yórk*) are alternative ways to emphasize *New York* and to deemphasize *tomorrow.* Either of these sentences would be appropriate in a discussion about possible activities for the next day. They would both be very strange in answer to the question *When are you going to New York?*

Some prepositional phrases can be moved about almost as easily as adverbs, and the reasons for moving them are similar. If we are talking about a building with a dentist's office, and someone wonders what floor it is on, it seems natural to say *The dentist's office is on the fifth floor*. Here *fifth floor* is marked with the definite article even though it is new information. This is because there can be only one fifth floor in the building. Nevertheless, its status as new information is suggested by its late position in the sentence. Only if the point is to tell someone what is found on the fifth floor, would it be more natural to say *On the fifth floor is a dentist's office*. Once again, the new information is given last. *A dentist's office is on the fifth floor* can sound peculiar because the indefinite article, *a*, ought to signal new information, but the initial position of *a dentist's office* suggests, instead, that it is old information. *On the fifth floor is the dentist's office* is reasonable only in a situation where both the floor and the office had already been mentioned and the only remaining new information to be conveyed is their connection with each other.

Topicalization

We have a limited ability in English to move almost any item to the beginning of the sentence and thereby to *topicalize* it. *That man, I can't stand* brings the object to the very front of the sentence, even before the subject. A topicalized phrase like *that man* usually refers to something that is already in awareness. Most likely the *man* has already been in the conversation, so it is old information, brought to the beginning. Under the right circumstances, a word can enter a conversation for the first time in a topicalized position. *Linguistics, she likes* could introduce *linguistics* if the sentence followed directly after *She hated philosophy*. Even here, however, the ability to topicalize *linguistics* depends on the subject of academic disciplines already being in awareness, even if not the particular discipline mentioned.

In English, topicalized phrases are only loosely integrated into the rest of the sentence, and they do not even fit easily into its intonational pattern. They have to be set off by the intonation in order to avoid any ambiguity about what is the subject of the sentence. In some languages topicalization is much freer and more thoroughly incorporated into the grammar. German, for instance, can be described as a "verb second" language, and it is more accurate to describe the phrase that precedes the verb as a "Topic" than as a "subject." Often, as in the following sentence, German has exactly the same word order as English.

Ich	*gab*	*Peter*	*das*	*Buch*	*gestern.*
I	gave	Peter	the	book	yesterday

German and English word order often coincide because the same noun phrase is often both Topic and Agent. When Topic and Agent are different, however, German permits an alternative word order that is quite impossible in English. In fact, any other noun phrase, or even an adverb, can become the Topic of a German sentence by being placed before the verb. As a result,

German allows the following sentences in addition to the one already given:

Das Buch gab ich Peter gestern.
Peter gab ich das Buch gestern.
Gestern gab ich Peter das Buch.

The most straightforward way to describe these German sentences is to say that the verb always comes second, while a single phrase, generally old or assumed information, precedes the verb. Often it is the Agent that is old information, and this means that it is often the Agent that is selected as the Topic. As a result, many German sentences, like many English sentences, begin with a subject that is both Agent and Topic. German, however, is much freer than English in allowing other noun phrases to displace the Agent from the Topic position.

In much of linguistic theory, the sentence has been taken to be the largest unit of analysis. Syntax has been thought of as the study of the constraints on sequences of words within a single sentence. Pragmatic considerations, however, force us to look at the way in which sentences constrain one another. We have to consider the entire discourse within which a sentence occurs, and we even need to look beyond the verbal context to the social context within which the discourse is set. Pragmatic requirements help us to understand why some sentences are more appropriate under some circumstances than others. Unlike a violation of syntactic rules, a violation of pragmatic constraints does not usually result in a totally ungrammatical sentence; it does result in a sentence that is odd in the circumstances. Once we take this larger context into account, we find new reasons for the varieties of sentences that occur in languages. Syntax can then be understood as responding to the pragmatic needs of conversation.

EASE OF PROCESSING

Although it may seem to be slightly paradoxical, some rules complicate the grammar of a language at the same time that they make the language easier for its speakers to use. One obvious example is the use of pronouns. Logically, languages should not really need pronouns at all. In place of a pronoun, a speaker could always substitute the full name or description of the person or thing referred to. Instead of saying *As John sauntered into the room he looked for the princess,* we could say *As John sauntered into the room John looked for the princess.* We might even regard a language that lacked pronouns as "simpler" than a language with pronouns, since it would dispense with a whole class of words and with all the rules that regulate their use. Since all languages have them, pronouns must offer important enough advantages to compensate for the added complexity they bring.

Pronouns are useful because they let us avoid a great deal of repetition. Once we have said *The little white kitten with the cute curly tail,* we can avoid saying the same thing over and over again by simply substituting *he*. A pronoun, then, is a bit like a variable in a mathematical system or in a computer programming language, a word that can be repeatedly redefined and that allows us to express a complicated concept with a very simple label. If we need to refer repeatedly to the same thing, it is easiest to abbreviate its full description by means of a single pronoun. A computer language or a mathematical notation that allows variables is formally more complex than a language that forbids them, but such a language also increases the user's freedom. In the same way, pronouns increase the complexity of natural languages, but they make it easier for us to talk.

Pronouns amount to abbreviations, but pronouns can, themselves, often be abbreviated or even omitted entirely. It is in the nature of pronouns to stand for old or familiar information, so they share the property of definiteness with demonstratives and definite articles. Since they express old information, many languages allow pronouns to be put into the background by being weakly stressed, and since they are so often unstressed, they become natural targets for phonological reduction. *I see 'er, Look at 'em, What'r yə doing?* attest to the contractions and reductions that English pronouns readily undergo. With sufficient phonological reduction, pronouns are often contracted and joined to adjacent words, and if they become fixed in position, they turn into affixes. Under some circumstances, pronouns can even be omitted entirely. Spanish allows subject pronouns to be omitted, and some languages allow pronouns to be omitted from all positions so long as the meaning remains clear.

Both the use of pronouns as substitutes for complex noun phrases and their phonological reduction and deletion amount to abbreviations that cut down on the time that is required to say something. Languages provide many other such devices. English uses *do* as a sort of "pro-verb" that substitutes for a more complete verb phrase as in *Jane likes to swim in salt water, and I do too*. This sentence is quicker to say than *Jane likes to swim in salt water, and I like to swim in salt water* and English speakers surely find it easier, but the rule that allows us to abbreviate in this way adds to the total complexity of English grammar. Even a simple conjunction can be regarded as a linguistic device for speeding things up. It is quicker to say *I like meat and potatoes but not vegetables* than to say *I like meat; I like potatoes; I do not like vegetables,* but the rule that allows us to reduce three separate sentences to the tighter construction of a single sentence must make the grammar more complex than it would otherwise have been.

We can also process language more easily if long or "heavy" elements are not allowed to distract us before shorter elements are taken care of. An element that is too long can interrupt the continuity of a sentence. *I gave all the long envelopes with the cute little flowers printed on them to you* may not be quite impossible, but it is surely more awkward than *I gave you all the long envelopes with the cute little flowers printed on them.* *I gave him it* is very nearly impossible in American English, but *I gave the little boy it* is even worse. A pronoun object like *it* is simply too short to follow a phrase even of such modest size as *the little boy*. On the other hand, *I gave the little boy a beautiful brown teddy bear* is entirely normal because *a beautiful brown teddy bear* is long enough to fit comfortably after *the little boy*. In all these cases, there is pressure to put the shorter element first and the longer element later. Presumably this conforms to the way in which we most easily process information. If the shorter element were to come last, we would have to hold the overall structure of the sentence in mind while waiting for it. If the short element is disposed of at the start, all one's processing powers can then be focused on the longer second element.

CLARITY AND ECONOMY

Syntax is among the resources that our language provides to convey our meanings. In particular, we have to use syntax in a way that will allow the hearer to understand how our words and phrases are related to each other. In one way or another every language has to accomplish this essential task, but languages differ greatly in their methods. No single means of doing the job is so clearly superior to all others that it wins out everywhere. Some of the alternatives can be seen by returning, once again, to cases and adpositions.

The semantic roles of noun phrases are often shown by distinctive adpositions, and it might seem that the most efficient language design would simply provide a single adposition for each conceivable semantic role. Every noun phrase could then be marked unambiguously as an Agent, Patient, Recipient, Benefactive, Locative, or as having some other semantic role. There would then be a direct and simple equivalence between meaning and form. Many languages approach this equivalence, with adpositions that reflect, to a considerable extent, the semantic roles of the nouns to which they are attached. Certainly the prepositions of English often correspond to the semantic roles of their noun phrases. But if there is a language with a perfect correspondence between semantic roles and either case markers or adpositions, it has yet to be discovered, and we have to wonder why languages make things so complicated.

Some of the complications arise from a conflict in goals. A requirement that every noun phrase should be labeled with a well-defined marker of its semantic role would clash with another desirable feature of language—economy. In many situations, an adposition or case marker would yield no helpful information. Intransitive verbs need to be accompanied by only a single noun phrase, and since the semantic role of this noun phrase can ordinarily be inferred from the verb, it hardly needs to be marked in any explicit way. What role except Agent could *Horace* fill in *Horace screamed*? To mark the semantic role of noun phrases such as this would be logical, but also redundant. It would detract from efficiency. As a result, in many languages, the noun phrase that is used with an intransitive verb takes no case marker at all, even though cases may be clearly marked elsewhere in the language. With transitive verbs that require two noun phrases, ambiguity can be avoided by marking just one of them, or even by fixing their relative word order, as in English. A requirement to mark both noun phrases could be a burdensome redundancy.

Even with more complex sentences, the plausible meanings that might be conveyed by a sequence of words may be so limited that it is unnecessary to mark the noun phrases explicitly. In sentences like *The bee stung the baby, I picked apples, Doreen glued the boards,* there is only one plausible relationship between the words. Babies do not ordinarily sting bees, nor do apples pick people, or boards glue anything at all. It is an unnecessary burden on the speaker to require every noun phrase in these sentences to be marked as Agent or Patient. Languages do provide ways of saying such things as *Apples pick people.* For fairy tales and science fiction we want this flexibility. We do not always need such flexibility, and most of the time we would rather avoid the complexity that allows the flexibility.

All languages have a large stock of adpositions that convey information about spatial position and movement. Some are highly "grammaticized" in the sense that their meanings are generalized and their choice is constrained primarily by the surrounding words. English *at, on,* and *in* are adpositions (prepositions) of this type. We meet someone *at* five o'clock, *in* the afternoon, *on* Tuesday, *in* March. A person can live *at* 3530, *on* Daleview Drive, *in* Ann Arbor. We cannot shuffle these prepositions with the nouns or select the prepositions in order to modulate our meaning. *On five o'clock at the afternoon in Tuesday* is simply wrong. The choice among these prepositions depends on the nouns with which they are used, not on their contrastive meaning.

We have many other locative prepositions with better defined meanings: *above, over, behind, below,* etc. We are freer to choose among these to fit the meaning we want to convey. When we need even more specific meanings, we can choose among a wide stock of fixed phrases that act very much like single prepositions: *next to, on top of, in front of.* Finally, when we want to be still more precise, we can freely construct a phrase of any desired degree of complexity and precision and use it in place of a regular preposition: *on the edge of, in the cracks between, a tiny bit before the middle of,* etc.

The variety of prepositions and of prepositionlike phrases, ranging from broadly generalized to minutely specific, allows us to be quick and concise when precision is unnecessary, but to be as precise as we want when that becomes important. We can probably process the highly grammaticized prepositions such as *in, on,* and *at* almost automatically. The most complex phrases need to be invented as we speak and decoded as we listen, so they must require considerably more effort. No system that defined a fixed number of semantic roles, and assigned a single marker for each of the roles, would give us this flexibility, however logical such a system might first appear.

To use prepositions in a way that avoided all ambiguity would carry an intolerable cost in complexity. *I cooked the applesauce for Matilda,* for instance, is ambiguous. The sentence can mean either *I cooked the applesauce in place of Matilda* or *I cooked the applesauce in order to give it to Matilda.* In most real communicative situations, ambiguities like this are easily resolved. If you are telling Jonathan not to eat the applesauce because you made it for his sister, it is not likely that your meaning will be misunderstood. Only occasionally is this ambiguity likely to present any problem, and when it does, we have the means to work our way around it. In most cases, economy encourages the speaker to use a simple form. More complex and explicit expressions are available when ambiguity threatens.

Real languages have to compromise between the need for clarity and the need for economy. They provide ways by which speakers can, if they are careful, avoid ambiguity, but they also permit enough to be left unsaid so that a slip into ambiguity is an ever-present danger. There is a kind of tension between the need to keep things explicit, clear, and unambiguous, and the desirability of keeping things simple. There are many alternate ways to stave off ambiguity, and languages differ greatly in the means that they use. It is easy to imagine ways to "improve" a language by making it less ambiguous and more logical, but this can generally be done only by placing an extra burden on the speakers. They would have to remember to put in all sorts of extra bits, most of which, in practical communication, are not really needed. It is equally easy to imagine other ways to "improve" a language by omitting redundancies so that it would be simpler for a speaker to use. This might also come at an unacceptable cost, however, for when too much is omitted, speakers might find it difficult to state their message with adequate precision. Hearers might then find it impossible to understand.

Every language requires some redundancy. No listener can hear and register every sound or every word that a speaker utters. The speaker must provide enough extra information to allow hearers to reconstruct the pieces that they miss. Too much redundancy, however, becomes a burden on everyone and, where little is lost, we are always ready to simplify. The rules that allow us to simplify, however, are themselves very complex, and the areas of redundancy, and ways of simplifying, vary widely from one language to another.

CHAPTER ELEVEN

Syntactic Typology

SIMILARITY AND VARIATION: NOUN PHRASES

The goal of linguistic typology is to chart out and find the reasons for the similarities and differences among the world's languages. Noun phrases are a good starting place for getting a feeling for syntactic similarities and differences.

All languages have noun phrases that serve in semantic roles such as Agent, Patient, and Instrument, and that can act as subjects and objects of verbs. Noun phrases are always built around a central noun, but they can have several additional constituents, including determiners, numbers, possessives, adjectives, and relative clauses. For example, the Garo translation of "Those two little houses on the hill" has constituents that correspond to most of those found in English, and it includes the typical constituents of noun phrases everywhere. ("SS" identifies a subordinating suffix that puts a verb into a form that can be used to modify a noun. "Cl" identifies a numeral classifier, the use of which will be described shortly.)

ua	*abri-o*	*dong-gipa*	*nok*	*chon-a*	*ge-gini*
that	hill-at	be-at–SS	house	little	Cl–two

'those two little houses on the hill'

1. Noun. English *house* and Garo *nok* are the **heads** of their noun phrases. Everything else could be omitted from the noun phrase more easily than this noun. All the other words modify the head.

2. Determiners. Words that have traditionally been called articles, such as *the* and *a*, and the words that have traditionally been called demonstratives, such as *this* and *those*, act in quite similar ways. Both are included among the "determiners." Like many other languages, English uses its determiners to help to mark the difference between old and new information in the way that was considered in Chapter 10. Typically, we use *a* to introduce new

information, while *the, this,* and *that* are more often used for information that
the speaker believes the hearer will be able to identify. Many languages,
including Garo, do without obligatory articles that correspond to English *a* and
the, but all have demonstratives. Demonstratives are "definite" (like the
definite article *the*), since they are used when the speaker believes that the
hearer will be able to identify the object referred to. Languages that lack
articles typically call on demonstratives when a definite meaning is essential.

Demonstratives typically suggest something about the location of the object
referred to, as do *this* and *that.* Both English *that* and Garo *ua* indicate things
that lie some distance from the speaker. Instead of the two-way distinction that
happens to be characteristic of both English and Garo, some languages make a
three-way distinction. They may have one word meaning 'this near me,' a
second meaning 'that near you,' and a third meaning 'that away from both of
us,' or they may have words that distinguish 'that at a middle distance,' from
'that farther away,' as well as a word for 'this close by.'

3. Possessives. Though not illustrated in this example, one possible noun-
phrase constituent is a possessive. In English we can say *my house* or *the old
man's house,* and Garo has close equivalents: *ang-ni nok* 'my house,' *budepa-
ni nok* 'old man's house.' Possession is shown in Garo by the suffix *-ni.* English
is a bit unusual in having two nearly equivalent ways of showing possession, as
in *the old man's house* and *the house of the old man.* Most languages get along
with a single construction, and in either case, a marker of possession often
comes between the words for the possessor and the possessed, as do both *-'s*
and *of,* as well as *-ni.*

4. Numbers. All languages have numbers, and most have elaborate counting
systems. Numbers are frequent constituents of noun phrases. Garo numbers
must always be attached to morphemes known as "numeral classifiers" that
are selected to fit the meaning of the noun. The Garo classifier *ge-* is used when
counting many physical objects that people make or build, including houses.
When counting people or animals, other classifiers replace *ge-. Sak-* is used
when counting people, *mang-* when counting animals: *nok ge-gini* 'two
houses,' *kok ge-gini* 'two baskets,' *mande sak-gini* 'two people,' *matchu
mang-gini* 'two cows.'

5. Adjectives. Nouns in all languages can be modified by words with meanings that correspond to English adjectives, but not all languages have a distinct
class of adjectives. In Garo all adjective-like modifiers are derived from verbs.
Thus *chon-a* is a verb meaning 'to be small,' but in the example sentence, it is
used to modify a noun, and it can be translated by an English adjective.

6. Relative clauses. All languages also have ways of modifying a noun with
what amounts to an entire sentence. Sentences that are used in this way are
called relative clauses, and speakers can use relative clauses to build up noun
phrases of any desired degree of complexity. Thus the English sentence *The
houses are on the hill* can be converted into the relative clause *that are on the
hill* by dropping one noun phrase and replacing it with *that.* This can then be
used, as it is or slightly abbreviated, to modify *the houses: houses (that are) on
the hill.*

Very short relative clauses give us a way to let verbs modify nouns. From a sentence like *The man mumbles,* we can produce a simple noun phrase like *the man who mumbles,* where the noun *man* is modified by the short relative clause, *who mumbles.* We can also convert much more complex English sentences into relative clauses. Thus, from *The man bought the chickens from the girl in the butcher shop* we can produce *the man who bought the chickens from the girl in the butcher shop,* in which the whole sentence has been turned into a noun phrase, and everything from *who* onward is a relative clause that modifies *man.* Complex noun phrases like this allow us to pull not only a verb, but everything that goes with the verb, into a noun phrase.

In Garo, as in English, relative clauses can pull more than just a verb into a noun phrase. Along with the verb, they can also bring along all its associated noun phrases. Thus from the sentence:

Nok   abri-o   dong-a
house   hill-on   is at-pres.
'The house is on the hill'

it is possible to form the noun phrase:

abri-o   dong-gipa   nok
hill-on   is at-Rel.   house
'the house that is on the hill'

The noun meaning 'hill,' and its locative case suffix *-o* are pulled into the relative clause along with the verb. In a language like Garo, which has no formal distinction between adjectives and verbs, we should not expect much difference between using a verb as a modifier and using it to form a relative clause. When Garo verbs are used as modifiers they often take a suffix *-gipa* instead of a tense marker such as *-a* 'present,' and the longer the modifier, the more likely it is to be marked with *-gipa.*

In most languages, perhaps in all, determiners, possessives, numbers, adjective-like modifiers, and relative clauses turn up as regular constituents of noun phrases. These phrases can become quite complex, and they are used, in turn, in a wide range of semantic and syntactic roles. They express Agents, Patients, and Instruments, and they appear not only as subjects and objects of verbs, but also in a variety of adpositional phrases. Noun phrases are usually easy to identify in a language and, as the similarity between English and Garo suggests, noun phrases in all languages have much in common.

At the same time, noun phrases also vary in several important ways from one language to another:

1. Word order. Although the constituents of noun phrases are similar everywhere, the order in which they occur is not. English word order is quite rigid. Possessives and determiners come first, followed by numbers, followed in turn by adjectives. Relative clauses always follow the noun. Garo word order is much freer. As in English, Garo demonstratives always come first, and Garo possessives must also precede the noun, but other constituents can either precede or follow the noun. Complex relative clauses most often precede, and numbers most often follow, but simple modifying verbs such as *chon-a* 'to be small' can occur almost as easily before as after. When a Garo noun phrase has many constituents, there seems to be a tendency to divide them so that neither side of the noun phrase gets overcrowded. In some other languages, everything precedes the noun, while in still others, everything follows. It is striking that when a demonstrative, number, and adjective all precede the noun, they seem always to occur in that order. When all of them follow the noun, the most common order is the exact reverse: noun–adjective–number–demonstrative. It might seem as if the demonstrative always belongs as far from the noun as possible. A few languages, however, use the demonstrative–number–adjective order even when the modifiers all follow the noun.

2. Internal markers of organization. Relative clauses are longer and more diverse than the other parts of a noun phrase. Their complexity more often makes it helpful to show their relationship to the head noun explicitly. The rigid word order of English helps to keep the organization of noun phrases clear, so we can keep explicit markers at a minimum. We do, sometimes, introduce relative clauses with a relative pronoun like *who, which,* or *that,* as in *the girl who was naughty* or *the mess that she made on the table.* In some circumstances these relative pronouns are required, in others they are optional.

Other languages use quite different devices for relating the parts of a Noun Phrase to each other. The Garo suffix -*gipa* shows explicitly that the verb to which it is attached is not the main verb of a sentence but, rather, a modifier of a nearby noun. The numeral classifiers of Garo are chosen to fit the meaning of the things being counted, and by pointing to the head noun, they relate the number to it, and so give some internal cohesion to the noun phrase.

In several European languages, such as French and Spanish, adjectives and articles must "agree" in gender and number with the noun that they modify. French nouns fall into two classes or "genders" known traditionally as "masculine" and "feminine." The French word for 'fork' happens to be feminine, while the word for 'knife' is masculine, and the forms of articles and adjectives have to be slightly different when used with these different words:

le   petit   couteau   blanc
the   little   knife   white
'the little white knife'

la   petite   fourchette blanche
the   little   fork   white
'the little white fork'

By relating the constituents of these noun phrases to each other, adjective agreement helps to give unity to the noun phrase.

The Bantu languages of eastern and southern Africa have more elaborate agreement than do European languages. Instead of the two or three categories of European genders, Swahili nouns are divided among a half dozen different classes, and all the modifiers take prefixes that agree with the class of the noun they modify. In some cases the constituents of a noun phrase seem almost to echo each other in a way that gives clear unity to the noun phrase.

wa-*tu*	**wa**-*zuri*	**wa**-*wili*	**wa**-*le*
people	good	two	those

'those two good people'

vi-*kapu*	**vi**-*zuri*	**vi**-*wili*	**vi**-*le*
baskets	good	two	those

'those two good baskets'

3. Relations to other parts of the sentence. The previous chapter described some of the techniques by which languages relate noun phrases to the verb and to the rest of the sentence. Word order can be exploited or verb agreement markers can point to particular noun phrases, but these are never enough to do the entire job by themselves. All languages also need ways to mark the role of some noun phrases more directly. Small sets of markers that are closely joined to the nouns are called **case markers.** Larger and more diverse sets of markers are known as **adpositions.** Both case markers and adpositions help to clarify the role of the noun phrase within the sentence. English uses prepositions to introduce many of its noun phrases and to show the roles that they play. Garo often uses case markers and postpositions, both of which come at the end of the noun phrase.

Although the order of items in a noun phrase is variable, and although languages use a variety of devices, both to link the constituents of a noun phrase to each other and to link noun phrases to the rest of the sentence, the similarities among the noun phrases of the world's languages are as striking as their differences. We could not even compare noun phrases systematically if their constituents were not so similar, and of course their formal similarity reflects the similar uses to which they are put.

NOUN PHRASE ACCESSIBILITY

The next few sections will review a few examples from a large number of typological studies that have been done in recent years, and one example that is particularly well known due to the work of Edward Keenan and Bernard Comrie concerns relative clauses. A relative clause allows constituents of any degree of complexity to be incorporated into a noun phrase. In effect, an entire sentence can be turned into a relative clause that modifies a noun. All languages have relative clauses, but they exhibit subtle differences in the way their relative clauses function.

Relative clauses are built from a sentence that has one or more noun phrases. In English it is generally possible to form a relative clause on any of its noun phrases. Consider *The burglar gave the fire extinguisher to the policeman in the vestibule*. This sentence has four noun phrases, *the burglar, the fire extinguisher, the policeman* and *the vestibule,* and it is possible to relativize on any one of the four:

> *the burglar who gave the fire extinguisher to the policeman in the vestibule*
> *the fire extinguisher that the burglar gave to the policeman in the vestibule*
> *the policeman who(m) the burglar gave the fire extinguisher to in the vestibule*
> *the vestibule that the burglar gave the policeman the fire extinguisher in*

In each case, one noun phrase from the original sentence has been extracted to become the head of a new noun phrase, while the rest of the sentence has been rearranged into a relative clause. In these examples, the relative clause is always introduced by *that* or *who,* but these "relative pronouns" can often be omitted in English. We can describe the possibilities by saying that the original sentence has been relativized, respectively, on the subject (*the burglar*), the object (*the fire extinguisher*), the indirect object (*the policeman*), and the prepositional phrase (*in the vestibule*).

Although all four of these relative clauses are possible in English, we may feel that some are more natural or easier to construct than others. In some other languages some kinds of relativization are impossible. All languages, it seems, have ways of relativizing on subjects (i.e., they have equivalents of *the burglar who gave the policeman the fire extinguisher in the vestibule*), but some allow no other kinds of relativization at all.

In Malagasy (which is one of the few known languages in which the basic word order is Verb-Object-Subject) we can start with this simple sentence:

Nahita   ny   vehivavy   ny   mpianatra
Saw   the   woman   the   student
'The student saw the woman.'

Only one kind of relative clause can be constructed from this sentence. The relative clause in this example is enclosed in brackets:

ny   mpianatra   [izay   nahita   ny   vehivavy]
the   student   Rel.   saw   the   woman
'the student [who saw the woman]'

Malagasy cannot relativize on *vehivavy* 'the woman,' and as a result it has no direct way of constructing a literal equivalent for the English noun phrase *the woman who(m) the student saw.*

In some other languages only subjects and objects can be relativized. The first of the following examples from Kinyarwanda, a Bantu language of Rwanda, illustrates relativization on the subject; the second illustrates relativization on the object:

N-a-bonye   *umugabo*   [*w-a-nditse*   *ibaruwa*].
I-past-see   man   Rel.-past-write   letter
'I saw the man [who wrote the letter].'

N-a-bonye   *ibaruwa*   [*Yohani*   *y-a-nditse.*]
I-past-see   letter   John   he-past-write
'I saw the letter [that John wrote].'

In still other languages it is possible to relativize on subjects, direct objects, and indirect objects but on no other noun phrases. In fact, there seems to be a clearly ordered hierarchy, with some noun phrases consistently easier to relativize than others. All languages allow relativization on subjects. Some of these also allow relativization on the direct object but no others. Some allow relativization of these two plus indirect objects. Still others, including English, also allow possessives to be relativized, as in *the book whose cover is red,* which is derived from *the book's cover is red.* This hierarchy can be summarized as Subject > Direct Object > Indirect Object > Possessive. Few languages allow relativization on noun phrases later on this hierarchy unless they also allow relativization on all the noun phrases that precede it. Even in English, we may feel that relativization is a bit easier on subjects than on other noun phrases. We may feel that the relative clause that modifies *burglar* comes more easily than the relative clause that modifies *policeman.* The ease with which relative clauses are formed offers one example of the way languages vary but do so only within limits. We would not even be able to compare languages in this manner unless relativization occurred everywhere in ways that are similar enough to be recognizable as the same phenomenon. More important, the patterns of relativization suggest that some logically imaginable language types do not, in fact, occur. We can easily imagine a language that allows indirect objects but not subjects to be relativized, but such languages appear not to exist. It seems that humans are restricted in the types of language that they can learn and use.

The fact that some languages limit the freedom of relativization leads to a disturbing question. How do languages manage without some kinds of relative clauses? Does this example suggest that some languages are richer in expressive power than others? To an English speaker it may seem harshly restrictive to forbid relativization on some kinds of noun phrases. Surely everyone must occasionally need to say things like *the woman who(m) the student saw,* in which a direct object is relativized. How do people manage when their language forbids this?

The answer seems to be that languages with restricted relativization compensate by allowing relatively free passivization. The relationship between relativization and passivization may not be immediately apparent, but consider what passives do: They move noun phrases about within a sentence. The

English passive moves one noun phrase out of the subject position before the verb and moves another noun phrase into the subject position. When *John ate the liverwurst* is made passive, the result is *The liverwurst was eaten by John.* Subject and object have changed places. Many languages have passive constructions that allow nouns other than the original subject to move into the subject position. In English, we can form a passive sentence and then relativize on this new subject: *the liverwurst that was eaten by John.* In English, of course, we do not have to passivize first, since we can relativize directly on the original object and produce *the liverwurst that John ate.* These alternative ways of relativizing on *liverwurst* result in nearly synonymous phrases except, perhaps, for a slight change in pragmatic emphasis.

Languages in which it is impossible to relativize on objects may be able to achieve nearly the same result by first moving the object into the subject position by means of a passive construction, and then relativizing on the new subject. Malagasy, again, offers an example. The following is an active (i.e., not passive) sentence (recall the Verb-Object-Subject order of Malagasy).

Nividy	*ny*	*vary*	*ho an'*	*ny*	*ankizy*	*ny*	*vehivavy.*
bought	the	rice	for	the	children	the	woman

'The woman bought the rice for the children.'

From this active sentence, the direct object, *rice,* can be brought into the subject position by means of a passive construction. A Malagasy hearer will recognize this as a passive because of the changed form of the verb. The new subject now comes last in the sentence.

Novidin'	*ny*	*vehivavy*	*ho an'*	*ny*	*ankizy*	*ny*	*vary.*
was-bought	the	woman	for	the	children	the	rice

'The rice was bought for the children by the woman.'

Having been moved to the subject position at the end of the sentence, *vary* 'rice' can now be easily relativized.

ny	*vary*	[*izay*	*novidin'*	*ny*	*vehivavy*	*ho*	*an'ny*	*ankizy*]
the	rice	that	was-bought	the	woman	for	the	children

'the rice that was bought for the children by the woman'

Malagasy turns out to be rich in passives. It is possible to use a different passive construction to move the Benefactive *ankizy* 'children' into the final, subject position of the sentence. Notice that the verb assumes a different form for this kind of passive.

Nividianan'	*ny*	*vehivavy*	*ny*	*vary*	*ny*	*ankizy.*
were-bought	the	woman	the	rice	the	children

'The children were bought rice by the woman.'

Now it is possible to relativize once again, this time on the new subject *ankizy* 'children,' and to produce a different relative clause.

ny	ankizy	[izay	nividianan'	ny	vehivavy	ny	vary]
the	children	that	were-bought	the	woman	the	rice

'the children who were bought rice by the woman'

As this example makes clear, the restrictions on relative clauses need not limit the expressive power of a language. Certainly the details of these constructions and the freedom with which they can be applied differ in many ways from the more familiar patterns of English, and yet, when we investigate further, we always seem to find that languages have the means to accomplish similar ends. If we are still tempted to feel that a language that forbids some kinds of relative clauses has less expressive power than English, we must balance our judgment by acknowledging that those same languages may have more flexible passives. As far as we are now able to judge, relativization and passivization, when used together, can achieve closely equivalent results in all languages, and we find no grounds for considering one language to be superior to another in overall expressive power.

VERB CLASSIFICATION

Noun phrases are grouped together with verbs to form clauses and sentences. A single sentence can have several noun phrases filling several syntactic and semantic roles, but each sentence usually has just one main verb. The main verb can be regarded as the center of the sentence, and different verbs call for differing constellations of semantic roles, such as Agent and Patient. Differing semantic roles, in turn, imply differing sets of syntactic roles. The traditional distinction between transitive and intransitive verbs amounts to a rudimentary classification of verbs, but languages have many more varieties of verbs than can be handled by this simple two-way division. Linguists are by no means agreed on the best way to classify verbs, or even on the most useful semantic roles to recognize. Nevertheless, they have proposed a number of classifications that are based on the semantic roles that verbs can take.

Perhaps all languages have a few verbs that, logically, should require no semantic roles at all. The "weather" verbs are the most obvious examples. When we say *It rained* or *It's snowing,* the verb tells us everything we need to know, and in some languages the verb can stand alone. We hardly know what *it* refers to in these English sentences, but it is forced on us by the English insistence that every sentence have a subject, whether or not it adds to the meaning. The *it* is part of the price we pay for our rigid word order. When nothing else is available, English needs a dummy subject like *it* just to keep its word order consistent.

Many verbs require, or at least permit, an Agent that is the initiator and controller of the action. In order to initiate and control, Agents have to be animate. Most agents are human beings; occasionally they can be animals. No other semantic role except the Agent is required with verbs such as *run, dance, sleep, groan, walk,* and *die,* and we call these "intransitives." *Cook, taste, lift, look at, open, hit, break, love, hate,* and scores of other verbs are most often used with both an Agent that takes the initiative and a Patient that receives the action: *He cooked the sauerkraut. We opened the horse radish.* Another set of verbs, including *give* and *bestow,* require not only an Agent and a Patient but also a Recipient, someone who receives the Patient: *We presented the gift to Gladys.* In addition to an Agent and a Patient, verbs such as *send* and *take* often have a third noun phrase that shows the goal or source of the action: *We sent the rice to China* and *They took the soup can from the cupboard.* In addition to an Agent and Patient, *put* requires a Locative noun phrase that shows where the Patient goes: *I put the car in the garage.*

For all these verbs the Agent might seem to be the normal subject, but some of them, and many others, can also be used without an Agent: *cook, boil, break, crack, open, splash.* All these verbs can be used either as transitives (with both an Agent and a Patient) or as intransitives (with the Patient alone): *I boil the water. The water boils. Christopher cracked the rocks. The rocks cracked. We are opening the box, the box is opening.* Since many English verbs can be used with varying constellations of semantic roles, any exhaustive classification of verbs would have to recognize some semantic roles as obligatory and some as optional. The details are often surprisingly idiosyncratic. *Crack* and *crush,* for example, have similar meanings, and both can be used with an Agent as subject and a Patient as object: *I cracked the rock, I crushed the rock.* Only *crack* can be used easily with the Patient as subject: *The rock cracked* is fine but **The rock crushed* is at least peculiar, if not quite impossible, at least if we mean that the rock itself got crushed.

Some verbs require an animate subject that is more of an Experiencer than an Agent: *see, hear, know, understand, think, want, feel.* It would be misleading to characterize the subjects of the following sentences as Agents: *Morris sees the problem. Bertha understands the explanation. Both of them want to know more. Morris* and *Bertha* are more acted upon than acting, but in English these Experiencer verbs seem not to be distinguished syntactically from Agent–Patient verbs such as *break.* We have a number of reciprocal verbs that allow the subject and object to be interchanged without affecting the meaning. *Meet, fight, quarrel, kiss,* and *marry* are verbs of this sort, as in *John met Mary* and *Mary met John.* With reciprocal verbs, English also allows the two nouns to be grouped together as the subject: *Mary and John met.* The polite English expressions for "making love" are generally reciprocal, as in *Mary and John made love;* the impolite expressions are more likely to formed with an Agent and a Patient.

We also have a group of verbs known as "stative" because many of them describe the state of things. Some of these describe position or location: *the bottle stood on the table, The rug lies on the floor, I am at the station.* In English, phrases formed from the verb *be* and an adjective can be considered as stative verbs: *to be red, to be intelligent,* etc. One characteristic of stative verbs is that they cannot be passivized: *The table was stood on by the bottle. Fit, cost,* and *resemble* are other stative verbs, and we can say *The shirt fits the boy* but not *The boy is fitted by the shirt; The chocolate costs a dollar* but not *A dollar is cost by the chocolate; She resembles her mother* but not *Her mother is resembled by her.*

In addition to the semantic roles that some verbs require, many others are optional. We can add Benefactives, Instrumentals, Locatives, and Temporals to most sentences. We usually use prepositions to identify these optional semantic roles in English, and we can pile up a large number of them in a single sentence: *Albert drew Norbert's picture for Mary with a piece of charcoal in the garden on Saturday.* This sentence has an Agent (*Albert*), a Patient (*Norbert's picture*), a Benefactive (*for Mary*), an Instrument (*with a piece of charcoal*), a Locative (*in the garden*), and a Temporal (*on Saturday*). Stylistically clumsy it may be, but sentences like this have to be counted as both grammatical and understandable.

The classification of verbs is made more complex by the ability of some verbs to be used with various kinds of **subordinate** clauses. A **clause** is a structured group of words that includes a verb. Since sentences are generally built around a verb, it is natural to think of all clauses as similar to sentences and even as constructed from sentences. Relative clauses are constructed from sentences so that they can modify a noun; subordinate clauses are constructed from sentences so that they can be subordinated to another sentence. Linguists often say that one sentence is **embedded** within another ''main'' sentence. It is not possible to treat subordination in detail here, but a few examples can suggest the ways in which subordination bears on verb classification.

Verbs such as *believe, think, hope, suggest* can take subordinate clauses that are introduced by *that* as in *I believe that he will come, I hope that he will stay away, I suggest that we tell him.* In these sentences, *he will come, he will stay away* and *we tell him* are clauses that have been subordinated to the verbs *believe, hope,* and *suggest* of the main sentences.

Verbs such as *wonder, doubt,* and *ask* can take subordinate clauses that are derived from questions. *I doubt if he will come* includes an embedded question derived from *Will he come? I wonder whether they have enough bread* includes the embedded question *Do they have enough bread? Twinkie asked Jonathan if he had taken out the garbage* includes the embedded question *Had he taken out the garbage?*

Verbs such as *cause, make, help, force, prevent, ask, tell,* and *forbid* can be followed by clauses in which subordination is not marked by *that* but is often marked instead by *to, from,* or the verb suffix *-ing. I asked him not to play on the lawn, I told him to get lost, I helped him to freeze the strawberries, I prevented her from making a fool of herself, I made them stop all that nonsense.* These all include subordinate clauses that have been embedded within a larger sentence. The details by which such subordination is accomplished are complex, but the important point to recognize is that different verbs require, or permit, different kinds of subordination.

As we study these details more closely, it almost seems that each English verb can occur only under its own unique set of conditions, different from every other verb. At the same time different languages show a number of similarities in the way verbs are used. The meanings of each verb encourage its use in particular constructions, so verbs of similar meanings in different languages should exhibit similarities in their use. The expectation is that universal semantic requirements will lead verbs of similar meanings in all languages to require similar semantic roles. These similarities in turn should help us to understand some of the syntactic uniformities among languages.

Much remains to be learned about the classification of verbs, even in a language as familiar as English, and even more remains to be learned about other languages. It does seem clear that any complete description of a language will have to indicate, very carefully, exactly which semantic roles and which kinds of subordination are allowed for each verb. This information will have to be included in the lexicon along with the other unique phonological, semantic, and syntactic properties of each word. Verb classification is a central feature of language design.

NOMINATIVE–ACCUSATIVE AND ERGATIVE–ABSOLUTIVE LANGUAGES

We have seen how important it is for a language to give the listener a secure means for distinguishing among the various semantic roles in a sentence. The listener has to be able to distinguish Agent from Patient, the actor from the acted on, to know who is benefiting and who is not. The semantic roles can be kept distinct in many ways, and a method that is different from anything known from familiar European languages is found in so-called "ergative–absolutive" languages.

One method that languages use to help the listener to identify the semantic roles of noun phrases is to mark them with case markers or adpositions. Since these are so widely used, languages ought to be able to achieve a kind of logical consistency if every noun phrase had to carry either a case marker or an adposition, but many languages allow a few noun phrases to slip through without one. One particular type of noun phrase that is often left unmarked by an adposition or case marker is the noun phrase that is used as the subject of an intransitive verb. Every language has many intransitive verbs (verbs that require only one associated noun phrase), as in *Lucy swims, Lucy worries, Lucy sleeps, Lucy laughs*. Simple economy offers a reasonable explanation for the tendency of these subjects to be left without an adposition or case marker. Why should speakers have to mark the noun phrase explicitly, when the sentence has no other noun phrase with which it might be confused?

Every language also has sentences built around transitive verbs, and these have two noun phrases, often an Agent and a Patient (e.g., *Lucy eats a crumpet, Lucy adores Schroeder*). Marking becomes more helpful when a sentence has two noun phrases. They can be distinguished by word order, as in

English, but when languages have freer word order, it is often helpful to mark at least one of the noun phrases with a case marker or adposition. However, just as economy makes it unnecessary to mark the single noun phrase of an intransitive sentence, economy should also discourage the marking of both noun phrases in a transitive sentence. Missing an opportunity for economy, some languages do mark both noun phrases of transitive sentences. Some even mark the single noun phrase of intransitive sentences, but the essential requirement is, somehow, to be able to differentiate the two noun phrases of a transitive sentence, at least in cases where there is a risk of ambiguity.

It seems almost always to be the case that *one* of the noun phrases of transitive sentences is treated in a way that parallels the subject of an intransitive sentence. In English and other familiar European languages, the Agents of typical transitive sentences are treated like the subjects of intransitive sentences. Thus we find it natural to use the same words in the same positions in both intransitive sentences (*I sleep, The women are tired, He dreams*) and in transitive sentences (*I chop wood, The women attack the problem, He avoids work*).

We can sidestep the question of the semantic role of the single noun phrase of an intransitive sentence and simply call it the "subject." Notice, then, that the Agents of English transitives and the subjects of intransitives have several similarities: (1) Both come before the verb; (2) Both govern verb agreement (determine whether or not the verb has the -*s* suffix); and (3) Both call for the nominative forms of pronouns (*I, we, he,* etc.). The Patient of a transitive verb is quite different: (1) It is placed after the verb; (2) It does not agree with the verb; and (3) It requires the objective form of pronouns (*me, us, him,* etc.). These facts can be summarized by describing both the subject of an intransitive sentence and the Agent of a transitive sentence as having the "nominative" case. The other noun phrase of a transitive sentence can then be called "accusative."

English speakers, and speakers of most other European languages, are so accustomed to using the same case (i.e., the same kind of noun phrase) both for the Agent of a transitive sentence and for the subject of an intransitive sentence that it is difficult, at first, to imagine any alternative. Logically, however, it should be possible to identify the subject (i.e., the *only* semantic role) of an intransitive sentence with the Patient, rather than with the Agent, of a transitive sentence and, in fact, many such languages exist. These are called **ergative/absolutive** languages, or simply **ergative** languages for short, to distinguish them from the **nominative/accusative** languages that are more familiar to Europeans and Americans. The term "ergative" names the case that is used for the Agent of a transitive verb. "Absolutive" is the name of the case that is used both for the subject of an intransitive verb and for the Patient of a transitive verb. A feeling for ergative constructions can be conveyed by means of pseudo-English sentences in which "by" is used as a marker of ergativity. Intransitive sentences, whose subjects are in the absolutive case, might look like these:

The window opens.
Me dream.
The wood rots.
The children eat.
Him swims.

Corresponding transitive sentences in which the Patient has the same case as the subject of intransitive sentences, and the ergative Agent is marked with *by,* would be formed like these:

The window opens by me. 'I open the window.'
Me bite by the dog. 'The dog bites me.'
The wood chops by the men. 'The men chop the wood.'
The children feed by the father. 'The father feeds the children.'
Him sees by you. 'You see him.'

These artificial sentences may remind an English speaker of passives, but that is a misleading impression, for the corresponding sentences of a real ergative language are not passives. Rather, the Patient in each transitive sentence simply duplicates the word order, case, and conditions of verb agreement of the subject of the intransitive sentences. More realistic examples can be taken from Dyirbal, an ergative language spoken by an aboriginal people of Australia. Intransitive Dyirbal sentences have their noun phrases in the Absolutive case. (Dyirbal nouns are accompanied by a classifier, represented in these sentences by *bayi* and *balan,* but these do not bear on the question of ergativity):

Bayi   yaṛa   banin^{y}u.
Class.   man-Abs.   came-here
'The man came here.'

Balan   d^{y}ugumbil   banin^{y}u.
Class.   woman-Abs.   came-here
'The woman came here.'

In a transitive sentence it is the Patient that takes the same form as the subject of the intransitive sentence. The Agent has the ergative case as shown by the case marker, -*ŋgu.*

Balan   d^{y}ugumbil   baŋgul   yaṛaŋgu   buṛan.
Class   woman-Abs.   Class.   man-Erg.   saw
'The man saw the woman.'

The contrast between ergative–absolutive and nominative–accusative languages gives us another example of the way in which languages can accomplish the same tasks with somewhat differing machinery. Everyone needs to have ways of talking about transitive and intransitive relationships. Everyone needs to distinguish Patients from Agents. Practical languages can meet these requirements in more than just one way.

WORD-ORDER TYPOLOGY

All languages have similar types of morphemes, words, and phrases. Everywhere, we find nouns, noun phrases, relative clauses, verbs, adpositions, determiners, possessives, adjectivelike modifiers of nouns, and question words. Most languages have prefixes or suffixes or both. Because languages must be spoken in one-dimensional time, these affixes, words, and phrases must occur in linear order, one after another. We would expect closely related words to occur near to one another, so it seems natural, for example, that adjectives are usually found close to the nouns they modify. On the other hand, there seems to be no obvious advantage in placing the adjective before the noun rather than after it, so it is hardly surprising that adjectives precede their nouns in some languages, while they follow in others. Verbs may occur first, last, or in the middle of a sentence. It takes only a brief exposure to a language remote from English to become aware of just how radically word order can vary.

Nevertheless, word-order variability is also limited in many ways. It was pointed out in the previous chapter that the subject of a sentence usually precedes the object. This means that most languages have VSO, SVO, or SOV as their basic word order. Languages with OSV, OVS, or VOS as their basic word order are unusual. In a sample of 30 languages, drawn from all parts of the world, Joseph Greenberg found many other limitations on permitted word orders.

Greenberg found, for example, that every verb-initial language in his sample has prepositions rather than postpositions. Every verb-final language, on the other hand, has postpositions. Verb-medial languages are divided, but the majority have prepositions. The number of these thirty languages with each combination of verb and adposition order is shown in Table 11–1.

The order of the constituents of a noun phrase also correlates with the position of the verb. Verb-final languages place the name of the possessor before the name of what is possessed (e.g., *Morton's pen*). Most verb-initial and verb-medial languages place the possessor after the possessed (e.g., *the pen of Morton*) (see Table 11–2). English is a partial, and unusual, exception,

Table 11–1
Prepositions and Verb Order

	VSO	SVO	SOV
Prepositions	6	10	0
Postpositions	0	3	11

Table 11–2
Possessives and Verb Order

	VSO	SVO	SOV
Possessed–Possessor	6	9	0
Possessor–Possessed	0	4	11

since English has constructions with both orders, but English was not one of the 30 languages in Greenberg's sample.

Table 11–3 shows that demonstratives are a bit more likely to precede their nouns than to follow, but this tendency is strong only in verb-final languages, and it is actually reversed in verb-initial languages.

Table 11–3
Demonstratives and Verb Order

	VSO	SVO	SOV
Noun–Demonstrative	4	6	2
Demonstrative–Noun	2	7	9

Table 11–4 shows that adjectives follow their noun in almost two thirds of the languages sampled, but they do so consistently only in verb-initial languages. They often precede the noun in SVO languages, and they are especially likely to precede in languages in which the verb comes last.

Table 11–4
Adjectives and Verb Order

	VSO	SVO	SOV
Noun–Adjective	6	8	5
Adjective–Noun	0	5	6

The position of the relative clause with respect to its noun correlates with verb order better than does the position of the adjective. Relative clauses almost always follow the noun in verb-initial and verb-medial languages, and they generally precede the noun in verb-final languages. Two languages in the sample allow relative clauses to occur on either side of the noun, and information is lacking for one language (see Table 11–5).

Taken together, Tables 11–3, 11–4, and 11–5 suggest that verb-final languages are more likely to have their modifiers before the noun, while verb-initial languages are more likely to have them after the noun. Verb-medial languages seem to compromise.

Table 11-5
Relative Clause Order

	VSO	SVO	SOV
Noun–Relative Clause	6	12	2
Relative Clause–Noun	0	0	7
Both	0	1	1

Still other regularities can be found. English questions formed with "question words" such as *who, when, where,* etc., deviate from the usual English word order, since the question word, whether subject, direct object, or the object of a preposition, is placed first in the sentence. We say *What did he destroy?* where *what* comes first even though it is the object of the verb. We say *Where did you hang it?* instead of *You hung it where?* although the latter would more closely parallel *You hung it in the closet.* English is not alone in putting question words first in a sentence, but some other languages keep them in the same spot as the corresponding noun phrase. A language of this type would have questions equivalent to *He destroyed what?* and *You hung it where?* Although this order is not impossible in English, it is not the most natural. Table 11–6 shows that the question word is much more likely to come first in VSO and SVO languages than in verb-final languages.

Table 11-6
Question Word Position

	VSO	SVO	SOV
Question word first	6	10	0
Question order same as Statement order	0	3	11

Many languages have inflected auxiliary verbs. English auxiliary verbs such as *have* and *be,* for instance, are inflected for tense (*has/had; is/was*). Inflected auxiliaries usually follow the main verb in SOV languages, but they usually precede the verb in VSO and SVO languages. Table 11–7 shows the position of the auxiliary in the 19 languages of the 30-language sample that have inflected auxiliary verbs.

Table 11-7
Inflected Auxiliary Verb Order

	VSO	SVO	SOV
Auxiliary–Verb	3	7	0
Verb–Auxiliary	0	1	8

Table 11-8
Prefixing and Suffixing

	VSO	SVO	SOV
Exclusively prefixing	0	1	0
Exclusively suffixing	0	2	11
Both	6	10	1

Finally, Table 11–8 shows the kinds of affixes found in languages of various types. Most verb-final languages have suffixes but no prefixes. Prefixes are more common in verb-initial and verb-medial languages than in verb-final languages, but few languages are totally without suffixes.

The figures in these tables express a complex and rather confusing set of interdependencies. Why should some constructions so often be found together? In some cases constructions seem to belong together because they are so similar. For example, a possessor, such as *king's* acts very much like an adjective since both possessors and adjectives narrow the meaning of the noun that they modify. Thus *the king's palace* and *the big palace* are parallel constructions, and a language seems to display a certain harmony if both possessors and adjectives are placed on the same side of the noun. At the same time, possessive constructions such as *of the king* are also parallel to prepositional phrases such as *to the king*. This second parallelism is expressed by the fact that almost all languages that have prepositions also place the possessor after the possessed. (This relationship is implied by Tables 11–1 and 11–2). In English, the *of* that marks possession is a preposition.

Since English has prepositions but also adjectives that precede the nouns, our possessive construction is pulled in opposite directions. Prepositions conform to the "of" construction, while English adjective order conforms to the "-'s" construction. Perhaps this helps to explain why we have two different ways of showing possession. A language with adjectives that follow the noun and prepositions could comfortably put all its possessors after the noun as well. Similarly postpositions and preceding adjectives would both conform to possessors that precede.

When the clear association of prepositions with verb-initial languages and of postpositions with verb-final languages is also taken into account, two constellations of constructions emerge as being in harmony with one another. On the one hand, VSO word order, prepositions, adjectives that follow nouns, and possessors that follow the possessed all fit together. A good many languages, including Welsh, Hebrew, Polynesian, and classical Arabic follow this pattern. Let us call these "Type A" languages. On the other hand, languages with exactly the opposite characteristics, verbs at the end, postpositions, adjectives before nouns, and possessors before the possessed, are also common: Armenian, Hindi, Korean, Hungarian, and Japanese. These can be called "Type B" languages. Many languages, to be sure, fail to fit perfectly into one

Table 11-9
Word Order Typology

Type A	Type B
Verb initial or medial	Verb final
Prepositions	Postpositions
Possessed–Possessor	Possessor–Possessed
Demonstrative–Noun or Noun–Demonstrative	Demonstrative–Noun
Noun–Adjective	Adjective–Noun or Noun–Adjective
Noun–Relative clause	Relative clause–Noun
Question word first	Question word not first
Auxiliary–Verb	Verb–Auxiliary
Prefixing and/or Suffixing	Suffixing

or the other of these extremes, and two variants are particularly common. French, Spanish, modern Greek, Thai, and Vietnamese are like Type A languages except that they have SVO rather than VSO order. Basque, Burmese, and Zuni are like Type B languages except that their adjectives precede, rather than follow, the noun. A considerable majority of the world's languages fit one of these four patterns. English, of course, does not.

An inspection of Tables 11-1 through 11-8 will show that several other constructions tend to correlate with the A/B distinction. These correlations make it tempting to see Types A and B as implying more than simply the orders of adposition, verb, adjective, and possessor, but as embracing many other constructions as well. A and B tend toward perfect opposites, and some linguists have suggested that languages tend to follow one of the two pervasive word-order patterns shown in Table 11-9.

It has even been suggested that languages are under some internal typological pressure to conform to one or another of these polar types. For instance, an SOV language that had prepositions might be under some sort of tension that could be resolved if either the position of the verb changed or prepositions were replaced by postpositions. The problem with this suggestion is that when the A/B distinction is expanded from the four characteristics we started with to include all the different word-order patterns that are listed in Table 11-9, relatively few languages any longer conform exactly to either type. Languages with most of the characteristics of Type A generally have at least one or two Type B characteristics, and vice versa. A possible explanation is that languages of a mixed type are in the process of change from one pure type to the other, but that implies that most languages are changing. The significance of the "polar" types is rather undermined if few languages are found at either pole. Perhaps the pressures to conform are not so strong after all.

Could it be that in moving toward consistency, languages run up against contradictory constraints? The perfect Type A language ought to have prefixes rather than suffixes, but suffixes are so much more common than prefixes in the world's languages that the pressure toward prefixing exerted by a Type A language may not be enough to overcome the opposing and more general pressure toward suffixing. This would suggest that we should not expect to find many "pure" Type A languages, if purity demands that they are exclusively prefixing. Conversely, we might expect a "pure" Type B language to have all its modifiers before the noun, but such languages are not common. A few languages do manage to put all their modifiers first, but more often, even in languages with verbs in the final position, a few modifiers follow the noun instead of preceding it. One of the functions of relative clauses is to allow a noun to have a very long modifier (e.g., *the man* [*that I saw trudging up the stairs at the same time that he* . . .]). It was suggested in Chapter 10 that there is some pressure toward moving long or "heavy" elements to the end of a construction, so that the shorter element can be processed first. That would suggest that even in a verb-final language, there may be some pressure to place long relative clauses after their nouns, in spite of the opposing pressure to move all modifiers to the front of the noun.

We may even wonder whether any constellation of word orders could be ideal. Can we find a single set of orders, all of which seem mutually compatible, and that serve to satisfy communicative needs in a maximally efficient manner? Perhaps every possible order is deficient in some way, and perhaps this is why no single word-order type has emerged as the single predominant pattern of all languages. As in other cases that we have considered, real languages represent various sorts of compromises. It may be that, in the face of contradictory pressures, a compromise is the best solution possible.

SIGNING AND SYNTAX

The syntax of American Sign Language (ASL), like the formation of its words described in Chapter 6, is distinguished from spoken language by the way in which it makes use of space. A manual language is, in some ways, more cumbersome than a spoken language, but by the ingenious use of the three dimensions of space it can compensate for its apparent limitations. One apparent problem about signing is that signed words can be produced at only about half the rate of spoken words. It may seem surprising, then, that signers are able to convey information at about the same rate as speakers. How do they overcome the apparent limitation on speed?

The signed words such as those that were described in Chapter 6 can be called "lexical signs," as a way of distinguishing them from other kinds of signs that will be described shortly. Most of the lexical signs are content words—nouns and verbs that refer to the things and actions that people want to talk about. When a sequence of these lexical signs is transcribed onto paper, it appears to have a rather telegraphic style. Content words are strung together but their organization is by no means apparent to a reader who has no knowledge of signing. Such strings seem to omit many of the subtleties of spoken sentences. The simple string of lexical signs, however, conveys only one part of the message that signers convey. People who are accustomed to spoken language, where both content and function words must occur in a single lineal sequence, may fail to notice that other things are happening simultaneously with the lexical signs. In addition to the main sequence of lexical signs, signers use at least three other types of visual and spatial signals. These give a syntactic organization to the lexical signs, they enrich the message, and they allow signing to have both a speed and subtlety that is comparable to a spoken language.

First, the individual lexical signs, especially the verbs, can be modulated in a variety of ways that enrich their use and their meanings. In spoken languages, inflections generally occur in linear sequence, either before or after the word that they modify. The modulations of ASL occur simultaneously with the sign they modify, but in other ways they act very much like the inflections of spoken language. They even carry meanings that inflections carry in many languages, though English happens to be a language in which most of these meanings require separate words. For example, Figure 11–1 shows the uninflected sign meaning to be SICK, which is made with the middle fingers of the hands bent, one of them tapping against the forehead. If the hands assume the same shape and are placed in the same location but are also moved in smooth circles, the meaning becomes 'prone to be sick.' Other lexical signs can be moved in similar circles, also with the meaning 'prone to be.' If the hands with the shape and location of SICK move back and forth rapidly and tensely the meaning becomes 'incessantly sick.' Other signs can be modulated in a similar way to give a similar meaning. ASL has several dozen ways of modulating lexical signs by various kinds of movement, and these add considerable subtlety to the message.

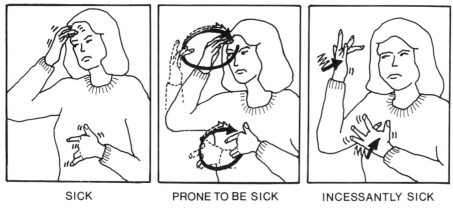

SICK   PRONE TO BE SICK   INCESSANTLY SICK

Figure 11–1
ASL sign for "sick" with modulations. From Klima and Bellugi (1979).

Second, signers use gestures of the face and head that augment the information conveyed by their manual signs. This is another way in which signing escapes the linearity of a language of sound. Signers can make a question by raising the eyebrows and by holding the head and shoulders forward, and raising the chin high enough to keep the face vertical. Negatives are often indicated with a lexical sign, but it is also possible to negate a sentence with a shake of the head. Tightly closed eyes give emphasis. More subtly, the syntactic structure of the sentence can be marked by the position of the head. A distinctive head tilt sets a relative clause off from its surroundings. Conditional clauses and other types of sentence embeddings can be marked in parallel ways. These gestures of the head and face punctuate the sequence of lexical signs in a way that is a bit reminiscent of the intonation of a spoken sentence.

Third, signers are able to use the space around them as a kind of stage in which to set the story they want to tell. The location of the participants in a conversation is exploited by orienting some signs toward them. Signs like GIVE and ASK are oriented so as to point both to the giver or asker and to the receiver or the one who is asked. In this way the meaning carried by spoken pronouns can be conveyed simultaneously with the verbs and need not be given by signs of their own. Even individuals who are not present can be assigned a space, and then other signs can be oriented to those spaces. Once Jim and Jane have been safely located in the signing space, GIVE can be oriented so as to show that it is *he* who is giving to *her,* rather than the other way around. Even the direction of gaze is enough to show which of several participants, whether physically present or simply located in space, is being referred to. The verbs of many spoken languages have person markers, so the ASL pattern is hardly unique, but in ASL the person markers occur simultaneously with the verb rather than as a separate affix in the way that is typical of spoken languages.

It was once supposed that sign language had little grammar, but the modulations of the lexical signs, the gestures of the face and head, and the use of space as a stage all enrich and give structure to the apparently telegraphic sequence of lexical signs. They allow many of the ideas for which English requires separate words to be made simultaneously with the lexical signs, and this allows information to be conveyed as rapidly with signs as with a spoken language. It was also once supposed that signs were nothing but pantomime and that sign languages everywhere were much alike. It is now clear that many mutually unintelligible sign languages are spoken around the world, but much remains to be learned about their similarities and differences, even about the degree to which they all exploit same kinds of modulations and facial gestures.

Like spoken languages, sign languages must be learned, and the most fluent signers are those who learn the language in childhood. Hearing people who learn to sign as adults rarely achieve anything like native fluency. People who are very deaf from birth have great difficulty learning to use a spoken language, so it is difficult to find skillful interpreters. One group of true bilinguals does exist, however. The hearing children of deaf parents often become fluent signers. Signing may even be their first language, but they also learn spoken language from older siblings or other relatives, or from neighboring children. They may, from an early age, act as interpreters for their parents, and they become the best adult interpreters.

The more we have learned about sign language, the greater is the impression of normality that it gives. Signing is used by people who are normal except for their ears, and their inability to learn to speak does not imply any lack of linguistic aptitude. If they participate in a community of deaf people, they develop a language that, while built according to somewhat different principles, fulfills all the same functions as spoken language. Signers can play with signs as speakers can play with words. They can, for example, sign the equivalent of puns. Forms of composed and expressive signing deserve to be regarded as poetry. Signers dream in signs and move their hands when they "talk" in their sleep. They "mutter" to themselves in sign, and move their hands when they talk to themselves, just as hearing people sometimes move their lips and even speak aloud to themselves. Deaf people plan conversations in signs. Deaf children who have learned signing as their first language have been observed signing to their toy animals, and signing to themselves when they think they are unobserved.

If we were not already convinced, signing would leave us with no doubt that human beings are, deeply and unchangeably, talking animals. People who cannot talk with their mouths find a way to talk with their hands. The ability of language to emerge almost as easily from the hands as from the mouth must persuade us that the basic organ of speech is not the vocal tract but the brain. People whose ears are good find it convenient to use their voices to talk. It is easier to combine with other activities, and it may be easier to listen to several people trying to speak at once than to watch several people who are trying to sign at once. Still, when ears are unavailable people find it possible to exploit an alternative medium, and our understanding of the human potential for language is greatly expanded by our new awareness of signing.

THE GROUND PLAN AGAIN

We have now surveyed enough examples to gain some feeling for the ways in which languages are similar and the ways in which they differ, and the examples should convey a sense of the fundamental ground plan to which all spoken languages conform. Even sign languages share much of the ground plan, though not all. All languages have a large class of verbs and another large class of nouns. In spoken languages, at least, nouns join with determiners, numbers, adjectives, and relative clauses to form noun phrases. Verbs frequently join with auxiliaries or with various sorts of affixes that express time relationships. Noun phrases in turn join with verbs to form clauses and sentences, with particular verbs calling for particular kinds of noun phrases. Some kinds of noun phrases, such as those marked by temporal and locative adpositions (e.g., *in the morning, at the dentist's*), act very much like adverbs in modifying the verb, but most languages also have more specialized adverbs (e.g., *tomorrow, there*) that perform a similar role although they lack the internal syntactic structure of adpositional phrases. All languages have ways of showing negation, of asking questions, and of issuing commands. All languages have devices, such as pronouns, that allow speakers to avoid repetition.

All languages also have a variety of grammatical devices that help to clarify the relationships among the nouns, verbs, and other content words of a sentence. In addition to word order, languages use case markers and adpositions that are attached to nouns or noun phrases, and many have markers of agreement that are attached to the verbs. Less frequently the constituents of a noun phrase must agree with each other. All these devices help to keep clear the relationships among the items within a clause or sentence. They are the means by which the necessarily linear sequence of words in a spoken sentence is organized into constituents and by which these constituents are given a hierarchical structure.

A clause is a construction that includes a verb. Many sentences consist of a single independent clause, but all languages also allow two or more clauses to be combined into larger and more complex sentences. We can recognize at least three ways of combining clauses. First, they can be strung together in a relatively simple sequence by various sorts of conjunctions, such as *and, but, before, while* or *then*. Second, they can be joined into tighter constructions when one sentence is embedded in such a way that it effectively becomes part of the larger sentence. Third, a sentence can be turned into a relative clause, which can be used to modify a noun, so that an entire sentence is turned into something that can act rather like an adjective. By using many of these constructions simultaneously, speakers can build up sentences of daunting complexity. Of course the details of how all this is done differ from one language to another, but all languages are built on a similar underlying plan.

We do not yet have entirely convincing explanations for all the word-order regularities that have been reviewed in this chapter, but we would not have been able to make these generalizations at all, if languages everywhere were not constructed in similar ways and used for similar purposes. If this seems to be an almost inevitable organization for a communication system, it is worth remembering that we know of other communication systems that are used to communicate different sorts of messages and that are built on very different plans. Neither the communication systems of animals nor the nonverbal human communication of laughs, cries, shrugs, and frowns can be made to fit into the syntactic categories that turn up so consistently in natural languages. Neither the calls of animals nor the shouts and cries of human beings can in any reasonable way be described as built up from nouns or verbs, let alone relative clauses or adpositions.

Computer and mathematical languages resemble human languages more closely, perhaps because, like natural languages, computer and mathematical languages are the products of human minds. However, even these artificially constructed languages lack many of the characteristics of natural languages. As long as we restrict ourselves to languages like English, Chinese, and Navajo, we work within a familiar world. Even our ability to describe the differences among these languages in detailed and precise ways testifies to their underlying similarity. The study of typological variability and the study of language universals support one another, for as we continue to chart the ways in which languages differ, we also come to understand the ways in which they are similar.

CHAPTER TWELVE

Syntactic Variation

REGIONAL VARIATION

Chapters 4 and 8 surveyed the ways in which the lexicon and phonology can vary from place to place, from social group to social group and from situation to situation. In this chapter we turn to variation in syntax. We will have no trouble finding examples of stylistic and social class variation in English syntax, but clear examples of regional variation are less easy to identify. When we listen to English speakers from the other side of the Atlantic, or from other parts of the world, it is usually their phonology or vocabulary that catches our attention. Syntax seems more uniform.

Our impression of syntactic uniformity is probably due to the example of written English. Virtually the same syntactic constructions are acceptable in writing throughout the English-speaking, and English-writing, world. The uniformity of written English syntax sets a standard by which we judge syntactic acceptability. When observations are limited to the syntax of written English, and to those varieties of formal spoken English that reflect written standards, we are unlikely to find extensive syntactic variation.

English speakers are relatively tolerant of varying pronunciations, accepting them as more or less equivalent in prestige. An Australian reads aloud with Australian pronunciation, and an North American reads from the same page with a North American pronunciation. Each of us imposes our own pronunciation on the same passage. It is not so easy to impose our own syntax on a string of written words, so we usually read them as they appear on paper. The syntactic conventions of written English even influence our judgments of spoken English. The greatest syntactic variation in English is found in the most colloquial forms of the spoken language. The differences among prestigious dialects seem insignificant; rarely are they great enough to cause misunderstanding. Still, even among prestigious dialects, enough differences can be found to show that no aspect of language is immune to variation.

In Britain, the auxiliary verb *do* can be used in a few places where it is quite impossible in America: *Did he pass his exams? Yes, he did do; Have you cleaned your room? Yes, I have done.* Although natural for British speakers, Americans are apt to find such expressions quite baffling. Americans are more likely than Britons to string verbs together with nothing between them. Most Americans can easily say the following sentences without the parenthesized words, while the extra words are needed in Britain: *We'll come (to) see you soon, Go (and) fix it now, I'll help (to) mow the lawn, We ordered that (to be) done immediately.* Words may be contracted in slightly different ways in Britain and America. British speakers are more likely than Americans to say *I'd have done that*; Americans find *I would've done that* more natural. British English allows *The soup has carrots in* and *I want some paper with lines on,* while Americans find such sentences incomplete without a concluding *it. I wonder that he did any work at all* sounds fine in Britain but would probably become *It's a wonder that he did any work at all* in America.

Some of the many minor idiomatic differences between British and American English touch on syntax without affecting it in any profound way. A few verbs have different past tense forms in Britain and America. British English speakers usually say *burnt, learnt, spilt,* and *spoilt,* while Americans generally regularize these as *burned, learned, spilled,* and *spoiled.* Conversely, where North Americans often say *dove, fit,* and *snuck,* British speakers more consistently use the regular *dived, fitted,* and *sneaked.* Where Americans say *gotten,* the British say *got,* as in *We would have got(ten) here sooner, if it hadn't been raining.*

The opposite shores of the Atlantic also have some subtle differences in modal verbs. *Shall* is a bit unusual and *shan't* almost unknown in North America, so that the British *Shall I drink it now?* becomes *Should I drink it now?* in America. *I should like that* becomes *I would like that.* The use of *would* in a habitual sense, as in *When I was young, I would go there every day* seems natural to Americans, but in Britain this sentence would probably be replaced by *When I was young, I went there every day,* or . . . *I used to go there every day.* The British *That will be the postman at the door* becomes the American's *That must be . . .,* or simply *That's the mailman at the door. Used, ought, need,* and *dare* act more like auxiliaries in Britain than in America so that *Used he to go there?, He used not to go there, Ought we to eat out?, Need you be so rude?* and *I daren't tell the truth* all sound better in Britain than they do in America.

The British *go to university* but, once there, they *go to a class.* Americans reverse this and *go to a university* but *go to class.* The impersonal pronoun *one* as in *One has to be careful,* or even *One must be honest with oneself,* is possible for some Britons, even in relatively informal speech, while it seems formal, even a bit pompous, to most Americans.

In addition to these transatlantic differences, a few minor syntactic differences also distinguish regional dialects of American English from one another. Speakers from some parts of the United States are able to use *anymore* in positive sentences where it is impossible for other speakers. Only in some dialects is *Anymore I come here to swim* a grammatical sentence. Some Americans find *I don't guess so* to be grammatical, while for others it is impossible.

These differences are trivial by comparison with the huge range of syntactic patterns that all English dialects share, but any impression of uniformity in English syntax is an illusion that is quickly dispelled when we turn away from prestigious dialects. As soon as we consider the dialects of varied social classes, we find marked syntactic variation. We will return to class differences in syntax after considering stylistic variation.

STYLISTIC VARIATION

Stylistic variation is as important in syntax as in phonology, but it takes such a different form that it may not, at first, appear to be the same phenomenon. We easily acknowledge different pronunciations as being "different ways of saying the same thing." Syntactic alternatives are not so easily regarded as "the same." Consider, nevertheless, the following eight sentences:

1. *I didn't give anything to her.*
2. *I did not give anything to her.*
3. *I gave nothing to her.*
4. *I didn't give her anything.*
5. *I gave her nothing.*
6. *I didn't give her nothing.*
7. *I didn't give her a thing.*
8. *She got nothing from me.*

These sentences all mean the same thing, or at least they can all be used to describe the same objective fact. They would all be true or false under the same conditions. Their connotations certainly vary, however, and we do not react to them all in just the same ways. In particular, they differ pragmatically. Some are more formal than others, and they express subtle differences in emphasis, attitude, and in what the speaker assumes that the hearer already knows.

Most people would probably accept the first sentence as an entirely natural and colloquial statement, readily identifiable as an easy contraction of the fuller, more formal, or more emphatic sentence 2. They might even be considered as variants of the "same" sentence. Sentence 3 is even more formal than 2, and it is not quite so clearly a form of the "same" sentence. Sentence 4, like sentence 1, is relaxed and colloquial, but *anything* and *her* have switched positions; this suggests a different pragmatic focus. Sentence 5 is quite formal and, like sentence 3, it might be more natural in writing than in speech. Several of the sentences are so colloquial that they might seem out of place in careful writing, but only sentence 6 clearly counts as "nonstandard." This is an example of a stigmatized construction that is rarely found in writing and that many people regard as "wrong," even in spoken language, but the sentence is readily understandable by all speakers of English. Since everyone can understand them, sentences like this must figure in some corner of everyone's linguistic competence, even of those who would never dream of uttering such a sentence themselves. As will be shown later, sentences like this are closely related to the other kinds of negative sentences.

Sentences 1 through 6 are all closely related. Sentences 7 and 8 seem more different. They are a bit more emphatic, or a bit more colorful or assertive, and we would be less likely to consider them as alternative forms of the same sentence. Nevertheless, speakers can use sentences 7 or 8 to convey the same factual information as the sentences 1 through 6, and the choice of 7 and 8 will also depend on what speakers choose to emphasize and on the attitudes they want to convey. Of course, these eight sentences do not exhaust the possibilities. There are many other ways to convey the same information, and for any other sentence, with any other meaning, an equally extensive set of alternatives could be proposed.

Why does a language give us so many options? Surely we could manage with something less flexible? The point is, of course, that we use our language for many other things than simply to convey factual information. As with our phonological and lexical options, our syntactic options respond to a whole range of pressures. In addition to communicating facts, we must provide continuity, introduce topics in coherent ways, and give the right emphasis to various parts of our statements. We want to say things in a way that is appropriate for the occasion, but we also want to express our attitude. The richness and variability of language gives us the freedom to pursue all these goals simultaneously. This richness requires many alternative ways to express any particular factual message.

SPOKEN AND WRITTEN STYLES

One important dimension of stylistic variability is the difference between spoken and written language. Writing is not simply spoken language transferred to paper. Writing is used for different purposes than speech, and the written medium imposes different constraints. The differences stand out with special clarity when we compare spontaneous informal conversation with relatively formal writing that is intended to convey factual information, but not all genres of spoken and written language are as different as these. Personal letters are, in some respects, more like conversation than are business letters or academic prose. The spoken language of radio and television shares many features with written styles. Prepared speeches are still closer to written language, even when they are not read from a written text. Fiction generally reflects spoken language more closely than does writing that is intended to convey factual information. Any thorough investigation of stylistic differences has to be sensitive to many variables, and the differences between speech and writing are just one of these. Nevertheless, spontaneous conversation on the one hand, and writing that is intended to convey factual information on the other, can be taken as representative or even typical forms of speech and writing respectively. They differ in a number of ways.

Formality

Most writing is distinctly more formal than spoken conversation. To be sure, spoken sermons tend to be very formal, and few kinds of language can be less formal than a scribbled grocery list, so we must not imagine that all the characteristics of writing are the result of its formality, but some of them certainly are.

Formality and informality are signaled in many ways. Different words are chosen in different situations, but syntactic features vary as well. Contractions such as *don't, can't,* and *I'll* are very nearly obligatory in relaxed spoken styles, but they are regarded as too informal for most serious writing. Other contractions such as *would've, gotta,* or *gonna* are even rarer on paper, but they are common in speech. Certain types of negation are unusual in informal spoken language but common in writing. Sentences such as *We have none* and *The men have nothing to do,* in which the negation is shown only by a word that follows the verb, are particularly characteristic of writing. When speaking, we more often use the casual *We don't have any* and *The men don't have anything to do.*

Planning

When speaking, we have to plan and talk simultaneously, and when we plan badly, that becomes apparent for all to hear. Writers have a chance to edit. They can clean up their sentences and make them conform more closely to well-defined standards. Although sentences are taken to be fundamental units in the linguistic study of syntax, it is not always easy to identify them in conversational language. We produce not only sentence fragments when speaking, but also many "run on" sentences. We string clauses together with conjunctions to produce monologs that are, from a formal point of view, almost endless sentences: . . . *so then I came back, and he looked pretty confused but I figured he would probably be okay, but then he didn't seem to start to look any better, and I finally decided that I would have to try something else, but I was nearly at my wits end, so. . . .*

Planned language allows the writer to produce more elaborate syntax. It is easier, when writing, to use formal syntactic devices to show the relation between the parts of a sentence. Relative and subordinate clauses and passives are more frequent in writing, and tenses are more varied. Spoken language tends to be characterized by much more repetition than does written language, including repetition of both words and types of constructions. Writers have more time to organize their ideas than do speakers, and they often manage to pack more information into the same amount of text.

It may also be the ability to plan that lets writers use a more varied vocabulary than speakers. In a million-word sample of written English, the 8000 most common words made up about 90% of the running vocabulary. In an equally extensive sample of spoken English, 90% of the vocabulary was accounted for by about 800 different words, only one tenth as many. Speakers have to use whatever words they can find quickly. Writers can take the time to search for variety.

Background Information

Speakers can judge the knowledge of their listeners more accurately than writers can judge the knowledge of their readers, and the knowledge that speaker and hearer share eases communication and makes it more rapid. Time and place, for example, can more often be taken for granted when talking than when writing. *This, that, here, there, now,* and *then* are all defined by reference to the immediate context in which they are used. When we write, place and time must be indicated in more elaborate ways than by such simple words. Spoken language also makes pronouns easier to use. In writing, pronouns almost always refer to people or things that have already been named: *Mary and John both heard the explosion. She rushed to the window but he froze in terror.* In speech, pronouns can be used more easily to refer to people or things that the speaker and hearer can both see or hear, and they need not have been mentioned earlier in the discourse: *Who's he?, What's she doing?*

Speakers can judge how much their hearers know and how much they need to know. *Did you see Mary today?* assumes that the hearer will be able to identify Mary. *One more please* assumes that the participants know what is being talked about. Perhaps both can see the sugar lumps, or the empty glasses. This kind of information cannot be assumed in most writing but must be carefully spelled out. Writers have to expect the background information of their readers to be quite varied, so they may have to provide more information than some readers will need. Writers do not have the benefit of bored or puzzled looks to help them judge whether they are moving too slowly or too quickly.

Turn-Taking and Interaction

In most conversations, speakers take regular turns as hearers. We have ways to show that we want a turn at talking, and other ways to show that we are ready to yield the floor. We may shift our posture or refocus our gaze when we are anxious to speak or ready to stop, but we are also adept at finding the pauses in someone else's turn and at inserting our own comments at appropriate breaks. We deliberately encourage others to talk when we ask questions. We expect others to take up the slack when we can think of nothing else to say.

When, during a conversation, we fail to understand, we can ask for repetition or clarification. When talking, we constantly adjust our language in re-

sponse to the signals we receive from others. We rely on one another's gestures, on eye contact, and on signs of understanding and misunderstandings.
Notes passed between two school children are interactive, but most written
language is composed at one time and read at another. Writers must anticipate
the potential misunderstandings of readers. They cannot wait for questions.

Personal Involvement

Conversation is more consistently marked than writing by signs of the personal
involvement of the participants. The pronouns *you* and *I* are used far more
often in conversation than in most forms of writing, and they emphasize the
involvement of the speaker and the hearer. Speakers constantly find ways to
indicate their attitude toward the topic of their conversation. By their intonation, their tone of voice, and their choice of words, they emphasize what they
find important. More often than writing, spoken language is marked by expressions of self-doubt, such as *I think, I suppose,* and *maybe.*

Conservatism

Spoken language fades the moment it is uttered. Before the invention of sound
recording, people never heard language that was as old as an hour. Writing, by
its nature, persists, and we expect to read passages that were written decades
and even centuries ago. As readers, we experience the writing of earlier years
so we form our sense of the written standard not just by the most current styles
but by older styles as well. Whether consciously or unconsciously, therefore,
writers tend to conform to a standard that is more enduring than that of daily
conversation. Knowing, or hoping, that their writing will be read for years in
the future, writers may try to avoid the linguistic idiosyncrasies of their own
day. They reach for enduring patterns, not those that they fear will soon be
forgotten. The shifting styles of spoken language are adopted only slowly on
paper.

Redundancy

Redundancy is the repetition of information. Speakers who say *Billy can't see
none of 'em* are redundant because they indicate negation twice. Speakers who
say *Egbert feeds his snake* are equally redundant because the suffixed *-s* of
feeds redundantly provides the information that the subject is third person
singular, information that is entirely clear both from the name *Egbert* and from
the pronoun *his.* We are sometimes admonished by our teachers to make our
language less redundant, but a certain amount of redundancy is essential for
understanding. We cannot catch every sound or even every word that a
speaker utters, so listeners always rely on the redundant parts of the message
to fill in the gaps. Without redundancy, a single misprint or the loss of a single
phoneme would destroy the message. All language, therefore, has to include

ample redundancy, but spoken and written language differ in the places where redundancy is found.

As we have seen, fast spoken language is characterized by phonological attrition and contraction. Another way of saying this is that fast speech entails a loss of redundancy. Words are more often spelled out fully in writing, and in this respect, writing is far more redundant than speech. The contractions of spoken language can even lead to the loss of entire words. *You've had enough, haven't you?* can be safely abbreviated to *Had enough, haven't you?* because both *you* and *have* are redundantly repeated in the final phrase, *haven't you?*, that marks this sentence as a question. Instead of *Do you want to go dancing?* we can say *You want to go dancing? Y'wanna go dancing?* or even *Wanna go dancing?* Instead of *Are you ready to go* we can say simply *Ready to go?*, and instead of *Have you gone to the store yet?* we can say *Gone to the store yet?* These words can be safely deleted because their information is expressed redundantly elsewhere. The intonation of the spoken language shows that these are questions, and since we usually address questions to the hearer, *you* adds little useful information.

By avoiding contractions and by retaining words that can be deleted in speech, written English is more redundant than spoken English, but in other ways the spoken language is more redundant. The intonation that always accompanies spoken language provides information that we do not represent directly in writing. Not only does intonation effectively distinguish questions from statements, as in the examples given in the last paragraph, but it also shows how words are grouped into phrases. Indeed, the structure of spoken discourse is usually punctuated in considerable detail by its intonation. The transition from one sentence to another is often shown as clearly by changes in the intonation as by the syntax. In some languages, including English, emphatic stress directs the hearer's attention to the most important parts of the discourse. Stress and intonation, however, are poorly represented by writing. Our periods and commas provide no more than a few hints about the intonation of the spoken language, so most of the information that is carried by intonation is lost from writing or it is conveyed by different means. Here is one place where spoken language is far more redundant than writing.

In addition, although we can delete some words from spoken English, we add other words. *A man is at the door* may be a satisfactory written sentence, but in conversation we would be more likely to say *There is a man at the door,* with an extra *there. I have the ball* may be replaced in speech by *I've got the ball,* where *have* is reduced to a contraction, but where the meaning is made clear by an added *got* that amounts to a second marker of possession. We may say *wash up the dishes* and *sweep up the floor,* but in writing we prefer the less redundant *wash the dishes* and *sweep the floor.* In casual speech, we may say *visit with a friend, head up a committee, refer back to an earlier topic, plan on a vacation* or *face up to a problem.* One of the tasks that teachers of English composition set for themselves is to encourage their students to remove "unnecessary redundancy" from their writing, by omitting the prepositions from *visit a friend, head a committee, refer to an earlier topic, plan a vacation,* and *face a problem.*

Perhaps words are always contracted more easily in spoken than in written language, and perhaps some words are always more readily deleted. Perhaps there is also less resistance, when speaking, to a few extra "redundant" words. If so, these differences exactly parallel a persistent pattern of linguistic change for, with the passage of time, phonological bits seem always to be ground away, slowly but relentlessly, until some words are lost completely. This gradual phonological erosion means that some information is lost, but ambiguity can be avoided by adding new words. Written language may be inherently conservative, always reflecting a somewhat earlier stage of the language in which some words maintain their older and fuller forms and other "redundant" words are not yet introduced. In the contractions, deletions, and extra "redundant" words of the spoken language we may see the direction in which our language is moving. We will return to this possibility in the next chapter.

NONSTANDARD ENGLISH

The greatest syntactic variability in English is found in the differences that divide the dialects of our social classes. Among these, Americans are most acutely aware of the characteristics that distinguish the dialect of many black Americans from the more prestigeful dialects of English that are known as "standard." While standard English is by no means entirely uniform, Americans do recognize some forms of their language as suitable for serious occasions. Radio and television networks try to use a generally neutral and inoffensive dialect, and network English can be taken as a good example of what Americans accept as standard. Linguists often refer to the quite different dialect that is spoken by some, though by no means all, black Americans as "Black English Vernacular," or "BEV." We need to be clear about how this term is used.

Most Americans, both black and white, believe that they can tell, even over the telephone, whether they are talking to a white person or to a black person, and it is true that even without looking at them, Americans can usually identify speakers as black or white. At the same time, it is important to insist that no one can make a correct identification every time, for even a few failures demonstrate that it is not biological race that is responsible for dialect differences. Black Americans who grow up in otherwise white communities learn the language of their community as readily as do their white neighbors. It is only because so many blacks grow up in a community of other blacks that dialect differences are perpetuated. It is easy, then, to show that it is not biology, but the division of the population into segregated communities, that keeps our dialects distinct. The idea that dialect differences arise from biological differences can be dismissed as a racist myth.

A second myth about dialect differences, one that is almost the reverse of the racist myth, is somewhat more difficult to dispose of. A good many well-meaning Americans are embarrassed by the apparent difference between the speech of blacks and whites. Perhaps it seems discriminatory to examine these differences, or even to talk about them. Perhaps it is imagined that the only possible explanation of language differences would be a racial one, and many people, both black and white, find such an explanation unacceptable. Perhaps there is fear that any acknowledgment of dialect differences might serve as an excuse for continued discrimination. People who are concerned about these issues may try to minimize, or even to deny, the existence of dialect differences. It is hardly possible to claim that most inner-city blacks speak identically to the whites in the surrounding suburbs, but these obvious differences may be explained away by claiming that the black dialect is simply southern American English, now transplanted to northern and western cities. In the face of the insistence of Southerners, both black and white, that they, too, can hear the difference, even this claim is difficult to maintain for long.

Careful linguistic observations have shown clearly that even in the deepest South, and even among people of equivalent social classes, the speech of whites and blacks is different. The differences cannot be wished away. Indeed, when we recognize the segregation that has always divided black and white communities in America, any linguist ought to expect dialect differences. They should be no more surprising than the dialect differences that divide Britain and America. Barriers to communication, whether regional or social, lead to dialect differences.

A term like "Black English Vernacular" means no more and no less than a term for a regional dialect such as "Irish English." It means that many black Americans, like many Irishmen and women, speak a form of English that is recognizably different from the English of other communities. It does *not* imply that every person of African descent speaks BEV, any more than that every person of Irish descent speaks Irish English. Nor does it mean that all blacks speak identically to one another. Dialect differences are found within the black community just as they are within Ireland. There is not just one "black dialect" that is sharply distinct from all "white dialects." Indeed, there is probably no feature of BEV that is not also used by some whites. It remains the case, however, that a number of linguistic characteristics are found *more often* among black speakers than among whites—exactly as some linguistic characteristics are found more often among Irish speakers than among other speakers of English. If we want to understand the problems that dialect differences pose for American society, we will do better to examine the differences carefully than to close our eyes to them in the hope that they will go away. The special characteristics of Black English extend to every aspect of the language, but it is syntactic differences that Americans are most often troubled by.

One characteristic of the speech of many black Americans is the absence of several suffixes that are expected in standard English. The third person singular -*s* is particularly likely to be absent. In standard dialects, -*s* distinguishes *he runs* from *I run*, but many people say *he run, he walk,* etc., as easily as they say *I run, I walk,* etc. Virtually no information is carried by this -*s*, since the subject of the verb shows everything a hearer could possibly want to know about person and number. The -*s*, in fact, is the final relic of a much fuller set of verb suffixes that was used in earlier forms of English, and its absence in some forms of BEV can be looked upon as the final logical step in a long historical process by which verb agreement has been removed from the language.

Some black speakers also lack the possessive -*'s* so that *the girl gloves* can be used where standard English calls for *the girl's gloves.* Here, something more meaningful than the third person singular seems to be missing, but the context, combined with a distinctive intonation that shows the relationship among the words is almost always enough to avoid ambiguity. Standard speakers who worry about the loss of meaning should realize that they, themselves, manage just fine without a distinctive possessive in the plural. *Boys'* in *the boys' gloves* is pronounced in exactly the same way as a simple plural, but the homophony of the plural, *boys,* and the possessive plural, *boys',* hardly ever results in ambiguity. Moreover, English has another possessive construction that is always available. *The gloves of the girl* can always be used as an unambiguous alternative to *the girl gloves.* In any case, the absence of a suffix does not imply the absence of the concept expressed by the suffix. The concept of possession is just as secure among BEV speakers as it is among speakers of any other dialect. It is simply expressed in a slightly different way.

Some black speakers, like some whites, also lack a few plurals that are almost always expressed in standard forms of American English today. Even without a plural -*s* there is no ambiguity about phrases like *five mile* and *two foot* since the number makes the meaning clear. In this case, the absence of the plural suffix actually perpetuates an older pattern of English grammar. Americans now tend to look on the lack of the plural -*s* in measure expressions as less than fully standard, but the absence of the plural continues to be more widely accepted in Britain.

Standard speakers regularly contract forms of the verb *be,* so that -*m, -s,* and -*re* become, in effect, suffixes that are attached to the subject of the sentence: *I'm done, He's working,* and *They're hungry.* Under the right circumstances, all English speakers can omit these contractions entirely, as in *what ya' doin'?* where the *are* can completely disappear. Many blacks delete these auxiliary verbs, particularly *is* and *are,* more freely than most white speakers. Indeed, some blacks can delete them wherever standard speakers can contract them. This results in sentences that sound odd to people whose experience has been limited to more standard forms of English: *He working now, They hungry.* The deletion of *is,* and *are* can be looked on as an extension of a pattern that is well established in other forms of English. All dialects allow *am, is,* and *are* to be contracted under many circumstances and to be deleted in a few; BEV simply allows deletion under a particularly wide range of circumstances.

English dialects differ in more fundamental ways in their patterns of negation. Schoolteachers have waged a long war on the so-called "double negative'' but many speakers, both black and white, successfully resist their teachers' injunctions. ''Multiple'' negation is really a better term than ''double negation'' since the number of negatives is by no means limited to two: *I don't see none of them nowhere.* People occasionally suggest that multiple negatives are illogical, since two negations are imagined to cancel each other and to result in a positive, as if negation acts like multiplication. By this criterion, triple negatives should be acceptable, since when three negatives are multiplied they still yield a negative, but of course *I don't see none of them nowhere* is as strongly stigmatized as any double negative. If one insists on comparing language and mathematics, addition might offer a better analogy than multiplication. If anything, two or three negatives in a sentence simply add up to a stronger negative. Only in the imagination of purists have multiple negatives ever seemed dangerously illogical.

Like the deletion of auxiliaries, nonstandard negation can be understood as resulting from an extension of patterns found in other dialects. The similarities among forms of negation in all dialects explain the fact that all speakers, however standard their speech, easily understand multiple negatives. They have to be counted as a part of everyone's receptive grammar. Any English speaker who was told by a lumber salesman *We don't have no more shingles* would only be foolish to wait expectantly for the shingles, cleverly calculating that the two negatives had canceled each other. Demonstrating just how similar multiple negation is to other kinds of English negation requires a digression to consider how negative sentences are formed in standard English dialects.

The most common way of negating sentences in any form of English is by attaching a *not* (or *-n't*) to the first word of the auxiliary.

I can see him. → I can't see him.
You are trying very hard. → *You aren't trying very hard.*
We will have been gone by then. → *We won't have been gone by then.*

When no auxiliary verb is available, a form of the verb *do* must be added to the sentence in order to support the *not*. In effect, the *do* gives the *-n't* a place where it can be attached.

I like to swim. → *I don't like to swim.*
He runs every day. → *He doesn't run every day.*
We went to dinner. → *We didn't go to dinner.*

One complicating aspect of English negation is illustrated by these sentences:

I have seen someone. → *I haven't seen anyone.*
You do something right. → *You don't do anything right.*

In these sentences, the *someone* and *something* of the positive sentences become *anyone* and *anything* when the sentences are made negative. In standard English, ''indefinite'' words (roughly those beginning with *some-, any-,* or *no-*) are changed from the *some-* form to the *any-* form when a sentence is made negative. (The rule is actually considerably more complex, but this first approximation will do for present purposes.)

Another complication is illustrated by these three sentences:

> *Something was good enough for him.* → *Nothing was good enough for him.*
>
> *Some of the boys do that.* → *None of the boys do that.*
>
> *Somebody can find some.* → *Nobody can find any.*

As these demonstrate, an English sentence with an indefinite word in the subject position is negated at the subject but not (in standard English) at the auxiliary. The indefinite subject changes to the negative form, but the auxiliary is unchanged. Later indefinite words are changed from their *some-* to their *any-* form. Taking all the sentences we have considered so far into account, English can be described as having the following Basic Rule of Negation:

Basic Rule of Negation: A sentence is made negative by adding a sign of negation at the *first possible position* in the sentence. If the subject is indefinite, it will be the subject that is made negative, otherwise the negative will be attached to the first word of the auxiliary. At the same time, later indefinite words must be converted to their *any-* form.

Standard English allows one other kind of negative sentence, the kind illustrated in *I have seen nothing* and *He wants none.* In these sentences, we no longer find a negative attached to an auxiliary, but the negative is shown, instead, by the form of the indefinite word, *nothing* or *none.* Such sentences are a bit stiff, more appropriate for formal writing than for easy colloquial speech, but no one can doubt their respectability. These sentences can be constructed according to a rule that we can call the Right Shift rule:

Right Shift Rule: If a negative sentence has an indefinite word following the verb, the negative can be *shifted* from the auxiliary to the next indefinite word.

The Right Shift rule is stated here in a way that implies that the Basic Rule of Negation must be applied first, and that the Right Shift rule is then applied to the output of the Basic Rule:

Positive sentence: They called someone.
Basic rule: They didn't call anyone.
Right Shift rule: They called no one.

The Right Shift rule accounts for such sentences as *He has none, I want nothing to do with it,* and *I gave none of them to anyone.* Notice that the rule will not produce **I gave any of them to no one,* since it allows the negative to be moved only as far as the *first* indefinite. The Right Shift rule yields sentences that mean almost the same thing as simple negative sentences, but their connotation is different. Sentences derived by means of the Right Shift rule are distinctly more formal than those that have undergone only the Basic Rule of Negation.

At last we are ready to return to nonstandard English. As all English speakers know, sentences such as *I don't see none, He can't hear nothing,* and

We didn't do nothing to no one are used by many speakers. These illustrate the simplest kind of English multiple negation, and they can be accounted for by a rule that is similar to the Right Shift rule, except that it copies negatives instead of shifting them. Like the Right Shift rule, it leaves the basic meaning of the sentence unchanged, but its social connotations are very different:

Right Copy Rule: If a negative sentence has one or more indefinite words following the verb, the negative can be *copied* from the first auxiliary to one or more of these indefinites.

Positive sentence:	They called someone.
Basic rule:	They didn't call anyone.
Right Copy rule:	They didn't call no one.

The Right Shift rule and the Right Copy rule differ in two ways. First, the Right Copy rule leaves a negative behind as part of the Auxiliary. Second, the Right Copy rule allows the negative to be copied repeatedly, rather than moved just one position. The two rules are, however, very much alike, for both of them begin with sentences that have been produced by the Basic Rule of negation, and both of them require later indefinite words to be changed into their negative form. In spite of their structural similarity, the two rules have sharply contrasting connotations, one being formal, almost pompous, the other so colloquial that it is widely regarded as "wrong." Clearly, what we regard as elegant and what we regard as "wrong" are matters of social convention and have nothing to do with the intrinsic properties of the linguistic forms.

Many speakers of English, both black and white, use sentences that conform to the Right Copy rule. A somewhat smaller number of speakers are able to form sentences that have both a negative indefinite subject and a negative in the auxiliary: *Nothing couldn't happen, Nobody didn't do nothing, Nothing don't never go right.* These can strike speakers of standard English as a bit more extreme than the sentences produced by the simple Right Copy rule, but the additional sentences can be accounted for by a rule that extends the Right Copy rule.

First Extension: If a sentence has a negative indefinite subject, the negative can be copied rightward *into* the auxiliary of the following verb.

Positive sentence:	Someone saw some fish.
Basic rule:	No one saw any fish.
Right Copy rule:	No one saw no fish.
First Extension:	No one didn't see no fish.

For some speakers a Second Extension of the Right Copy rule is also possible. Most of these speakers are black, and, when pulled out of context, the sentences that are produced by means of this Second Extension differ enough from standard forms of English to make the meaning obscure for some other speakers. For the sake of authenticity, here are some actual sentences that William Labov has quoted from black teenagers in New York City. They are given with their translations into standard English.

Well, wasn't much I couldn't do. 'Well, there wasn't much I could do.'
I told you, I don't believe there's no God. 'I told you, I don't believe there's any God.'
It ain't no cat can't get in no coop. 'There isn't any cat that can get in any coop.'

Speakers who have been segregated within a standard speaking community sometimes find it difficult to believe that these translations are correct, but within the context in which they were spoken their meaning cannot be in doubt. The third sentence, for instance, was used when describing pigeon coops that some boys kept on the roofs of their houses. The sentence was used when insisting on the strength of the coops and the safety of the pigeons.

These sentences differ from those given earlier, in containing embedded sentences. They can be paraphrased as *There wasn't much [that I could do], I told you I don't believe [that there's a God], There isn't any cat [that can get in any coop].* In each case, the words in brackets form an embedded sentence (because they contain their own verbs) and, in the BEV versions, the negative has been copied from its position in the outer sentence *into* the embedded sentence. This Second Extension of the Right Copy rule can be stated as follows:

Second Extension: A negative can be copied from an outer sentence into a sentence that is embedded within it.

With each extension of the rules, the form of the language diverges a bit further from standard English. No English speaker has trouble understanding sentences that fit the basic form of the Right Copy rule, but sentences produced by the Second Extension can be confusing to standard speakers. Different groups of speakers use different constellations of rules, and this allows several overlapping dialects to be distinguished.

1. Standard Colloquial. Speakers of standard colloquial English make free use of the Basic Rule of negation, of course, but they avoid all forms of the Right Copy rule. Even the Right Shift rule is used only sparingly in informal standard English.

2. Standard Literary English. A more formal dialect or style, literary English, allows the Right Shift rule to be freely added to the Basic Rule of negation, but all forms of Right Copying are strictly avoided.

3. Nonstandard Type 1. Many speakers, both black and white, who use the Right Copy rule never use either of the extensions. For such speakers, the Right Copy rule is usually optional. This means that *I don't have any* and *I don't have none* are both possible sentences. The difference between them is stylistic, and sentences with more than one negative may have a bit of extra emphasis. Some speakers use multiple negatives more often in casual and friendly circumstances than in more formal situations.

4. Nonstandard Type 2. Some speakers use the First Extension of the Right Copy rule, but not the second. For such speakers, both the basic form of the

Right Copy rule and its First Extension are usually optional. This dialect includes both black and white speakers.

5. Nonstandard Type 3. Still other speakers can use the Second Extension of the Right Copy rule, though it always remains optional. There seems to be no dialect of English in which speakers always copy negatives into embedded sentences whenever they have the chance. For some of these speakers, however, the basic Right Copy rule is no longer optional. This is a way of saying that whenever these speakers have a chance to copy a negative from an auxiliary to a later indefinite within the same clause, they always do so. Since they never use sentences such as *I don't have any,* these have to count as ungrammatical within their dialect. Most speakers of this dialect are black, and it is characteristic of some inner-city communities.

The dialect differences, and the rules that each follows, always or optionally, are summarized in the Table 12–1. A glance at the table demonstrates the overlapping character of the dialects. As dialects move further from standard English, more types of negation become possible until, finally, some rules that are never used in standard English are required in some other dialects. Americans will not be surprised to learn that there is a close correlation between these dialects and social class. The lower one descends in the social class system, the more negatives one is likely to find. Socially adjacent dialects differ only in minor ways, but the extremes are sufficiently different to cause occasional misunderstandings.

It is important to insist again, however, that there is nothing less logical about dialects with multiple negation than about dialects that allow only a single negative in each sentence. The same ideas can be expressed by everyone. All dialects offer parallel resources and, as far as we can tell, none offers any greater scope for self-expression than any other. It might be argued that the dialect with the most options should be counted as the richest. By this criterion, a dialect that allows, but does not require, Right Copying, and thus allows both *I don't see any* and *I don't see none* would offer its speakers a stylistic resource that is missing from both standard English and nonstandard type 3, which allow only one form of the sentence. If all the options of a dialect

Table 12–1
Social Dialects and English Negation

	Standard colloquial English	Standard literary English	Non-standard Type 1	Non-standard Type 2	Non-standard Type 3
1. Basic rule of negation	(The basic rule is used in all styles and dialects)				
2. Right-shift rule	(Optional but largely confined to literary and formal styles)				
3. Right-copy rule	Not used	Not used	Optional	Optional	Always
4. First extension	Not used	Not used	Not used	Optional	Optional
5. Second extension	Not used	Not used	Not used	Not used	Optional

could be taken into account, however, it seems unlikely that any dialect would emerge richer than any other.

As a wider range of English social dialects have come under closer linguistic scrutiny, it has repeatedly been found that, whatever their differences, they always have equivalent ways of conveying the same messages. As with negation, moreover, the ways of expressing ideas in the various dialects of English are always closely related. Sentences such as *I wondered was something the matter* or *I asked him did he care* may sound a bit odd to inexperienced standard speakers, but they are closely related to their standard equivalents: *I wondered whether something was the matter* and *I asked him if he cared*. These are sentences with embedded questions. In standard English, embedded questions are marked by either *if* or *whether*. In some nonstandard dialects, embedding is marked, instead, by reversing the order of the subject and first auxiliary of the embedded sentence. Instead of adding *whether* to *something was the matter,* some speakers mark the embedding with a word order change: *was something the matter.* We have no reason to judge one of these methods to be more efficient or more logical than the other.

Of course the linguistic equivalence of different syntactic constructions does not stop prejudice from being focused upon them. Class and syntactic patterns are clearly correlated, and people recognize the correlation. Perhaps it is inevitable that the language of prestigious people comes to be admired, not because it is intrinsically superior, but simply because it is is used by the "right people." Reciprocally, the language of those who are scorned is also likely to be scorned. For many Americans today, it is no longer respectable to express open prejudice against blacks, but some white Americans who would never admit to having such a prejudice will still express a strong distaste for the language that many black people use. Sadly, this is likely to reveal a suppressed prejudice against the speakers.

Nonstandard forms of English are by no means confined to blacks. It is more accurate to say that nonstandard English is characteristic of poor people than of any particular ethnic group, but since so many blacks are found among America's poor, they also suffer disproportionately from the attitudes toward nonstandard dialects. We could dismiss the linguistic attitudes as merely foolish and confused if they did not so often result in discrimination against minority and lower-income people, especially disadvantaged school children. When the dialect features of the lower class come to be defined as "wrong," and when schools exert great efforts to eradicate them, we thoughtlessly denigrate the children and their parents, and even the community where this dialect is the norm.

Ideally the attitudes of our society should change to be more accepting of dialect variation, but neither students nor educators can wait for that fine day. Less ideally, but possibly more realistically, students might be helped to learn standard English without requiring them to reject their own dialect. Unfortunately, it has been terribly difficult to foster one dialect without implying scorn for the other. This means that schools face a terrible dilemma. If too much time is spent trying to teach children something that is nothing more than verbal etiquette, the schools divert precious resources from other more important areas of education. On the other hand, if children do not learn a less stigmatized dialect, they are all too likely to suffer discrimination in later education and in the job market. A good many linguists have come to believe that too much insistence on standard English in the early grades does more harm than good. Corrections of small children's language have never been very effective in changing their speech, and attacks upon the natural speech of the community contribute to the alienation that so many lower-class children feel toward school. Help may be more effective with high school students who understand the realities of the world around them, but learning a new dialect is always difficult. If the solution to these dilemmas were easy, the problem would long ago have been solved.

VARIATION

In every language, some constructions vary while others do not, but the areas of freedom differ from one language to another. It may be difficult to imagine that the unvarying features of one's own language have flourishing options elsewhere, but every language has its own areas of freedom. English speakers find it natural that direct and indirect objects can occur in either order, as in *Jennifer gave Roberto a birthday cake* or *Jennifer gave a birthday cake to Roberto*. On the other hand, English speakers, whose language rigidly requires adjectives to precede their noun, may find it hard to imagine a language in which the order could be optional, but Tagalog is such a language. English possessive pronouns always occur before the name of the thing possessed (*my mother*), but in Norwegian it is possible to put the equivalent words in either order: *moren min* or *min mor*.

It is not only word order that can be free. Even the items that are required and those that are optional vary from one language to another. Subject pronouns can be omitted from Spanish but they are required in English. In our optional contractions, we see an alternation between free words and bound morphemes. In the choice between *dived* and *dove* we see the alternation between irregular and regular morphology. Nothing in language is safe from variation.

It is the variability of language that opens the possibility for change. Change never comes abruptly, but develops slowly as the proportion of a new variant gradually rises and as the older variant gradually recedes. At any one time, a language may appear to be a reasonably stable system since so many of its features are fixed. This is, however, a deceptive stability, for all languages have points of variation, and over any long period we always find changes. It is these changes, building on the underlying variability of language, to which we turn in the next chapter.

CHAPTER THIRTEEN

Syntactic Change

INTRODUCTION

In the nineteenth century, the comparative method gave a firm basis to the study of phonological change. Our understanding of syntactic change has developed more slowly, but it is as universal, as relentless, and as unmistakable as phonological change. Not only do the differences among related languages show us that their syntax, like their phonology, has diverged from the more uniform syntax of their common ancestor, but written records of ancient languages give us concrete examples of their otherwise forgotten syntax.

Several types of syntactic change can be distinguished, and each of these will be considered in more detail in the next sections of this chapter.

1. Grammaticalization. With the passage of time, loosely joined words may be gradually drawn into more tightly defined syntactic constructions. This tightening of syntax may be shown by more unified intonation, by more rigid word order, and by a more consistent use of grammatical markers that organize the words. The process by which words are drawn into increasingly rigid syntactic constructions is called **grammaticalization.** We can watch grammaticalization when children learn their first language, for sequences of words that they string quite loosely at first come later to fit tightly together. In a much longer perspective, we can also infer grammaticalization to have taken place in the history of particular languages. We can look upon grammaticalization as the first stage of syntax, as the starting point for a long cycle of subsequent change.

2. Content words become function words. As grammaticalization proceeds, function words will be needed to show the relationship among the content words. In the cases we know best, function words such as determiners, pronouns, prepositions, and auxiliary verbs have developed gradually from content words such as nouns and verbs. A few content words lose much of their semantic reference to the external world, and come to be used, instead, in a specialized syntactic role.

3. Function words become affixes. As time passes, some function words lose more and more of their freedom. Their word order may become fixed and they may lose their stress. A weakly stressed function word with a fixed position can easily become attached to a neighboring word as a prefix or suffix. Its fate then becomes irrevocably tied with that word.

4. Loss of affixes. Phonological reduction works relentlessly on affixes so that their fate is frequently to become less and less distinct from one another, and then finally to disappear. As affixes become less distinct they become less capable of performing a useful service for the language, and their functions must then be assumed by other words or morphemes. Thus the weakening and loss of affixes is likely to entail compensatory changes in other parts of the language.

These four processes act persistently and simultaneously. At any one time, different processes are generally working on different constructions, so we cannot characterize a whole language as passing through a particular point in a cycle. Nevertheless, individual constructions do pass from one "stage" to another. In any language we are likely to see a few constructions in each stage of the cycle, and taken together they represent a continuing process by which the constituents of a language become gradually more tightly glued together and then less distinct from one another, until they finally lose their separate identities and disappear. As some constituents shrink, new higher-level constructions have to be created in compensation. We will start to consider this cycle more carefully at the stage of grammaticalization.

GRAMMATICALIZATION

English allows some phrases to be added to the beginning of a sentence without quite incorporating them into the sentence as part of single united construction. We can name someone or describe an object, and then say something about it:

> *People who smoke? I've had enough of them.*
> *Mushy liberals! They don't have any better answers than the conservatives.*
> *That old man, what's he doing?*

It is not entirely clear whether or not these initial phrases are part of the sentences that follow. The phrases are not full sentences themselves, but they are likely to be said with an intonation that sets them off quite sharply from what follows. The ambivalent status of these phrases is suggested by the possibility of choosing varying punctuation. The phrases and their associated sentences are hardly more closely related than two successive sentences, and the construction has barely begun the process of grammaticalization.

In some varieties of informal and nonstandard English, similar phrases have been drawn a bit more closely into the sentence. The so called "double subject" construction can be widely heard in both Black English Vernacular (BEV), and the dialect of many white Americans.

Mr. Smith, he don't live here no more.
My mother, she has the flu.
Those old guys, they don't bother us.

Speakers of prestigious forms of English may look on these sentences as inelegant and redundant, but some speakers use double subjects frequently. The introductory phrases are closely enough attached to the remainder of the sentence to allow a reasonably unified intonation. If every subject that was not, itself, a pronoun were followed by a pronoun, as they are in these examples, then the pronouns would start to look like markers of verb agreement. They could even turn into verb prefixes that agree with the subject in person and number. This is exactly how agreement markers were created in many languages.

French has a construction that is very similar to the nonstandard English double subject, but it is less stigmatized:

Le   gendarme,   il   n'a   rien   dit.
The   policeman,   he   not-has   nothing   said
'The policeman didn't say anything.'

Moi,   je   n'en   veux   pas.
Me,   I   not-some   want   not
'I don't want any.'

As the second of these examples demonstrates, even a subject pronoun such as *je* 'I' can be anticipated and given emphasis by an earlier emphatic pronoun: *moi*. The intonation of these French sentences is more unified than the intonation of the parallel English sentences, suggesting that the introductory phrase or pronoun has become more tightly bound to the rest of the sentence. Even in French this is a colloquial rather than a literary construction, but it is far better established than in English. This series of examples suggests a kind of evolution in which very loosely attached phrases are gradually grammaticized by being more and more firmly attached to the following sentence.

A somewhat later stage of grammaticalization can be seen in a different English example. In expressions such as *I'll go find the mustard* two verbs follow each other in close association. It seems plausible to derive such sentences from two shorter sentences that are joined by a conjunction, *I'll go, and I'll find the mustard*. All languages probably have ways of getting rid of the redundant second pronoun to yield sentences equivalent to *I'll go and find the mustard*. When *and* is also omitted, the two verbs are brought together, and speakers may begin to interpret the first verb, *go*, as if it is subordinated to the second verb *find*. *Go* begins to act just a bit like an auxiliary verb. The

American sequences of paired verbs that were mentioned in the previous chapter such as *We'll come see you* and *Go fix it now* represent a slightly more grammaticized stage than their British English equivalents, *We'll come to see you* and *Go and fix it now*.

These examples suggest that when words and phrases regularly occur in sequence, they are likely to acquire an increasingly structured relationship. By introducing new constructions, grammaticalization may compensate for changes taking place elsewhere in the language. As will be described in Chapters 14 and 15, grammaticalization can also be observed in child and adult language learners, and it can be seen with special clarity as pidgin languages develop into creoles.

FROM CONTENT WORDS TO FUNCTION WORDS

Content words are the nouns, verbs, and adjectives that refer to the world outside of language. Function words include a language's pronouns, determiners, adpositions, and auxiliary verbs, and their reference to anything beyond the language itself is less clear. By showing how content words are related to each other, function words provide the skeleton of a sentence. When the origin of function words is known, we generally find that they have evolved from content words. It is unusual for content words to develop from function words.

The Beijing dialect of Chinese has a number of verbs that seem to be in the process of developing into prepositions. One of these, *yòng,* in some circumstances, means 'to use':

Wŏ   yòng   jiăndao.
I   use   scissors.

Often, however, *yòng* is more naturally translated by the preposition 'with.'

Wŏ   yòng   jiăndao   jiăn   zhĭ.
I   with   scissors   cut   paper
'I cut paper with scissors.'

The Chinese word *gĕi* can be used as a verb meaning 'give,' but in some circumstances it acts like a preposition meaning 'to' or 'for the benefit of.'

Wŏ   gĕi   tā   săn.
I   give   him   umbrella
'I give him an umbrella.'

Wŏ   jiè   gĕi   tā   săn.
I   lend   to   him   umbrella
'I lend an umbrella to him.'

The meanings of 'use' and 'with' are clearly related. So are the meanings of 'give' and 'to.' It is not difficult to understand how words could be used in both senses, but the process by which verbs like these become prepositions can be a long one. Enough is known about the history of Chinese to confirm the suspicion that these words began as verbs, and their use as prepositions has been a relatively recent development. If the trend continues, their use as verbs might gradually decline until they are finally used only as prepositions.

Adpositions can be derived from nouns as well as from verbs. In Garo, locations can be indicated by constructions like the following:

ang-ni   *ki?saŋ-o*
me-possessive   buttocks-at
'at my behind, behind me'

As a noun, *ki?saŋ* is a straightforward body part term meaning 'rump, buttocks,' but it is regularly used in phrases like this to give the sense of 'in back of,' 'behind.' Garo has other constructions that are syntactically identical, but that have a less clear referent, anatomical or otherwise.

u?-ni   *ja?man-o*
that-possessive   after-at
'after that, then'

In this phrase, *ja?man-o* has the form of a noun, as shown by the locative suffix *-o,* which ordinarily attaches only to nouns. Unlike *ki?saŋ* 'buttocks,' which can be used freely as an ordinary noun, however, *ja?man* rarely occurs except in this construction, and it rarely occurs without the *-o*. It cannot be used freely with other case markers than *-o,* and this suffix seems to be in the process of becoming glued permanently to the word. *Ja?man-o* is joined to the preceding noun in what appears to be a possessive construction (something like 'that's after,' 'at the after of that'), but it has moved at least part way toward becoming a postposition. It might be regarded as a postposition governed by the possessive case, which is marked by *-ni*. Earlier forms of Garo did not leave written records, so we cannot confirm this origin of *ja?man-o,* but the most plausible inference is that certain nouns have gradually taken over the role of postpositions.

A different example can be taken from Latin, a language that did not have articles but that did have demonstrative adjectives. Like the English demonstratives, *this* and *that,* the Latin demonstratives conveyed a definite meaning at the same time that they indicated a location. Languages that lack articles often allow demonstratives to be pressed into service when a definite meaning is essential. Latin demonstratives could be used in this way, and as Latin evolved, its demonstratives were converted into the definite articles of the modern Romance languages. Two things were needed for this conversion. First, under many circumstances the words became obligatory. Second, their reference to a particular location (near, far, etc.) was lost so that all that remained was definiteness. The Latin demonstrative *ille* 'that, away from both you and me' originally contrasted with both *hic* 'this, near me' and *iste* 'that, near you.' In the dialects that evolved toward French, *hic* and *iste* gradually stopped being used as demonstratives. This meant that they no longer contrasted with *ille,* and this deprived *ille* of its ability to indicate a specific location. *Ille* was also worn down phonologically until it was transformed into the articles of the modern Romance languages: French *le,* Spanish *el,* and Italian *il.* Articles have developed in much the same way in many other groups of languages.

Just as demonstratives have been pressed into service as definite articles, so numerals for 'one' have regularly been converted into indefinite articles. Even the English indefinite article, *a/an,* is ultimately related to the numeral *one,* and in many European languages the indefinite article and the word for 'one' are even more similar. Neither French *un* nor German *ein,* both meaning 'a,' hides its origin as a numeral.

Tense markers in many languages have developed from verbs with meanings such as 'go, come, start, finish, know, want, possess, exist.' Several verbs in English have moved in the direction of tense markers. *Will* still retains something of its older meaning of 'want, desire,' but it is now more often used to show the future tense. More recently, English has developed an additional marker of the future from the verb *go,* as in *I am going to eat dinner at five o'clock.* French not only has a construction that parallels English *going to,* but a second construction with *venir* 'come' that indicates the recent past.

Je vais manger.
I go to-eat
'I am going to eat.'

Je viens de manger.
I come of to-eat
'I have just eaten.'

English *have* can still mean 'possess' and *be* can still mean 'exist,' but both *have* and *be* are so deeply involved in our tense system that their older meanings of possession and existence sometimes disappear: *The birds have gone. Why can't they be content?* When we need to be clear about possession and existence we often use less ambiguous words like *possess, own,* and *exist.*

Content words can also develop into pronouns. Second person pronouns occasionally develop from respectful phrases such as 'honorable one.' The Burmese adapted an old word for 'slave,' *čúndó,* as a polite and humble way of saying 'I.' Gradually the older pronoun for 'I' was used less often until, in many circumstances, it came to be regarded as quite rude. At the same time the newer *čúndó* lost its older sense of 'slave' and turned into an ordinary pronoun. With repeated use, words or phrases like *čúndó* may come to suggest no more respect or humility than the earlier pronouns they replaced. Third person pronouns, like articles, sometimes develop from demonstrative pronouns. Demonstratives, in turn, sometimes develop from locational adverbs meaning 'here' and 'there.' Some dialects of English use expressions like *this here desk*

and *that there house* in which a locational adverb reinforces the demonstrative.

Thus content words are regularly pressed into service as auxiliary verbs,
articles, demonstratives, pronouns, and adpositions. A few such shifts are
likely to be in progress in any language that we investigate, but a single change
can take as long as several centuries to complete.

FROM FUNCTION WORDS TO AFFIXES

Function words may gradually lose their independent existence, and become
glued to neighboring words as prefixes or suffixes. The process can be a long
one, and it is sometimes useful to recognize an intermediate stage. Linguists
use the word **clitic** for something that is less independent than a word, but not
as dependent as an affix.

The origin of English *-n't* remains transparent since, under many circumstances, *not* and *-n't* can be used in identical constructions: *He could not have
come, He couldn't have come.* This looks like a rather simple phonological
reduction, but in a few circumstances *-n't* is now the only possible form: *Can't
we stop now? He's had enough, hasn't he?* Uncontracted equivalents of these
sentences are, at best, problematic: *Can not we stop now?* is nearly impossible
and even *Can we not stop now* is distinctly stilted. We are taught in school that
the formal equivalent of *He's had enough, hasn't he?* is *He has had enough,
has he not?* but this requires the *not* to be moved from its ordinary contracted
position, and it is, in any case, somewhat artificial. English *-n't,* then, has been
converted part way to a suffix, and the conversion has gone a good deal further
in colloquial English than in the formal written language. For formal writing,
we learn to expand *-n't* back to an independent word, but in everyday speech,
sentences like *I would not have done that if I had not been there,* where the *not*
retains its independent form, must be quite rare. English *-n't* has become a
clitic, if not yet quite a suffix.

A number of other words are so regularly contracted in spoken colloquial
English that they seem to have developed part-way toward affixes. Forms such
as *would've* and *could've* are so consistently used in spoken English that
people sometimes spell them as 'would of' and 'could of.' The contractions
seem to be loosing their association with the full word, *have,* from which they
were originally derived. Perhaps it is only our writing system, where contractions are considered inelegant, that keeps it alive as a separate word. We say
I'd've done it but he wouldn't've even if we write *I would have done it but he
would not have.*

When words are contracted they lose prominence, and they are likely to lose
their ability to be stressed. When this happens, speakers may want to emphasize an idea but find themselves blocked by a contracted form that can no
longer be given the necessary stress. In such cases, it may be possible to
supply the emphasis by means of extra words. If these extra words are used

frequently enough, they too are drawn into the syntax. Today, *got* is often used to reinforce the reduced and abbreviated contractions of *have*. We say *I've got enough* and *What've you got?* when it might seem that *I have enough* and *What do you have?* would do as well. We may be advised in school to avoid *got* in such sentences, for it still seems redundant and unnecessary. Still, as *have* is more regularly contracted, and as it loses its possessive meaning, its remaining phonetic substance seems insufficient to carry the full meaning of possession. Speakers then emphasize that meaning by adding *got*. Gradually, of course, even the *got* begins to lose its older meaning. Its more specific meaning of 'obtained, fetched' is weakened until it conveys only a generalized sense of possession. *Got* even begins to turn into a new auxiliary verb. In some circumstances, such as *It got eaten up already, got* loses even its possessive meaning, and it is reduced to nothing but a marker of a colloquial form of the passive.

As words are shortened and abbreviated, new pieces may be needed to give them more substance, but when they first begin to be used, reinforced phrases like *have got, this here,* and *that there* are likely to seem inelegant and redundant. With time, some of these reinforcements become fixed, only to be further worn away in later centuries. The Indo-European ancestor of Latin is reconstructed as having had a word **in* meaning 'in.' By the time of Latin, this had been joined by a second syllable to form *intus* 'within, inside.' This in turn was expanded by the addition of *de* to form *deintus,* which, by phonological reduction, evolved into modern French *dans* 'in.' In modern French this has been expanded yet again into still another word, *dedans* 'inside.' The Indo-European **in* has received three successive reinforcements, but the reinforcements have always had to compete with phonological erosion.

Spoken English appears to represent a somewhat later stage of linguistic evolution than does written English. We are freer about making contractions in speech than in writing, and the contractions surely represent a later stage of the language. At the same time, extra words that are regarded as too inelegant or too redundant for the written language find their way into colloquial speech. It would be rash to imagine that all the colloquial forms of spoken English will become fixed in the standard language of later centuries, but we may get some hints about the future by looking at colloquial forms. Certainly many of the forms that came to be accepted in the Romance languages were already anticipated in the "vulgar Latin" that was the daily spoken language of the Roman Empire.

As function words are reduced to affixes, any possibility of giving them stress is likely to disappear and they then become ever more susceptible to phonological reduction. We presume that the tense and person suffixes of Latin were derived, ultimately, from independent words that gradually became glued to the end of verbs. By the stage of Latin these had fused together quite tightly but, as seen in Table 13–1, affixes with identifiable independent meanings could still be recognized.

In these examples, a number of distinct morphemes that indicate tense and person can be easily distinguished. The imperfect tense is clearly shown by the

Table 13-1
Latin Person-Tense Suffixes

	Present indicative	Imperfect indicative	Future indicative
I	amō	amābam	amābō
thou	amās	amābās	amābis
he, she	amat	amābat	amābit
we	amāmus	amābāmus	amābimus
you	amātis	amābātis	amābitis
they	amant	amābant	amābunt

suffix *-ba-* or *-bā-*, while the future is generally indicated by *-bi-*. The suffixes *-s, -t, -mus,* and *-tis* are found in all tenses, and they unmistakably identify person and number. In the first person singular and in the third person plural, however, tense markers and person markers have begun to fuse. In *amō* 'I love' the tense and person markers fuse into a single indivisible *-ō,* and this even absorbs the *a* that appears in other forms of the verb root. In subsequent centuries, as Latin evolved into the Romance languages, the originally separate parts of these endings gradually lost their individual identities. Additional irregularities developed, and the distinctions among the endings began to be lost.

As distinctions are lost, an affix system becomes a less reliable means for conveying information. When essential meanings become obscure, speakers have to resort to other means of making themselves clear. The increasing use of alternative expressions may, in turn, reduce the functional importance of the affixes and lower their resistance to further erosion. Once the distinctions among affixes begin to break down and alternative ways of expressing the meanings become established, the affixes, with their increasing irregularities, become something of a burden. They may survive for a time as redundant forms, but the way has been paved for their complete loss.

THE LOSS OF AFFIXES

With the passage of time, affixes can be gradually worn away until nothing at all is left. Erosion can take place anywhere in a word, but the end is particularly vulnerable. Since suffixes are more common than prefixes, phonological erosion can easily nibble away an important part of a language's grammatical apparatus.

Two distinct kinds of changes can contribute to the decline and loss of affixes: phonological change and analogical change. Phonological change occurs when a class of sounds changes in a regular fashion. Sounds that were once distinctive may lose their contrast and, as a result, affixes that were once different come to be pronounced alike. Analogical change occurs when one form changes to fit the pattern of another form. We notice children introducing analogical changes when they regularize irregular plurals or past tenses. The child who says *Both my foots are stucked* forms a plural of *foot* and a past tense form of *stick* on the analogy of many other plurals and pasts. Childish innovations like these are usually later corrected, and leave no permanent changes in the language, but a few analogical changes spread until they replace older irregular forms. The present competition of *dreamed/dreamt* and *dived/dove* may gradually allow regular forms to win out over irregular forms. Analogical change is a less regular process than phonological change, but it often happens that analogy favors the most common patterns of the language, so that these spread at the expense of less common patterns. In this way, the number of irregular forms is reduced, and the language is made more regular.

Old English nouns had suffixes that showed not only the distinction between singular and plural, but also the distinction between nominative, accusative, dative, and genitive cases, roughly the difference between subject, direct object, indirect object, and possessive. Even in the earliest recorded forms of Old English, the eight logically possible combinations of case and number were no longer uniformly distinguished, and no Old English noun had more than six distinct forms. The nominative plural and accusative plural were usually the same, and some nouns had many other identical forms. The Old English number and case marking system had already undergone some erosion from what must have been a more complete set of earlier distinctions, but it was still much fuller than that of Modern English.

Old English nouns fell into several different classes ("declensions"), each of which was characterized by its own distinctive set of suffixes. The declensions were quite varied, and this added greatly to the complexity of the system. So many of the cases had become identical to each other that the meanings that cases sometimes convey must already have needed the support of prepositions and fixed word order. The case forms of the Old English words that meant 'dog,' 'animal,' 'foot' and 'love' that are shown in Table 13–2. The words that once meant 'dog' and 'animal' have narrowed in meaning and turned into *hound* and *deer* in modern English.

Table 13–2
Old English Nouns

	Dog	Animal	Foot	Love
Singular				
Nom.	hund	dēor	fōt	lufu
Acc.	hund	dēor	fōt	lufe
Gen.	hundes	dēores	fōtes	lufe
Dat.	hunde	dēore	fēt	lufe
Plural				
Nom.–Acc.	hundas	dēor	fēt	lufa
Gen.	hunda	dēor	fōta	lufa
Dat.	hundum	dēorum	fōtum	lufum

As the centuries passed, both phonological and analogical changes contributed to the further undermining of the case system. The most important phonological change came when several vowels lost their contrast in unstressed syllables. Case suffixes were unstressed, and the vowels that had once distinguished different cases could no longer do the job. This meant that the suffixes were no longer capable of conveying different meanings. For example, the genitive singular -as as in *hundas* 'dog's' and the nominative/accusative -es as in *hundes* 'dogs' both came to be pronounced as [-əs]. The vowel was later lost giving the identical *hound's* and *hounds* of modern English. The loss of contrast among unstressed vowels was also a major factor in the loss of English grammatical gender. Different genders had once been kept separate by distinctive suffixes, and when the suffixes stopped being distinctive the gender differences disappeared.

Analogical changes worked along with phonological changes, and they helped to reduce the differences among the declensions. The genitive singular suffix of many nouns was -es, pronounced [-əs], and this form gradually spread until it became the universal marker of the genitive, the ancestor of modern -'s. In the same way, the nominative–accusative plural of the largest declension was -as, also pronounced [-əs], and it also spread to other words and to other cases, until it finally became the nearly universal marker of the plural, the ancestor of modern -s. Only a handful of older, now irregular, plurals survived this massive leveling: *foot/feet, child/children, deer/deer,* and a very few of others.

Verbs have undergone even more vigorous erosion than nouns. The complexities of the Old English verb can be seen in Table 13–3, which gives the forms of the verb *fremman* 'to support.' The same forces of phonological and analogical change that reduced the case system of the nouns went to work on the verbs until this entire array of suffixes was finally reduced to just four forms in the modern language. The modern -d of the past tense can be seen foreshadowed in the Old English preterite (past), but the modern -ing is derived from an old marker of verbal nouns, -ung, as in *leornung* 'learning, knowledge.' The only survivor of person marking in modern English is the third person singular -s, which derives from northern English dialects that won out in competition with the southern forms shown in the table. The decline of the second person singular pronouns, *thou* and *thy,* nudged along the simplification of verb inflection, for when the second person singular pronouns dropped out of use, so did the verb forms that were once used with them. Only in deliberately archaic contexts are forms like *thou goeth, thou eateth, thou keepeth* still used.

In some forms of nonstandard English the verbs have been leveled even more than in standard varieties. As was discussed in Chapter 12, the third person singular verb suffix is often lost in some forms of Black English Vernacular and, somewhat less commonly, the possessive -'s can be lost as well. It is entirely reasonable to look on these losses as carrying the historical trends of English to a further stage. Perhaps they anticipate the future direction of all forms of English.

Table 13–3
Old English *Fremman* (to Support)

Present system		
Indicative		
ic	fremme	'I support'
ðu	fremest	'you (singular) support'
hē, hēo, hit	fremeð	'he, she, it supports'
wē, gē, hī	fremmað	'we, you (plural), they support'
Subjunctive		
Singular	fremme	'I, you (sg.), he, she, it support'
Plural	fremmen	'we, you (pl.), they support'
Imperative		
Singular	freme	'(you sg.) support'
Plural	fremað	'(you pl.) support'
Infinitive	fremman	'to support'
Gerund	tō fremmenne	'to support'
Participle	fremmende	'supporting'
Preterit (past) system		
Indicative		
ic	fremede	'I supported'
ðu	fremedest	'you (sg.) supported'
hē, hēo, hit	fremede	'he, she, it supported'
wē, gē, hī	fremedon	'we, you (pl.), they supported'
Subjunctive		
Singular	fremede	'I, you (sg.), he, she, it supported'
Plural	fremeden	'we, you (pl.), they supported'
Past participle	fremed	'supported'

The apparatus of noun cases and verb suffixes could not have been lost without compensating changes in other parts of the language. Word order has become less free, and prepositions have taken over some of the work of the lost cases. In the same way, verbal auxiliaries have spread as the older inflected tenses have weakened. As has often happened, new and separate words took over a job that disappearing affixes could no longer handle by themselves. We will see further examples of the same process when we consider pidgin languages.

INTERRELATED RESTRUCTURING: FROM LATIN TO FRENCH

The Romance languages have left a continuous stream of written records that has lasted for more than two thousand years. No group of languages has a better known history. Many of the kinds of changes that have been reviewed in the earlier sections of this chapter can be seen in the two thousand-year transformation of Latin into French. A survey of some of these changes will show their interrelations and demonstrate how extensive the restructuring of a language can be.

In the written language of the classical Latin authors, word order was far less rigid than in English or in the modern Romance languages, but the favored position for the verb was sentence final. Latin nouns had case suffixes that distinguished subjects, objects, and some other types of noun phrases so securely that order was free to make pragmatic distinctions. In its free word order, Latin was like modern Russian (see Chapter 10), and it also resembled Russian in lacking definite and indefinite articles.

Like all languages, Latin had a full complement of pronouns, and both pronouns and nouns were inflected for case. Latin verbs had suffixes that indicated the person (first, second, or third) and number (singular or plural) of the subject. The person and number of the subject were generally shown unambiguously by the verb suffix, and this helped to allow a subject pronoun to be omitted without risking any loss of meaning. Independent subject pronouns were generally used only when some special emphasis was needed.

Almost all of this has changed in modern French. The verb has moved away from final position. Person suffixes on the verb no longer reliably indicate the subject, and subject pronouns have become obligatory. Case marking of nouns has been lost, but word order has become more rigid, and both definite and indefinite articles have developed. While we can find no single initiating cause for all these changes, it is certainly plausible to see them as interrelated.

We know something about language variation even from Roman times, for texts survive that reflect the colloquial language of daily life more closely than do the more formal "classical" texts. This "vulgar Latin" already anticipated some features of the later Romance languages. The verb was less regularly placed in the final position, and demonstratives were more often used with nouns. When the demonstratives lost their ability to distinguish "near" from "far," they became definite articles. A form of the numeral "one" was appropriated as an indefinite article. In Classical Latin, as in Old English, some case endings had become identical to one another, so their ability to distinguish different semantic and syntactic roles of their nouns was already weakening. In succeeding centuries the case endings withered still further and, except for the pronouns, the cases have left no trace in modern French or in the other Romance languages. The increasing rigidity of word order compensated for the loss of case marking by providing an alternate means for indicating the functions of noun phrases.

Like English, modern French requires a subject. If the subject is not a noun, a French sentence needs a subject pronoun. It is tempting to guess that subject pronouns came to be required as compensation for the withering away of person markings on the verb. When person and number were no longer securely shown by the verb ending, pronoun subjects might take their place. Two problems raise doubts about this plausible suspicion, however. First, as long as the context makes the meaning clear, some languages get along easily without requiring any explicit indication of the subject at all, so it is not obvious that any compensation was needed for the lost person suffixes. Second, subjects very likely became obligatory before the person suffixes were lost and, if this was the case, the withering away of the person markers could hardly explain the obligatory subjects. We can even speculate that it could have been the presence of a secure subject that allowed the older person suffixes of the verb to wither, rather than the reverse. In any case the two processes must surely have been related, and the result, as seen in modern French, is that the person and number of the subject are more clearly shown by the subject pronoun than by a verb suffix.

Pronouns changed in other ways. All unstressed pronouns came to be placed before the verb in French, and they acquired an absolutely rigid order. They are still written as separate words, but if French were an unwritten language that was being transcribed for the first time, the unstressed pronouns would almost surely be interpreted as clitics or even as verb prefixes. Like most prefixes and suffixes, they occur in a fixed order. Nothing else except for *ne* 'not' can be inserted among them, and since the order of *ne* is as rigid as that of the pronouns, it can be regarded as an additional prefix or clitic. Like affixes in many languages, *ne* and the pronouns are unstressed, and in rapid speech many of their vowels are reduced almost to the vanishing point. In the following example, /ɥ/ stands for a labiopalatal approximant.

/jənələlɥidɔnəre pa/
| *je* | *ne* | *le* | *lui* | *donnerai* | *pas.* |
| I | not | it | to-him | give-will | not |

'I will not give it to him.'

French shows a tendency to develop several other kinds of prefixes than just these unstressed pronouns. French spelling usually indicates plurality with a suffixed -*s*: *livre, livres* 'book, books'; *homme, hommes* 'man, men.' This final -*s* is usually silent, however, so that, in the spoken language, it does not reliably convey plurality. French nouns, however, are almost always preceded by an article, a demonstrative, or a possessive pronoun, and these always indicate number. *Le* and *la* (pronounced /lə, la/ or /l-/) are the masculine and feminine singular definite articles, while *les* (pronounced either /le/ or /lez/ depending on what follows) is the plural definite article. Thus we have /ləlivr, lelivr/ *le livre, les livres* 'the book, the books,' and /lɔm, lezɔm/ *l'homme, les hommes* 'the man, the men,' as the singular and plural forms. In the spoken language, it is usually the prefixed article, demonstrative, or possessive pronoun, rather than the archaic and disappearing plural suffix, that now indicates plurality.

As a result, plurality in modern spoken French is shown more effectively by what precedes the noun than by what follows. French has a few adjectives that can intervene between the article and the noun, and these adjectives prevent us from regarding the articles as simple prefixes, but they are moving in that direction. At any rate, with nouns, as with verbs, we see a tendency for information to be moved from a suffixed to a prefixed position. Suffixation withers, but prefixation flourishes.

Tense suffixes were characteristic of earlier stages of Romance, but in spoken French, even tense is now more securely indicated by auxiliary verbs that precede the main verb than by suffixes that follow it. The old tense suffixes continue to be spelled in distinctive ways, but so many of them are now pronounced identically that they are losing their ability to convey real information in speech. The old past tense, for instance, survives in literary French, but it has virtually disappeared from the colloquial language and been replaced by a tense formed with an auxiliary verb.

Literary:

Il	*me*	*donna*	*le*	*livre.*
He	me	give-past	the	book

'He gave me the book.'

Colloquial:

Il	*m'a*	*donné*	*le*	*livre.*
He	me-have	given	the	book

'He gave me the book.'

French also has two competing ways of expressing the future, one that uses a tense suffix, and a somewhat less formal one that uses an auxiliary verb before the main verb. In spite of their spelling, the *donner* of the colloquial future, and the *donné* of the colloquial past are pronounced identically. This means that the tense difference is shown only by what precedes the verb.

Literary:

Je	*vous*	*donnerai*	*le*	*livre.*
I	to-you	give-fut.	the	book

'I will give you the book.'

Colloquial:

Je	*vais*	*vous*	*donner*	*le*	*livre.*
I	going	to-you	give-inf.	the	book

'I am going to give you the book.'

Informal spoken French shows a few additional characteristics that seem to carry these trends even further. The prefixed pronouns cannot be used alone or given stress, so French has developed a distinctive set of emphatic pronouns, known as the "disjunctive" pronouns, that are used where emphasis is needed. The disjunctive pronouns can occur in isolation (as when answering a question), as objects of prepositions (*à moi* 'to me,' *avec toi* 'with you'), and in other circumstances where pronouns must be stressed. Disjunctive pronouns are never found in the preverbal position where only the unstressed clitic pronouns occur, but in spoken French, it is now possible to use stressed disjunctive pronouns *in addition to* the unstressed cliticized pronouns.

Stressed disjunctive pronouns can occur initially, in a topicalized position:

Moi, *je* *n'en* *veux* *pas.*
Me, I not-some want not
'As for me, I don't want any.'

They can also be placed after the verb, where they seem better incorporated into the intonation of the sentence, and to have become more grammaticalized.

Il *dort* *lui.*
he sleeps he
'He sleeps.'

In colloquial spoken French, it is even possible to use nouns along with unstressed pronoun prefixes.

/jəlem mwa mari/
je *l'aime* *moi* *Marie.*
I her-love I Marie
'I love Marie.'

/jələlчie dɔne mwa ləlivr a pʲɛr/
Je *le* *lui* *ai* *donné,* *moi,* *le* *livre,* *à* *Pierre.*
I it to-him have given I the book to Pierre
'I gave the book to Pierre.'

In sentences like these, the unstressed pronoun prefixes are reduced to little more than markers of subject and object agreement. They have become person prefixes on the verb, while the nouns and the stressed disjunctive pronouns that follow the verb carry most of the information. Sentences like these are more likely to be found in the colloquial French of daily life than in literary French, where they are still regarded as rather inelegant. Just as vulgar Latin anticipated later developments of the Romance languages, however, so spoken French may well anticipate the future direction of change.

If we consider the entire development from classical Latin through vulgar Latin and Old French to modern written French and finally to the most colloquial spoken French, we first see the old Latin person suffixes withering away while independent pronouns become required, even in the subject position. Then, in a repetition of the cycle, these independent pronouns have gradually been converted into pronoun prefixes, and another new set of pronouns has arisen to help carry the information when emphasis is needed. These newest pronouns are now more often placed after the verb than before it.

Since so many nouns and, increasingly, even stressed disjunctive pronouns now follow the verb, some scholars have suggested that French is becoming a verb-initial language. As is characteristic of such languages, French relies heavily on prefixes. Person and tense markers precede the verb, while the plurals precede the noun. The typological pattern of modern colloquial French has become almost the reverse of that of classical Latin.

CAUSES OF SYNTACTIC CHANGE

With syntax, as with phonology, we know more about *how* changes take place than about *why* they take place. We should, however, conclude this review of syntax by considering some of the explanations that linguists have offered for change.

Simplification

Some syntactic changes appear to simplify the language. When redundancies are eliminated, speaking becomes a bit easier. When analogical changes iron out complex morphological irregularities, the result looks like a simpler and more orderly language. But simplification never quite succeeds. As quickly as some complexities are eliminated from a language, others are introduced, and as far as we can tell, no language is significantly more or less complex than any other. If simplification were the predominant force for syntactic change, all complexities should long ago have been squeezed out of our languages, and we would now be blessed with a maximally simple and efficient communication system. Nor should we forget that what is simple for the speaker may not be simple for the hearer. The very intricacies that make talking so complex introduce redundancies that can help a hearer to understand.

Imperfect Learning by Children

Since each child must learn the language anew, imperfect learning might encourage a drift toward new grammatical patterns. The simplification of complex morphological systems may be, in part, the result of imperfect learning. As new structures take over old jobs, each generation of learners may be less and less successful at controlling the old forms. If each successive generation learns these old forms less well, they will finally disappear. We can speculate that as the English case system began to break down, it could have reached the point where children would no longer have been able to understand it well enough to find it helpful or to use it effectively themselves. They would have had to use alternative methods to convey their meanings, and the final remnants of the older case system would then have become entirely expendable.

Imperfect learning, however, risks amounting to little more than a mechanism by which simplification could have occurred. Children eventually overcome nearly all their early regularizations, so we must be careful about crediting them with too much influence. All the problems that make simplification problematic as an explanation for change also beset imperfect learning. Languages do not grow forever simpler. If the children of each generation introduce a few simplifications, somebody must also be busily adding compensating complexities.

Filling out a Pattern; Typological Consistency

The patterns of word-order typology that were reviewed in Chapter 11 suggest that a language whose word-order types contradict each other could be under pressure to change toward a more harmonious set of patterns. If the verbs of a language move from sentence-final to either medial or initial position, we might expect postpositions to give way to prepositions, and noun modifiers might begin to shift to the position after their nouns. Prefixation might take over from suffixation. Many of the changes that have occurred in the development from Latin to French can be interpreted as preserving, or reestablishing, harmonious word-order patterns.

On the other hand, if typological pressure is effective in promoting harmonious word orders, it is puzzling to find that languages so regularly have disharmonious patterns. In relatively few languages do all constructions conform to one another. In almost every language, at least one or two constructions seem to be out of place with the others. If typological pressure is significant, there must also be important opposing mechanisms that reintroduce disharmony.

Phonological Erosion

One mechanism that may introduce disharmony is phonological erosion. Some linguists have even suggested that phonological erosion is the prime mover that initiates the cycle of syntactic change. Most verb-final languages, for example, have suffixes and postpositions, but modifiers, such as demonstratives and adjectives, tend to precede their nouns. If noun suffixes, in such a language, are ground away, as suffixes often are, it could be that the only thing available to take over their function would be the modifiers that precede the nouns. Some of these could then be gradually reduced to noun prefixes. Disappearing case suffixes, for example, could have their job taken over by prepositions, and plural suffixes could give way to prefixed ways of showing number. In this way the language could move from a primarily suffixing and postpositional language to a primarily prefixing and prepositional language. Such changes would introduce disharmonies into the language, and these, in turn, could bring new pressures for change in other parts of the system.

Linguists are by no means agreed on the importance of phonological erosion in inaugurating change. If typological pressures are really as strong as some linguists have suggested, it might seem more reasonable to expect that phonological erosion would be resisted in places where it threatened to introduce a violation of typological patterns. To some linguists, a wholesale reorganization of word order seems to be an excessively drastic means of adjusting to the loss of a few affixes.

Borrowing

Neighboring but unrelated languages often show syntactic similarities that can be explained only by borrowing. Syntactic borrowing requires more time and closer contact between languages than lexical borrowing, but under the right circumstances borrowing can influence syntax as profoundly as it can influence the lexicon.

The syntax of one language can influence another in two different ways. First, under conditions of strong social pressure, there is no limit at all on what can be borrowed. Over a long enough period, languages can gradually grow more and more like their neighbors. Second, and more dramatically, if an entire population shifts from one language to another, the new speakers may carry syntactic patterns from their older native language into their newly learned one, just as they carry phonological patterns. A shifting population that lacks close contact with native speakers of the language they are learning may find it easier to leave the vocabulary of its old language behind than to abandon its syntax.

Neighboring Indo-European and Dravidian languages in India have such similar syntax that sentences can sometimes be translated word for word, and even morpheme for morpheme. The following sentences come from a dialect of Marathi, an Indo-European language closely related to Hindi, and an adjacent dialect of Kannada, an unrelated Dravidian language.

Kannada:	*hog-*	*i*	*wənd*	*kudri*	*turg*	*maR*	*i*		*aw*	*tənd*
Marathi:	*ja-*	*un*	*ek*	*ghoRa*	*cori*	*kar-*	*un*		*təw*	*anla*
	go	having	one	horse	theft	take	having		he	brought

'Having gone and having stolen a horse, he brought it back.'

Marathi and Kannada belong to language families that, so far as we know, are unrelated. The syntactic parallels between these dialects cannot be due to a common origin, and it strains credulity to suppose that they are simply accidental. Since the languages have been in contact for centuries and since there is widespread bilingualism in the area from which these examples are drawn, there has been ample opportunity for the languages to influence one another. As people have switched from one language to the other, the patterns of the two languages have influenced each other profoundly.

In spite of distinct antecedents, languages spoken in the same region of the world often share grammatical features. We must, therefore, recognize borrowing as one process that can cause syntax to change, but borrowing cannot explain most syntactic changes. Borrowing, after all, can only cause languages to become more similar to one another, and we have no reason to suppose that the languages of the world have grown less diverse in the long course of their history. Other mechanisms must be at work that counteract the homogenizing influence of borrowing and that lead languages to become more diverse.

Innovation and Cleverness

Borrowing and imitation are obvious and reasonably well understood processes, but we sometimes fail to recognize the opposing pressures of inventiveness and imagination. We do not always want to sound just like others. We reward and admire those who are innovative, and their innovations are, in turn, imitated by others. New forms cannot diverge too far from old ones, but cautious innovations are possible, even in syntax, and they can accumulate into significant changes. Changes do not come suddenly in syntax any more than they do in phonology. Rather, change occurs almost imperceptibly as people come gradually to favor some forms, while other forms go into a correspondingly gradual decline.

Social Connotations

Like phonological patterns, syntactic patterns acquire social connotations. The most heavily stigmatized forms in American English are found in nonstandard dialects. The pressures toward standardization may bring some reduction in syntactic variability, but social pressures can also lead toward greater diversity. For some people, standard English seems overly refined, even sissyish. To assert their masculinity, some young men avoid the delicate speech of their oppressors. The imaginative innovations by which people set themselves apart from each other are more obvious in vocabulary than in syntax. It is relatively easy to learn new words in order to distinguish one's own group. When members of another group borrow these terms, new ones can always be invented. The push–pull mechanism of competitive borrowing and innovation can stimulate rapid lexical change, and we can at least speculate that a similar mechanism might move syntax. Members of one group could emphasize new syntactic forms in order to demonstrate their difference from another group. If these forms were widely imitated, new forms would have to be invented by those who wished to maintain their distinctive status. The study of such mechanisms in syntax has hardly begun.

Why Not Change?

Finally, some of the mystery of change may be dispelled by turning the question around once more: Why should languages stay the same? Always phrasing the question as a search for the causes of change reveals a bias. The normal state of language is not necessarily stability. To be sure, a degree of stability is needed if we are to communicate. Adjacent generations must be able to understand each other. Still we can tolerate considerable variability in syntax, and perhaps we should reserve our surprise for the degree to which languages do, in fact, maintain considerable consistency, not merely across generations but even across centuries. Today we may want to read documents that were written several centuries ago, but before writing began, there was no need for language to be more stable than would allow communication across the span of a single long lifetime. Why should a language *not* change?

THE RESTLESS CYCLE

The examples of syntactic change that have been reviewed in this chapter give us a picture that is reminiscent of the view of phonological change offered in Chapter 8. Like phonology, syntax seems always to be just a bit unstable, almost restless. In expressing themselves, speakers can always select among a range of choices, and change occurs as the proportion of one alternative rises at the expense of a competitor. Nothing in language is completely stable, but each language has its points of special variability. Constructions that seem rock solid in English may be paralleled by highly variable constructions in another language.

As the centuries pass, some syntactic choices are made with increasing regularity while others become less popular. As the balance shifts and as changes accumulate, syntax, like phonology, moves further and further from its origins, and it may come to differ in every way from its ancestor of a few thousand years earlier. At one stage, affixes may be so thoroughly worn away that most words are uninflected, but at another stage, separate words may join together and give rise to new sets of affixes. If we knew the details of a language through enough millennia, we might be able to watch it swinging restlessly from one pattern to another and then back again, always changing, but never progressing.

For as far as we are able to tell, no set of syntactic forms does a better job, overall, than any other set. The tasks for which we use syntax can be accomplished in many ways. Just as *bread* can equally well be called *pain* (French) or *roti* (Hindi) or by any other sequence of sounds that the speakers agree on, and just as words can be kept in contrast by many alternative phonological distinctions, it also makes little difference whether the verb is placed first, middle, or last, so long as the conventions are consistent enough to allow understanding. We are unable to detect differences in efficiency between languages that have extensive affixing and those that do not. Whether adjectival meanings are expressed by verbs, by nouns, or by a separate adjective class seems to make no difference in the ability of people to make their meanings clear.

Since there are many alternative ways of reaching the same goals, syntax can vary widely from one language to another, and languages of one type can gradually change to languages of another type. The limits of syntactic variation and the limits on how far and in what way a language can change, like the limits of all other kinds of linguistic variation, must be set by the nature of the human mind, by the limits on what we are able to learn, and by the limits on what we are able to use.

PART FOUR

Growth

INTRODUCTION TO PART FOUR

The three earlier parts of this book each concluded with a section on language change, but the changes considered in those chapters left a linguistic system of the same fundamental type, a human language with all the familiar characteristics of other human languages. This final set of chapters describes changes of a different kind, changes in which older forms of language grow into forms of a fundamentally different kind. Some of these new forms are more flexible, more complex, or more versatile than those that went before. Some even allow new social relationships to emerge that had not been possible earlier.

The languages known as "pidgins" and "creoles," that grow up in communities where people come from a variety of backgrounds and where no single well-established language is readily available, are described in Chapter 14. Chapter 15 deals with the growth of language in children and suggests briefly how second-language learning may differ from first-language learning. Chapter 16 offers some comparisons between human language and other human and animal communication and considers the evolutionary origins of human language. Finally, Chapter 17 surveys the development of writing, printing, and electronic communication, and considers the impact of these technologies both on language and on the societies in which they are used.

CHAPTER FOURTEEN

Pidgin and Creole Languages

PIDGINS

Languages generally change at a stately pace. Changes accumulate from decade to decade, but not even a century is normally enough to move a language beyond intelligibility. Under conditions of sufficient social upheaval, however, changes can come much more rapidly. The languages that develop under the most extreme conditions are known as **pidgins** and **creoles,** and they are different enough from other languages to challenge a number of our usual conceptions about language.

Any tourist who has haggled over the price of a piece of pottery, in a language that he barely knows, has taken the first steps toward the invention of a pidgin language. What matters, when haggling, is meaning. Grammatical niceties, such as affixes and function words, are easily sloughed off. Rough and ready pronunciation will suffice. What does matter are a few understandable words. *How much? Five pesos. Too much. How much you say? Three pesos. Okay.* Or: *Bus station where? There, one kilometer, big house, left.* Those who overcome their embarrassment at reverting to something just a bit like the language of a two-year-old soon learn to communicate a surprising amount with a few dozen words.

The tourist's jargon dies as soon as he boards his plane for home, but when people with no common language are thrown together for longer periods, they gradually build a richer and more stable language on beginnings that are no less humble. They exploit useful bits of the languages they already know, but they often piece these bits together in unconventional ways. The classic situation for the establishment of a pidgin is a community of laborers who live far from home and who speak a variety of mutually incomprehensible languages, as in the early slave communities of west Africa and the New World. Here, men and women with many different languages were forced to live and work together. The pidgin languages of these communities were always used primarily among native speakers of African languages. Europeans occasionally learned enough pidgin to let them talk with their slaves, but communication between master and slave was always limited, and what the Africans needed most was a way of talking with each other.

None of their many African languages was widely enough known to serve as a common language in the slave communities, nor could any African language be used with the white masters. A few useful words from African languages generally found their way into the pidgin, but the largest part of the vocabulary was drawn from whatever European language was spoken in the area. Portuguese, Spanish, French, Dutch, or English provided most of the words for these communities, but the urgent need to communicate ran far ahead of any opportunity to learn the conventional phonology or syntax of a European language. Thus it was in phonology and in syntax that the influence of the speakers' native languages were strongest. People whose main concern was to make themselves understood carried older habits into their new language, and it was inevitable that both the pronunciation and grammatical patterns of African languages would deeply affect the pidgin. The result was the invention of a medium of communication that drew most of its vocabulary from a colonial language, but whose pronunciation might conform more closely to African habits and whose words were joined together in ways that were remote from any European standard.

A pidgin is, by definition, a language that is native to no one. Generally this means that no one feels strongly about its correctness or its purity. A pidgin is used for practical ends. If people pronounce the words in varied ways, or arrange them in varied orders, it matters little as long as they can make themselves understood. Nor are pidgins, at least when first devised, likely to be used for as wide a range of purposes as most languages. Pidgins may lack the elaborated registers that other languages use for oratory and verbal art. In a community of displaced laborers, even the topics of conversation may be restricted by the limited range of vocabulary that people control.

A language with a restricted vocabulary and a restricted range of styles, and a language whose speakers are tolerant of extreme variation, will also be a language that is relatively easy to learn. People who are thrown together in a mixed community may start with no more words or syntax than the pottery-buying tourist. Newcomers can speak with chaotic variation, carrying much of their native pronunciation, and even their native syntax, into their attempts at the pidgin. Soon, however, as more topics need to be discussed and as people gain practice, conventions arise even in a pidgin. Gradually, the pidgin stabilizes. It acquires a conventional lexicon and increasingly consistent patterns of pronunciation and syntax, but as long as a pidgin remains a second language for everyone, it is likely to stay relatively simple and be more variable than most languages.

The era of European colonialism gave us the best-known pidgin languages. Pidgins were once widely used in the mixed communities of African ancestry on both sides of the Atlantic, and in the nineteenth century, as the European presence in the Pacific grew stronger, pidgins arose there as well. The most important pidgin spoken today is known as Tok Pisin, and it is widely used in Papua New Guinea. New Guinea is estimated to have as many as 700 distinct native languages. Such diversity could survive only as long as most people passed their lives near their places of birth. In the latter part of the nineteenth century, the influence of the world beyond New Guinea was felt, and radical changes began. Mixed crews on coastal vessels, employees of colonial officers, and especially, laborers on the spreading plantations needed to talk to each other. Pidgin English provided a common language that made this possible, and Tok Pisin has spread and flourished ever since. It is now used by more than half a million people, more than twice as many as any other language spoken in Papua New Guinea. With less grammatical complexity than most languages, it continues to be regarded by those who speak it as relatively easy to learn. Its simplicity more than offsets any disadvantage arising from its relatively restricted stock of words. Tok Pisin serves admirably today as one of the official languages of Papua New Guinea. It is regularly used in parliament, and it is an important medium for publication.

The following example of Tok Pisin suggests the ways in which it is similar to and different from English (Hall, 1966, pp. 149–50).

naw mi stap rabawl. mi stap lɔŋ bɪglajn, mi kətim kopra. naw wənfɛlə mastər bɪlɔŋ kəmpəni ɛm i-kɪčim mi, mi kuk lɔŋ ɛm gɛn. mastər kɪŋ . mi stap. naw ɔl mastər i-kɪk, naw ɔl i-kɪkɪm ɛm, naw leg bɪlɔŋ ɛm i-sweləp. ɔl mastər tæsɔl i-kɪk, naw ɔl i-kɪkɪm ɛm.

Then I stayed in Rabaul. I was in the work-group, cutting copra. Then a white man from the company took me as a cook again. Mr. King. I stayed there. Now all the white men were playing football, and they kicked him, so that his leg swelled up. The white men were just kicking, and kicked him.

Even this short passage illustrates a number of the characteristic features of Tok Pisin. First, most of the words are derived from English, but their meanings have often diverged rather sharply from the originals, and they are arranged in ways that deviate markedly from other forms of English. Consider, for example, the personal pronouns. A few pronouns are used in the passage, and the complete inventory of Tok Pisin pronouns consists of *mi* 'I, me'; *ju* 'you, singular'; *em* 'he, him, she, her, it' (from 'him'); *ɔl* 'they, them' (from 'all'); *jufɛlə* 'you plural'; *mifɛlə* 'we exclusive, she and I, they and I', etc. but not including the person spoken to; *jumi* 'we inclusive, you and I' including the person spoken to. All these pronouns are based on English words, but they have been organized into a system that is quite different from English. The English distinction between subject and object pronouns has been lost, and the English words have been given meanings that bring them closer to the pronouns of a number of New Guinea languages. Thus the distinction, widespread in New Guinea, between inclusive and exclusive 'we,' has been taken into Tok

Pisin, while the distinction between 'he and she' has been lost. It is as if English words have been mobilized to fit New Guinea patterns. This surely makes the language easier for the people of New Guinea to learn than other forms of English would be.

Earlier forms of Tok Pisin did not have obligatory articles, but the meanings that we convey by articles can sometimes be suggested by other words. *ɔl*, derived from English 'all,' serves not only as a pronoun, but also, as in the passage, as a plural definite article (*ɔl mastər*, 'the white men'). *wənfɛlə* 'one' could be used where English would have an indefinite article. *-fɛlə* is often added to both numbers and adjectives. This derives from English *fellow*, but in Tok Pisin it has become a suffix that shows its word to be a modifier: *gʊdfɛlə* 'good,' *bɪgfɛlə* 'big', *blækfɛlə* 'black.'

The grammatical markers on verbs deviate even more radically from other kinds of English. When used with third person subjects, verbs are generally prefixed with *i-*, originally from 'he.' *maʃin i-bəgərəp* 'the machine is wrecked.' The suffix *-ɪm* marks a verb as transitive: *mi rid* 'I read'; *mi rid-ɪm buk* 'I read a book'; *me rid-ɪm* 'I read it'. The verb in *ɛm i-sɪŋawt-ɪm meri* 'she calls the woman' is marked by both the person prefix, *i-*, and the transitive suffix, *-im*. Although most Tok Pisin words come from English, its syntax is so radically different that we may question whether it should be regarded as a form of English at all. In a number of respects it is closer to the other languages of New Guinea.

Although the vocabulary of pidgin languages may be limited, imaginative compounding can make up for some of the limitations, as suggested by these words from Tok Pisin:

gras	grass
mausgras	moustache
gras bilong fes	beard
gras bilong hed	head hair
gras bilong pisin	feather
gras antap long ai	eyebrow
gras nogut	weed
han	hand, arm
han bilong diwai	branch of a tree
han bilong pisin	wing of a bird

The best-known pidgins developed in communities where a single colonial language played a dominant role. This language, known as the **superstrate** language, would generally provide the bulk of the pidgin's vocabulary, but the morphology of the superstrate language was often cast aside. Plurals and tense markers generally disappear in pidgin languages as do distinctions of gender. Complexities such as markers of verbal or adjective agreement are generally stripped away, and irregular morphology is likely to be radically regularized. By dispensing with idiosyncratic affixes, words can generally be used in fixed, unchanging, forms.

The native languages of the pidgin speakers are known as the **substrate** languages, and their influence on the pidgin is likely to be strongly felt in syntax. Pidgins have been somewhat superficially characterized as joining the syntax of one language (the substrate) and the vocabulary of another (the superstrate). In fact, both vocabulary and syntax generally show the influence of more than a single language, and both have to be regarded as mixed, but it is true that the influence of the superstrate is often strongest in vocabulary. Since the speakers have diverse language backgrounds, no single substrate language is so clearly dominant in syntax as the superstrate generally is in vocabulary. Nevertheless, where the native languages resemble each other, as did many of the west African languages of the earliest slaves, these exert a collective influence on the syntax of a developing pidgin.

Pronunciation, like syntax, is likely to reflect the phonology of the substrate languages. Where these have characteristics in common, the speakers can use sounds from the substrate languages even when using words from the superstrate. Where the substrate languages differ, the least common or most difficult phones of particular languages are likely to be avoided, but speakers manage quite well with those phones that are widely represented in their various native languages.

CREOLES

The longer and more regularly a pidgin is used, the more it tends to stabilize. As its speakers become more skillful, its conventions become fixed, but its final stabilization comes only when children grow up in community where a pidgin serves as the primary medium of communication or even as the only common language. A pidgin can become the neighborhood language, and when parents share no other language, it may even be the language of their home. In such cases, children need to create their own native language from a pidgin that had not previously been a native language for anyone. The adults who speak the pidgin are unlikely to be as fluent as the models on whom most children base their language. We give the name **creole** to a language that began as a pidgin, but that has later been converted into the mother tongue of a new generation of speakers. By using different words, we imply that creoles and pidgins are different kinds of languages. Acquired as a first and native language, a creole comes to be spoken with all the fluency of any other first language. It may be the only language of its new speakers, and they will have to use it for all the varied purposes of any other language. Children who appropriate a pidgin as their first language need a medium for word play, for joking, for poetry, and for story telling, even if not for written literature. The vocabulary expands as the language is extended to embrace a more varied subject matter. For most speakers in Papua New Guinea, Tok Pisin is still a second language, but in some communities, it is now being creolized as children learn it as their first language.

Once established, a creole is learned and used like any other natural language. It can change in the same way, and it can become differentiated into social and regional dialects. It can develop stylistic variation. If the complexity of language is limited only by the complexity of the human mind, we should expect creoles to grow to be as complex as any other natural language. An unstandardized pidgin that is used for limited purposes may remain simpler than other languages. Creoles regain complexity. It is not in complexity or in the variety of uses to which they are put that creoles are different from other languages, but rather in the discontinuity of their history.

As a creole becomes established, stabilized constructions replace the looser and more variable constructions of its pidgin predecessor. A clear example is the development of the Tok Pisin future marker, variously pronounced *baimbai, bai,* or *bə.* This began as the English *by and by,* and at first it was an optional adverb, often placed at the beginning of a sentence. It gave speakers a clear and simple way of indicating future time during a period when control over the conventional English tense system was hardly possible. To turn *by and by* into a grammatical marker of the future, several changes were needed.

First, *baimbai* or one of its abbreviated alternatives began to be used redundantly even when another adverb of time, such as *bihain* 'later' (from English *behind*) was also used: *bihain bai i kambek gen* 'later it will come back again.' In fact, *bai* has become an increasingly obligatory marker of future time, and by becoming obligatory it acts less like an adverb, and more like a tense marker.

Second, *bai* has moved closer to the verb, and its position has become more fixed. The ancestral *baimbai* often occurred before the subject, at the beginning of a sentence, although like many adverbs, its position was variable. Today, when the subject is a Noun Phrase, *bai* usually occurs after the subject and directly before the verb. With most pronoun subjects, *bai* occurs before the pronoun, but the third person singular pronoun, *em,* acts more like a noun and the *bai* follows. Thus the position of *bai* has come to be fixed by the syntax, another trait more characteristic of a tense marker than an adverb.

Finally, *by and by* has been abbreviated. It seems to have been pronounced *baimbai* almost from the beginning, and pidgin speakers can still be heard to pronounce it this way. *Bai* developed later as a short alternative to *baimbai,* and *bai* is the most abbreviated form ordinarily used by adults who have learned Tok Pisin as a second language. Children who have learned it as their first language sometimes reduce the word still further to *bə.* As the phrase was abbreviated, it also tended to lose stress, and *bə* is so weakly stressed that it almost loses its status as a separate syllable. In this way also it has become less like an adverb and more like a grammatical marker or even a prefix.

The transformation of *by and by* into *bə* is an example of grammaticalization. Ordinarily, we expect many centuries to be pass before an entire phrase is reduced to less than a full syllable, but creolization can telescope the process into a single generation. Pidginization and creolization can have the effect of radically accelerating linguistic change, and they give us an opportunity to observe ongoing changes with unusual clarity.

The collapse of *by and by* into *bə* is just one small example of a pervasive process. In the first crisis of communication, when people are groping for simple ways to express themselves, much of the grammatical apparatus is swept away. Meanings are conveyed by full words, rather than by affixes. Later as the pidgin becomes stabilized and creolized, new grammatical apparatus is created. This new grammar may have little to do with the grammar of the superstrate language from which most of the vocabulary is derived, but it does not duplicate the grammar of any single substrate language either. Just where this new grammar comes from is one of the most fascinating questions that has been raised by students of pidgin and creole languages.

SIMILARITIES AMONG CREOLES

Although pidgins and creoles have been spoken in widely separated parts of the world, and although they have been influenced by a very wide range of languages, they seem to share a number of characteristics. Some linguists believe that, in their syntax, creoles resemble each other more closely than they resemble either the superstrate languages or the substrate languages that have influenced them. Linguists have pointed, for instance, to the creole equivalents of verbs like English *be,* which are known as "copulas." English *be* has at least four distinct uses, and many creoles have a different construction for each of them.

1. **Adjectival verbs.** English sentences such as *he is tired* require a form of *be* to link the predicate adjective (*tired*) to the subject (*he*). In many creoles, the adjectives themselves act as verbs, and they require no additional linking verb. This is the case in Guyanese Creole, an English-based creole spoken in Guyana on the northern coast of South America. (Calling it "English based" means that English was the superstrate language from which most of its vocabulary was drawn.) In Guyanese Creole *i wiiri* 'he is tired' (from English *weary*) is formed in exactly the same way as *i wok* 'he works.'

2. **Progressives.** English progressive tenses are constructed with a form of *be* together with the suffix *-ing,* as in *he is working.* English-based creoles often lack English *-ing,* but most creoles do have an equivalent for our progressive. Their progressives are often formed by means of a special word placed before the verb. The Guyanese Creole sentences just cited can both be made progressive by means of the preverbal marker *a*: *i a wiiri* 'he is getting tired,' *i a wok* 'he is working.'

3. **Locatives.** English requires a form of *be* in sentences that indicate location, as in *he is in Chicago.* Many creoles have a specialized verb used only for this purpose. Such verbs might be translated as 'to be at.' Thus in Miskito Coast Creole, spoken on the Atlantic coast of Nicaragua, *De gyorld-em aal de pan di veranda* 'The girls were all on the veranda' the second *de,* though presumably derived from English *there,* acts as a verb and means 'to be at.' (The *-em* of *gyorld-em* is an example of a common creole plural marker derived from the plural pronoun, 'them.')

4. Equatives. The true copula equates a subject and another noun phrase, as in *John is a fool*. The creole verbs corresponding to this equative 'be' are generally quite different from locative 'be,' and they are used in much more restricted circumstances than English *be*. In Miskito Coast Creole *dat a di fos sang* 'That is the first song' the equative *a* may derive from English *are* but it is used only in the specific equative sense.

Many creoles also have a set of preverbal markers that indicate time relationships. In particular, three such markers seem to be found in a surprising number of creoles. They always come just before the verb, and when two or three are used together, they seem always to occur in a fixed order. The first is a tense marker that can correspond either to the simple past (e.g., *he went*), or the past perfect (e.g., *he had gone*). The next is the progressive marker. An example is the Guyanese *a* illustrated earlier. The third confers a meaning that has been called "irrealis." It indicates that the action described by the following verb is not real, or is not yet real. Verbs preceded by the irrealis marker most often correspond to the English future or conditional: *he will come, he would come*. The future has not yet happened, so it is not yet real, and conditionals may never happen at all. It has been claimed that creoles as distant in time and space as the eighteenth and nineteenth century Atlantic and twentieth century Hawaii all had three markers with these meanings, and that they occurred in the same order.

Many creoles are characterized by serial verbs that follow each other directly with no explicit marker of their syntactic relation. Miskito Coast Creole *aal di waari ron kom bai me*, literally, 'all the wild-boars ran came by me,' might be expressed in English as 'came running by me.' Possession is frequently indicated by the simple juxtaposition of the name of the possessor and the name of the possessed, with nothing that corresponds to English -'*s*: Miskito Coast *di uman biebi* 'the woman's baby.' Many creoles spoken around the Atlantic often have just six pronouns, three singular and three plural. They often lack the typical European distinction of gender (*he, she* and *it*), but even creoles with predominantly English vocabulary usually make a distinction between singular and plural second-person pronouns, *you* singular and *you* plural. Distinctive possessive pronouns (*my, our*, etc.) and distinctive objective pronouns (*me, us*, etc.) are generally lacking.

The words that express these devices in various creoles are quite varied. The grammatical morphemes and function words of creoles, like the content words, generally derive from a European source. Creoles that draw their vocabulary from French, of course, tend to have grammatical morphemes from French. Wherever they come from, their meanings have often been quite radically changed as they have been adapted to the needs of creole speakers, but the syntactic patterns into which they fit seem to be surprisingly similar.

The similarities among creoles go beyond anything that we would expect to arise by mere chance. They cry out for an explanation, and several have been offered. First and most obviously, we must recognize historical connections both among the pidgin languages and among the languages that have influenced them. The historical ties are closer for creoles spoken around the Atlantic than for those spoken in the Pacific, and the Atlantic creoles may have the most similarities. Most of the characteristics of the Atlantic creoles that distinguish them from the European superstrate languages have parallels in the African languages of the regions from which slaves were drawn. Serial verbs, preverbal markers, six-member pronoun systems, and distinctions among various equivalents of the copula are all common in west African languages. It is hardly plausible to look for the "origin" of any of these features in any specific African language, for no single language was important enough to have imposed its patterns throughout the pidgin- and creole-speaking world. Nevertheless, the majority of the slaves spoke languages belonging to the Niger–Kordofanian family, and these shared enough characteristics to have had a strong collective influence. The most obvious explanation for the similarities among the creoles is that they arose when a group of similar substrate (African) languages came into contact with a group of similar superstrate (European) languages under similar conditions. We should not be surprised when the result is a group of similar pidgins and creoles.

The Atlantic pidgins and creoles show enough phonological similarity to west African languages to suggest that these substratum languages have had considerable influence. Unusual European sounds, such as the English interdentals (θ, ð) and the French front rounded vowels (y, ø) are rarely preserved in English-based or French-based pidgins and creoles, but the unusual sounds of west African languages have sometimes survived. Prenasalized consonants and labio-velars, almost unknown in Europe but common in west Africa, appear in some pidgins and creoles, and even tones, characteristic of many west African languages but unknown in the European superstrate languages, are reported in a few creoles. Many pidgins and creoles approximate the seven-vowel system that is common in west Africa. The syllables of many west African languages approximate a CV (consonant-vowel) pattern, final consonants being quite rare. In many pidgins and creoles, words drawn from the superstrate languages have their final consonant clusters simplified, and many final consonants are lost. Medial-consonant clusters may be either simplified, or separated by intrusive vowels. In this way, even though the vocabulary is drawn primarily from the European superstrate, the syllable structure of the pidgins and creoles comes to approximate that of the west African substrate.

Attributing the common characteristics of pidgins and creoles to substrate influence is not always entirely satisfying, however, for the resemblances, in some cases, seem too specific. The lexical resemblances among the languages are sufficient to make it clear that there was considerable contact among them. At the time when the Atlantic pidgins were being formed, travel around the American and African shores was common enough to let one region influence another. Pidgins already established in one place must have been carried to new areas, and it should not be imagined that pidgins developed everywhere in complete independence of one another. Even the pidgins and creoles spoken in the Pacific may have been influenced by people who were already familiar with Atlantic pidgins. Sailors accustomed to speaking pidgins in Atlantic ports could have carried their habits to the other side of the world.

Some linguists have been so impressed by the similarities among the languages that they have wondered whether all pidgins and creoles might not be derived from a single ancestral pidgin, and some have suggested that the earliest pidgin drew its vocabulary from Portuguese, the first European language to have a strong presence in west Africa. Whatever the apparent superstrate language, some Portuguese words are found in most surviving pidgins and creoles, and these have been interpreted as evidence for their Portuguese antecedents. *Pickaninny* 'child' and *savvy* 'know, be able to,' for instance, are derived ultimately from Portuguese but they are widespread in pidgins and creoles of all sorts.

How could a pidgin whose vocabulary is drawn primarily from English or French trace its antecedents to a Portuguese pidgin? A few linguists have suggested that pidgins might be able to change their vocabulary, or "relexify," when brought under the influence of a new colonial language. Speakers of a pidgin with predominantly Portuguese vocabulary who found themselves under English dominance might substitute English words for the older Portuguese. With sufficiently massive borrowing, the vocabulary of the language might change even while the syntax remained stable. This would help to account for the syntactic similarities among pidgins, and among the creoles derived from them, at the same time that it would account for their great lexical differences.

These historical explanations for the similarities among pidgins and creoles have not satisfied everyone. They seem particularly forced when trying to explain the resemblances between Atlantic and Pacific creoles. These are, after all, spoken by people with very different language backgrounds. Could their similarities be attributed, instead, to the similarities of the situations in which pidgins and creoles arose? Could they even be the result of universal human linguistic abilities that constrain the form of newly invented languages?

It seems natural that people who are forced together without a common language will exploit the aspects of phonology that the largest number of them share. The less usual, and presumably more difficult, phones might easily be lost. Those that survive would be the phones that are found in the widest variety of languages. Could there be a similar selection of widespread syntactic features? People who struggle to communicate in poorly known languages may have only a limited range of available strategies. Unstressed affixes from the superstrate language may be difficult to hear clearly and therefore difficult to learn. When the meanings conveyed by these affixes are essential, speakers may use full words in their place. Adverbs can replace tenses. A word meaning 'many' can be used instead of the plurals. The numeral 'one' can substitute for the indefinite article. When a definite meaning is essential, demonstratives can serve in place of definite articles.

The strongest claims for universal patterns of creole formation have come from the linguist Derek Bickerton. Resting his case on specific similarities that he sees in creoles spoken throughout the world, Bickerton argues that human beings are endowed with a "bio-program" that gives us the propensity to create particular linguistic structures. This bio-program has some similarity to the inbuilt "Language Acquisition Device" that Chomsky has offered as the explanation for the ability of all humans to learn a language, but Bickerton's bio-program is more specific. Bickerton argues that even such specific traits as preverbal markers of past, progressive, and irrealis rest on our genetically endowed linguistic aptitudes. These syntactic devices are not found in all the world's languages, but Bickerton attributes this to historical changes that have pulled the languages away from the most "natural" form that a language might have. Every language is buffeted by historical circumstances that pull it away from the patterns laid down by the bio-program, but there are limits to how far a language can be pulled. A language could not deviate too far from the patterns of the bio-program without becoming impossible to learn or use. Before that happens a language would have to develop new patterns that align it once more with the underlying human bio-program.

Under the extreme conditions of creole formation, when children grow up in a community without even a stabilized pidgin, the children will be forced to create what amounts to a new language, and in these conditions, Bickerton argues, they will have no choice but to fall back on their bio-program and to develop a language that is close to the form for which our brains are most directly adapted. It is not surprising, therefore, that creoles everywhere exhibit similar characteristics, since all are products of similar human minds. By examining creoles then, we might have a chance to uncover the linguistic patterns for which the human mind is best adapted.

Bickerton's arguments remain controversial. Few other linguists accept them in full. Nevertheless, they raise fascinating questions. Can we regard some linguistic structures as more "natural" than others, as conforming more closely to undistorted human nature? To what extent do the similarities among pidgins and creoles arise from the particular forms of the antecedent languages, and to what extent are they due to the similarities of the situation, or even to the universal nature of the human mind? Are creoles such original inventions that they give us a privileged view of human nature? Bickerton's argument suggests that pidgins and creoles could have a unique role in helping us to understand the mind of the talking ape.

DECREOLIZATION AND THE CREOLE ORIGIN OF BLACK ENGLISH VERNACULAR

Millions of people today speak languages that are unquestionably creoles. These languages are concentrated most densely in the Caribbean where, on some islands, a large proportion of the population is of African descent. Most of the people of Haiti speak a French-based creole, and most Jamaicans speak a form of creole English. Today, these creoles exist in the shadow of standards that are set in France, Britain, and the United States, and they are strongly influenced by these standards. Most formal schooling, most broadcasting, and most writing aims at a standard that is quite different from daily conversation. People become accustomed to hearing a standardized language in formal circumstances, and people with ambitions or pretensions may try, more or less successfully, to adapt their own language to it. Creoles share enough with the standard language to mislead people into regarding them as merely corrupted versions of the standard. As people let words, grammatical forms, and even pronunciations from the standard language filter into their own speech, a range of intermediate styles comes to bridge the gap between the standardized language at one extreme and the creole at the other. The upper class, with better education and wider contacts, moves closer to the standard, especially in formal circumstances. A less standardized creole remains the comfortable language for the family and informal conversation, especially among less educated people. Linguists refer to the least standardized forms as the **basilect,** and to the most standardized forms toward which people sometimes aim as the **acrolect.** Intermediate forms, inevitably, are called the **mesolect.** The social stratification of these postcolonial societies comes to be mirrored by their stratified language.

Speakers may cherish the basilectal creole for its familiarity and intimacy, but if the standard language is the language of education, writing, government, and power, it will influence all forms of the language. To show their sophistication and status, people incorporate features of the acrolect into their language, or they slide back and forth along the continuum, adapting their language to the situation and the topic. Not everyone controls the entire range. Those at the bottom may be able to move only part way up from the basilect toward the mesolect. Those who can easily control the standard may drift part way down the scale when relaxing with close friends, but they may lack full competence in the basilect.

This situation invites borrowing from the standard. As prestige forms filter down from the acrolect through the mesolect and even to the basilect, the creole becomes less distinctive. A time could come when, in the absence of historical records, we would no longer be certain whether a language should be considered a creole at all. After it has been strongly enough influenced by the standard language it might more reasonably be regarded as simply a dialect of that language. The creole background of the dialect could be obscured.

Today, the dialect of lower-class black Americans can hardly be considered a creole, but a number of linguists believe that we cannot understand the special characteristics of Black English Vernacular unless we recognize some creole influence in its history. The only unmistakable creole surviving within the United States is "Sea Island Creole," sometimes known as "Gullah," spoken on the islands along the coast of South Carolina. Other dialects spoken by black Americans, whether in the rural South or the urban North, are too much like other forms of English to count as creoles, but they do share enough with the creoles of the Sea Islands and the Caribbean to suggest some shared history. Final consonant clusters are often simplified in BEV, and the deletion of final consonants is common. Final-consonant weakening and loss recall the creole tendency toward CV syllables. The weakening of suffixes in BEV resembles the creole tendency to lose inflections. Many BEV speakers do not distinguish between *you/your* or *they/their,* and this recalls the loss of distinctive possessive pronouns in creole English. Many English-based creoles, like BEV, are rich in multiple negation.

Still, even if BEV has creole antecedents, it has moved too close to other forms of English to be considered a creole any longer. Linguists speak of the process by which a creole is pulled back into the standard language as "decreolization." This might be looked on as the final step in a long process that begins with pidginization, moves through creolization, and ends when the language finally dissolves back into the standard. This is not, however, the inevitable fate of all creoles. Under the right historical circumstances, a creole should be able to develop into an independent language, quite separate from the superstrate from which it once drew its vocabulary. It is the condition of the modern world, where former colonial languages retain great prestige, that gives them the power to influence and absorb the creoles.

LANGUAGE MIXING AND FAMILY TREES

Linguists like to draw family trees that display the genetic relationship among languages. The best known family tree shows ancestral Indo-European splitting decisively into its subgroups, and these subgroups splitting in turn into smaller and smaller subdivisions until, finally, the twigs of the tree represent the modern languages. Our trees summarize a mass of information, but they would be impossible to draw without one crucial assumption: that languages do not mix. If languages could easily mix, then a single language, like a single human being, could have more than just one parent, and the branches of the family tree would not only divide but rejoin. Instead of a tree, the diagram of related languages would be a network.

For most languages, the assumption that languages cannot mix works well enough. Languages certainly borrow from one another, and heavy borrowing can obscure linguistic relationships, but most linguists, most of the time, have believed that if we can learn enough about the languages, we should be able to peel away the levels of borrowing and uncover the "true" underlying genetic relationships. In spite of extensive borrowing from Romance languages, for example, English, at its core, remains a thoroughly Germanic language. There can be no doubt about where English belongs on the Indo-European family tree.

Pidgin and creole languages offer the most serious challenge to the linguistic faith that languages cannot mix. Tok Pisin is not merely one additional dialect of English to be set beside the dialects of Britain, America, and Australia. It does not have the kind of continuity with earlier forms of English that other dialects have, and in both phonology and syntax, it shows far deeper influence from other languages than fits easily with the assumption that mixing is impossible. Can we find a place for Tok Pisin on the family tree of languages? If so, where does it belong?

We can be clearer about the place for pidgin languages if we recall the two very different ways in which one language can influence another. In classic borrowing, speakers simply draw on the resources of another language. Most often they appropriate words, but sometimes they take over some features of syntax or phonology as well, and they incorporate these into their own language. Most borrowing hardly disturbs the equilibrium or continuity of the language. When a community of speakers **shifts** its language, however, we should expect rather different results. People who are badly outnumbered or people who are ruled by a powerful minority may abandon their old language in favor of the language of the majority or dominant group. When people shift their language in this way, it is no longer words that are most easily transferred. Shifting speakers may be quite successful at learning the vocabulary of their new language and in avoiding the vocabulary of their old one. They may be much less successful at overcoming their ingrained phonological and syntactic habits.

Borrowing and language shift can both occur under varying degrees of pressure and with correspondingly varied results. With light borrowing, words from another language are incorporated easily into the native syntax and adjusted to native pronunciation, and they have virtually no effect on the wider structures of the language. If a larger number of words are borrowed, they may bring along some new phonology or even a bit of syntax. Enough Latin words have been borrowed into English to bring along their plurals. Latin plurals compete with English rivals in *stadia/stadiums, formulae/formulas,* and *indices/indexes,* but many people feel most comfortable with Latin plurals in *cacti, stimuli, alumnae,* and *strata.* Latin has had sufficient prestige to influence English in other ways. Split infinitives occur in English when a word, often an adverb, is inserted between the infinitive marker, *to,* and the verb, as in *he was able to gradually see better.* Split infinitives have always been used in informal English, but because the Latin infinitive suffix cannot been separated from the verb root, English writers have been advised to avoid splitting them in English as well. Many English writers try.

A few eccentric plurals and some discomfort about split infinitives hardly amount to an upheaval in English, but when language contact becomes more intense, and especially when the number of bilingual speakers grows, traits from another language can penetrate more deeply. Increasingly skillful bilinguals may be quite successful at preserving the original pronunciation of borrowed words. They may even introduce new contrasts into the borrowing language. Whole phrases can be taken over, and with them come elements of syntax. Function words begin to follow content words. When the pressure of another language is sufficiently intense, there seems to be no limit to what can be borrowed. Until the First World War, Greek was widely spoken in Asia Minor (modern Turkey) but Greek speakers were often bilingual in Turkish, and Turkish had extensive influence on Asia Minor Greek. Grammatical gender and adjective agreement are characteristic of other kinds of Greek, but they were lost in Asia Minor. Word order was modified in the direction of Turkish, and Asia Minor Greek even developed vowel harmony, an important characteristic in Turkish, but rare in Indo-European languages.

Overwhelming cultural pressure can end in several ways. The speakers may finally shift to the dominant language and let their own language die. Many languages are dying today as children fail to learn the language of their parents. Sometimes the shift takes several generations to complete, but the final result ·nay be the same. More interesting are the rarer cases in which the population ⸱lings stubbornly to its older language even after becoming fluent in a new language. As the new language grows in importance, the older language may be used only in restricted circumstances, and this may narrow its range of stylistic variation. If some speakers lack fluency in the older language, their attempts to use it will be marked by phonological and syntactic influence from the new language. With diminished use, children may fail to learn some of the rarer and more difficult features of the older grammar. Finally, the older language may be reduced to little more than a stubborn residue of vocabulary, cherished as an in-group symbol but embedded in a language that is, in most respects, closer to the dominant one. Anglo-Romani, the "language" of English Gypsies, has reached this point. In most respects it is like English, but it has a stock of non-English vocabulary. Its special words are valued both as a means of maintaining secrecy and as a symbol of group solidarity. Anglo-Romani shows the result of overwhelming borrowing, and we may wonder whether a secure place for Anglo-Romani can be found on the family tree of languages.

When a population shifts its language, the consequences are often quite different, but no less dramatic. When the numbers of a shifting population are small and when access to the dominant language is easy, little is likely to survive from the old language. Immigrant groups in the United States have often lost their languages within a single generation, retaining little more than a few words for their ethnic foods or rituals. The language of the first American generation may be indistinguishable from that of other Americans.

As the relative size of the shifting population rises, and as their opportunity for contact with native speakers of the new language falls, more elements of the older language are likely to be carried over into the new one. The English spoken in India, even by people who grow up with English as their first language, shows the pervasive influence of the indigenous Indian languages. The pronunciation of Indian English has more in common with older Indian languages than with the English of London, and the syntactic influence of Indian languages is by no means trivial. English in India varies from the stumbling attempts of school children to a close approximation to British standards, of course, but most English used in India, even by fluent speakers, shows extensive influence from the older languages of India.

The difference between Indian English and a pidgin or a creole language is one of degree. Like pidgin languages, Indian English was formed by people who lacked wide and easy access to native speakers. The learners could not avoid carrying their older habits into their new language. The process did not take place suddenly in India, and it did not result in a language that we would want to call a pidgin, but whenever language shift occurs, there is the opportunity for the older language to influence the new. Pidgins and creoles can be understood as simply the most dramatic outcome of language shift, the end point on a range of possible outcomes.

At their most extreme, both borrowing and shift can lead to such altered languages that we can no longer reasonably regard them as having continuity with earlier languages. Neither Anglo-Romani nor Tok Pisin has the degree of continuity with any earlier language to let them be fitted neatly onto a family tree with other languages. We will do best to regard them as new languages, inventive responses to extreme social conditions. At the same time, both are simply extreme examples of the ways in which languages can influence each other. Language shift does not interrupt the continuity of a language when learners, in particular children, have free access to the new language, nor is continuity interrupted by moderate borrowing. But either massive borrowing or sudden language shift can result in forms of language that are so altered as to be most reasonably regarded as new inventions.

The best-known examples of pidgin and creole languages all grew out of the experience of European colonialism. They are the linguistic reflection of a period in history when European power was dominant in the world, but the linguistic processes that give rise to pidgins and creoles need not have been confined to the colonial era. We know of pidgins, or pidgin-like languages, that were based on non-European languages. A pidgin based on Assamese, an Indo-European (but not European) language spoken in northeastern India, is used by the linguistically diverse people of the state of Nagaland that lies along the Burma border. A pidgin known as Chinook Jargon was spoken along the northwest Pacific coast of North America. It was based largely on the Native American languages of its region, and it was used as a trade language until this century by both whites and Native Americans. Whenever people have come together with a need to communicate but without the opportunity to master each other's languages, one option has been to devise a pidgin. If the right circumstances were found, creoles may have developed from pidgins at many times in the past. We have to accept these processes as well within the "normal" linguistic capacity of human beings.

The kinds of discontinuities known to take place during pidginization have occasionally been invoked to explain ancient historical changes. The Germanic languages are sufficiently different from other Indo-European languages to have encouraged a few linguists to suggest that Germanic might have originated as a form of creole Indo-European. If the ancient inhabitants of northern Europe had contact with some kind of Indo-European but no chance to learn it perfectly, they might still have developed a pidgin Indo-European and this could then have been creolized and become the ancestor of the later Germanic languages. There is no convincing way to test this guess, and most linguists consider the phonological correspondences between Germanic and the other Indo-European languages too regular to suggest this kind of discontinuity. Nevertheless, we cannot rule out the possibility of creolization in the early ancestry of some modern languages. Pidginization and creolization may have contributed to the diversity that we find among the languages of the world today.

In addition to the problems that pidgins and creoles present for family trees of languages, they challenge a number of other beliefs about language. Are pidgin speakers able to make the confident distinction between grammatical and ungrammatical sentences that formal syntax depends on? Pidgins are so variable, so subject to change and improvisation, that a clear division between grammatical and ungrammatical seems unlikely. Nor do pidgins appear to be so tightly rule-governed as other languages. This does not stop them from being used effectively, and pidgins ought to make us wonder whether other languages have to be regarded as tightly rule-governed formal systems either. If creoles really lie close to a human bio-program, do we have to recognize that some languages are more "natural" than others? If pidgins are really simpler than other languages, does this make them less flexible, less able to convey people's meanings than other languages? Can we be confident that the creoles that derive from pidgins have resources equivalent to other languages? It has been an article of linguistic faith that all languages are essentially equal in expressive power, but perhaps we should not too casually dismiss the challenge that pidgins and creoles pose to this faith. The speed with which these languages change also challenges our understanding of linguistic change at the same time that it gives us a unique opportunity for observing change.

CHAPTER FIFTEEN

First and Second Language Learning

CHILD LANGUAGE

Parents have always delighted in their children's first words. Like their first smiles, the words announce that this small creature is on the way to becoming a human being. Starting slowly, with just one word at a time, language acquisition seems to gather speed until, magically, a talking and thinking person emerges. In recent decades admiring parents have been joined by a growing army of devoted linguists who, with pencil and tape recorder in hand, have preserved the words of small children, hoping to understand more about the most mysterious aspect of human maturation.

The first scholars to take an interest in child language were not linguists, however, but developmental psychologists. The acquisition of language is so central to child development that no one who is interested in the growth of either cognitive or social skills can fail take an interest in language, but psychologists and linguists have approached child language from very different perspectives. Developmental psychologists have always been deeply concerned with individual differences, and this interest was carried over to their study of child language. They have wanted, for example, to understand and to measure intelligence, and studies of intelligence have always taken language into account. Measurement of language ability is an important component of most general intelligence tests, and measuring either general intelligence or some narrower type of verbal aptitude necessarily implies a concern with individual differences.

Studies of child language by linguists blossomed in the 1960s, and linguists brought their own rather different set of interests and assumptions to their work. Unlike developmental psychologists, linguists brought an expectation of uniformity to the study of child language. Linguists have often pointed out that all normal people successfully learn to speak, and they take it for granted that everyone with the same dialect speaks in pretty much the same way. To linguists, the interesting thing about child language seemed to be the common path that children follow, rather than the ways in which children vary. The first linguists who studied child language were not much interested in individual differences and sometimes not even much aware of them.

The 1960s were years of exciting new discoveries in syntax, and for a number of years linguists who worked with child language focused on the acquisition of syntax. Since the syntax of languages was generally studied as a rather autonomous topic, its acquisition also tended to be seen as rather autonomous. This meant that linguists were more likely to ask how syntax unfolds than to examine the social conditions that might foster its unfolding. More recently, both the presumption of uniformity and the presumption of syntactic autonomy have been taken less for granted. Linguists have become more aware of individual variation in the way children learn their language, and they have become increasingly concerned with the social environment in which language is learned.

Among the reasons for the interest that linguists have had in child language is Chomsky's concern with the paradox of language acquisition. As pointed out in Chapter 9, Chomsky argues that the input received by children is inadequate to explain language acquisition. Since children grow into fluent speakers, Chomsky contends that much of language must be built into the child's mind from the start. Unfortunately children cannot be persuaded to offer judgments about grammaticality, so empirical studies of child language are inevitably limited to observations of linguistic performance. Since Chomsky regards performance as much less interesting than competence, his ideas hardly seem to encourage the empirical study of children who talk. Thus, it may seem a bit surprising that a good many linguists have done their best to test a succession of Chomskyan proposals by listening to what children say.

However, a desire to test the predictions of Chomskyan universal grammar is not the only reason for a fascination with child language. When we observe child language we are forced to struggle with the old but still important problem of the interaction between native endowment and learning, between heredity and environment. Chomsky has insisted on the contribution of the inherited mind, but languages still have to be learned. Even if the universal features of language can be attributed to the mind, languages also differ from one another, and the unique features of each language must be learned. Sorting out what is native and what must be learned is always difficult, but language is a promising field in which to try.

Neither developing cognition and nor developing social interaction can be studied apart from the role of language in maturation, so linguists have an important contribution to make to the study of child development. Some parallels can be drawn between the changes that come to a language in the course of its history and the very much more rapid changes that take place during a single child's growth. We may be able to expand our understanding of slow historical change by watching the rapid changes of children. Mature language is the end product of a complex developmental process, and the final form that languages take must be constrained by that process. An understanding of the form of adult language ought to be illuminated by an understanding of how each individual acquires it. Our understanding of how meaning is organized in language can be deepened by observing the way in which children learn the meanings of words and sentences. The importance of the social context in which language is learned poses a challenge to claims about the autonomy of our language capacity. Finally, more than any other subfield of linguistics, child language forces us to pay attention to the differences among individuals. Psychologists may still be able to teach linguists that individual differences deserve our attention. We should be able to work on all these questions by examining the circumstances in which children acquire their language, by trying to find out how much they understand, and by listening carefully to what they say.

EARLY WORDS

Even before children use recognizable words, they begin to communicate in increasingly human ways. The child who enjoys passing a spoon back and forth with a parent is learning something about taking turns, a skill that will soon be needed in conversation. With gestures and with tone of voice children make their needs known. They learn to call attention to themselves or to what interests them, and they learn to pay attention to others. They also exercise their vocal organs by babbling, and they imitate the speech sounds of others. They may produce long stretches of babbling that strangely echo the intonation of their community's language. They seem to invent whole sentences even before they have words. All this babbling sounds as if it is a preparation for language.

The first specifically linguistic task that children face is to identify a few of the recurring chunks of the language they hear, and to recognize how these chunks are used. As children learn to point correctly when plied with such questions as *where is your nose?* and *where is your doll?*, they show a growing ability to relate meanings to sounds, and parents are usually convinced that their children understand a great deal well before they say much. They may respond correctly to quite complex verbal instructions, though they may understand as much from the situation as from the words they hear. Even an understanding of the situation, of course, demonstrates a growing ability to communicate and cooperate.

Sometime between a few months before their first birthday and a few months after it, most children begin to use a few of their noises with enough consistency to qualify as words. Their first ''words'' may not be conventional words of the adult language, but that hardly matters. Some children use only a part of a word, often including the stressed syllable, and use it in place of the entire word: *nana* 'banana.' They may also create "words" from longer stretches of the adult language. *Allgone* has to count as a single word for a child who has not yet learned to use either *all* or *gone* alone. Parents and older children are skillful at interpreting their children's earliest experiments and, as child and parent work together to negotiate the meaning, parents also have much to learn. When parents read meaning into the child's babbles, they help to invent new words. A baby's invented words may be taken over by the whole family, and occasionally they even spread to the community. In many unrelated languages, the words for 'mother' and 'father' resemble our own *mama* and *papa*. [m], [p], and [a] are among the earliest sounds that most children articulate, and parents everywhere seem to have been eager to interpret their children's early babbles as names for themselves.

Considerable experience is needed to bring meanings into line with the adult language. American children often use *doggie* for any four-legged animal. One child was observed to extend the word *fly* to all kinds of small objects: any small insect, a toad, specks of dirt, dust, crumbs of bread, the child's own toes. Extended meanings like these show that, from the time they start to speak, children do more than simply parrot the language they hear. They use words in unconventional ways, and they use their language to devise new messages.

A child's earliest words are all firmly anchored in the concrete world of experience. Many of these words are names for the most salient physical objects of a child's world: *mommy, doggie, cookie, milk*. These are nouns in the adult language but there is no reason to read adult parts of speech into early child language. Along with names come words such as *hot, allgone,* and *bye bye,* not nouns in the adult language but also words that can be learned without the help of other words. With no previous language, children can learn to associate the sound of *bye bye* with waving and with the situation in which someone leaves. They can learn to associate *hot* with a painful sensation, and *allgone* with disappearance.

Even when children are able to say no more than one word at a time, adults often interpret their utterances as if they are entire sentences. Intonation distinguishes *mommy!* meaning "mommy come here," or *mommy?* meaning "is that mommy coming?," from a more neutral *mommy* that just means "that is my mommy." Children can name objects, to their own and their parents' satisfaction, but they can also call, greet, repeat, request, demand, and protest. They even ask rudimentary questions and respond with rudimentary answers. They use their words within a particular setting, of course, and parents use the evidence provided by the setting to interpret what their children say. The parents' interpretation, in turn, can influence the meaning that children give to their words.

From the start, children use their words to actively communicate. They even engage in rudimentary conversations. One 20-month-old child who was still limited to single words repeated *kʰa* several times and, when the adult with whom she was talking did not understand, she said *gɔɔ, go*. This was not understood either, and she then said *bəiʃ* no less than nine times. The adult, puzzled, said *What? Oh, bicycle? Is that what you said?* But the child said *na'* which, at last, was understood correctly as 'no.' Fortunately, the conversation, for that is what it was, had been recorded on tape and the child's meaning was sorted out later. The noise of a car driving by outside could be heard on the tape shortly before her first *kʰa*. The adult had not noticed the noise until listening to the tape, but the child had, and she tried to call attention to it. When she failed to make herself understood she described what the car did: 'go.' When that still did not work she tried 'bus.' That, too, failed, but she was able to inform her partner that he had guessed wrong. Clearly this child was doing much more than uttering disconnected single words. Her words were related to each other, and they were clearly an attempt at a conversation about a topic that she found interesting.

Conversations with children are often more successful than this one, of course, and adults work as hard as the children to make them successful. For one thing, adults ask a great many questions. These may coax children to talk, but questions can also be used to call attention to a topic even when no verbal reply is expected: *Can you see the fish, Jimmy?* Once the child is paying attention, a comment can be made: *See? It's swimming.* Adults and children may cooperate so closely that one can almost be said to finish a statement that the other begins. A child who offers a single word as topic of conversation, *spoon,* may elicit *it fell down, didn't it?* Children are constantly encouraged to enter into dialogues, and their language grows in cooperation with older speakers.

TWO WORDS

Vocabulary often grows quite slowly at first. Several months may be needed just to accumulate the first 15 or 20 words, but at that point, children sometimes gain speed adding as many as 30 to 50 words each month. Soon they are also likely to begin to use two words in sequence, the first hint of syntax. Observers of children generally find it useful to recognize a "two-word stage," during which children use two words with increasing ease but still have trouble with longer sequences. The time when the two-word stage begins is variable, but 18 months is a rough average.

Children appear to make use of at least two strategies for overcoming their limitation to single words, and the same two strategies continue to be used later. First, with what is sometimes known as the "bottom-up" strategy, they join words that they already know. This does not necessarily happen suddenly, but as children learn to use words more easily, they also use them more often and at closer intervals. At first a pause still separates the words, and each is given its own separate intonation. These are still two distinct words that happen to be said in succession. Gradually, however, children reduce the pause between the words and use a more unified intonation until the two words are finally joined in a single construction. When children form unified phrases that they have not heard from others, like *up chair* or *allgone bread* they show their ability to invent new expressions to convey their meaning.

When children use the second, or "top-down," strategy they start by learning longer chunks of the language as units, and only later separate the chunks into their parts. It is not only set phrases like *allgone* and *goodnight* that are learned as wholes, but also phrases that, in the adult language, are clearly formed from two distinct words. *All clean, all dressed, all well, big train, big hug, big boy, nice boy,* and dozens of others enter some children's vocabulary as rote learned units, in effect as single words. Later, children extract the common element from their partially similar "words" and begin to join the parts more freely in new constructions. After learning a number of set phrases such as *big boy, big truck,* and *big hat,* children seem able to make a generalization, extract the *big* as a separate piece, and then use it freely with other words.

In their willingness to imitate longer stretches of language, children who use the top-down strategy may seem more adventurous than bottom-up learners but, whatever their origin in the adult language, many long memorized chunks have to be interpreted as single words for a child. Top-down learners sometimes learn long idiomatic phrases, and even some of the phones from affixes and function words may survive in such phrases. One child learned his older brother's phrase "I want to tell you something" as a single unanalyzed, but useful, expression. He pronounced it as [ayteiusints]. At first, it was only a single "word" to the child, but it could serve as raw material for later analysis. Its parts could be incorporated into an expanding syntactic system.

Most children use both the bottom-up and top-down strategies, but some rely more on one or more on the other. Those who rely most heavily on the bottom-up strategy tend to start with relatively short words. They often learn the names for many objects, words that are nouns in the adult language. They may then build up more complex phrases by adding modifiers and possessive words to these names: *my dog, big dog,* and eventually even *my big dog.* Top-down learners tend to use more pronouns than bottom-up learners but fewer words that are nouns in the adult language. Function words may seem to appear earlier, but mimicking the sounds of function words, when these are fixed within longer units, does not necessarily imply understanding. Nevertheless, when these longer units begin to be broken into their parts, the function words may emerge in the right spots and, eventually, with the right meaning. Top-down learners use what appear to be complete sentences sooner than bottom-up learners. These, however, are extreme types. Most children combine building up with breaking down.

By whatever combination of strategies they are learned, two-word sequences give children more freedom of expression and allow a richer exchange of information than had been possible earlier, but listeners still need the help of the context to understand the child's meaning. Parents interpret their children's two-word utterances very freely. Thus a child used *mommy sock* to mean 'it is mommy's sock' on one occasion, but on another the same words meant 'mommy is putting on my sock.' This child had more to say than she had means of expression.

Word pairs can be used to express many different semantic relationships, and even at the two-word stage many children maintain reasonably consistent word order: possessor and possessed (*my bib*), modifier and modified (*big block*), object and location (*shoe here*), action and location (*run here*), actor and action (*baby fall*), action and object (*spill water*), among many others. Children gain freedom in constructing new phrases that follow these patterns. A child may, for example, learn to construct possessive phrases from a large number of possessives (*my, mommy, doggie,* etc.) together with an even larger number of names for objects. As a child accumulates more phrases of this sort, it is tempting to see them as forerunners of the syntactic constructions of the adult language (possessive pronoun with noun, etc.) but small children are not limited by the syntactic categories of adults. Some children use *more* as easily with prepositions (*more up*) or with verbs (*more jump*) as with nouns (*more bread*). This freedom suggests that the syntactic categories of the adult language are not yet relevant for the child. It seems more reasonable to understand children's two word utterances as being formed from semantic categories such as actor, action, and location, than from the syntactic classes of the adult language.

Children need to use words long before they have enough experience to perfect their pronunciation but, as their vocabulary grows, phonology has to improve as well. The larger the number of words that are used, the more crucial are the means for keeping them distinct. Children do not all acquire their sound systems in just the same way, but some patterns are common. Whatever language is being learned, simple stops and nasals usually come early. Bilabials are likely to come before velars. The early consonants are used with a restricted number of vowels. Low unrounded [a], high-front unrounded [i], and high-back rounded [u] are maximally distinct from each other, and they often come early. Children usually start with syllables that consist of a single initial consonant followed by a single vowel. Frequently, children repeat pairs of identical syllables, both in babbling and in words like *mama* and *papa*. Starting with these simple beginnings, the child's range of sounds gradually expands. Sometimes by learning a single contrast, children learn to keep several pairs of phonemes distinct simultaneously. [p] may become distinct from [b], [t] from [d], and [k] from [g] at the same time, all due to the mastery of a single distinctive feature. If they are learning a language with syllable-final consonants or consonant clusters, these will be gradually added, but several years are needed to master the entire phonological system of a language.

It is striking that the speech sounds that typically come early—stops, nasals, [i], [a], and [u]—are among the most universally distributed sounds in the world's languages. Conversely, phones with the most restricted distribution tend to be among the last that children master. Each language seems to have a few phones that are characteristically learned late. English-speaking children often have the most trouble with the retroflex [ɹ] and with the interdental fricatives, [θ] and [ð], and these are also somewhat unusual sounds in the world's languages. The parallel between the order of acquisition and frequency in the world's languages suggests a range of articulatory difficulty, with [p], [b], [a], etc., at one end, and [ɹ], [θ], and [ð] at the other. [ž] also tends to be late among English speakers, however, and this probably has more to do with its comparative rarity than with its difficulty. The similarity between children's early syllables and the distribution of syllable types in the world's languages suggest that syllables with a single initial consonant, a single vowel, and no final consonant are the easiest to learn.

ELABORATION

Two-word sequences provide for no more than the bare beginnings of syntax, but they give children something with which to build. Sometimes children seem able to combine short sequences or to nest one inside another, and in that way to build up more complex utterances. A child who can form two-word sequences from an *actor* and an *action*, such as *Billy eat, me find, mommy see,* and who can form other two-word sequences from an *action* and an *object,* such as *eat bread, find ball, see book,* may begin to combine these as *actor–action–object: Billy eat bread, me find ball,* and *Mommy see book.* One child learned to use two-word sequences of two different types, both of which began with *up.* In *up Daddy* the meaning was 'Daddy should get up,' while *up bed* meant 'up from bed.' The child then learned to combine them as either *up Daddy bed* or *up bed Daddy* 'Daddy, get up from bed!' The fact that *up* stayed securely in first place suggests continuity with the earlier word pairs in which *up* was always first.

As more kinds of word sequences are learned, they begin to fall into patterns. A child may learn that words like *big* and *little* can be used with the names for all sorts of tangible objects. Independently she may also learn that *hot* can also be used with the names for objects. Later, when she grasps that *big, little, hot,* and various other words that also refer to qualities, can all be used with many of the same object names, a rudimentary class of adjectives is born.

Through the years of early childhood the average number of words or morphemes per utterance grows steadily. Some children, inclined toward a bottom-up strategy, gain considerable skill at combining content words into larger constructions, and only later fill in the chinks between the words with the affixes and function words of the adult language. Some of these children speak in a way that is a bit reminiscent of a pidgin language that has little morphological apparatus. With a top-down strategy, long and relatively complex phrases are memorized, and the child then learns to substitute the parts within these phrases. Both strategies allow more and more words and morphemes to be combined in increasingly complex patterns.

As a child's language moves beyond the two-word stage, changes come more quickly so it becomes more difficult to follow the steps in detail, but the development of negations and questions has been studied carefully. These offer good examples of one way that a language can grow. For many English-speaking children, the first negative sentences are easily formed with an initial *no*: *No sit there, No the sun shining, No fall, No play that.* Children do not hear such sentences from adults so they cannot learn them by imitation, but they are adept at learning the meaning of *no*, and it offers a straightforward means for expressing negation. Attaching the word at the very beginning of a sentence surely represents an easy way to accomplish the child's purpose, and it matters not at all that adults find it ungrammatical.

A bit later, children learn other negative words, and they begin to move their negatives away from the beginning of the sentence. This brings some sentences into line with adult patterns, though others are still deviant: *I can't catch you, I don't want it, That no fish school, There no squirrels, He no bite you.* Changes like these allow negation to be expressed in more subtle ways than had been possible earlier. Particular parts of sentences sometimes need to be negated, not merely the sentence as a whole. For many children, *can't* and *don't* probably begin as unanalyzable negative words. *Can't* expresses 'inability,' probably a more useful concept for most children than 'ability.' The positive form, *can*, may only appear later. The negative sentences of this stage have moved closer to the adult forms, but several refinements are still needed. Children must learn additional negative words, such as *isn't* and *wasn't*, and they must learn the connection between these and the uncontracted *is, was*, and *not*. They have to figure out how to use *do* and *did* as dummy auxiliaries onto which a negative can be grafted when no other auxiliary is available. They have to learn to reject sentences such as *I didn't see something* in favor of *I didn't see anything.*

Questions may pass through a similar sequence of steps. For many children, the earliest questions are simply formed with a rising intonation. This allows a child to ask a yes–no question even while not yet capable of more than a single word at a time. A few question words, most often *what, where*, and *who*, are also likely to be learned quite early and, like the earliest negatives, these are often attached to the beginning of an otherwise unremarkable phrase: *Where my mittens?, What you eat?* These questions deviate from adult usage, but they allow children to express themselves, and to engage in dialogue. When auxiliary verbs first appear, they often keep their usual position even when used with a question word: *What he can ride in?, Why kitty can't stand up?* Getting in both a question word and an auxiliary is enough of a challenge at first. Subtleties like rearranging word order have to wait.

Negations and questions are examples of the gradual grammaticalization of a child's constructions. The earliest constructions are formed by the simplest of syntactic devices. A word, or even an intonation, is simply attached to an otherwise unchanged utterance. Gradually, the constructions become more regular and more condensed. Statements that can only be said in loose succession at first, are brought into a single, well-defined construction. As word order becomes fixed and morphology more consistent, some words can be contracted or even omitted. Phonological reductions are possible. Constructions that are often repeated become quicker and more automatic. Grammaticalization may take centuries in the ordinary historical development of a language, and it may take decades as a pidgin develops into a creole. When we listen to children, we can watch grammaticalization take place in the course of months.

When learning a language like English, syntax is more important than morphology, and it generally comes first, but children must eventually learn the inflectional apparatus of the language as well. The order in which children learn inflectional suffixes depends on their regularity, frequency, phonetic salience, and semantic transparency. The progressive verb suffix -ing is often the first inflection to be learned by English-speaking children. Not only does -ing carry a more essential meaning than a suffix such as the third person singular -s, but its frequency is high, and it is completely regular. In addition, -ing consists of a full syllable, so it is phonetically more salient than most English suffixes. Suffixes with clear and simple meanings generally come before those with subtle or variable meanings. Thus, in spite of their phonetic identity, children who are learning English generally learn the plural -s before they learn the possessive -'s, partly because the plural is more common, but also because its meaning is more transparent.

Frequency, regularity, phonetic salience, and semantic transparency do not always coincide. Irregular past-tense forms are often learned before regular -ed. This is because the irregular verbs are among the most common English verbs, and the irregular pasts tend to be more distinct phonetically than pasts with regular -ed. Children can learn such forms as went, fell, and ate as independent words without relying on any general rule for deriving them. When children finally learn a rule for forming the regular past, many of them begin, for the first time, to attach -ed to words where it does not belong. Thus children with a well-established went may suddenly begin to say goed. Only later do they sort out the difference between regular and irregular verbs and return to went. Here, as in many other cases, children take the first steps toward learning a construction by memorizing fixed examples. Along with irregular pasts like went, children presumably learn a number of regular pasts like stopped, listened, and coasted as independent words. Once enough regular pasts have been learned, children can finally generalize from the known examples and act according to an unconscious rule. They create the pasts of other verbs, even of verbs for which adults would not use the regular past.

Children learning English and other European languages do not generally gain control over affixes until they have already learned to join words in fairly complex ways, but this is due partly to the nature of these languages. In English, and to an only slightly lesser extent in most other European languages, syntax is more important for conveying meaning than is morphology. Turkish, by contrast, has many suffixes that consist of full syllables, and these are very regular and carry essential meaning. It is hardly surprising that children who learn Turkish learn to use affixes at an earlier stage than do children who learn English.

We know more about the first few years of language acquisition than about its later stages. The early stages develop more dramatically so they are more exciting to study, but the attention that has been given to the early years also reflects a myth about the time when language is mastered. Five-year-olds are sometimes said to have already learned most of their language. If this were correct, subsequent learning would certainly be less interesting to study; in fact, five-year-olds still have a great deal to learn. The myth of the masterful five-year-old may have arisen because children of this age avoid the most obvious errors of their younger brothers and sisters. Most five-year-olds have their phonology under good control, and they no longer make many obvious morphological or syntactic errors. Avoiding errors, however, is not the same as mastering the language. If they avoid errors it is partly because they avoid complex constructions in which errors would be most likely. Much of the syntax of complex sentences remains well beyond the capacity of five-year-olds, and it takes many more years of practice and experience to master it. A five-year-old's vocabulary will have to keep expanding throughout childhood. Indeed, language learning does not end with childhood. New words and even new ways of putting words together continue to be learned as long as the mind remains active.

LEARNING, TEACHING, AND KNOWING

Observing children and describing the path that they follow as they learn to speak is only the first step in trying to understand how they do it. This section will review a few of the ways in which psychologists and linguists have tried to account for language acquisition.

The most obvious "explanation" for language learning is that children simply imitate what they hear, but this is hardly enough. Quite apart from the fact that imitation is itself a rather mysterious ability, it is clear that children do much more than repeat what others say. The child who uses *doggie* for all four-legged animals, and the child who says *no sit there*, are not simply imitating. They are using words in their own imaginative ways.

Perhaps it is the regularization of irregular morphology that shows the child's own contribution most clearly. In order to regularize irregular plurals and past tenses and to produce such words as *mens, goed,* or *eated,* children need to learn the relationship between regular pairs such as *boy/boys, sew/sewed,* and *heat/heated.* They have to distinguish the varying pronunciations of these suffixes and figure out what governs the choice among them. This seems to require an ability to make, unconsciously, linguistic generalizations of considerable abstraction. More creativity is certainly needed to invent *goed* than to repeat *went.* Children who say *eated* or *foots* give the best possible evidence of their linguistic skills, and they show us that they can do much more than simply imitate. This is not to deny the contribution of imitation to language learning. In their eagerness to imitate speech sounds, children are very different from the young of other animals. Human children could hardly learn a language without imitation, but anyone who did no more than imitate what others had said would talk only in the limited sense that a parrot is said to talk. Imitation is only a first step.

The type of learning theory that was developed within behaviorist psychology adds little to imitation in explaining language acquisition. This kind of behaviorist learning theory was often tested by experiments with animals. By systematic rewards and punishments, it could be demonstrated that animals, and in simple experimental situations human beings as well, could be taught to respond to various sorts of stimuli. Responses that were rewarded, whether by a pellet of food or by simple approval, were strengthened. Responses that were punished became weaker.

Language, however, is not a simple kind of behavior, and any situation or "stimulus" can elicit so many different responses that there is no way to relate particular stimuli to particular responses. We can say too many different things and say them in too many different ways ever to figure out what stimulates what. Much of what people say has no identifiable stimulus at all. Behaviorist learning theory is particularly deficient in explaining the acquisition of syntax, for people who talk to small children rarely comment on, or correct, children's syntax, and it is difficult to see that children are ever rewarded for good syntax or punished for their mistakes. A child who says *That a doggie* while pointing to a cat, may be told *That isn't a doggie, it's a cat.* She is not likely to be told *You shouldn't say 'That a doggie,' say 'That is a doggie' instead.* It is probably just as well that we do not often try to correct the syntax of small children, for they can be very stubborn. One linguist reports the following conversation between a father and his child (Braine, 1971, p. 161):

Child: Want other one spoon, Daddy.
Father: You mean, you want the other spoon.
Child: Yes, I want other one spoon, please Daddy.
Father: Can you say "the other spoon"?
Child: Other . . . one . . . spoon.
Father: Say "other."
Child: Other
Father: "Spoon."
Child: Spoon.
Father: "Other spoon."
Child: Other . . . spoon. Now give me other one spoon.

If syntax is not taught by correction, reward, or punishment, are there other ways in which adults help children to learn? Middle-class American adults modify their language when speaking to children, and they do so in ways that seem to offer help. When talking with small children, American adults and older children have been observed to raise their pitch level, exaggerate their intonation, simplify the phonology of some words, keep their sentences relatively short and simple, and use a high proportion of questions and imperatives. The syntax used with children is likely to be more complex than the syntax that the children use themselves, but it may be no more than about 6 months ahead. It probably offers a challenge, and a model toward which to move, but it is not so complex as to be beyond reach. Middle-class American parents restrict the range of their vocabulary and reduce their syntactic complexity, and they tirelessly repeat themselves. Indeed, some adults modify their speech so extensively when speaking to children that many students of child language suspect that Chomsky was much too quick when he characterized the language that children hear as seriously distorted by performance errors. In fact, children may receive not merely warm encouragement to imitate but many hours of repetitive drill. Middle-class parents surely enjoy the word games that they play with their children every bit as much as the children do, and these games seem well designed to help children to learn.

Parents also expand on what their children say. If a child says *kitty want milk,* a parent may immediately say *Does the kitty want some milk?* and in that way give a prompt demonstration of how *the* and *some* are used, and how statements are turned into questions. Parents gradually increase the complexity of their expansions as the child's language improves. They repeat what the child says but say it in a way that is a bit more complex and that conforms more closely to mature speech. The expansions seem to be sufficiently complex to challenge the child but not so complex as to be beyond reach. Some observers have felt that expansions of this sort are an important way of providing children with a model of more complete language.

The topics of conversation between adults and child also deserve attention. Much of the earliest talk with children is restricted to an exceedingly narrow range of topics: the names for concrete objects that can be seen, heard, or touched, and comments about what the child is doing and what is happening to her. Sentences tend to be short and in the present tense, and the meanings are largely inferable from the surrounding context. These topics seem to be ideally suited for the earliest lessons in language. Adults and older children are also very sensitive to the child's own initiatives. They respond to the child's calls for attention. They accept topics introduced by the child, and they test to see whether the child has understood. When children do not appear to understand, adults reduce the length of their own sentences, offer alternative wording, and struggle to make themselves clear. All this appears ideally suited for language instruction.

This, at least, is the kind of language that characterizes middle-class American and European parents. It is by no means certain, however, that this kind of language is essential to language acquisition, and members of some other societies apparently have quite different beliefs about what is needed if their children's language is to develop properly. Some people are reported to wait to talk to their children until they are old enough to be competent conversational partners. Their children have ample opportunity to listen to the language, but adults apparently offer young children much less direct help with language than seems natural to middle-class Americans. The Kaluli, a people of New Guinea, feel that it would be wrong to modify their own speech when talking to children, but they do feel that their children need instruction. Kaluli instruction takes the form of supplying words and sentences for the child to repeat. Small children are led through practice conversations in which they are instructed to repeat a series of sentences, many of them probably well beyond their ability to understand. Children are believed to need such practice in order to develop their skills. We are only beginning to find out what others believe about language learning, and about the kind of help they feel their children need. Children everywhere learn to speak their language fluently, and language seems to be learned under a wide range of conditions. We do not yet know just what is essential and what is not.

We do not know how much the modified language that middle-class Americans use with their children helps, but the behavior of caretakers cannot possibly explain everything that children do. Chimpanzees treated like children do not learn to talk and, sooner or later, we are forced back on the minds of the children themselves. What is it about children that allows them to learn a language? What sort of a mind does a language learner need? What does a learner have to know? These are the most difficult questions we can ask about child language, and several kinds of answers have been proposed.

In the 1960s, Chomsky suggested that children come to the task of learning a language with something he called a Language Acquisition Device, or LAD. The specific nature of this "device" was left rather vague at first, but Chomsky proposed that children engage in a kind of unconscious hypotheses testing. The LAD, it was thought, might provide hypotheses that children could test against the data of the language that they hear. Perhaps children even act just a bit like linguists. Perhaps they search (unconsciously of course) through the data provided by the language around them, form hypotheses that seem to explain this data, and then test their hypotheses by forming new sentences. In order to move progressively closer to the adult language, children would have to reject or modify any hypotheses that result in sentences that do not fit the language. In view of the long years that linguists have spent trying to understand grammar, however, Chomsky has always argued that children must have a head start, already having been given a great deal of specific, though unconscious, linguistic knowledge by their genetic inheritance.

More recently, Chomsky's ideas have been given substance by the principles and parameters approach that was briefly described in Chapter 9. The mind, Chomsky says, comes to the task of language learning equipped with certain universal principles that are needed for all languages. Children need to have the parameters of their minds set to conform to the language of their community. Since Chomsky has been concerned primarily with the core aspects of syntax, he has had little to say about the more variable and peripheral features of language that have to be learned.

At least two other linguists have tried to describe the child's built-in abilities from other points of view. Dan Slobin suggests that children appear to work with a number of "operating strategies" as they look for order in the language around them. It is good strategy, for instance, to "pay attention to the ends of words" since many languages hang important bits on their ends. Children also seem to operate with the expectation that similar stretches of sounds will have consistent meaning. This is not always an entirely reliable expectation, but it is surely a good working assumption. Another reasonable strategy is to "avoid exceptions." This suggests that it is sensible to expect forms and constructions to be regular until forced by the evidence to conclude otherwise. To "avoid interruptions" is also a sensible strategy, for it should lead children to expect the significant meaningful units of the language to occur without being interrupted by other meaningful units. Slobin has proposed a large number of such operating strategies and, collectively, they offer a kind of description of the expectations that children bring to the task of language learning.

Derek Bickerton takes a still different approach. He suggests that the same bio-program that he credits with molding creole languages guides all children as they learn their first language. Bickerton's built-in bio-program has some superficial similarities with Chomsky's built-in principles, but Bickerton's bio-program is based on empirical observation of language learners, and on what they learn easily and what they learn with more difficulty. Chomsky's proposals are logical inferences that follow from an investigation of adult language competence, and they have no grounding in direct observations of children. Bickerton believes that some linguistic structures are closer than others to the natural tendencies of the human mind, and the bio-program should predispose children toward these structures. He argues that children will learn easily, almost automatically, those features of their language that happen to correspond to the underlying bio-program. He suggests, for example, that children rarely make mistakes with the English progressive tenses (such as *is going, were going*) because their use is laid down by the bio-program. Where the language deviates from the bio-program, he expects children to learn more slowly and to learn with more difficulty. If this is a valid way of describing our inborn abilities, then identifying the bio-program that we start with might seem to be a relatively straightforward process. We should be able to investigate how children learn various languages and various syntactic patterns within these languages, note which structures are learned easily and which cause more difficulty, and conclude that the easily learned patterns belong to the bio-program.

The logic of this method of judging syntactic difficulty is the same as the logic of judging phonetic difficulty by observing the order in which children learn phones. Early learned forms are judged to be closer to the bio-program. In practice, extending this logic to syntax is beset with difficulties. First, a structure whose meaning conforms closely to the bio-program might still be syntactically complex. Even if we are willing to agree that the progressive is, somehow, provided by the bio-program, different languages could still differ in the formal complexity of their progressive structures. It would be surprising if structures of different complexity were learned with equal ease just because they happen to express the same idea. Possibly children everywhere develop the need to express semantic concepts such as negation, progressivity, transitivity, and causation in much the same order. If children learning one language take longer to learn the structures for a particular concept than do children learning another language, that would suggest that the structures of the first language are more complex. Unfortunately, it is not easy to determine either the age at which children need to express a semantic concept, or the age at which a linguistic structure is learned. When, in the course of acquiring English negations and questions, would we conclude that a child had "learned" them? Individual children who are learning the same language acquire particular structures of their language at quite varied ages, and we would need a large sample of children from each language before we could have any confidence about interlanguage age differences. All these factors help to explain why the task of measuring the complexity of syntactic structures, or of judging their conformity with any sort of bio-program, has not yet proceeded far enough to give most linguists confidence that it would even be a promising undertaking.

Linguists have had many conflicting ideas about how children learn their language, but most of the arguments reduce to a disagreement about the relative contributions of the child's own mind on the one hand, and of the environment in which learning takes place on the other. It is abundantly clear that both are essential. A child could not learn a language without an inborn eagerness to attach meanings to sounds. Surely it is by their inborn nature that children are able to learn phonological contrasts, to attach intonation to segmental phones, to distinguish meanings by word order, and to recognize structure in strings of morphemes. At the same time it is equally clear that a child could not learn to speak without living in a community and interacting with other people. If children really can be credited with inventing creoles, it is not literally true that children need to be in contact with a fully developed language in order to acquire a language of their own. Deaf children who live in a family of hearing people and who are isolated from any sign language seem to develop their own set of signs in order to deal with their family members. Here, even more dramatically than with a creole, a language can, apparently, be invented where none existed before. Even in these cases, however, languages are developed, or invented, only in a community of interacting people. There is no reason to believe that an isolated child could ever develop a language alone. If languages are invented, they are invented by a community and not by a single individual.

To master an established language people require many years of participation in a community where the language is used. Linguists differ in their judgment about the relative importance of the mind and of the community, but we will surely learn more by watching and listening to children than by posing the argument too simply. Arguing whether language is built in or learned is a distraction. Certainly it is both.

SECOND LANGUAGE LEARNING

Common wisdom in the United States holds that children are more adept than adults at learning a second language. The younger the child, the more easily is learning supposed to take place. Many of us have enviously watched children who are thrown into foreign schools and who appear to adjust easily to a new language. It is part of American folklore that even if immigrant parents never become proficient in the language of their new home, their children have no trouble. Generations of immigrants to America have relied on their children as interpreters. Only a small minority of adult second language learners ever learn enough to pass themselves off as native speakers.

This popular view of children's skill has received scholarly support from linguists who have been impressed by Chomsky's arguments about the nature of the LAD. The stages through which children pass as they learn their first language seem to have the kind of regularity that we expect in physical maturation. Crawling, walking with support, walking independently, and running follow each other in fixed succession. Children who are temporarily disabled during the critical age for learning some physical skill may never be able to learn it properly. Similarly, some linguists have argued that the LAD functions properly only during a critical age of childhood. Anyone who is not exposed to language during the critical age may risk a permanent handicap. It has even been claimed that, at about the time of puberty, specific maturational changes take place that bring a decisive end to the ability to acquire a language in the natural manner of a younger child. Adults, whose LADs have decayed, simply cannot expect to learn a language as easily as a child.

This argument is certainly comforting to the many adults who grow discouraged by their own slow progress in a second language, but not all the evidence supports the superiority of children. Nor does everyone share the American confidence in children. Scandinavian educators, concerned about the difficulties faced by the children of recent immigrants, generally take it for granted that children have an especially traumatic time with their new language. Some immigrant children are said to sit mutely in class, sometimes for many years, without managing to learn very much of the school language. Even American educators routinely expect college students to learn as much in one year of foreign language instruction as high school students learn in two, hardly evidence that the LAD deteriorates between high school age and college.

English-speaking children who were learning a new language by attending local schools in Holland and Switzerland were tested for several kinds of linguistic skills. After an equivalent number of months of immersion, the older children did consistently better than their younger brothers and sisters. How can the clear superiority of the older children be reconciled with the widespread impression that younger children move more quickly? Our casual impressions probably come from the differing standards by which we judge children of varied ages. We judge eight-year-olds to speak perfectly when they achieve an eight-year-old level. We expect more of 18-year-olds. It may take less time for eight-year-olds to reach their own age level, but 18-year-olds learn more in the same amount of time.

Only in phonology is there much evidence that adults face a genuine disadvantage. Adults who master most aspects of a second language may never outgrow their foreign accent. Even here there are exceptions, but phonetic habits do seem particularly resistant to change. There is considerable mystery about why some people learn pronunciation so much more easily than others. One study concluded that the most successful mimics are people who had a "warm mothering experience" but who had never belonged to a tight adolescent peer group. The logic of these odd findings is that a warm mothering experience is supposed to give people such basic security that a strange phonology poses no threat. By escaping peer-group pressure, a commitment to narrow norms is avoided. Whether or not explanations like this have any value, phonology does seem to lie especially close to a person's self-identity. Many second-language learners may feel quite threatened by being pushed to leave their familiar phonology behind. Since most adults do not plan to be spies, this ought not matter very much, but it remains a fact that foreign accents often persist, and they may lead us to exaggerate the disability of adult learners. Even when they learn everything else perfectly, we still hear their accent, so we lower our judgment of their success.

The problems faced by adult second-language learners are probably more social than linguistic. Adults are less willing than children to subject themselves to the kind of social environment that most successfully fosters language. If adults were willing to immerse themselves full-time in a foreign culture, living in a foreign family and trying to do little except soak up the language, one suspects that they might be able to achieve the linguistic skills required for kindergarten in even less than the 5 years that we allot to children. Few adults are willing to spend even a single year in the kind of full-time language immersion that we accept as normal for children. Even if willing, an adult cannot easily find the right sort of environment for such learning. We let 16-year-old exchange students sit in their high school classrooms while they wait for their language to grow. If they don't learn much else, we console ourselves with the thought that at least they will learn the language. Adults are too impatient. They have other things to do, and they do not easily find a community of adults that will accept them and encourage their increasing competence.

The most serious problem for adults may be their more ambitious goals. The needs of small children can be satisfied with a limited vocabulary and relatively simple sentences. Children are usually content with a single dialect and a relatively undifferentiated style. Adults can expect to meet people from a variety of backgrounds who speak with a variety of styles and dialects. Adults want to read books that are written for adults, and they want to talk about a wide range of topics. Adults, in short, are dissatisfied with anything less than the level of mastery achieved in their first language only after decades of busy talk and schooling. They are rarely willing to invest even a twentieth as much time on a second language. Adults may seriously underestimate the complexity of a language and fail to appreciate the sheer volume of facts that they need to learn. They become discouraged, and they give up.

Native speakers of English face one final problem: Too many other people already know English. When the practical chores of life can be accomplished without the struggle to learn another language, the temptation not to try is great. When others speak such fine English, it is embarrassing to pull out one's schoolgirl French. Children taken abroad by their high-status, English-speaking parents may move easily into a welcoming monolingual community. Educated adults are more likely to move into a community where English is already widely used and where no one has much hope that the visitor will be able to learn the new language. Many adults find it impossible to resist these expectations. Low-status immigrants, whether adults or children, may not be accepted into any community at all. As a result, they may never be able to get the kind of experience that they need for learning a new language.

Adult second-language learners differ from children in two other ways, but it is difficult to know how much bearing these have on language learning. First, adults more regularly submit themselves to formal instruction. We must hope that formal instruction will speed up learning, but we should admit the possibility that it may also cause problems. If, for instance, adults would profit from passing through a stage that is more or less analogous to a young child's baby talk, where the syntax of many sentences deviates from adult standards, pedagogical insistence on correct forms might actually slow learning down.

Second, adults already know one language, and they carry over all sorts of patterns from their first language into their second. Possibly the first language interferes enough with the new language to slow its acquisition. However, since older child second-language learners manage to overcome interference from their first language, the knowledge of one language is not inevitably a barrier against a second. Some studies even suggest that adults who come from quite varied language backgrounds all tend to have the same kinds of problems with a new language. If second-language learners, whatever their background, make the same kinds of mistakes, it may be because the first language does not really make much difference.

Finally the failures should not be allowed to hide the triumphs. If there were really a critical age after which language acquisition becomes much more difficult, we should be puzzled by the considerable number of adults who manage to gain ease and fluency in a second or third language. In fact, with the single but important exception of pronunciation, there is no convincing evidence that adults are any less capable than children of learning a language. With an equivalent amount of time and effort, adults generally learn more.

The result of successful second-language learning should be bilingualism, a state that is sometimes regarded as a bit exotic in the predominantly monolingual English-speaking world, but a state that is taken for granted in many other places. In some parts of the world children routinely grow up with two or more languages. Where diverse tribal languages jostle one another, most people may take their spouses from another language group, so almost everyone grows up learning at least two languages, that of the mother and that of the father. People then learn the languages of other neighbors simply to carry on normal life.

Bilingualism is not an all-or-none matter. A second language may be useful at any level of proficiency from a few labored phrases to comfortable fluency. If people counted as "bilingual" only if they controlled their languages with equal ease in all situations, few people would deserve to be called bilingual. More often, speakers use their languages for different purposes and in different situations. One language may be used at home, another at work, and speakers may find it awkward or even impossible to use one language in a situation in which they have grown accustomed to the other. Some Filipinos have said that it is best to talk politics in English, and to worship in Spanish, but to make love in Tagalog. Whether or not someone deserves to be called bilingual depends as much on the situations in which the languages are used as on linguistic skill. In some situations, even a modest ability may be enough to allow a speaker to perform adequately in a second language. In a different situation, a much higher level of proficiency may still fall short of being useful.

Americans seem ambivalent about bilingualism. On the one hand, a disturbingly low rate of success does not stop us from pushing students through foreign-language classes in our schools and colleges. We warmly admire the rare educated American who has lived abroad and learned to survive in a foreign language. On the other hand, Americans have been so scornful of the language abilities of immigrants that we have allowed most of their rich linguistic heritage to be lost within a single generation. Children who grow up in bilingual homes have been made to feel ashamed rather than proud of their own bilingualism. We have failed to take advantage of the linguistic abilities of some of our citizens, even as we have struggled to give others a minimal competence in a foreign language.

Our linguistic prejudices show most clearly in the recent movement to formalize the status of English as our official language. English has never before been given official status in the United States. Bilingual schools and even schools with a medium of instruction other than English have flourished during some periods of American history. The proportion of non-English speakers in the United States is considerably lower today than during some periods of the nineteenth century, and there is no indication that the children and grandchildren of our recent immigrants are any slower to learn English than were their predecessors a century ago. Nevertheless, some people now act as if English is threatened by the new immigration. In an era when it is no longer respectable to express open prejudice against ethnic minorities, language has become a convenient substitute target for intolerance. People who would never admit to prejudice against Mexicans may nevertheless profess alarm at some imagined threat from Spanish. For linguists, it seems obvious that our country would be a richer and more interesting place to live if we could glory in the diversity of our linguistic heritage rather than forcing a uniform standard on everyone. The place of English in the United States, and in the world, is far too secure to be threatened by immigration. The children and grandchildren of today's immigrants will only add to the strength of English, for they will swell the numbers of native English speakers. Other languages may need to be defended against English. English has no need for protection by legislation.

CHAPTER SIXTEEN

Language and the Human Species

ANIMAL AND HUMAN COMMUNICATION

At one time or another, everyone seems to have observed that, of all the things that distinguish human beings from other animals, nothing is as significant as our ability to learn and to use language. Language is so important to us, and so special, that we cannot help wondering how talking humans could possibly have evolved from mute animals. Evidence that might help us to find out is meager. Writing, our only direct evidence of older forms of language, began no earlier than five or six thousand years ago, and even with a generous estimate, the comparative method of linguistics is unlikely to carry us back more than two or three times as far. By contrast, the bones of *Homo sapiens* who lived at least thirty thousand years ago are hardly distinguishable from the bones of modern humans. We cannot imagine that such modern-looking people would not also have had languages of the same type as those we know today. We must presume, therefore, that languages like our own have existed for at least two or three times as long as linguistic evidence can lead us. Few linguists believe that linguistic reconstruction will ever tell us very much about the earlier evolutionary stages of language. Can we find other evidence?

We can make some good guesses about the communication system of our prelinguistic ancestors by observing how our animal relatives communicate. Along with monkeys and apes, human beings belong to the Primate order of mammals, and both our bodies and our behavior are grounded in primate patterns. Each modern primate species, to be sure, has evolved its own characteristic set of communicative signals. All these signals must diverge to some extent from the signals used by our common ancestor, and it must never be imagined that the communication system of any living species exactly preserves the features of animals who were ancestral to humans. Neverthe-less, the communication systems of various primate species are similar enough, in general outline if not in specific detail, to suggest a pattern of primate com-munication that was probably characteristic of our common ancestor as well.

Many primate species are adapted to life in the trees. Odors are less helpful for tree-dwelling than for ground-dwelling animals and, like other primate noses, ours cannot match the information-gathering ability of the noses of dogs or of many other mammals. But primates have good eyes and good ears and, like other mammals, they use their eyes and ears to receive the signals of at least three important modes of communication: vocal calls, facial expressions, and bodily postures and gestures. We are all familiar with the barks, snarls, and wagging tails of dogs, and with the meows, bare-toothed hisses, and arched backs of cats. When we watch monkeys and apes, we soon recognize their special calls, facial expressions, and gestures as well. Each species, of course, has its own repertory of signals, but primates, like other mammals, use their voices, their faces, and their bodies to produce them.

A good many primate signals are enough like our own to be easily under-stood. They certainly rest on evolutionary homologies, our shared genetic ancestry. Like confident or threatening humans, primates convey confidence by swaggering and by holding themselves straight in a way that makes them seem larger than they really are. Submissive animals crouch or lie down and make themselves look small. When attacking, or when making a confident threat, chimpanzees frown tensely with a narrowed mouth, a gesture reminis-cent of a silent human glare. Infants of many primate species, including hu-mans, pout when begging, opening their eyes wide and drawing their mouth forward into an "o". Many primates show alertness by widening their eyes. Even smiling and laughing have some parallels in other primate species. Mon-keys and apes spread their mouths wide in a kind of grin, both in fear and in greeting, with the subordinate animal generally grinning more intensely. Domi-nant chimpanzees may grin at a timid subordinate animal in what appears to be a gesture of reassurance. Smiles may be used more reciprocally when humans greet each other, but we can recognize an old primate gesture in the nervous grin of a subordinate human. In a number of species, the corners of the mouth are drawn up, the eyebrows raised, and the eyes are sometimes narrowed when engaging in rough-and-tumble play. Among chimps, this is accompanied by panting grunts that are related to human laughter.

Like other mammalian signals, primate postures, calls, and facial expres-sions often convey rich information about the inner emotional state of the animal, but they generally say nothing at all about the state of the surrounding world. We do, however, know of at least one set of primate calls that does convey genuine and important information about the environment. Wild ver-vet monkeys of Kenya have three distinct alarm calls, each of which can be used in ways that alert other animals to a particular enemy: a series of short tones for leopards, low-pitched staccato grunts for eagles, and what are de-scribed as high-pitched "chatters" for pythons. When an animal gives one of these calls, other animals become defensive. On hearing a leopard alarm, they run to take cover in the trees. Eagle alarms cause them to look up, to run into dense brush, or both. Snake alarms cause them to look down toward the ground. Vervets respond appropriately to recorded calls even when no dangerous animal is actually in the neighborhood, so it is clear that they do not need to see a threatening animal themselves. It is tempting to interpret these alarm calls as meaning something like "watch out for the snake" or "watch out for the leopard," though this may give the caller more credit than is deserved. Still, even if the call simply expresses the animal's own fright, other animals are certainly able to interpret these calls and use them to their own advantage. They can profit from information about the environment that is conveyed by another animal's voice. We know of no signals used by wild mammals that come closer to human language than these vervet alarm calls.

Many other animal messages do have clear parallels with those of human language. Greetings, reassurances, entreaties, demands, warnings, and threats pass reciprocally between communicating individuals of many species. Animals have to coordinate some of their activities, and they must communicate in order to do so. They display emotions such as anger, contentment, hunger, and sexual interest, all sentiments that can be conveyed with human language. Primates are relatively noisy animals, and they are highly social. Their cries are one means of coordinating their activities, and our own prehuman ancestors must have been equally social and equally vocal. It is natural to look on primate calls, specialized to convey particular meanings, as a foundation upon which language could have been built. We are right to be impressed by the parallels between human language and animal communication but, at the same time, we must also acknowledge the differences. Since it is the unique characteristics of language that present us with the greatest evolutionary puzzles, it is the differences that will be stressed here. What, then, is special about language, and what differentiates it from communication among other primates?

To begin with, primate communication, like other mammalian communication, seems to be shaped almost entirely by the inborn nature of the animal. We can agree that our ability to learn a human language is also inborn, but we still need to learn one particular language. Nonhuman primates seem not to need to learn their communication system any more than they need to learn to digest their food. So far as we are able to tell, the cries and gestures of chimpanzees, as much as the barks of dogs or the meows of cats, are set by the hereditary nature of the species. Each species has its own distinctive inborn patterns of communication, but the individuals of each species share their communication system because they share the same genetic heritage.

Since the patterns of mammalian communication are not learned, we find no mammalian parallels to our own dialect and language differences. Rather surprisingly, we do find such parallels among birds. Individuals of many bird species are born with the potential for a range of songs, but they have to perfect their own song by mimicking the songs of their neighbors. Birds of many species have some ability to mimic, though only a few are as versatile as parrots and mynas, with their ability to mimic even human voices. Because some features of their calls must be learned by imitation, different varieties of songs become established among different local populations of the same species. It seems entirely reasonable to call these local varieties "dialects," and birds that live near each other tend, like neighboring humans, to share a dialect. Distinctive dialects, we presume, allow birds of these species to distinguish intruders from familiar neighbors.

So far as we know, dialects of this sort are entirely missing from nonhuman mammalian communication. This sets language dramatically apart from the communication system of our nearest relatives. Our brains have certainly evolved in a way that makes us capable of learning and using a language, but we are not programmed for a particular language. Like some birds, but unlike other mammals, we perfect our communication system only by listening to other individuals.

When we study primate communication, we are tempted to focus on vocal cries, for these seem closest to our own language, but this may betray a biased human concern with our voices. The vocal medium is so important to us that we may exaggerate its importance among animals. The three modalities of cries, facial expressions, and bodily postures are combined more intimately in animal communication than in language. We can hear a dog's bark, and this may persuade us that barking is an auditory signal, but barking can also be seen. Even a deaf dog should be able to recognize the barking of another dog. A cat's arched back is so regularly combined with a hiss and bared teeth that the entire combination has to be seen as forming a single complex signal. Any attempt to pull apart the visible and auditory aspects of animal signaling is a bit artificial.

Human language is more clearly confined to its single channel than is animal communication. Although language is often accompanied by gestures and by facial expressions, the contribution of these "nonverbal" gestures to language is relatively small. We can, after all, understand language in the dark or over the telephone. We can treat the spoken channel of language as reasonably self-contained and independent. The single spoken channel can even be translated into the single visible channel of writing.

Animal calls and gestures are also more limited than language in the information that they can communicate. Language is sometimes said to be unusual in permitting "displacement," the communication of information about things that are distant in time or space. Displacement is not totally absent from animal communication, for animals as low on the evolutionary hierarchy as bees are able to "dance" in a way that points to the location of distant sources of nectar. Hive-mates are able to interpret these "dances" and then fly off and find the nectar. Bee dancing is exceptional, however, and most animals exchange little information about anything that is out of sight, or that happened in the past, or that might happen in the future.

Most animals are even more limited than the restriction on displacement suggests, for they do not even communicate much about their immediate surroundings. Vervet monkeys alert other animals to specific dangers, but we find this remarkable precisely because it is such an exception to the more usual information that is conveyed by mammalian, and even primate, messages. Not only are apes unable to convey ideas like "there is a banana behind that tree" or "there was a banana there yesterday," but they are unable even to suggest the idea of "I see a banana right there on the ground." They can, to be sure, show their interest in the banana simply by the direction of their gaze. This may draw attention to the banana, but it does not name or describe it, and the gaze may not even be intended as communication. Most mammalian communication, like the gaze toward a banana, concerns the inner state of the signalers, or suggests their intentions. Mammals are very good at expressing their anger, their playfulness, their hunger, or their sexual interest. While they can threaten to attack or acknowledge their subordination, they can say very little about the state of the world outside their own bodies.

Human beings have no trouble at all describing the world around them, or describing past, future, and distant worlds. Our ability to state facts about the world even allows us to state untrue "facts," to make up fantasies, to invent imaginary worlds, to make mistakes, to lie. We can talk about a wide range of topics because the vocabulary of a natural language is incomparably larger than the repertory of signals used in any known system of animal communication. Not even apes distinguish more than a few dozen calls and gestures. People easily marshal tens of thousands of words, and these allow us to speak about all sorts of topics and to do so with a subtlety that is well beyond the reach of even the most intelligent animal.

Human language is also far more productive than any system of animal communication. We can always make up new sentences in order to state new facts and to talk about new things. It is not even clear just what it would mean for an animal to make up a new signal or to convey a new message. Their cries and their gestures do not combine into the kinds of tight syntactic structures that allow us to distinguish clearly between a repetition and a new construction. Animals repeat their cries and gestures without ever saying anything that is really new. The creativity of language is made possible by its enormous vocabulary and its recursive grammar. We know of no parallel in animal communication.

The words of our large vocabulary are kept distinct from one another by means of a phonological system that is built with contrasting phonemes and distinctive features. This makes language a digital rather than an analog system of communication. Once again, we know of nothing in mammalian communication that exploits such a coding system. Our phonology allows languages to have what has been called a "dual level of patterning," one level consisting of distinctive but meaningless sounds, the second consisting of the meaningful morphemes and words that are constructed from these sounds. Somehow, in the course of human evolution, we acquired an entirely new method of distinguishing communicative noises. Animal cries that grade into each other were supplemented by words that are kept in contrast by distinctive phonological features.

The need to learn language, the wider range of messages that language allows, its huge vocabulary, its productivity, its dual level of patterning, and its specialized exploitation of a single channel all combine to make language a very different form of communication from any other that we know about, certainly very different from anything known among primates.

SIGNING APES

In addition to observing animals as they communicate in their natural surroundings, we can also train them in the laboratory to see how much they can learn with our help. The great apes, particularly the chimpanzees, are so much like human beings that the temptation to try to teach them language is irresistible. In a classic experiment, Keith and Catherine Hayes brought a chimpanzee infant named Viki into their home and, in everything from baby food to diapers, they treated her like a human child. In physical skills, Viki developed faster than human children, but even though she was given every conceivable encouragement to learn English, 6 years of careful guidance yielded nothing but approximations to three words: *mama, papa,* and *cup.* Even these were pronounced with so much difficulty and in such a distorted way that innocent observers could be excused for failing to recognize them as words. They were hardly more than tricks that a relatively intelligent animal had been trained to perform. Even a dog can be trained to bark on command, and it is not clear that Viki's "words" amounted to more than trained barking. The failure of Viki to learn any significant amount of language invited the conclusion that chimps simply lack any verbal capacity.

More recently, several experimenters have tried to teach other kinds of language to apes. The most famous experiment is that of Beatrice and Alan Gardner, who undertook to teach the sign language of the deaf to a young chimpanzee named Washoe. Chimpanzees have bodies, in particular hands and arms, that are very much like our own, and the Gardners noticed the ease with which young chimpanzees imitate human gestures. Chimps seem to be as aware as we are of the similarity of their bodies and ours. Although they are unwilling or unable to imitate the sounds of speech, chimpanzees spontaneously imitate our gestures. The Gardners reasoned that Viki's failure with language could have been due to the modality of the language that was being pushed on her, rather than a failure of her mind. Chimps, they suggested, simply do not have the kind of control over their vocal apparatus that would allow it to be used for language. They might be more successful with their hands and arms.

Washoe was raised among people who spoke with her only in American Sign Language (ASL), and she was encouraged in every way to make signs herself. She had ample opportunity to imitate signs, and her teachers would sometimes hold her hands and form them into the sign they wanted her to make. She was guided, coaxed, and rewarded as her gestures came to approximate the conventional signs of ASL. She made her first four signs when she was approximately 1½ years old, 6 months after coming to the Gardners, and for the next several years her repertory of signs grew steadily. She learned many names for physical objects (*flower, toothbrush, key, dog*), but she also learned signs that the Gardners translate with English adjectives (*sweet, dirty, more*), or verbs (*tickle, open, gimme, listen*). Like a human child, she seemed able to associate a sign not only with a particular object, but also to extend its use to other similar objects. Having learned to use the sign *key* for one particular key, she was able to use it for other keys as well.

Washoe stayed with the Gardners for 3 years, until she was about 4 years old. At that time she was reported to be able to use, with understanding, about 85 signs. Her training then continued with other teachers, and her vocabulary reached about 160 signs. She could make the appropriate sign for an object when she was shown its picture, and she certainly liked the candy with which she was rewarded for doing so. She learned considerably more than skeptics of the experiment had predicted, and for a while it almost seemed that we might soon be able to ask Washoe how it feels to be a chimpanzee.

When she still had no more than a dozen signs, Washoe began to combine them into sequences. She even used sequences that she had never seen, such as "gimme-tickle." She signed "open-food-drink" in a way that was interpreted to refer to the refrigerator, although humans always described it as "cold-box." Most of her combinations included signs for "please, hurry, gimme" or "more," suggesting that she most often signed to express her wishes. She signed "go-sweet" when hoping to be carried to a raspberry bush, "open-flower" to be let through a gate to a flower garden, "open-key" for a locked door and "listen eat" at the sound of an alarm clock that signaled meal time. Even longer sequences such as *you me go out* or even *you me go out hurry* were used when she wanted to go out with someone and was encouraging their speedy action. On one famous occasion she saw a swan and signed *water bird,* and she has sometimes been credited with having invented a new name.

These combinations look a bit like phrases or sentences, but not everyone has been willing to accept them as evidence for syntactic ability. Although Washoe sometimes joined signs into rather long sequences, some skeptical observers have doubted her ability to join them in consistent patterns. They have wondered if her sequences amounted to more than jumbles of unrelated signs. Even *water bird* could have resulted from naming two different objects in succession, not from giving a new name to a swan. The evidence is not entirely clear, but Washoe does not seem to have been as successful as children at keeping the order of her signs consistent, and her signing was often characterized by repetitions in which signs tumbled out in what seems, at least to some observers, to have been a rather haphazard way. She used an unusually large number of signs such as "gimme" or "dirty" that have been called "wild cards," and that she seemed to toss in more or less at random.

These signs padded out her sequences without adding significantly to their meaning. She was less likely to initiate conversations or to use signs spontaneously than human children, and a high proportion of her utterances were instrumental, used to get things that she wanted, rather than to convey information. She would sign that she wanted to be tickled, to be pushed on a swing, or to be given another piece of candy, but she did not seek, or volunteer, information. Of course children also use language to get what they want, but more than Washoe, they also use language for other purposes.

Another experiment, this one with a young chimpanzee named Nim Chimpsky and raised in New York by Herbert Terrace and his associates, has added to the skepticism. Like Washoe, Nim learned to use more than 100 signs, but his signing differed in significant ways from the language of a human child. Children show a steady increase in the average length of their utterances. Nim used occasional long sequences, but the average length stayed low. Apparently one or two signs were enough to convey what Nim wanted to communicate. Even when he did use longer sequences they seemed to say no more than his two-sign sequences. His most frequent sequences were *play me* and *play me Nim,* the latter communicating nothing more than the former. He once gave an impressive 16 sign sequence: *give orange me give eat orange me eat orange give me eat orange give me you.* He was certainly eager for the orange, but except for some added emphasis, the information conveyed by these 16 signs, was already clear after the first two or three. Such jumbles of signs do not seem to offer much evidence of structured syntax, and none of the signing chimpanzees has gained any ability with the more subtle aspects of ASL. Their vocabulary remains tiny by comparison with human signers, and they have shown no hint of the kinds of modulations or stage setting that are described in Chapter 11, and that are essential components of ASL.

Perhaps the most severe challenge to the claims made on behalf of signing chimps is the charge that a large proportion of their signing is done in direct imitation of their teachers. Washoe's teachers signed constantly when in her presence. They knew that children learn language by immersion, so they made the reasonable assumption that the best way for Washoe to learn would be to immerse her in signing. Washoe was able not only to see, but also to imitate, the signing of her human companions. She was even encouraged to do so. Far fewer of her utterances were spontaneous and original than we expect from children.

The most skeptical observers have even wondered whether Washoe's signing was much more impressive than the tricks of a well-trained dog. Dogs can learn to follow the commands of a trainer, and they can learn to perform tricks in order to get rewards. We are not surprised by a dog that has learned to beg for a treat. No one doubts the intelligence of chimps, and since their hands and arms are so much like our own, we should not be surprised that they are better than dogs at learning our tricks. Whether the differences are great enough to bring them significantly closer to language remains controversial.

It is difficult to stay neutral about these experiments. Everyone seems to carry strong biases into their interpretations of chimpanzee signing. Some people really want chimps to be able to talk, and they are generous in crediting them with human-like behavior. Others resist blurring the line that divides us from animals, and they may fail to give Washoe and Nim the credit they deserve. If we define "language" narrowly enough, we can make certain that apes will never use language. Whenever apes learn enough to threaten our unique nature, we may be tempted to redefine the challenge, and in that way keep them at a safe distance from ourselves.

Other apes than Washoe and Nim have been taught signs, and still others have been taught to communicate in a variety of artificial "languages" that require colored plastic chips to be manipulated, or buttons on a console to be pushed. Apes are quicker to learn these systems than other animals, and the experiments are expanding our understanding of the background from which the human intellect developed, but by human standards the range of topics about which an ape has any interest in communicating appears to be exceedingly narrow. Syntactic ability is hard to find. Most linguists today continue to believe that a wide gulf divides human language from anything that an ape, or any other animal, can learn. Nevertheless, Washoe and other apes have surely learned more than most linguists would have predicted before the experiments began. We may be surprised again.

HUMAN NONVERBAL COMMUNICATION

We focus so often on language that we sometimes forget that human beings have other ways to communicate than just by talking and writing. We also have a complex system of nonverbal communication of cries, gestures, and facial expressions, and these resemble mammalian communication considerably more closely than does language. Our cries, laughs, groans, frowns, and smiles, along with the postures and movements of our body, exploit the same modalities as primate communication, and from fear and rage to hunger and high spirits, we use these modalities to display the same range of emotions as other animals.

Like nonhuman signals, the signals of human nonverbal communication often combine the channels of sight and sound. A human laugh, like a dog's bark, can be both seen and heard. When we say "he laughed but his eyes were not laughing" we acknowledge the essential gestural component of a laugh. Like mammalian communication, our nonverbal communication seems to be more narrowly constrained by our genetic inheritance than is language. Nowhere do smiles have the meaning of our sobs. Nowhere do sobs routinely indicate joy. Like the cries and facial expressions of any mammalian species, the relative uniformity of human nonverbal communication is certainly due to our shared biological nature. A dog can bark, and we can laugh because the genetic inheritance of the two species provides for barking and laughing.

To be sure, no human behavior is immune to the molding of culture. We are the most malleable of animals, and the traditions of our particular cultures add refinements even to the inherited cries and gestures of our nonverbal communication. Laughs and cries do not mean *exactly* the same thing in every culture. Still, they are far more uniform than words. Without long exposure to the Chinese language, we understand nothing at all that is said in Chinese. We understand a great deal of the gestural language of China from the moment we arrive in Beijing.

We use our nonverbal communication to convey the same kinds of information that animals convey. Our cries (laughter, sighs, groans, coos, screams, sobs, etc.) and our facial expressions (frowns, scowls, grins, pouts, narrowed eyes, raised eyebrows, etc.) are best suited to indicate our emotions. With subtlety and precision, but without a single word, we display the exact degree of our anger, fear, boredom, curiosity, satisfaction, or hunger. For some of our most important messages, mere language is far less eloquent than gentle sighs and melting glances.

On the other hand, our nonverbal communication is almost useless for conveying facts about the world outside of our own bodies. Without language, or some communication system based closely on language, we cannot tell someone what happened yesterday. We cannot describe the state of the world on the other side of the mountain. We cannot agree on where or when to meet for lunch. We cannot even describe the state of affairs that is visible in our immediate surroundings. We are hardly more capable than a chimpanzee of using our nonverbal communication to say "I see a banana right there on the ground." Like animal communication, our communication of cries and gestures is essentially nonproductive. We cannot create new gestural messages in the way that we can create new sentences. If it makes any sense at all to count the number of human cries and gestures, the number is certainly tiny compared to the size of our vocabulary.

Our nonverbal communication also lacks the dual level of patterning that is characteristic of language. It has nothing that corresponds to the principle of contrast that is so central to language. Rather, like animal systems of communication, our nonverbal communication is built on analog rather than digital principles. We can chuckle, giggle, laugh, and guffaw. These differ in their sounds, and each "means" something different. Nevertheless, they grade into each other without sharp boundaries. We have no trouble producing something that is halfway between a giggle and a laugh or halfway between a laugh and a guffaw, and what is intermediate in sound is also intermediate in meaning. In language there can be no such intermediate forms. We cannot compromise between *like* and *love* as we can compromise between a grin and a tender smile. We say one word or we say another word, and it simply makes no sense imagine a halfway point between them.

The distinction that has been drawn here between language and human nonverbal communication may seem too stark. Humans are complex animals, and it would be surprising if language and nonverbal communication did not, at times, seem to overlap. We do use some kinds of signals that may appear to be intermediate but, when these are examined closely, each falls rather clearly on one side or the other of the boundary between language and nonverbal communication. The sign language of the deaf, for instance, is gestural rather than vocal, but it is rich and flexible like any true language, and it is not limited in its expressive powers as is our ordinary nonverbal communication. Sign language is productive, it must be learned, and its hand shapes, positions, and movements can be combined in a large number of ways to produce a large vocabulary and an unlimited number of sentences. Sign language is certainly a language, rather than a form of nonverbal communication.

Even those of us who are not deaf use some gestures that are more like language than like our smiles and frowns. When people use the "V for Victory" sign, or stick out their tongues in sassy defiance, they use symbols that have a specific meaning and that must be specifically learned. These gestures are more like spoken words than like smiles or frowns, and they are not used by people in all cultures. Not even nods or head shakes are used everywhere, and both their lack of universality and their specific meanings distinguish nods and head shakes from the universal human gestures of laughs and cries.

The deepest interpenetration of language and nonverbal communication may come with intonation. We count intonation as a part of phonology, but it can convey messages that are, in part, independent of the meaning of the words. In particular, intonation conveys a great deal about the emotional state of the speaker. Quite apart from the words we choose, we show our anger, excitement, or pleasure by our "tone of voice." We do not have to know Swedish to hear the anger in the voices of quarreling Swedes. The emotional features of intonation are carried by analog rather than digital signals, and they express the same emotions as nonverbal cries. These emotions can be heard in the voices of children who have not yet learned to talk. Some aspects of intonation amount to an invasion of language by features of our nonverbal communication.

Neither the conventional and language-like gestures of nods and head shakes nor the expression of emotion through linguistic intonation should obscure the gulf that divides language from nonverbal communication. Our cries and gestures must be recognized as forming a typical primate, even mammalian, system of communication. The evolutionary continuities between animal communication and human nonverbal communication are obvious. To the extent that language is different from our nonverbal communication, it is also different from all other mammalian communication. The unique features of language divide it sharply from other human and non-human communication, and it is the unique features of language that present us with the riddles of linguistic evolution.

FOSSILS AND BRAINS

The bones of fossil humans of the last thirty thousand years look like our own, but as we move back through the preceding two or three million years of prehistoric time, the remains of our ancestors look less and less modern. Most relevant to language was the evolving brain, and the earlier we go, the smaller were the skulls that contained those brains. The earliest known fossils that were securely on our side of the division between humans and apes were the Australopithecines who already lived in Africa three million years ago. Though they walked upright as we do, their brains were not much larger than those of modern chimpanzees, less than half as large as modern human brains. Since the Australopithecines had smaller bodies than either modern chimpanzees or humans, the size of their brains relative to the size of their bodies had already moved to an intermediate position, but even on a relative scale, their brains were much smaller than our own. Since the time of the Australopithecines, the human brains have grown steadily larger.

Among modern human populations we find no correlation between brain size and any measure that we have devised for intelligence or linguistic ability, but it seems hard to deny the connection between the inexorable 3-million-year growth of the human brain on the one hand, and increasing intelligence and increasing skill with language on the other. The interior markings on fossil skulls have been scrutinized in the hope of finding hints about the evolving organization of the brain and about the kind of language these brains might have permitted, but we know so little, even about how the brains of modern humans produce language, that any attempt to read the markings on fossil skulls remains a speculative and controversial undertaking. We do not really know how large a brain or what kind of brain is needed for language.

Fossils have also been examined in the hope of learning something about the evolution of the vocal tract, for the human vocal tract has been strikingly modified from that of other primates. The human larynx (the "Adam's apple"), which contains the vocal cords, is positioned lower in the vocal tract than is the larynx of other primate species. The low position of our larynx has a serious consequence, because it results in a dangerous crossing of the trachea and esophagus, the wind pipe and the upper part of the digestive tract. Other primates, like other mammals and even newborn human infants, can breathe at the same time that they swallow. This is possible because the air can pass unobstructed around the esophagus. Food is less likely to get misdirected into the air passage, so animals are unlikely to choke. Death by choking on food is a real danger for human beings, and only a strong and competing evolutionary advantage could have permitted such a danger to arise. The only apparent advantage of the low position of the larynx is to expand the pharynx, the space just above. This improves the resonance characteristics of the vocal tract, and the modified arrangement seems to allow us to produce a greater number of distinctive vowels.

At approximately the rear point of the velum, the human vocal tract is bent at a sharper angle than the vocal tract of other primates. The bend reduces the efficiency of breathing, but it also seems to contribute to the versatile resonance needed for speech. The Neanderthals, who survived in Europe until suddenly replaced by fully modern *Homo sapiens* about thirty-five thousand years ago, were much more like ourselves than the earlier Australopithecines were, but even the Neanderthals may have had a higher larynx and a less-bent vocal tract than we do. A few linguists have concluded that this made them incapable of using a language of a modern type. Other linguists remain skeptical of this evidence. Not only are the fossils sufficiently few and fragmentary to make some observers mistrust the reconstructions, but it is not certain that different resonance properties of the vocal tract would rule out a complex language, even if it sounded different from our own. If a language had enough consonants, it ought to be able to dispense with a large number of vowels. Neanderthal brains, oddly, were, on the average, slightly larger than ours, and those large brains may have produced fine speech in spite of a slightly different vocal tract.

To most linguists, after all, it is the brain rather than the vocal tract that is the primary organ of speech. Deaf signers manage to speak without using their vocal tract at all. However much the human vocal tract may be adapted to speech, the adaptation of the brain matters more. Except for the steady expansion of the brain's size, fossils, unfortunately, give little evidence for the brain's potentiality for language. Can we learn more by studying our own brains or by comparing our brains to those of other animals?

At about 1400 cm^3, our brains are about three times the size of chimpanzee brains, but only a quarter the size of elephant brains. Clearly size has to be judged in proportion to the total size of the animal. Even in proportion to our general body size, however, we come out high, for our brains are still more than twice as large as would be expected for an ordinary primate with a body size equivalent to ours. Are our brains unique in other ways than size? The human brain shares its general anatomy with other primate brains, but it is not simply a puffed-up version, for some parts have expanded more dramatically than others. The cerebellum (the rear part of the brain), and the neocortex of the cerebrum (the outer layer of main front and upper part) have expanded the most (see Figure 16–1). Within the neocortex it is especially the so-called association areas that have expanded. In lower mammals most of the neocortex is taken up with basic sensory and motor functions. The less specialized association areas are larger in primates, and they are especially large in humans. It is these association areas that are credited with much of the human ability to learn. Even these differences in proportions, however, do not amount to a radical change from the pattern of other primate brains. Primates differ from other mammals in much the same way that humans differ from other primates. Other primates with relatively large brains show expansion of the cerebellum and the neocortex, just as we do. Our brains are larger than those of any other primate, and ours have expanded most in the same areas where the brains of other large primates expand, even if more modestly. In

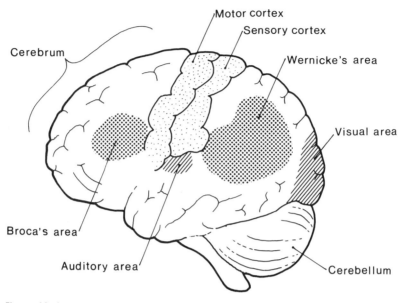

Figure 16-1
Speech centers of the human brain.

every respect our brain carries general primate tendencies particularly far. Our brain looks like an ultraprimate brain. Nothing about its size or proportions gives any hint about the source of our linguistic ability. For that we must turn to quite different evidence.

It is a grim fact that the best evidence for the way the brain handles language comes from people with war injuries, accidents, or strokes. People whose brains have been injured sometimes have great difficulty with language, a condition known as **aphasia.** It is striking that fewer than 5% of the brain injuries that lead to aphasia result from damage to the right cerebral hemisphere, so it easy to conclude that the left side of the brain has the main responsibility for language. Two regions on the left side, known respectively as *Broca's area* and *Wernicke's area,* are particularly vulnerable. The areas do not have sharp boundaries, but the closer the injury is to one of these areas, the more likely it is to result in aphasia. The syndrome known as Broca's aphasia, which arises when Broca's area has been damaged, is characterized by halting, labored speech. Patients have particular trouble with grammatical elements. They seem to be able to find content words, especially nouns, but they have extreme difficulty organizing these into sentences. Damage to Wernicke's area results in quite different symptoms. Patients with Wernicke's aphasia have trouble understanding language. They may speak with considerable fluency and with relatively good syntax, but much of what they say makes little sense. They have trouble with content words and may be very limited in their ability to express clear ideas. The study of brain-damaged patients seems to show that certain language functions are localized in specific parts of the brain, but the picture is far from simple. Young children who suffer brain injuries are more likely to regain speech functions than are older patients. Apparently other parts of an immature brain are able to take over language functions when they have to. Adults no longer have so much flexibility.

Many linguists have proposed models for the way in which the brain might process language. To produce and understand language seems to require a considerable number of discrete operations, and it is tempting to guess that the brain handles these varied operations in some sort of discrete way. Unfortunately, it is not yet possible to relate the features of the linguists' models to features of the brain's anatomy. The evidence for localization of language functions provided by brain-damaged patients is tantalizing, but it tells us little about the specific mechanisms by which language is stored or processed. Nothing that we know about the brain, for example, helps us to understand how the lexicon is stored or accessed, or where or how grammatical rules are processed. We cannot even begin to search for the features of universal grammar that Chomsky and others attribute to the brain. We do not yet know of any specific anatomical differences between human and ape brains that can be credited for our ability to talk.

LANGUAGE IN AN EVOLVING SPECIES

We do not know when the first hints of language began, but from the evidence of prehistoric archeology we can draw plausible inferences about the social and biological conditions that might have encouraged improved communication. The human story begins with descent from the trees. Because apes must grasp branches and even swing from them, they need better manual dexterity and a more upright posture than other mammals. Our own arboreal ancestors certainly shared these traits, but it now seems clear that the decisive step that started human evolution along its unique path was the fully upright posture that came with life on the ground. The result of upright posture was the liberation of the hands and arms for other duties than locomotion. Walking on two legs does not, by itself, confer an unambiguous advantage. Anyone who has tried to catch an uncooperative cat or dog must recognize the superior sprinting ability of a four-legged animal. As early humans became committed to bipedal locomotion, however, their hands became free to hold, carry, and manipulate objects. Walking upright implies spending less time in the trees and more time on the ground than our even earlier ancestors had done, and this was a dangerous environment where the hands and arms might find important new tasks. Even a badly thrown rock or an awkwardly wielded club must have been a great comfort when facing a hungry predator. Life on the ground might not have been possible at all without hands and arms that could manage simple weapons.

Freeing the hands for tools also frees them to carry infants and food. Apes need all four limbs to clamber through the trees, so their infants must take responsibility for their own safety. Human infants can trust their parents to hold them, so humans can be born at a less-mature stage than apes. Once food could be carried, different members of a family or band could begin to specialize in different kinds of food collection, but they would have needed a way to agree about where to meet, and they would have needed to be sufficiently cooperative to exchange their products. All this cooperation must have required better communication.

Chimpanzee mothers and children receive little help from males. One infant is all that a mother can cope with at one time, so a chimpanzee mother cannot risk another birth until her previous child is independent. As a result, chimps are slow to reproduce. Births are widely spaced, and the young cannot be quite so leisurely about growing up as human young, since they must get out of the way to make room for a younger sibling. Humans overcome this limitation by persuading the father to help out. If a human father does not actually handle his children, he can at least be expected to provide them, and their mother, with some of their food. This creates a family with two parents, and such a family can support several dependent children at the same time. Human children can be spaced more closely and still have a longer period of dependence and more time to learn than ape young. All of these changes imply more cooperation, better planning, a higher intelligence, and more opportunities to learn. These, in turn, must have encouraged a growing ability to communicate.

Once our ancestors began to rely on tools and weapons, there must have been intense selective pressure in favor of individuals who were good at learning to manufacture and use them, but the evidence for better tools is slow to appear. We can recognize manufactured stone tools from as early as 2.5 million years ago, but for the next million years tools remained crude with little evidence of deliberate design. More consistently shaped tools appear about 1.5 million years ago. More symmetry and regularity suggest clearer planning and an abstract concept of the tool's form. The stone worker must have known what he was aiming for. After another million years had passed, about half a million years ago, manufacturing techniques became more elaborate, and it was then that the human species finally expanded beyond the warm and temperate regions of the world. This population expansion implies growing technological skills.

Through these two million years there is evidence of gradually developing technology, but we must also be impressed by its slow pace. Living in a world of ceaseless innovation, we can scarcely imagine the passing of tens of thousands of generations with such meager evidence of cultural change. Of course, only the most durable goods have survived from the first two million years of tool making, but we must still wonder if people whose stone tools changed so slowly could possibly have been enough like ourselves to have anything that we would recognize as language. Does consistent tool design suggest some sort of abstract conceptual ability that might also hint at an ability with language?

Or does the slow rate of change suggest an animal so unlike ourselves that the cultural learning required for language would have been impossible?

From about 200,000 years ago we find more differentiated tool design. Burials appeared, along with the first hints of art. Changes came more quickly. As tools grew more complex, language would have been helpful for describing them and perhaps for teaching others to make them, but it is difficult to guess what level of complexity in archeological tool assemblages implies language. Stone-working techniques might have been learned simply by imitating others. Even today, much of the technology of nonindustrial societies is passed down more by imitation than by deliberate verbal instruction.

The few million years of human evolution have been far too short to build all of language into our genetic inheritance. This is not to deny that many important and specific traits of language are provided by our genes, but even the most generous genetic estimate still leaves much to be learned, including, for instance, the entire lexicon. Once the domestication of fathers allowed families to care for several dependent children at the same time, the period of maturation could take even more time, and learning could be extended over a longer period. A growing need to coordinate activities, both within the family and among the families of a larger band, together with slower maturation and a greater potential for learning, must all have conspired to encourage a form of communication that had to be learned and that was, therefore, startlingly different from the communication systems of other primates. The human species must have undergone stringent selection for the capacity to learn increasingly refined language. A few million years is not much time for human and chimpanzee communication to have diverged so far.

THE EARLIEST LANGUAGE AND GROWING COMPLEXITY

As part of the folklore of their discipline, linguists recall a number of quaint theories about how language might have begun. There was the bow-wow theory (that it all began with animal cries), the ding-dong theory (that it began with singing), and the heave-ho theory (that it began as a way to coordinate work). None of these theories has much to support or to recommend it, but a theory that has been taken more seriously in recent decades has been influenced by our growing understanding of deaf signing. If apes are better at learning sign language than spoken language, might some sort of gestural language have preceded vocal language?

The gestural theory has a certain plausible appeal, but we really do not know how the earliest stage of language began, and it is hard to know what sort of evidence we might marshal in order to find out. Like the bow-wow and ding-dong theories, the gestural theory concerns the initial stage of language, and this is, in some ways, the most puzzling step of all. Nevertheless another and somewhat different question deserves to be asked as well: Once a rudimentary language was launched, what sorts of selective pressures might have fostered its increasing complexity? This question is sometimes dismissed as unimportant. It has been argued that language came as a single package, introduced by a single mutation, so that our ancestors either had it or did not have it. But surely language is too complex to have developed in a single jump. We can witness the gradual development of language ourselves by watching children as they pass through a series of intermediate stages on the way to fully adult language. We do not have to imagine that a child's language recapitulates the stages of the species' evolution, but the fact that we can observe the transitional stages of a child's language should, at least, help us to imagine possible transitional stages of evolutionary history. Indeed, language could have grown gradually more complex over a period of many thousands, or even millions, of years. It is, therefore, reasonable to ask what sorts of pressures could have propelled it from what must have been simple beginnings toward the highly complex and modulated medium that we know today.

Evolution proceeds when genes give enough advantage to some individuals to let them produce and raise more children than their contemporaries. Only in this way can some genes spread at the expense of others. Can we imagine that the ability to use more complex language than their contemporaries could have given some individuals enough advantage to let them raise more children?

We may be a bit skeptical of the advantages that a finely nuanced language offers for subsistence or cooperation. The technology of pre-modern society probably requires little verbal instruction, for it can be learned largely by observation and imitation. Even the essential cooperation needed for technology and subsistence should be manageable with a very much simpler language than ours. The social role of language seems more important, and we have to recognize that language is used in competition as well as in cooperation. In premodern societies, perhaps even in our own, language in its delicately nuanced forms is used not so much for basic subsistence tasks as for establishing, maintaining, and refining social relationships. It is when dealing with people, not material objects, that people call on their richest linguistic resources. It is in defining themselves in relation to others and in conducting interpersonal negotiations, in competing, manipulating, and scheming to get their own way that the most subtle features of language become important. People need language for arguing their case, for claiming their rights, for leaving just the right degree of ambiguity, for outdoing their rivals in many intricate forms of verbal competition, for talking their way out of tight spots. When disputes grow dangerous, people need language as an alternative to violence.

The social and competitive aspects of language should confer a selective advantage on the linguistically skilled individual. If language ability can be used as a weapon by which to gain power over others, it becomes a means for gaining access to resources. Resources have been dangerously limited in most human societies, so access to richer-than-average resources implies a greater-than-average ability to keep children alive. If skillful language helped some individuals to gain more resources than others, it is not so absurd to guess that there could have been biological selection in favor of those genes that conferred more skill with language.

This is not an argument that most linguists find congenial. We like to think of language as a tool for cooperation, not as a means by which some individuals gain an advantage over others. Nevertheless, if the ability to use complex language was to evolve, it must have conferred advantages, and it is in the social sphere of human life that the advantages seem most clear.

This argument leaves many questions unanswered. It tells us nothing about the particular steps that language might have passed through on its way to the intricate system we know today. It also leaves us unable to say why other animals did *not* develop language. The advantages that we attribute to language should have been advantageous to many species other than our own. Other animals, one would suppose, could have profited from both the closer cooperation and the competitive advantage that language allows, but no other species gained the ability to speak. We do not know what was unique about human beings that set us off on our distinctive evolutionary path.

LINGUISTIC EVIDENCE

Linguists are generally skeptical about accepting data from the languages we know about as evidence of earlier evolutionary stages. Some people have tried, of course, to assign languages to different stages of development. Languages like Latin, which have complex morphological apparatus, have sometimes been looked on as highly developed. To consider Latin as highly evolved, however, implies that the Romance daughters of Latin, with their simpler morphology, have deteriorated seriously since the time of the Romans, hardly flattering to speakers of French and Spanish. Other people have been more inclined to praise the relatively simple morphology of languages like English or Chinese. To some, this kind of morphology seems cleaner and more logical than the intricacies of Latin. Both judgments reveal more about the prejudices of the observers than they do about the quality of the languages. More recently a few linguists have suggested that syntactic complexity, if not morphological complexity, may be related to social complexity. It has been claimed, for example, that complex forms of subordinating constructions are found only in the languages of complex societies. The languages of nonliterate people, by contrast, are said to be limited to coordination. Differences of this sort are probably attributable to writing, however. Writing can be planned, so subordinate constructions are much easier when writing than when speaking. It is hardly fair to compare the writing of complex societies with the spoken language of simpler societies. The ordinary spoken languages of people who have writing are probably as deficient in subordinate constructions as the spoken languages of nonliterate people. Most linguists remain skeptical about judging any language spoken today as more primitive or more developed than any other.

Can we consider some specific linguistic features as relatively advanced even if we cannot rank entire languages along a developmental scale? We might try to identify relatively evolved features by looking for those that depend on the previous existence of other features. If feature B cannot exist without feature A, we might conclude that A must have developed first. Front-rounded vowels, for instance, seem never to be found except in languages that also have front-*un*rounded vowels. If front-rounded vowels cannot exist alone, we might conclude that front-unrounded vowels must have come first in linguistic prehistory. The fact that front-unrounded vowels are much more common among the world's languages than front-rounded vowels suggests that they are, in some sense, easier to articulate, and this might also lead us to suspect that they came first. This does not require us to conclude that languages with front-rounded vowels are, in general, more advanced than others, since they may be less advanced in other respects. Each language could have its own areas of development. It can also happen that languages can lose front-rounded vowels, so change is not just one way.

There is one other serious problem about interpreting uncommon features like front-rounded vowels as evolutionarily advanced. We can easily imagine a time when our forebears were still incapable of some modern sounds, but these individuals have to be regarded as genetically different animals than we are. We cannot be certain that what comes most easily to us would also have come most easily to them. These hypothetical ancestors might have had no trouble at all with front-rounded vowels even while stumbling badly with front-unrounded ones. Still, an exploration of which sounds are most common in the world's languages and of which sounds are prerequisites for others has seemed, to some linguists, to be one of the few plausible means of guessing about which sounds came first in evolutionary history.

A parallel argument is possible for syntax but even more risky. When we considered relative clauses in Chapter 11, we saw that some kinds of relativization presuppose others. Relativization on the subject is most common, followed by relativization on the direct object, on the indirect object, and then on other syntactic roles. Languages permit relativization on phrases low on this hierarchy only if they permit relativization on all those above it. The relativization hierarchy might lead us to guess that, in the course of linguistic evolution, relativization came first on subjects and then spread progressively down the hierarchy to other syntactic roles. Only in this way would disharmonious languages with relativization on incompatible roles have been avoided. Since some modern languages relativize on more roles than others, the implication would be that some languages are more "advanced" than others, at least with respect to this feature.

It is a mistake, however, to consider relativization in isolation from other aspects of the syntax. We saw in Chapter 11 that languages that are poor in relativization tend to be rich in passives, and passives provide a mechanism that can compensate for missing relative clauses. As soon as we consider passivization and relativization together, it no longer seems clear that one type of language has any claim at all to being "advanced." Most linguists would prefer to regard different syntactic patterns as simply alternative ways to solve problems, no one of which is more or less advanced than any other.

The area of language about which it is easiest to imagine a steady evolutionary progression is vocabulary. Over the course of thousands and even millions of years, the capacity of the human mind to store and retrieve words has certainly increased dramatically. It is plausible to suppose that it increased at a fairly steady pace over a very long period, perhaps in proportion to the expanding size of the brain. Do we, however, find evidence among modern languages for differences in vocabulary size? The problems that make vocabulary difficult to count were reviewed in Chapter 2, but in one area, color terminology, a correlation does exist between the number of *basic* terms and the level of the society's technological complexity. Languages with only a few basic color terms do have alternative means for talking about colors, but if many areas of vocabulary expand in parallel with technological complexity as clearly as color terminology seems to expand, we might still have grounds for calling some languages more complex, or even more advanced, than others. Even if one area of terminology really is impoverished, however, a language may well compensate with a rich terminology in other areas. One example is the very large botanical vocabulary of the Hanunóo, hill farmers of the Philippines, that was noted in Chapter 2. We know that people easily develop new vocabulary whenever they have a need to talk about a new subject. We have not yet found a way to measure vocabulary size that would give us any basis for judging one language as, over all, more developed than another.

Thus using modern languages to provide a scale by which to extrapolate backwards to possible earlier and less-developed stages of language does not seem promising. We may still be tempted by two other lines of linguistic evidence: child language on the one hand, and pidgins and creoles on the other. Pidgin languages are, in some respects, simpler than other languages. If pidgins and creoles give us evidence of a human bio-program, it is conceivable that they could resemble an earlier stage of human language, a stage at which language had not yet been pulled away from the bio-program by the complex forces of history. The problems with such a view probably do not have to be spelled out.

We may be even more tempted by analogies between child language and linguistic evolution. There is a sense in which each human child must cross the same boundary that the entire species once crossed. Children begin life with their animal functions in good working order, but newborn infants do little that is specifically human. They eat, digest, and sleep, and they communicate their needs with cries, but so do all mammals. We can only speculate about the steps taken by the species as it acquired the ability to use language, but we can watch children as they acquire first words and then sentences along with all the other distinctive social and intellectual skills that go with talking.

We must not assume that a child passes through the same linguistic stages as the species once did, however. It is reasonable enough to look on the stages of a child's language as being a preparation for the full linguistic competence of adulthood, but we must never imagine that the intermediate evolutionary stages of language were a preparation for the "full" language we use today. Simple though the "languages" of some of our more remote ancestors may have been, they were the full communication systems of those who used them. Nevertheless, children do show us one path that leads from animal-like communication to full human language, and they demonstrate a whole series of intermediate forms of communication. We cannot observe the language of small children and simultaneously maintain that the gap between animal and human communication is unbridgeable. Every child bridges it.

LANGUAGE AND COGNITION

We are so accustomed to thinking of language as a system by which we communicate with other people that we are in danger of forgetting that we also use language as a private tool for sorting out our own thoughts. We may even spend more of our lives using language privately—thinking through problems and carrying on interior monologues—than we do speaking and listening to others. Not even sleep stops language. We may debate about whether or not we dream in color; no one doubts that we can dream in language.

Language and the workings of the human mind are so intricately interdependent that we even find it difficult to imagine what it would be like to think without language. How, we wonder, does a dog, an infant, or even a deaf mute who has never been exposed to signing manage to think? We feel that we need language to keep our thoughts in order. We need to give things names in order to keep them distinct in our minds. We manipulate words in lieu of manipulating the objects or performing the actions for which our words stand. It is considerably more difficult to draw a line between language and thought than to draw a line between language and nonverbal communication.

It has always seemed natural to study animal communication when looking for the evolutionary antecedents of language, but we might do even better to consider the workings of animal and human minds. Many of the cognitive prerequisites for language are well established among mammals, and they are particularly clear among apes. We might ask how apes use their minds, and how selection among our prelinguistic hominoid ancestors might have fostered increasingly refined cognition. We might look on language as a component of a growing intelligence rather than as an extension of an animal call system.

The single most crucial step on the way toward language may have been the ability to use symbols. A **symbol** is a conventional label that stands for something else, for an object or event in the world, perhaps, or for a mental image of an object or event. We can also recognize **signs,** like the panting of a dog, but signs have an inherent relationship to the thing they stand for. We learn that a dog is tired or hot because it pants, but panting is a physiological response to heat. A symbol has no such inherent connection with its meaning. Any arbitrary symbol can be assigned any arbitrary meaning. The words of human languages are symbols, and developing the ability to learn and use symbols was essential for the development of language.

Whether the first symbols were spoken or gestural does not seem crucial, but in some way and at some time, people began to assign conventional names to things and to use these names to convey meanings to others. This was a revolutionary event, but it was an event that rested crucially on cognitive abilities that are much older than language: the ability to recognize individuals, the ability to classify these individuals, and the ability to abstract away from some details so that objects and events can be recognized as the "same" in spite of their differences.

All mammals can classify. Dogs surely recognize some things as dogs, others as cats, and still others as people, or bones, or trees. Certainly dogs act differently toward representatives of these various classes. They also act consistently toward particular members of these classes. They recognize their own master, and they recognize a familiar cat. The obvious ability of animals to recognize both particular individuals and classes of individuals is an ability that is essential for naming, and thus for language.

Chimpanzees do better than monkeys or other mammals at sorting tasks that require classification. The young chimpanzee, Viki, was able to sort spoons, forks, screws, and buttons, and she could even separate pictures of animals from inanimate objects, people from animals, and adults from children. Apes are also better than other animals at solving the kinds of problems that humans devise for them. But, however clever apes are at the kinds of sorting and problem-solving challenges we burden them with, humans are even better. Once our ancestors stood up and adjusted to upright posture, the most consistent direction of human evolution was toward increasing intelligence, including a refined ability to classify the objects and events in the world, and the ability to manipulate concepts mentally as a way of solving problems. In the new environmental and ecological niches that humans entered, intelligence allowed people to learn new discriminations, to become more adaptable to varying kinds of surroundings, to substitute cunning for brawn. The several million years during which the brain expanded attest to the pressures that must have selected, steadily and insistently, ever more intelligent individuals.

Subtler discriminations, more insightful planning, and more elaborate learning ability might all have been assisted if the evolving mind had some symbol-like capacity or could make use of some sort of proto-symbols. These would have been useful as a way of grouping together whatever could be treated as the same, but keeping distinct what had to be separated. All animals must group some things and discriminate others, but grouping and discriminating are what symbols do best. Our earliest protosymbols might have been purely private, used internally as a means of keeping ideas from becoming tangled, but at some point some individuals might have found it helpful to make some external sign, gestural or vocal, as a reminder of the categories that they were trying to keep straight.

Symbolizing, then, could have begun, less as a way of communicating with other individuals, than as a way of organizing an individual's own thoughts. If some individuals ever used perceptible gestures or noises that reflected their mental images, other individuals would have found it advantageous to be able to understand them, and strong selective pressures would have favored those individuals who could understand the sounds or movements of others. From such beginnings it would have been but a small step to shared symbols that could be deliberately used to communicate. By such a scenario, symbols would develop from tools for manipulating ideas, but once externalized, these offshoots of the mind would come to be shared to allow the meeting of minds that is so characteristic of language as we know it. Symbols would have become a window on the mind, a way to gain an understanding of what others are thinking. Once externalized, symbols would inevitably become mixed with the nonverbal forms of communication already in use. The two systems could be expected to overlap and merge in a number of ways, but the evolutionary origins of the systems could have been quite separate.

Chimpanzees, and probably the other great apes, appear to have moved a good distance along this hypothetical evolutionary path, and perhaps we will learn more about the evolution of language by investigating how apes use their minds than by studying their calls or by arguing about their syntactic ability. Washoe and the other apes who have been taught to sign or to manipulate other symbols may persuade us that they have the ability to learn these symbols, although there is no evidence that they use symbols in their natural habitat. The chimpanzee ability to learn gestural or plastic symbols, however, would be mysterious if it did not rest on skills that were useful to an animal in its natural surroundings. Since chimpanzees are good at classifying and problem solving, it is plausible to suppose that they have better means than other animals of keeping track of mental representations of both objects and classes of objects. Their internal mental processes must depend on something more or less like symbols, for without such a cognitive base, it seems hard to imagine why chimpanzees would be able to learn symbols, or at least come so close to learning symbols, under human tutelage. Chimpanzees in the wild do not, as far as we can tell, externalize symbols in a way that would allow another animal to "read" them, but their handling of symbols when instructed by humans suggests they are not far from that ability.

Intelligence would have been at a premium in a species whose members had minds similar to those of chimpanzees but who were leaving the security of the trees behind and who were struggling to solve new and more varied problems in an unfamiliar and more threatening savannah environment. Selection would insistently favor those who could foresee and solve problems and those who could learn by experience. The most intelligent individuals, using all the mental resources at their command, might have begun to make movements or noises as a means of helping to keep track of the many variables that entered into the puzzles presented by their world. As soon as others began to understand these movements or noises, the path toward language would have been opened. At once there would have been a new selective pressure for ever better communicative ability. A better ability to communicate would have fed back to select for a better mental ability as well. Always, better language would have been associated with a better mind, a better ability to classify, a better ability to remember, a better ability to anticipate and to solve problems. Symbols that were revolutionizing the organization of the mind could also come to be used for communicating with other minds. Primate calls may have had very little to do with any of this process.

This scenario is nothing if not speculative, but we need to speculate if we are to have ideas about what kind of evidence to look for next. At a minimum, this argument should make us cautious about too easily assuming that language could have come from nowhere except from primate calls.

THE EFFECTS OF LANGUAGE

Whatever selective pressures may have encouraged the evolution of the human capacity for language, and whatever stages developing language may have passed through, we can have no doubt that language has helped to turn human beings into a unique species, strangely different from any other that has existed on earth. Little that is human is not, in some degree, dependent on language, and in concluding this chapter we can consider a few of the ways that language has helped to make us different.

Language modulates every human relationship. Even the vocabulary we use to describe our relationships suggests how important a place language has in our dealings with people. We *accuse, advise, answer, challenge, claim, demand, deny, discuss, describe, encourage, explain, flirt, insult, invite, joke, lie, negotiate, object, promise, pretend, question, reject, request, refuse, teach, learn, threaten, warn, woo,* and a great deal more, all with the help of language. Language lubricates, when it does not clog, all the wheels of human interaction.

The extra complexity that language introduces into our personal relationships lets us pursue more complex strategies and build more complex societies than can any other animal. Language gives us the means to keep track of distant kinsmen, and this gives us an extensive set of potential allies. Many animals recognize close kin, and we know many examples of related animals assisting one another, but humans can reckon relationships further and organize relationships in more complex ways than any other species. Kinship must have been the primary principle by which people organized themselves in the societies in which human evolution occurred, and as language grew more complex, so could kinship systems. Later, the ability to keep track of large numbers of people was a prerequisite for the even more complex societies that we live in today.

Language can help us to avoid, or at least to postpone, violence. Chimpanzees often live in peace with their fellows. Males can cooperate and even form close alliances with one another. But males sometimes quarrel viciously, and we now know that they are also capable of grisly violence, even of what, in human terms, we are tempted to call "murder." Males compete, and sometimes they fight over access to resources and especially over females. Two or more individuals sometimes gang up on another, and in extreme cases allied males have been known to kill an outnumbered enemy.

If we find this behavior disturbing, it is because it is all too familiar from our own human experience, but we do have one means that apes lack, of avoiding, or at least postponing, this kind of violence. An outnumbered man who is threatened with death by his enemies is no more capable of physical self-defense than an outnumbered chimpanzee, but he may be able to remind his attackers that, even if he is killed, he has brothers back home who will avenge his death. People can talk through the consequences of their actions. They can calculate possible outcomes, and sometimes this lets them substitute talk for violence. Whether the overall level of human violence is lower as a result of such calculations is surely doubtful. Perhaps we succeed only in postponing violence so that we can finally focus it into the particularly destructive episodes that we call "war," for if language allows us to avoid some kinds of relatively small-scale violence, it also gives us the means to organize our societies for our own unique forms of mass slaughter. Still, the difference between animal and human potential is clear.

Language is an unusual form of behavior in being both *shared* with other individuals and *learned*. Shared behavior and learned behavior are both widespread among animals, but behavior that is simultaneously shared and learned is not common. Communication would not be possible if its principles were not shared with other individuals, of course, but most animal forms of communication are, as we have seen, inherited as part of the genetic endowment of each individual, so they do not have to be learned. Many other aspects of an animal's behavior do require learning, but most of these do not have to be shared in the way that a communication system must be shared. In many species, for example, each animal learns its territorial boundaries, but since animals have separate territories, their territorial knowledge varies and does not need to be generally shared.

The few million years within which the ability to use language evolved was not enough time to build all the characteristics of a language into the genetic inheritance of the species. The only way we could acquire such a complex skill as language in this relatively short period was to rely on learning to complete the job. The brain had to evolve in a way that would allow it to learn a language, but many of the details could be left to learning rather than being built into our genes. Unlike mammalian communication, then, a language has to be learned. Unlike territorial knowledge, the knowledge of a language also has to be shared with other individuals.

The songs of some birds are the best-known animal example of behavior that is both shared and learned. It is hardly a coincidence that bird songs, like language, are used for communication, for it is their communicative use that requires the songs to be shared. Since the songs of some species of birds also have a learned component, they are, like language, traditional. They can be passed on from one individual to another, and individual birds that live in the same neighborhood share features of their dialect. It is this double quality of being both learned and shared that makes language, like bird songs, a traditional form of behavior, a kind of behavior that is subject to cultural variation. Because we must talk with each other, we need a language that resembles the language of our neighbors and our kinsmen. Because language must be learned, people who have no need to communicate can learn very different languages.

By evolving into the kind of animal that is capable of sustaining differing linguistic traditions, we may also have become the kind of animal that can sustain other kinds of variable traditions. We are, of course, capable of passing on cultural traditions of every sort. Not only our language but also our kinship practices, our religion, our ideas about government, our art, and our technology—everything we do or care about—is culturally variable. It is tempting for a linguist to speculate that it was the need to learn the cultural tradition of language that has given us, as a byproduct, the ability to learn and share so much else.

Linguists sometimes suggest that learning a language amounts to building a theory of the language. Like little linguists, children have to discover the nature of their community's language. They are exposed to a mass of quite raw data and make increasingly successful generalizations about the way in which this data is organized. We can imagine children to be making a series of hypotheses or guesses about how the language works, and then testing these guesses as they grope toward a more refined theory of the language. This amounts to theory building, and if this is a fair way to characterize the way in which we learn language, it suggests that the ability to build theories might be another byproduct of language.

When we speak of building theories, we think first of scientific theories, but even people who lack modern science have always been inveterate constructors of theories. The deliberate search for theories and the deliberate testing of these theories against data that we know as "science" is a relatively recent and still rather unusual intellectual enterprise. Other theories that are less deliberately constructed and tested are known everywhere. We now give the name "religion" to many of the theories that have helped humans to explain the world and to understand the place of human beings in the world, but like scientific theories, the doctrines that we label religious help people to make sense of the vagaries of nature and of humankind. They bring a kind of order to the world that lies around and within us and that is not always as orderly as we would like. A linguist must be tempted by the idea that it could have been language, and the necessity of building a theory of language, that turned us into such enthusiastic builders of theories. Human beings are unable to refrain from searching for explanations.

Perhaps this is claiming too much for language. Admittedly it expresses a language-centered view of humankind, a view that may be especially appealing to linguists. It is not too much to recognize the importance of language to all theory building and to point out that we always use language when we state and teach our theories. Simple technology can be conveyed by demonstration and imitation. Theories about the nature of the world must be conveyed by language. Religious doctrines, as much as scientific theories, must always be expressed in language. The most elegant of modern theories are now stated in mathematical form, but even this amounts to a special kind of language. Only a talking animal could have invented such a refined form of language as mathematics.

Language even gives us the power to create our own worlds. We give names to the objects in the world around us, but we also bring other things into existence by the very act of naming. We create elaborate kinship systems and cosmologies. We populate our world with ghosts, spirits, elves, and all manner of gods. We invent concepts like *honor* and *truth, good* and *evil.* None of these could exist without the language that lets us name them and describe their features. Unlike simple technology, these ideas cannot be taught by pointing, but only through the medium of language. Nevertheless, these ideas become as real and important to us as the tangible objects that we can see and touch, so important that people have been willing to die for them.

CHAPTER SEVENTEEN

Language and Civilization

WRITING

The first 16 chapters of this book have been concerned almost exclusively with spoken language. Now, at last, something also needs to be said about writing and about the effects of writing. This chapter will consider a few of the techniques that allow languages to be conveyed in other ways than by speech, including not only writing by hand but also by printing and electronics. It will also suggest a few of the effects that these varied media have had on the societies in which we live.

Someone who lacked all knowledge of writing, but who wanted to convey a message by painting on a cave wall or by scratching on birch bark, would probably start by drawing pictures. Pictures might offer a promising way to communicate ideas before an abstract representation of a spoken language could even be imagined. Many nonliterate people have used pictures as an aid to their memory or as a means to suggest a story. Even today, when the spoken language of the reader cannot be known, we still use diagrams and pictures. Pictorial directions for operating new gadgets, as well as the international conventions for highway signs, can be understood equally well, or badly, by speakers of English, Hungarian, or Japanese. No one, however, has been ingenious enough to devise a system of pictures and diagrams that can express everything that we express with words. As a result, the most flexible forms of written communication have always been based on spoken language, and the word "writing" can most usefully be reserved for systems in which the symbols represent either the words or the sounds of speech. Pictorial systems, like highway signs, in which the symbols stand for ideas rather than for language, are best excluded from the definition of writing.

Spoken language is built up from units of increasing scope, from distinctive features, phonemes, and syllables, through morphemes and words, to sentences and even longer stretches of discourse. We can use the word **graph** to refer to any unit of a written language and, in principle, a single graph could be used to represent any stretch of speech from a distinctive feature to an entire sentence or more. Since there is no limit to the number of sentences in a language, it would, of course, be quite impossible to have a unique graph for every possible sentence. Some writing systems have had distinct symbols for many thousands of words, but even words occur in so many tens of thousands that no practical writing system could have a separate graph for every one of them. Languages have fewer morphemes than they have words, so a distinct graph for each morpheme is a more realistic possibility.

Writing in which the graphs stand for meaningful units of language, whether words or morphemes, is called **logographic.** If a purely logographic script were to come close to representing everything that can be said in the spoken language, it would need thousands of distinct graphs for the thousands of distinct morphemes of the spoken language, a daunting challenge to human memory. Memory can be helped by pictorial graphs that suggest the meaning of the words or morphemes they stand for, and pictorial symbols seem to be an easy way to enlarge the repertory of graphs. Pictures are not enough, however, because many of the most common morphemes of any spoken language, in particular the functional morphemes that bind the content words together, are difficult or impossible to represent by pictures. A flexible writing system needs symbols for function words and for words with abstract meanings that cannot easily be pictured. These can be represented by arbitrary graphs, but learning hundreds or thousands of them becomes a terrible burden for anyone who wants to be literate.

The only way to ease this burden is to reach down to the phonological level of the language, and to symbolize its sounds. At a minimum, all the practical writing systems that we know about have supplemented their logographs with at least a few symbols that represent the sounds of language. The graphs of some writing systems represent entire syllables, and others represent units of approximately the scope of a phoneme, but in either case, such writing systems are called **phonographic.** Phonographic writing demands a considerably more abstract analysis of the spoken language than does logographic writing. Nevertheless, the difficulty of devising separate symbols for thousands of nonpicturable words and morphemes pushes every practical writing system to exploit the phonographic principle.

The simplest way to represent the sounds of nonpicturable words is by rebus writing reminiscent of children's games. *I* can be represented by a picture of an *eye, can* by a picture of a (tin) *can,* and *not* by a picture of a *knot.* An entire phrase of nonpicturable words can then be easily expressed in pictures, as in Figure 17–1.

Rebus writing was the crucial first step that permitted nonpicturable words and morphemes to be symbolized by their sounds. All early systems of full

Figure 17–1
Rebus writing.

writing used some rebuses, so all were partially phonographic, though they continued to use many logographs as well. Such scripts remained mixed. Logographs were sometimes sufficiently pictorial to suggest their meaning, but they implied nothing about pronunciation. From the time of the earliest full writing, however, logographs were supplemented by other written symbols that represented sounds.

The earliest known writing is from Sumer, an early urban civilization of lower Mesopotamia, located in modern Iraq. Like later Mesopotamians, the Sumerians wrote by impressing marks on clay, the only local material that they possessed in abundance. Sumerian writing began a bit before 3000 BC, and the first column of Figure 17–2 shows the earliest form of several of its graphs. Sumerian writing had the peculiarity that a single graph was sometimes made to stand for several different words of related meaning. Thus a star-like graph stood for both *an* 'heaven' and *dingir* 'god.' The words *ka* 'mouth,' and *dug* 'speak' could both be shown by a head with the area of the mouth highlighted. A single graph was used for both *sal* 'pudendum' and *munus* 'woman.' Some words were symbolized by combining graphs for other words. The graph for *geme* 'slave girl' suggests a 'woman from the mountains.' The graphs for 'eat' and for 'drink' combine a head with, respectively, the graph for 'food' (perhaps a picture of a bowl) and the graph for 'water.' The pictorial nature of these graphs is obvious. Pictures were easier to learn than arbitrary symbols, but the pictures stood for words, units of the spoken language, not for abstract ideas.

In some of the earliest Sumerian writing, the function words were not represented at all. This resulted in a sort of telegraphic style in which the content words had to convey all the meaning, but early Sumerian writing was used primarily for administrative and commercial purposes, such as for lists, inventories, and records of commercial transactions. The writers were able to record these matters with little or no grammatical apparatus.

As the use of writing expanded, a fuller representation of the language was needed, and the rebus principle was exploited. The graph for the word *a* that meant 'water' was also used for the homophonous but less easily picturable word *a* that meant 'in.' The graph for *ti* 'arrow' was extended to the similar sounding *til* 'life.' Phonographic symbols like these were used extensively for place names, and they also began to be added to logographic symbols to avoid

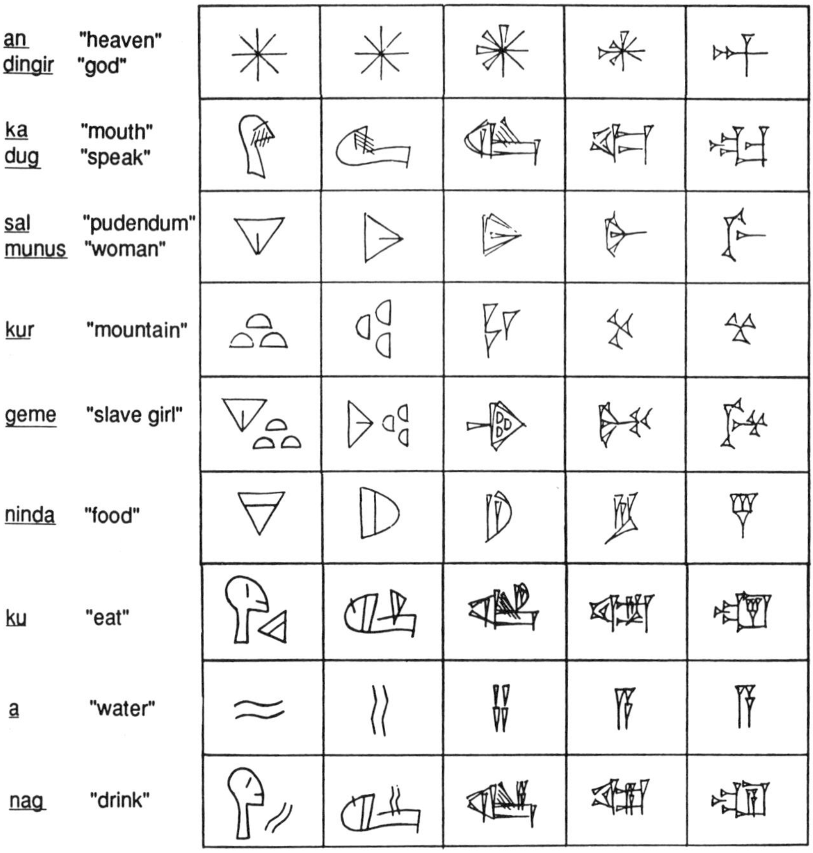

an dingir	"heaven" "god"					
ka dug	"mouth" "speak"					
sal munus	"pudendum" "woman"					
kur	"mountain"					
geme	"slave girl"					
ninda	"food"					
ku	"eat"					
a	"water"					
nag	"drink"					

Figure 17–2
Sumerian written symbols. From Kramer (1963).

ambiguities. Thus *an* 'heaven' and *dingir* 'god' were both represented by the same logographic picture of a star, but they could be differentiated by adding the phonographic symbols for *na* or *ra,* which suggested the final sounds of *an* and *dingir,* respectively.

Early Sumerian writing, then, gave both pictorial and phonological hints about which word a graph might stand for, but with the passage of time, the pictorial value of the graphs was gradually eroded. Figure 17–2 shows Sumerian graphs at several successive stages. For reasons that remain obscure, the graphs were first rotated by 90 degrees, as shown in the second column. Then in the first half of the third millennium BC, a blunt stylus replaced the older pointed stylus as the writing instrument, and the new stylus encouraged the more stylized forms of "cuneiform" writing shown in the third column. This consisted of wedge-shaped impressions in the clay that were not easily used to construct realistic pictures. The final column in Fig. 17–2 shows the forms used in about 1800 BC, the period that left the largest number of Sumerian literary documents. By this time, the graphs had been stylized well beyond any possible recognition. Ease of rapid writing triumphed over the ease of recognition. The same transformation from pictorial to arbitrary graphs occurred several times in the history of writing. The Egyptian hieroglyphics that were carved in stone on monuments stayed conservative enough to retain their pictorial quality, but cursive equivalents of the hieroglyphics were written on papyrus, and these became totally obscure. Deprived of pictorial aids to memory and with many hundreds of arbitrary graphs, the writing systems of the ancient Near East were formidably difficult to learn.

Chinese writing began somewhat later than Sumerian writing, and scholars are not agreed about whether it developed in full independence from the Near East. It is possible that the idea of writing traveled to China from the Near East, but the graphs used for Chinese show no specific similarities with earlier written graphs, and Chinese writing may be an entirely independent invention. In any case, the development of Chinese writing does show a number of striking parallels with Sumerian and other forms of early Near Eastern writing.

The oldest surviving examples of written Chinese were scratched on bones and tortoise shells that were used in divination. These date from between 1200 and 1400 BC, but the system was so elaborate by then that it must already have passed through a long period of development. As shown in Figure 17–3, many of the earliest Chinese characters were pictorial. By the time the writing system assumed its permanent form, at about the beginning of the modern era, the characters had been adapted to rapid writing with a brush, and most of them had become highly stylized. Only a tiny proportion of modern characters retain any trace of pictorial representation. 口 *kŏu* "mouth" is a picture of a mouth that has been squared off to conform to the angular style of written Chinese. 人 *rén* 'man' represents a pair of human legs. 門 *mén* 'door, gate' still looks a bit like a pair of swinging doors. 木 *mù* 'tree' has a vertical trunk and some branches. A few other characters are diagrammatic, if not exactly pictorial: 一 *yi* 'one,' 二 *èr* 'two,' 三 *sàn* 'three,' 上 *shàng* 'above,' 下 *syà* 'below.' A few characters suggest more complex pictures. 日 *ri* 'sun' is a conventionalized sun, kept distinct from 'mouth' by the central horizontal line. 東 *dong* 'east' shows the sun behind a tree, as it might be seen at dawn.

As is true of many tone languages, Chinese syllables are salient phonological units, and Chinese characters almost always represent exactly one syllable. Typically, these syllables are meaningful units of the language, sometimes words, sometimes morphemes that form parts of larger words, so the characters usually stand for meaningful bits of the language. No more than the Sumerians could the Chinese get along without representing their sounds, however, and like the Sumerians they resorted to the rebus principle. It is a principle that can still be seen in many modern characters.

The great majority of the characters have two parts. One part, known as the "radical," sometimes gives a hint about the meaning of the syllable it represents. The other part is a "phonetic" sign that, somewhat more often, gives a

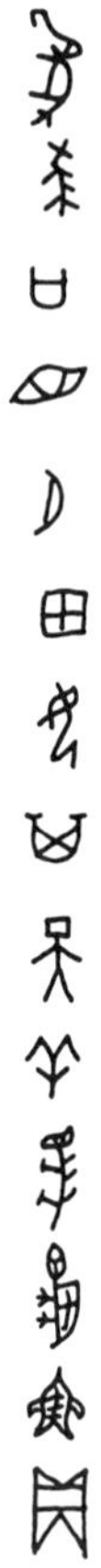

	ancient graph	modern character	modern pronunciation	meaning
1.	象	象	xiàng	"elephant"
2.	求	求	qiú	"pelt"
3.	口	口	kǒu	"opening, orifice, mouth"
4.	目	目	mù	"eye"
5.	月	月	yuè	"moon, month"
6.	田	田	tián	"(cultivated) field"
7.	女	女	nǚ	"(kneeling) woman"
8.	其	其	qí	"(winnowing) basket"
9.	天	天	tiān	"overhead" > "sky, heaven"
10.	羊	羊	yáng	"sheep, ram"
11.	馬	馬	mǎ	"horse"
12.	龜	龜	guī	"turtle"
13.	魚	魚	yú	"fish"
14.	鼎	鼎	dǐng	"tripod, cauldron"

Figure 17–3
Early and modern Chinese written symbols. From Boltz, (1986).

hint about its pronunciation. 們 *mén* is a plural marker for pronouns. It can be used with 我 *wǒ* 'I,' to form the plural pronoun 我們 *wǒ mén* 'we.' The left part of 們 is the radical, and it is a modification of the character for 'man,' in which the human legs of 人 *rén* have been stylized beyond recognition. Characters with this radical often stand for words that have something to do with people. The phonetic of 們 is at the right, and when used by itself as 門 it is *mén* 'door.' Here is the rebus principle at work, for 們 can be understood as suggesting ''a morpheme that sounds like the word for 'door' but that has something to do with people." Of the two parts, the phonetic half gives the better hint of what the morpheme might be, and it is misleading to suppose that a character like 們 is simply a logographic symbol that stands for a morpheme meaning plural. It is more accurate to say that it is a phonographic symbol that stands for the syllable pronounced *mén*, but that is kept distinct from a homophonous syllable by its radical. 悶 *mèn* 'melancholy, depressed' combines the same phonetic sign with a radical meaning 'heart' that is tucked in at the bottom of the phonetic. This word differs in pronunciation from 'door' only in tone, and the character suggests "the word that sounds rather like 'door' but that stands for something to do with the emotions." 問 *wèn* 'ask about' has the same phonetic sign, but its radical is a mouth, appropriate for a character whose meaning concerns language.

The fact that each character stands for one syllable and that syllables are often meaningful units of the language, along with the manner in which the characters are arranged on paper, has contributed to the misleading idea that Chinese is a "monosyllabic" language. In fact Chinese has many words and even a good many morphemes that are more than one syllable long and, unless an abbreviation is used, these words need to be represented by more than one character. Like any language, Chinese has a great many homophonous syllables, and the most difficult aspect of Chinese writing is that these homophonous syllables are written with many different characters, depending on which word they appear in. It is as if in writing English we needed to write *can* in different ways not only in 'tin *can*' and '*can*not' but also in 'un *can*ny' and '*can*dy.' On the analogy with Chinese, we might use the same phonetic for each of these syllables, but in each case we would have to join it to a different radical. This means that a character can never be chosen on the basis of pronunciation alone. In favorable cases a reader can sometimes use the phonetic half of a character to figure out what syllable it stands for. A writer needs to remember the radical as well.

In the course of the millennia in which Chinese has been written, most characters have become as stylized as Sumerian graphs, so that pictorial hints no longer offer any help to the reader. The pronunciation of the language has undergone extensive changes since the writing was established, and this has also undermined the reliability of the phonetic signs. As a result, many characters have become entirely arbitrary representations of their syllables, and anyone who wants to become literate must simply memorize them. The many thousands of characters used in Chinese writing are a serious burden on the learner's memory, but it would be wrong to imagine that Chinese is a purely logographic writing system. A reader who encounters an unknown character has a better chance of identifying it from its phonetic half than from its radical. To the extent that the characters represent sounds, however, they represent entire syllables rather than phonemes. Phonographic writing systems in which entire syllables are symbolized are called **syllabaries** to distinguish them from alphabetic systems in which the units symbolized are closer to phonemes. Chinese writing uses an imperfect syllabary rather than an alphabet.

People with no vested interest in a writing system such as Chinese or the similarly complex writing systems of the ancient Near East may despair at the conservatism of people who cling to cumbersome and archaic conventions. Simple phonographic scripts have been designed for Chinese that would be much easier to learn than the traditional characters, but not even the upheaval of Chinese communism was enough to do more than legitimize a number of simplified characters that can be made with fewer strokes than the older forms. English speakers, who live with a cumbersome spelling system that takes years to master, should have no trouble understanding the forces that make writing conservative. English-speaking adults who are already comfortably literate have a vested interest in their traditional system of writing, and they would gain nothing by a new spelling. Children, foreigners, and the poorly educated would profit, but it is not they who have the power to introduce the changes. To most literate speakers of English, simplified spelling looks childish, and they want no part of it. They are even likely to have gained a fondness for their familiar script, and they can always find reasons for rejecting crass simplifications. Every Chinese character is a work of art, and no one lightly abandons ancient art. In some cases, the very complexity of a writing system is valued, for it protects the power of those who have already mastered it. People who have spent years learning to read and write may have no desire to share their precious skills with large numbers of new readers. Most literate Chinese are no more attracted by the prospect of a revised orthography than are most literate speakers of English.

We should, moreover, be cautious about too easily seeing a writing system like Chinese as a terrible handicap. The Japanese, whose writing system has elements that make it, in some respects, even more complex than Chinese, have achieved a literacy rate higher than that of the United States. Clearly, a purely alphabetic and phonographic writing system is not a prerequisite for formidable educational achievement. The Chinese writing system, moreover, has one great virtue that no purely phonographic script could match. Several mutually unintelligible spoken languages are used in China, but their speakers all write in the same way. Modern Chinese writing is better adapted to Mandarin than to other Chinese "dialects," but written Chinese does serve as a unifying national language in a way that would be far more difficult for a purely phonographic writing system that was unambiguously based on a single dialect. Today, literate Chinese can understand each other's writing, even when they cannot understand each other's speech. A "better" phonographic script could undermine the Chinese sense of their own linguistic unity.

WRITING AND THE URBAN REVOLUTION

Writing began in Sumer in the centuries just before 3000 BC, and it appeared in Egypt soon after. This was the time when people first began to live in communities that were large enough to be called cities. Specialists in technical crafts, in ceremony, and in government lived in these cities. A division of labor was developed and a system of trade and exchange invented that, for the first time, allowed some of these city dwellers to abandon farming and to rely on food imported from the surrounding villages. Writing was a central component of this transformation in human life that we call the Urban Revolution, and writing helped to allow the emergence of new ideas and new forms of society. The earliest writing reflected the new economic order in which goods were stockpiled and exchanged. It was in no way "literary," but mostly concerned buying and selling, rent and taxes. It was inventories, bills of sale, and lists of goods and their prices that were recorded.

Along with economic and administrative records, the earliest surviving examples of writing include lists of words. These amounted to the first dictionaries, and they were probably made by students or for the benefit of students. They were a means of imparting the complex skills of literacy, for reading and writing required a kind of formal education that was different from anything village farmers had ever needed. The skills of a farmer could be learned by watching and imitating. Literacy required schools, and ever since the time of the Sumerians, schools have always had reading and writing at the core of their curriculum. Only a few specialists mastered the early scripts, but they, or the people who employed and controlled them, gained power at the expense of the unlettered majority. In a society where no one could write, illiteracy was no hardship. When a small minority could monopolize writing, this minority acquired a new means of control.

The cities of the ancient Near East were the first human communities that were too large for everyone to have close personal ties with everyone else. Disputes among urban strangers could no longer be settled by methods suitable for village neighbors. Where long-standing tradition and intimate mutual acquaintance could not be taken for granted, codified rules became a useful way to define human relationships, and law codes were soon set down in writing.

Law codes were a response to the impersonalization of the new cities, but writing had other implications that led to an increased recognition of the individual and thus had effects that were quite the opposite of impersonalization. The stories and myths of an oral tradition can be repeated many times by word of mouth, but the name of the original author is usually quickly forgotten. Even in our own literate times, oral jokes circulate so anonymously that we rarely know or care where they started or who composed them. When a language is written down, it can more easily carry its author's name. A written text can be copied, just as a spoken story can be repeated, but the author's name is more likely to travel with something written. Writing can give a new recognition to the individual composer of words.

Ideas that are codified in writing can encourage a new kind of dogmatism. People may develop a mystical faith in the written word. When something has been written, especially if it can be attributed to revered ancestors, people can be persuaded that it must represent a special kind of truth. When writing becomes a substitute for feeble human memory, it can be called on to give dogmatic support for traditional precedents. The written word can be used uncritically to justify beliefs and actions. When historical precedent looms in the background, it can become more difficult to adjust action to the pragmatic needs of the moment.

At the same time, and even in a somewhat contradictory way, writing can be a tool that supports clear critical thinking. The force of an orator's personality or social position may limit the ability of listeners to resist persuasion. Once the orator's words are written down, their persuasive power must rely more on logic and accurate facts, for the contradictions of a weak argument are more easily perceived when written than when only presented orally. Written facts can be more easily checked. Poor logic and internal contradictions stand out more clearly. A reader can survey an argument carefully, consider it from various angles, and think through its implications. Thus even though writing could foster dogma, it could also sharpen critical thinking, and it could even foster a degree of skepticism.

With the storage and accumulation of knowledge that came with writing, systematic science became possible. Astronomical tables were compiled, eclipses predicted, and the foundations of mathematics, established. The amount of stored knowledge began to grow, and its growth has never stopped. A new division of knowledge accompanied the new division of labor. Ever since the time when knowledge first began to accumulate in writing, each human being has been limited to an ever-shrinking proportion of the total that is known.

Linguists have always insisted that spoken language occurs both logically and chronologically prior to writing. All writing is, to a large extent, based on speaking and secondary to it. Nevertheless, once a writing system has become well established, it develops a tradition and a momentum of its own. It can acquire considerable independence from the spoken language on which it was originally based, and even the earliest writing systems influenced the spoken languages that they represented. From the beginning of writing, languages and dialects that had written forms gained in prestige at the expense of those that were only spoken. People had an extra incentive to learn languages that were written, for they offered more than just a way of talking with a few more people. A written language gave access to existing records and offered people a way to keep their own records. It is convenient to be able to keep records in one's own language, but if records are to be read by others, it is even more important to keep them in a language that others will understand. Often it is desirable to write in the language that is accessible to the largest number of readers. People even find it practical or prestigious to speak a language that is written. Writing, therefore, has always encouraged a few languages to spread at the expense of others.

Even today, the greatest linguistic diversity is found in the areas of the world where writing has come most recently. New Guinea and sub-Saharan Africa both have hundreds of distinct languages. Writing was missing from most of the Americas until the European conquest, and both North and South America were linguistically heterogeneous. Europe, the Near East, and the Far East, where writing has a long history, have fewer languages, each spoken by larger numbers of people. India and Southeast Asia lie between these extremes. They have a few languages with long literary traditions, each spoken by many millions of people, but hundreds of other languages survive in marginal areas where writing has only recently penetrated.

Every written language began by representing a spoken language. Talk came first; writing started as a way of recording talk. Nevertheless, people often come to look on the marks on paper, clay, papyrus, or parchment as more "real" than the sounds of their own voices. With its prestige and its relative permanence, people easily come to think of the written language as more basic, even "better" or more "correct," than the ephemeral language of speech. Where their own spoken forms differ from the conventions of writing, people may feel that it is their spoken language that is wrong, and they may try to change their speech to adjust to the norms of writing. In this way writing also affects spoken language and encourages its standardization. From its first invention, writing has always strengthened some languages, some dialects, some grammatical patterns, some words, and even some pronunciations. Competing forms have been correspondingly undermined.

THE ALPHABET

In centuries preceding 1000 BC, speakers of Semitic languages who lived east of the Mediterranean Sea invented the alphabet, the first fully phonographic writing system and the direct ancestor of the alphabet we still use today. Most Semitic alphabets, among them Phoenician and Hebrew, had just 22 letters (see Figure 17–4). The letters occurred in a fixed order, and each was named by a word that began with the sound represented by the letter, as if the names of our first three letters were *apple, box,* and *cat.* The first letter of the Semitic alphabets stood for a glottal stop. The Hebrew name for this letter was *ʔālep,* and the name came from the word *ʔelep* 'ox' that began with a glottal stop. The shapes of the letters may originally have been conventionalized pictures of the same objects, or at least it is tempting to see pictures in a few of them. The word for 'eye' was *ʕaijin.* It is easy to see a picture of an eye in the circle that stood for a pharyngeal consonant, and whose name was also *ʕaijin.*

The 22 letters of the early Semitic alphabets all stood for consonants, but these were enough to write all the words of the language. This was a brilliant simplification from the thousands of symbols required by older logographic scripts. Symbols that stood for entire morphemes or words were dispensed with in favor of a mere 22 letters. To people who are accustomed to writing vowels as well as consonants, scripts that are limited to consonants must seem to be seriously handicapped: *Hwvr y cn stll rd wrtng tht dsnt hv vls, thgh t cn b rthr dfclt t frst f y rnt ccstmd t sch wrtng.* It would be hopeless to read the same sentence with only the vowels: *oee ou a i ea ii a oe ae owe ou i a e ae iiu a i i ou a auoe o u ii.* Consonants are more salient than vowels (when children first learn to write, they more often omit vowels than consonants), and in spite of occasional ambiguities, it is entirely possible to represent a language without symbols for the vowels. If we imagine that adding vowels to consonants gives us a complete representation of the sounds of our language, we should remember that we are no better at transcribing stress and intonation than the early Semitic writers were at transcribing vowels. No system of writing represents all the sounds of the spoken language.

It is probably no accident that the alphabet was developed on the margins of the older states where earlier scripts were already well established. The people who invented and used the new alphabet must have known about older, more prestigious and complex forms of writing, but they had no vested interest in them. They used their alphabet for mundane practical record keeping, where an easily learned system had clear advantages. Today, three thousand years after its invention, several of the 22 Phoenician letters can still be recognized in our own alphabet. As shown in Figure 17–4, many of our letters have similar shapes, and several still have similar phonetic values. Even the order of the letters has survived.

The Greeks took over the Semitic alphabet and adapted it to their own, quite different, language. The earliest Greek alphabets retained the shapes of the Semitic letters, their standard order, and even many of their names. Most of the letters also retained their approximate phonetic value, but the Semitic languages had several consonant sounds that were not found in Greek, and the symbols for these consonants could be reassigned to new sounds. For example, Greek had no glottal stop and no need of a symbol for it. The Semitic *ʔālep,* could then be redefined as a vowel. It became the Greek *alpha* and, later, our own *A*. Similarly, the fifth letter of the Phoenician alphabet stood for a breathy h-like consonant that the Greeks did not have, so it could also be redefined as a vowel. It became the Greek *epsilon* and the ancestor of our own *E*. With the invention of vowels, the Greeks developed a writing system that had the most important characteristics of modern European alphabets.

The Greeks passed the alphabet on to the Etruscans, and from the Etruscans, it reached the Romans. The Romans developed a monumental letter style, used especially for carving on stone, and this style has been retained virtually unchanged until today. We quite properly refer to our own alphabet as "Roman," though several letters have been added since Roman times. The Romans used *I* and *V* to represent both vowels and consonants, but in the Middle Ages, alternative forms of these letters were developed. *I* eventually split into modern *I* and *J,* while *V* split three ways into *U, V,* and *W.*

Of greater importance was the separation of upper- and lower-case letters. Most well-established writing systems develop somewhat distinct styles for quick handwriting and for careful monumental inscriptions. Different letter shapes are appropriate for stone, clay, and parchment, and for chisel, stylus, brush, and pen, but neither Phoenicians, ancient Greeks, nor Romans ever mixed two different styles in the same document. Our modern lower-case or

Semitic			Hebrew		Greek			Roman
↟	ʔ	ʔelep 'ox'	א	ʔālep	A	alpha	/ă, ā/	A
⌐	b	bajit 'house'	ב	bēt	B	beta	/b/	B
∧	g	gāmāl 'camel'	ג	gīmel	Γ	gamma	/g/	C
△	d	delet 'door'	ד	dālet	Δ	delta	/d/	D
⋻	h	?	ה	hē	E	epsilon	/ĕ/	E
Y	w	wāw 'hook'	ו	wāw	F	wau	/w/	F
I	z	zajin 'weapon'	ז	zajin	Z	zeta	/z/	G
Ⱶ	ħ	?	ח	ħēt	H	eta	/ǣ/	H
⊕	ṭ	?	ט	ṭēt	Θ	theta	/tʰ/	
⟨	j	jād 'hand'	י	jōd	I	iota	/ĭ, ī/	I
⟩	k	kap 'cupped hand'	כ ך	kāp	K	kappa	/k/	K
ℓ	l	lāmad 'to study'	ל	lāmed	Λ	lambda	/l/	L
⟩⟩	m	majim 'water'	מ ם	mēm	M	mu	/m/	M
⟩	n	ʔnūn 'fish'	נ ן	nūn	N	nu	/n/	N
⧧	s	ʔsāmak 'fulcrum'	ס	sāmek	Ξ	xi	/ks/	
o	ʕ	ʕajin 'eye'	ע	ʕajin	O	omicron	/o/	O
⟩	p	pe 'mouth'	פ ף	pē	Π	pi	/p/	P
⟩⟩	ç	?	צ ץ	çādē	M	san	/s/	
φ	q	qōp 'ape'	ק	qōp	Ϙ	koppa	/k/	Q
⟨	r	rōš 'head'	ר	rēš	P	rho	/r/	R
w	š,ś	śēn 'tooth'	ש	šin	Σ	sigma	/s/	S
✝	t	tāw 'mark'	ת	tāw	T	tau	/t/	T
					Υ	upsilon	/ y̆, ȳ /	Y
					Φ	phi	/pʰ/	
					X	chi	/kʰ/	X
					Ψ	psi	/ps/	Y
					Ω	omega	/ō/	Z

Figure 17–4
The alphabet. From Sampson (1985).

"minuscule" letters are derived from an earlier cursive style that was used for writing on parchment. Upper-case or "majuscule" letters are derived from the Roman monumental style. "Capital" letters first found their way into manuscripts as elaborate or decorative initials, but they were gradually mixed with minuscule letters until they became an essential part of our written language. Curiously it is now possible to write some short documents entirely in upper case letters, the style that was originally restricted to monuments, while documents are almost never written entirely in lower-case letters, the style once used for manuscripts.

The alphabet traveled not only westward and northward to Rome and Western Europe, but to the northeast and southeast as well. The modern Cyrillic alphabet, used for Russian, Bulgarian, and Serbian, is derived more directly from Greek than is our Roman alphabet. A number of Cyrillic letters still have a recognizably Greek shape. Derivatives of Greek pi π, rho ρ, and delta Δ can be seen in the name of the Russian newspaper:ПРАВДА 'PRAVDA.' Arabic and Hebrew, the two most important living Semitic languages, are written with more radically modified versions of the old Semitic alphabet. Arabic writing developed from a flowing cursive style and, even when Arabic is printed, the letters are connected as letters often are in handwriting. Hebrew evolved into a very different squared-up style, but the Arabic and the Hebrew alphabets both derive directly from earlier Semitic alphabets, and lack the innovations introduced by the Greeks. All the basic letters of both Arabic and Hebrew are still consonants just as they were in the earliest alphabets.

The alphabets of Europe and the Near East are all closely related, but by the third century BC, a quite different alphabet had been developed in northern India. This was then carried to the rest of the sub-continent and farther eastward to Southeast Asia, just as the Semitic alphabet was carried from the Near East to Europe. The unknown designers of the earliest Indian alphabet may have known about the alphabet already in use in the Near East, but the letters they designed had different shapes, and they were organized in an original way. The Devanagari alphabet, used today to write both Sanskrit and modern Hindi, is a typical example.

The basic Devanagari letters stand both for a consonant and for what is known as an "inherent" vowel. This vowel is conventionally transliterated into Roman script as *a*, and it is known as "short *a*," but it is pronounced, in Hindi, almost like a schwa. Each Devanagari letter, then, stands for an entire syllable, not just a single consonant, and the first consonant of the alphabet, क, is more accurately transliterated as *ka* than as simple *k*. These Devanagari syllable signs are arranged in a logical order that has nothing in common with the random order of the Semitic alphabet or its direct descendants. The Devanagari consonants are always set out in a table (see Figure 17–5) in which the rows represent the point of articulation and the columns represent the features of voicing, aspiration, and nasalization. The first row consists of the five velar consonants: voiceless, voiceless aspirated, voiced, voiced aspirated, and nasal, respectively. Next come rows for the five palatals, the five dentals, the five retroflexes, and the five bilabials. These are followed by a less-orderly list of liquids and sibilants.

In order to indicate a different vowel than the inherent *a*, any one of several accentlike marks can be placed before, after, above or below these basic Devanagari letters: का *kā* (long *a*), के *ke*, कु *ku*, चि *či*, नी *nī*. Notice that wherever the vowel marks are written, they always represent the vowel that follows the consonant in speech, and the combination of a consonant letter with a vowel sign represents one syllable. Devanagari does not really constitute a syllabary, however, since most of its symbols are further analyzable into vowels and consonants.

श्र a, श्रा ā, इ i, ई ī, उ u, ऊ ū, ऋ r̥, ॡ r̥̄, ॢ l̥,

ए e, ऐ ai, श्रो o, श्रौ au.

Velars	क	ख	ग	घ	ङ
	ka	kʰa	ga	gʰa	ŋa
Affricates	च	छ	ज	झ	ञ
	ča	čʰa	ǰa	ǰʰa	ɲa
Retroflexes	ट	ठ	ड	ढ	ण
	ṭa	ṭʰa	ḍa	ḍʰa	ŋa
Dentals	त	थ	द	ध	न
	t̪a	t̪ʰa	d̪a	d̪ʰa	n̪a
Bilabials	प	फ	ब	भ	म
	pa	pʰa	ba	bha	ma
Semivowels	य	र	ल्ल	व	
	ya	ra	la	va	
Sibilants	श	ष	स	ह	
	sa	sa	sa	ha	

Figure 17–5
The Devanagari alphabet. From Gonda (1966).

It is worth pointing out that most writing systems come closer to representing syllables than did the Ancient Greek alphabet or its direct descendents, Roman and Cyrillic. This may suggest something about the perceptual salience, or even the psychological reality, of syllables. Linguists who were accustomed to a writing system in which syllables were more prominently represented than in ours might have been less enthusiastic about a theoretical unit like the phoneme, for a phoneme amounts to a spoken analog of the type of letter found in western alphabets. If the field of linguistics had arisen in a society that used a syllabary instead of an alphabet, syllables might have seemed more important than phonemes.

The Devanagari consonant and vowel graphs would be adequate for a language in which every syllable consisted of just one consonant followed by just one vowel, but Sanskrit and Hindi are phonologically more complex than this. One problem is that the usual vowel signs can represent only vowels that follow consonants, and the script needs some way to indicate word-initial vowels where the vowel sign has no available consonant sign to hang on to. Devanagari accomplishes this with a special set of initial-vowel graphs. When the Devanagari alphabet is displayed in a chart, the vowel graphs used for initials are always written in a separate area from the consonants, as in Figure 17–6. Another problem arises with consonant clusters. Since, even in the absence of an explicit vowel symbol, each consonant graph implies a following inherent schwa, two successive consonant letters indicate two syllables rather than a cluster. Clusters, therefore, are represented by special symbols, constructed by stacking two consonants vertically (e.g., क्न *kna,* from क *ka* and न *na*), by joining them horizontally (क्त्य *ktya,* from क *ka,* त *ta,* and य *ya*), or by adding an extra mark to a letter (e.g., प्र *pra,* from प *pa,* with a small tick added for *r*). In all cases, the cluster is represented by a single complex symbol that can, in turn, be joined by one of the vowel signs. With these conventions, Devanagari and the many related alphabets of India and Southeast Asia provide writing systems that represent the vowels and consonants of their languages as accurately as any European alphabet.

From the moment when it was invented, alphabetic writing was far easier to learn than its more cumbersome predecessors. No longer was writing so easily monopolized by a small group of specialists. Even simple merchants could now keep written records. As long as writing was the domain of specialists, it brought power. Those who monopolized writing had an instrument of control, and it has sometimes been argued that writing helped to foster the autocratic political systems that characterized much of the ancient Near East. The alphabet, by contrast, has been looked on as a democratizing invention because it distributed the power of writing among a wider proportion of the population. Greek democracy grew and flourished in what was probably the most literate society that had existed up to that time. On the other hand, alphabetic writing has been used, and continues to be used, in many societies that are anything but democratic, so alphabetic writing is hardly a sufficient condition for democracy. Nevertheless, if widespread literacy is necessary for democracy, we should cherish the alphabet that makes literacy easiest.

HANGŬL WRITING OF KOREA

In the fifteenth century, King Sejong of Korea appointed a committee to assist him in designing a new script that would be well suited to the country's language, and usable by ordinary people. The committee did its work brilliantly, and produced the script that is known today as Hangŭl. It is unique among the world's writing systems, in combining aspects of featural, phonemic, and syllabic representation.

Like Devanagari, Hangŭl makes a basic distinction between vowels and consonants. The consonants have more compact geometric shapes and, remarkably, the simplest consonant graphs were designed to suggest the manner in which the sounds are articulated. The symbol for *n* represents the tongue tip pointing upward; the symbol for *g* is a stylized representation of the tongue humped up at the back; *m* is shaped like the Chinese character for "mouth"; *s* represents a tooth. The circle that can represent either ŋ or nothing at all has the shape of the throat in cross section.

Most of these basic symbols stand for continuants: *s* or one of the nasals. In Korean, as in English, however, ŋ never occurs initially and, probably for this

Consonants

	bilabial	apical	sibilant	velar	laryngal
lax continuant	ㅁ m	ㄴ n	ㅅ s		ㅇ ŋ/–
lax stop	ㅂ b	ㄷ d	ㅈ ɟ	ㄱ g	
tense aspirated stop	ㅍ pʰ	ㅌ tʰ	ㅊ cʰ	ㅋ kʰ	ㅎ h
tense continuant			ㅆ s		
tense unaspirated stop	ㅃ p	ㄸ t	ㅉ c	ㄲ k	
liquid		ㄹ l			

Vowels

	front		back	
	unrounded	rounded	unrounded	rounded
high	i ㅣ		ɯ ㅡ	u ㅜ
mid	e ㅔ	ø ㅚ	ʏ ㅓ	o ㅗ
low	æ ㅐ		a ㅏ	

Figure 17–6
Hangŭl "alphabet." From Sampson (1985).

reason, it is treated differently from the other nasals. Instead of being assigned to the nasal, the simplest velar symbol stands for a lax stop, *g* (it is more accurate to distinguish Korean consonants as lax, aspirated, and tense, than by their voicing). Graphs for two of the lax consonants, *d*, and *ɟ* (a palatal stop) are made by adding a horizontal line to the symbol for the corresponding continuant. The bilabial lax stop *b* is written differently, perhaps because *m* was felt already to have enough horizontal lines. The tense aspirated stops are made by adding a second horizontal bar, the bilabial, once again, being an exception. Finally, the tense unaspirated stops are shown by doubling the symbols for the lax consonants. Korean readers may not be aware of the articulatory logic of their own graphs, but it is entirely reasonable to interpret the single and double horizontal bars as graphs that symbolize different consonant classes, or what linguists would call distinctive phonetic "features."

The circle that indicates ŋ when it is at the end of a syllable is also used as a sort of dummy holder of the initial position when a syllable has no initial consonant at all. When double horizontal bars are added to this circle that means "nothing," the resulting graph indicates pure aspiration: *h*.

As can be seen in Figure 17–6, the graphs for vowels are more linear than those for consonants. The symbols for the back vowels and *i* are built around either a vertical or horizontal bar, sometimes modified by a short tick at

Constituents	Syllable	Pronunciation	Meaning
ㅏ	아	/a/	(a suffix)
ㄷ ㅏ	다	/da/	all
ㅏ ㄹ	알	/al/	egg
ㄷ ㅏ ㄹ	달	/dal/	moon;sweet
ㄷ ㅏ ㄹ ㄱ	닭	/dalg/	hen

Figure 17–7
Formation of Hangŭl syllables. From Taylor (1980).

the middle. The graph for *u* has a longer tick than the others, and it was probably lengthened to satisfy the aesthetic sense of people who were already accustomed to Chinese writing, where a horizontal bar with a single small tick below would look absurd. The graphs for front vowels other than *i* are formed by adding the graph for *i* to the corresponding back vowel. Thus the vertical "i" bar can be regarded as a featural sign meaning "front."

The Hangŭl vowel and consonant graphs shown in Figure 17–6, like the letters of our own alphabet, represent units with approximately the scope of a phoneme. These Hangŭl graphs, however, not only have an internal structure that our own letters lack, but they are also grouped in a very different way from the simple lineal ordering of western alphabetic writing. Hangŭl was designed by people who could write Chinese, and they grouped their "letters" into blocks, each of which, like a Chinese character, stood for one syllable. To the indiscriminating western eye, these blocks look a bit like Chinese characters, but they are constructed systematically from smaller parts and, unlike Chinese characters, they give an exact representation of the syllable's pronunciation. The way in which syllables are built up from their parts can be seen in Figure 17–7.

The Hangŭl script is simple enough to be learned in a single day, but it can be used to transcribe any Korean word. It can be used for words of other languages with no more difficulty than our own alphabet. Figures 17–6 and 17–7 should give enough information to allow the English word "ungentlemanliness" to emerge from the following sample of Hangŭl:

언젠틀먼리네스

The invention of the Hangŭl script was a stunning intellectual achievement. Hangŭl is more logical and systematic than any other writing system in general use. Not surprisingly, perhaps, it was at first scorned by scholars who were trained in Chinese. It was too coarse, too vulgarly simple, useful only for the common people who could manage nothing more refined. It was regarded exactly as most literate speakers of English regard simplified spelling today. For most of the centuries since its invention, Hangŭl coexisted with the far more prestigious Chinese writing, but in the twentieth century, Hangŭl has finally come into its own. South Koreans continue to mix some Chinese characters into predominantly Hangŭl text, rather as we sometimes mix logographic characters, such as the digits or even & or %, among our phonographic letters. The North Koreans have eliminated all Chinese characters from their writing, and even in the South the trend is in the same direction. It must be admitted that Hangŭl is more difficult to print than the lineally arranged Roman letters. Each syllable sign needs to be cast separately, so a Hangŭl type font needs many hundreds of distinct "sorts," as many as there are distinct syllables in the spoken language. Nevertheless, the ease of learning to read and write in Hangŭl must have made it easier for Korea to achieve a high rate of literacy. Perhaps it has contributed to Korea's rapid economic growth.

PRINTING AND THE MODERN ERA

Korea should be famous not only for its remarkable Hangŭl script, but also for its contribution to the history of printing. Printing with movable type was invented in China, but it was exploited seriously for the first time in thirteenth century Korea. When printing with movable type, the individual pieces of type are inscribed with just one letter or character. The pieces can be separated after use and then reassembled to print another document. Movable type was used in Korea two centuries before printing burst on Europe, but it was in Europe that its revolutionary implications were realized.

By the fifteenth century, Europe was ready for printing. Manuscripts were already in heavy demand, and printing was quickly accepted as a way to produce, more cheaply and efficiently, the same kinds of documents that were already being copied by hand. Once printing was shown to be practical, it quickly replaced hand copying. Itinerant printers, who carried their skills in their heads and in their hands, spread across Europe and, within a few decades, the production of books was transformed. Printing greatly increased the supply of books, and it encouraged the spread of literacy to a wider segment of the population than had ever been literate before, but it brought other, less obvious, changes as well. The techniques of the jeweler were needed in order to cast metal type. Even the trade in rags was transformed to provide raw material for the paper that was needed in ever-larger quantities. The hand presses that were used for most of the centuries of printing required heavy and dirty manual labor, but alone among manual craftsmen, printers had to be literate, and printers became the elite of manual workers. They had closer ties to the learned professions than did any other craftsmen.

Setting words in type was a laborious task, and it was hardly worth the effort for a mere dozen copies. Once the type was set, however, it was easy to produce 100, 200, or even a few thousand copies. Thus printing implied a sharp distinction between the handwritten "manuscript" that existed only as a single copy and a "published" piece that had been set up in type and turned out by the hundreds. The technology of printing did not encourage "editions" of five or twenty, so there could be no ambiguity about what was published and what was not. Once words were set in print, both authors and printers had an interest in protecting their investment, and authors had a stake in their own words. The labor required to copy a manuscript had been so great that it could hardly have occurred to an author that an income might be earned by copying one's compositions and selling them. Printing made this a real possibility, and for the first time in history, a few people could earn a living by writing and selling their words. Copyright laws, made valuable only by the technology of printing, protected these new rights.

Printing was by no means the sole cause of the social transformations that we associate with the beginning of the modern era. China and Korea had known printing with movable type long before the introduction of printing in Europe, but the Far East did not experience the revolutionary social changes that came to the West. Nevertheless, the scientific revolution, the age of discoveries, and the Reformation all got underway in the decades that followed the introduction of printing in Europe, and it is difficult to imagine any of these without the printing press.

Printing allowed far more reliable distribution of scientific data and theories than had ever before been possible. Copernicus, born in 1473, only a quarter of a century after European printing began, worked with printed versions of astronomical tables. Printing gave him access to a wider selection of tables than earlier astronomers ever had, and he did not have to spend interminable hours copying them himself. A medieval astronomer would have been lucky to have a single astronomical manuscript available for reference. Copernicus had several printed texts. He could compare them and seek ways to reconcile their contradictions. His revolutionary theories could, in their turn, be distributed in print so that others could build upon them.

Classical texts of anatomy, botany, and geography were also reproduced in the early days of printing, and they became much more widely accessible than they had been earlier. Their contents could then be more easily checked against the observable facts of nature. During earlier periods when manuscripts were scarce and jealously guarded, it had been difficult to check the texts for accuracy, but printers now actively sought additions and corrections to older works. A midwife presumed to correct information in the classical anatomical works of Galen. Botanical specimens were collected and observed in order to correct and expand older descriptions. The reports of sea captains were solicited so that maps could be extended and improved. The age of discoveries, inaugurated within a half-century following the introduction of printing in Europe with the voyages of Columbus to the New World and of Vasco da Gama around Africa to India, would have been far more difficult without the maps and travelers' reports whose distribution was made possible by printing.

The sixteenth-century arguments of the Reformation were conducted in print, and they could never have had the same impact in a society that was limited to manuscripts. The 95 theses that Luther is supposed to have tacked to the church door in Wittenberg in 1517 are remembered as a symbol of the Reformation. More significant were the 300,000 copies of Luther's publications that were sold by 1520. Luther's theses are said to have been known throughout Germany within a fortnight and throughout Europe within a month, a speed inconceivable without the printing press.

If printing played a part in the transformation of society, it also, like writing before it, influenced the spoken languages. The alphabet, by itself, was not enough to allow reading to grow into more than a minority skill, and throughout the Middle Ages, literacy remained largely a monopoly of the clergy. Most people would have had little use for reading and writing, even if they had known how. Throughout Europe, the few who were literate did most of their reading and writing in Latin, and until the effects of printing began to be felt, Latin remained the chief literary language of the Western world. Once printing made books more widely available, more people found literacy worth the effort. Even people whose Latin was shaky, including a growing number of women, sometimes learned to read. To satisfy the needs of people who found it easier to read in a language that was closer to their own spoken tongue, more and more books began to be printed in the vernacular languages.

Although writing, printing, and reading in the vernaculars increased, books could not be printed in every local dialect. A few vernacular dialects became favored vehicles for printing, and their importance grew not only at the expense of Latin but also at the expense of the many dialects that did not acquire a printed literature. As long as Latin remained the language of education and learning, people felt free to use their own local dialects for daily purposes. They could even write these dialects on some occasions. Printers, however, had to settle on certain dialects as the standard for printed books. In France, the choice went to the dialect of Paris. It became the standard, while the other vernacular dialects of France began a long decline. A single written form of German became established as standard throughout the Germanic-speaking regions of modern Germany, Austria, and Switzerland. Only on the peripheries did alternative written standards survive: Dutch and Flemish in the low countries in the west, and Yiddish among the Jewish minority in the east. Almost five thousand years earlier, writing had strengthened some languages at the expense of others. Now printing drove the same process further, strengthening those dialects that happened to be represented in print, and at the same time marginalizing others.

Political unity could speed the establishment of a single dominant dialect, but political disunity did not always prevent it. Standard printed French, Spanish, Portuguese, and Italian reached out to divide the Romance-speaking areas of Western Europe. Printing even brought prestige to the spoken dialects on which the printed standards were based. The spoken dialects of London and Paris were imitated by speakers in other parts of England and France. Political unification came more slowly to Germany and Italy, and no single German or Italian city had as much prestige as Paris and London. As a result, it took longer for national spoken standards to emerge in Germany and Italy, but the effects of standardization were finally felt throughout Europe.

Linguists like to define a "language" as a set of mutually intelligible "dialects." If two people can understand each other, linguists generally consider them to speak the same language. The popular definition of a language has always been different. For most people other than linguists, a language embraces the spoken forms of all those people who recognize the same written standard. Thus the mutually unintelligible varieties of speech that are used in China are popularly referred to as dialects because all literate Chinese use the same written form. Conversely, Norwegian, Swedish, and Danish, although mutually intelligible, are popularly counted as different languages, because the Norwegians, Swedes, and Danes use different conventions when they write. Norway is even said to have two different languages because it has two different written standards that compete as ways of transcribing the many, but easily mutually comprehensible, spoken dialects of Norway. Even nonliterate tribal people are sometimes said to speak dialects although these dialects may, by the criteria of linguists, be unrelated languages. Thus in popular usage, the term *language* depends on the existence of a written standard. Dialects, or even the sets of mutually comprehensible dialects that linguists want to call languages, can no more be counted than can the number of waves that cover a pond. If we are able to count the languages of Europe today, it is because we count written standards, and because European written standards are relatively few in number and clearly distinct from one another. It was printing that imposed its standards upon the endless dialectal diversity of the countryside.

Printing made written material far more widely available than ever before, and from the time when printing first began in Europe, an ever-increasing number of people have found it useful to learn to read. As the literate proportion of the population grew, the shrinking minority that remained illiterate became increasingly marginalized. Universal schooling, the expansion of knowledge that fills our libraries, modern science and technology, and the tools for both construction and destruction that these entail, are all inconceivable without the printing press. These, by a kind of inexorable logic, have led us, in turn, to still another revolution in communications, a revolution that promises, or threatens, still another set of radical changes in our society.

THE INFORMATION AGE

We express the vanity of our era when we say that we are passing through an "information revolution," but we may well be correct in guessing that the changes made possible by telecommunications and by computerized manipulation of information may finally be as important as the changes brought by the earlier communications revolutions of writing and printing. Computers allow us to organize, process, and analyze information in ways that could hardly have been imagined a few decades ago. With modern telecommunications we can move this information instantaneously anywhere in the world.

As a symbol for the beginning of the information age we might pick the mid-nineteenth century, when a telegraph line was strung from New York to Texas.

Before this time, messages could rarely move more quickly than the speed of a galloping horse. Once telegraph wires went up, it was suddenly possible to communicate instantaneously across thousands of miles. Depending on a laborious string of dots and dashes, early telegraphy was, by modern standards, impossibly cumbersome. The wire from New York to Texas could carry only a tiny fraction of the information carried by a modern cable, but when it was first installed people wondered how the line could be kept busy. What did the people of New York and Texas have to say to each other that would make the line practical? We have learned, since then, that people can find plenty to talk about once they have the means, and ever since the first telegraph wires were strung, the lines of communication that reach across the land, under the seas, and up and down from satellites, have been spun into a tighter and tighter web.

Modern sages are fond of pointing out that telecommunications and computers are merging into a single information system. The sages point less often to a third component of the information age, the humble photocopier, but the copier does join with our more sophisticated electronic machinery to make the spread of information easier than ever before. Predictions about where these technologies will lead us are hazardous, but it is fun to speculate.

The communication system toward which we may be heading is easy enough to imagine. Every desk may carry a machine that combines a telephone, keyboard, screen, and printer. With the help of this machine, we would be able to connect our own desk, by satellite or by cable, to any other desk in the world, and to send and receive messages by voice, written words, or the visual images of facsimile printing or the television screen.

Many people still feel little need for this electronic desk. Breathless predictions that every home would soon be cabled to an electronic network have had to be regularly postponed, but what will happen when telephone books become obsolete? Long-distance telephone rates keep falling, and we can look forward to the time when it will be no more expensive for an Englishman to call Melbourne than to call Manchester. Those who protest that they have no one to talk to in Melbourne might remind themselves of the skeptics who doubted that New Yorkers and Texans could keep that first telegraph wire busy. As soon as we can call the world, we will want to call the world. We will face a problem, however, because we will never be able to collect enough telephone books to find all the numbers. The only way to inform callers about distant telephone numbers will be by a computerized information system. Everyone who owns a telephone may need to learn how to find numbers in an electronic data bank.

More radical would be the collapse of first-class mail under the competition of facsimile and electronic messages. In 1986, it was already both cheaper and faster to send electronic messages between Europe and America than to send airmail letters. As more and more people learn to send their written messages electronically, first-class mail may be undermined. The unit costs of sending a letter may rise until it finally becomes uneconomical to maintain the present mail system. Electronics may then become the only practical way to send written messages, and everyone who wants to write a letter will have to join the network.

Electronics is already revolutionizing newspaper publishing. Old-fashioned typesetting has been replaced by word processing. Long-distance data transmission has allowed a few national and even world newspapers to grow, while competition with television has undermined local newspapers. Other forms of publishing can be expected to change as radically. Copyright laws were a social response to the technology of printing. They could be enforced when printing implied a sharp distinction between a single-copy manuscript and a published edition of many hundreds or even thousands of copies. Computer printing and photocopying have wiped out the distinction. "Editions" of two, five, twenty, or fifty have become easy and commonplace. The line between what is, and what is not, published has become hopelessly blurred. Small editions circulate informally, while conventional publication grows steadily more expensive. When a $75 book can be privately photocopied for $10, the temptation to break the copyright law becomes irresistible. More photocopying means lower sales of printed books, shorter print runs, higher unit costs, higher prices, and an ever-greater temptation to use the copier. The final result may be that conventional publication for many specialized books will become uneconomical.

At the same time, electronic word processing has dramatically eased the task of writing and rewriting. Typesetting programs allow individual authors, sitting at their computers, to produce copy that is ready for photoduplication. The ease and flexibility of electronic word processing will certainly mean that more and more books will be written, and the ease of reproduction means that, in one form or another, more and more will be published. It has been estimated that half the books that have ever been published in all of human history have appeared since 1950. As word processing and photo-duplication become easier, the flood of the written word can only keep rising.

Marshall McLuhan popularized the idea that, with telephones replacing the mail and television replacing newspapers and magazines, we are leaving the age of the written word and entering a new age of oral communication. If McLuhan had paused to glance at the piles of computer printouts that gush from every government, business, and university computing center, he would have had to admit that, whatever is happening, the end of the written word is hardly upon us. On the contrary, computers and photocopiers make writing, printing, and the production of multiple copies far easier than ever before. Instead of returning to orality, we are in danger of drowning in paper.

As more authors with better word processing programs, printers, and photocopiers produce more "publications," libraries will no longer be able to build shelves fast enough to hold them all. Unless they drastically restrict their collections, even large research libraries will have to revolutionize their storage system. Books and journals can be shrunk to microfilm or microfiche, but even these will grow in bulk, and libraries will more often be forced to move to electronic storage. Most publication will, in any case, pass through an electronic stage of word processing, and it will become more efficient to store data and texts in electronic form, sending them to a screen or a printer only when needed. We can look forward to more "demand" publishing, as publishers learn to produce copies only on order, avoiding overly optimistic print runs and the storage of large inventories.

Even more important than the changes in style of publication and information exchange are the changes we can expect in the distribution of power. A computer can give the user an exhilarating sense of power. It can be glorious to manipulate huge banks of information simply by typing a few keys in one's own home, to fire off an electronic message across the oceans, to set a printer to work in a distant city. But the power felt by the individual user rests on the vast industry that produces and maintains both the hardware and the software on which the individual is totally dependent. Our society will be shaped by how power is wielded within this industry.

In a world where almost infinite information is available at the touch of a key, no single person can survey more than a tiny fraction of the total. Who will organize this information? Who will control its distribution? Who will control the data banks? Who will decide which information is easy to reach and which information gets buried? Those who manage electronic information will have the same sorts of power now held by those who manage the mass media, the editors, movie moguls, and television executives who decide what we read and watch. This is enormous power, and we can look forward to intense struggles over these new information resources.

The implications of electronic information range from the trivial to the frightening. At the trivial end is the looming problem of electronic junk mail. If I can send an electronic message instantaneously to anyone in the world, then anyone can send one to me. Advertisers, fund raisers, and ambitious politicians have a glorious opportunity to distribute "urgent" appeals, and to make the receiver pay for the paper the appeals are printed on. Most of us do not want all those messages, and we will need to learn how to defend ourselves against the onslaught.

Electronic information has more frightening implications than junk mail. Electronics gives large institutions an advantage over small. Paper work used to grow even faster than the size of an organization, and this put a limit on centralization, but large organizations can now keep records much more efficiently than they could in the past. Errorless electronic record keeping encourages larger and larger banks, manufacturing concerns, and retail organizations. Centralization of power and decision making also allows centralized governments to interfere with more aspects of our lives.

More and more of our daily activities are recorded electronically. Our grades in school, our grocery purchases, our phone calls, the tickets we buy for travel and our hotel accommodations when we get there, all find their way into banks of electronic data. We face the time when all this information can be collected and scrutinized. Difficult decisions will have to be made about what information should be public and what should remain private. None of us wants to let everyone know about every purchase we make, but we easily forget, as we flash our credit card at the checkout line, that someone, somewhere, is able to find out exactly what we buy and to deduce what we eat for breakfast. Many decades will pass before we sort out the conflicting needs of the individual for privacy, and of a free society for the open distribution of information.

We also face a problem of simple information overload. When a committee must make a decision in any well-ordered bureaucracy today, the committee members are presented with a well-ordered stack of photocopied documents containing all the background information required for a careful and informed decision. The photocopier allows the relevant information to be more easily and thoroughly assembled than ever in the past, and anyone who has faith in bureaucracies must believe that decisions will improve as information becomes more accessible. If one uses both arms it is sometimes still possible to lift these stacks of documents off the table, but busy committee members fool themselves if they believe they can absorb all the information the stacks contain. The photocopier works too quickly. The availability of the data seems to promise that decisions can be made more rationally, but this can be an illusion. The illusion may even be dangerous if it lets us defend decisions as if they have been wise, when they have really involved the same kinds of guesswork as decisions in the past.

No one will be able to handle all the information that computers and the photocopier will make available. We will need ways to sort the information so as to make what we need accessible. How it is sorted, who controls the sorting, and how it is made available to the user are questions that will deeply affect the distribution of power. The most disadvantaged will be the new illiterates, those people who, for whatever reason, fail to learn to handle the new media. No one was illiterate before writing was invented, but when some people learned to write, others were left behind. Now, when some can manipulate information electronically, others will be as seriously excluded as the old illiterates. We face the danger of an increasingly imbalanced distribution of power, with more and more decisions made centrally, while large numbers of people are effectively excluded.

Finally, we should return to language itself and ask what implications the information revolution holds for the way we speak. Both writing and printing encouraged the spread of some languages at the expense of others, and the new information technology seems destined to do the same. Before the invention of writing, languages of a few hundred speakers could be viable systems of communication. Writing raised the minimum to at least a few thousand or tens of thousands. Printing meant that only those languages with speakers counting in the hundreds of thousands could be taken seriously enough to be taught and learned as "real" languages. Electronics seems destined to raise this minimum, at least to a few million, perhaps to many million. A global communication system may require a single global language.

The period since the Second World War is the first period of human history when just one dominant world language has been recognized everywhere. British power followed by American power spread the English language around the globe, and it now has no close competitor. French remains the first foreign language in a few former French colonies of Africa. Minority people in the former Soviet Union, China, and Brazil may have to learn Russian, Chinese, or Portuguese before they learn English. For most others, for continental Europeans, most Africans, most Russians, most Asians, and most Latin Americans, the first foreign language is English. Only in English-speaking countries do students face a problem when deciding which foreign language to study. For others, English is generally the obvious choice. When Japanese, Finns, Nigerians, and Brazilians travel to each other's countries, they generally use English. Any scholar who hopes for more than a local readership is now almost forced to write in English. The spread of English into more and more areas of life seems inexorable. Other languages are being correspondingly restricted.

It has been said that the language of international physics is "broken" English. English is also the language of the oil industry, of air traffic control, of the environmental movement, of international motorcycle racing, and of telecommunications and computing. Authors of programming languages strive to give the users commands in "natural" language, but they act as if the most natural of all languages is English. No technical problem prevents the substitution of Portuguese or Swahili for the English commands of FORTRAN or PASCAL, but people who learn to program generally know enough English to make the effort to translate them superfluous. Whatever their own native language, programmers usually expect their computers to be most fluent in English.

Does this mean that other languages are destined to yield ground to English and finally die out? Those who cherish linguistic diversity can be confident that a good many languages will survive at least for our own lifetime, but languages with limited numbers of speakers are disappearing steadily, and languages with large numbers of speakers are everywhere gaining at the expense of others. In Central and South America, Portuguese and Spanish spread at the expense of Native American languages. Russian used to spread at the expense of the minority languages of the former Soviet Union. Mandarin spreads at the expense of the other languages of China. English spreads at the expense of every other language in the world.

The communication system being spun from cables and satellite links today, like any communication system, belongs to a community. Although this community is worldwide, it is as much in need of a mutually comprehensible language as is any other community. We have no trouble understanding and sympathizing with the decisions of individual speakers as they reach for the practical advantages of English. Only with English can a Ghanaian telephone to Burma or a Burmese send a fax back to Ghana. It is no wonder that both Burmese and Ghanaians are eager to learn English. We can understand why millions of people the world over want to learn the international language.

Nevertheless, linguists who delight in the diversity of the world's languages will always mourn the passing of so many of them. A world with only a few widespread languages, to say nothing of a world reduced to the bland uniformity of universal English, seems an unattractive prospect to people who make the study of language their specialty. Every language is the product of thousands of years of human conversation, the irreplaceable bearer of its people's culture. Every language gives testimony to the power of the human intellect. With each language that dies out, as with each plant or animal species that humans exterminate, the world becomes a poorer and less interesting place in which to live. It is the most mournful task of linguistics to record as much as possible of the world's linguistic wealth before it is too late.

BIBLIOGRAPHIC NOTES

CHAPTER 2. MEANING AND THE LEXICON

The figure for the extent of Hanunóo botanical vocabulary is given in Conklin (1962). The example of verbs of sensation is drawn from Viberg (1984). The example of Spanish and Atsugewi verbs of motion is based on Talmy (1985). Body-part terms in many languages are discussed by E. Andersen (1978). Palaung pronouns are treated somwhat more fully in Burling (1970), which also has a considerably fuller treatment of componential analysis. The discussion of color terms is based on Berlin and Kay (1969). The scholar who has done the most to make us aware of the importance of prototypes is Eleanor Rosch. See Rosch (1975), and Rosch and Lloyd, eds. (1978). I first heard the example of "breakfast" from Charles Fillmore. Lakoff (1987) discusses many aspects of word meanings, including prototype theory, and I take the example of *over* from this book, but Lakoff credits Brugman (1981) for the analysis. Lakoff and Johnson (1980) deal with some of the more pervasive metaphors of our language. The sentences using the word *axon* are from Kalil (1969). The influence of language on world view and culture is an ancient and terribly tangled subject. The name most closely associated with the view that language constrains our view of the world is Benjamin Lee Whorf, and his articles can be found in Whorf (1964). The Palaung and Norwegian examples are taken from my field work or personal experience.

CHAPTER 3. MORPHOLOGY

Morphology is an old and well-established subject in linguistics, and it has been discussed in many places. Bauer (1983) offers a very solid and up-to-date treatment of the subject. Dixon (1977) has a stimulating discussion of the ways in which adjective meanings are conveyed in a variety of languages. The examples of Bontok infixes and Ilocano reduplication come from H. A. Gleason (1961), and the long Eskimo word is from Anderson (1985). The Arabic example is based on Mitchell (1962). Langacker (1987) gives a name to "conventional expressions," and some of my examples are drawn from his book. Carey (1978) is often cited on vocabulary size, but Ellegård's discussion (1960) shows why vocabulary is so difficult to count. The Garo examples in this chapter are from my own field work.

CHAPTER 4. LEXICAL VARIATION AND CHANGE

American regionalisms are treated in Cassidy (1985). Social dialects are discussed extensively in Labov's various books and papers, but he deals less with the lexicon than with syntax and phonology. Weinreich (1953) is the classic work on the influence that one language can have on another, but Thomason and Kaufman (1988) is a more recent treatment of the subject. A number of my examples of English words that have acquired increasingly abstract meanings come from Traugott (1989). I draw on Watkins (1985) both for my discussion of the reconstruction of Proto-Indo-European culture, and for the example of the etymology of *foot*. Renfrew (1988) proposes the association of Indo-European with agriculture. A standard work on the classification of world languages is Voegelin and Voegelin (1977), but see also Grimes (1988), which is more up to date in certain respects, and Ruhlen (1987), which is easier to use. My population figures are from the 1990 World Almanac and Book of Facts. Greenberg (1987) presents the arguments for a radically revised classification of Amerindian languages.

CHAPTER FIVE: PHONETICS

Several good introductions to phonetics are available. Ladefoged (1982) can be warmly recommended for a lucid and far more extensive survey of phonetics than is allowed by the space available in this chapter. See also Catford (1988). Ladefoged (1971) offers an extensive treatment of acoustic phonetics. Pullum and Ladusaw (1986) is the best and most complete source for information on phonetic characters.

CHAPTER SIX: PHONOLOGY

As with phonetics, a number of good general textbooks of phonology are available. Lass (1984) is both clear and thoughtful, but it is not elementary, and it is weak in the treatment of tone, intonation, and autosegmental phonology. Distinctive feature theory was presented in an early form in Jakobson and Halle (1956), and applied specifically to English in Chomsky and Halle (1968). I have drawn on Ladefoged (1982) for a number of examples of minimal pairs in languages other than English, and have taken other examples from my own field experience. Hawaiian phonemes are described in Kahananui and Anthony (1970), and Navajo phonemes in Reichard (1951). An excellent source on American Sign Language is Klima and Bellugi (1979). A number of articles on autosegmental phonology can be found in van der Hulst and Smith (1982). The Mende example is from Leben (1978). The treatment of English word stress is based on that of Goldsmith (1981). Turkish vowel harmony has often served to illustrate phonological processes, and my examples come from Mardin (1976). The basis for generative phonology, which receives a brief introduction here in the section called "Alternations and Underlying Forms," was laid by Chomsky and Halle (1968). Two textbooks written from the point of view of generative phonology are Anderson (1974), and Kenstowicz and Kisseberth (1979). Goldsmith (1989) deals with several more modern approaches to phonology.

CHAPTER SEVEN: PHONOLOGICAL VARIATION

Francis (1983) and Chambers and Trudgill (1980) are good surveys of dialectology. The former is strongest on traditional geographical dialectology, the latter on social dialectology. William Labov should be credited for much of the recent interest in variability. He investigated social dialects in New York City (1966), and he did pioneering work on Black English Vernacular (1970, 1972a). The graph of "r" in New York City is from Labov (1964). On British English pronunciation, see Jones (1957), and on American English, see Kenyon and Knott (1953), both a bit out of date but both rich in valuable detail. Work on fast phonology is scattered and not easily accessible, but Lass (1984) makes some interesting observations. American dialect geography is treated in Kurath (1949).

CHAPTER EIGHT: PHONOLOGICAL CHANGE

Although more than half a century old, the chapters dealing with historical linguistics in Bloomfield's *Language* (1933) still provide a solid introduction to the comparative method. A number of good textbooks focus specifically on historical linguistics and develop the subject in far fuller detail than is possible here, including W. P. Lehmann (1973), Anttila (1989), and Bynon (1977). Among much else, these all treat such well-known events as the Great Vowel Shift and Grimm's Law. My example from the Bodo languages was given more fully in Burling (1959). Pyles and Algeo (1982) give a clear introduction to the phonological changes that have taken place in the history of English. English dialects are treated more fully in the sources referred to in the notes for Chapter 4. The northern cities chain shift, and much else, is described in great detail in Labov *et al.* (1972). Greenberg (1966) describes the origin of nasal vowels from the loss of final nasals. Haudricourt (1961) gives extensive data on the origins of tones.

CHAPTER NINE. GENERATIVE GRAMMAR

The generative upheaval of linguistics began in 1957 with the publication of Chomsky's *Syntactic Structures* and gathered force and redirection with his *Aspects of the Theory of Syntax* (1965). Many publications have followed (see bibliography). Cook (1988) is a brief and unusually clear introduction to Chomsky's more recent proposals that are known as "Government and Binding." Lightfoot (1983) is an even more accessible introduction that emphasizes the biological basis of language but is less thorough in other respects than Cook. Radford (1988) gives a more technical and textbook treatment of modern Chomskyan linguistics, and offers a clear and systematic treatment of many topics of recent concern. Newmeyer (1980, 1983) has written on the history of generative–transformational linguistics. Gazdar *et al.* (1985) and Bresnan (1978) suggest formal approaches to syntax that differ from Chomsky's in important ways. Hockett (1968), though already old by the standards of formal syntax, is a thoughtful critique of Chomsky's generative grammar, and deserves to be taken more seriously than it has been.

CHAPTER TEN. THE FUNCTIONS OF SYNTAX

A good deal of the functional–typological view of syntax that is reviewed in this chapter and the next owes its origins to a remarkable article by Joseph Greenberg (1963). The four volumes of Greenberg *et al.* (1978) collect a large number of important articles developing the functional and typological approach. Comrie (1981) is good introductory survey of syntactic typology. Givón (1979, 1984) and Dik (1978) are more technical treatments of typological and functional problems. Stockwell (1977) gives a good outline of the tasks that a language needs to accomplish. I rely heavily on Ekerot (1979) for my discussion of pragmatic factors in syntax. Books edited by Shopen (1979a,b) provide good descriptions of particular languages. I am indebted to Frances Trix for the Arabic and Turkish examples that begin this chapter, and to Paz Naylor for the Tagalog example. The Russian example is modified from an example in Comrie (1981). The Chinese and Bemba examples are from Givón (1979), as are the statistics of definite and indefinite articles in subject and object position. The Swahili examples are from Hinnebusch (1979). Garo examples are from my own field experience.

CHAPTER ELEVEN. SYNTACTIC TYPOLOGY

Several of the sources listed for Chapter Seven could as well have been cited here, since typological and functional approaches have been closely associated. The beginnings of a good deal of modern linguistic typology can be seen in a book edited by Greenberg (1963). Greenberg's own article in that book gives the data on word-order typology that are summarized in this chapter. Hawkins (1983) gives a more elaborate analysis of word-order universals. The three volumes of Shopen (1985) contain detailed articles discussing the typology of many aspects of syntax. Noun-phrase accessibility and the formation of relative clauses are described by Keenan and Comrie (1979), and summarized in Comrie (1981). The Kinyarwanda example is based on Gary and Keenan (1977). Several linguists have offered classifications of verbs according to the types of noun phrases with which they are used, among them Dik (1978), Givón (1984), and Gazdar et al. (1985). All these classifications owe more than is sometimes acknowledged to Fillmore (1968). Ergativity has been the subject of extensive literature, and the Dyirbal example was given in Dixon (1979). I take the examples of Malagasy passivization from Comrie (1981). The Swahili example is from H. A. Gleason (1961). On deaf signing, see Klima and Bellugi (1979).

CHAPTER TWELVE. SYNTACTIC VARIATION

The study of syntactic variation has been slower to develop than the study of phonological variation, but work in the area is now accelerating. For my description of the differences between British and American English, I depend on the detailed description of Trudgill and Hannah (1985). The differences between written and oral language have been recently rediscovered by linguists, and Chafe and Tannen (1987) give a good review of work done in this area. Biber (1988) gives a detailed analysis of the differences among several spoken and written English genres. Ochs (1979) reviews the related question of the difference between planned and unplanned discourse. See also Tannen (1984) and Chafe (1982). Kučera and Francis (1967) analyze a million-word sample of written English. Dahl (1979) gives comparable data for a sample of spoken English. As with phonology, the study of social differences in grammar owes a great deal to the work of William Labov, particularly to his work with black New York teenagers. Labov (1970) is a relatively accessible survey of this work, while the articles in Labov (1972a) are somewhat more technical. The sentences exhibiting the second extension of the Right Copy rule appeared first in Labov *et al.* (1968). Burling (1973) is an introductory survey of the characteristics of black English.

CHAPTER THIRTEEN. SYNTACTIC CHANGE

As with syntactic typology, the recent study of syntactic change has been inspired by the work of Joseph Greenberg. This began with Greenberg (1963), and several of his other important articles on syntactic change are listed in the bibliography. Two books edited by Li (1975, 1977) contain important articles on the subject. Vennemann (1974, 1975) develops and extends the implications of Greenberg's fundamental ideas. My treatment of grammaticalization in this chapter owes a great deal to C. Lehmann (1982), and the Chinese examples are from his work. My discussion of French historical syntax is based entirely on Harris (1978). A clear and readily accessible survey of the linguistic history of English can be found in Pyles and Algeo (1982). The example of Marathi–Kannada convergence is from Gumperz (1969).

CHAPTER 14. PIDGIN AND CREOLE LANGUAGES

Pidgins and creoles have been studied and described since in the nineteenth century, but the modern linguistic fascination with them extends back hardly more than 3 decades. Hall's still readable introduction (1966) can already be regarded as an "early" synthesis. The Tok Pisin paragraph given here is taken from his book. Hymes (1971) collected many of the best articles of the first modern wave of attention to these languages. Since then, a mass of linguistic work has been done, both on particular pidgin and creole languages and on the implication of these languages for linguistic theory. Holm (1988) gives a fine survey of these languages, and the examples given in this chapter from Miskito Coast Creole are taken from his book. Holm is stronger on the Atlantic creoles than on those from the Pacific. Mühlhäusler (1986) is stronger on those from the Pacific. Romaine (1988) provides still another general treatment, and is the source of the examples of Tok Pisin vocabulary. Sankoff (1980) gathers a number of excellent articles on Tok Pisin, including a discussion of *baimbai* on which I draw. Rickford (1987) is a solid study of creole development. Bickerton's stimulating but controversial book (1981) presents the case for a universal bioprogram as the causative factor lying behind the (apparently) universal characteristics of creole languages. The examples from Guyanese Creole are from Bickerton. Dillard (1972) argues forcefully for the creole antecedents of American Black English vernacular. Thomason and Kaufman (1988) consider pidgins and creoles within a more general context of borrowing and language shift.

CHAPTER 15. FIRST AND SECOND LANGUAGE LEARNING

The study of child language has exploded in volume in the last 2 decades, and a number of introductory and general reviews of the subject are available. See, for example, McNeill (1970), Brown (1973), Elliot (1981), and J. B. Gleason (1985). Recent work is well described in the articles in Fletcher and Garman (1986). Eve Clark has done important work on the development of lexical meaning (1975, 1977), and the example of the extension of the meaning of *fly* is hers. The example of *mommy sock* comes from Bloom (1970). Social and interactional aspects of acquisition are stressed in the articles on Ochs and Schieffelin (1979), and Snow (1986) gives a fine review of recent work. Ochs *et al.* (1979) describe the cooperation of adult and child in producing utterances. The child who talked about the car is described by Scollon (1979). The difference between top-down and bottom-up strategies is well developed by Peters (1983, 1986). Ferguson has helped us to understand the development of phonology. See, for instance, Ferguson and Farwell (1975). Slobin (1985) is a massive report on a massive comparative study of langauge acquisition in a number of different languages. I take the Kaluli example from Schieffelin (1979). Heath (1983) describes striking differences in the linguistic socialization of children in different cultural communities. Children's negatives and questions are analyzed by Klima and Bellugi (1966). The child who insisted on *other one spoon* was quoted in Braine (1971). An early statement hypothesizing a Language Acquisition Device is in Chomsky (1966). Lenneberg (1967) makes the strongest case for a critical age after which language-learning capacity is supposed to decline. Slobin (1973) offers the view that children make use of operating strategies for working their way into a language. Bickerton (1981) makes intriguing suggestions about things to look for in child language that might test the relevance of the bio-program for our understanding of how children learn to talk. I have given a fuller discussion of the differences between first and second language acquisition in Burling (1981), which appears along with a number of other articles dealing with one or another aspect of the subject in Winitz (1981). Ervin-Tripp (1974), and Snow and Hoefnagel-Höhle (1978) give convincing evidence that older children learn a new language more quickly than their younger brothers and sisters. Dulay and Burt (1974) argue that first-language interference is not a major source of second-language errors.

CHAPTER 16. LANGUAGE AND THE HUMAN SPECIES

Material on the origin of language is scattered, but the volume is huge. Stoss (1976) is a short introduction to language evolution, and Harnad *et al.* (1976) is a much larger and more technical collection of papers on every conceivable aspect of the subject. Hockett's ideas about language evolution have been extremely influential, and are summarized in Hockett (1960). Smutts *et al.* (1987) includes articles on all aspects of primate behavior including communication. Cries and facial expressions of several species of primates are very clearly described and compared in Jolly (1985). Vervet monkey alarm calls are described by Seyfarth *et al.* (1980). The work with Washoe the signing ape is reported in Gardner and Gardner (1969), while skepticism about apes' ability to learn signing is expressed in Terrace *et al.* (1979) and Seidenberg and Pettito (1979). Fossil evidence for language is reviewed by Holloway (1983). Lieberman (1984) argues strongly for the recent evolution of the vocal tract, but on this topic, Laitman (1983) should also be consulted. Much of the interest in the brain and language was stimulated by Lenneberg (1967). Passingham (1982) is excellent on the brain and on differences between humans and other primates. Spuhler (1977) gives a good review of what is known about language and the brain. Krantz (1980) develops the idea that language could have been an invention. Archeological evidence is reviewed by Isaac (1976). The most stimulating discussions of language evolution by linguists that I have seen are the relevant chapters in Bickerton (1981) and in Givón (1979).

CHAPTER 17. LANGUAGE AND CIVILIZATION

Gelb (1963) and Diringer (1953) are the standard sources on the history and techniques of writing, but I would recommend a more recent book by Sampson (1985), which is linguistically oriented and excellent. DeFrancis (1989) is also good, and it corrects Sampson in useful ways, particularly with respect to Chinese, though I find it unnecessarily polemical. Boltz (1986) describes early Chinese writing, and Kramer (1963) describes early Sumerian. Kroeber (1948) has a wonderful account of the spread of the alphabet that I have long admired. On Korean, I have drawn both on the chapter in Sampson (1985) and Taylor (1980). On the social and personal implications of writing, I draw heavily on Jack Goody's rich writing on the subject: Goody (1977, 1986, 1987), Goody and Watt (1963). See also Havelock (1982) and Scribner and Cole (1981). Febvre and Martin (1976) and Eisenstein (1979) both tell wonderful stories of the history and implications of printing, with Febvre and Martin strongest on the technological side of book making, and Eisenstein strongest on the social implications.

BIBLIOGRAPHY

Andersen, Elaine S. "Body Part Terminology," in Greenberg, Joseph H., Charles A. Ferguson, and Edith A. Moravcsik (eds.), *Universals of Human Language,* Vol. 3, *Word Structure.* Stanford, California: Stanford University Press, 1978, pp. 335–368.

Anderson, Stephen R. *The Organization of Phonology.* New York: Academic Press, 1974.

Anderson, Stephen R. "Inflectional Morphology," in Shopen, Timothy (ed.), *Language Typology and Syntactic Description,* Vol. III, *Grammatical Categories and the Lexicon.* Cambridge, England: Cambridge University Press, 1985, pp. 150–201.

Anttila, Raimo. *Historical and Comparative Linguistics.* 2nd Rev. Ed. Amsterdam and Philadelphia: John Benjamins, 1989.

Bauer, Laurie. *English Word Formation.* Cambridge, England: Cambridge University Press, 1983.

Berlin, Brent, and Paul Kay. *Basic Color Terms: Their Universality and Evolution.* Berkeley, California: University of California Press, 1969.

Biber, Douglas. *Variation across Speech and Writing.* Cambridge, England: Cambridge University Press, 1988.

Bickerton, Derek. *Roots of Language.* Ann Arbor, Michigan: Karoma, 1981.

Bloom, Lois. *Language Development: Form and Function in Emerging Grammars.* Cambridge, Massachusetts: MIT Press, 1970.

Bloomfield, Leonard. *Language.* New York: Holt, 1933.

Boltz, William G. "Early Chinese Writing." *World Archaeology,* Vol. 17, 1986, pp. 420–436.

Braine, M. D. S. "The Acquisition of Language in Infant and Child," in Reed, C. E. (ed). *The Learning of Language.* New York: Appleton-Century-Crofts, 1971, pp. 7–96.

Bresnan, Joan W. "A Realistic Transformational Grammar," in Halle, Morris, Joan Bresnan, and George A. Miller (eds). *Linguistic Theory and Psychological Reality.* Cambridge, Massachusetts: MIT Press, 1978, pp. 1–59.

Brown, Roger. *A First Language: The Early Stages.* Cambridge, Massachusetts: Harvard University Press, 1973.

Brugman, Claudia. *Story of Over.* M.A. thesis, University of California, Berkeley, 1982. (Available from the Indiana University Linguistics Club.)

Burling, Robbins. "Proto-Bodo." *Language,* Vol. 35, 1959, pp. 433–453.

Burling, Robbins. *Man's Many Voices: Language in its Cultural Context.* New York: Holt, Rinehart & Winston, 1970.

Burling, Robbins. *English in Black and White.* New York: Holt, Rinehart & Winston, 1973.

Burling, Robbins. "Social Constraints on Adult Language Learning," in Winitz, Harris (ed.), *Native Language and Foreign Language Acquisition.* New York: Annals of the New York Academy of Science, Vol. 379, 1981, pp. 279–290.

Bynon, Theodora. *Historical Linguistics*. Cambridge, England: Cambridge University Press, 1977.

Carey, Susan. "The Child as a Word Learner," in Halle, Morris, Joan Bresnan, and George A. Miller (eds.), *Linguistic Theory and Psychological Reality*. Cambridge, Massachusetts: MIT Press, 1978, pp. 264–293.

Cassidy, Frederic G. (ed.). *Dictionary of American Regional English*. Cambridge, Massachusetts: Belknap Press, 1985.

Catford, J. G. *A Practical Introduction to Phonetics*. Oxford, England: Clarendon Press, 1988.

Chafe, Wallace. "Integration and Involvement in Speaking, Writing and Oral Literature," in Tannen, Deborah (ed.), *Spoken and Written Language: Exploring Orality and Literacy*. Norwood, New Jersey: Ablex, 1982, pp. 35–53.

Chafe, Wallace, and Deborah Tannen. "The Relation between Written and Spoken Language." *Annual Review of Anthropology*, Vol. 16, 1987, pp. 183–407.

Chambers, J. K., and Peter Trudgill. *Dialectology*. Cambridge, England: Cambridge University Press, 1980.

Chomsky, Noam. *Syntactic Structures*. The Hague, The Netherlands: Mouton, 1957.

Chomsky, Noam. *Aspects of the Theory of Syntax*. Cambridge, Massachusetts: MIT Press, 1965.

Chomsky, Noam. *Language and Mind*. New York: Harcourt, Brace & World, 1968.

Chomsky, Noam. *Lectures on Government and Binding*. Dordrecht, The Netherlands: Foris, 1981.

Chomsky, Noam. *Knowledge of Language: Its Nature, Origin and Use*. New York: Praeger, 1986.

Chomsky, Noam, and Morris Halle. *The Sound Patterns of English*. New York: Harper & Row, 1968.

Clark, Eve V. "Knowledge, Context, and Strategy in the Acquisition of Meaning," in Dato, D. P. (ed.), *Georgetown University Round Table on Language and Linguistics 1975*. Washington, D.C.: Georgetown University Press, 1975, pp. 77–98.

Clark, Eve V. "Strategies and the Mapping Problem in First-Language Acquisition," in Macnamara, John (ed.), *Language Learning and Thought*. New York: Academic Press, 1977, pp. 147–168.

Clark, Virginia P., Paul A. Eschholz, and Alfred F. Rosa. *Language: Introductory Readings*, 3rd Ed. New York: St. Martin's Press, 1981.

Comrie, Bernard. *Language Universals and Language Typology*. Chicago: University of Chicago Press, 1981.

Conklin, Harold C. "Lexicographical Treatment of Folk Taxonomies." *International Journal of American Linguistics*, Vol. 28.2 (Part IV), 1962, pp. 119–141.

Cook, V. J. *Chomsky's Universal Grammar*. Oxford, England: Basil Blackwell, 1988.

Dahl, Hartvig. *Word Frequencies of Spoken American English*. Detroit, Michigan: Gale Research Company, 1979.

DeFrancis, John. *Visible Speech: The Diverse Oneness of Writing Systems*. Honolulu, Hawaii: University of Hawaii Press, 1989.

Dik, Simon. *Functional Grammar*. Amsterdam: North Holland, 1978.

Dillard, Joseph L. *Black English: Its History and Usage in the United States*. New York: Random House, 1972.

Diringer, D. *The Alphabet*, 2nd Rev. Ed. New York: Philosophical Library, 1953.

Dixon, Robert M. W. *The Dyirbal Language of North Queensland*. Cambridge, England: Cambridge University Press, 1972.

Dixon, Robert M. W. "Where have all the Adjectives Gone?" *Studies in Language,* Vol. 1, 1977, pp. 19–80.

Dixon, Robert M. W. "Ergativity." *Language.* Vol. 55, 1979, pp. 59–138.

Dulay, Heidi C., and Marina K. Burt. "Natural Sequences in Child Second-Language Acquisition." *Language Learning,* Vol. 24(1), 1974, pp. 37–53.

Eisenstein, Elizabeth. *The Printing Press as an Agent of Change: Communications and Cultural Transformations in Early Modern Europe.* 2 Vols. Cambridge, England: Cambridge University Press, 1979.

Ekerot, Lars Johan. "Syntax och Informationsstruktur," in Kenneth Hyltenstram (ed.), *Svenska i invandrarperspektiv,* Lund, Sweden: Liber Läromedel, 1979, pp. 79–108.

Ellegård, Alvar. "Estimating Vocabulary Size." *WORD,* Vol. 16, 1960, pp. 219–244.

Elliot, Alison J. *Child Language.* Cambridge, England: Cambridge University Press, 1981.

Ervin-Trip, Susan. "Is Second Language Learning like the First?" *TESOL Quarterly,* Vol. 8(2), 1974, pp. 111–127.

Febvre, Lucien, and Henri-Jean Martin. *The Coming of the Book.* Atlantic Highlands, New Jersey: Humanities Press, 1976.

Ferguson, Charles A., and Carol B. Farwell. "Words and Sounds in Early Language Acquisition." *Language,* Vol. 51, 1975, pp. 419–439.

Fillmore, Charles. "The Case for Case," in Bach, Emmon, and Robert T. Harms. *Universals in Linguistic Theory.* New York: Holt, Rinehart & Winston, 1968, pp. 1–88.

Fletcher, Paul, and Michael Garman (eds.). *Language Acquisition: Studies in First Language Development,* 2nd Ed. Cambridge, England: Cambridge University Press, 1986.

Francis, W. Nelson. *Dialectology: An Introduction.* London and New York: Longman, 1983.

Gardner, R. Allen, and Beatrice T. Gardner. "Teaching Sign Language to an Ape." *Science,* Vol. 165, 1969, pp. 664–672.

Gary, Judith Olmsted, and Edward L. Keenan. "On Collapsing Grammatical Relations in Universal Grammar," in Peter Cole and Jerold M. Sadock (eds). *Syntax and Semantics,* Vol. 8. New York: Academic Press, 1977, pp. 83–120.

Gazdar, Gerald, Ewan Klein, Geoffrey Pullum, and Ivan Sag. *Generalized Phrase Structure Grammar.* Cambridge, Massachusetts: Harvard University Press, 1985.

Gelb, I. J. *A Study of Writing.* Chicago, Illinois: University of Chicago Press, 1963.

Givón, Talmy. *On Understanding Grammar.* New York: Academic Press, 1979.

Givón, Talmy. *Syntax: A Functional–Typological Introduction.* Amsterdam: Benjamins, 1984.

Gleason, Henry Allan, Jr. *Workbook in Descriptive Linguistics.* New York: Holt, Rinehart & Winston, 1961.

Gleason, Jean Berko. *The Development of Language.* Columbus, Ohio: Merrill, 1985.

Goldsmith, John. "English as a Tone Language," in D. Goyvaerts (ed.), *Phonology in the 1980s.* Ghent, Belgium: E. Story-Scientia, 1981, pp. 287–308.

Goldsmith, John. *Autosegmental and Metrical Phonology.* New York: Blackwell, 1989.

Gonda, Jan. *A Concise Elementary Grammar of the Sanskrit Language.* Leiden, The Netherlands: E. J. Brill, 1966.

Goody, Jack. *The Domestication of the Savage Mind*. Cambridge, England: Cambridge University Press, 1977.

Goody, Jack. *The Logic of Writing and the Organization of Society*. Cambridge, England: Cambridge University Press, 1986.

Goody, Jack. *The Interface between the Written and the Oral*. Cambridge, England: Cambridge University Press, 1987.

Goody, Jack, and I. P. Watt. "The Consequences of Literacy." *Comparative Studies in History and Society,* Vol. 5, 1963, pp. 304–345.

Greenberg, Joseph H. "Synchronic and Diachronic Universals in Phonology." *Language,* Vol. 42, 1966, pp. 508–517.

Greenberg, Joseph H. "Some Methods of Dynamic Comparison in Linguistics," in Jaan Puhvel (ed.), *Substance and Structure of Language*. Berkeley, California: University of California Press, 1969, pp. 147–203.

Greenberg, Joseph H. "How Does a Language Acquire Gender Markers?" in Greenberg, Joseph H., Charles A. Ferguson, and Edith A. Moravcsik (eds.), *Universals of Human Language,* Vol. 3, *Word Structure*. Stanford, California: Stanford University Press, 1978, pp. 249–295.

Greenberg, Joseph H. (ed.). *Universals of Language*. Cambridge, Massachusetts: MIT Press, 1963.

Greenberg, Joseph H. "Some Universals of Grammar with Particular Reference to the Order of Meaningful Elements," in J. H. Greenberg (ed.), *Universals of Language*. Cambridge, Massachusetts: MIT Press, 1963.

Greenberg, Joseph H. *Language in the Americas*. Stanford, California: Stanford University Press, 1987.

Greenberg, Joseph H., Charles A. Ferguson, and Edith A. Moravcsik (eds.). *Universals of Human Language,* 4 Vols. Stanford, California: Stanford University Press, 1978.

Grimes, Barbara F. (ed.). *Ethnologue: Languages of the World,* 11th Ed. Dallas, Texas: Summer Institute of Linguistics, 1988.

Gumperz, John J. "Communication in Multilingual Communities," in Tyler, Stephen (ed.), *Cognitive Anthropology*. New York: Holt, Rinehart & Winston, 1969, pp. 435–439.

Hall, Robert A., Jr. *Pidgin and Creole Languages*. Ithaca, New York: Cornell University Press, 1966.

Harnad, Stephen R., Horst D. Steklis, and Jane Lancaster (eds.). *Origins and Evolution of Language and Speech*. Annals of the New York Academy of Sciences, Vol. 280, New York: New York Academy of Sciences, 1976.

Harris, Martin. *The Evolution of French Syntax: A Comparative Approach*. London: Longman, 1978.

Haudricourt, André-G. "Bipartition et Tripartition des Systèmes de Tons dans Quelques Language d'Extrême-Orient." *Bullitin de la Société Linguistique de Paris,* Vol. 56, 1961, pp. 163–180.

Havelock, E. *The Literate Revolution in Greece and Its Cultural Consequences*. Princeton, New Jersey: Princeton University Press, 1982.

Hawkins, John A. *Word Order Universals*. New York: Academic Press, 1983.

Heath, Shirley Brice. *Ways with Words*. Cambridge, England: Cambridge University Press, 1983.

Hinnebusch, Thomas J. "Swahili," in Shopen, Timothy (ed.), *Languages and Their Status*. Cambridge, Massachusetts: Winthrop Publishers, 1979, pp. 209–293.

Hockett, Charles. "The Origin of Speech." *Scientific American,* Vol. 203, October, 1960, pp. 88–96.

Hockett, Charles F. *The State of the Art,* (Janua Linguarum, series minor, 73). The Hague, The Netherlands: Mouton, 1968.

Holloway, Ralph L. "Human Paleontological Evidence Relevant to Language Behavior." *Human Neurobiology,* Vol. 2, 1983, pp. 105–14.

Holm, John. *Pidgins and Creoles. Vol. I: Theory and Structure.* Cambridge, England: Cambridge University Press, 1988.

Hulst, Harry van der, and Norval Smith (eds.). *The Structure of Phonological Representations,* 2 Vols. Dordrecht, The Netherlands: Foris Publications, 1982.

Hymes, Dell (ed.). *Pidginization and Creolization of Languages.* Cambridge, England: Cambridge University Press, 1971.

Isaac, Glynn L. "Stages of Cultural Elaboration in the Pleistocene: Possible Archeological Indicators of the Development of Language," in Harnad, Stephen R., Horst D. Steklis, and Jane Lancaster (eds.), *Origins and Evolution of Language and Speech,* Annals of the New York Academy of Sciences, Vol. 280. New York: New York Academy of Sciences, 1976, pp. 275–288.

Jakobson, Roman, and Morris Halle. *Fundamentals of Language.* The Hague, The Netherlands: Mouton, 1956.

Jolly, Alison. *The Evolution of Primate Behavior.* 2nd Ed. New York: Macmillan, 1985.

Jones, Daniel. *An Outline of English Phonetics.* Cambridge, Massachusetts: Heffer, 1957.

Kahananui, Dorothy, and Alberta P. Anthony. *Let's Speak Hawaiian.* Honolulu, Hawaii: University of Hawaii Press, 1970.

Kalil, Ronald. "Synapse Formation in the Developing Brain." *Scientific American,* Vol. 261, December, 1989, pp. 76–85.

Keenan, Edward L., and Bernard Comrie. "Noun Phrase Accessibility and Universal Grammar." *Language,* 55, 1979, pp. 333–351.

Kenstowicz, Michael, and Charles Kisseberth. *Generative Phonology: Description and Theory.* New York: Academic Press, 1979.

Kenyon, J. S., and T. A. Knott. *A Pronouncing Dictionary of American English.* Springfield, Massachusetts: G. & C. Merriam, 1953.

Klima, Edward S., and Ursula Bellugi. "Syntactic Regulation in the Speech of Children," in Lyons, John and R. J. Wales (eds.), *Psycholinguistics Papers.* Edinburgh, Scotland: Edinburgh University Press, 1966, pp. 183–208.

Klima, Edward S., and Ursula Bellugi. *The Signs of Language.* Cambridge, Massachusetts: Harvard University Press, 1979.

Kramer, Samuel N. *The Sumerians: Their History, Culture, and Character.* Chicago, Illinois: University of Chicago Press, 1963.

Krantz, Grover S. "Sapienization and Speech," *Current Anthropology,* Vol. 21, 1980, pp. 773–792.

Kroeber, Alfred L. *Anthropology.* New York: Harcourt, Brace, 1948.

Kučera, Henry, and W. Nelson Francis. *Computational Analysis of Present-Day American English.* Providence, Rhode Island: Brown University Press, 1967.

Kurath, Hans. *A Word Geography of the Eastern United States.* Ann Arbor, Michigan: University of Michigan Press, 1949.

Labov, William. "Phonological Correlates of Social Stratification," in Gumperz, John J. and Dell Hymes (eds), *The Ethnography of Communication.* Special Publication of the American Anthropologist: Vol. 66, No. 6, 1964, pp. 164–176.

Labov, William. *The Social Stratification of English in New York City.* Washington, D.C.: Center for Applied Linguistics, 1966.

Labov, William. *Language in the Inner City.* Philadelphia, Pennsylvania: University of Pennsylvania Press, 1972a.

Labov, William. *Sociolinguistic Patterns.* Philadelphia, Pennsylvania: University of Pennsylvania Press, 1972b.

Labov, William. *The Study of Nonstandard English.* Champaign, Illinois: National Council of Teachers of English, 1970.

Labov, William, Paul Cohen, Clarence Robins, and John Lewis. *A Study of the Non-standard English of Negro and Puerto Rican Speakers in New York City,* Vol. I, *Phonological and Grammatical Analysis;* Vol. II, *The Use of Language in the Speech Community,* Final Report, Cooperative Research Project No. 3288. Washington, D.C.: Office of Education, 1968.

Labov, William, Malcah Yaeger, and Richard Steiner. *A Quantitative Study of Sound Change in Progress,* Vols. I and II. Philadelphia, Pennsylvania: U.S. Regional Survey, 1972.

Ladefoged, Peter. *Elements of Acoustic Phonetics.* Chicago, Illinois: University of Chicago Press, 1971.

Ladefoged, Peter. *A Course in Phonetics.* 2nd Ed. New York: Harcourt Brace Jovanovich, 1982.

Laitman, Jeffrey T. "The Evolution of the Hominid Upper Respiratory System and Implications for the Origins of Speech," in Eric de Grolier (ed.), *Glossogenics: The Origin and Evolution of Language.* New York: Harwood Academic Publishers, 1983, pp. 63–90.

Lakoff, George, and Mark Johnson. *Metaphors We Live By.* Chicago, Illinois: University of Chicago Press, 1980.

Lakoff, George. *Women, Fire, and Dangerous Things.* Chicago, Illinois: University of Chicago Press, 1987.

Langacker, Ronald W. *Foundations of Cognitive Grammar.* Stanford, California: Stanford University Press, 1987.

Lass, Roger. *Phonology: An Introduction to Basic Concepts.* Cambridge, England: Cambridge University Press, 1984.

Leben, William R. "The Representation of Tone," in Victoria Fromkin (ed.), *Tone: A Linguistic Survey.* New York: Academic Press, 1978, pp. 177–219.

Lehmann, Christian. *Thoughts on Grammaticalization: A Programmatic Sketch.* Köln, Germany: AKUP, Arbeiten des Kölner Universalien-Projekts, 1982.

Lehmann, Winifred P. *Syntactic Typology: Studies in the Phenomenology of Language.* Austin, Texas: University of Texas Press, 1978.

Lehmann, Winifred P. *Historical Linguistics: An Introduction.* New York: Holt, Rinehart & Winston, 1973.

Lenneberg, Eric. *Biological Foundations of Language.* New York: John Wiley, 1967.

Li, Charles N. (ed.). *Word Order and Word Order Change.* Austin, Texas: University of Texas Press, 1975.

Li, Charles N. (ed). *Subject and Topic.* New York: Academic Press, 1976.

Li, Charles N. (ed.). *Mechanisms of Syntactic Change.* Austin, Texas: University of Texas Press, 1977.

Lieberman, Phillip. *The Biology and Evolution of Language.* Cambridge, Massachusetts: Harvard University Press, 1984.

Lightfoot, David. *The Language Lottery.* Cambridge, Massachusetts: MIT Press, 1983.

Mardin, Yusuf. *Colloquial Turkish*. Istanbul: Haset Kitapevi, ca. 1976.

McNeill, David. *The Acquisition of Language: The Study of Developmental Psycholinguistics*. New York: Harper & Row, 1970.

Mitchell, T. F. *Colloquial Arabic*. London: Hodder and Stoughton, 1962.

Mühlhäusler, Peter. *Pidgin and Creole Linguistics*. Oxford, England: Blackwell, 1986.

Newmeyer, Frederick J. *Grammatical Theory: Its Limits and Its Possibilities*. Chicago, Illinois: University of Chicago Press, 1983.

Newmeyer, Frederick J. *Linguistic Theory in America: The First Quarter Century of Generative Transformational Grammar*. New York: Academic Press, 1980.

Ochs, Elinor. "Planned and Unplanned Discourse," in Talmy Givón (ed.), *Syntax and Semantics*, Vol. 12, *Discourse and Syntax*. New York: Academic Press, 1979, pp. 51–80.

Ochs, Elinor, and Bambi B. Schieffelin (eds.). *Developmental Pragmatics*. New York: Academic Press, 1979.

Ochs, Elinor, Bambi B. Schieffelin, and Martha L. Platt. "Propositions across Utterances and Speakers," in Ochs, Elinor, and Bambi B. Schieffelin (eds.), *Developmental Pragmatics*. New York: Academic Press, 1979, pp. 251–268.

Passingham, R. E. *The Human Primate*. Oxford and San Francisco: W. H. Freeman, 1982.

Peters, Ann M. *The Units of Language Acquisition*. Cambridge, England: Cambridge University Press, 1983.

Peters, Ann M. "Early Syntax," in Fletcher, Paul, and Michael Garman (eds.), *Language Acquisition: Studies in First Language Development,* 2nd Ed. Cambridge, England: Cambridge University Press, 1986, pp. 307–325.

Pullum, Geoffrey K., and William A. Ladusaw. *Phonetic Symbol Guide*. Chicago, Illinois: University of Chicago Press, 1986.

Pyles, Thomas, and John Algeo. *The Origins and Development of the English Language,* 3rd Ed. New York: Harcourt Brace Jovanovich, 1982.

Radford, Andrew. *Transformational Grammar*. Cambridge, England: Cambridge University Press, 1981.

Reichard, Gladys. *Navaho Grammar*. New York: J. J. Augustin, 1951.

Renfrew, A. Colin. *Archaeology and Language: The Puzzle of Indo-European Origins*. Cambridge, England: Cambridge University Press, 1988.

Rickford, John R. *Dimensions of a Creole Continuum*. Stanford, California: Stanford University Press, 1987.

Romaine, Suzanne. *Pidgin and Creole Languages*. New York: Longman, 1988.

Rosch, Eleanor. "Cognitive Representations of Semantic Categories." *Journal of Experimental Psychology: General,* Vol. 104, 1975, pp.192–233.

Rosch, Eleanor, and B. B. Lloyd (eds). *Cognition and Categorization*. Hillsdale, New Jersey: Lawrence Erlbaum, 1978.

Ruhlen, Merritt. *A Guide to the World's Languages*. Stanford, California: Stanford University Press, 1987.

Sampson, Geoffrey. *Writing Systems: A Linguistic Introduction*. Stanford, California: Stanford University Press, 1985.

Sankoff, Gillian. *The Social Life of Language*. Philadelphia, Pennsylvania: University of Pennsylvania Press, 1980.

Schieffelin, Bambi B. "Getting it Together: An Ethnographic Approach to the Study of the Development of Communicative Competence," in Ochs, Elinor, and Bambi B. Schieffelin (eds.), *Developmental Pragmatics*. New York: Academic Press, 1979, pp. 73–108.

Scollon, Ronald. "A Real Early Stage: An Unzippered Consideration of a Dissertation on Child Language," in Ochs, Elinor, and Bambi B. Schieffelin (eds.), *Developmental Pragmatics*. New York: Academic Press, 1979, pp. 215–227.

Scribner, Sylvia and Michael Cole. *The Psychology of Literacy*. Cambridge, Massachusetts: Harvard University Press, 1981.

Seidenberg, Mark S., and Laura A. Petitto. "Signing Behavior in Apes: A Critical Review." *Cognition*, Vol. 7, 1979, pp. 177–215.

Seyfarth, Robert M., Dorothy L. Cheney, and Peter Marler. "Monkey Responses to Three Different Alarm Calls: Evidence of Predator Classification and Semantic Communication." *Science*, Vol. 210, 1980, pp. 801–803.

Shopen, Timothy (ed.). *Languages and Their Speakers*. Cambridge, Massachusetts: Winthrop, 1979a.

Shopen, Timothy (ed.). *Languages and Their Status*. Cambridge, Massachusetts: Winthrop, 1979b.

Shopen, Timothy (ed.). *Language Typology and Syntactic Description*. (3 Vols.) Cambridge, England: Cambridge University Press, 1985.

Slobin, Dan Isaac. "Cognitive Prerequisites for the Acquisition of Grammar," in Ferguson, Charles A., and Dan I. Slobin (eds.), *Studies of Child Language Development*. New York: Holt, Rinehart & Winston, 1973, pp. 175–208.

Slobin, Dan Isaac. *The Crosslinguistic Study of Language Acquisition*, Vol. 1, *The Data;* Vol. 2, *Theoretical Issues*. Hillsdale, New Jersey: Erlbaum, 1985.

Smuts, Barbara B., Dorothy L. Cheney, Robert M. Seyfarth, Richard Wrangham, and Thomas T. Strubsaker (eds.). *Primate Societies*. Chicago: University of Chicago Press, 1987.

Snow, Catherine E. and M. Hoefnagel-Höhle. "The Critical Period for Language Acquisition: Evidence from Second Language Learning." *Child Development*, Vol. 49, 1978, pp. 1114–1128.

Snow, Catherine. "Conversations with Children," in Fletcher, Paul and Michael Garman (eds.), *Language Acquisition: Studies in First Language Development*, 2nd Ed. Cambridge, England: Cambridge University Press, 1986, pp. 69–89.

Spuhler, James. "Biology, Speech, and Language." *Annual Review of Anthropology 1977*. Palo Alto, California: Annual Reviews, 1977, pp. 509–561.

Stockwell, Robert. *Foundations of Syntactic Theory*. Englewood Cliffs, N. J.: Prentice-Hall, 1977.

Stross, Brian. *The Origin and Evolution of Language*. Dubuque, Iowa: Wm. C. Brown, 1976.

Talmy, Leonard. "Lexicalization Patterns: Semantic Structure in Lexical Forms," in Timothy Shopen (ed.), *Language Typology and Syntactic Description*, Vol. III, *Grammatical Categories and the Lexicon*. Cambridge, England: Cambridge University Press, 1985, pp. 57–149.

Tannen, Deborah. *Conversational Style: Analyzing Talk among Friends*. Norwood, N. J.: Ablex, 1984.

Taylor, Insup. "The Korean Writing System: An Alphabet? A Syllabary? A Logography?" in Kolers, Paul A., Merald E. Wrolstad, and Herman Bouma (eds.), *Processing of Visible Language 2*. New York: Plenum Press, 1980, pp. 67–82.

Terrace, Herbert S., Laura A. Petitto, Richard J. Sanders, and Thomas G. Bever. "Can an Ape Create a Sentence?" *Science*, Vol. 206, 1979, pp. 891–902.

Thomason, Sarah Grey, and Terrace Kaufman. *Language Contact, Creolization, and Genetic Linguistics*. Berkeley and Los Angeles: University of California Press, 1988.

Traugott, Elizabeth Closs. "On the Rise of Epistemic Meanings in English: An Example of Subjectification in Semantic Change." *Language,* Vol. 65, 1989, pp. 31–55.

Trudgill, Peter, and Jean Hannah. *International English: A Guide to Varieties of Standard English.* London, England: Edward Arnold, 1985.

Vennemann, Theo. "Topics, Subjects, and Word Order: From SXV to SVX via TVX," in Anderson, John M., and Charles Jones (eds.), *Historical Linguistics.* North Holland Linguistic Series 12. Amsterdam: North Holland, 1974, pp. 339–376.

Venneman, Theo. "An Explanation of Drift," in Li, Charles N. (ed.). *Word Order and Word Order Change.* Austin, Texas: University of Texas Press, 1975, pp. 269–305.

Viberg, Åke. "The Verbs of Perception: A Typological Study" in Butterworth, Brian, Bernard Comrie, and Östen Dahl (eds.), *Explanations for Language Universals.* Berlin, New York, Amsterdam: Mouton, 1984, pp. 123–162.

Voegelin, C. F., and F. M. Voegelin. *Classification and Index of the World's Languages.* New York: Elsevier, 1977.

Watkins, Calvert (ed.). *The American Heritage Dictionary of Indo-European Roots.* Boston: Houghton Mifflin, 1985.

Whorf, Benjamin L. *Language, Thought, and Reality.* Cambridge, Massachusetts: MIT Press, 1964.

Weinreich, Uriel. *Languages in Contact.* New York: Linguistic Circle of New York, 1953.

Winitz, Harris (ed.). *Native Language and Foreign Language Acquisition.* Annals of the New York Academy of Science, Vol. 379, New York: New York Academy of Sciences, 1981.

The World Almanac and Book of Facts. 1990. New York: Pharos Books. 1989.

INDEX

Pages in **boldface** type include definitions.
Pages in *italics* have particularly full treatments of the topics.